ANNUAL EDITIONS

Anthropology
Twenty-Eighth Edition

05/06

EDITOR
Elvio Angeloni
Pasadena City College

Elvio Angeloni received a B.A. from UCLA in 1963, an M.A. in anthropology from UCLA in 1965, and an M.A. in communication arts from Loyola Marymount University in 1976. He has produced several films, including *Little Warrior*, winner of the Cinemedia VI Best Bicentennial Theme, and *Broken Battles*, shown on PBS. He most recently served as an academic adviser on the instructional television series *Faces of Culture*.

McGraw-Hill/Dushkin
2460 Kerper Boulevard, Dubuque, Iowa 52001

Visit us on the Internet
http://www.dushkin.com

Credits

1. **Anthropological Perspectives**
   Unit photo—© *Saudi Aramco World*/PADIA/T. F. Walters.
2. **Culture and Communication**
   Unit photo—© Getty Images/Connie Coleman.
3. **The Organization of Society and Culture**
   Unit photo—© CORBIS/Royalty-Free.
4. **Other Families, Other Ways**
   Unit photo—© *Saudi Aramco World*/PADIA/Brynn Bruijn.
5. **Gender and Status**
   Unit photo—© *Saudi Aramco World*/PADIA/Nik Wheeler.
6. **Religion, Belief, and Ritual**
   Unit photo—© 2004 by PhotoDisc, Inc.
7. **Sociocultural Change: The Impact of the West**
   Unit photo—© *Saudi Aramco World*/PADIA/Robert Azzi.

Copyright

Cataloging in Publication Data
Main entry under title: Annual Editions: Anthropology. 2005/2006.
1. Anthropology—Periodicals. I. Angeloni, Elvio, *comp.* II. Title: Anthropology.
ISBN 0–07–310840–5   658'.05   ISSN 1091–613X

Twenty-Eighth Edition

Cover image © Adalberto Rios Szalay/Sexto Sol/Getty Imges and Photo.com
Printed in the United States of America   1234567890QPDQPD987654   Printed on Recycled Paper

To the Reader

In publishing ANNUAL EDITIONS we recognize the enormous role played by the magazines, newspapers, and journals of the public press in providing current, first-rate educational information in a broad spectrum of interest areas. Many of these articles are appropriate for students, researchers, and professionals seeking accurate, current material to help bridge the gap between principles and theories and the real world. These articles, however, become more useful for study when those of lasting value are carefully collected, organized, and reproduced in a low-cost format, which provides easy and permanent access when the material is needed. That is the role played by ANNUAL EDITIONS.

This twenty-eighth edition of Annual Editions: Anthropology contains a variety of articles on contemporary issues in social and cultural anthropology. In contrast to the broad range of topics and minimum depth typical of standard textbooks, this anthology provides an opportunity to read firsthand accounts by anthropologists of their own research. In allowing scholars to speak for themselves about the issues on which they are expert, we are better able to understand the kind of questions anthropologists ask, the ways in which they ask them, and how they go about searching for answers. Indeed, where there is disagreement among anthropologists, this format allows the readers to draw their own conclusions.

Given the very broad scope of anthropology—in time, space, and subject matter—the present collection of highly readable articles has been selected according to certain criteria. The articles have been chosen from both professional and nonprofessional publications for the purpose of supplementing the standard textbook in cultural anthropology that is used in introductory courses. Some of the articles are considered classics in the field, while others have been selected for their timely relevance.

Included in this volume are a number of features designed to make it useful for students, researchers, and professionals in the field of anthropology. While the articles are arranged along the lines of broadly unifying themes, the topic guide can be used to establish specific reading assignments tailored to the needs of a particular course of study. Other useful features include the table of contents abstracts, which summarize each article and present key concepts in italics. In addition, each unit is preceded by an overview, which provides a background for informed reading of the articles, emphasizes critical issues, and presents key points to consider. Finally, there are World Wide Web sites that can be used to further explore the topics.

Annual Editions: Anthropology 05/06 will continue to be updated annually. Those involved in producing the volume wish to make the next one as useful and effective as possible. Your criticism and advice are always welcome. Please fill out the postage-paid article rating form on the last page of the book and let us know your opinions. Any anthology can be improved. This continues to be—annually.

Elvio Angeloni

Elvio Angeloni
Editor
evangeloni@paccd.cc.ca.us

Contents

UNIT 1
Anthropological Perspectives

UNIT 2
Culture and Communication

The concepts in bold italics are developed in the article. For further expansion, please refer to the Topic Guide.

UNIT 3
The Organization of Society and Culture

The concepts in bold italics are developed in the article. For further expansion, please refer to the Topic Guide.

UNIT 4
Other Families, Other Ways

The concepts in bold italics are developed in the article. For further expansion, please refer to the Topic Guide.

UNIT 5
Gender and Status

UNIT 6
Religion, Belief and Ritual

The concepts in bold italics are developed in the article. For further expansion, please refer to the Topic Guide.

UNIT 7
Sociocultural Change: The Impact of the West

The concepts in bold italics are developed in the article. For further expansion, please refer to the Topic Guide.

The concepts in bold italics are developed in the article. For further expansion, please refer to the Topic Guide.

Topic Guide

This topic guide suggests how the selections in this book relate to the subjects covered in your course. You may want to use the topics listed on these pages to search the Web more easily.

On the following pages a number of Web sites have been gathered specifically for this book. They are arranged to reflect the units of this *Annual Edition*. You can link to these sites by going to the DUSHKIN ONLINE support site at *http://www.dushkin.com/online/*.

ALL THE ARTICLES THAT RELATE TO EACH TOPIC ARE LISTED BELOW THE BOLD-FACED TERM.

Acculturation
19. Dowry Deaths in India: 'Let Only Your Corpse Come Out of That House'
20. Who Needs Love! In Japan, Many Couples Don't
26. Eyes of the Ngangas: Ethnomedicine and Power in Central African Republic
28. Shamans
33. The Arrow of Disease
34. The Price of Progress
36. Egypt's Young and Restless
39. A Pacific Haze: Alcohol and Drugs in Oceania
40. When Will America Be Discovered?

Aggression
12. Prehistory of Warfare
19. Dowry Deaths in India: 'Let Only Your Corpse Come Out of That House'
33. The Arrow of Disease
37. The Surprises of Suicide Terrorism
41. The Last Americans

Altruism
3. Eating Christmas in the Kalahari
11. Too Many Bananas, Not Enough Pineapples, and No Watermelon at All: Three Object Lessons in Living With Reciprocity

Child care
4. Coping with Culture Clash
14. How Many Fathers Are Best for a Child?
16. Death Without Weeping
17. Our Babies, Ourselves
24. Where Fat Is a Mark of Beauty

Children
14. How Many Fathers Are Best for a Child?
16. Death Without Weeping
17. Our Babies, Ourselves
24. Where Fat Is a Mark of Beauty

Communication
4. Coping with Culture Clash
5. Fighting for Our Lives
6. "I Can't Even Open My Mouth"
7. Shakespeare in the Bush
8. Body Art As Visual Language

Cooperation
3. Eating Christmas in the Kalahari
11. Too Many Bananas, Not Enough Pineapples, and No Watermelon at All: Three Object Lessons in Living With Reciprocity

Cross-cultural experience
1. Doing Fieldwork Among the Yanomamö
2. Doctor, Lawyer, Indian Chief
3. Eating Christmas in the Kalahari
4. Coping with Culture Clash
7. Shakespeare in the Bush

9. Understanding Eskimo Science
11. Too Many Bananas, Not Enough Pineapples, and No Watermelon at All: Three Object Lessons in Living With Reciprocity
13. The Founding Indian Fathers
16. Death Without Weeping
17. Our Babies, Ourselves
18. Arranging a Marriage in India
26. Eyes of the Ngangas: Ethnomedicine and Power in Central African Republic
28. Shamans

Cultural change
12. Prehistory of Warfare
17. Our Babies, Ourselves
19. Dowry Deaths in India: 'Let Only Your Corpse Come Out of That House'
20. Who Needs Love! In Japan, Many Couples Don't
28. Shamans
32. Why Can't People Feed Themselves?
33. The Arrow of Disease
34. The Price of Progress
35. The Social Psychology of Modern Slavery
36. Egypt's Young and Restless
37. The Surprises of Suicide Terrorism
39. A Pacific Haze: Alcohol and Drugs in Oceania
40. When Will America Be Discovered?
41. The Last Americans

Cultural diversity
4. Coping with Culture Clash
8. Body Art As Visual Language
14. How Many Fathers Are Best for a Child?
17. Our Babies, Ourselves
18. Arranging a Marriage in India
22. The Berdache Tradition
26. Eyes of the Ngangas: Ethnomedicine and Power in Central African Republic
28. Shamans

Cultural identity
8. Body Art As Visual Language
13. The Founding Indian Fathers
17. Our Babies, Ourselves
24. Where Fat Is a Mark of Beauty
27. The Adaptive Value of Religious Ritual

Cultural relativity
1. Doing Fieldwork Among the Yanomamö
3. Eating Christmas in the Kalahari
4. Coping with Culture Clash
8. Body Art As Visual Language
13. The Founding Indian Fathers
17. Our Babies, Ourselves
18. Arranging a Marriage in India
26. Eyes of the Ngangas: Ethnomedicine and Power in Central African Republic
30. Body Ritual Among the Nacirema

World Wide Web Sites

The following World Wide Web sites have been carefully researched and selected to support the articles found in this reader. The easiest way to access these selected sites is to go to our DUSHKIN ONLINE support site at *http://www.dushkin.com/online/*.

AE: Anthropology 05/06

The following sites were available at the time of publication. Visit our Web site—we update DUSHKIN ONLINE regularly to reflect any changes.

General Sources

American Anthropologist
http://www.aaanet.org

Check out this site—the home page of the American Anthropology Association—for general information about the field of anthropology as well as access to a wide variety of articles.

Anthropology Links
http://www.gmu.edu/departments/anthropology/anthrframe.html

George Mason University's Department of Anthropology Web site provides a number of interesting links.

Latin American Studies
http://www.library.arizona.edu/research.htm

Click on Latin American Studies to access an extensive list of resources—links to encyclopedias, journals, indexes, almanacs, and handbooks, and to the Latin American Network Information Center and Internet Resources for Latin American Studies.

Web Resources for Visual Anthropology
http://www.usc.edu/dept/elab/urlist/index.html

This UR-List offers a mouse-click selection of Web resources by cross-indexing 375 anthropological sites according to 22 subject categories.

UNIT 1: Anthropological Perspectives

American Indian Sites on the Internet
http://www.library.arizona.edu/library/teams/sst/anthro/web/indians.html

This Web page points out a number of Internet sites of interest to different kinds of anthropologists.

Archaeology and Anthropology Computing and Study Skills
http://www.bodley.ox.ac.uk/isca/CASShome.html

Consult this site of the Institute of Social and Cultural Anthropology to learn about ways to use the computer as an aid in conducting fieldwork, methodology, and analysis.

The Crisis in Anthropology
http://www.comma2000.com/max-gluckman/index.html

The differences between anthropologists' perspectives are made clear in this first Max Gluckman Memorial Lecture, delivered by Professor Bruce Kapferer on May 17, 1997.

Introduction to Anthropological Fieldwork and Ethnography
http://web.mit.edu/dumit/www/syl-anth.html

This class outline can serve as an invaluable resource for conducting anthropological fieldwork. Addressing such topics as The Interview and Power Relations in the Field, the site identifies many important books and articles for further reading.

Theory in Anthropology
http://www.indiana.edu/~wanthro/theory.htm

These Web pages cover subdisciplines within anthropology, changes in perspectives over time, and prominent theorists, reflecting 30 years of dramatic changes in the field.

UNIT 2: Culture and Communication

Exploratorium Magazine: "The Evolution of Languages"
http://www.exploratorium.edu/exploring/language

Where did languages come from and how did they evolve? This educational site explains the history and origin of language. You can also investigate words, word stems, and the similarities between different languages.

Hypertext and Ethnography
http://www.umanitoba.ca/anthropology/tutor/aaa_presentation.html

Presented by Brian Schwimmer of the University of Manitoba, this site will be of great value to people who are interested in culture and communication. Schwimmer addresses such topics as multivocality and complex symbolization.

Language Extinction
http://www.colorado.edu/iec/alis/articles/langext.htm

"An often overlooked fact in the ecological race against environmental extinction is that many of the world's languages are disappearing at an alarming rate." This article investigates language extinction and its possible consequences.

Showcase Anthropology
http://www.anthropology.wisc.edu/chaysimire/

Examples of documents that make innovative use of the Web as a tool for "an anthropology of the future"—one consisting of multimedia representations in a nonlinear and interactive form—are provided on this Web site.

UNIT 3: The Organization of Society and Culture

Huarochiri, a Peruvian Culture in Time
http://wiscinfo.doit.wisc.edu/chaysimire/

Take a tour of this Andean province, visit Tupicocha (a modern village), and learn about the ancient Quechua Book and Khipus, a unique legacy.

Smithsonian Institution Web Site
http://www.si.edu

Looking through this site, which provides access to many of the enormous resources of the Smithsonian, will give a sense of the scope of anthropological inquiry today.

Sociology Guy's Anthropology Links
http://www.trinity.edu/~mkearl/anthro.html

This list of anthropology resources on the Web is suggested by a sociology professor at Trinity University and includes cultures of Asia, Africa, the Middle East; Aztecan, Mayan, and aboriginal cultures; sections on Mythology, Folklore, Legends, and Archaeology; plus much more.

www.dushkin.com/online/

What Is Culture?
http://www.wsu.edu:8001/vcwsu/commons/topics/culture/culture-index.html

Here is a source for everything you might want to know about "culture," starting with a baseline definition.

UNIT 4: Other Families, Other Ways

Kinship and Social Organization
http://www.umanitoba.ca/anthropology/tutor/kinmenu.html

Kinship, marriage systems, residence rules, incest taboos, and cousin marriages are explored in this kinship tutorial.

UNIT 5: Gender and Status

Arranged Marriages
http://women3rdworld.miningco.com/cs/arrangedmarriage/

This site, provided by ABOUT, contains a number of papers on arranged marriages. It also has links to other related women's issues, subjects, and forums.

Bonobo Sex and Society
http://songweaver.com/info/bonobos.html

This site includes a *Scientific American* article discussing a primate's behavior that challenges traditional assumptions about male supremacy in human evolution.

FGM Research
http://www.amnesty.org/ailib/intcam/femgen/fgm1.htm

Dedicated to research pertaining to Female Genital Mutilation (FGM), this site presents a variety of perspectives: psychological, cultural, sexual, human rights, and so on.

OMIM Home Page-Online Mendelian Inheritance in Man
http://www3.ncbi.nlm.nih.gov/omim/

This National Center for Biotechnology Information database is a catalog of human genes and genetic disorders. It contains text, pictures, and reference information.

Reflections on Sinai Bedouin Women
http://www.sherryart.com/women/bedouin.html

Social anthropologist Ann Gardner tells something of her culture shock while first living with a Sinai Bedouin family as a teenager. She provides links to sites about organization of society and culture, particularly with regard to women.

UNIT 6: Religion, Belief and Ritual

Anthropology Resources Page
http://www.usd.edu/anth/

Many topics can be accessed from this University of South Dakota Web site. Repatriation and reburial are just two.

Masks
http://www.mpm.edu/collect/mask.html

This article, reprinted from *Lore* magazine, Fall 1989 issue, is an essay on masks, written by George Ulrich, which describes the importance of masks throughout the cultural history of the world.

Philosophy of Religion: Magic, Ritual, and Symbolism
http://www.kcmetro.cc.mo.us/longview/socsci/philosophy/religion/magic.htm

This site presents course notes for a Philosophy of Religion class in which the roles of magic, ritual, and symbolism are examined. Links to many helpful reading options are provided.

Yahoo: Society and Culture: Death
http://dir.yahoo.com/Society_and_Culture/Death_and_Dying/

This Yahoo site has an extensive index to diverse issues related to how different people approach death, such as beliefs about euthanasia, reincarnation, and burial.

UNIT 7: Sociocultural Change: The Impact of the West

Human Rights and Humanitarian Assistance
http://www.etown.edu/vl/humrts.html

Through this site you can conduct research into a number of human rights topics and issues affecting indigenous peoples in the modern era.

The Indigenous Rights Movement in the Pacific
http://www.inmotionmagazine.com/pacific.html

This article addresses issues that pertain to the problems of the Pacific Island peoples as a result of U.S. colonial expansion in the Pacific and Caribbean 100 years ago.

RomNews Network—Online
http://www.romnews.com/community/index.php

This is a Web site dedicated to news and information for and about the Roma (European Gypsies). Visit here to learn more about their culture and the discrimination they constantly face.

WWW Virtual Library: Indigenous Studies
http://www.cwis.org/wwwvl/indig-vl.html

This site presents resources collected by the Center for World Indigenous Studies (CWIS) in Africa, Asia and the Middle East, Central and South America, Europe, and the Pacific.

We highly recommend that you review our Web site for expanded information and our other product lines. We are continually updating and adding links to our Web site in order to offer you the most usable and useful information that will support and expand the value of your Annual Editions. You can reach us at: *http://www.dushkin.com/annualeditions/*.

World Map

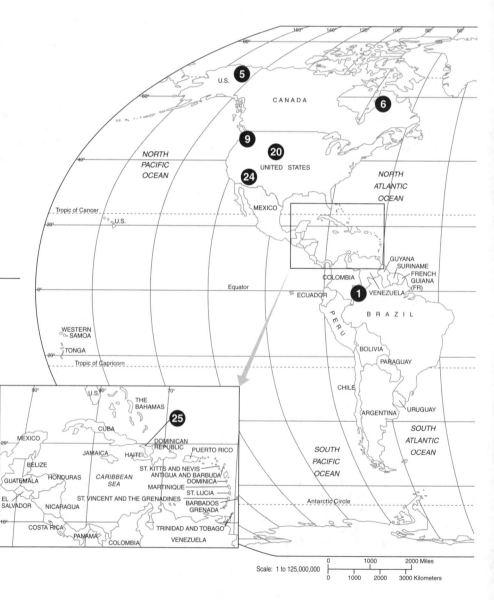

Scale: 1 to 125,000,000

0   1000   2000 Miles

0   1000   2000   3000 Kilometers

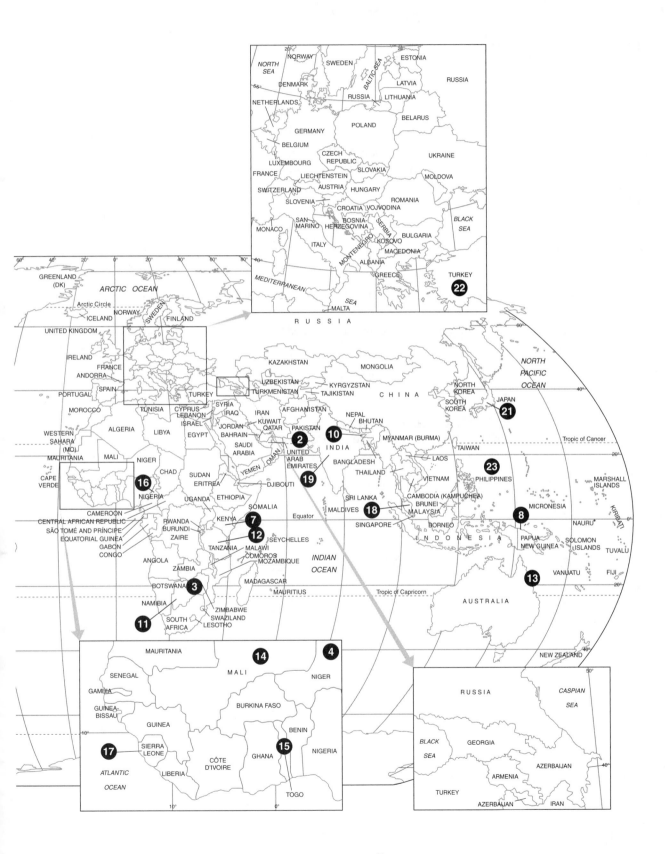

UNIT 1
Anthropological Perspectives

Unit Selections

1. **Doing Fieldwork Among the Yąnomamö**, Napoleon A. Chagnon
2. **Doctor, Lawyer, Indian Chief**, Richard Kurin
3. **Eating Christmas in the Kalahari**, Richard Borshay Lee
4. **Coping with Culture Clash**, Anver Versi

Key Points to Consider

- What is culture shock?

- How can anthropologists who become personally involved with a community through participant observation maintain their objectivity as scientists?

- In what ways do the results of fieldwork depend on the kinds of questions asked?

- In what sense is sharing intrinsic to egalitarianism?

- How can culture clash be avoided when conducting international business?

 **Links: www.dushkin.com/online/**
These sites are annotated in the World Wide Web pages.

American Indian Sites on the Internet
http://www.library.arizona.edu/library/teams/sst/anthro/web/indians.html

Archaeology and Anthropology Computing and Study Skills
http://www.bodley.ox.ac.uk/isca/CASShome.html

The Crisis in Anthropology
http://www.comma2000.com/max-gluckman/index.html

Introduction to Anthropological Fieldwork and Ethnography
http://web.mit.edu/dumit/www/syl-anth.html

Theory in Anthropology
http://www.indiana.edu/~wanthro/theory.htm

For at least a century, the goals of anthropology have been to describe societies and cultures throughout the world and to compare the differences and similarities among them. Anthropologists study in a variety of settings and situations, ranging from small hamlets and villages to neighborhoods and corporate offices of major urban centers throughout the world. They study hunters and gatherers, peasants, farmers, labor leaders, politicians, and bureaucrats. They examine religious life in Latin America as well as revolutionary movements.

Wherever practicable, anthropologists take on the role of "participant observer." Through active involvement in the lifeways of people, they hope to gain an insider's perspective without sacrificing the objectivity of the trained scientist. Sometimes the conditions for achieving such a goal seem to form an almost insurmountable barrier, but anthropologists call on persistence, adaptability, and imagination to overcome the odds against them.

The diversity of focus in anthropology means that it is earmarked less by its particular subject matter than by its perspective. Although the discipline relates to both the biological and social sciences, anthropologists know that the boundaries drawn between disciplines are highly artificial. For example, while in theory it is possible to examine only the social organization of a family unit or the organization of political power in a nation-state, in reality it is impossible to separate the biological from the social, from the economic, from the political. The explanatory perspective of anthropology, as the articles in this unit demonstrate, is to seek out interrelationships among all these factors. The first three articles in this section illustrate varying degrees of difficulty that an anthropologist may encounter in taking on the role of the participant observer. Napoleon Chagnon's essay, "Doing Fieldwork Among the Yąnomamö," shows the hardships imposed by certain physical conditions and the vast differences in values and attitudes to be bridged by the anthropologist just to get along.

Even the realm of international business is not a "one-size-fits-all phenomenon," as Anver Versi points out in "Coping with Culture Clash." In fact, an inability to understand one another's business culture can cost multinationals billions of dollars.

Richard Kurin, in "Doctor, Lawyer, Indian Chief," and Richard Lee, in "Eating Christmas in the Kalahari," apparently had few problems with the physical conditions and the personalities of the people they were studying. However, they were not completely accepted by the communities until they modified their behavior to conform to the expectations of their hosts and found ways to participate as equals in the socioeconomic exchange systems.

Much is at stake in these discussions as we attempt to achieve a more objective understanding of the diversity of peoples' ways. After all, the purpose of anthropology is not only to describe and explain, but also to develop a special vision of the world in which cultural alternatives (past, present, and future) can be measured against one another and used as guides for human action.

Doing Fieldwork among the Yąnomamö[1]

Napoleon A. Chagnon

VIGNETTE

The Yąnomamö are thinly scattered over a vast and verdant tropical forest, living in small villages that are separated by many miles of unoccupied land. They have no writing, but they have a rich and complex language. Their clothing is more decorative than protective. Well-dressed men sport nothing more than a few cotton strings around their wrists, ankles, and waists. They tie the foreskins of their penises to the waist string. Women dress about the same. Much of their daily life revolves around gardening, hunting, collecting wild foods, collecting firewood, fetching water, visiting with each other, gossiping, and making the few material possessions they own: baskets, hammocks, bows, arrows, and colorful pigments with which they paint their bodies. Life is relatively easy in the sense that they can 'earn a living' with about three hours' work per day. Most of what they eat they cultivate in their gardens, and most of that is plantains—a kind of cooking banana that is usually eaten green, either roasted on the coals or boiled in pots. Their meat comes from a large variety of game animals, hunted daily by the men. It is usually roasted on coals or smoked, and is always well done. Their villages are round and open—and very public. One can hear, see, and smell almost everything that goes on anywhere in the village. Privacy is rare, but sexual discreetness is possible in the garden or at night while others sleep. The villages can be as small as 40 to 50 people or as large as 300 people, but in all cases there are many more children and babies than there are adults. This is true of most primitive populations and of our own demographic past. Life expectancy is short.

The Yąnomamö fall into the category of Tropical Forest Indians called 'foot people.' They avoid large rivers and live in interfluvial plains of the major rivers. They have neighbors to the north, Carib-speaking Ye'kwana, who are true 'river people': They make elegant, large dug-out canoes and travel extensively along the major waterways. For the Yąnomamö, a large stream is an obstacle and can be crossed only in the dry season. Thus, they have traditionally avoided larger rivers and, because of this, contact with outsiders who usually come by river.

They enjoy taking trips when the jungle abounds with seasonally ripe wild fruits and vegetables. Then, the large village—the *shabono*—is abandoned for a few weeks and everyone camps out for from one to several days away from the village and garden. On these trips, they make temporary huts from poles, vines, and leaves, each family making a separate hut.

Two major seasons dominate their annual cycle: the wet season, which inundates the low-lying jungle, making travel difficult, and the dry season—the time of visiting other villages to feast, trade, and politic with allies. The dry season is also the time when raiders can travel and strike silently at their unsuspecting enemies. The Yąnomamö are still conducting intervillage warfare, a phenomenon that affects all aspects of their social organization, settlement pattern, and daily routines. It is not simply 'ritualistic' war: At least one-fourth of all adult males die violently in the area I lived in.

Social life is organized around those same principles utilized by all tribesmen: kinship relationships, descent from ancestors, marriage exchanges between kinship/descent groups, and the transient charisma of distinguished headmen who attempt to keep order in the village and whose responsibility it is to determine the village's relationships with those in other villages. Their positions are largely the result of kinship and marriage patterns; they come from the largest kinship groups within the village. They can, by their personal wit, wisdom, and charisma, become autocrats, but most of them are largely 'greaters' among equals. They, too, must clear gardens, plant crops, collect wild foods, and hunt. They are simultaneously peacemakers and valiant warriors. Peacemaking often requires the threat or actual use of force, and most headmen have an acquired reputation for being *waiteri*: fierce.

The social dynamics within villages are involved with giving and receiving marriageable girls. Marriages are arranged by older kin, usually men, who are brothers, uncles, and the father. It is a political process, for girls are promised in marriage while they are young, and the men who do this attempt to create alliances with other men via marriage exchanges. There is a shortage of women due in part to a sex-ratio imbalance in the younger age categories, but also complicated by the fact that some men have multiple wives. Most fighting within the village stems from sexual affairs or failure to deliver a promised woman—or out-and-out seizure of a married woman by some other man. This can lead to internal fighting and conflict of such an intensity that villages split up and fission, each group then becoming a new village and, often, enemies to each other.

But their conflicts are not blind, uncontrolled violence. They have a series of graded forms of violence that ranges from chest-pounding and club-fighting duels to out-and-out shooting to kill. This gives them a good deal of flexibility in settling disputes without immediate resort to lethal violence. In addition, they have developed patterns of alliance and friendship that serve to limit violence—trading and feasting with others in order to become friends. These alliances can, and often do, result in intervillage exchanges of marriageable women, which leads to additional amity between villages. No good thing lasts forever, and most alliances crumble. Old friends become hostile and, occasionally, treacherous. Each village must therefore be keenly aware that its neighbors are fickle and must behave accordingly. The thin line between friendship and animosity must be traversed by the village leaders, whose political acumen and strategies are both admirable and complex.

Each village, then, is a replica of all others in a broad sense. But each village is part of a larger political, demographic, and ecological process, and it is difficult to attempt to understand the village without knowing something of the larger forces that affect it and its particular history with all its neighbors.

COLLECTING THE DATA IN THE FIELD

I have now spent over 60 months with Yąnomamö, during which time I gradually learned their language and, up to a point, submerged myself in their culture and way of life.[2] As my research progressed, the thing that impressed me most was the importance that aggression played in shaping their culture. I had the opportunity to witness a good many incidents that expressed individual vindictiveness on the one hand and collective bellicosity on the other hand. These

ranged in seriousness from the ordinary incidents of wife beating and chest pounding to dueling and organized raids by parties that set out with the intention of ambushing and killing men from enemy villages. One of the villages was raided approximately twenty-five times during my first 15 months of fieldwork—six times by the group among whom I was living. And, the history of every village I investigated, from 1964 to 1991, was intimately bound up in patterns of warfare with neighbors that shaped its politics and determined where it was found at any point in time and how it dealt with its current neighbors.

The fact that the Yąnomamö have lived in a chronic state of warfare is reflected in their mythology, ceremonies, settlement pattern, political behavior, and marriage practices. Accordingly, I have organized this case study in such a way that students can appreciate the effects of warfare on Yąnomamö culture in general and on their social organization and political relationships in particular.

I collected the data under somewhat trying circumstances, some of which I will describe to give a rough idea of what is generally meant when anthropologists speak of 'culture shock' and 'fieldwork.' It should be borne in mind, however, that each field situation is in many respects unique, so that the problems I encountered do not necessarily exhaust the range of possible problems other anthropologists have confronted in other areas. There are a few problems, however, that seem to be nearly universal among anthropological fieldworkers, particularly those having to do with eating, bathing, sleeping, lack of privacy, loneliness, or discovering that the people you are living with have a lower opinion of you than you have of them or you yourself are not as culturally or emotionally 'flexible' as you assumed.

The Yąnomamö can be difficult people to live with at times, but I have spoken to colleagues who have had difficulties living in the communities they studied. These things vary from society to society, and probably from one anthropologist to the next. I have also done limited fieldwork among the Yąnomamö's northern neighbors, the Carib-speaking Ye'kwana Indians. By contrast to many

experiences I had among the Yąnomamö, the Ye'kwana were very pleasant and charming, all of them anxious to help me and honor bound to show any visitor the numerous courtesies of their system of etiquette. In short, they approached the image of 'primitive man' that I had conjured up in my mind before doing fieldwork, a kind of 'Rousseauian' view, and it was sheer pleasure to work with them. Other anthropologists have also noted sharp contrasts in the people they study from one field situation to another. One of the most startling examples of this is in the work of Colin Turnbull, who first studied the Ituri Pygmies (1965, 1983) and found them delightful to live with, but then studied the Ik (1972) of the desolate outcroppings of the Kenya/Uganda/Sudan border region, a people he had difficulty coping with intellectually, emotionally, and physically. While it is possible that the anthropologist's reactions to a particular people are personal and idiosyncratic, it nevertheless remains true that there are enormous differences between whole peoples, differences that affect the anthropologist in often dramatic ways.

Hence, what I say about some of my experiences is probably equally true of the experiences of many other fieldworkers. I describe some of them here for the benefit of future anthropologists—because I think I could have profited by reading about the pitfalls and field problems of my own teachers. At the very least I might have been able to avoid some of my more stupid errors. In this regard there is a growing body of excellent descriptive work on field research. Students who plan to make a career in anthropology should consult these works, which cover a wide range of field situations in the ethnographic present.[3]

The Longest Day: The First One

My first day in the field illustrated to me what my teachers meant when they spoke of 'culture shock.' I had traveled in a small, aluminum rowboat propelled by a large outboard motor for two and a half days. This took me from the territorial capital, a small town on the Orinoco River, deep into Yąnomamö country. On the morning of the third day we reached a small mission settlement, the field 'headquarters' of a group of Americans who were working in two Yąnomamö villages. The missionaries had come out of these villages to hold their annual conference on the progress of their mission work and were conducting their meetings when I arrived. We picked up a passenger at the mission station, James P. Barker, the first non-Yąnomamö to make a sustained, permanent contact with the tribe (in 1950). He had just returned from a year's furlough in the United States, where I had earlier visited him before leaving for Venezuela. He agreed to accompany me to the village I had selected for my base of operations to introduce me to the Indians. This village was also his own home base, but he had not been there for over a year and did not plan to join me for another three months. Mr. Barker had been living with this particular group about five years.

We arrived at the village, Bisaasi-teri, about 2:00 P.M. and docked the boat along the muddy bank at the terminus of the path used by Yąnomamö to fetch their drinking water. It was hot and muggy, and my clothing was soaked with perspiration. It clung uncomfortably to my body, as it did thereafter for the remainder of the work. The small biting gnats, *bareto*, were out in astronomical numbers, for it was the beginning of the dry season. My face and hands were swollen from the venom of their numerous stings. In just a few moments I was to meet my first Yąnomamö, my first primitive man. What would he be like? I had visions of entering the village and seeing 125 social facts running about altruistically calling each other kinship terms and sharing food, each waiting and anxious to have me collect his genealogy. I would wear them out in turn. Would they like me? This was important to me; I wanted them to be so fond of me that they would adopt me into their kinship system and way of life. I had heard that successful anthropologists always get adopted by their people. I had learned during my seven years of anthropological training at the University of Michigan that kinship was equivalent to society in primitive tribes and that it was a moral way of life, 'moral' being something 'good' and 'desirable.' I was determined to work my way into their moral system of kinship and become a member of their society—to be 'accepted' by them.

How Did They Accept You?

My heart began to pound as we approached the village and heard the buzz of activity within the circular compound. Mr. Barker commented that he was anxious to see if any changes had taken place while he was away and wondered how many of them had died during his absence. I nervously felt my back pocket to make sure that my notebook was still there and felt personally more secure when I touched it.

The entrance to the village was covered over with brush and dry palm leaves. We pushed them aside to expose the low opening to the village. The excitement of meeting my first Yąnomamö was almost unbearable as I duck-waddled through the low passage into the village clearing.

I looked up and gasped when I saw a dozen burly, naked, sweaty, hideous men staring at us down the shafts of their drawn arrows! Immense wads of green tobacco were stuck between their lower teeth and lips making them look even more hideous, and strands of dark-green slime dripped or hung from their nostrils—strands so long that they clung to their pectoral muscles or drizzled down their chins. We arrived at the village while the men were blowing a hallucinogenic drug up their noses. One of the side effects of the drug is a runny nose. The mucus is always saturated with the green powder and they usually let it run freely from their nostrils. My next discovery was that there were a dozen or so vicious, underfed dogs snapping at my legs, circling me as if I were to be their next meal. I just stood there holding my notebook, helpless and pathetic. Then the stench of the decaying vegetation and filth hit me and I almost got sick. I was horrified. What kind of welcome was this for the person who came here to live with you and learn your way of life, to become friends with you? They put their weapons down when they recognized Barker and returned to their chanting, keeping a nervous eye on the village entrances.

We had arrived just after a serious fight. Seven women had been abducted the day before by a neighboring group, and the local men and their guests had just that morning recovered five of them in a brutal club fight that nearly ended in a shooting war. The abductors, angry because they had lost five of their seven new captives, vowed to raid the Bisaasi-teri. When we arrived and entered the village unexpectedly, the Indians feared that we were the raiders. On several occasions during the next two hours the men in the village jumped to their feet, armed themselves, nocked their arrows and waited nervously for the noise outside the village to be identified. My enthusiasm for collecting ethnographic facts diminished in proportion to the number of times such an alarm was raised. In fact, I was relieved when Barker suggested that we sleep across the river for the evening. It would be safer over there.

As we walked down the path to the boat, I pondered the wisdom of having decided to spend a year and a half with these people before I had even seen what they were like. I am not ashamed to admit that had there been a diplomatic way out, I would have ended my fieldwork then and there. I did not look forward to the next day—and months—when I would be left alone with the Yąnomamö; I did not speak a word of their language, and they were decidedly different from what I had imagined them to be. The whole situation was depressing, and I wondered why I ever decided to switch from physics and engineering in the first place. I had not eaten all day, I was soaking wet from perspiration, the *bareto* were biting me, and I was covered with red pigment, the result of a dozen or so complete examinations I had been given by as many very pushy Yąnomamö men. These examinations capped an otherwise grim day. The men would blow their noses into their hands, flick as much of the mucus off that would separate in a snap of the wrist, wipe the residue into their hair, and then carefully examine my face, arms, legs, hair, and the contents of my pockets. I asked Barker how to say, 'Your hands are dirty'; my comments were met by the Yąnomamö in the following way: They would 'clean' their hands by spitting a quantity of slimy tobacco juice into them, rub them together, grin, and then proceed with the examination.

Mr. Barker and I crossed the river and slung our hammocks. When he pulled his hammock out of a rubber bag, a heavy disagreeable odor of mildewed cotton and stale wood smoke came with it. 'Even the missionaries are filthy,' I thought to myself. Within two weeks, everything I owned smelled the same way, and I lived with that odor for the remainder of the fieldwork. My own habits of personal cleanliness declined to such levels that I didn't even mind being examined by the Yąnomamö, as I was not much cleaner than they were after I had adjusted to the circumstances. It is difficult to blow your nose gracefully when you are stark naked and the invention of handkerchiefs is millenia away.

Life in the Jungle: Oatmeal, Peanut Butter, and Bugs

It isn't easy to plop down in the Amazon Basin for a year and get immediately into the anthropological swing of things. You have been told about horrible diseases, snakes, jaguars, electric eels, little spiny fish that will swim up your urine into your penis, quicksand, and getting lost. Some of the dangers are real, but your imagination makes them more real and threatening than many of them really are. What my teachers never bothered to advise me about, however, was the mundane, nonexciting, and trivial stuff—like eating, defecating, sleeping, or keeping clean. These turned out to be the bane of my existence during the first several months of field research. I set up my household in Barker's abandoned mud hut, a few yards from the village of Bisaasi-teri, and immediately set to work building my own mud/thatch hut with the help of the Yąnomamö. Meanwhile, I had to eat and try to do my 'field research.' I soon discovered that it was an enormously time-consuming task to maintain my own body in the manner to which it had grown accustomed in the relatively antiseptic environment of the northern United States. Either I could be relatively well fed and relatively comfortable in a fresh change of clothes and do very little fieldwork, or I could do considerably more fieldwork and be less well fed and less comfortable.

It is appalling how complicated it can be to make oatmeal in the jungle. First, I had to make two trips to the river to haul the water. Next, I had to prime my kerosene stove with alcohol to get it burning, a tricky procedure when you are trying to mix powdered milk and fill a coffee pot at the same time. The alcohol prime always burned out before I could turn the kerosene on, and I would have to start all over. Or, I would turn the kerosene on, optimistically hoping that the Coleman element was still hot enough to vaporize the fuel, and start a small fire in my palm-thatched hut as the liquid kerosene squirted all over the table and walls and then ignited. Many amused Yąnomamö onlookers quickly learned the English phrase 'Oh, Shit!' and, once they discovered that the phrase offended and irritated the missionaries, they used it as often as they could in their presence. I usually had to start over with the alcohol. Then I had to boil the oatmeal and pick the bugs out of it. All my supplies, of course, were carefully stored in rat-proof, moisture-proof, and insect-proof containers, not one of which ever served its purpose adequately. Just taking things out of the multiplicity of containers and repacking them afterward was a minor project in itself. By the time I had hauled the water to cook with, unpacked my food, prepared the oatmeal, milk, and coffee, heated water for dishes, washed and dried the dishes, repacked the food in the containers, stored the containers in locked trunks, and cleaned up my mess, the ceremony of preparing breakfast had brought me almost up to lunch time!

Eating three meals a day was simply out of the question. I solved the problem by eating a single meal that could be prepared in a single container, or, at most, in two containers, washed my dishes only when there were no clean ones left, using cold river water, and wore each change of clothing at least a week to cut down on my laundry problem—a courageous undertaking in the tropics. I reeked like a jockstrap that had been left to mildew in the bottom of some dark gym locker. I also became less concerned about sharing my provisions with the rats, insects, Yąnomamö, and the elements, thereby eliminating the need for my complicated storage process. I was able to last most of the day on *café con leche*, heavily sugared espresso coffee diluted about five to one with hot milk. I would prepare this in the evening and store it in a large thermos. Frequently, my single meal was no more complicated than a can of sardines and a package of soggy crackers. But at least two or three times a week I would do something 'special' and sophisticated, like make a batch of oatmeal or boil rice and add a can of tuna fish or tomato paste to it. I even saved time by devising a water system that obviated the trips to the river. I had a few sheets of tin roofing brought in and made a rain water trap; I caught the water on the tin surface, funneled it into an empty gasoline drum, and then ran a plastic hose from the drum to my hut. When the drum was exhausted in the dry season, I would get a few Yąnomamö boys to fill it with buckets of water from the river, 'paying' them with crackers, of which they grew all too fond all too soon.

I ate much less when I traveled with the Yąnomamö to visit other villages. Most of the time my travel diet consisted of roasted or boiled green plantains (cooking bananas) that I obtained from the Yąnomamö, but I always carried a few cans of sardines with me in case I got lost or stayed away longer than I had planned. I found peanut butter and crackers a very nourishing 'trail' meal, and a simple one to prepare. It was nutritious and portable, and only one tool was required to make the meal: a hunting knife that could be cleaned by wiping the blade on a convenient leaf. More importantly, it was one of the few foods the Yąnomamö would let me eat in relative peace. It looked suspiciously like animal feces to them, an impression I encouraged. I referred to the peanut butter as the feces of babies or 'cattle.' They found this disgusting and repugnant. They did not know what 'cattle' were, but were increasingly aware that I ate several canned products of such an animal. Tin cans were thought of as containers made of 'machete skins,' but how the cows got inside was always a mystery to them. I went out of my way to describe my foods in such a way as to make them sound unpalatable to them, for it gave me some peace of mind while I ate: They wouldn't beg for a share of something that was too horrible to contemplate. Fieldworkers develop strange defense mechanisms and strategies, and this was one of my own forms of adaptation to the fieldwork. On another occasion I was eating a can of frankfurters and growing very weary of the demands from one of the onlookers for a share in my meal. When he finally asked what I was eating, I replied: 'Beef.' He then asked: 'Shaki![4] What part of the animal are you eating?' To which I replied, 'Guess.' He muttered a contemptuous epithet, but stopped asking for a share. He got back at me later, as we shall see.

Meals were a problem in a way that had nothing to do with the inconvenience of preparing them. Food sharing is important to the Yąnomamö in the context of displaying friendship. 'I am hungry!' is almost a form of greeting with them. I could not possibly have brought enough food with me to feed the entire village, yet they seemed to overlook this logistic fact as they begged for my food. What became fixed in their minds was the fact that I did not share my food with whomsoever was present—usually a small crowd—at each and every meal. Nor could I easily enter their system of reciprocity with respect to food. Every time one of them 'gave' me something 'freely,' he would dog me for months to 'pay him back,' not necessarily with food but with knives, fishhooks, axes, and so on. Thus, if I accepted a plantain from someone in a different village while I was on a visit, he would most likely visit me in the future and demand a machete as payment for the time that he 'fed' me. I usually reacted to these kinds of demands by giving a banana, the customary reciprocity in their culture—food for food—but this would be a disappointment for the individual who had nursed visions of that single plantain growing into a machete over time. Many years after beginning my fieldwork, I was approached by one of the prominent men who demanded a machete for a piece of meat he claimed he had given me five or six years earlier.

Despite the fact that most of them knew I would not share my food with

them at their request, some of them always showed up at my hut during mealtime. I gradually resigned myself to this and learned to ignore their persistent demands while I ate. Some of them would get angry because I failed to give in, but most of them accepted it as just a peculiarity of the subhuman foreigner who had come to live among them. If or when I did accede to a request for a share of my food, my hut quickly filled with Yąnomamö, each demanding their share of the food that I had just given to one of them. Their begging for food was not provoked by hunger, but by a desire to try something new and to attempt to establish a coercive relationship in which I would accede to a demand. If one received something, all others would immediately have to test the system to see if they, too, could coerce me.

A few of them went out of their way to make my meals downright unpleasant—to spite me for not sharing, especially if it was a food that they had tried before and liked, or a food that was part of their own cuisine. For example, I was eating a cracker with peanut butter and honey one day. The Yąnomamö will do almost anything for honey, one of the most prized delicacies in their own diet. One of my cynical onlookers—the fellow who had earlier watched me eating frankfurters—immediately recognized the honey and knew that I would not share the tiny precious bottle. It would be futile to even ask. Instead, he glared at me and queried icily, 'Shaki! What kind of animal semen are you pouring onto your food and eating?' His question had the desired effect and my meal ended.

Finally, there was the problem of being lonely and separated from your own kind, especially your family. I tried to overcome this by seeking personal friendships among the Yąnomamö. This usually complicated the matter because all my 'friends' simply used my confidence to gain privileged access to my hut and my cache of steel tools and trade goods—and looted me when I wasn't looking. I would be bitterly disappointed that my erstwhile friend thought no more of me than to finesse our personal relationship exclusively with the intention of getting at my locked up possessions, and my depression would hit new lows every

time I discovered this. The loss of the possessions bothered me much less than the shock that I was, as far as most of them were concerned, nothing more than a source of desirable items. No holds were barred in relieving me of these, since I was considered something subhuman, a non-Yąnomamö.

The hardest thing to learn to live with was the incessant, passioned, and often aggressive demands they would make. It would become so unbearable at times that I would have to lock myself in my hut periodically just to escape from it. Privacy is one of our culture's most satisfying achievements, one you never think about until you suddenly have none. It is like not appreciating how good your left thumb feels until someone hits it with a hammer. But I did not want privacy for its own sake; rather, I simply had to get away from the begging. Day and night for almost the entire time I lived with the Yąnomamö, I was plagued by such demands as: 'Give me a knife, I am poor!'; 'If you don't take me with you on your next trip to Widokaiyateri, I'll chop a hole in your canoe!'; 'Take us hunting up the Mavaca River with your shotgun or we won't help you!'; 'Give me some matches so I can trade with the Reyaboböwei-teri, and be quick about it or I'll hit you!'; 'Share your food with me, or I'll burn your hut!'; 'Give me a flashlight so I can hunt at night!'; 'Give me all your medicine, I itch all over!'; 'Give me an ax or I'll break into your hut when you are away and steal all of them!' And so I was bombarded by such demands day after day, month after month, until I could not bear to see a Yąnomamö at times.

It was not as difficult to become calloused to the incessant begging as it was to ignore the sense of urgency, the impassioned tone of voice and whining, or the intimidation and aggression with which many of the demands were made. It was likewise difficult to adjust to the fact that the Yąnomamö refused to accept 'No' for an answer until or unless it seethed with passion and intimidation—which it did after a few months. So persistent and characteristic is the begging that the early 'semiofficial' maps made by the Venezuelan Malaria Control Service *(Malariología)* designated the site of their first permanent field station, next to the village of Bisaasi-teri, as *Yababuhii:* 'Gimme.' I had to become like the Yąnomamö to be able to get along with them on their terms: somewhat sly, aggressive, intimidating, and pushy.

It became indelibly clear to me shortly after I arrived there that had I failed to adjust in this fashion I would have lost six months of supplies to them in a single day or would have spent most of my time ferrying them around in my canoe or taking them on long hunting trips. As it was, I did spend a considerable amount of time doing these things and did succumb often to their outrageous demands for axes and machetes, at least at first, for things changed as I became more fluent in their language and learned how to defend myself socially as well as verbally. More importantly, had I failed to demonstrate that I could not be pushed around beyond a certain point, I would have been the subject of far more ridicule, theft, and practical jokes than was the actual case. In short, I had to acquire a certain proficiency in their style of interpersonal politics and to learn how to imply subtly that certain potentially undesirable, but unspecified, consequences might follow if they did such and such to me. They do this to each other incessantly in order to establish precisely the point at which they cannot goad or intimidate an individual any further without precipitating some kind of retaliation. As soon as I realized this and gradually acquired the self-confidence to adopt this strategy, it became clear that much of the intimidation was calculated to determine my flash point or my 'last ditch' position—and I got along much better with them. Indeed, I even regained some lost ground. It was sort of like a political, interpersonal game that everyone had to play, but one in which each individual sooner or later had to give evidence that his bluffs and implied threats could be backed up with a sanction. I suspect that the frequency of wife beating is a component in this syndrome, since men can display their *waiteri* (ferocity) and 'show' others that they are capable of great violence. Beating a wife with a club is one way of displaying ferocity, one that does not expose the man

to much danger—unless the wife has concerned, aggressive brothers in the village who will come to her aid. Apparently an important thing in wife beating is that the man has displayed his presumed potential for violence and the intended message is that other men ought to treat him with circumspection, caution, and even deference.

After six months, the level of Yąnomamö demand was tolerable in Bisaasi-teri, the village I used for my base of operations. We had adjusted somewhat to each other and knew what to expect with regard to demands for food, trade goods, and favors. Had I elected to remain in just one Yąnomamö village for the entire duration of my first 15 months of fieldwork, the experience would have been far more enjoyable than it actually was. However, as I began to understand the social and political dynamics of this village, it became patently obvious that I would have to travel to many other villages to determine the demographic bases and political histories that lay behind what I could understand in the village of Bisaasi-teri. I began making regular trips to some dozen neighboring Yąnomamö villages as my language fluency improved. I collected local genealogies there, or rechecked and cross-checked those I had collected elsewhere. Hence, the intensity of begging was relatively constant and relatively high for the duration of my fieldwork, for I had to establish my personal position in each village I visited and revisited.

For the most part, my own 'fierceness' took the form of shouting back at the Yąnomamö as loudly and as passionately as they shouted at me, especially at first, when I did not know much of the language. As I became more fluent and learned more about their political tactics, I became more sophisticated in the art of bluffing and brinksmanship. For example, I paid one young man a machete (then worth about $2.50) to cut a palm tree and help me make boards from the wood. I used these to fashion a flooring in the bottom of my dugout canoe to keep my possessions out of the water that always seeped into the canoe and sloshed around. That afternoon I was working with one of my informants in the village.

The long-awaited mission supply boat arrived and most of the Yąnomamö ran out of the village to see the supplies and try to beg items from the crew. I continued to work in the village for another hour or so and then went down to the river to visit with the men on the supply boat. When I reached the river I noticed, with anger and frustration, that the Yąnomamö had chopped up all my new floor boards to use as crude paddles to get their own canoes across the river to the supply boat.[5] I knew that if I ignored this abuse I would have invited the Yąnomamö to take even greater liberties with my possessions in the future. I got into my canoe, crossed the river, and docked amidst their flimsy, leaky craft. I shouted loudly to them, attracting their attention. They were somewhat sheepish, but all had mischievous grins on their impish faces. A few of them came down to the canoe, where I proceeded with a spirited lecture that revealed my anger at their audacity and license. I explained that I had just that morning paid one of them a machete for bringing me the palmwood, how hard I had worked to shape each board and place it in the canoe, how carefully and painstakingly I had tied each one in with vines, how much I had perspired, how many *bareto* bites I had suffered, and so on. Then, with exaggerated drama and finality, I withdrew my hunting knife as their grins disappeared and cut each one of their canoes loose and set it into the strong current of the Orinoco River where it was immediately swept up and carried downstream. I left without looking back and huffed over to the other side of the river to resume my work.

They managed to borrow another canoe and, after some effort, recovered their dugouts. Later, the headman of the village told me, with an approving chuckle, that I had done the correct thing. Everyone in the village, except, of course, the culprits, supported and defended my actions—and my status increased as a consequence.

Whenever I defended myself in such ways I got along much better with the Yąnomamö and gradually acquired the respect of many of them. A good deal of their demeanor toward me was directed with the forethought of establishing the point at which I would draw the line and react defensively. Many of them, years later, reminisced about the early days of my fieldwork when I was timid and *mohode* ("stupid") and a little afraid of them, those golden days when it was easy to bully me into giving my goods away for almost nothing.

Theft was the most persistent situation that required some sort of defensive action. I simply could not keep everything I owned locked in trunks, and the Yąnomamö came into my hut and left at will. I eventually developed a very effective strategy for recovering almost all the stolen items: I would simply ask a child who took the item and then I would confiscate that person's hammock when he was not around, giving a spirited lecture to all who could hear on the antisociality of thievery as I stalked off in a faked rage with the thief's hammock slung over my shoulder. Nobody ever attempted to stop me from doing this, and almost all of them told me that my technique for recovering my possessions was ingenious. By nightfall the thief would appear at my hut with the stolen item or send it over with someone else to make an exchange to recover his hammock. He would be heckled by his covillagers for having got caught and for being embarrassed into returning my item for his hammock. The explanation was usually, 'I just borrowed your ax! I wouldn't think of stealing it!'

Collecting Yąnomamö Genealogies and Reproductive Histories

My purpose for living among Yąnomamö was to systematically collect certain kinds of information on genealogy, reproduction, marriage practices, kinship, settlement patterns, migrations, and politics. Much of the fundamental data was genealogical—who was the parent of whom, tracing these connections as far back in time as Yąnomamö knowledge and memory permitted. Since 'primitive' society is organized largely by kinship relationships, figuring out the social organization of the Yąnomamö essentially meant collecting extensive data on genealogies, marriage, and reproduction. This turned out to be a staggering and very frustrating problem. I could not have deliberately picked a more difficult

people to work with in this regard. They have very stringent name taboos and eschew mentioning the names of prominent living people as well as all deceased friends and relatives. They attempt to name people in such a way that when the person dies and they can no longer use his or her name, the loss of the word in their language is not inconvenient. Hence, they name people for specific and minute parts of things, such as 'toenail of sloth,' 'whisker of howler monkey,' and so on, thereby being able to retain the words 'toenail' or 'whisker' but somewhat handicapped in referring to these anatomical parts of sloths and monkeys respectively. The taboo is maintained even for the living, for one mark of prestige is the courtesy others show you by not using your name publicly. This is particularly true for men, who are much more competitive for status than women in this culture, and it is fascinating to watch boys grow into young men, demanding to be called either by a kinship term in public, or by a teknonymous reference such as 'brother of Himotoma.' The more effective they are at getting others to avoid using their names, the more public acknowledgment there is that they are of high esteem and social standing. Helena Valero, a Brazilian woman who was captured as a child by a Yąnomamö raiding party, was married for many years to a Yąnomamö headman before she discovered what his name was (Biocca, 1970; Valero, 1984). The sanctions behind the taboo are more complex than just this, for they involve a combination of fear, respect, admiration, political deference, and honor.

At first I tried to use kinship terms alone to collect genealogies, but Yąnomamö kinship terms, like the kinship terms in all systems, are ambiguous at some point because they include so many possible relatives (as the term 'uncle' does in our own kinship system). Again, their system of kin classification merges many relatives that we 'separate' by using different terms: They call both their actual father and their father's brother by a single term, whereas we call one 'father' and the other 'uncle.' I was forced, therefore, to resort to personal names to collect unambiguous genealogies or 'pedigrees.' They quickly grasped what I was up to and that I was

determined to learn everyone's 'true name,' which amounted to an invasion of their system of prestige and etiquette, if not a flagrant violation of it. They reacted to this in a brilliant but devastating manner: They invented false names for everybody in the village and systematically learned them, freely revealing to me the 'true' identities of everyone. I smugly thought I had cracked the system and enthusiastically constructed elaborate genealogies over a period of some five months. They enjoyed watching me learn their names and kinship relationships. I naively assumed that I would get the 'truth' to each question and the best information by working in public. This set the stage for converting my serious project into an amusing hoax of the grandest proportions. Each 'informant' would try to outdo his peers by inventing a name even more preposterous or ridiculous than what I had been given by someone earlier, the explanations for discrepancies being 'Well, he has two names and this is the other one.' They even fabricated devilishly improbable genealogical relationships, such as someone being married to his grandmother, or worse yet, to his mother-in-law, a grotesque and horrifying prospect to the Yąnomamö. I would collect the desired names and relationships by having my informant whisper the name of the person softly into my ear, noting that he or she was the parent of such and such or the child of such and such, and so on. Everyone who was observing my work would then insist that I repeat the name aloud, roaring in hysterical laughter as I clumsily pronounced the name, sometimes laughing until tears streamed down their faces. The 'named' person would usually react with annoyance and hiss some untranslatable epithet at me, which served to reassure me that I had the 'true' name. I conscientiously checked and rechecked the names and relationships with multiple informants, pleased to see the inconsistencies disappear as my genealogy sheets filled with those desirable little triangles and circles, thousands of them.

My anthropological bubble was burst when I visited a village about 10 hours' walk to the southwest of Bisaasi-teri some five months after I had begun collecting genealogies on the Bisaasi-teri. I was chatting with the local headman of this village and happened to casually drop the name of the wife of the Bisaasi-teri headman. A stunned silence followed, and then a villagewide roar of uncontrollable laughter, choking, gasping, and howling followed. It seems that I thought the Bisaasi-teri headman was married to a woman named "hairy cunt." It also seems that the Bisaasi-teri headman was called 'long dong' and his brother 'eagle shit.' The Bisaasi-teri headman had a son called "asshole" and a daughter called 'fart breath.' And so on. Blood welled up my temples as I realized that I had nothing but nonsense to show for my five months' of dedicated genealogical effort, and I had to throw away almost all the information I had collected on this the most basic set of data I had come there to get. I understood at that point why the Bisaasi-teri laughed so hard when they made me repeat the names of their covillagers, and why the 'named' person would react with anger and annoyance as I pronounced his 'name' aloud.

I was forced to change research strategy—to make an understatement to describe this serious situation. The first thing I did was to begin working in private with my informants to eliminate the horseplay and distraction that attended public sessions. Once I did this, my informants, who did not know what others were telling me, began to agree with each other and I managed to begin learning the 'real' names, starting first with children and gradually moving to adult women and then, cautiously, adult men, a sequence that reflected the relative degree of intransigence at revealing names of people. As I built up a core of accurate genealogies and relationships—a core that all independent informants had verified repetitiously—I could 'test' any new informant by soliciting his or her opinion and knowledge about these 'core' people whose names and relationships I was confident were accurate. I was, in this fashion, able to immediately weed out the mischievous informants who persisted in trying to deceive me. Still, I had great difficulty getting the names of dead kinsmen, the only accurate way to extend genealogies back in

time. Even my best informants continued to falsify names of the deceased, especially closely related deceased. The falsifications at this point were not serious and turned out to be readily corrected as my interviewing methods improved (see below). Most of the deceptions were of the sort where the informant would give me the name of a living man as the father of some child whose actual father was dead, a response that enabled the informant to avoid using the name of a deceased kinsman or friend.

The quality of a genealogy depends in part on the number of generations it embraces, and the name taboo prevented me from making any substantial progress in learning about the deceased ancestors of the present population. Without this information, I could not, for example, document marriage patterns and interfamilial alliances through time. I had to rely on older informants for this information, but these were the most reluctant informants of all for this data. As I became more proficient in the language and more skilled at detecting fabrications, any informants became better at deception. One old man was particularly cunning and persuasive, following a sort of Mark Twain policy that the most effective lie is a sincere lie. He specialized in making a ceremony out of false names for dead ancestors. He would look around nervously to make sure nobody was listening outside my hut, enjoin me never to mention the name again, become very anxious and spooky, and grab me by the head to whisper a secret name into my ear. I was always elated after a session with him, because I managed to add several generations of ancestors for particular members of the village. Others steadfastly refused to give me such information. To show my gratitude, I paid him quadruple the rate that I had been paying the others. When word got around that I had increased the pay for genealogical and demographic information, volunteers began pouring into my hut to 'work' for me, assuring me of their changed ways and keen desire to divest themselves of the 'truth.'

Enter Rerebawä: Inmarried Tough Guy

I discovered that the old man was lying quite by accident. A club fight broke out in the village one day, the result of a dispute over the possession of a woman.

She had been promised to a young man in the village, a man named Rerebawä, who was particularly aggressive. He had married into Bisaasi-teri and was doing his 'bride service'—a period of several years during which he had to provide game for his wife's father and mother, provide them with wild foods he might collect, and help them in certain gardening and other tasks. Rerebawä had already been given one of the daughters in marriage and was promised her younger sister as his second wife. He was enraged when the younger sister, then about 16 years old, began having an affair with another young man in the village, Bäkotawä, making no attempt to conceal it. Rerebawä challenged Bäkotawä to a club fight. He swaggered boisterously out to the duel with his 10-foot-long club, a roof-pole he had cut from the house on the spur of the moment, as is the usual procedure. He hurled insult after insult at both Bäkotawä and his father, trying to goad them into a fight. His insults were bitter and nasty. They tolerated them for a few moments, but Rerebawä's biting insults provoked them to rage. Finally, they stormed angrily out of their hammocks and ripped out roof-poles, now returning the insults verbally, and rushed to the village clearing. Rerebawä continued to insult them, goading them into striking him on the head with their equally long clubs. Had either of them struck his head—which he held out conspicuously for them to swing at—he would then have the right to take his turn on their heads with his club. His opponents were intimidated by his fury, and simply backed down, refusing to strike him, and the argument ended. He had intimidated them into submission. All three retired pompously to their respective hammocks, exchanging nasty insults as they departed. But Rerebawä had won the showdown and thereafter swaggered around the village, insulting the two men behind their backs at every opportunity. He was genuinely angry with them, to the point of calling the older man by the name of his long-deceased father. I quickly seized on this incident as an opportunity to collect an accurate genealogy and confidentially asked Rerebawä about his adversary's ancestors. Rerebawä had been particularly 'pushy' with me up to this point, but we soon became warm friends and staunch allies: We were both 'outsiders' in Bisaasi-teri and, although he was a Yąnomamö, he nevertheless had to put up with some considerable amount of pointed teasing and scorn from the locals, as all inmarried 'sons-in-law' must. He gave me the information I requested of his adversary's deceased ancestors, almost with devilish glee. I asked about dead ancestors of other people in the village and got prompt, un-equivocal answers: He was angry with everyone in the village. When I compared his answers to those of the old man, it was obvious that one of them was lying. I then challenged his answers. He explained, in a sort of 'you damned fool, don't you know better?' tone of voice that everyone in the village knew the old man was lying to me and gloating over it when I was out of earshot. The names the old man had given to me were names of dead ancestors of the members of a village so far away that he thought I would never have occasion to check them out authoritatively. As it turned out, Rerebawä knew most of the people in that distant village and recognized the names given by the old man.

I then went over all my Bisaasi-teri genealogies with Rerebawä, genealogies I had presumed to be close to their final form. I had to revise them all because of the numerous lies and falsifications they contained, much of it provided by the sly old man. Once again, after months of work, I had to recheck everything with Rerebawä's aid. Only the living members of the nuclear families turned out to be accurate; the deceased ancestors were mostly fabrications.

Discouraging as it was to have to re-check everything all over again, it was a major turning point in my fieldwork. Thereafter, I began taking advantage of local arguments and animosities in se-lecting my informants, and used more extensively informants who had married into the village in the recent past. I also began traveling more regularly to other villages at this time to check on genealo-gies, seeking out villages whose members were on strained terms with the people about whom I wanted informa-tion. I would then return to my base in

the village of Bisaasi-teri and check with local informants the accuracy of the new information. I had to be careful in this work and scrupulously select my local informants in such a way that I would not be inquiring about *their* closely related kin. Thus, for each of my local infor-mants, I had to make lists of names of certain deceased people that I dared not mention in their presence. But despite this precaution, I would occasionally hit a new name that would put some infor-mants into a rage, or into a surly mood, such as that of a dead 'brother' or 'sis-ter'[6] whose existence had not been indi-cated to me by other informants. This usually terminated my day's work with that informant, for he or she would be too touchy or upset to continue any further, and I would be reluctant to take a chance on accidentally discovering another dead close kinsman soon after discovering the first.

These were unpleasant experiences, and occasionally dangerous as well, de-pending on the temperament of my infor-mant. On one occasion I was planning to visit a village that had been raided recently by one of their enemies. A woman, whose name I had on my cen-sus list for that village, had been killed by the raiders. Killing women is consid-ered to be bad form in Yąnomamö war-fare, but this woman was deliberately killed for revenge. The raiders were un-able to bushwhack some man who stepped out of the village at dawn to uri-nate, so they shot a volley of arrows over the roof into the village and beat a hasty retreat. Unfortunately, one of the arrows struck and killed a woman, an accident. For that reason, her village's raiders *de-liberately* sought out and killed a woman in retaliation—whose name was on my list. My reason for going to the village was to update my census data on a name-by-name basis and estimate the ages of all the residents. I knew I had the name of the dead woman in my list, but nobody would dare to utter her name so I could remove it. I knew that I would be in very serious trouble if I got to the village and said her name aloud, and I desperately wanted to remove it from my list. I called on one of my regular and usually cooper-ative informants and asked him to tell me the woman's name. He refused ada-

mantly, explaining that she was a close relative—and was angry that I even raised the topic with him. I then asked him if he would let me whisper the names of *all* the women of that village in his ear, and he would simply have to nod when I hit the right name. We had been 'friends' for some time, and I thought I was able to predict his reaction, and thought that our friendship was good enough to use this procedure. He agreed to the procedure, and I began whispering the names of the women, one by one. We were alone in my hut so that nobody would know what we were doing and no-body could hear us. I read the names softly, continuing to the next when his response was a negative. When I ulti-mately hit the dead woman's name, he flew out of his chair, enraged and trem-bling violently, his arm raised to strike me: 'You son-of-a-bitch!' he screamed. 'If you say her name in my presence again, I'll kill you in an instant!' I sat there, bewildered, shocked, and con-fused. And frightened, as much because of his reaction, but also because I could imagine what might happen to me should I unknowingly visit a village to check ge-nealogy accuracy without knowing that someone had just died there or had been shot by raiders since my last visit. I re-flected on the several articles I had read as a graduate student that explained the 'genealogical method,' but could not re-call anything about its being a potentially lethal undertaking. My furious informant left my hut, never again to be invited back to be an informant. I had other sim-ilar experiences in different villages, but I was always fortunate in that the dead person had been dead for some time, or was not very closely related to the indi-vidual into whose ear I whispered the forbidden name. I was usually cautioned by one of the men to desist from saying any more names lest I get people 'an-gry.'[7]

Kaobawä: The Bisaasi-teri Headman Volunteers to Help Me

I had been working on the genealogies for nearly a year when another individual came to my aid. It was Kaobawä, the headman of Upper Bisaasi-teri. The vil-lage of Bisaasi-teri was split into two components, each with its own garden and own circular house. Both were in sight of each other. However, the intensity and frequency of internal bickering and argumentation was so high that they decided to split into two separate groups but remain close to each other for protection in case they were raided. One group was downstream from the other; I refer to that group as the 'Lower' Bisaasi-teri and call Kaobawä's group 'Upper' (upstream) Bisaasi-teri, a convenience they themselves adopted after separating from each other. I spent most of my time with the members of Kaobawä's group, some 200 people when I first arrived there. I did not have much contact with Kaobawä during the early months of my work. He was a somewhat retiring, quiet man, and among the Yąnomamö, the outsider has little time to notice the rare quiet ones when most everyone else is in the front row, pushing and demanding attention. He showed up at my hut one day after all the others had left. He had come to volunteer to help me with the genealogies. He was 'poor,' he explained, and needed a machete. He would work only on the condition that I did not ask him about his own parents and other very close kinsmen who had died. He also added that he would not lie to me as the others had done in the past.

This was perhaps the single most important event in my first 15 months of field research, for out of this fortuitous circumstance evolved a very warm friendship, and among the many things following from it was a wealth of accurate information on the political history of Kaobawä's village and related villages, highly detailed genealogical information, sincere and useful advice to me, and hundreds of valuable insights into the Yąnomamö way of life. Kaobawä's familiarity with his group's history and his candidness were remarkable. His knowledge of details was almost encyclopedic, his memory almost photographic. More than that, he was enthusiastic about making sure I learned the truth, and he encouraged me, indeed, *demanded that* I learn all details I might otherwise have ignored. If there were subtle details he could not recite on the spot, he would advise me to wait until he could check things out with someone else in the village. He would often do this

clandestinely, giving me a report the next day, telling me who revealed the new information and whether or not he thought they were in a position to know it. With the information provided by Kaobawä and Rerebawä, I made enormous gains in understanding village interrelationships based on common ancestors and political histories and became lifelong friends with both. And both men knew that I had to learn about his recently deceased kin from the other one. It was one of those quiet understandings we all had but none of us could mention.

Once again I went over the genealogies with Kaobawä to recheck them, a considerable task by this time. They included about two thousand names, representing several generations of individuals from four different villages. Rerebawä's information was very accurate, and Kaobawä's contribution enabled me to trace the genealogies further back in time. Thus, after nearly a year of intensive effort on genealogies, Yąnomamö demographic patterns and social organization began to make a good deal of sense to me. Only at this point did the patterns through time begin to emerge in the data, and I could begin to understand how kinship groups took form, exchanged women in marriage over several generations, and only then did the fissioning of larger villages into smaller ones emerge as a chronic and important feature of Yąnomamö social, political, demographic, economic, and ecological adaptation. At this point I was able to begin formulating more sophisticated questions, for there was now a pattern to work from and one to flesh out. Without the help of Rerebawä and Kaobawä it would have taken much longer to make sense of the plethora of details I had collected from not only them, but dozens of other informants as well.

I spent a good deal of time with these two men and their families, and got to know them much better than I knew most Yąnomamö. They frequently gave their information in a way which related themselves to the topic under discussion. We became warm friends as time passed, and the formal 'informant/anthropologist' relationship faded into the background. Eventually, we simply stopped

'keeping track' of work and pay. They would both spend hours talking with me, leaving without asking for anything. When they wanted something, they would ask for it no matter what the relative balance of reciprocity between us might have been at that point....

For many of the customary things that anthropologists try to communicate about another culture, these two men and their families might be considered to be 'exemplary' or 'typical.' For other things, they are exceptional in many regards, but the reader will, even knowing some of the exceptions, understand Yąnomamö culture more intimately by being familiar with a few examples.

Kaobawä was about 40 years old when I first came to his village in 1964. I say "about 40" because the Yąnomamö numeration system has only three numbers: one, two, and more-than-two. It is hard to give accurate ages or dates for events when the informants have no means in their language to reveal such detail. Kaobawä is the headman of his village, meaning that he has somewhat more responsibility in political dealings with other Yąnomamö groups, and very little control over those who live in his group except when the village is being raided by enemies. We will learn more about political leadership and warfare in a later chapter, but most of the time men like Kaobawä are like the North American Indian 'chief' whose authority was characterized in the following fashion: "One word from the chief, and each man does as he pleases." There are different 'styles' of political leadership among the Yąnomamö. Some leaders are mild, quiet, inconspicuous most of the time, but intensely competent. They act parsimoniously, but when they do, people listen and conform. Other men are more tyrannical, despotic, pushy, flamboyant, and unpleasant to all around them. They shout orders frequently, are prone to beat their wives, or pick on weaker men. Some are very violent. I have met headmen who run the entire spectrum between these polar types, for I have visited some 60 Yąnomamö villages. Kaobawä stands at the mild, quietly competent end of the spectrum. He has had six wives thus far—and temporary affairs with as many more, at least one of which resulted in a child that is publicly acknowledged as his child. When I first met him he had just two wives: Bahimi and Koamashima. Bahimi had two living children when I first met her; many others had died. She was the older and enduring wife, as much a friend to him as a mate. Their relationship was as close to what we think of as 'love' in our culture as I have seen among the Yąnomamö. His second wife was a girl of about 20 years, Koamashima. She had a new baby boy when I first met her, her first child. There was speculation that Kaobawä was planning to give Koamashima to one of his younger brothers who had no wife; he occasionally allows his younger brother to have sex with Koamashima, but only if he asks in advance. Kaobawä gave another wife to one of his other brothers because she was *beshi* ("horny"). In fact, this earlier wife had been married to two other men, both of whom discarded her because of her infidelity. Kaobawä had one daughter by her. However, the girl is being raised by Kaobawä's brother, though acknowledged to be Kaobawä's child.

Bahimi, his oldest wife, is about five years younger than he. She is his cross-cousin—his mother's brother's daughter. Ideally, all Yąnomamö men should marry a cross-cousin.... Bahimi was pregnant when I began my field work, but she destroyed the infant when it was born—a boy in this case—explaining tearfully that she had no choice. The new baby would have competed for milk with Ariwari, her youngest child, who was still nursing. Rather than expose Ariwari to the dangers and uncertainty of an early weaning, she chose to terminate the newborn instead. By Yąnomamö standards, this has been a very warm, enduring marriage. Kaobawä claims he beats Bahimi only 'once in a while, and only lightly' and she, for her part, never has affairs with other men.

Kaobawä is a quiet, intense, wise, and unobtrusive man. It came as something of a surprise to me when I learned that he was the headman of his village, for he stayed at the sidelines while others would surround me and press their demands on me. He leads more by example than by coercion. He can afford to be this

way at his age, for he established his reputation for being forthright and as fierce as the situation required when he was younger, and the other men respect him. He also has five mature brothers or half-brothers in his village, men he can count on for support. He also has several other mature 'brothers' (parallel cousins, whom he must refer to as 'brothers' in his kinship system) in the village who frequently come to his aid, but not as often as his 'real' brothers do. Kaobawä has also given a number of his sisters to other men in the village and has promised his young (8-year-old) daughter in marriage to a young man who, for that reason, is obliged to help him. In short, his 'natural' or 'kinship' following is large, and partially because of this support, he does not have to display his aggressiveness to remind his peers of his position.

Rerebawä is a very different kind of person. He is much younger—perhaps in his early twenties. He has just one wife, but they have already had three children. He is from a village called Karohi-teri, located about five hours' walk up the Orinoco, slightly inland off to the east of the river itself. Kaobawä's village enjoys amicable relationships with Rerebawä's, and it is for this reason that marriage alliances of the kind represented by Rerebawä's marriage into Kaobawä's village occur between the two groups. Rerebawä told me that he came to Bisaasi-teri because there were no eligible women from him to marry in his own village, a fact that I later was able to document when I did a census of his village and a preliminary analysis of its social organization. Rerebawä is perhaps more typical than Kaobawä in the sense that he is chronically concerned about his personal reputation for aggressiveness and goes out of his way to be noticed, even if he has to act tough. He gave me a hard time during my early months of fieldwork, intimidating, teasing, and insulting me frequently. He is, however, much braver than the other men his age and is quite prepared to back up his threats with immediate action—as in the club fight incident just described above. Moreover, he is fascinated with political relationships and knows the details of intervillage relationships over a large area of the tribe. In this respect he shows all the attributes of being a headman, although

he has too many competent brothers in his own village to expect to move easily into the leadership position there.

He does not intend to stay in Kaobawä's group and refuses to make his own garden—a commitment that would reveal something of an intended long-term residence. He feels that he has adequately discharged his obligations to his wife's parents by providing them with fresh game, which he has done for several years. They should let him take his wife and return to his own village with her, but they refuse and try to entice him to remain permanently in Bisaasi-teri to continue to provide them with game when they are old. It is for this reason that they promised to give him their second daughter, their only other child, in marriage. Unfortunately, the girl was opposed to the marriage and ultimately married another man, a rare instance where the woman in the marriage had this much influence on the choice of her husband.

Although Rerebawä has displayed his ferocity in many ways, one incident in particular illustrates what his character can be like. Before he left his own village to take his new wife in Bisaasi-teri, he had an affair with the wife of an older brother. When it was discovered, his brother attacked him with a club. Rerebawä responded furiously: He grabbed an ax and drove his brother out of the village after soundly beating him with the blunt side of the single-bit ax. His brother was so intimidated by the thrashing and promise of more to come that he did not return to the village for several days. I visited this village with Kabawä shortly after this event had taken place; Rerebawä was with me as my guide. He made it a point to introduce me to this man. He approached his hammock, grabbed him by the wrist, and dragged him out on the ground: 'This is the brother whose wife I screwed when he wasn't around!' A deadly insult, one that would usually provoke a bloody club fight among more valiant Yąnomamö. The man did nothing. He slunk sheepishly back into his hammock, shamed, but relieved to have Rerebawä release his grip.

Even though Rerebawä is fierce and capable of considerable nastiness, he has a charming, witty side as well. He has a biting sense of humor and can entertain the group for hours with jokes and clever manipulations of language. And, he is one of few Yąnomamö that I feel I can trust. I recall indelibly my return to Bisaasi-teri after being away a year—the occasion of my second field trip to the Yąnomamö. When I reached Bisaasi-teri, Rerebawä was in his own village visiting his kinsmen. Word reached him that I had returned, and he paddled downstream immediately to see me. He greeted me with an immense bear hug and exclaimed, with tears welling up in his eyes, 'Shaki! Why did you stay away so long? Did you not know that my will was so cold while you were gone that I could not at times eat for want of seeing you again?' I, too, felt the same way about him—then, and now.

Of all the Yąnomamö I know, he is the most genuine and the most devoted to his culture's ways and values. I admire him for that, although I cannot say that I subscribe to or endorse some of these values. By contrast, Kaobawä is older and wiser, a polished diplomat. He sees his own culture in a slightly different light and seems even to question aspects of it. Thus, while many of his peers enthusiastically accept the 'explanations' of things given in myths, he occasionally reflects on them—even laughing at some of the most preposterous of them.... Probably more of the Yąnomamö are like Rerebawä than like Kaobawä , or at least try to be. ....

NOTES

1. The word Yąnomamö is nasalized through its entire length, indicated by the diacritical mark ',''. When this mark appears on any Yąnomamö word, the whole word is nasalized. The vowel 'ö' represents a sound that does not occur in the English language. It is similar to the umlaut 'ö' in the German language or the 'oe' equivalent, as in the poet Goethe's name. Unfortunately, many presses and typesetters simply eliminate diacritical marks, and this has led to multiple spellings of the word Yąnomamö—and multiple mispronunciations. Some anthropologists have chosen to introduce a slightly different spelling of the word Yąnomamö since I began writing about them, such as Yąnomami, leading to additional misspellings as their diacriticals are characteristically eliminated by presses, and to the *incorrect* pronunciation 'Yąnoma-meee.' Vowels indicated as 'ä' are pronounced as the 'uh' sound in the word 'duck'. Thus, the name Kaobawä would be pronounced 'cow-ba-wuh,' but entirely nasalized.

2. I spent a total of 60 months among the Yąnomamö between 1964 and 1991. The first edition of this case study was based on the first 15 months I spent among them in Venezuela. I have, at the time of this writing, made 20 field trips to the Yąnomamö and this edition reflects the new information and understandings I have acquired over the years. I plan to return regularly to continue what has now turned into a lifelong study.

3. See Spindler (1970) for a general discussion of field research by anthropologists who have worked in other cultures. Nancy Howell has recently written a very useful book (1990) on some of the medical, personal, and environmental hazards of doing field research, which includes a selected bibliography on other fieldwork programs.

4. They could not pronounce "Chagnon." It sounded to them like their name for a pesky bee, shaki, and that is what they called me: pesky, noisome bee.

5. The Yąnomamö in this region acquired canoes very recently. The missionaries would purchase them from the Ye'kwana Indians to the north for money, and then trade them to the Yąnomamö in exchange for labor, produce, or 'informant' work in translating. It should be emphasized that those Yąnomamö who lived on navigable portions of the Upper Orinoco River moved there recently from the deep forest in order to have contact with the missionaries and acquire the trade goods the missionaries (and their supply system) brought.

6. Rarely were there actual brothers or sisters. In Yąnomamö kinship classifications, certain kinds of cousins are classified as siblings. See Chapter 4.

7. Over time, as I became more and more 'accepted' by the Yąnomamö, they became less and less concerned about my genealogical inquiries and now, provide me with this information quite willingly because I have been very discrete with it. Now, when I revisit familiar villages I am called aside by someone who whispers to me things like, "Don't ask about so-and-so's father."

Doctor, Lawyer, Indian Chief

As Punjabi villagers say, "You never really know who a man is until you know who his grandfather and his ancestors were"

Richard Kurin

I was full of confidence when—equipped with a scholarly proposal, blessings from my advisers, and generous research grants—I set out to study village social structure in the Punjab province of Pakistan. But after looking for an appropriate fieldwork site for several weeks without success, I began to think that my research project would never get off the ground. Daily I would seek out villages aboard my puttering motor scooter, traversing the dusty dirt roads, footpaths, and irrigation ditches that crisscross the Punjab. But I couldn't seem to find a village amenable to study. The major problem was that the villagers I did approach were baffled by my presence. They could not understand why anyone would travel ten thousand miles from home to a foreign country in order to live in a poor village, interview illiterate peasants, and then write a book about it. Life, they were sure, was to be lived, not written about. Besides, they thought, what of any importance could they possibly tell me? Committed as I was to ethnographic research, I readily understood their viewpoint. I was a *babu log*—literally, a noble; figuratively, a clerk; and simply, a person of the city. I rode a motor scooter, wore tight-fitting clothing, and spoke Urdu, a language associated with the urban literary elite. Obviously, I

did not belong, and the villagers simply did not see me fitting into their society.

The Punjab, a region about the size of Colorado, straddles the northern border of India and Pakistan. Partitioned between the two countries in 1947, the Punjab now consists of a western province, inhabited by Muslims, and an eastern one, populated in the main by Sikhs and Hindus. As its name implies—*punj* meaning "five" and *ab* meaning "rivers"—the region is endowed with plentiful resources to support widespread agriculture and a large rural population. The Punjab has traditionally supplied grains, produce, and dairy products to the peoples of neighboring and considerably more arid states, earning it a reputation as the breadbasket of southern Asia.

Given this predilection for agriculture, Punjabis like to emphasize that they are earthy people, having values they see as consonant with rural life. These values include an appreciation of, and trust in, nature; simplicity and directness of expression; an awareness of the basic drives and desires that motivate men (namely, *zan, zar, zamin*—"women, wealth, land"); a concern with honor and shame as abiding principles of social organization; and for Muslims, a deep faith in Allah and the teachings of his prophet Mohammed.

Besides being known for its fertile soils, life-giving rivers, and superlative agriculturists, the Punjab is also perceived as a zone of transitional culture, a region that has experienced repeated invasions of people from western and central Asia into the Indian subcontinent. Over the last four thousand years, numerous groups, among them Scythians, Parthians, Huns, Greeks, Moguls, Persians, Afghans, and Turks, have entered the subcontinent through the Punjab in search of bountiful land, riches, or power. Although Punjabis—notably Rajputs, Sikhs, and Jats—have a reputation for courage and fortitude on the battlefield, their primary, self-professed strength has been their ability to incorporate new, exogenous elements into their society with a minimum of conflict. Punjabis are proud that theirs is a multiethnic society in which diverse groups have been largely unified by a common language and by common customs and traditions.

Given this background, I had not expected much difficulty in locating a village in which to settle and conduct my research. As an anthropologist, I viewed myself as an "earthy" social scientist who, being concerned with basics, would have a good deal in common with rural Punjabis. True, I might be looked on as an invader of a sort; but I was benevolent, and sensing this, villagers were sure to incorporate me into their society with even greater ease than was the case for the would-be conquering armies that had preceded me. Indeed, they would welcome me with open arms.

I was wrong. The villages whom I approached attributed my desire to live with them either to neurotic delusions or nefarious ulterior motives. Perhaps, so the arguments went, I was really after women, land, or wealth.

On the day I had decided would be my last in search of a village, I was driving along a road when I saw a farmer running through a rice field waving me down. I stopped and he climbed on the scooter. Figuring I had nothing to lose, I began to explain why I wanted to live in a village. To my surprise and delight, he was very receptive, and after sharing a pomegranate milkshake at a roadside shop, he invited me to his home. His name was Allah Ditta, which means "God given," and I took this as a sign that I had indeed found my village.

"My" village turned out to be a settlement of about fifteen hundred people, mostly of the Nunari qaum, or "tribe." The Nunaris engage primarily in agriculture (wheat, rice, sugar cane, and cotton), and most families own small plots of land. Members of the Bhatti tribe constitute the largest minority in the village. Although traditionally a warrior tribe, the Bhattis serve in the main as the village artisans and craftsmen.

On my first day in the village I tried explaining in great detail the purposes of my study to the village elders and clan leaders. Despite my efforts, most of the elders were perplexed about why I wanted to live in their village. As a guest, I was entitled to the hospitality traditionally bestowed by Muslim peoples of Asia, and during the first evening I was assigned a place to stay. But I was an enigma, for guests leave, and I wanted to remain. I was also perceived as being strange, for I was both a non-Muslim and a non-Punjabi, a type of person not heretofore encountered by most of the villagers. Although I tried to temper my behavior, there was little I could say or do to dissuade my hosts from the view that I embodied the antithesis of Punjabi

values. While I was able to converse in their language, Jatki, a dialect of western Punjabi, I was only able to do so with the ability of a four-year-old. This achievement fell far short of speaking the t'et', or "genuine form," of the villagers. Their idiom is rich with the terminology of agricultural operations and rural life. It is unpretentious, uninflected, and direct, and villagers hold high opinions of those who are good with words, who can speak to a point and be convincing. Needless to say, my infantile babble realized none of these characteristics and evoked no such respect.

Similarly, even though I wore indigenous dress, I was inept at tying my lungi, or pant cloth. The fact that my lungi occasionally fell off and revealed what was underneath gave my neighbors reason to believe that I indeed had no shame and could not control the passions of my nafs, or "libidinous nature."

This image of a doltish, shameless infidel barely capable of caring for himself lasted for the first week of my residence in the village. My inability to distinguish among the five varieties of rice and four varieties of lentil grown in the village illustrated that I knew or cared little about nature and agricultural enterprise. This display of ignorance only served to confirm the general consensus that the mysterious morsels I ate from tin cans labeled "Chef Boy-ar-Dee" were not really food at all. Additionally, I did not oil and henna my hair, shave my armpits, or perform ablutions, thereby convincing some commentators that I was a member of a species of subhuman beings, possessing little in the form of either common or moral sense. That the villagers did not quite grant me the status of a person was reflected by their not according me a proper name. In the Punjab, a person's name is equated with honor and respect and is symbolized by his turban. A man who does not have a name, or whose name is not recognized by his neighbors, is unworthy of respect. For such a man, his turban is said to be either nonexistent or to lie in the dust at the feet of others. To be given a name is to have one's head crowned by a turban, an acknowledgment that one leads a responsible and respectable life. Although I repeatedly introduced myself as "Rashid Karim," a

fairly decent Pakistani rendering of Richard Kurin, just about all the villagers insisted on calling me Angrez ("Englishman"), thus denying me full personhood and implicitly refusing to grant me the right to wear a turban.

As I began to pick up the vernacular, to question villagers about their clan and kinship structure and trace out relationships between different families, my image began to change. My drawings of kinship diagrams and preliminary census mappings were looked upon not only with wonder but also suspicion. My neighbors now began to think there might be a method to my madness. And so there was. Now I had become a spy. Of course it took a week for people to figure out whom I was supposedly spying for. Located as they were at a crossroads of Asia, at a nexus of conflicting geopolitical interests, they had many possibilities to consider. There was a good deal of disagreement on the issue, with the vast majority maintaining that I was either an American, Russian, or Indian spy. A small, but nonetheless vocal, minority held steadfastly to the belief that I was a Chinese spy. I thought it all rather humorous until one day a group confronted me in the main square in front of the nine-by-nine-foot mud hut that I had rented. The leader spoke up and accused me of spying. The remainder of the group grumbled jahsus! jahsus! ("spy! spy!"), and I realized that this ad hoc committee of inquiry had the potential of becoming a mob.

To be sure, the villagers had good reason to be suspicious. For one, the times were tense in Pakistan—a national political crisis gripped the country and the populace had been anxious for months over the uncertainty of elections and effective governmental functions. Second, keenly aware of their history, some of the villagers did not have to go too far to imagine that I was at the vanguard of some invading group that had designs upon their land. Such intrigues, with far greater sophistication, had been played out before by nations seeking to expand their power into the Punjab. That I possessed a gold seal letter (which no one save myself could read) from the University of Chicago to the effect that I was pursuing legitimate studies was not enough to convince the crowd that I was indeed an innocent scholar.

I repeatedly denied the charge, but to no avail. The shouts of *jahsus! jahsus!* prevailed. Confronted with this I had no choice.

"Okay," I said. "I admit it. I am a spy!"

The crowd quieted for my long-awaited confession.

"I am a spy and am here to study this village, so that when my country attacks you we will be prepared. You see, we will not bomb Lahore or Karachi or Islamabad. Why should we waste our bombs on millions of people, on factories, dams, airports, and harbors? No, it is far more advantageous to bomb this strategic small village replete with its mud huts, livestock, Persian wheels, and one light bulb. And when we bomb this village, it is imperative that we know how Allah Ditta is related to Abdullah, and who owns the land near the well, and what your marriage customs are."

Silence hung over the crowd, and then one by one the assemblage began to disperse. My sarcasm had worked. The spy charges were defused. But I was no hero in light of my performance, and so I was once again relegated to the status of a nonperson without an identity in the village.

I remained in limbo for the next week, and although I continued my attempts to collect information about village life, I had my doubts as to whether I would ever be accepted by the villagers. And then, through no effort of my own, there was a breakthrough, this time due to another Allah Ditta, a relative of the village headman and one of my leading accusers during my spying days.

I was sitting on my woven string bed on my porch when Allah Ditta approached, leading his son by the neck. "Oh, *Angrez!*" he yelled, "this worthless son of mine is doing poorly in school. He is supposed to be learning English, but he is failing. He has a good mind, but he's lazy. And his teacher is no help, being more intent upon drinking tea and singing film songs than upon teaching English. Oh son of an Englishman, do you know English?"

"Yes, I know English," I replied, "after all, I am an *Angrez.*"

"Teach him," Allah Ditta blurted out, without any sense of making a tactful request.

And so, I spent the next hour with the boy, reviewing his lessons and correcting his pronunciation and grammar. As I did so, villagers stopped to watch and listen, and by the end of the hour, nearly one hundred people had gathered around, engrossed by this tutoring session. They were stupefied. I was an effective teacher, and I actually seemed to know English. The boy responded well, and the crowd reached a new consensus. I had a brain. And in recognition of this achievement I was given a name—"Ustad Rashid," or Richard the Teacher.

Achieving the status of a teacher was only the beginning of my success. The next morning I awoke to find the village sugar vendor at my door. He had a headache and wanted to know if I could cure him.

"Why do you think I can help you?" I asked.

Bhai Khan answered, "Because you are a *ustad*, you have a great deal of knowledge."

The logic was certainly compelling. If I could teach English, I should be able to cure a headache. I gave him two aspirins.

An hour later, my fame had spread. Bhai Khan had been cured, and he did not hesitate to let others know that it was the *ustad* who had been responsible. By the next day, and in fact for the remainder of my stay, I was to see an average of twenty-five to thirty patients a day. I was asked to cure everything from coughs and colds to typhoid, elephantiasis, and impotency. Upon establishing a flourishing and free medical practice, I received another title, *hakim*, or "physician." I was not yet an anthropologist, but I was on my way.

A few days later I took on yet another role. One of my research interests involved tracing out patterns of land ownership and inheritance. While working on the problem of figuring out who owned what, I was approached by the village watchman. He claimed he had been swindled in a land deal and requested my help. As the accused was not another villager, I agreed to present the watchman's case to the local authorities.

Somehow, my efforts managed to achieve results. The plaintiff's grievance was redressed, and I was given yet another title in the village—*wakil*, or "lawyer." And in the weeks that followed, I was steadily called upon to read, translate, and advise upon various court orders that affected the lives of the villagers.

My roles as teacher, doctor, and lawyer not only provided me with an identity but also facilitated my integration into the economic structure of the community. As my imputed skills offered my neighbors services not readily available in the village, I was drawn into exchange relationships known as *seipi*. *Seipi* refers to the barter system of goods and services among village farmers, craftsmen, artisans, and other specialists. Every morning Roshan the milkman would deliver fresh milk to my hut. Every other day Hajam Ali the barber would stop by and give me a shave. My next-door neighbor, Nura the cobbler, would repair my sandals when required. Ghulam the horse-cart driver would transport me to town when my motor scooter was in disrepair. The parents of my students would send me sweets and sometimes delicious meals. In return, none of my neighbors asked for direct payment for the specific actions performed. Rather, as they told me, they would call upon me when they had need of my services. And they did. Nura needed cough syrup for his children, the milkman's brother needed a job contact in the city, students wanted to continue their lessons, and so on. Through *seipi* relations, various neighbors gave goods and services to me, and I to them.

Even so, I knew that by Punjabi standards I could never be truly accepted into village life because I was not a member of either the Nunari or Bhatti tribe. As the villagers would say, "You never really know who a man is until you know who his grandfather and his ancestors were." And to know a person's grandfather or ancestors properly, you had to be a member of the same or a closely allied tribe.

The Nunari tribe is composed of a number of groups. The nucleus consists of four clans—Naul, Vadel, Sadan, and More—each named for one of four brothers thought to have originally founded the tribe. Clan members are said to be related by blood ties, also called *pag da sak*, or "ties of the turban." In sharing the turban, members of each clan share the same name. Other clans, unrelated by ties of blood to these four, have become attached to this nucleus through a history of marital relations or of continuous political and economic interdependence. Marital relations, called *gag da sak*, or "ties of the skirt," are conceived of as relations in which alienable turbans (skirts) in the form of women are exchanged with other, non-turban-sharing groups. Similarly, ties of political and economic domination and subordination are thought of as relations in which the turban of the client is given to that of the patron. A major part of my research work was concerned with reconstructing how the four brothers formed the Nunari tribe, how additional clans became associated with it, and how clan and tribal identity were defined by nomenclature, codes of honor, and the symbols of sharing and exchanging turbans.

To approach these issues I set out to reconstruct the genealogical relationships within the tribe and between the various clans. I elicited genealogies from many of the villagers and questioned older informants about the history of the Nunari tribe. Most knew only bits and pieces of this history, and after several months of interviews and research, I was directed to the tribal genealogists. These people, usually not Nunaris themselves, perform the service of memorizing and then orally relating the history of the tribe and the relationships among its members. The genealogist in the village was an aged and arthritic man named Hedayat, who in his later years was engaged in teaching the Nunari genealogy to his son, who would then carry out the traditional and hereditary duties of his position.

The villagers claimed that Hedayat knew every generation of the Nunari from the present to the founding brothers and even beyond. So I invited Hedayat to my hut and explained my purpose.

"Do you know Allah Ditta son of Rohm?" I asked.

"Yes, of course," he replied.

"Who was Rohm's father?" I continued.

"Shahadat Mohammad," he answered.

"And his father?"

"Hamid."

"And his?"

"Chigatah," he snapped without hesitation.

I was now quite excited, for no one else in the village had been able to recall an ancestor of this generation. My estimate was that Chigatah had been born sometime between 1850 and 1870. But Hedayat went on.

"Chigatah's father was Kamal. And Kamal's father was Nanak. And Nanak's father was Sikhu. And before him was Dargai, and before him Maiy. And before him was Siddiq. And Siddiq's father was Nur. And Nur's Asmat. And Asmat was of Channa. And Channa of Nau. And Nau of Bhatta. And Bhatta was the son of Koduk."

Hedayat had now recounted sixteen generations of lineal ascendants related through the turban. Koduk was probably born in the sixteenth century. But still Hedayat continued.

"Sigun was the father of Koduk. And Man the father of Sigun. And before Man was his father Maneswar. And Maneswar's father was the founder of the clan, Naul."

This then was a line of the Naul clan of the Nunari tribe, ascending twenty-one generations from the present descendants (Allah Ditta's son) to the founder, one of four brothers who lived perhaps in the fifteenth century. I asked Hedayat to recite genealogies of the other Nunari clans, and he did, with some blanks here and there, ending with Vadel, More, and Saddan, the other three brothers who formed the tribal nucleus. I then asked the obvious question, "Hedayat, who was the father of these four brothers? Who is the founding ancestor of the Nunari tribe?"

"The father of these brothers was not a Muslim. He was an Indian rajput [chief]. The tribe actually begins with the conversion of the four brothers," Hedayat explained.

"Well then," I replied, "who was this Indian chief?"

"He was a famous and noble chief who fought against the Moguls. His name was Raja Kurin, who lived in a massive fort in Kurinnagar, about twenty-seven miles from Delhi."

"What!" I asked, both startled and unsure of what I had heard.

"Raja Kurin is the father of the brothers who make up—"

"But his name! It's the same as mine," I stammered. "Hedayat, my name is Richard Kurin. What a coincidence! Here I am living with your tribe thousands of miles from my home and it turns out that I have the same name as the founder of the tribe! Do you think I might be related to Raja Kurin and the Nunaris?"

Hedayat looked at me, but only for an instant. Redoing his turban, he tilted his head skyward, smiled, and asked, "What is the name of your father?"

I had come a long way. I now had a name that could be recognized and respected, and as I answered Hedayat, I knew that I had finally and irrevocably fit into "my" village. Whether by fortuitous circumstances or by careful manipulation, my neighbors had found a way to take an invading city person intent on studying their life and transform him into one of their own, a full person entitled to wear a turban for participating in, and being identified with, that life. As has gone on for centuries in the region, once again the new and exogenous had been recast into something Punjabi.

Epilogue: There is no positive evidence linking the Nunaris to a historical Raja Kurin, although there are several famous personages identified by that name (also transcribed as Karan and Kurran). Estimated from the genealogy recited by Hedayat, the founding of the tribe by four brothers appears to have occurred sometime between 440 and 640 years ago, depending on the interval assumed for each generation. On that basis, the most likely candidate for Nunari progenitor (actual or imputed) is Raja Karan, ruler of Anhilvara (Gujerat), who was defeated by the Khilji Ala-ud-Din in 1297 and again in 1307. Although this is slightly earlier than suggested by the genealogical data, such genealogies are often telescoped or otherwise unreliable.

Nevertheless, several aspects of Hedayat's account make this association doubtful. Hedayat clearly identifies Raja Kurin's conquerors as Moguls, whereas the Gujerati Raja Karan was defeated by the Khiljis. Second, Hedayat places the Nunari ancestor's kingdom only twenty-seven miles from Delhi. The Gujerati Raja Karan ruled several kingdoms, none closer than several hundred miles to Delhi.

Other circumstances, however, offer support for this identification of the Nunari ancestor. According to Hedayat, Raja Kurin's father was named Kam Deo. Although the historical figure was the son of Serung Deo, the use of "Deo," a popular title for the rajas of the Vaghela and Solonki dynasties, does seem to place the Nunari fonder in the context of medieval Gujerat. Furthermore, Hedayat clearly identifies the saint (*pir*) said to have initiated the conversion of the Nunaris to Islam. This saint, Mukhdum-i-Jehaniyan, was a contemporary of the historical Raja Karan.

Also of interest, but as yet unexplained, is that several other groups living in Nunari settlement areas specifically claim to be descended from Raja Karan of Gujerat, who is said to have migrated northward into the Punjab after his defeat. Controverting this theory, the available evidence indicates that Raja Karan fled, not toward the Punjab, but rather southward to the Deccan, and that his patriline ended with him. It is his daughter, Deval Devi who is remembered: she is the celebrated heroine of "Ashiqa," a famous Urdu poem written by Amir Khusrau in 1316. She was married to Khizr Khan, the son of Karan's conqueror; nothing is known of her progeny.

Richard Kurin is the Deputy Director of Folklife Programs at the Smithsonian Institution.

Eating Christmas in the Kalahari

Richard Borshay Lee

The !Kung Bushmen's knowledge of Christmas is thirdhand. The London Missionary Society brought the holiday to the southern Tswana tribes in the early nineteenth century. Later, native catechists spread the idea far and wide among the Bantu-speaking pastoralists, even in the remotest corners of the Kalahari Desert. The Bushmen's idea of the Christmas story, stripped to its essentials, is "praise the birth of white man's god-chief"; what keeps their interest in the holiday high is the Tswana-Herero custom of slaughtering an ox for his Bushmen neighbors as an annual goodwill gesture. Since the 1930's, part of the Bushmen's annual round of activities has included a December congregation at the cattle posts for trading, marriage brokering, and several days of trance-dance feasting at which the local Tswana headman is host.

As a social anthropologist working with !Kung Bushmen, I found that the Christmas ox custom suited my purposes. I had come to the Kalahari to study the hunting and gathering subsistence economy of the !Kung, and to accomplish this it was essential not to provide them with food, share my own food, or interfere in any way with their food-gathering activities. While liberal handouts of tobacco and medical supplies were appreciated, they were scarcely adequate to erase the glaring disparity in wealth between the anthropologist, who maintained a two-month inventory of canned goods, and the Bushmen, who rarely had a day's supply of food on hand. My approach, while paying off in terms of data, left me open to frequent accusations of stinginess and hard-heartedness. By their lights, I was a miser.

The Christmas ox was to be my way of saying thank you for the cooperation of the past year; and since it was to be our last Christmas in the field, I determined to slaughter the largest, meatiest ox that money could buy, insuring that the feast and trance-dance would be a success.

Through December I kept my eyes open at the wells as the cattle were brought down for watering. Several animals were offered, but none had quite the grossness that I had in mind. Then, ten days before the holiday, a Herero friend led an ox of astonishing size and mass up to our camp. It was solid black, stood five feet high at the shoulder, had a five-foot span of horns, and must have weighed 1,200 pounds on the hoof. Food consumption calculations are my specialty, and I quickly figured that bones and viscera aside, there was enough meat—at least four pounds—for every man, woman, and child of the 150 Bushmen in the vicinity of /ai/ai who were expected at the feast.

Having found the right animal at last, I paid the Herero £20 ($56) and asked him to keep the beast with his herd until Christmas day. The next morning word spread among the people that the big solid black one was the ox chosen by /ontah (my Bushman name; it means, roughly, "whitey") for the Christmas feast. That afternoon I received the first delegation. Ben!a, an outspoken sixty-year-old mother of five, came to the point slowly.

"Where were you planning to eat Christmas?"

"Right here at /ai/ai," I replied.

"Alone or with others?"

"I expect to invite all the people to eat Christmas with me."

"Eat what?"

"I have purchased Yehave's black ox, and I am going to slaughter and cook it."

"That's what we were told at the well but refused to believe it until we heard it from yourself."

"Well, it's the black one," I replied expansively, although wondering what she was driving at.

"Oh, no!" Ben!a groaned, turning to her group. "They were right." Turning back to me she asked, "Do you expect us to eat that bag of bones?"

"Bag of bones! It's the biggest ox at /ai/ai."

"Big, yes, but old. And thin. Everybody knows there's no meat on that old ox. What did you expect us to eat off it, the horns?"

Everybody chuckled at Ben!a's one-liner as they walked away, but all I could manage was a weak grin.

That evening it was the turn of the young men. They came to sit at our evening fire. /gaugo, about my age, spoke to me man-to-man.

"/ontah, you have always been square with us," he lied. "What has happened to change your heart? That sack of guts and bones of Yehave's will hardly feed one camp, let alone all the Bushmen around ai/ai." And he proceeded to enumerate the seven camps in the /ai/ai vicinity, family by family. "Perhaps you have forgotten that we are not few, but many. Or are you too blind to tell the difference between a proper cow and an old wreck? That ox is thin to the point of death."

"Look, you guys," I retorted, "that is a beautiful animal, and I'm sure you will eat it with pleasure at Christmas."

"Of course we will eat it; it's food. But it won't fill us up to the point where we will have enough strength to dance. We will eat and go home to bed with stomachs rumbling."

That night as we turned in, I asked my wife, Nancy: "What did you think of the black ox?"

"It looked enormous to me. Why?"

"Well, about eight different people have told me I got gypped; that the ox is nothing but bones."

"What's the angle?" Nancy asked. "Did they have a better one to sell?"

"No, they just said that it was going to be a grim Christmas because there won't be enough meat to go around. Maybe I'll get an independent judge to look at the beast in the morning."

Bright and early, Halingisi, a Tswana cattle owner, appeared at our camp. But before I could ask him to give me his opinion on Yehave's black ox, he gave me the eye signal that indicated a confidential chat. We left the camp and sat down.

"/ontah, I'm surprised at you: you've lived here for three years and still haven't learned anything about cattle."

"But what else can a person do but choose the biggest, strongest animal one can find?" I retorted.

"Look, just because an animal is big doesn't mean that it has plenty of meat on it. The black one was a beauty when it was younger, but now it is thin to the point of death."

"Well I've already bought it. What can I do at this stage?"

"Bought it already? I thought you were just considering it. Well, you'll have to kill it and serve it, I suppose. But don't expect much of a dance to follow."

My spirits dropped rapidly. I could believe that Ben!a and /gaugo just might be putting me on about the black ox, but

Halingisi seemed to be an impartial critic. I went around that day feeling as though I had bought a lemon of a used car.

In the afternoon it was Tomazo's turn. Tomazo is a fine hunter, a top trance performer… and one of my most reliable informants. He approached the subject of the Christmas cow as part of my continuing Bushman education.

"My friend, the way it is with us Bushmen," he began, "is that we love meat. And even more than that, we love fat. When we hunt we always search for the fat ones, the ones dripping with layers of white fat: fat that turns into a clear, thick oil in the cooking pot, fat that slides down your gullet, fills your stomach and gives you a roaring diarrhea," he rhapsodized.

"So, feeling as we do," he continued, "it gives us pain to be served such a scrawny thing as Yehave's black ox. It is big, yes, and no doubt its giant bones are good for soup, but fat is what we really crave and so we will eat Christmas this year with a heavy heart."

The prospect of a gloomy Christmas now had me worried, so I asked Tomazo what I could do about it.

"Look for a fat one, a young one… smaller, but fat. Fat enough to make us //gom ('evacuate the bowels'), then we will be happy."

My suspicions were aroused when Tomazo said that he happened to know of a young, fat, barren cow that the owner was willing to part with. Was Tomazo working on commission, I wondered? But I dispelled this unworthy thought when we approached the Herero owner of the cow in question and found that he had decided not to sell.

The scrawny wreck of a Christmas ox now became the talk of the /ai/ai water hole and was the first news told to the outlying groups as they began to come in from the bush for the feast. What finally convinced me that real trouble might be brewing was the visit from u!au, an old conservative with a reputation for fierceness. His nickname meant spear and referred to an incident thirty years ago in which he had speared a man to death. He had an intense manner; fixing me with his eyes, he said in clipped tones:

"I have only just heard about the black ox today, or else I would have come here earlier. /ontah, do you honestly think you can serve meat like that to people and avoid a fight?" He paused, letting the implications sink in. "I don't mean fight you, /ontah; you are a white man. I mean a fight between Bushmen. There are many fierce ones here, and with such a small quantity of meat to distribute, how can you give everybody a fair share? Someone is sure to accuse another of taking too much or hogging all the choice pieces. Then you will see what happens when some go hungry while others eat."

The possibility of at least a serious argument struck me as all too real. I had witnessed the tension that surrounds the distribution of meat from a kudu or gemsbok kill, and had documented many arguments that sprang up from a real or imagined slight in meat distribution. The owners of a kill may spend up to two hours arranging and rearranging the piles of meat under the gaze of a circle of recipients before handing them out. And I also knew that the Christmas feast at /ai/ai would be bringing together groups that had feuded in the past.

Convinced now of the gravity of the situation, I went in earnest to search for a second cow; but all my inquiries failed to turn one up.

The Christmas feast was evidently going to be a disaster, and the incessant complaints about the meagerness of the ox had already taken the fun out of it for me. Moreover, I was getting bored with the wisecracks, and after losing my temper a few times, I resolved to serve the beast anyway. If the meat fell short, the hell with it. In the Bushmen idiom, I announced to all who would listen:

"I am a poor man and blind. If I have chosen one that is too old and too thin, we will eat it anyway and see if there is enough meat there to quiet the rumbling of our stomachs."

On hearing this speech, Ben!a offered me a rare word of comfort. "It's thin," she said philosophically, "but the bones will make a good soup."

At dawn Christmas morning, instinct told me to turn over the butchering and cooking to a friend and take off with Nancy to spend Christmas alone in the bush. But curiosity kept me from retreating. I wanted to see what such a scrawny ox looked like on butchering and if there *was* going to be a fight, I wanted to catch every word of it. Anthropologists are incurable that way.

The great beast was driven up to our dancing ground, and a shot in the forehead dropped it in its tracks. Then, freshly cut branches were heaped around the fallen carcass to receive the meat. Ten men volunteered to help with the cutting. I asked /gaugo to make the breast bone cut. This cut, which begins the butchering process for most large game, offers easy access for removal of the viscera. But it also allows the hunter to spot-check the amount of fat on the animal. A fat game animal carries a white layer up to an inch thick on the chest, while in a thin one, the knife will quickly cut to bone. All eyes fixed on his hand as /gaugo, dwarfed by the great carcass, knelt to the breast. The first cut opened a pool of solid white in the black skin. The second and third cut widened and deepened the creamy white. Still no bone. It was pure fat; it must have been two inches thick.

"Hey /gau," I burst out, "that ox is loaded with fat. What's this about the ox being too thin to bother eating? Are you out of your mind?"

"Fat?" /gau shot back, "You call that fat? This wreck is thin, sick, dead!" And he broke out laughing. So did everyone else. They rolled on the ground, paralyzed with laughter. Everybody laughed except me; I was thinking.

I ran back to the tent and burst in just as Nancy was getting up. "Hey, the black ox. It's fat as hell! They were kidding about it being too thin to eat. It was a joke or something. A put-on. Everyone is really delighted with it!"

"Some joke," my wife replied. "It was so funny that you were ready to pack up and leave /ai/ai."

If it had indeed been a joke, it had been an extraordinarily convincing one, and tinged, I thought, with more than a touch of malice as many jokes are. Nevertheless, that it was a joke lifted my spirits considerably, and I returned to the butchering site where the shape of the ox was rapidly disappearing under the axes and knives of the butchers. The atmosphere had become festive. Grinning broadly, their arms covered with blood well past the elbow, men packed chunks of meat into the big cast-iron cooking pots, fifty pounds to the load, and muttered and chuckled all the while about the thinness and worthlessness of the animal and /ontah's poor judgment.

We danced and ate that ox two days and two nights; we cooked and distributed fourteen potfuls of meat and no one went home hungry and no fights broke out.

But the "joke" stayed in my mind. I had a growing feeling that something important had happened in my relationship with the Bushmen and that the clue lay in the meaning of the joke. Several days later, when most of the people had dispersed back to the bush camps, I raised the question with Hakekgose, a Tswana man who had grown up among the !Kung, married a !Kung girl, and who probably knew their culture better than any other non-Bushman.

"With us whites," I began, "Christmas is supposed to be the day of friendship and brotherly love. What I can't figure out is why the Bushmen went to such lengths to criticize and belittle the ox I had bought for the feast. The animal was perfectly good and their jokes and wisecracks practically ruined the holiday for me."

"So it really did bother you," said Hakekgose. "Well, that's the way they always talk. When I take my rifle and go hunting with them, if I miss, they laugh at me for the rest of the day. But even if I hit and bring one down, it's no better. To them, the kill is always too small or too old or too thin; and as we sit down on the kill site to cook and eat the liver, they keep grumbling, even with their mouths full of meat. They say things like, 'Oh this is awful! What a worthless animal! Whatever made me think that this Tswana rascal could hunt!'"

"Is this the way outsiders are treated?" I asked.

"No, it is their custom; they talk that way to each other too. Go and ask them."

/gaugo had been one of the most enthusiastic in making me feel bad about the merit of the Christmas ox. I sought him out first.

"Why did you tell me the black ox was worthless, when you could see that it was loaded with fat and meat?"

"It is our way," he said smiling. "We always like to fool people about that. Say there is a Bushman who has been hunting. He must not come home and announce like a braggard, 'I have killed a big one in the bush!' He must first sit down in silence until I or someone else comes up to his fire and asks, 'What did you see today?' He replies quietly, 'Ah, I'm no good for hunting. I saw nothing at all [pause] just a little tiny one.' Then I smile to myself," /gaugo continued, "because I know he has killed something big."

"In the morning we make up a party of four or five people to cut up and carry the meat back to the camp. When we arrive at the kill we examine it and cry out, 'You mean to say you have dragged us all the way out here in order to make us cart home your pile of bones? Oh, if I had known it was this thin I wouldn't have come.' Another one pipes up, 'People, to think I gave up a nice day in the shade for this. At home we may be hungry but at least we have nice cool water to drink.' If the horns are big, someone says, 'Did you think that somehow you were going to boil down the horns for soup?'

"To all this you must respond in kind. 'I agree,' you say, 'this one is not worth the effort; let's just cook the liver for strength and leave the rest for the hyenas. It is not too late to hunt today and even a duiker or a steenbok would be better than this mess.'

"Then you set to work nevertheless; butcher the animal, carry the meat back to the camp and everyone eats," /gaugo concluded.

Things were beginning to make sense. Next, I went to Tomazo. He corroborated /gaugo's story of the obligatory insults over a kill and added a few details of his own.

"But," I asked, "why insult a man after he has gone to all that trouble to track and kill an animal and when he is going to share the meat with you so that your children will have something to eat?"

"Arrogance," was his cryptic answer.

"Arrogance?"

"Yes, when a young man kills much meat he comes to think of himself as a chief or a big man, and he thinks of the rest of us as his servants or inferiors. We can't accept this. We refuse one who boasts, for someday his pride will make him kill somebody. So we always speak of his meat as worthless. This way we cool his heart and make him gentle."

"But why didn't you tell me this before?" I asked Tomazo with some heat.

"Because you never asked me," said Tomazo, echoing the refrain that has come to haunt every field ethnographer.

The pieces now fell into place. I had known for a long time that in situations of social conflict with Bushmen I held all the cards. I was the only source of tobacco in a thousand square miles, and I was not incapable of cutting an individual off for non-cooperation. Though my boycott never lasted longer than a few days, it was an indication of my strength. People resented my presence at the water

hole, yet simultaneously dreaded my leaving. In short I was a perfect target for the charge of arrogance and for the Bushmen tactic of enforcing humility.

I had been taught an object lesson by the Bushmen; it had come from an unexpected corner and had hurt me in a vulnerable area. For the big black ox was to be the one totally generous, unstinting act of my year at /ai/ai, and I was quite unprepared for the reaction I received.

As I read it, their message was this: There are no totally generous acts. All "acts" have an element of calculation. One black ox slaughtered at Christmas does not wipe out a year of careful manipulation of gifts given to serve your own ends. After all, to kill an animal and share the meat with people is really no more than Bushmen do for each other every day and with far less fanfare.

In the end, I had to admire how the Bushmen had played out the farce—collectively straight-faced to the end. Curi-

ously, the episode reminded me of the *Good Soldier Schweik* and his marvelous encounters with authority. Like Schweik, the Bushmen had retained a thorough-going skepticism of good intentions. Was it this independence of spirit, I wondered, that had kept them culturally viable in the face of generations of contact with more powerful societies, both black and white? The thought that the Bushmen were alive and well in the Kalahari was strangely comforting. Perhaps, armed with that independence and with their superb knowledge of their environment, they might yet survive the future.

Richard Borshay Lee is a full professor of anthropology at the University of Toronto. He has done extensive fieldwork in southern Africa, is coeditor of Man the Hunter *(1968) and* Kalahari Hunter-Gatherers *(1976), and author of* The !Kung San: Men, Women, and Work in a Foraging Society.

Reprinted with permission from *Natural History*, December 1969. © 1969 by Natural History Magazine.

Coping with culture clash

Abstract: *Culture clash has cost international companies billions of dollars in lost business and led to the sinking of otherwise sea-worthy enterprises. It took a long time for international business to realize that business culture is not a one-size-fits-all phenomenon. The inability to understand another's business culture has cost multinationals so much that many have now put culture awareness at the top of their management agenda. Africa is probably at the top of the pile in the culture-clash stakes.*

Anver Versi

Have you ever felt like pulling out your hair in frustration because somebody you are doing business with in another country keeps messing you about? They don't return your calls promptly, they do not stick to the schedule, they say they will do something today and then don't do it for several days, they make unreasonable demands, they are rude in their communications—the list can go on and on. "Why can't people just get on with business normally instead of making life more difficult than it already is?" is the exasperated cry from any number of executives.

The trouble, as more and more international executives are finding out is that both parties are 'getting on with business normally' but what is normal for one is abnormal for another.

Another phrase for this is 'culture clash' or 'culture shock'. Culture clash has cost international companies billions of dollars in lost business and led to the sinking of otherwise sea-worthy enterprises. It took a long time for international business to realise that business culture is not a one-size-fits-all phenomenon. Different parts of the world have different business cultures and these are so normal as far as they are concerned that they just cannot understand why anybody else would want to do things differently. There is a name for this—it is called ethnocentrism.

My way is the right way! Ethnocentrism means 'my way is the right way' but since it is subconscious, you are not aware of it—you simply think of it as 'normal' so when people do things differently, you start to pull your hair out because 'you just can't understand why they are messing me about'.

This inability to understand the other's business culture has cost multinationals so much that many have now put 'culture awareness' at the top of their management agenda. In the US it is called 'diversity awareness' and it is considered so important that diversity gurus are being paid as much as $50,000 per session to speak at conferences.

Africa is probably at the top of the pile in the culture-clash stakes. Take for example the time-fixation of Westerners or people of Western origin. They are always looking at their watches and become very upset when someone does not keep an appointment. They talk of 'African time' which means that the person you are expecting will be there when he is there—never mind what time he said he would come. He may come early, on time, later or even tomorrow. He is here, so what is the problem?

This might seem a trivial issue but it excellently typifies the culture-clash between the West and Africa. It has long, now dimly remembered roots. The Western 'time culture' grew out of two factors. One is the short growing and harvesting season (spring and summer) before the dead winter months. This leads to a sense of urgency and therefore the conservation of time.

Clocking in, clocking out

The second and more important factor was industrialisation and mass production. Work was broken down into simple, repeated, mechanical tasks. Management was involved trying to produce as many units as possible within a time frame. It was a question of clocking in and clocking out. Management watched the clock to see how many units were produced per hour, workers watched the clock to see when their shift was over. Although machinery has now mostly replaced people, the habit has remained.

Another legacy of industrialisation was that tasks became more important than the people performing them. This gave rise to a system of depersonalisation—the position or post was what counted, not who filled it. Institutions thus became more important than personalities.

In Africa on the other hand, with year round growth possible, it was ridiculous to split time into hours and minutes. You thought in terms of seasons, of periods of rainfall. You waited for the crop to ripen. You used the time in between to carry out urgent chores, or fulfilling your social and communal obligations. The crops would grow when they would, the rain would come when it did—there was little you could do to hasten the process. But the needs of people around you were urgent so you gave them priority.

We see these traits today in modern Africa just as we see the culture clash between the time-starved Westerner and the time-rich African. Who is to say which is the better business culture? And if the point of business is to enhance the quality of life, and if the African feels it is more important to make a detour to visit his sick mother before meeting the Westerner to discuss something which will not happen for a long time, who can quarrel with him?

Each has his value system and his priorities and both are justified within their cultural environments.

These different culture clashes are not limited to business. In the West generally, who you are is not important, what is important is your function.

In Africa, who you are is more important than what you do. After all, anybody can do what you do—but what you do only becomes meaningful because you are doing it. And what is the point of doing something, or obtaining a position of influence if you cannot help your relations, your friends and your neighbours?

Individualism versus collectivism

In the West, individualism rules because the state acts as your 'family'; in Africa collectivism rules because only your relatives will look after you in trouble.

As the diversity gurus in the US are finding out, if you understand where the other person is coming from culturally, you can work out a modus operandi. If you don't, you will not only lose your hair, but maybe also your shirt. So a good rule might be: when in Africa, do as Africans do.

From *African Business*, May 2002, p. 8. © 2002 by African Business. Reprinted by permission of I.C. Publications, Ltd.

UNIT 2
Culture and Communication

Unit Selections

5. **Fighting for Our Lives**, Deborah Tannen
6. **"I Can't Even Open My Mouth"**, Deborah Tannen
7. **Shakespeare in the Bush**, Laura Bohannan
8. **Body Art As Visual Language**, Enid Schildkrout

Key Points to Consider

- How can language restrict our thought processes?

- In what ways is communication difficult in a cross-cultural situation?

- How has the "argument culture" affected the way we conduct ourselves vis-à-vis others?

- Does body art express individuality, conformity or both?

- How has this section enhanced your ability to communicate more effectively?

 **Links: www.dushkin.com/online/**
These sites are annotated in the World Wide Web pages.

Exploratorium Magazine: "The Evolution of Languages"
   http://www.exploratorium.edu/exploring/language
Hypertext and Ethnography
   http://www.umanitoba.ca/anthropology/tutor/aaa_presentation.html
Language Extinction
   http://www.colorado.edu/iec/alis/articles/langext.htm
Showcase Anthropology
   http://www.anthropology.wisc.edu/chaysimire/

Anthropologists are interested in all aspects of human behavior and how they interrelate with each other. Language is a form of such behavior (albeit primarily verbal behavior) and, therefore, worthy of study. Although it changes over time, language is patterned and passed down from one generation to the next through learning, not instinct. In keeping with the idea that language is integral to human social interaction, it has long been recognized that human communication through language is by its nature different from the kind of communication found among other animals. Central to this difference is the fact that humans communicate abstractly, with symbols that have meaning independent of the immediate sensory experiences of either the sender or the receiver of messages. Thus, for instance, humans are able to refer to the future and the past instead of just the here and now.

Recent experiments have shown that anthropoid apes can be taught a small portion of Ameslan or American Sign Language. It must be remembered, however, that their very rudimentary ability has to be tapped by painstaking human effort, and that the degree of difference between apes and humans serves only to emphasize the peculiarly human need for and development of language.

Just as the abstract quality of symbols lifts our thoughts beyond immediate sense perception, it also inhibits our ability to think about and convey the full meaning of our personal experience. No categorical term can do justice to its referents—the variety of forms to which the term refers. The degree to which this is an obstacle to clarity of thought and communication relates to the degree of abstraction in the symbols involved. The word "chair," for instance, would not present much difficulty, since it has objective referents. However, consider the trouble we have in thinking and communicating with words whose referents are not tied to immediate sense perception—words such as "freedom," "democracy," and "justice." Deborah Tannen's discussion of the "argument culture" (in "Fighting for our Lives") is a prime example of this. At best, the likely result is symbolic confusion: an inability to think or communicate in objectively definable symbols. At worst, language may be used to purposefully obfuscate.

A related issue has to do with the fact that languages differ as to what is relatively easy to express within the restrictions of their particular vocabularies. Thus, although a given language may not have enough words to cope with a new situation or a new field of activity, the typical solution is to invent words or to borrow them. In this way, it may be said that any language can be used to teach anything. This point is illustrated by Laura Bohannan's attempt to convey the "true" meaning of Shakespeare's *Hamlet* to the West African Tiv (see "Shakespeare in the Bush"). Much of her task was devoted to finding the most appropriate words in the Tiv language to convey her Western thoughts. At least part of her failure was due to the fact that some of the words are just not there, and her inventions were unacceptable to the Tiv.

In a somewhat different manner, Deborah Tannen, in "I Can't Even Open My Mouth," points out that there are subtleties to language that cannot be found in a dictionary and whose meaning can only be interpreted in the context of the social situation.

Taken collectively, the articles in this unit show how symbolic confusion may occur between individuals or groups. In addition, they demonstrate the tremendous potential of recent research to enhance effective communication among all of us.

FIGHTING FOR OUR LIVES

Deborah Tannen, Ph.D.

This is not another book about civility. "Civility" suggests a superficial, pinky-in-the-air veneer of politeness spread thin over human relations like a layer of marmalade over toast. This book is about a pervasive warlike atmosphere that makes us approach public dialogue, and just about anything we need to accomplish, as if it were a fight. It is a tendency in Western culture in general, and in the United States in particular, that has a long history and a deep, thick, and far-ranging root system. It has served us well in many ways but in recent years has become so exaggerated that it is getting in the way of solving our problems. Our spirits are corroded by living in an atmosphere of unrelenting contention—an argument culture.

The argument culture urges us to approach the world—and the people in it—in an adversarial frame of mind. It rests on the assumption that opposition is the best way to get anything done: The best way to discuss an idea is to set up a debate; the best way to cover news is to find spokespeople who express the most extreme, polarized views and present them as "both sides"; the best way to settle disputes is litigation that pits one party against the other; the best way to begin an essay is to attack someone; and the best way to show you're really thinking is to criticize.

Our public interactions have become more and more like having an argument with a spouse. Conflict can't be avoided in our public lives any more than we can avoid conflict with people we love. One of the great strengths of our society is that we can express these conflicts openly. But just as spouses have to learn ways of settling their differences without inflicting real damage on each other, so we, as a society, have to find constructive ways of resolving disputes and differences. Public discourse requires *making* an argument for a point of view, not *having* an argument—as in having a fight.

The war on drugs, the war on cancer, the battle of the sexes, politicians' turf battles—in the argument culture, war metaphors pervade our talk and shape our thinking. Nearly everything is framed as a battle or game in which winning or losing is the main concern. These all have their uses and their place, but they are not the only way—and often not the best way—to understand and approach our world. Conflict and opposition are as necessary as cooperation and agreement, but the scale is off balance, with conflict and opposition overweighted. In this book, I show how deeply entrenched the argument culture is, the forms it takes, and how it affects us every day—sometimes in useful ways, but often creating more problems than it solves, causing rather than avoiding damage. As a sociolinguist, a social scientist, I am trained to observe and explain language and its role in human relations, and that is my biggest job here. But I will also point toward other ways for us to talk to each other and get things done in our public lives.

THE BATTLE OF THE SEXES

My interest in the topic of opposition in public discourse intensified in the years following the publication of *You Just Don't Understand,* my book about communication between women and men. In the first year I appeared on many television and radio shows and was interviewed for many print articles in newspapers and magazines. For the most part, that coverage was extremely fair, and I was—and remain—indebted to the many journalists who found my ideas interesting enough to make them known to viewers, listeners, and readers. But from time to time—more often than I expected—I encountered producers who insisted on setting up a television show as a fight (either between the host and me or between another guest and me) and print journalists who made multiple phone calls to my colleagues, trying to find someone who would criticize my work. This got me thinking about what kind of information comes across on shows and in articles that take this approach, compared to those that approach topics in other ways.

At the same time, my experience of the academic world that had long been my intellectual home began to change. For the most part, other scholars, like most journalists, were welcoming and respectful in their responses to my work, even if they disagreed on specific points or had alternative views to suggest. But about a year after *You Just Don't Understand* became a best-seller—the wheels of academia grind more slowly than those of the popular press—I began reading attacks on my work that completely misrepresented it. I had been in academia for over fifteen years by then, and had valued my interaction with other researchers as one of the greatest rewards of academic life. Why, I wondered, would someone represent me as having said things I had never said or as having failed to say things I had said?

The answer crystallized when I put the question to a writer who I felt had misrepresented my work: "Why do you need to make others wrong for you to be right?" Her response: "It's an argument!" Aha, I thought, that explains it. When you're having an argument with someone, your goal is not to listen and understand. Instead, you use every tactic you can think of—including distorting what your opponent just said—in order to win the argument.

Not only the level of attention *You Just Don't Understand* received but, even more, the subject of women and men, triggered the tendency to polarize. This tendency to stage a fight on television or in print was posited on the conviction that opposition leads to truth. Sometimes it does. But the trouble is, sometimes it doesn't. I was asked at the start of more than one talk show or print interview, "What is the most controversial thing about your book?" Opposition does not lead to truth when the most controversial thing is not the most important.

The conviction that opposition leads to truth can tempt not only members of the press but just about anyone seeking to attract an audience to frame discussions as a fight between irreconcilable opposites. Even the Smithsonian Institution, to celebrate its 150th anniversary, sponsored a series of talks billed as debates. They invited me to take part in one titled "The Battle of the Sexes." The organizer preempted my objection: "I know you won't be happy with this title, but we want to get people interested." This is one of many assumptions I question in this book: Is it necessary to frame an interchange as a battle to get people interested? And even if doing so succeeds in capturing attention, does it risk dampening interest in the long run, as audiences weary of the din and begin to hunger for more substance?

THOUGHT-PROVOKING
OR JUST PROVOCATIVE?

In the spring of 1995, Horizons Theatre in Arlington, Virginia, produced two one-act plays I had written about family relationships. The director, wanting to contribute to the reconciliation between Blacks and Jews, mounted my plays in repertory with two one-act plays by an African American playwright, Caleen Sinnette Jennings. We had both written plays about three sisters that explored the ethnic identities of our families (Jewish for me, African-American for her) and the relationship between those identities and the American context in which we grew up. To stir interest in the plays and to explore the parallels between her work and mine, the theater planned a public dialogue between Jennings and me, to be held before the plays opened.

As production got under way, I attended the audition of actors for my plays. After the auditions ended, just before everyone headed home, the theater's public relations volunteer distributed copies of the flyer announcing the public dialogue that she had readied for distribution. I was horrified. The flyer announced that Caleen and I would discuss "how past traumas create understanding and conflict between Blacks and Jews today." The flyer was trying to grab by the throat the issue that we wished to address indirectly. Yes, we were concerned with conflicts between Blacks and Jews, but neither of us is an authority on that conflict, and we had no intention of expounding on it. We hoped to do our part to ameliorate the conflict by focusing on commonalities. Our plays had many resonances between them. We wanted to talk about our work and let the resonances speak for themselves.

Fortunately, we were able to stop the flyers before they were distributed and devise new ones that promised something we could deliver: "a discussion of heritage, identity, and complex family relationships in African-American and Jewish-American culture as represented in their plays." Jennings noticed that the original flyer said the evening would be "provocative" and changed it to "thought-provoking." What a world of difference is implied in that small change: how much better to make people think, rather than simply to "provoke" them—as often as not, to anger.

It is easy to understand why conflict is so often highlighted: Writers of headlines or promotional copy want to catch attention and attract an audience. They are usually under time pressure, which lures them to established, conventionalized ways of expressing ideas in the absence of leisure to think up entirely new ones. The promise of controversy seems an easy and natural way to rouse interest. But serious consequences are often unintended: Stirring up animosities to get a rise out of people, though easy and "provocative," can open old wounds or create new ones that are hard to heal. This is one of many dangers inherent in the argument culture.

FOR THE SAKE OF ARGUMENT

In the argument culture, criticism, attack, or opposition are the predominant if not the the only ways of responding to people or ideas. I use the phrase "culture of critique" to capture this aspect. "Critique" in this sense is not a general term for analysis or interpretation but rather a synonym for criticism.

It is the *automatic* nature of this response that I am calling attention to—and calling into question. Sometimes passionate opposition, strong verbal attack, are appropriate and called for. No one knows this better than those who have lived under repressive regimes that forbid public opposition. The Yugoslavian-born poet Charles Simic is one. "There are moments in life," he writes, "when true invective is called for, when it becomes an absolute necessity, out of a deep sense of justice, to denounce, mock, vituperate, lash out, in the strongest possible language." I applaud and endorse this view. There are times when it is necessary and right to fight—to defend your country or yourself, to argue for right against wrong or against offensive or dangerous ideas or actions.

What I question is the ubiquity, the knee-jerk nature, of approaching almost any issue, problem, or public person in an adversarial way. One of the dangers of the habitual use of adversarial rhetoric is a kind of verbal inflation—a rhetorical boy who cried wolf: The legitimate, necessary denunciation is muted, even lost, in the general cacophony of oppositional shouting. What I question is using opposition to accomplish *every* goal, even those that do not require fighting but might also (or better) be accomplished by other means, such as exploring, expanding, discussing, investigating, and the exchanging of ideas suggested by the word "dialogue." I am questioning the assumption that *everything* is a matter of polarized opposites, the proverbial "two sides to every question" that we think embodies open-mindedness and expansive thinking.

In a word, the type of opposition I am questioning is what I call "agonism." I use this term, which derives from the Greek word for "contest," *agonia,* to mean an automatic warlike stance—not the literal opposition of fighting against an attacker or the unavoidable opposition that arises organically in response to conflicting ideas or actions. An agonistic response, to me, is a kind of programmed contentiousness—a prepatterned, unthinking use of fighting to accomplish goals that do not necessarily require it.

HOW USEFUL ARE FIGHTS?

Noticing that public discourse so often takes the form of heated arguments—of having a fight—made me ask how useful it is in our personal lives to settle differences by arguing. Given what I know about having arguments in private life, I had to conclude that it is, in many cases, not very useful.

In close relationships it is possible to find ways of arguing that result in better understanding and solving problems. But with most arguments, little is resolved, worked out, or achieved when two people get angrier and less rational by the minute. When you're having an argument with someone, you're usually not trying to understand what the other person is saying, or what in their experience leads them to say it. Instead, you're readying your response: listening for weaknesses in logic to leap on, points you can distort to make the other person look bad and yourself look good. Sometimes you know, on some back burner of your mind, that you're doing this—that there's a kernel of truth in what your adversary is saying and a bit of unfair twisting in what you're saying. Sometimes you do this because you're angry, but sometimes it's just the temptation to take aim at a point made along the way because it's an easy target.

Here's an example of how this happened in an argument between a couple who had been married for over fifty years. The husband wanted to join an HMO by signing over their Medicare benefits to save money. The wife objected because it would mean she could no longer see the doctor she knew and trusted. In arguing her point of view, she said, "I like Dr. B. He knows me, he's interested in me. He calls me by my first name." The husband parried the last point: "I don't like that. He's much younger than we are. He shouldn't be calling us by first name." But the form of address Dr. B. uses was irrelevant. The wife was trying to communicate that she felt comfortable with the doctor she knew, that she had a relationship with him. His calling her by first name was just one of a list of details she was marshaling to explain her comfort with him. Picking on this one detail did not change her view—and did not address her concern. It was just a way to win the argument.

We all are guilty, at times, of seizing on irrelevant details, distorting someone else's position the better to oppose it, when we're arguing with those we're closest to. But we are rarely dependent on these fights as sources of information. The same tactics are common when public discourse is carried out on the model of personal fights. And the results are dangerous when listeners are looking to these interchanges to get needed information or practical results.

Fights have winners and losers. If you're fighting to win, the temptation is great to deny facts that support your opponent's views and to filter what you know, saying only what supports your side. In the extreme form, it encourages people to misrepresent or even to lie. We accept this risk because we believe we can tell when someone is lying. The problem is, we can't.

Paul Ekman, a psychologist at the University of California, San Francisco, studies lying. He set up experiments in which individuals were videotaped talking about their emotions, actions, or beliefs—some truthfully, some not. He has shown these videotapes to thousands of people, asking them to identify the liars and also to say how sure they were about their judgments. His findings are chilling: Most people performed not much better than chance, and those who did the worst had just as much confidence in their judgments as the few who were really able to detect lies. Intrigued by the implications of this research in various walks of life, Dr. Ekman repeated this experiment with groups of people whose jobs require them to sniff out lies: judges, lawyers, police, psychotherapists, and employees of the CIA, FBI, and ATF (Bureau of Alcohol, Tobacco, and Firearms). They were no better at detecting who was telling the truth than the rest of us. The only group that did significantly better were members of the U.S. Secret Service. This finding gives some comfort when it comes to the Secret Service but not much when it comes to every other facet of public life.

TWO SIDES TO EVERY QUESTION

Our determination to pursue truth by setting up a fight between two sides leads us to believe that every issue has two sides—no more, no less: If both sides are given a forum to confront each other, all the relevant information will emerge, and the best case will be made for each side. But opposition does not lead to truth when an issue is not composed of two opposing sides but is a crystal of many sides. Often the truth is in the complex middle, not the oversimplified extremes.

We love using the word "debate" as a way of representing issues: the abortion debate, the health care debate, the affirmative action debate—even "the great backpacking vs. car camping debate." The ubiquity of this word in itself shows our tendency to conceptualize issues in a way that predisposes public discussion to be polarized, framed as two opposing sides that give each other no ground. There are many problems with this approach. If you begin with the assumption that there *must* be an "other side," you may end up scouring the margins of science or the fringes of lunacy to find it. As a result, proven facts, such as what we know about how the earth and its inhabitants evolved, are set on a par with claims that are known to have no basis in fact, such as creationism.

The conviction that there are two sides to every story can prompt writers or producers to dig up an "other side," so kooks who state outright falsehoods are given a platform in public discourse. This accounts, in part, for the bizarre phenomenon of Holocaust denial. Deniers, as Emory University professor Deborah Lipstadt shows, have been successful in gaining television airtime and campus newspaper coverage by masquerading as "the other side" in a "debate."

Appearance in print or on television has a way of lending legitimacy, so baseless claims take on a mantle of possibility. Lipstadt shows how Holocaust deniers dispute established facts of history, and then reasonable spokespersons use their having been disputed as a basis for questioning known facts. The actor Robert Mitchum, for example, interviewed in *Esquire,* expressed doubt about the Holocaust. When the interviewer asked about the slaughter of six million Jews, Mitchum replied, "I don't know. People dispute that." Continual reference to "the other side" results in a pervasive conviction that everything has another side—with the result that people begin to doubt the existence of any facts at all.

THE EXPENSE OF TIME AND SPIRIT

Lipstadt's book meticulously exposes the methods used by deniers to falsify the overwhelming historic evidence that the Holocaust occurred. That a scholar had to invest years of her professional life writing a book unraveling efforts to deny something that was about as well known and well documented as any historical fact has ever been—while those who personally experienced and witnessed it are still alive—is testament to another way that the argument culture limits our knowledge rather than expanding it. Talent and effort was wasted when individuals who have been unfairly attacked must spend years of their creative lives defending themselves rather than advancing their work. The entire society loses their creative efforts. This is what happened with scientist Robert Gallo.

Dr. Gallo is the American virologist who codiscovered the AIDS virus. He is also the one who developed the technique for studying T-cells, which made that discovery possible. And Gallo's work was seminal in developing the test to detect the AIDS virus in blood, the first and for a long time the only means known of stemming the tide of death from AIDS. But in 1989, Gallo became the object of a four-year investigation into allegations that he had stolen the AIDS virus from Luc Montagnier of the Pasteur Institute in Paris, who had independently identified the AIDS virus. Simultaneous investigations by the National Institutes of Health, the office of Michigan Congressman John Dingell, and the National Academy of Sciences barreled ahead long after Gallo and Montagnier settled the dispute to their mutual satisfaction. In 1993 the investigations concluded that Gallo had done nothing wrong. Nothing. But this exoneration cannot be considered a happy ending. Never mind the personal suffering of Gallo, who was reviled when he should have been heralded as a hero. Never mind that, in his words, "These were the most painful years and horrible years of my life." The dreadful, unconscionable result of the fruitless investigations is that Gallo had to spend four years fighting the accusations instead of fighting AIDS.

The investigations, according to journalist Nicholas Wade, were sparked by an article about Gallo written in the currently popular spirit of demonography: not to praise the person it features but to bury him—to show his weaknesses, his villainous side. The implication that Gallo has stolen the AIDS virus was created to fill a requirement of the discourse: In demonography, writers must find negative sides of their subjects to display for readers who enjoy seeing heroes transformed into villains. The suspicion led to investigations, and the investigations became a juggernaut that acquired a life of its own, fed by the enthusiasm for attack on public figures that is the culture of critique.

METAPHORS: WE ARE WHAT WE SPEAK

Perhaps one reason suspicions of Robert Gallo were so zealously investigated is that the scenario of an ambitious scientist ready to do anything to defeat a rival appeals to our sense of story; it is the kind of narrative we are ready to believe. Culture, in a sense, is an environment of narratives that we hear repeatedly until they seem to make self-evident sense in explaining human behavior. Thinking of human interactions as battles is a metaphorical frame through which we learn to regard the world and the people in it.

All language uses metaphors to express ideas; some metaphoric words and expressions are novel, made up for the occasion, but more are calcified in the language. They are simply the way we think it is natural to express ideas. We don't think of them as metaphors. Someone who says, "Be careful: You aren't a cat, you don't have nine lives," is explicitly comparing you to a cat, because the cat is named in words. But what if someone says, "Don't pussyfoot around; get to the point"? There is no explicit comparison to a cat, but the comparison is there nonetheless, implied in the word "pussyfoot." This expression probably developed as a reference to the movement of a cat cautiously circling a suspicious object. I doubt that individuals using the word "pussyfoot" think consciously of cats. More often than not, we use expressions without thinking about their metaphoric implications. But that doesn't mean those implications are not influencing us.

At a meeting, a general discussion became so animated that a participant who wanted to comment prefaced his remark by saying, "I'd like to leap into the fray." Another participant called out, "Or share your thoughts." Everyone laughed. By suggesting a different phrasing, she called attention to what would probably have otherwise gone unnoticed: "Leap into the fray" characterized the lively discussion as a metaphorical battle.

Americans talk about almost everything as if it were a war. A book about the history of linguistics is called *The Linguistics Wars.* A magazine article about claims that science is not completely objective is titled "The Science Wars." One about breast cancer detection is "The Mammogram War"; about competition among caterers, "Party Wars"—and on and on in a potentially endless list. Politics, of course, is a prime candidate. One of innumerable possible examples, the headline of a story reporting that the Democratic National Convention nominated Bill Clinton to run for a second term declares, "DEMOCRATS SEND CLINTON INTO BATTLE FOR A 2D TERM." But medicine is as frequent a candidate, as we talk about battling and conquering disease.

Headlines are intentionally devised to attract attention, but we all use military or attack imagery in everyday expressions without thinking about it: "Take a shot at it," "I don't want to be shot down," "He went off half cocked," "That's half the battle."

Why does it matter that our public discourse is filled with military metaphors? Aren't they just words? Why not talk about something that matters—like actions?

Because words matter. When we think we are using language, language is using us. As linguist Dwight Bolinger put it (employing a military metaphor), language is like a loaded gun: It can be fired intentionally, but it can wound or kill just as surely when fired accidentally. The terms in which we talk about something shape the way we think about it—and even what we see.

The power of words to shape perception has been proven by researchers in controlled experiments. Psychologist Elizabeth Loftus and John Palmer, for example, found that the terms in which people are asked to recall something affect what they recall. The researchers showed subjects a film of two cars colliding, then asked how fast the cars were going; one week later, they asked whether there had been any broken glass. Some subjects were asked, "About how fast were the cars going when they smashed into each other?" Those who read the question with the verb "smashed" estimated that the cars were going faster. They were also more likely to "remember" having seen broken glass. (There wasn't any.)

This is how language works. It invisibly molds our way of thinking about people, actions, and the world around us. Military metaphors train us to think about—and see—everything in terms of fighting, conflict, and war. This perspective then limits our imaginations when we consider what we can do about situations we would like to understand or change.

Even in science, common metaphors that are taken for granted influence how researchers think about natural phenomena. Evelyn Fox Keller describes a case in which acceptance of a metaphor led scientists to see something that was not there. A mathematical biologist, Keller outlines the fascinating behavior of cellular slime mold. This unique mold can take two completely different forms: It can exist as single-cell organisms, or the separate cells can come together to form multicellular aggregates. The puzzle facing scientists was: What triggers aggregation? In other words, what makes the single cells join together? Scientist focused their investigations by asking what entity issued the order to start aggregating. They first called this bosslike entity a "founder cell," and later a "pacemaker cell," even though no one had seen any evidence for the existence of such a cell. Proceeding nonetheless from the assumption that such a cell must exist, they ignored evidence to the contrary: For example, when the center of the aggregate is removed, other centers form.

Scientists studying slime mold did not examine the interrelationship between the cells and their environment, nor the interrelationship between the functional systems within each cell, because they were busy looking for the pacemaker cell, which, as eventually became evident, did not exist. Instead, under conditions of nutritional deprivation, each individual cell begins to feel the urge to merge with others to form the conglomerate. It is a reaction of the cells to their environment, not to the orders of a boss. Keller recounts this tale to illustrate her insight that we tend to view nature through our understanding of human relations as hierarchical. In her words, "We risk imposing on nature the very stories we like to hear." In other words, the conceptual metaphor of hierarchical governance made scientists "see" something—a pacemaker cell—that wasn't there.

Among the stories many Americans most like to hear are war stories. According to historian Michael Sherry, the American war movie developed during World War II and has been with us ever since. He shows that movies not explicitly about war were also war movies at heart, such as westerns with their good guy–bad guy battles settled with guns. *High Noon,* for example, which became a model for later westerns, was an allegory of the Second World War: The happy ending hinges on the pacifist taking up arms. We can also see this story line in contemporary adventure films: Think of *Star Wars,* with its stirring finale in which Han Solo, having professed no interest in or taste for battle, returns at the last moment to destroy the enemy and save the day. And precisely the same theme is found in a contemporary low-budget independent film, *Sling Blade,* in which a peace-loving retarded man becomes a hero at the end by murdering the man who has been tormenting the family he has come to love.

PUT UP YOUR DUKES

If war provides the metaphors through which we view the world and each other, we come to view others—and ourselves—as warriors in battle. Almost any human encounter can be framed as a fight between two opponents. Looking at it this way brings particular aspects of the event into focus and obscures others.

Framing interactions as fights affects not only the participants but also the viewers. At a performance, the audience, as well as the performers, can be transformed. This effect was noted by a reviewer in *The New York Times,* commenting on a musical event:

> **Showdown at Lincoln Center.** Jazz's ideological war of the last several years led to a pitched battle in August between John Lincoln Collier, the writer, and Wynton Marsalis, the trumpeter, in a debate at Lincoln Center. Mr. Marsalis demolished Mr. Collier, point after point after point, but what made the debate unpleasant was the crowd's blood lust; humiliation, not elucidation, was the desired end.

Military imagery pervades this account: the difference of opinions between Collier and Marsalis was an "ideological war," and the "debate" was a "pitched battle" in which Marsalis "demolished" Collier (not his arguments, but him). What the commentator regrets, however, is that the audience got swept up in the mood instigated by the way the debate was carried out: "the crowd's blood lust" for Collier's defeat.

This is one of the most dangerous aspects of regarding intellectual interchange as a fight. It contributes to an atmosphere of animosity that spreads like a fever. In a society that includes people who express their anger by shooting, the result of demonizing those with whom we disagree can be truly tragic.

But do audiences necessarily harbor within themselves a "blood lust," or is it stirred in them by the performances they are offered? Another arts event was set up as a debate between a playwright and a theater director. In this case, the metaphor through which the debate was viewed was not war but boxing—a sport that is in itself, like a debate, a metaphorical battle that pitches one side against the other in an all-out effort to win. A headline describing the event set the frame: "AND IN THIS CORNER...," followed by the subhead "A Black Playwright and White Critic Duke It Out." The story then reports:

> the face-off between August Wilson, the most successful black playwright in the American theater, and Robert Brustein, longtime drama critic for The New Republic and artistic director of the American Repertory Theatre in Cambridge, Mass. These two heavyweights had been battling in print since last June....
>
> Entering from opposite sides of the stage, the two men shook hands and came out fighting—or at least sparring.

Wilson, the article explains, had given a speech in which he opposed Black performers taking "white" roles in color-blind casting; Brustein had written a column disagreeing; and both followed up with further responses to each other.

According to the article, "The drama of the Wilson-Brustein confrontation lies in their mutual intransigence." No one would question that audiences crave drama. But is intransigence the most appealing source of drama? I happened to hear this debate broadcast on the radio. The line that triggered the loudest cheers from the audience was the final question put to the two men by the moderator, Anna Deavere Smith: "What did you each learn from the other in this debate?" The loud applause was evidence that the audience did not crave intransigence. They wanted to see another kind of drama: the drama of change—change that comes from genuinely listening to someone with a different point of view, not the transitory drama of two intransigent positions in stalemate.

To encourage the staging of more dramas of change and fewer of intransigence, we need new metaphors to supplement and complement the pervasive war and boxing match metaphors through which we take it for granted issues and events are best talked about and viewed.

MUD SPLATTERS

Our fondness for the fight scenario leads us to frame many complex human interactions as a battle between two sides. This then shapes the way we understand what happened and how we regard the participants. One unfortunate result is that fights make a mess in which everyone is muddied. The person attacked is often deemed just as guilty as the attacker.

The injustice of this is clear if you think back to childhood. Many of us still harbor anger as we recall a time (or many times) a sibling or playmate started a fight—but both of us got blamed. Actions occur in a stream, each a response to what came before. Where you punctuate them can change their meaning just as you can change the meaning of a sentence by punctuating it in one place or another.

Like a parent despairing of trying to sort out which child started a fight, people often respond to those involved in a

public dispute as if both were equally guilty. When champion figure skater Nancy Kerrigan was struck on the knee shortly before the 1994 Olympics in Norway and the then-husband of another champion skater, Tonya Harding, implicated his wife in planning the attack, the event was characterized as a fight between two skaters that obscured their differing roles. As both skaters headed for the Olympic competition, their potential meeting was described as a "long-anticipated figure-skating shootout." Two years later, the event was referred to not as "the attack on Nancy Kerrigan" but as "the rivalry surrounding Tonya Harding and Nancy Kerrigan."

By a similar process, the Senate Judiciary Committee hearings to consider the nomination of Clarence Thomas for Supreme Court justice at which Anita Hill was called to testify are regularly referred to as the "Hill-Thomas hearings," obscuring the very different roles played by Hill and Thomas. Although testimony by Anita Hill was the occasion for reopening the hearings, they were still the Clarence Thomas confirmation hearings: Their purpose was to evaluate Thomas's candidacy. Framing these hearings as a two-sides dispute between Hill and Thomas allowed the senators to focus their investigation on cross-examining Hill rather than seeking other sorts of evidence, for example by consulting experts on sexual harassment to ascertain whether Hill's account seemed plausible.

SLASH-AND-BURN THINKING

Approaching situations like warriors in battle leads to the assumption that intellectual inquiry, too, is a game of attack, counterattack, and self-defense. In this spirit, critical thinking is synonymous with criticizing. In many classrooms, students are encouraged to read someone's life work, then rip it to shreds. Though criticism is one form of critical thinking—and an essential one—so are integrating ideas from disparate fields and examining the context out of which ideas grew. Opposition does not lead to the whole truth when we ask only "What's wrong with this?" and never "What can we use from this in building a new theory, a new understanding?"

There are many ways that unrelenting criticism is destructive in itself. In innumerable small dramas mirroring what happened to Robert Gallo (but on a much more modest scale), our most creative thinkers can waste time and effort responding to critics motivated less by a genuine concern about weaknesses in their work than by a desire to find something to attack. All of society loses when creative people are discouraged from their pursuits by unfair criticism. (This is particularly likely to happen since, as Kay Redfield Jamison shows in her book *Touched with Fire*, many of those who are unusually creative are also unusually sensitive; their sensitivity often drives their creativity.)

If the criticism is unwarranted, many will say, you are free to argue against it, to defend yourself. But there are problems with this, too. Not only does self-defense take time and draw off energy that would better be spent on new creative work, but any move to defend yourself makes you appear, well, defensive. For example, when an author wrote a letter to the editor protesting a review he considered unfair, the reviewer (who is typically given the last word) turned the very fact that the author defended himself into a weapon with which to attack again. The reviewer's response began, "I haven't much time to waste on the kind of writer who squanders his talent drafting angry letters to reviewers."

The argument culture limits the information we get rather than broadening it in another way. When a certain kind of interaction is the norm, those who feel comfortable with that type of interaction are drawn to participate, and those who do not feel comfortable with it recoil and go elsewhere. If public discourse included a broad range of types, we would be making room for individuals with different temperaments to take part and contribute their perspectives and insights. But when debate, opposition, and fights overwhelmingly predominate, those who enjoy verbal sparring are likely to take part—by calling in to talk shows, writing letters to the editor or articles, becoming journalists—and those who cannot comfortably take part in oppositional discourse, or do not wish to, are likely to opt out.

This winnowing process is easy to see in apprenticeship programs such as acting school, law school, and graduate school. A woman who was identified in her university drama program as showing exceptional promise was encouraged to go to New York to study acting. Full of enthusiasm, she was accepted by a famous acting school where the teaching method entailed the teacher screaming at students, goading and insulting them as a way to bring out the best in them. This worked well with many of the students but not with her. Rather than rising to the occasion when attacked, she cringed, becoming less able to draw on her talent, not more. After a year, she dropped out. It could be that she simply didn't have what it took—but this will never be known, because the adversarial style of teaching did not allow her to show what talent she had.

POLARIZING COMPLEXITY: NATURE OR NURTURE?

Few issues come with two neat, and neatly opposed, sides. Again, I have seen this in the domain of gender. One common polarization is an opposition between two sources of differences between women and men: "culture," or "nurture," on one hand and "biology," or "nature," on the other.

Shortly after the publication of *You Just Don't Understand,* I was asked by a journalist what question I most often encountered about women's and men's conversational styles. I told her, "Whether the differences I describe are biological or cultural." The journalist laughed. Puzzled, I asked why this made her laugh. She explained that she had always been so certain that any significant differences are cultural rather than biological in origin that the question struck her as absurd. So I should not have been surprised when I read, in the article she wrote, that the two questions I am most frequently asked are "Why do women nag?" and "Why won't men ask for directions?" Her ideological certainty that the question I am most frequently asked was absurd led her to ignore my answer and get a fact wrong in her report of my experience.

Some people are convinced that any significant differences between men and women are entirely or overwhelmingly due to cultural influences—the way we treat girls and boys, and men's

dominance of women in society. Others are convinced that any significant differences are entirely or overwhelmingly due to biology: the physical facts of female and male bodies, hormones, and reproductive functions. Many problems are caused by framing the question as a dichotomy: Are behaviors that pattern by sex biological or cultural? This polarization encourages those on one side to demonize those who take the other view, which leads in turn to misrepresenting the work of those who are assigned to the opposing camp. Finally, and most devastatingly, it prevents us from exploring the interaction of biological and cultural factors—factors that must, and can only, be understood together. By posing the question as either/or, we reinforce a false assumption that biological and cultural factors are separable and preclude the investigations that would help us understand their interrelationship. When a problem is posed in a way that polarizes, the solution is often obscured before the search is under way.

WHO'S UP? WHO'S DOWN?

Related to polarization is another aspect of the argument culture: our obsession with ratings and rankings. Magazines offer the 10, 50, or 100 best of everything: restaurants, mutual funds, hospitals, even judges. Newsmagazines tell us Who's up, Who's down, as in *Newsweek*'s "Conventional Wisdom Watch" and *Time*'s "Winners and Losers." Rankings and ratings pit restaurants, products, schools, and people against each other on a single scale, obscuring the myriad differences among them. Maybe a small Thai restaurant in one neighborhood can't really be compared to a pricey French one in another, any more than judges with a vast range of abilities and beliefs can be compared on a single scale. And timing can skew results: Ohio State University protested to *Time* magazine when its football team was ranked at the bottom of a scale because only 29 percent of the team graduated. The year before it would have ranked among the top six with 72 percent.

After a political debate, analysts comment not on what the candidates said but on the question "Who won?" After the president delivers an important speech, such as the State of the Union Address, expert commentators are asked to give it a grade. Like ranking, grading establishes a competition. The biggest problem with asking what grade the president's speech deserves, or who won and who lost a campaign debate, is what is not asked and is therefore not answered: What was said, and what is the significance of this for the country?

AN ETHIC OF AGGRESSION

In an argument culture aggressive tactics are valued for their own sake. For example, a woman called in to a talk show on which I was a guest to say, "When I'm in a place where a man is smoking, and three's a no-smoking sign, instead of saying to him 'You aren't allowed to smoke in here. Put that out,' I say, 'I'm awfully sorry, but I have asthma, so your smoking makes it hard for me to breathe. Would you mind terribly not smoking?' Whenever I say this, the man is extremely polite and solicitous, and he puts his cigarette out, and I say, 'Oh, thank you, thank you!' as if he's done a wonderful thing for me. Why do I do that?"

I think this woman expected me to say that she needs assertiveness training to learn to confront smokers in a more aggressive manner. Instead, I told her that there was nothing wrong with her style of getting the man to stop smoking. She gave him a face-saving way of doing what she asked, one that allowed him to feel chivalrous rather than chastised. This is kind to him, but it is also kind to herself, since it is more likely to lead to the result she desires. If she tried to alter his behavior by reminding him of the rules, he might well rebel: "Who made you the enforcer? Mind your own business!" Indeed, who gives any of us the authority to set others straight when we think they're breaking rules?

Another caller disagreed with me, saying the first caller's style was "self-abasing" and there was no reason for her to use it. But I persisted: There is nothing necessarily destructive about conventional self-effacement. Human relations depend on the agreement to use such verbal conventions. I believe the mistake this caller was making—a mistake many of us make—was to confuse *ritual* self-effacement with the literal kind. All human relations require us to find ways to get what we want from others without seeming to dominate them. Allowing others to feel they are doing what you want for a reason less humiliating to them fulfills this need.

Thinking of yourself as the wronged party who is victimized by a lawbreaking boor makes it harder to see the value of this method. But suppose you are the person addicted to smoking who lights up (knowingly or not) in a no-smoking zone. Would you like strangers to yell at you to stop smoking, or would you rather be allowed to save face by being asked politely to stop in order to help them out? Or imagine yourself having broken a rule inadvertently (which is not to imply rules are broken only by mistake; it is only to say that sometimes they are). Would you like some stranger to swoop down on you and begin berating you, or would you rather be asked politely to comply?

As this example shows, conflicts can sometimes be resolved without confrontational tactics, but current conventional wisdom often devalues less confrontational tactics even if they work well, favoring more aggressive strategies even if they get less favorable results. It's as if we value a fight for its own sake, not for its effectiveness in resolving disputes.

This ethic shows up in many contexts. In a review of a contentious book, for example, a reviewer wrote, "Always provocative, sometimes infuriating, this collection reminds us that the purpose of art is not to confirm and coddle but to provoke and confront." This false dichotomy encapsulates the belief that if you are not provoking and confronting, then you are conforming and coddling—as if there weren't myriad other ways to question and learn. What about exploring, exposing, delving, analyzing, understanding, moving, connecting, integrating, illuminating… or any of innumerable verbs that capture other aspects of what art can do?

THE BROADER PICTURE

The increasingly adversarial spirit of our contemporary lives is fundamentally related to a phenomenon that has been much remarked upon in recent years: the breakdown of a sense of community. In this spirit, distinguished journalist and author Orville

Schell points out that in his day journalists routinely based their writing on a sense of connection to their subjects—and that this sense of connection is missing from much that is written by journalists today. Quite the contrary, a spirit of demonography often prevails that has just the opposite effect: Far from encouraging us to feel connected to the subjects, it encourages us to feel critical, superior—and, as a result, distanced. The cumulative effect is that citizens feel more and more cut off from the people in public life they read about.

The argument culture dovetails with a general disconnection and breakdown of community in another way as well. Community norms and pressures exercise a restraint on the expression of hostility and destruction. Many cultures have rituals to channel and contain aggressive impulses, especially those of adolescent males. In just this spirit, at the 1996 Republican National Convention, both Colin Powell and Bob Dole talked about growing up in small communities where everyone knew who they were. This meant that many people would look out for them, but also that if they did something wrong, it would get back to their parents. Many Americans grew up in ethnic neighborhoods that worked the same way. If a young man stole something, committed vandalism, or broke a rule or law, it would be reported to his relatives, who would punish him or tell him how his actions were shaming the family. American culture today often lacks these brakes.

Community is a blend of connections and authority, and we are losing both. As Robert Bly shows in his book by that title, we now have a *Sibling Society:* Citizens are like squabbling siblings with no authority figures who can command enough respect to contain and channel their aggressive impulses. It is as if every day is a day with a substitute teacher who cannot control the class and maintain order.

The argument culture is both a product of and a contributor to this alienation, separating people, disconnecting them from each other and from those who are or might have been their leaders.

WHAT OTHER WAY IS THERE?

Philosopher John Dewey said, on his ninetieth birthday, "Democracy begins in conversation." I fear that it gets derailed in polarized debate.

In conversation we form the interpersonal ties that bind individuals together in personal relationships; in public discourse, we form similar ties on a larger scale, binding individuals into a community. In conversation, we exchange the many types of information we need to live our lives as members of a community. In public discourse, we exchange the information that citizens in a democracy need in order to decide how to vote. If public discourse provides entertainment first and foremost—and if entertainment is first and foremost watching fights—then citizens do not get the information they need to make meaningful use of their right to vote.

Of course it is the responsibility of intellectuals to explore potential weaknesses in others' arguments, and of journalists to represent serious opposition when it exists. But when opposition becomes the overwhelming avenue of inquiry—a formula that *requires* another side to be found or a criticism to be voiced; when the lust for opposition privileges extreme views and obscures complexity; when our eagerness to find weaknesses blinds us to strengths; when the atmosphere of animosity precludes respect and poisons our relations with one another; then the argument culture is doing more damage than good.

I offer this book not as a formal assault in the argument culture. That would be in the spirit of attack that I am questioning. It is an attempt to examine the argument culture—our use of attack, opposition, and debate in public discourse—to ask, What are its limits as well as its strengths? How has it served us well, but also how has it failed us? How is it related to culture and gender? What other options do we have?

I do not believe we should put aside the argument model of public discourse entirely, but we need to rethink whether this is the *only* way, or *always* the best way, to carry out our affairs. A step toward broadening our repertoires would be to pioneer reform by experimenting with metaphors other than sports and war, and with formats other than debate for framing the exchange of ideas. The change might be as simple as introducing a plural form. Instead of asking "What's the other side?" we might ask instead, "What are the other sides?" Instead of insisting on hearing "both sides," we might insist on hearing "all sides."

Another option is to expand our notion of "debate" to include more dialogue. This does not mean there can be no negativity, criticism, or disagreement. It simply means we can be more creative in our ways of managing all of these, which are inevitable and useful. In dialogue, each statement that one person makes is qualified by a statement made by someone else, until the series of statements and qualifications moves everyone closer to a fuller truth. Dialogue does not preclude negativity. Even saying "I agree" makes sense only against the background assumption that you might disagree. In dialogue, there is opposition, yes, but no head-on collision. Smashing heads does not open minds.

There are times when we need to disagree, criticize, oppose, and attack—to hold debates and view issues as polarized battles. Even cooperation, after all, is not the absence of conflict but a means of managing conflict. My goal is not a make-nice false veneer of agreement or a dangerous ignoring of true opposition. I'm questioning the *automatic* use of adversarial formats—the assumption that it's *always* best to address problems and issues by fighting over them. I'm hoping for a broader repertoire of ways to talk to each other and address issues vital to us.

NOTES

Note: Sources referred to by short form are cited in full in the References.
[Numbers indicate page numbers of original document. Ed]

7. "*culture of critique*": I first introduced this term in an op-ed essay, "The Triumph of the Yell," *The New York Times,* Jan. 14, 1994, p. A29.

7. "*There are moments*": Charles Simic, "In Praise of Invective," *Harper's,* Aug. 1997, pp. 24, 26–27; the quote is from p. 26. The article is excerpted from *Orphan Factory* (Ann Arbor:

University of Michigan Press, 1997). I am grateful to Amitai Etizioni for calling this article to my attention.

8. Both the term "agonism" and the phrase "programmed contentiousness" come from Walter Ong, *Fighting for Life.*

10. "*the great backpacking vs. car camping debate*": Steven Hendrix, "Hatchback vs. Backpack," *The Washington Post Weekend,* Mar. 1, 1996, p. 6.

11. *creationism*: See, for example, Jessica Mathews, "Creationism Makes a Comeback," *The Washington Post,* Apr. 8, 1996, p. A21.

11. "*People dispute that*": Lipstadt, *Denying the Holocaust,* p. 15. Lipstadt cites *Esquire,* Feb. 1983, for the interview with Mitchum.

12. *Gallo had to spend*: See Nicholas Wade, "Method and Madness: The Vindication of Robert Gallo," *The New York Times Magazine,* Dec. 26, 1993, p. 12, and Elaine Richman, "The Once and Future King," *The Sciences,* Nov.–Dec. 1996, pp. 12–15. The investigations of Gallo were among a series of overly zealous investigations of suspected scientific misconduct—all of which ended in the exoneration of the accused, but not before they had caused immense personal anguish and professional setbacks. Others similarly victimized were Gallo's colleague Mike Popovic, immunologist Thereza Imanishi-Kari, and her coauthor (not accused of wrongdoing but harmed as a result of his defense of her), Nobel Prize winner David Baltimore. On Popovic, see Malcolm Gladwell, "Science Friction," *The Washington Post Magazine,* Dec. 6, 1992, pp. 18–21, 49–51. On Imanishi-Kari and Baltimore, see *The New Yorker,* May 27, 1996, pp. 94–98ff.

14. *potentially endless list:* Randy Allen Harris, *The Linguistics Wars* (New York: Oxford University Press, 1993); "The Science Wars," *Newsweek,* Apr. 21, 1997, p. 54; "The Mammogram War," *Newsweek,* Feb. 24, 1997, p. 54; "Party Wars," *New York,* June 2, 1997, cover. The subhead of the latter reads, "In the battle to feed New York's elite, the top caterers are taking off their white gloves and sharpening their knives."

14. "DEMOCRATS SEND CLINTON": *The New York Times,* Aug. 29, 1996, p. A1.

15. "*We risk imposing*": Keller, *Reflections on Gender and Science,* p. 157. Another such case is explained by paleontologist Stephen Jay Gould in his book *Wonderful Life* about the Burgess shale—a spectacular deposit of 530-million-year-old fossils. In 1909, the first scientist to study these fossils missed the significance of the find, because he "shoehorned every last Burgess animal into a modern group, viewing the fauna collectively as a set of primitive or ancestral versions of later, improved forms" (p. 24). Years later, observers looked at the Burgess shale fossils with a fresh eye and saw a very different reality: a panoply of life forms, far more diverse and numerous than what exists today. The early scientists missed what was right before their eyes because, Gould shows, they proceeded from a metaphoric understanding of evolution as a linear march of progress from the ancient and primitive to the modern and complex, with humans the inevitable, most complex apex. Accepting the metaphor of "the cone of increasing diversity" prevented the early scientists from seeing what was really there.

16. *"Showdown at Lincoln Center"*: Peter Watrous, "The Year in the Arts: Pop & Jazz/1994," *The New York Times,* Dec. 25, 1994, sec. 2, p. 36.

17. *"the face-off between"*: Jack Kroll, "And in This Corner…," *Newsweek,* Feb. 10, 1997, p. 65.

18. *a fight between two skaters:* Though Harding was demonized somewhat more as an unfeminine, boorish "Wicked Witch of the West" (George Vecsey, "Let's Begin the Legal Olympics," *The New York Times,* Feb. 13, 1994, sec. 8, p. 1.), Kerrigan was also demonized as cold and aloof, an "ice princess."

18. *"long-anticipated figure-skating shootout"*: Jere Longman, "Kerrigan Glides Through Compulsory Interviews," *The New York Times,* Feb. 13, 1994, sec. 8, p. 9.

18. *"the rivalry surrounding"*: Paul Farhi, "For NBC, Games Not Just for Guys; Network Tailors Its Coverage to Entice Women to Watch," *The Washington Post,* July 26, 1996, p. A1.

20. *"I haven't time"*: *The Washington Post Book World,* June 16, 1996, p. 14.

21. *even judges: Washingtonian,* June 1996, ranked judges.

22. *Ohio State University protested:* Letter to the editor by Malcolm S. Baroway, Executive Director, University Communications, *Time,* Oct. 3, 1994, p. 14.

22. Overlaid on the talk show example is the gender issue: The woman who called wished she had the courage to stand up to a man and saw her habitual way of speaking as evidence of her insecurity. This interpretation is suggested by our assumptions about women and men. Many people, researchers included, start from the assumption that women are insecure, so ways they speak are scrutinized for evidence of insecurity. The result is often a failure to understand or appreciate women's styles on their own terms, so women are misinterpreted as defective men.

23. *"Always provocative, sometimes infuriating"*: Jill Nelson, "Fighting Words," review of Ishmael Reed, *Airing Dirty Laundry, The New York Times Book Review,* Feb. 13, 1994, p. 28.

24. *In this spirit:* John Krich, "To Teach Is Glorious: A Conversation with the New Dean of Cal's Journalism School," Orville Schell, *Express,* Aug. 23, 1996, pp. 1, 14–16, 18, 20–22. The remark is from p. 15.

24. *Many cultures have rituals:* See Schlegel and Barry, *Adolescence.*

25. *"Democracy begins in conversation"*: *Dialogue on John Dewey,* Corliss Lamont, ed. (New York: Horizon Press, 1959), p. 88. Thanks to Pete Becker for this reference.

26. *In dialogue, there is:* This insight comes from Walter Ong, who writes, "There is opposition here but no head-on collision, which stops dialogue. (Of course, sometimes dialogue has to be stopped, but that is another story.)" (*Fighting for Life,* p. 32).

REFERENCES

Gould, Stephen Jay. *Wonderful Life: The Burgess Shale and the Nature of History* (New York: W. W. Norton, 1989).

Keller, Evelyn Fox. *Reflections on Gender and Science* (New Haven: Yale University Press, 1985).

Krich, John. "To Teach Is Glorious: A Conversation with the New Dean of Cal's Journalism School, Orville Schell." *Express,* Aug. 23, 1996, pp. 1, 14–16, 18, 20–22.

Lipstadt, Deborah. *Denying the Holocaust: The Growing Assault on Truth and Memory* (New York: Free Press, 1993).

Ong, Walter J. *Fighting for Life: Contest, Sexuality, and Consciousness* (Ithaca, N.Y.: Cornell University Press, 1981).

Schlegel, Alice, and Herbert Barry III. *Adolescence: An Anthropological Inquiry* (New York: Free Press, 1991).

DEBORAH TANNEN is best known as the author of *You Just Don't Understand: Women and Men in Conversation,* which was on *The New York Times* bestseller list for nearly four years, including eight months as number one, and has been translated into twenty-four languages. Her book, *Talking from 9 to 5: Women and Men in the Workplace: Language, Sex, and Power,* was a *New York Times* Business bestseller. She has written for and been featured in *The New York Times, Newsweek, Time, USA Today, People,* and *The Washington Post.* Her many national television and radio appearances include *20/20, 48 Hours,* CBS News, ABC *World News Tonight,* and *Good Morning America.* She is one of only three University Professors at Georgetown University in Washington, D.C., where she is on the Linguistics Department faculty. *The Argument Culture* is her sixteenth book.

Deborah Tannen has also published short stories, essays, and poems. Her first play, *An Act of Devotion,* is included in *Best Short Plays 1993–1994.* It was produced, together with her play *Sisters,* by Horizons Theatre in Arlington, VA.

"I Can't Even Open My Mouth"

Separating Messages from Metamessages in Family Talk

"DO YOU REALLY need another piece of cake?" Donna asks George.

"You bet I do," he replies, with that edge to his voice that implies, "If I wasn't sure I needed it before, I am darned sure now."

Donna feels hamstrung. She knows that George is going to say later that he wished he hadn't had that second piece of cake.

"Why are you always watching what I eat?" George asks.

"I was just watching out for you," Donna replies. "I only say it because I love you."

Elizabeth, in her late twenties, is happy to be making Thanksgiving dinner for her extended family in her own home. Her mother, who is visiting, is helping out in the kitchen. As Elizabeth prepares the stuffing for the turkey, her mother remarks, "Oh, you put onions in the stuffing?"

Feeling suddenly as if she were sixteen years old again, Elizabeth turns on her mother and says, "*I'm* making the stuffing, Mom. Why do you have to criticize everything I do?"

"I didn't criticize," her mother replies. "I just asked a question. What's got into you? I can't even open my mouth."

The allure of family—which is, at heart, the allure of love—is to have someone who knows you so well that you don't have to explain yourself. It is the promise of someone who cares enough about you to protect you against the world of strangers who do not wish you well. Yet, by an odd and cruel twist, it is the family itself that often causes pain. Those we love are looking at us so close-up that they see all

our blemishes—see them as if through a magnifying glass. Family members have innumerable opportunities to witness our faults and feel they have a right to point them out. Often their intention is to help us improve. They feel, as Donna did, "I only say it because I love you."

Family members also have a long shared history, so everything we say in a conversation today echoes with meanings from the past. If you have a tendency to be late, your parent, sibling, or spouse may say, "We have to leave at eight"—and then add, "It's really important. Don't be late. Please start your shower at seven, not seven-thirty!" These extra injunctions are demeaning and interfering, but they are based on experience. At the same time, having experienced negative judgments in the past, we develop a sixth sense to sniff out criticism in almost anything a loved one says—even an innocent question about ingredients in the stuffing. That's why Elizabeth's mother ends up feeling as if she can't even open her mouth—and Elizabeth ends up feeling criticized.

When we are children our family constitutes the world. When we grow up, family members—not only our spouses but also our grown-up children and adult sisters and brothers—keep this larger-than-life aura. We overreact to their judgments because it feels as if they were handed down by the Supreme Court and are unassailable assessments of our value as human beings. We bristle because these judgments seem unjust; or because we sense a kernel of truth we would rather not face; or because we fear that if someone who knows us so well

judges us harshly we must really be guilty, so we risk losing not only that person's love but everyone else's, too. Along with this heavy load of implications comes a dark resentment that a loved one is judging us at all—and has such power to wound.

"I still fight with my father," a man who had reached a high position in journalism said to me. "He's been dead twenty-one years." I asked for an example. "He'd tell me that I had to comb my hair and dress better, that I'd learn when I grew up that appearance is important." When he said this I noticed that his hair was uncombed, and the tails of his faded shirt were creeping out from the waist of his pants. He went on, "I told him I'd ignore that. And now sometimes when I'm going somewhere important, I'll look in the mirror and think—I'll say to him in my mind, 'See? I *am* a success and it didn't matter.'"

This man's "fights" with his father are about approval. No matter what age we've reached, no matter whether our parents are alive or dead, whether we were close to them or not, there are times when theirs are the eyes through which we view ourselves, theirs the standards against which we measure ourselves when we wonder whether we have measured up. The criticism of parents carries extra weight, even when children are adults.

I CARE, THEREFORE I CRITICIZE

Some family members feel they have not only a right but an obligation to tell you when they think you're doing something wrong. A woman from Thailand recalls that when she was in her late teens and early twenties, her mother frequently had talks with her in which she tried to set her daughter straight. "At the end of each lecture," the woman says, "my mother would always tell me, 'I have to complain about you because I am your mother and I love you. Nobody else will talk to you the way I do because they don't care.'"

It sometimes seems that family members operate under the tenet "I care, therefore I criticize." To the one who is being told to do things differently, what comes through loudest and clearest is the criticism. But the one offering suggestions and judgments is usually focused on the caring. A mother, for example, was expressing concern about her daughter's boyfriend: He didn't have a serious job, he didn't seem to want one, and she didn't think he was a good prospect for marriage. The daughter protested that her mother disapproved of everyone she dated. Her mother responded indignantly, "Would you rather I didn't care?"

As family members we wonder why our parents, children, siblings, and spouses are so critical of us. But as family members we also feel frustrated because comments we make in the spirit of caring are taken as criticizing.

Both sentiments are explained by the double meaning of giving advice: a loving sign of caring, a hurtful sign of criticizing. It's impossible to say which is right; both meanings are there. Sorting out the ambiguous meanings of caring and criticizing is difficult because language works on two levels: the message and the metamessage. Separating these levels—and being aware of both—is crucial to improving communication in the family.

THE INTIMATE CRITIC: WHEN METAMESSAGES HURT

Because those closest to us have front-row seats to view our faults, we quickly react—sometimes overreact—to any hint of criticism. The result can be downright comic, as in Phyllis Richman's novel *Who's Afraid of Virginia Ham?* One scene, a conversation between the narrator and her adult daughter, Lily, shows how criticism can be the metronome providing the beat for the family theme song. The dialogue goes like this:

LILY: Am I too critical of people?
MOTHER: What people? Me?
LILY: Mamma, don't be so self-centered.
MOTHER: Lily, don't be so critical.
LILY: I knew it. You do think I'm critical. Mamma, why do you always have to find something wrong with me?

The mother then protests that it was Lily who asked if she was too critical, and now she's criticizing her mother for answering. Lily responds, "I can't follow this. Sometimes you're impossibly hard to talk to."

It turns out that Lily is upset because her boyfriend, Brian, told her she is too critical of him. She made a great effort to stop criticizing, but now she's having a hard time keeping her resolve. He gave her a sexy outfit for her birthday—it's expensive and beautiful—but the generous gift made her angry because she took it as criticism of the way she usually dresses.

In this brief exchange Richman captures the layers of meaning that can make the most well-intentioned comment or action a source of conflict and hurt among family members. Key to understanding why Lily finds the conversation so hard to follow—and her mother so hard to talk to—is separating messages from metamessages. The *message* is the meaning of the words and sentences spoken, what anyone with a dictionary and a grammar book could figure out. Two people in a conversation usually agree on what the message is. The *metamessage* is meaning that is not said—at least not in so many words—but that we glean from every aspect of context: the way something is said, who is saying it, or the fact that it is said at all.

Because they do not reside in the words themselves, metamessages are hard to deal with. Yet they are often the source of both comfort and hurt. The message (as I've said) is the word meaning while the metamessage is the heart meaning—the meaning that we react to most strongly, that triggers emotion.

When Lily asked her mother if she was too critical of people, the message was a question about Lily's own personality. But her mother responded to what she perceived as the metamessage: that Lily was feeling critical of *her*. This was probably based on experience: Her daughter had been critical of her in the past. If Lily had responded to the message alone, she would have answered, "No, not you. I was thinking of Brian." But she, too, is reacting to a metamessage—that her mother had made herself the point of a comment that was not about her mother at all. Perhaps Lily's resentment was also triggered because her mother still looms so large in her life.

The mixing up of message and metamessage also explains Lily's confused response to the gift of sexy clothing from her boyfriend. The message is the gift. But what made Lily angry was what she thought the gift implied: that Brian finds the way she usually dresses not sexy enough—and unattractive. This implication is the metamessage, and it is what made Lily critical of the gift, of Brian, and of herself. Metamessages speak louder than messages, so this is what Lily reacted to most strongly.

It's impossible to know whether Brian intended this metamessage. It's possible that he wishes Lily would dress differently; it's also possible that he likes the way she dresses just fine but simply thought this particular outfit would look good on her. That's what makes metamessages so difficult to pinpoint and talk about: They're implicit, not explicit.

When we talk about messages, we are talking about the meanings of words. But when we talk about metamessages, we are talking about relationships. And when family members react to each other's comments, it's metamessages they are usually responding to. Richman's dialogue is funny because it shows how we all get confused between messages and metamessages when we talk to those we are close to. But when it happens in the context of a relationship we care about, our reactions often lead to hurt rather than to humor.

In all the conversations that follow, both in this chapter and throughout the book, a key to improving relationships within the family is distinguishing the message from the metamessage, and being clear about which one you are reacting to. One way you can do this is *metacommunicating*—talking about communication.

"WHAT'S WRONG WITH FRENCH BREAD?" TRY METACOMMUNICATING

The movie *Divorce American Style* begins with Debbie Reynolds and Dick Van Dyke preparing for dinner guests—and arguing. She lodges a complaint: that all he does is criticize. He protests that he doesn't. She says she can't discuss it right then because she has to take the French bread out of the oven. He asks, "French bread?"

A simple question, right? Not even a question, just an observation. But on hearing it Debbie Reynolds turns on him, hands on hips, ready for battle: "What's wrong with French bread?" she asks, her voice full of challenge.

"Nothing," he says, all innocence. "It's just that I really like those little dinner rolls you usually make." This is like the bell that sets in motion a boxing match, which is stopped by another bell—the one at the front door announcing their guests have arrived.

Did he criticize or didn't he? On the message level, no. He simply asked a question to confirm what type of bread she was preparing. But on the metamessage level, yes. If he were satisfied with her choice of bread, he would not comment, except perhaps to compliment. Still, you might ask, So what? So what if he prefers the dinner rolls she usually makes to French bread? Why is it such a big deal? The big deal is explained by her original complaint: She feels that he is *always* criticizing—always telling her to do things differently than she chose to do them.

The big deal, in a larger sense, is a paradox of family: We depend on those closest to us to see our best side, and often they do. But because they are so close, they also see our worst side. You want the one you love to be an intimate ally who reassures you that you're doing things right, but sometimes you find instead an intimate critic who implies, time and again, that you're doing things

wrong. It's the cumulative effect of minor, innocent suggestions that creates major problems. You will never work things out if you continue to talk about the message—about French bread versus dinner rolls—rather than the metamessage—the implication that your partner is dissatisfied with everything you do. (*Divorce American Style* was made in 1967; that it still rings true today is evidence of how common—and how recalcitrant—such conversational quagmires are.)

One way to approach a dilemma like this is to *metacommunicate*—to talk about ways of talking. He might *say* that he feels he can't open his mouth to make a suggestion or comment because she takes everything as criticism. She might *say* that she feels he's always dissatisfied with what she does, rather than turn on him in a challenging way. Once they both understand this dynamic, they will come up with their own ideas about how to address it. For example, he might decide to preface his question with a disclaimer: "I'm not criticizing the French bread." Or maybe he *does* want to make a request—a direct one—that she please make dinner rolls because he likes them. They might also set a limit on how many actions of hers he can question in a day. The important thing is to talk about the metamessage she is reacting to: that having too many of her actions questioned makes her feel that her partner in life has changed into an in-house inspection agent, on the lookout for wrong moves.

LIVING WITH THE RECYCLING POLICE

"This is recyclable," Helen exclaims, brandishing a small gray cylinder that was once at the center of a roll of toilet paper. There she stops, as if the damning evidence is sufficient to rest her case.

"I know it's recyclable," says Samuel. "You don't have to tell me." He approves of recycling and generally practices it, if not quite as enthusiastically (he would say obsessively) as Helen. But this time he slipped: In a moment of haste he tossed the cardboard toilet paper tube into the wastebasket. Now Helen has found it and wants to know why it was there. "You can't go through the

garbage looking for things I threw away," Samuel protests. "Our relationship is more important than a toilet paper carcass."

"I'm not talking about our relationship," Helen protests. "I'm talking about recycling."

Helen was right: She *was* talking about recycling. But Samuel was right, too. If you feel like you're living with the recycling police—or the diet police, or the neatness police—someone who assumes the role of judge of your actions and repeatedly finds you guilty—it takes the joy out of living together. Sometimes it even makes you wish, for a fleeting moment, that you lived alone, in peace. In that sense, Samuel was talking about the relationship.

Helen was focusing on the message: the benefits of recycling. Samuel was focusing on the metamessage: the implication he perceives that Helen is enforcing rules and telling him he broke one. Perhaps, too, he is reacting to the metamessage of moral superiority in Helen's being the more fervent recycler. Because messages lie in words, Helen's position is more obviously defensible. But it's metamessages that have clout, because they stir emotions, and emotions are the currency of relationships.

In understanding Samuel's reaction, it's also crucial to bear in mind that the meaning of Helen's remark resides not just in the conversation of the moment but in the resonance of all the conversations on the subject they've had in their years together—as well as the conversations Samuel had before that, especially while growing up in his own family. Furthermore, it's her *repeatedly* remarking on what he does or does not recycle that gives Samuel the impression that living with Helen is like living with the recycling police.

GIVE ME CONNECTION, GIVE ME CONTROL

There is another dimension to this argument—another aspect of communication that complicates everything we say to each other but that is especially powerful in families. That is our simultaneous but conflicting desires for connection and for control.

In her view Helen is simply calling her husband's attention to a small oversight in their mutual pursuit of a moral good—an expression of their connection. Their shared policy on recycling reflects their shared life: his trash is her trash. But Samuel feels that by installing herself as the judge of his actions, she is placing herself one-up. In protest he accuses, "You're trying to control me."

Both connection and control are at the heart of family. There is no relationship as close—and none as deeply hierarchical—as the relationship between parent and child, or between older and younger sibling. To understand what goes on when family members talk to each other, you have to understand how the forces of connection and control reflect both closeness and hierarchy in a family.

"He's like family," my mother says of someone she likes. Underlying this remark is the assumption that *family* connotes closeness, being connected to each other. We all seek connection: It makes us feel safe; it makes us feel loved. But being close means you care about what those you are close to think. Whatever you do has an impact on them, so you have to take their needs and preferences into account. This gives them power to control your actions, limiting your independence and making you feel hemmed in.

Parents and older siblings have power over children and younger siblings as a result of their age and their roles in the family. At the same time, *ways of talking create power.* Younger siblings or children can make life wonderful or miserable for older siblings or parents by what they say—or refuse to say. Some family members increase their chances of getting their way by frequently speaking up, or by speaking more loudly and more forcefully. Some increase their influence by holding their tongues, so others become more and more concerned about winning them over.

"Don't tell me what to do. Don't try to control me" are frequent protests within families. It is automatic for many of us to think in terms of power relations and to see others' incursions on our freedom as control maneuvers. We are less likely to think of them as connection maneuvers, but they often are that, too. At every moment we're struggling not only for control but also for love, approval, and involvement. What's tough is that the *same* actions and comments can be either control maneuvers or connection maneuvers—or, as in most cases, both at once.

CONTROL MANEUVER OR CONNECTION MANEUVER?

"Don't start eating yet," Louis says to Claudia as he walks out of the kitchen. "I'll be right there."

Famished, Claudia eyes the pizza before her. The aroma of tomato sauce and melted cheese is so sweet, her mouth thinks she has taken a bite. But Louis, always slow-moving, does not return, and the pizza is cooling. Claudia feels a bit like their dog Muffin when she was being trained: "Wait!" the instructor told Muffin, as the hungry dog poised pitifully beside her bowl of food. After pausing long enough to be convinced Muffin would wait forever, the trainer would say, "Okay!" Only then would Muffin fall into the food.

Was Louis intentionally taking his time in order to prove he could make Claudia wait no matter how hungry she was? Or was he just eager for them to sit down to dinner together? In other words, when he said, "Don't start eating yet," was it a control maneuver, to make her adjust to his pace and timing, or a connection maneuver, to preserve their evening ritual of sharing food? The answer is, it was both. Eating together is one of the most evocative rituals that bond individuals as a family. At the same time, the requirement that they sit down to dinner together gave Louis the power to make Claudia wait. So the need for connection entailed control, and controlling each other is in itself a kind of connection.

Control and connection are intertwined, often conflicting forces that thread through everything said in a family. These dual forces explain the double meaning of caring and criticizing. Giving advice, suggesting changes, and making observations are signs of caring when looked at through the lens of connection. But looked at through the lens of control, they are put-downs, interfering with our desire to manage our own lives and actions, telling us to do things differently than we choose to do them. That's why caring and criticizing are tied up like a knot.

The drives toward connection and toward control are the forces that underlie our reactions to metamessages. So the second step in improving communication in the family—after distinguishing between message and metamessage—is understanding the double meaning of control and connection. Once these multiple layers are sorted out and brought into focus, talking about ways of talking—metacommunicating—can help solve family problems rather than making them worse.

SMALL SPARK, BIG EXPLOSION

Given the intricacies of messages and metamessages, and of connection and control, the tiniest suggestion or correction can spark an explosion fueled by the stored energy of a history of criticism. One day, for example, Vivian was washing dishes. She tried to fix the drain cup in an open position so it would catch debris and still allow water to drain, but it kept falling into the closed position. With a mental shrug of her shoulders, she decided to leave it, since she didn't have many dishes to wash and the amount of water that would fill the sink wouldn't be that great. But a moment later her husband, Mel, happened by and glanced at the sink. "You should keep the drain open," he said, "so the water can drain."

This sounds innocent enough in the telling. Vivian could have said, "I tried, but it kept slipping in, so I figured it didn't matter that much." Or she could have said, "It's irritating to feel that you're looking over my shoulder all the time, telling me to do things differently from the way I'm doing them." This was, in fact, what she was feeling—and why she experienced, in reaction to Mel's suggestion, a small eruption of anger that she had to expend effort to suppress.

Vivian was surprised at what she did say. She made up a reason and implied she had acted on purpose: "I figured it would be easier to clean the strainer if I let it drain all at once." This thought *had* occurred to her when she decided not to struggle any longer to balance the drain cup in an open position, though it wasn't true that she did it on purpose for that reason. But by justifying her actions, Vivian gave Mel the opening to argue for his method, which he did.

"The whole sink gets dirty if you let it fill up with water," Mel said. Vivian decided to let it drop and remained silent. Had she spoken up, the result would probably have been an argument.

Throughout this interchange Vivian and Mel focused on the message: When you wash the dishes, should the drain cup be open or closed? Just laying out the dilemma in these terms shows how ridiculous it is to argue about. Wars are being fought; people are dying; accident or illness could throw this family into turmoil at any moment. The position of the drain cup in the sink is not a major factor in their lives. But the conversation wasn't really about the message—the drain cup—at least not for Vivian.

Mel probably thought he was just making a suggestion about the drain cup, and in the immediate context he was. But messages always bring metamessages in tow: In the context of the history of their relationship, Mel's comment was not so much about a drain cup as it was about Vivian's ability to do things right and Mel's role as judge of her actions.

This was clear to Vivian, which is why she bristled at his comment, but it was less clear to Mel. Our field of vision is different depending on whether we're criticizing or being criticized. The critic tends to focus on the message: "I just made a suggestion. Why are you so touchy?" The one who feels criticized, however, is responding to the metamessage, which is harder to explain. If Vivian had complained, "You're always telling me how to do things," Mel would surely have felt, and might well have said, "I can't even open my mouth."

At the same time, connection and control are in play. Mel's assumption that he and Vivian are on the same team makes him feel comfortable giving her pointers. Furthermore, if a problem develops with the sink's drainage, he's the one who will have to fix it. Their lives are intertwined; that's where the connec-

tion lies. But if Vivian feels she can't even wash dishes without Mel telling her to do it differently, then it seems to her that he is trying to control her. It's as if she has a boss to answer to in her own kitchen.

Vivian might explain her reaction in terms of metamessages. Understanding and respecting her perspective, Mel might decide to limit his suggestions and corrections. Or Vivian might decide that she is overinterpreting the metamessage and make an effort to focus more on the message, taking some of Mel's suggestions and ignoring others. Once they both understand the metamessages as well as the messages they are communicating and reacting to, they can metacommunicate: talk about each other's ways of talking and how they might talk differently to avoid hurt and recriminations.

"WOULDN'T YOU RATHER HAVE SALMON?"

Irene and David are looking over their menus in a restaurant. David says he will order a steak. Irene says, "Did you notice they also have salmon?"

This question exasperates David; he protests, "Will you please stop criticizing what I eat?"

Irene feels unfairly accused: "I didn't criticize. I just pointed out something on the menu I thought you might like."

The question "Did you notice they also have salmon?" is not, on the message level, a criticism. It could easily be friendly and helpful, calling attention to a menu item her husband might have missed. But, again, conversations between spouses—or between any two people who have a history—are always part of an ongoing relationship. David knows that Irene thinks he eats too much red meat, too much dessert, and, generally speaking, too much.

Against the background of this aspect of their relationship, any indication that Irene is noticing what he is eating is a reminder to David that she disapproves of his eating habits. That's why the question "Do you really want to have dessert?" will be heard as "You shouldn't have dessert," and the observation "That's a big piece of cake" will commu-

nicate "That piece of cake is too big," regardless of how they're intended. The impression of disapproval comes not from the message—the words spoken—but from the metamessage, which grows out of their shared history.

It's possible that Irene really was not feeling disapproval when she pointed out the salmon on the menu, but it's also possible that she was and preferred not to admit it. Asking a question is a handy way of expressing disapproval without seeming to. But to the extent that the disapproval comes through, such indirect means of communicating can make for more arguments, and more hurt feelings on both sides. Irene sees David overreacting to an innocent, even helpful, remark, and he sees her hounding him about what he eats and then denying having done so. Suppose he had announced he was going to order salmon. Would she have said, "Did you notice they also have steak?" Not likely. It is reasonable, in this context, to interpret any alternative suggestion to an announced decision as dissatisfaction with that decision.

Though Irene and David's argument has much in common with the previous examples, the salmon versus steak decision is weightier than French bread versus dinner rolls, recycling, or drain cups. Irene feels that David's health—maybe even his life—is at stake. He has high cholesterol, and his father died young of a heart attack. Irene has good reason to want David to eat less red meat. She loves him, and his health and life are irrevocably intertwined with hers. Here is another paradox of family: A blessing of being close is knowing that someone cares about you: cares what you do and what happens to you. But caring also means interference and disapproval.

In other words, here again is the paradox of connection and control. From the perspective of control, Irene is judging and interfering; from the perspective of connection, she is simply recognizing that her life and David's are intertwined. This potent brew is family: Just knowing that someone has the closeness to care and the right to pass judgment—and that you care so much about that judgment—creates resentment that can turn into anger.

CRYING LITERAL MEANING: HOW NOT TO RESOLVE ARGUMENTS

When Irene protested, "I didn't criticize," she was crying literal meaning: taking refuge in the message level of talk, ducking the metamessage. All of us do that when we want to avoid a fight but still get our point across. In many cases this defense is sincere, though it does not justify ignoring or denying the metamessage someone else may have perceived. If the person we're talking to believes it wasn't "just a suggestion," keeping the conversation focused on the message can result in interchanges that sound like a tape loop playing over and over. Let's look more closely at an actual conversation in which this happened—one that was taped by the people who had it.

Sitting at the dining room table, Evelyn is filling out an application. Because Joel is the one who has access to a copy machine at work, the last step of the process will rest on his shoulders. Evelyn explains, "Okay, so you'll have to attach the voided check here, after you make the Xerox copy. Okay?" Joel takes the papers, but Evelyn goes on: "Okay just—Please get that out tomorrow. I'm counting on you, hon. I'm counting on you, love."

Joel reacts with annoyance: "Oh, for Pete's sake."

Evelyn is miffed in turn: "What do you mean by that?"

Joel turns her words back on her: "What do *you* mean by that?"

The question "What do you mean by that?" is a challenge. When communication runs smoothly, the meanings of words are self-evident, or at least we assume they are. (We may discover later that we misinterpreted them.) Although "What do you mean?" might be an innocent request for clarification, adding "by that" usually signals not so much that you didn't understand what the other person meant but that you understood—all too well—the *implication* of the words, and you didn't like it.

Evelyn cries literal meaning. She sticks to the message: "Oh, honey, I just mean I'm *counting* on you."

Joel calls attention to the metamessage: "Yes, but you say it in a way that suggests I can't be counted on."

Evelyn protests, accurately, "I never said that."

But Joel points to evidence of the metamessage: "I'm talking about your *tone*."

I suspect Joel was using *tone* as a catchall way of describing the metamessage level of talk. Moreover, it probably wasn't only the way Evelyn spoke—her tone—that he was reacting to but the fact that Evelyn said it at all. If she really felt she could count on him, she would just hand over the task. "I'm counting on you" is what people say to reinforce the importance of doing something when they believe extra reinforcement is needed. Here, the shared history of the relationship adds meaning to the metamessage as well. Joel has reason to believe that Evelyn feels she can't count on him.

Later in the same conversation, Joel takes a turn crying literal meaning. He unplugs the radio from the wall in the kitchen and brings it into the dining room so they can listen to the news. He sets it on the table and turns it on.

"Why aren't you using the plug?" Evelyn asks. "Why waste the batteries?" This sparks a heated discussion about the relative importance of saving batteries. Evelyn then suggests, "Well, we could plug it in right here," and offers Joel the wire.

Joel shoots her a look.

Evelyn protests, "Why are you giving me a dirty look?"

And Joel cries literal meaning: "I'm not!" After all, you can't prove a facial expression; it's not in the message.

"You are!" Evelyn insists, reacting to the metamessage: "Just because I'm handing this to you to plug in."

I have no doubt that Joel did look at Evelyn with annoyance or worse, but not because she handed him a plug—that would be literal meaning, too. He was surely reacting to the metamessage of being corrected, of her judging his actions. For her part, Evelyn probably felt Joel was irrationally refusing to plug in the radio when an electrical outlet was staring them in the face.

How to sort through this jumble of messages and metamessages? The message level is a draw. Some people prefer the convenience of letting the radio run on batteries when it's moved from its normal

perch to a temporary one. Others find it obviously reasonable to plug the radio in when there's an outlet handy, to save batteries. Convenience or frugality, take your pick. We all do. But when you live with someone else—caution! It may seem natural to suggest that others do things the way you would do them, but that is taking account only of the message. Giving the metamessage its due, the expense in spirit and goodwill is more costly than batteries. Being corrected all the time is wearying. And it's even more frustrating when you try to talk about what you believe they implied and they cry literal meaning—denying having "said" what you know they communicated.

Consider, too, the role of connection and control. Telling someone what to do is a control maneuver. But it is also a connection maneuver: Your lives are intertwined, and anything one person does has an impact on the other. In the earlier example, when Evelyn said, "I'm counting on you," I suspect some readers sympathized with Joel and others with Evelyn, depending on their own experience with people they've lived with. Does it affect your reaction to learn that Joel forgot to mail the application? Evelyn had good reason, based on years of living with Joel, to have doubts about whether he would remember to do what he said he would do.

Given this shared history, it might have been more constructive for Evelyn to admit that she did not feel she could completely count on Joel, rather than cry literal meaning and deny the metamessage of her words. Taking into account Joel's forgetfulness—or maybe his being overburdened at work—they could devise a plan: Joel might write himself a reminder and place it strategically in his briefcase. Or Evelyn might consider mailing the form herself, even though that would mean a trip to make copies. Whatever they decide, they stand a better chance of avoiding arguments—and getting the application mailed on time—if they acknowledge their metamessages and the reasons motivating them.

WHO BURNED THE POPCORN?

Living together means coordinating so many tasks, it's inevitable that family members will have different ideas of how to perform those tasks. In addition, everyone makes mistakes; sometimes the dish breaks, you forget to mail the application, the drain cup falls into the closed position. At work, lines of responsibility and authority are clear (at least in principle). But in a family—especially when adults are trying to share responsibilities and authority—there are fewer and fewer domains that belong solely to one person. As couples share responsibility for more and more tasks, they also develop unique and firm opinions about how those tasks should be done—and a belief in their right to express their opinions.

Even the most mundane activity, such as making popcorn (unless you buy the microwave type or an electric popper), can spark conflict. First, it takes a little going, and people have their own ideas of how to do it best. Second, popcorn is often made in the evening, when everyone's tired. Add to that the paradox of connection and control—wanting the person you love to approve of what you do, yet having someone right there to witness and judge mistakes—and you have a potful of kernels sizzling in oil, ready to pop right out of the pot.

More than one couple have told me of arguments about how to make popcorn. One such argument broke out between another couple who were taping their conversations. Since their words were recorded, we have a rare opportunity to listen in on a conversation very much like innumerable ones that vanish into air in homes all around the country. And we have the chance to think about how it could have been handled differently.

The seed of trouble is planted when Molly is in the kitchen and Kevin is watching their four-year-old son, Benny. Kevin calls out, "Molly! Mol! Let's switch. You take care of him. I'll do whatever you're doing."

"I'm making popcorn," Molly calls back. "You always burn it."

Molly's reply is, first and foremost, a sign of resistance. She doesn't want to switch jobs with Kevin. Maybe she's had enough of a four-year-old's company and is looking forward to being on her own in the kitchen. Maybe she is enjoying making popcorn. And maybe her reason is truly the one she gives: She

doesn't want Kevin to make the popcorn because he always burns it. Whatever her motivation, Molly resists the switch Kevin proposes by impugning his ability to make popcorn. And this comes across as a call to arms.

Kevin protests, "No I don't! I never burn it. I make it perfect." He joins Molly in the kitchen and peers over her shoulder. "You making popcorn? In the big pot?" (Remember this line; it will become important later.)

"Yes," Molly says, "but you're going to ruin it."

"No I won't," Kevin says. "I'll get it just right." With that they make the switch. Kevin becomes the popcorn chef, Molly the caretaker. But she is not a happy caretaker.

Seeing a way she can be both caretaker and popcorn chef, Molly asks Benny, "You want to help Mommy make popcorn? Let's not let Daddy do it. Come on."

Hearing this, Kevin insists, "I know how to make popcorn!" Then he ups the ante: "I can make popcorn better than you can!" After that the argument heats up faster than the popcorn. "I cook every kernel!" Kevin says.

"No you won't," says Molly.

"I will too! It's never burned!" Kevin defends himself. And he adds, "It always burns when you do it!"

"Don't make excuses!"

"There's a trick to it," he says.

And she says, "I know the trick!"

"No you don't," he retorts, "'cause you always burn it."

"I do not!" she says. "What are you, crazy?"

It is possible that Kevin is right—that Molly, not he, is the one who always burns the popcorn. It is also possible that Molly is right—that he always burns the popcorn, that she doesn't, and that he has turned the accusation back onto her as a self-defense strategy. Move 1: I am not guilty. Move 2: You are guilty.

In any case, Kevin continues as popcorn chef. After a while Molly returns to the kitchen. "Just heat it!" she tells Kevin. "Heat it! No, I don't want you—"

"It's going, it's going," Kevin assures her. "Hear it?"

Molly is not reassured, because she does not like what she hears. "It's too

slow," she says. "It's all soaking in. You hear that little—"

"It's not soaking in," Kevin insists. "It's fine."

"It's just a few kernels," Molly disagrees.

But Kevin is adamant: "All the popcorn is being popped!"

Acting on her mounting unease about the sounds coming from the popping corn, Molly makes another suggestion. She reminds Kevin, "You gotta take the trash outside."

But Kevin isn't buying. "I can't," he says. "I'm doing the popcorn." And he declines Molly's offer to watch it while he takes out the trash.

In the end Molly gets to say, "See, what'd I tell you?" But Kevin doesn't see the burned popcorn as a reason to admit fault. Remember his earlier question, "In the big pot?" Now he protests, "Well, I never *use* this pot, I use the other pot."

Molly comes back, "It's not the pot! It's you!"

"It's the pot," Kevin persists. "It doesn't heat up properly. If it did, then it would get hot." But pots can't really be at fault; those who choose pots can. So Kevin accuses, "You should have let me do it from the start."

"You *did* it from the start!" Molly says.

"No, I didn't," says Kevin. "You chose this pan. I would've chosen a different pan." So it's the pot's fault, and Molly's fault for choosing the pot.

This interchange is almost funny, especially for those of us—most of us, I'd bet—who have found ourselves in similar clashes.

How could Kevin and Molly have avoided this argument? Things might have turned out better if they had talked about their motivations: Is either one of them eager to get a brief respite from caring for Benny? If so, is there another way they can accomplish that goal? (Perhaps they could set Benny up with a task he enjoys on his own.) With this motivation out in the open, Molly might have declined to switch places when Kevin proposed it, saying something like, "I'm making popcorn. I'm enjoying making it. I'd rather not switch." The justification Molly used, "You always burn it," may have seemed to her a better tactic because it claims her right to keep making popcorn on the basis of the family good rather than her own preference. But the metamessage of incompetence can come across as provocative, in addition to being hurtful.

It's understandable that Kevin would be offended to have his popcorn-making skills impugned, but he would have done better to avoid the temptation to counter-attack by insisting he does it better, that it's Molly who burns it. He could have prevented the argument rather than esca-late it if he had metacommunicated: "You can make the popcorn if you want," he might have said, "but you don't have to say I can't do it." For both Molly and Kevin—as for any two people negotiating who's going to do what—metacommuni-cating is a way to avoid the flying metamessages of incompetence.

"I KNOW A THING OR TWO"

One of the most hurtful metamessages, and one of the most frequent, that family talk entails is the implication of incom-petence—even (if not especially) when children grow up. Now that we're adults we feel we should be entitled to make our own decisions, lead our own lives, imperfect though they may be. But we still want to feel that our parents are proud of us, that they believe in our com-petence. That's the metamessage we yearn for. Indeed, it's because we want their approval so much that we find the opposite metamessage—that they don't trust our competence—so distressing.

Martin and Gail knew that Gail's mother tended to be critical of whatever they did, so they put off letting her see their new home until the purchase was fi-nal. Once the deal was sealed they showed her, with pride, the home they had chosen while the previous owner's furni-ture was still in it. They were sure she would be impressed by the house they were now able to afford, as well as its spotless condition. But she managed to find something to criticize—even if it was invisible: "They may've told you it's in move-in condition," she said with author-ity, "but I know a thing or two, and when they take those pictures off the wall, there will be holes!" Even though they were fa-

miliar with her tendency to find fault, Gail and Martin were flummoxed.

The aspect of the house Gail's mother found to criticize was profoundly insig-nificant: Every home has pictures on the wall, every picture taken down leaves holes, and holes are easily spackled in and painted over. It seems that Gail's mother was really reaching to find some-thing about their new home to criticize. From the perspective of control, it would be easy to conclude that Gail's mother was trying to take the role of expert in or-der to put them down, or even to spoil the joy of their momentous purchase. But consider the perspective of connection. Pointing out a problem that her children might not have noticed shows that she can still be of use, even though they are grown and have found this wonderful house without her help. She was being protective, watching out for them, mak-ing sure no one pulled the wool over their eyes.

Because control and connection are inextricably intertwined, protection im-plies incompetence. If Gail and Martin need her mother's guidance, they are in-capable of taking care of themselves. Though Gail's mother may well have been reacting to—and trying to over-come—the metamessage that they don't need her anymore, the metamessage they heard is that she can't approve whole-heartedly of anything they do.

"SHE KNEW WHAT WAS RIGHT"

In addition to concern about their chil-dren's choice of home, parents often have strong opinions about adult children's partners, jobs, and—especially—how they treat their own children. Raising chil-dren is something at which parents self-evidently have more experience, but metamessages of criticism in this area, though particularly common, are also par-ticularly hurtful, because young parents want so much to be good parents.

A woman of seventy still recalls the pain she felt when her children were small and her mother-in-law regarded her as an incompetent parent. It started in the first week of her first child's life. Her mother-in-law had come to help—and didn't want to go home. Finally, her fa-

ther-in-law told his wife it was time to leave the young couple on their own. Un-convinced, she said outright—in front of her son and his wife—"I can't trust them with the baby."

Usually signs of distrust are more subtle. For example, during a dinner con-versation among three sisters and their mother, the sisters were discussing what the toddlers like to eat. When one said that her two-year-old liked fish, their mother cautioned, "Watch the bones." How easy it would be to take offense (though there was no indication this woman did): "You think I'm such an in-competent mother that I'm going to let my child swallow fish bones?" Yet the grandmother's comment was her way of making a contribution to the conversa-tion—one that exercises her lifelong re-sponsibility of protecting children.

It is easy to scoff at the mother-in-law who did not want to leave her son and his wife alone with their own baby. But con-sider the predicament of parents who be-come grandparents and see (or believe they see) their beloved grandchildren treated in ways they feel are hurtful. One woman told me that she loves being a grandmother—but the hardest part is having to bite her tongue when her daughter-in-law treats her child in a way the grandmother feels is misguided, un-fair, or even harmful. "You see your chil-dren doing things you think aren't right," she commented, "but at least they're adults; they'll suffer the consequences. But a child is so defenseless."

In some cases grandparents really do know best. My parents recall with linger-ing guilt a time they refused to take a grandparent's advice—and later wished they had. When their first child, my sister Naomi, was born, my parents, like many of their generation, relied on expert ad-vice for guidance in what was best for their child. At the time, the experts coun-seled that, once bedtime comes, a child who cries should not be picked up. After all, the reasoning went, that would sim-ply encourage the baby to cry rather than go to sleep.

One night when she was about a year old, Naomi was crying after being put to sleep in her crib. My mother's mother, who lived with my parents, wanted to go in and pick her up, but my parents wouldn't let her. "It tore us apart to hear her cry," my father recalls, "but we wanted to do what was best for her." It later turned out that Naomi was crying because she was sick. My parents cringe when they tell this story. "My mother pleaded with us to pick her up," my mother says. "She knew what was right."

I'M GROWN UP NOW

Often a parent's criticism is hurtful—or makes us angry—even when we know it is right, maybe especially if we sense it is right. That comes clear in the following example.

Two couples were having dinner together. One husband, Barry, was telling about how he had finally—at the age of forty-five—learned to ignore his mother's criticism. His mother, he said, had commented that he is too invested in wanting the latest computer gizmo, the most up-to-date laptop, regardless of whether he needs it. At that point his wife interrupted. "It's true, you are," she said—and laughed. He laughed, too: "I know it's true." Then he went back to his story and continued, unfazed, about how in the past he would have been hurt by his mother's comment and would have tried to justify himself to her, but this time he just let it pass. How easily Barry acknowledged the validity of his mother's criticism—when it was his wife making it. Yet acknowledging that the criticism was valid didn't change his view of his mother's comment one whit: He still thought she was wrong to criticize him.

When we grow up we feel we should be free from our parents' judgment (even though we still want their approval). Ironically, there is often extra urgency in parents' tendency to judge children's behavior when children are adults, because parents have a lot riding on how their children turn out. If the results are good, everything they did as parents gets a seal of approval. My father, for example, recalls that as a young married man he visited an older cousin, a woman he did not know well. After a short time the cousin

remarked, "Your mother did a good job." Apparently, my father had favorably impressed her, but instead of complimenting him, she credited his mother.

By the same token, if their adult children have problems—if they seem irresponsible or make wrong decisions—parents feel their life's work of child rearing has been a failure, and those around them feel that way, too. This gives extra intensity to parents' desire to set their children straight. But it also can blind them to the impact of their corrections and suggestions, just as those in power often underestimate the power they wield.

When adult children move into their own homes, the lid is lifted off the pressure cooker of family interaction, though the pot may still be simmering on the range. If they move far away—as more and more do—visits turn into intense interactions during which the pressure cooker lid is clicked back in place and the steam builds up once again. Many adult children feel like they're kids again when they stay with their parents. And parents often feel the same way: that their adult children are acting like kids. Visits become immersion courses in return-to-family.

Parents with children living at home have the ultimate power—asking their children to move out. But visiting adult children have a new power of their own: They can threaten not to return, or to stay somewhere else. Margaret was thrilled that her daughter Amanda, who lives in Oregon, would be coming home for a visit to the family farm in Minnesota. It had been nearly a year since Margaret had seen her grandchildren, and she was eager to get reacquainted with them. But near the end of the visit, there was a flare-up. Margaret questioned whether Amanda's children should be allowed to run outside barefoot. Margaret thought it was dangerous; Amanda thought it was harmless. And Amanda unsheathed her sword: "This isn't working," she said. "Next time I won't stay at the farm. I'll find somewhere else to stay." Because Margaret wants connection—time with

her daughter and grandchildren—the ability to dole out that connection gives her daughter power that used to be in Margaret's hands.

THE PARADOX OF FAMILY

When I was a child I walked to elementary school along Coney Island Avenue in Brooklyn, praying that if a war came I'd be home with my family when it happened. During my childhood in the 1950s my teachers periodically surprised the class by calling out, "Take cover!" At that cry we all ducked under our desks and curled up in the way we had been taught: elbows and knees tucked in, heads down, hands clasped over our necks. With the possibility of a nuclear attack made vivid by these exercises, I walked to school in dread—not of war but of the possibility that it might strike when I was away from my family.

But there is another side to family, the one I have been exploring in this chapter. My nephew Joshua Marx, at thirteen, pointed out this paradox: "If you live with someone for too long, you notice things about them," he said. "That's the reason you don't like your parents, your brother. There's a kid I know who said about his friend, 'Wouldn't it be cool if we were brothers?' and I said, 'Then you'd hate him.'"

We look to communication as a way through the minefield of this paradox. And often talking helps. But communication itself is a minefield because of the complex workings of message and metamessage. Distinguishing messages from metamessages, and taking into account the underlying needs for connection and control, provides a basis for metacommunicating. With these insights as foundation, we can delve further into the intricacies of family talk. Given our shared and individual histories of talk in relationships, and the enormous promise of love, understanding, and listening that family holds out, it's worth the struggle to continue juggling—and talking.

Shakespeare in the Bush

Laura Bohannan

Just before I left Oxford for the Tiv in West Africa, conversation turned to the season at Stratford. "You Americans," said a friend, "often have difficulty with Shakespeare. He was, after all, a very English poet, and one can easily misinterpret the universal by misunderstanding the particular."

I protested that human nature is pretty much the same the whole world over; at least the general plot and motivation of the greater tragedies would always be clear—everywhere—although some details of custom might have to be explained and difficulties of translation might produce other slight changes. To end an argument we could not conclude, my friend gave me a copy of *Hamlet* to study in the African bush: it would, he hoped, lift my mind above its primitive surroundings, and possibly I might, by prolonged meditation, achieve the grace of correct interpretation.

It was my second field trip to that African tribe, and I thought myself ready to live in one of its remote sections—an area difficult to cross even on foot. I eventually settled on the hillock of a very knowledgeable old man, the head of a homestead of some hundred and forty people, all of whom were either his close relatives or their wives and children. Like the other elders of the vicinity, the old man spent most of his time performing ceremonies seldom seen these days in the more accessible parts of the tribe. I was delighted. Soon there would be three months of enforced isolation and leisure, between the harvest that takes place just before the rising of the swamps and the clearing of new farms when the water goes down. Then, I thought, they would have even more time to perform ceremonies and explain them to me.

I was quite mistaken. Most of the ceremonies demanded the presence of elders from several homesteads. As the swamps rose, the old men found it too difficult to walk from one homestead to the next, and the ceremonies gradually ceased. As the swamps rose even higher, all activities but one came to an end. The women brewed beer from maize and millet. Men, women, and children sat on their hillocks and drank it.

People began to drink at dawn. By midmorning the whole homestead was singing, dancing, and drumming. When it rained, people had to sit inside their huts: there they drank and sang or they drank and told stories. In any case, by noon or before, I either had to join the party or retire to my own hut and my books. "One does not discuss serious matters when there is beer. Come, drink with us." Since I lacked their capacity for the thick native beer, I spent more and more time with *Hamlet*. Before the end of the second month, grace descended on me. I was quite sure that *Hamlet* had only one possible interpretation, and that one universally obvious.

Early every morning, in the hope of having some serious talk before the beer party, I used to call on the old man at his reception hut—a circle of posts supporting a thatched roof above a low mud wall to keep out wind and rain. One day I crawled through the low doorway and found most of the men of the homestead sitting huddled in their ragged cloths on stools, low plank beds, and reclining chairs, warming themselves against the chill of the rain around a smoky fire. In the center were three pots of beer. The party had started.

The old man greeted me cordially. "Sit down and drink." I accepted a large calabash full of beer, poured some into a small drinking gourd, and tossed it down. Then I poured some more into the same gourd for the man second in seniority to my host before I handed my calabash over to a young man for further distribution. Important people shouldn't ladle beer themselves.

"It is better like this," the old man said, looking at me approvingly and plucking at the thatch that had caught in my hair. "You should sit and drink with us more often. Your servants tell me that when you are not with us, you sit inside your hut looking at a paper."

The old man was acquainted with four kinds of "papers": tax receipts, bride price receipts, court fee receipts, and letters. The messenger who brought him letters from the chief used them mainly as a badge of office, for he always knew what was in them and told the old man. Personal letters for the few who had relatives in the government or mission stations were kept until someone went to a large market where there was a letter writer and reader. Since my arrival, letters were brought to me to be read. A few men also brought me bride price receipts, privately, with requests to change the figures to a higher sum. I found moral arguments were of no avail, since in-laws are fair game, and the technical hazards of forgery difficult to explain to an illiterate people. I did not wish them to think me silly enough to look at any such papers for days on end, and I hastily explained that my "paper" was one of the "things of long ago" of my country.

"Ah," said the old man. "Tell us."

I protested that I was not a storyteller. Story telling is a skilled art among them; their standards are high, and the audiences critical—and vocal in their criticism. I protested in vain. This morning they wanted to hear a story while they drank. They threatened to tell me no more stories until I told them one of mine. Finally, the old man promised that no one would criticize my style "for we know you are struggling with our language." "But," put in one of the elders, "you must explain what we do not understand, as we do when we tell you our stories." Realizing that here was my chance to prove *Hamlet* universally intelligible, I agreed.

The old man handed me some more beer to help me on with my storytelling. Men filled their long wooden pipes and knocked coals from the fire to place in the pipe bowls; then, puffing contentedly, they sat back to listen. I began in the proper style, "Not yesterday, not yesterday, but long ago, a thing occurred. One night three men were keeping watch outside the homestead of the great chief, when suddenly they saw the former chief approach them."

"Why was he no longer their chief?"

"He was dead," I explained. "That is why they were troubled and afraid when they saw him."

"Impossible," began one of the elders, handing his pipe on to his neighbor, who interrupted, "Of course it wasn't the dead chief. It was an omen sent by a witch. Go on."

Slightly shaken, I continued. "One of these three was a man who knew things"—the closest translation for scholar, but unfortunately it also meant witch. The second elder looked triumphantly at the first. "So he spoke to the dead chief saying, 'Tell us what we must do so you may rest in your grave,' but the dead chief did not answer. He vanished, and they could see him no more. Then the man who knew things—his name was Horatio—said this event was the affair of the dead chief's son, Hamlet."

There was a general shaking of heads round the circle. "Had the dead chief no living brothers? Or was this son the chief?"

"No," I replied. "That is, he had one living brother who became the chief when the elder brother died."

The old men muttered: such omens were matters for chiefs and elders, not for youngsters; no good could come of going behind a chief's back; clearly Horatio was not a man who knew things.

"Yes, he was," I insisted, shooing a chicken away from my beer. "In our country the son is next to the father. The dead chief's younger brother had become the great chief. He had also married his elder brother's widow only about a month after the funeral."

"He did well," the old man beamed and announced to the others, "I told you that if we knew more about Europeans, we would find they really were very like us. In our country also," he added to me, "the younger brother marries the elder brother's widow and becomes the father of his children. Now, if your uncle, who married your widowed mother, is your father's full brother, then he will be a real father to you. Did Hamlet's father and uncle have one mother?"

His question barely penetrated my mind; I was too upset and thrown too far off balance by having one of the most important elements of *Hamlet* knocked straight out of the picture. Rather uncertainly I said that I thought they had the same mother, but I wasn't sure—the story didn't say. The old man told me severely that these genealogical details made all the difference and that when I got home I must ask the elders about it. He shouted out the door to one of his younger wives to bring his goatskin bag.

Determined to save what I could of the mother motif, I took a deep breath and began again. "The son Hamlet was very sad because his mother had married again so quickly. There was no need for her to do so, and it is our custom for a widow not to go to her next husband until she has mourned for two years."

"Two years is too long," objected the wife, who had appeared with the old man's battered goatskin bag. "Who will hoe your farms for you while you have no husband?"

"Hamlet," I retorted without thinking, "was old enough to hoe his mother's farms himself. There was no need for her to remarry." No one looked convinced. I

gave up. "His mother and the great chief told Hamlet not to be sad, for the great chief himself would be a father to Hamlet. Furthermore, Hamlet would be the next chief: therefore he must stay to learn the things of a chief. Hamlet agreed to remain, and all the rest went off to drink beer."

While I paused, perplexed at how to render Hamlet's disgusted soliloquy to an audience convinced that Claudius and Gertrude had behaved in the best possible manner, one of the younger men asked me who had married the other wives of the dead chief.

"He had no other wives," I told him.

"But a chief must have many wives! How else can he brew beer and prepare food for all his guests?"

I said firmly that in our country even chiefs had only one wife, that they had servants to do their work, and that they paid them from tax money.

It was better, they returned, for a chief to have many wives and sons who would help him hoe his farms and feed his people; then everyone loved the chief who gave much and took nothing—taxes were a bad thing.

I agreed with the last comment, but for the rest fell back on their favorite way of fobbing off my questions: "That is the way it is done, so that is how we do it."

I decided to skip the soliloquy. Even if Claudius was here thought quite right to marry his brother's widow, there remained the poison motif, and I knew they would disapprove of fratricide. More hopefully I resumed, "That night Hamlet kept watch with the three who had seen his dead father. The dead chief again appeared, and although the others were afraid, Hamlet followed his dead father off to one side. When they were alone, Hamlet's dead father spoke."

"Omens can't talk!" The old man was emphatic.

"Hamlet's dead father wasn't an omen. Seeing him might have been an omen, but he was not." My audience looked as confused as I sounded. "It *was* Hamlet's dead father. It was a thing we call a 'ghost.'" I had to use the English word, for unlike many of the neighboring tribes, these people didn't believe in the survival after death of any individuating part of the personality.

"What is a 'ghost?' An omen?"

"No, a 'ghost' is someone who is dead but who walks around and can talk, and people can hear him and see him but not touch him."

They objected. "One can touch zombis."

"No, no! It was not a dead body the witches had animated to sacrifice and eat. No one else made Hamlet's dead father walk. He did it himself."

"Dead men can't walk," protested my audience as one man.

I was quite willing to compromise. "A 'ghost' is the dead man's shadow."

But again they objected. "Dead men cast no shadows."

"They do in my country," I snapped.

The old man quelled the babble of disbelief that arose immediately and told me with that insincere, but courteous, agreement one extends to the fancies of the young, ignorant, and superstitious, "No doubt in your country the dead can also walk without being zombis." From the depths of his bag he produced a withered fragment of kola nut, bit off one end to show it wasn't poisoned, and handed me the rest as a peace offering.

"Anyhow," I resumed, "Hamlet's dead father said that his own brother, the one who became chief, had poisoned him. He wanted Hamlet to avenge him. Hamlet believed this in his heart, for he did not like his father's brother." I took another swallow of beer. "In the country of the great chief, living in the same homestead, for it was a very large one, was an important elder who was often with the chief to advise and help him. His name was Polonius. Hamlet was courting his daughter, but her father and her brother… [I cast hastily about for some tribal analogy] warned her not to let Hamlet visit her when she was alone on her farm, for he would be a great chief and so could not marry her."

"Why not?" asked the wife, who had settled down on the edge of the old man's chair. He frowned at her for asking stupid questions and growled, "They lived in the same homestead."

"That was not the reason," I informed them. "Polonius was a stranger who lived in the homestead because he helped the chief, not because he was a relative."

"Then why couldn't Hamlet marry her?"

"He could have," I explained, "but Polonius didn't think he would. After all, Hamlet was a man of great importance who ought to marry a chief's daughter, for in his country a man could have only one wife. Polonius was afraid that if Hamlet made love to his daughter, then no one else would give a high price for her."

"That might be true," remarked one of the shrewder elders, "but a chief's son would give his mistress's father enough presents and patronage to more than make up the difference. Polonius sounds like a fool to me."

"Many people think he was," I agreed. "Meanwhile Polonius sent his son Laertes off to Paris to learn the things of that country, for it was the homestead of a very great chief indeed. Because he was afraid that Laertes might waste a lot of money on beer and women and gambling, or get into trouble by fighting, he sent one of his servants to Paris secretly, to spy out what Laertes was doing. One day Hamlet came upon Polonius's daughter Ophelia. He behaved so oddly he frightened her. Indeed"—I was fumbling for words to express the dubious quality of Hamlet's madness—"the chief and many others had also noticed that when Hamlet talked one could understand the words but not what they meant. Many people thought that he had become mad." My audience suddenly became much more attentive. "The great chief wanted to know what was wrong with Hamlet, so he sent for two of Hamlet's age mates [school friends would have taken long explanation] to talk to Hamlet and find out what troubled his heart. Hamlet, seeing that they had been bribed by the chief to betray him, told them nothing. Polonius, however, insisted that Hamlet was mad because he had been forbidden to see Ophelia, whom he loved."

"Why," inquired a bewildered voice, "should anyone bewitch Hamlet on that account?"

"Bewitch him?"

"Yes, only witchcraft can make anyone mad, unless, of course, one sees the beings that lurk in the forest."

I stopped being a storyteller, took out my notebook and demanded to be told more about these two causes of madness. Even while they spoke and I jotted notes, I tried to calculate the effect of this new factor on the plot. Hamlet had not been exposed to the beings that lurk in the forests. Only his relatives in the male line could bewitch him. Barring relatives not mentioned by Shakespeare, it had to be Claudius who was attempting to harm him. And, of course, it was.

For the moment I staved off questions by saying that the great chief also refused to believe that Hamlet was mad for the love of Ophelia and nothing else. "He was sure that something much more important was troubling Hamlet's heart."

"Now Hamlet's age mates," I continued, "had brought with them a famous storyteller. Hamlet decided to have this man tell the chief and all his homestead a story about a man who had poisoned his brother because he desired his brother's wife and wished to be chief himself. Hamlet was sure the great chief could not hear the story without making a sign if he was indeed guilty, and then he would discover whether his dead father had told him the truth."

The old man interrupted, with deep cunning, "Why should a father lie to his son?" he asked.

I hedged: "Hamlet wasn't sure that it really was his dead father." It was impossible to say anything, in that language, about devil-inspired visions.

"You mean," he said, "it actually was an omen, and he knew witches sometimes send false ones. Hamlet was a fool not to go to one skilled in reading omens and divining the truth in the first place. A man-who-sees-the-truth could have told him how his father died, if he really had been poisoned, and if there was witchcraft in it; then Hamlet could have called the elders to settle the matter."

The shrewd elder ventured to disagree. "Because his father's brother was a great chief, one-who-sees-the-truth might therefore have been afraid to tell it. I think it was for that reason that a friend of Hamlet's father—a witch and an elder—sent an omen so his friend's son would know. Was the omen true?"

"Yes," I said, abandoning ghosts and the devil; a witch-sent omen it would have to be. "It was true, for when the storyteller was telling his tale before all the homestead, the great chief rose in fear. Afraid that Hamlet knew his secret he planned to have him killed."

The stage set of the next bit presented some difficulties of translation. I began cautiously. "The great chief told Hamlet's mother to find out from her son what he knew. But because a woman's children are always first in her heart, he had the important elder Polonius hide behind a cloth that hung against the wall of Hamlet's mother's sleeping hut. Hamlet started to scold his mother for what she had done."

There was a shocked murmur from everyone. A man should never scold his mother.

"She called out in fear, and Polonius moved behind the cloth. Shouting, 'A rat!' Hamlet took his machete and slashed through the cloth." I paused for dramatic effect. "He had killed Polonius!"

The old men looked at each other in supreme disgust. "That Polonius truly was a fool and a man who knew nothing! What child would not know enough to shout, 'It's me!'" With a pang, I remembered that these people are ardent hunters, always armed with bow, arrow, and machete; at the first rustle in the grass an arrow is aimed and ready, and the hunter shouts "Game!" If no human voice answers immediately, the arrow speeds on its way. Like a good hunter Hamlet had shouted, "A rat!"

I rushed in to save Polonius's reputation. "Polonius did speak. Hamlet heard him. But he thought it was the chief and wished to kill him earlier that evening...." I broke down, unable to describe to these pagans, who had no belief in individual afterlife, the difference between dying at one's prayers and dying "unhousell'd, disappointed, unaneled."

This time I had shocked my audience seriously. "For a man to raise his hand against his father's brother and the one who has become his father—that is a terrible thing. The elders ought to let such a man be bewitched."

I nibbled at my kola nut in some perplexity, then pointed out that after all the man had killed Hamlet's father.

"No," pronounced the old man, speaking less to me than to the young men sitting behind the elders. "If your father's brother has killed your father, you must appeal to your father's age mates; *they* may avenge him. No man may use violence against his senior relatives." Another thought struck him. "But if his father's brother had indeed been wicked enough to bewitch Hamlet and make him mad that would be a good story indeed, for it would be his fault that Hamlet, being mad, no longer had any sense and thus was ready to kill his father's brother."

There was a murmur of applause. *Hamlet* was again a good story to them, but it no longer seemed quite the same story to me. As I thought over the coming complications of plot and motive, I lost courage and decided to skim over dangerous ground quickly.

"The great chief," I went on, "was not sorry that Hamlet had killed Polonius. It gave him a reason to send Hamlet away, with his two treacherous mates, with letters to a chief of a far country, saying that Hamlet should be killed. But Hamlet changed the writing on their papers, so that the chief killed his age mates instead." I encountered a reproachful glare from one of the men whom I had told undetectable forgery was not merely immoral but beyond human skill. I looked the other way.

"Before Hamlet could return, Laertes came back for his father's funeral. The great chief told him Hamlet had killed Polonius. Laertes swore to kill Hamlet because of this, and because his sister Ophelia, hearing her father had been killed by the man she loved, went mad and drowned in the river."

"Have you already forgotten what we told you?" The old man was reproachful. "One cannot take vengeance on a madman; Hamlet killed Polonius in his madness. As for the girl, she not only went mad, she was drowned. Only witches can make people drown. Water itself can't hurt anything. It is merely something one drinks and bathes in."

I began to get cross. "If you don't like the story, I'll stop."

The old man made soothing noises and himself poured me some more beer. "You tell the story well, and we are lis-

tening. But it is clear that the elders of your country have never told you what the story really means. No, don't interrupt! We believe you when you say your marriage customs are different, or your clothes and weapons. But people are the same everywhere; therefore, there are always witches and it is we, the elders, who know how witches work. We told you it was the great chief who wished to kill Hamlet, and now your own words have proved us right. Who were Ophelia's male relatives?"

"There were only her father and her brother." *Hamlet* was clearly out of my hands.

"There must have been many more; this also you must ask of your elders when you get back to your country. From what you tell us, since Polonius was dead, it must have been Laertes who killed Ophelia, although I do not see the reason for it."

We had emptied one pot of beer, and the old men argued the point with slightly tipsy interest. Finally one of them demanded of me, "What did the servant of Polonius say on his return?"

With difficulty I recollected Reynaldo and his mission. "I don't think he did return before Polonius was killed."

"Listen," said the elder, "and I will tell you how it was and how your story will go, then you may tell me if I am right. Polonius knew his son would get into trouble, and so he did. He had many fines to pay for fighting, and debts from gambling. But he had only two ways of getting money quickly. One was to marry off his sister at once, but it is difficult to find a man who will marry a woman desired by the son of a chief. For if the chief's heir commits adultery with your wife, what can you do? Only a fool calls a case against a man who will someday be his judge. Therefore Laertes had to take the second way: he killed his sister by witchcraft, drowning her so he could secretly sell her body to the witches."

I raised an objection. "They found her body and buried it. Indeed Laertes jumped into the grave to see his sister once more—so, you see, the body was truly there. Hamlet, who had just come back, jumped in after him."

"What did I tell you?" The elder appealed to the others. "Laertes was up to no good with his sister's body. Hamlet prevented him, because the chief's heir, like a chief, does not wish any other man to grow rich and powerful. Laertes would be angry, because he would have killed his sister without benefit to himself. In our country he would try to kill Hamlet for that reason. Is this not what happened?"

"More or less," I admitted. "When the great chief found Hamlet was still alive, he encouraged Laertes to try to kill Hamlet and arranged a fight with machetes between them. In the fight both the young men were wounded to death. Hamlet's mother drank the poisoned beer that the chief meant for Hamlet in case he won the fight. When he saw his mother die of poison, Hamlet, dying, managed to kill his father's brother with his machete."

"You see, I was right!" exclaimed the elder.

"That was a very good story," added the old man, "and you told it with very few mistakes. There was just one more error, at the very end. The poison Hamlet's mother drank was obviously meant for the survivor of the fight, whichever it was. If Laertes had won, the great chief would have poisoned him, for no one would know that he arranged Hamlet's death. Then, too, he need not fear Laertes' witchcraft; it takes a strong heart to kill one's only sister by witchcraft.

"Sometime," concluded the old man, gathering his ragged toga about him, "you must tell us some more stories of your country. We, who are elders, will instruct you in their true meaning, so that when you return to your own land your elders will see that you have not been sitting in the bush, but among those who know things and who have taught you wisdom."

Laura Bohannan is a former professor of anthropology at the University of Illinois, at Chicago.

From *Natural History,* August/September 1966. © 1966 by Laura Bohannan. Reprinted by permission.

BODY ART AS VISUAL LANGUAGE

by Enid Schildkrout

[Editor's Note: Enid Schildkrout curated an exhibition titled "Body Art: Marks of Identity" that was on display at the American Museum of Natural History in New York from November 29, 1999 through May 29, 2000. Exhibition texts, illustrations, and the floor-plan can be viewed at www.anthro.amnh.org.]

Body art is not just the latest fashion. In fact, if the impulse to create art is one of the defining signs of humanity, the body may well have been the first canvas. Alongside paintings on cave walls created by early humans over 30,000 years ago, we find handprints and ochre deposits suggesting body painting. Some of the earliest mummies known—like the "Ice Man" from the Italian-Austrian Alps, known as Otzi, and others from central Asia, the Andes, Egypt and Europe—date back to 5000 years. People were buried with ornaments that would have been worn through body piercings, and remains of others show intentionally elongated or flattened skulls. Head shaping was practiced 5000 years ago in Chile and until the 18th century in France. Stone and ceramic figurines found in ancient graves depict people with every kind of body art known today. People have always marked their bodies with signs of individuality, social status, and cultural identity.

THE LANGUAGE OF BODY ART

There is no culture in which people do not, or did not paint, pierce, tattoo, reshape, or simply adorn their bodies. Fashions change and forms of body art come and go, but people everywhere do something or other to "package" their appearance. No sane or civilized person goes out in the raw; everyone grooms, dresses, or adorns some part of their body to present to the world. Body art communicates a person's status in society; displays accomplishments; and encodes memories, desires, and life histories.

Body art is a visual language. To understand it one needs to know the vocabulary, including the shared symbols, myths, and social values that are written on the body. From tattoos to top hats, body art makes a statement about the person who wears it. But body art is often misunderstood and misinterpreted because its messages do not necessarily translate across cultures. Elaborately pictorial Japanese tattooing started among men in certain occupational groups and depicts the exploits of a gangster hero drawn from a Chinese epic. The tattoos have more meaning to those who know the stories underlying the images than they do to people unfamiliar with the tales. Traditional Polynesian tattooing is mainly geometric and denotes rank and political status but more recently has been used to define ethnic identity within Pacific island societies.

In an increasingly global world, designs, motifs, even techniques of body modification move across cultural boundaries, but in the process their original meanings are often lost. An animal crest worn as a tattoo, carved into a totem pole, or woven into a blanket may signify membership in a particular clan among Indians on the Northwest Coast of North America, but when worn by people outside these cultures, the designs may simply refer to the wearer's identification with an alternative way of life. Polynesian or Indonesian tattoo designs worn by Westerners are admired for the beauty of their graphic qualities, but their original cultural meanings are rarely understood. A tattoo from Borneo was once worn to light the path of a person's soul after death, but in New York or Berlin it becomes a sign of rebellion from "coat and tie" culture.

Because body art is such an obvious way of signaling cultural differences, people often use it to identify, exoticize, and ostracize others. Tattoos, scarification, or head shaping may be a sign of high status in one culture and low status in another, but to a total outsider these practices may appear to be simply "mutilation." From the earliest voyages of discovery to contemporary tourism, travelers of all sorts—explorers and missionaries, soldiers and sailors, traders and tourists—have brought back images of the people they meet. These depictions sometimes reveal as much about the people looking at the body art as about the people making and wearing it. Some early images of Europeans and Americans by non-Westerners emphasized elaborate clothing and facial hair. Alternatively, Western images of Africans, Polynesians and Native Americans focused on the absence of clothes and the presence of tattoos, body paint and patterns of scars. Representations of body art in engravings, paintings, photographs and film are powerful visual metaphors that have been used both to record cultural differences and to proclaim one group's supposed superiority over another.

BODY ART: PERMANENT AND EPHEMERAL

Most people think that permanent modification of the skin, muscles, and bones is what body art is all about. But if one looks at body art as a form of communication, there is no logical reason to separate permanent forms of body art, like tattoos, scarification, piercing, or plastic surgery, from temporary forms, such as makeup, clothing, or hairstyles. Punks and sideshow artists may have what appears to be extreme body art, but everyone does it in one way or another. All of these modifications convey information about a person's identity.

Nonetheless, some forms of body art are undeniably more permanent than others. The decision to display a tattoo is obviously different from the decision to change the color of one's lipstick or dye one's hair. Tattooing, piercing, and scarification are more likely to be ways of signaling one's place in society, or an irreversible life passage like the change from childhood to adulthood. Temporary forms of body art, like clothing, ornaments and painting, more often mark a moment or simply follow a fashion. But these dichotomies don't stand up to close scrutiny across cultures: tattoos and scarification marks are often done to celebrate an event and dying or cutting one's hair, while temporary, may signal a life-changing event, such as a wedding or a funeral.

ULTURAL IDEALS OF BEAUTY

Ideas of beauty vary from one culture to another. Some anthropologists and psychologists believe that babies in all cultures respond positively to certain kinds of faces. The beautiful body is often associated with the healthy body and non-threatening facial expressions and gestures. But this does not mean that beauty is defined the same way in all cultures. People's ideas about the way a healthy person should look are not the same in all cultures: some see fat as an indication of health and wealth while others feel quite the opposite. People in some cultures admire and respect signs of aging, while others do all they can to hide gray hair and wrinkles.

Notwithstanding the fact that parents often make decisions for their children, like whether or not to pierce the ears of infants, in general I would maintain that to be considered art and not just a marking, body art has to have some measure of freedom and intentionality in its creation. The brands put on enslaved people, or the numbers tattooed on concentration camp victims, or the scars left from an unwanted injury are body markings not body art.

CULTURAL SIGNIFICANCE OF BODY ART

Body art takes on specific meanings in different cultures. It can serve as a link with ancestors, deities, or spirits. Besides being decorative, tattoos, paint, and scars can mediate the relationships between people and the supernatural world. The decorated body can serve as a shield to repel evil or as a means of attracting good fortune. Tattoos in central Borneo had the same designs as objects of everyday use and shielded people from dangerous spirits. Selk'nam men in Tierra del Fuego painted their bodies to transform themselves into spirits for initiation ceremonies. Australian Aborigines painted similar designs on cave walls and their bodies to indicate the location of sacred places revealed in dreams.

Transitions in status and identity, for example the transition between childhood and adulthood, are often seen as times of danger. Body art protects a vulnerable person, whether an initiate, a bride, or a deceased person, in this transitional phase. To ensure her good fortune, an Indian bride's hands and feet are covered in henna designs that also emphasize her beauty. For protection during initiation, a central African Chokwe girl's body is covered in white kaolin. In many societies, both the dead and those who mourn them are covered with paints and powders for decoration and protection.

Worldwide travel, large-scale migrations, and increasing access to global networks of communication mean that body art today is a kaleidoscopic mix of traditional practices and new inventions. Materials, designs, and practices move from one cultural context to another. Traditional body art practices are given new meanings as they move across cultural and social boundaries.

Body art is always changing, and in some form or another always engaging: it allows people to reinvent themselves—to rebel, to follow fashion, or to play and experiment with new identities. Like performance artists and actors, people in everyday life use body art to cross boundaries of gender, national identity, and cultural stereotypes.

Body art can be an expression of individuality, but it can also be an expression of group identity. Body art is about conformity and rebellion, freedom and authority. Its messages and meanings only make sense in the context of culture, but because it is such a personal art form, it continually challenges cultural assumptions about the ideal, the desirable, and the appropriately presented body.

BODY ART TECHNIQUES

Body Painting

Body painting, the most ephemeral and flexible of all body art, has the greatest potential for transforming a person into something else—a spirit, a work of art, another gender, even a map to a sacred place including the afterlife. It can be simply a way of emphasizing a person's visual appeal, a serious statement of allegiance, or a protective and empowering coating.

Natural clays and pigments made from a great variety of plants and minerals are often mixed with vegetable oils and animal fat to make body paint. These include red and yellow ochre (iron rich clay), red cam wood, cinnabar, gold dust, many roots, fruits and flowers, cedar bark, white kaolin, chalk, and temporary skin dyes made from indigo and henna leaves. People all over the world adorn the living and also treat the dead with body paint.

The colors of body paint often have symbolic significance, varying from culture to culture. Some clays and body paints are felt to have protective and auspicious properties, making them ideal for use in initiation rituals, for weddings, and for funerals— all occasions of transition from one life stage to another.

Historically, body paints and dyes have been important trade items. Indians of North America exchanged many valuable items for vermilion, which is mercuric sulphide (an artificial equivalent of the natural dye made from cinnabar). Mixed with red lead by European traders, it could cause or sometimes caused mercury poisoning in the wearer.

Makeup

Makeup consists of removable substances—paint, powders, and dyes—applied to enhance or transform appearance. Commonly part of regular grooming, makeup varies according to changing definitions of beauty. For vanity and social acceptance, or for medicinal or ritual purposes, people regularly transform every visible part of their body. They have tanned or whitened skin; changed the color of their lips, eyes, teeth, and hair; and added or removed "beauty" spots.

From the 10th to the 19th century, Japanese married women and courtesans blackened their teeth with a paste made from a mixture of tea and sake soaked in iron scraps; black teeth were considered beautiful and sexually appealing.

Makeup can accentuate the contrast between men and women, camouflage perceived imperfections or signify a special occasion or ritual state. Makeup, like clothing and hairstyles, allows people to reinvent themselves in everyday life.

Rituals and ceremonies often require people to wear certain kinds of makeup, clothing, or hairstyles to indicate that a person is taking on a new identity (representing an ancestor or a spirit in a masquerade, for example) or transforming his or her social identity as in an initiation ceremony, wedding, graduation or naming ceremony. Male Japanese actors in Kabuki theater represent women by using strictly codified paints and motifs, and the designs and motifs of Chinese theatrical makeup indicate the identity of a character.

Hair

Hair is one the easiest and most obvious parts of the body subject to change, and combing and washing hair is part of everyday grooming in most cultures. Styles of combing, braiding, parting, and wrapping hair can signify status and gender, age and ritual status, or membership in a certain group.

Hair often has powerful symbolic significance. Covering the head can be a sign of piety and respect, whether in a place of worship or all the time. Orthodox Jewish women shave their heads but also cover them with wigs or scarves. Muslim women in many parts of the world cover their heads, and sometimes cover their faces too, with scarves or veils. Sikh men in India never cut their hair and cover their heads with turbans. And the Queen of England is rarely seen without a hat.

Cutting hair is a ritual act in some cultures and heads are often shaved during rituals that signify the passage from one life stage to another. Hair itself, once cut, can be used as a symbolic substance. Being part, and yet not part, of a person, living or dead, hair can take on the symbolic power of the person. Some Native Americans formerly attached hair from enemies to war shirts, while warriors in Borneo formerly attached hair from captured enemies to war shields.

Reversing the normal treatment of hair, whatever that is in a particular culture, can be a sign of rebellion or of special status. Adopting the uncombed hair of the Rastafarians can be a sign of rebellion among some people, while for Rastafarians it is a sign of membership in a particular religious group. In many cultures people in mourning deliberately do not comb or wash their hair for a period of time, thereby showing that they are temporarily not part of normal everyday life.

What we do with our hair is a way of expressing our identity, and it is easy to look around and see how hair color, cut, style, and its very presence or absence, tells others much about how we want to be seen.

Body Shaping

The shape of the human body changes throughout life, but in many cultures people have found ways to permanently or temporarily sculpt the body. To conform to culturally defined ideals of male and female beauty, people have bound the soft bones of babies' skulls or children's feet, stretched their necks with rings, removed ribs to achieve tiny waists, and most commonly today, sculpted the body through plastic surgery.

Becoming fat is a sign of health, wealth and fertility in some societies, and fattening is sometimes part of a girl's coming of age ceremony. Tiny waists, small feet, and large or small breasts and buttocks have been prized or scorned as ideals of female beauty. Less common are ways of shaping men's bodies but developing muscles, shaping the head, or gaining weight are ways in which cultural ideals of male beauty and power have been expressed.

Head shaping is still done in parts of South America. For the Inka of South America and the Maya of Central America and Mexico, a specially shaped head once signified nobility. Because the skull bones of infants and children are not completely fused, the application of pressure with pads, boards, bindings, or massage results in a gently shaped head that can be a mark of high status or local identity.

While Western plastic surgery developed first as a way of correcting the injuries of war, particularly after WW II, today people use plastic surgery to smooth their skin, remove unwanted fat, and reshape parts of their bodies.

Scarification

Permanent patterns of scars on the skin, inscribed onto the body through scarification, can be signs of beauty and indicators of status. In some cultures, a smooth, unmarked skin represents an ideal of beauty, but people in many other cultures see smooth skin as a naked, unattractive surface. Scarification, also called cicatrisation, alters skin texture by cutting the skin and controlling the body's healing process. The cuts are treated to prevent infection and to enhance the scars' visibility. Deep cuts leave visible incisions after the skin heals, while inserting substances like clay or ash in the cuts results in permanently raised wheals or bumps, known as keloids. Substances inserted into the wounds may result in changes in skin color, creating marks similar to tattoos. Cutting elaborate and extensive decorative patterns into the skin usually indicates a permanent change in a person's status. Because scarification is painful, the richly scarred person is often honored for endurance and courage. Branding is a form of scarification that creates a scar after the surface of the skin has been burned. Branding was done in some societies as a part of a rite of passage, but in western Europe and elsewhere branding, as well as some forms of tattoo, were widely used to mark captives, enslaved peoples, and criminals. Recently, some individuals and members of fraternities on U.S. college campuses have adopted branding as a radical form of decoration and self-identification.

Tattooing

Tattoo is the insertion of ink or some other pigment through the outer covering of the body, the epidermis, into the dermis, the second layer of skin. Tattooists use a sharp implement to puncture the skin and thus make an indelible mark, design, or picture on the body. The resulting patterns or figures vary according to the purpose of the tattoo and the materials available for its coloration.

Different groups and cultures have used a variety of techniques in this process. Traditional Polynesian tattooists punctured the skin by tapping a needle with a small hammer. The Japanese work by hand but with bundles of needles set in wooden handles. Since the late 19th century, the electric tattoo machine and related technological advances in equipment have revolutionized tattoo in the West, expanding the range of possible designs, the colors available, and the ease with which a tattoo can be applied to the body. Prisoners have used materials as disparate as guitar strings and reconstructed electric shavers to create tattoos. Tattoos are usually intended as permanent markings, and it is only recently through the use of expensive laser techniques that they can be removed.

While often decorative, tattoos send important cultural messages. The "text" on the skin can be read as a commitment to some group, an emblem of a rite of passage, a personal or a fashion statement. In fact, cosmetic tattooing of eyebrows and eyeliner is one of the fastest growing of all tattoo enterprises. Tattoos can also signify bravery and commitment to a long, painful process—as is the case with Japanese full body tattooing or Māori body and facial patterns. Though there have been numerous religious and social injunctions against tattooing, marking the body in this way has been one of the most persistent and universal forms of body art.

Piercing

Body piercing, which allows ornaments to be worn in the body, has been a widespread practice since ancient times. Piercing involves long-term insertion of an object through the skin in a way that permits healing around the opening. Most commonly pierced are the soft tissues of the face, but many peoples, past and present, have also pierced the genitals and the chest. Ear, nose and lip ornaments, as well as pierced figurines, have been found in ancient burials of the Inka and Moche of Peru, the Aztecs and Maya of ancient Mexico, and in graves of central Asian, European and Mediterranean peoples.

The act of piercing is often part of a ritual change of status. Bleeding that occurs during piercing is sometimes thought of as an offering to gods, spirits or ancestors. Particular ornaments may be restricted to certain groups—men or women, rulers or priests—or may be inserted as part of a ceremony marking a change in status. Because ornaments can be made of precious and rare materials, they may signal privilege and wealth.

Enid Schildkrout is chair and curator in the Division of Anthropology at the American Museum of Natural History in New York City and founding editor of Faces magazine.

UNIT 3

The Organization of Society and Culture

Unit Selections

Key Points to Consider

- What traditional Inuit (Eskimo) practices do you find contrary to values professed in your society but important to Eskimo survival under certain circumstances?

- What can contemporary hunter-collector societies tell us about the quality of life in the prehistoric past?

- What are the rules of reciprocity?

- Under what circumstances do people conduct warfare and why do they stop fighting?

- To what extent are modern American political institutions based upon Native American traditions?

 **Links: www.dushkin.com/online/**
These sites are annotated in the World Wide Web pages.

Huarochiri, a Peruvian Culture in Time
http://wiscinfo.doit.wisc.edu/chaysimire/

Smithsonian Institution Web Site
http://www.si.edu

Sociology Guy's Anthropology Links
http://www.trinity.edu/~mkearl/anthro.html

What Is Culture?
http://www.wsu.edu:8001/vcwsu/commons/topics/culture/culture-index.html

Human beings do not interact with one another or think about their world in random fashion. Instead, they engage in both structured and recurrent physical and mental activities. In this section, such patterns of behavior and thought—referred to here as the organization of society and culture—may be seen in a number of different contexts, from the hunting tactics of the Inupiaq Eskimos of the Arctic (see "Understanding Eskimo Science") to the cattle-herding Masai of East Africa (in "Mystique of the Masai").

Of special importance are the ways in which people make a living—in other words, the production, distribution, and consumption of goods and services. It is only by knowing the basic subsistence systems that we can hope to gain insight into the other levels of social and cultural phenomena, for, as anthropologists have found, they are all inextricably bound together.

Noting the various aspects of a sociocultural system in harmonious balance, however, does not imply an anthropological seal of approval. To understand infanticide (killing of the newborn) in the manner that it is practiced among some peoples is neither to condone nor to condemn it. The adaptive patterns that have been in existence for a long time, such as many of the patterns of hunters and gatherers, probably owe their existence to their contributions to long-term human survival. Anthropologists, however, are not content with the data derived from individual experience. On the contrary, personal descriptions must become the basis for sound anthropological theory. Otherwise, they remain meaningless, isolated relics of culture in the manner of museum pieces. Thus, in "Too Many Bananas, Not Enough Pineapples, and No Watermelon at All: Three Object Lessons in Living With Reciprocity," David Counts provides us with ground rules for reciprocity that were derived from his own particular field experience and yet are cross-culturally applicable. "Prehistory of Warfare" by Steven A. LeBlanc expresses that constant striving in anthropology to develop a general perspective from particular events by showing how environmental circumstances and shifts in technology may result in marked changes in lifestyle and centralization of political power and warfare. Finally, "The Founding Indian Fathers" by Jack Weatherford shows how the American form of government did not just appear out of nowhere, but has its roots in the Native American past.

While the articles in this unit are to some extent descriptive, they also serve to challenge both academic and commonsense notions about why people behave and think as they do. They remind us that assumptions are never really safe. Anytime anthropologists can be kept on their toes, their field as a whole is the better for it.

Understanding Eskimo Science

Traditional hunters' insights into the natural world are worth rediscovering.

Richard Nelson

Just below the Arctic Circle in the boreal forest of interior Alaska; an amber afternoon in mid-November; the temperature -20°; the air adrift with frost crystals, presaging the onset of deeper cold.

Five men—Koyukon Indians—lean over the carcass of an exceptionally large black bear. For two days they've traversed the Koyukuk River valley, searching for bears that have recently entered hibernation dens. The animals are in prime condition at this season but extremely hard to find. Den entrances, hidden beneath 18 inches of powdery snow, are betrayed only by the subtlest of clues—patches where no grass protrudes from the surface because it's been clawed away for insulation, faint concavities hinting of footprint depressions in the moss below.

Earlier this morning the hunters took a yearling bear. In accordance with Koyukon tradition, they followed elaborate rules for the proper treatment of killed animals. For example, the bear's feet were removed first, to keep its spirit from wandering. Also, certain parts were to be eaten away from the village, at a kind of funeral feast. All the rest would be eaten either at home or at community events, as people here have done for countless generations.

Koyukon hunters know that an animal's life ebbs slowly, that it remains aware and sensitive to how people treat its body. This is especially true for the potent and demanding spirit of the bear.

The leader of the hunting group is Moses Sam, a man in his 60s who has trapped in this territory since childhood. He is known for his detailed knowledge of the land and for his extraordinary success as a bear hunter. "No one else has that kind of luck with bears," I've been told. "Some people are born with it. He always takes good care of his animals—respects them. That's how he keeps his luck."

Moses pulls a small knife from his pocket, kneels beside the bear's head, and carefully slits the clear domes of its eyes. "Now," he explains softly, "the bear won't see if one of us makes a mistake or does something wrong."

Contemporary Americans are likely to find this story exotic, but over the course of time episodes like this have been utterly commonplace, the essence of people's relationship to the natural world. After all, for 99 percent of human history we lived exclusively as hunter-gatherers; by comparison, agriculture has existed only for a moment and urban societies scarcely more than a blink.

From this perspective, much of human experience over the past several million years lies beyond our grasp. Probably no society has been so deeply alienated as ours from the community of nature, has viewed the natural world from a greater distance of mind, has lapsed into a murkier comprehension of its connections with the sustaining environment. Because of this, we have great difficulty understanding our rootedness to earth, our affinities with nonhuman life.

I believe it's essential that we learn from traditional societies, especially those whose livelihood depends on the harvest of a wild environment—hunters, fishers, trappers, and gatherers. These people have accumulated bodies of knowledge much like our own sciences. And they can give us vital insights about responsible membership in the community of life, insights founded on a wisdom we'd long forgotten and now are beginning to rediscover.

Since the mid-1960s I have worked as an ethnographer in Alaska, living intermittently in remote northern communities and recording native traditions centered around the natural world. I spent about two years in Koyukon Indian villages and just over a year with Inupiaq Eskimos on the Arctic coast—traveling by dog team and snowmobile, recording traditional knowledge, and learning the hunter's way.

Eskimos have long inhabited some of the harshest environments on earth, and they are among the most exquisitely adapted of all human groups. Because plant life is so scarce in their northern terrain, Eskimos depend more than any other people on hunting.

Eskimos are famous for the cleverness of their technology—kayaks, harpoons, skin clothing, snow houses, dog teams. But I believe their greatest genius, and the basis of their success, lies in the less tangible realm of the intellect—the nexus of mind and nature. For what repeatedly struck me above all else was their profound knowledge of the environment.

Several times, when my Inupiaq hunting companion did something especially clever, he'd point to his head and declare: "You see—Eskimo scientist!" At first I took it as hyperbole, but as time went by I realized he was speaking the truth. Scientists had often come to his village, and he saw in them a familiar commitment to the empirical method.

Traditional Inupiaq hunters spend a lifetime acquiring knowledge—from others in the community and from their own observations. If they are to survive, they must have absolutely reliable information. When I first went to live with Inupiaq people, I doubted many things they told me. But the longer I stayed, the more I trusted their teachings.

For example, hunters say that ringed seals surfacing in open leads—wide cracks in the sea ice—can reliably forecast the weather. Because an unexpected gale might set people adrift on the pack ice, accurate prediction is a matter of life and death. When seals rise chest-high in the water, snout pointed skyward, not going anywhere in particular, it indicates stable weather, the Inupiaq say. But if they surface briefly, head low, snout parallel to the water, and show themselves only once or twice, watch for a sudden storm. And take special heed if you've also noticed the sled dogs howling incessantly, stars twinkling erratically, or the current running strong from the south. As time passed, my own experiences with seals and winter storms affirmed what the Eskimos said.

Like a young Inupiaq in training, I gradually grew less skeptical and started to apply what I was told. For example, had I ever been rushed by a polar bear, I would have jumped away to the animal's *right* side. Inupiaq elders say polar bears are left-handed, so you have a slightly better chance to avoid their right paw, which is slower and less accurate. I'm pleased to say I never had the chance for a field test. But in judging assertions like this, remember that Eskimos have had close contact with polar bears for several thousand years.

The Inupiaq hunter possesses as much knowledge as a highly trained scientist in our own society

During winter, ringed and bearded seals maintain tunnel-like breathing holes in ice that is many feet thick. These holes are often capped with an igloo-shaped dome created by water sloshing onto the surface when the animal enters from below. Inupiaq elders told me that polar bears are clever enough to excavate around the base of this dome, leaving it perfectly intact but weak enough that a hard swat will shatter the ice and smash the seal's skull. I couldn't help wondering if this were really true; but then a younger man told me he'd recently followed the tracks of a bear that had excavated one seal hole after another, exactly as the elders had described.

In the village where I lived, the most respected hunter was Igruk, a man in his 70s. He had an extraordinary sense of animals—a gift for understanding and predicting their behavior. Although he was no longer quick and strong, he joined a crew hunting bowhead whales during the spring migration, his main role being that of adviser. Each time Igruk spotted a whale coming from the south, he counted the number of blows, timed how long it stayed down, and noted the distance it traveled along the open lead, until it vanished toward the north. This way he learned to predict, with uncanny accuracy, where hunters could expect the whale to resurface.

I believe the expert Inupiaq hunter possesses as much knowledge as a highly trained scientist in our own society, although the information may be of a different sort. Volumes could be written on the behavior, ecology, and utilization of Arctic animals—polar bear, walrus, bowhead whale, beluga, bearded seal, ringed seal, caribou, musk ox, and others—based entirely on Eskimo knowledge.

Comparable bodies of knowledge existed in every Native American culture before the time of Columbus. Since then, even in the far north, Western education and cultural change have steadily eroded these traditions. Reflecting on a time before Europeans arrived, we can imagine the whole array of North American animal species—deer, elk, black bear, wolf, mountain lion, beaver, coyote, Canada goose, ruffed grouse, passenger pigeon, northern pike—each known in hundreds of different ways by tribal communities; the entire continent, sheathed in intricate webs of knowledge. Taken as a whole, this composed a vast intellectual legacy, born of intimacy with the natural world. Sadly, not more than a hint of it has ever been recorded.

Like other Native Americans, the Inupiaq acquired their knowledge through gradual accretion of naturalistic observations—year after year, lifetime after lifetime, generation after generation, century after century. Modern science often relies on other techniques—specialized full-time observation, controlled experiments, captive-animal studies, technological devices like radio collars—which can provide similar information much more quickly.

Yet Eskimo people have learned not only *about* animals but also *from* them. Polar bears hunt seals not only by waiting at their winter breathing holes, but also by stalking seals that crawl up on the ice to bask in the spring warmth. Both methods depend on being silent, staying downwind, keeping out of sight, and moving only when the seal is asleep or distracted. According to the elders, a stalking bear will even use one paw to cover its conspicuous black nose.

Inupiaq methods for hunting seals, both at breathing holes and atop the spring ice, are nearly identical to those of the polar bear. Is this a case of independent invention? Or did ancestral Eskimos learn the techniques by watching polar bears, who had perfected an adaptation to the sea-ice-environment long before humans arrived in the Arctic?

The hunter's genius centers on knowing an animal's behavior so well he can turn it to his advantage. For instance, Igruk once saw a polar bear far off across flat ice, where he couldn't stalk it without being seen. But he knew an old technique of mimicking a seal. He lay down in plain sight, conspicuous in his dark parka and pants, then lifted and dropped his head like a seal, scratched the ice, and imitated flippers with his hands. The bear mistook his pursuer for prey. Each time Igruk lifted his head the animal kept still; whenever Igruk "slept" the bear crept closer. When it came near enough, a gunshot pierced the snowy silence. That night, polar bear meat was shared among the villagers.

A traditional hunter like Igruk plumbs the depths of his intellect—his capacity to manipulate complex knowledge. But he also delves into his animal nature, drawing from intuitions of sense and body and heart: feeling the wind's touch, listening for the tick of moving ice, peering from crannies, hiding as if he himself were the hunted. He moves in a world of eyes, where everything watches—the bear, the seal, the wind, the moon and stars, the drifting ice, the silent waters below. He is beholden to powers we have long forgotten or ignored.

In Western society we rest comfortably on our own accepted truths about the nature of nature. We treat the environment as if it were numb to our presence and blind to our behavior. Yet despite our certainty on this matter, accounts of traditional people throughout the world reveal that most of humankind has concluded otherwise. Perhaps our scientific method really does follow the path to a single, absolute truth. But there may be wisdom in accepting other possibilities and opening ourselves to different views of the world.

I remember asking a Koyukon man about the behavior and temperament of the Canada goose. He described it as a gentle and good-natured animal, then added: "Even if [a goose] had the power to knock you over, I don't think it would do it."

For me, his words carried a deep metaphorical wisdom. They exemplified the Koyukon people's own restraint toward the world around them. And they offered a contrast to our culture, in which possessing the power to overwhelm the en-vironment has long been sufficient justification for its use.

"Each animal knows way more than you do," a Koyukon Indian elder was fond of telling me.

We often think of this continent as having been a pristine wilderness when the first Europeans arrived. Yet for at least 12,000 years, and possibly twice that long, Native American people had inhabited and intensively utilized the land; had gathered, hunted, fished, settled, and cultivated; had learned the terrain in all its details, infusing it with meaning and memory; and had shaped every aspect of their life around it. That humans could sustain membership in a natural community for such an enormous span of time without profoundly degrading it fairly staggers the imagination. And it gives strong testimony to the adaptation of mind—the braiding together of knowledge and ideology—that linked North America's indigenous people with their environment.

A Koyukon elder, who took it upon himself to be my teacher, was fond of telling me: "Each animal knows way more than you do." He spoke as if it summarized all that he understood and believed.

This statement epitomizes relationships to the natural world among many Native American people. And it goes far in explaining the diversity and fecundity of life on our continent when the first sailing ship approached these shores.

There's been much discussion in recent years about what biologist E. O. Wilson has termed "biophilia"—a deep, pervasive, ubiquitous, all-embracing affinity for nonhuman life. Evidence for this "instinct" may be elusive in Western cultures, but not among traditional societies. People like the Koyukon manifest biophilia in virtually all dimensions of their existence. Connectedness with non-human life infuses the whole spectrum of their thought, behavior, and belief.

It's often said that a fish might have no concept of water, never having left it. In the same way, traditional peoples might never stand far enough outside themselves to imagine a generalized concept of biophilia. Perhaps it would be impossible for people to intimately bound with the natural world, people who recognize that all nature is our own embracing community. Perhaps, to bring a word like *biophilia* into their language, they would first need to separate themselves from nature.

In April 1971 I was in a whaling camp several miles off the Arctic coast with a group of Inupiaq hunters, including Igruk, who understood animals so well he almost seemed to enter their minds.

Onshore winds had closed the lead that migrating whales usually follow, but one large opening remained, and here the Inupiaq men placed their camp. For a couple of days there had been no whales, so everyone stayed inside the warm tent, talking and relaxing. The old man rested on a soft bed of caribou skins with his eyes closed. Then, suddenly, he interrupted the conversation: "I think a whale is coming, and perhaps it will surface very close...."

To my amazement everyone jumped into action, although none had seen or heard anything except Igruk's words. Only he stayed behind, while the others rushed for the water's edge. I was last to leave the tent. Seconds after I stepped outside, a broad, shining back cleaved the still water near the opposite side of the opening, accompanied by the burst of a whale's blow.

Later, when I asked how he'd known, Igruk said, "There was a ringing inside my ears." I have no explanation other than his; I can only report what I saw. None of the Inupiaq crew members even commented afterward, as if nothing out of the ordinary had happened.

This article originally appeared in *Audubon* magazine, September/October 1993, pp. 102–109. Adapted from *Biophilia* by Richard Nelson, 1993.
Published by Island Press. © 1993 by Richard Nelson. Reprinted by permission of Susan Bergholz Literary Services, New York. All rights reserved.

Mystique of the Masai

Pastoral as well as warlike, they have persisted in maintaining their unique way of life

Ettagale Blauer

The noble bearing, self-assurance, and great beauty of the Masai of East Africa have been remarked upon from the time the first Europeans encountered them on the plains of what are now Kenya and Tanzania. (The word 'Masai' derives from their spoken language, Maa.) Historically, the Masai have lived among the wild animals on the rolling plains of the Rift Valley, one of the most beautiful parts of Africa. Here, the last great herds still roam freely across the plains in their semiannual migrations.

Although the appearance of people usually marks the decline of the game, it is precisely the presence of the Masai that has guaranteed the existence of these vast herds. Elsewhere in Kenya and Tanzania, and certainly throughout the rest of Africa, the herds that once roamed the lands have been decimated. But the Masai are not hunters, whom they call *iltorrobo*—poor men—because they don't have cattle. The Masai do not crave animal trophies, they do not value rhinoceros horns for aphrodisiacs, meat is not part of their usual diet, and they don't farm the land, believing it to be a sacrilege to break the earth. Traditionally, where Masai live, the game is unmolested.

In contrast to their peaceful and harmonious relationship to the wildlife, however, the Masai are warlike in relationship to the neighboring tribes, conducting cattle raids where they take women as well as cattle for their prizes, and they have been fiercely independent in resisting the attempts of colonial governments to change or subdue them. Although less numerous than the neighboring Kikuyu, the Masai have a strong feeling of being "chosen" people, and have been stubborn in maintaining their tribal identity.

However, that traditional tribal way of life is threatened by the exploding populations of Kenya and Tanzania (41 million people), who covet the vast open spaces of Masai Mara, Masai Amboseli, and the Serengeti Plain. Today, more than half of the Masai live in Kenya, with a style of life that requires extensive territory for cattle herds to roam in search of water and pastureland, and the freedom to hold ceremonies that mark the passage from one stage of life to the next. The Masai's need for land for their huge herds of cattle is not appreciated by people who value the land more for agriculture than for pasturage and for herds of wild animals.

The Masai live in countries that are attractive to tourists and whose leaders have embraced the values and life-style of the Western world. These two facts make it increasingly difficult for the Masai to live according to traditional patterns. The pressure to change in Kenya comes in part from their proximity to urban centers, especially the capital city of Nairobi, whose name is a Masai word meaning cool water.

Still, many Masai live in traditional homes and dress in wraps of bright cloth or leather, decorated with beaded jewelry, their cattle nearby. But the essence of the Masai culture—the creation of age-sets whose roles in life are clearly delineated—is under constant attack. In both Kenya and Tanzania, the governments continually try to "civilize" the Masai, to stop cattle raiding, and especially to put an end to the *morani*—the warriors—who are seen as the most disruptive of the age-sets.

TRADITIONAL LIFE

Masai legends trace the culture back some 300 years, and are recited according to age-groups, allowing fifteen years for each group. But anthropologists believe they arrived in the region some 1,000 years ago, having migrated from southern Ethiopia. As a racial group, they are considered a Nilo-Hamitic mix. Although deep brown in color, their features are not negroid. (Their extensive use of ochre may give their skin the look of American Indians but that is purely cosmetic.)

Traditional Masai people are governed by one guiding principle: that all the cattle on earth are theirs, that they were put there for them by *Ngai*, who is the god of both heaven and earth, existing also in the rains which bring the precious grass to feed the cattle. Any cattle they do not presently own are only temporarily out of their care, and must be recaptured. The Masai do not steal material objects; theft for them is a separate matter from raiding cattle, which is seen as the *return* of cattle to their rightful owners. From this basic belief, an entire culture has grown. The grass that feeds the cattle and the ground on which it grows are sacred; to the Masai, it is sacrilege to break the ground for any reason, whether

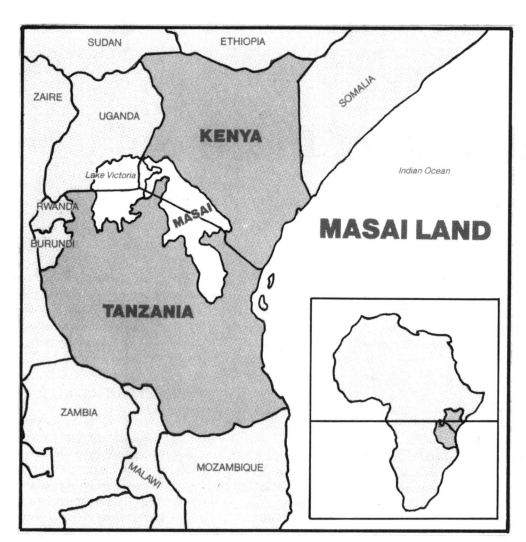

A map of Masai Land. The Masai's traditional territory exists within the two countries of Kenya and Tanzania.

to grow food or to dig for water, or even to bury the dead.

Cattle provide their sole sustenance: milk and blood to drink, and the meat feast when permitted. Meat eating is restricted to ceremonial occasions, or when it is needed for gaining strength, such as when a woman gives birth or someone is recovering from an illness. When they do eat meat at a ceremony they consume their own oxen, which are sacrificed for a particular reason and in the approved way. Hunting and killing for meat are not Masai activities. It is this total dependence on their cattle, and their disdain for the meat of game animals, that permits them to coexist with the game, and which, in turn, has kept intact the great herds of the Masai Mara and the Serengeti Plain. Their extraordinary diet of milk, blood, and occasionally, meat,

keeps them sleek and fit, and Westerners have often noted their physical condition with admiration.

In 1925 Norman Leys wrote, "Physically they are among the handsomest of mankind, with slender bones, narrow hips and shoulders and most beautifully rounded muscles and limbs." That same description holds today. The Masai live on about 1,300 calories a day, as opposed to our consumption of nearly 3,000. They are invariably lean.

Traditional nomadic life of the Masai, however, was ferocious and warlike in relation to other tribes. The warriors *(morani)* built *manyattas*, a type of shelter, throughout the lands and used each for a few months at a time, then moved to another area when the grazing was used up. As the seasons changed, they would return to those manyattas. They often

went out raiding cattle from neighboring tribes whom they terrorized with their great ferocity.

A large part of that aggressiveness is now attributed to drugs; the morani worked themselves into a frenzy as they prepared for a raid, using the leaves and barks of certain trees known to create such moods. A soup was made of fat, water, and the bark of two trees, *il kitosloswa* and *il kiluretti*. From the description, these seem to act as hallucinogens. As early as the 1840s, Europeans understood that the morani's extremely aggressive behavior derived from drug use. Drugs were used for endurance and for strength throughout warriorhood. During a meat feast, which could last a month, they took stimulants throughout, raising them to a virtual frenzy. This, combined with the natural excitement attendant to crowd behavior, made them formidable foes.

Having gained this supernatural energy and courage, they were ready to go cattle raiding among other tribes. To capture the cattle, the men of the other tribe had to be killed. Women were never touched in battle, but were taken to Masailand to become Masai wives. The rate of intermarriage was great during these years. Today, intermarriage is less frequent and the result mostly of chance meetings with other people. It is likely that intermarriage has actually prolonged the life of the Masai as a people; many observers from the early 1900s remarked upon the high rate of syphilis among the Masai, attributable to their habit of taking multiple sexual partners. Their birthrate is notably lower than the explosive population growth of the other peoples of Kenya and Tanzania. Still, they have increased from about 25,000 people at the turn of the century to the estimated 300,000–400,000 they are said to number today.

While the ceaseless cycle of their nomadic life has been sharply curtailed, many still cross the border between the two countries as they have for hundreds of years, leading their cattle to water and grazing lands according to the demands of the wet and dry seasons. They are in tune with the animals that migrate from the Serengeti Plain in Tanzania to Masai Mara in Kenya, and back again.

MALE AGE-SETS

The life of a traditional Masai male follows a well-ordered progression through a series of life stages.

Masai children enjoy their early years as coddled and adored love objects. They are raised communally, with great affection. Children are a great blessing in Africa. Among the Masai, with the lack of emphasis on paternity, and with a woman's prestige tied to her children, natural love for children is enhanced by their desirability in the society. Children are also desired because they bring additional cattle to a family, either as bride-price in the case of girls or by raiding in the case of boys.

During their early years, children play and imitate the actions of the elders, a natural school in which they learn the rituals and daily life practices of their people. Learning how to be a Masai is the lifework of every one in the community. Infant mortality in Africa remains high; catastrophic diseases introduced by Europeans, such as smallpox, nearly wiped them out. That memory is alive in their oral traditions; having children is a protection against the loss of the entire culture, which they know from experience could easily happen. Africans believe that you must live to see your face reflected in that of a child; given the high infant mortality rate, the only way to protect that human chain is by having as many children as possible.

For boys, each stage of life embraces an age-group created at an elaborate ceremony, the highlight of their lives being the elevation to moran. Once initiated, they learn their age-group's specific duties and privileges. Males pass through four stages: childhood, boyhood, warriorhood, and elderhood. Warriors, divided into junior and senior, form one generation, or age-set.

Four major ceremonies mark the passage from one group to another: boys who are going to be circumcised participate in the *Alamal Lenkapaata* ceremony, preparation for circumcision; *Emorata* is followed by initiation into warriorhood—status of moran; the passage from warrior to elderhood is marked by the *Eunoto* ceremony; and total elderhood is confirmed by the *Olngesherr*. All ceremonies have in common ritual head shaving, continual blessings, slaughter of an animal, ceremonial painting of face or body, singing, dancing, and feasting. *Laibons*—spiritual advisers—must be present at all ceremonies, and the entire tribe devotes itself to these preparations.

Circumcision is a rite of passage and more for teenage boys. It determines the role the boy will play throughout his life, as leader or follower. How he conducts himself during circumcision is keenly observed by all; a boy who cries out during the painful operation is branded a coward and shunned for a long time; his mother is disgraced. A boy who is brave, and who had led an exemplary life, becomes the leader of his age-group.

It takes months of work to prepare for these ceremonies so the exact date of such an event is rarely known until the last minute. Westerners, with contacts into the Masai community, often stay ready for weeks, hoping to be on hand when such a ceremony is about to take place. Each such ceremony may well be the last, it is thought.

Before they can be circumcised, boys must prove themselves ready. They tend the cattle—the Masai's only wealth—and guard them from predators whose tracks they learn to recognize. They know their cattle individually, the way we know people. Each animal has a name and is treated as a personality. When they feel they are ready, the boys approach the junior elders and ask them to open a new circumcision period. If this is approved, they begin a series of rituals, among them the Alamal Lenkapaata, the last step before the formal initiation. The boys must have a liabon, a leader with the power to predict the future, to guide them in their decisions. He creates a name for this new generation. The boys decorate themselves with chalky paint, and spend the night out in the open. The elders sing and celebrate and dance through the night to honor the boys.

An Alamal Lenkapaata held in 1983 was probably the most recent to mark the opening of a new age-set. Ceremonies were held in Ewaso Ngiro, in the Rift Valley. As boys joined into groups and danced, they raised a cloud of dust around themselves. All day long, groups would form and dance, then break apart and later start again.

Under a tree, elders from many areas gathered together and their discussion was very intense. John Galaty, professor of anthropology from McGill University in Montreal, who has studied the Masai extensively, flew in specifically to attend this ceremony. He is fluent in Masai and translated the elders' talk. "We are lucky," they said, "to be able to have this ceremony. The government does not want us to have it. We have to be very careful. The young men have to be warned that there should be no cattle raiding." And there wasn't any.

An ox was slaughtered, for meat eating is a vital element of this ceremony.

The boys who were taking part cut off hunks of meat which they cooked over an open fire. Though there was a hut set aside for them, the boys spent little time sleeping. The next day, all the elders gathered to receive gifts of sugar and salt from John Keen, a member of Kenya's parliament, and himself a Masai. (Kenya has many Masai in government, including the Minister of Finance, George Saitoti.) The dancing, the meat eating, all the elements of the ceremony continued for several days. If this had been a wealthy group, they might have kept up the celebration for as long as a month.

Once this ceremony is concluded, the boys are allowed to hold councils and to discuss important matters. They choose one from their own group to be their representative. The Alamal Lenkapaata ceremony includes every boy of suitable age, preparing him for circumcision and then warriorhood. The circumcisions will take place over the next few years, beginning with the older boys in this group. The age difference may be considerable in any age-group since these ceremonies are held infrequently; once a circumcision period ends, though, it may not be opened again for many years.

THE MORAN

The Masai who exemplifies his tribe is the moran. This is the time of life that expresses the essence of the Masai—bravery, willingness to defend their people and their cattle against all threats, confidence to go out on cattle raids to increase their own herds, and ability to stand up to threats even from Europeans, whose superior weapons subdued the Masai but never subjugated them. The Masai moran is the essence of that almost mythical being, the noble savage, a description invented by Europeans but here actually lived out. With his spear, his elaborately braided and reddened hair, his bountiful beaded jewelry, his beautiful body and proud bearing, the moran is the symbol of everything that is attractive about the Masai. When a young man becomes a moran, his entire culture looks upon him with reverence.

The life a moran enjoys as his birthright is centered on cattle raiding, enhancing his appearance, and sex. The need to perform actual work, such as building fences, rescuing a cow that has gone astray, and standing ready to defend their homeland—Masailand—is only occasionally required. Much of his time is devoted to the glorification of his appearance. His body is a living showcase of Masai art.

From the moment a boy undergoes the circumcision ceremony, he looks ahead to the time when he will be a moran. He grows his hair long so it can be braided into myriad tiny plaits, thickened with ochre and lat. The age-mates spend hours at this, the whole outdoors being their salon. As they work, they chat, always building the bonds between them. Their beaded jewelry is made by their girlfriends. Their bare legs are ever-changing canvases on which they trace patterns, using white chalk and ochre. Though nearly naked, they are a medley of patterns and colors.

After being circumcised, the young men "float" in society for up to two years, traveling in loose groups and living in temporary shelters called *inkangitie*. After that time they can build a manyatta. Before fully becoming a moran, however, they must enter a "holy house" at a special ceremony. Only a young man who has not slept with a circumcised woman can enter the holy house. The fear of violating this taboo is very strong, and young men who do not enter the house are beaten by their parents and carry the disrespect of the tribe all their lives.

The dancing of the morani celebrates everything that they consider beautiful and strong: morani dance competitively by jumping straight into the air, knees straight, over and over again, each leap trying to go higher than the last, as they sing and chant and encourage each other. The morani also dance with their young girlfriends. Each couple performs sinuous motions repeatedly, then breaks off and another couple takes their place. A hypnotic rhythm develops as they follow the chanting and hand clapping of their mates.

Although they are now forbidden by the governments of Kenya and Tanzania to kill a lion—a traditional test of manhood—or to go cattle raiding, they retain all the trappings of a warrior, without the possibility of practicing their skill. They occasionally manage a cattle raid, but even without it, they still live with pride and dignity. Masai remain morani for about fifteen years, building up unusually strong relationships among their age-mates with whom they live during that time. Hundreds of boys may become morani at one time.

Traditionally, every fifteen years saw the advent of a new generation of warriors. Now, both colonial governments and independent black-ruled governments have tampered with this social process, and have been successful in reducing the time men spend as warriors. By forcing this change, the governments hope to mold the Masai male into a more tractable citizen, especially by forbidding such disruptive activities as lion killing and cattle raiding. But tinkering with the Masai system can have unforeseen and undesirable consequences. It takes a certain number of years before a moran is ready to take on the duties of that age-group. They need time to build up herds of cattle to be used for bride-price and to learn to perform the decision-making tasks expected. This change also leaves the younger boys without warriors to keep them in check, and to guide them through the years leading up to the circumcision ceremony.

More significantly, since 1978 it has been illegal to build a manyatta, and warriors from that time have been left with no place to live. Their mothers cannot live with them, they cannot tend their cattle or increase their herds, they have no wives or jobs. Since, once they become warriors, they are not allowed to enter another person's house to eat, they are forced to steal other peoples' cattle and live off the land.

Circumcision exists for women as well as for men. From the age of nine until puberty, young girls live with the morani as sexual partners; it is an accepted part of Masai life that girls do not reach puberty as virgins. It is because of this practice that syphilis causes the most serious problems for the Masai. The girls, unfamiliar with their bodies, contract the disease and leave it untreated until sterility results. This sexual activity changes dramatically when a girl reaches puberty. At that time, she is circumcised and forbidden to stay with the warriors. This is to prevent her from becoming pregnant before she is married. As soon as she recovers from the circumcision, or clitoridectomy, an operation that destroys her ability to experience orgasm, she is considered ready for marriage. Circumcision is seen as a means of equalizing men and women. By removing any vestige of the appearance of the organs of the opposite sex, it purifies the gender. Although female circumcision has long been banned by the Kenyan government, few girls manage to escape the operation.

While the entire tribe devotes itself to the rituals that perpetuate the male age-set system, girls travel individually through life in their roles as lovers, wives, and child bearers, in all instances subservient to the boys and men. They have no comparable age-set system and hence do not develop the intensely felt friendships of the men who move through life together in groups, and who, during the period of senior warriorhood live together, away from their families.

It is during this period that the mothers move away from their homes. They build manyattas in which they live with their sons who have achieved the status of senior morani, along with their sons' girlfriends, and away from their own small children. The husbands, other wives, and the other women of the tribe, take care of these children.

The male-female relationship is dictated according to the male age-sets. When a newly circumcised girl marries, she joins the household of her husband's family, and likely will be one among several of his wives. Her role is to milk the cows, to build the house, and to bear children, especially male children. Only through childbirth can she achieve high status; all men, on the other hand, achieve status simply by graduating from one age-set to the next.

A childless Masai woman is virtually without a role in her society. One of the rarest ceremonies among the Masai is a blessing for women who have not given birth and for women who want more children. While the women play a peripheral role in the men's ceremonies, the men are vital to the women's, for it is a man who blesses the women. To prepare for the ritual, the women brew great quantities of beer and offer beer and lambs to the men who are to bless them.

In their preparation for this ceremony, and in conducting matters that pertain to their lives, the women talk things out democratically, as do the men. They gather in the fields and each woman presents her views. Not until all who want to speak have done so does the group move toward a consensus. As with the men, a good speaker is highly valued and her views are listened to attentively. But these sessions are restricted to women's issues; the men have the final say over all matters relating to the tribe. Boys may gather in councils as soon as they have completed the Alamal Lenkapaata; girls don't have similar opportunities. They follow their lovers, the morani, devotedly, yet as soon as they reach the age when they can marry, they are wrenched out of this love relationship and given in marriage to much older men, men who have cattle for bride-price.

Because morani do not marry until they are elevated to elderhood, girls must accept husbands who are easily twice their age. But just as the husband has more than one wife, she will have lovers, who are permitted as long as they are members of her husband's circumcision group, not the age group for whom she was a girlfriend. This is often the cause of tension among the Masai. All the children she bears are considered to be her husband's even though they may not be his biologically. While incest taboos are clearly observed and various other taboos also pertain, multiple partners are expected. Polygamy in Masailand (and anywhere it prevails) dictates that some men will not marry at all. These men are likely to be those without cattle, men who cannot bring bride-price. For the less traditional, the payment of bride-price is sometimes made in cash, rather than in cattle, and to earn money, men go to the cities to seek work. Masai tend to find jobs that permit them to be outside and free; for this reason, many of the night watchmen in the capital city of Nairobi are Masai. They sit around fires at night, chatting, in an urban version of their life in the countryside....

RAIDING, THEFT, AND THE LAW

Though now subject to national laws, the Masai do not turn to official bodies or courts for redress. They settle their own disputes democratically, each man giving his opinion until the matter at hand is settled. Men decide all matters for the tribe (women do not take part in these discussions), and they operate virtually without chiefs. The overriding concern is to be fair in the resolution of problems because kinship ties the Masai together in every aspect of their lives. Once a decision is made, punishment is always levied in the form of a fine. The Masai have no jails, nor do they inflict physical punishment. For a people who value cattle as much as they do, there is no greater sacrifice than to give up some of their animals.

The introduction of schools is another encroachment upon traditional life which was opposed by the Masai. While most African societies resisted sending their children to school, the Masai reacted with particular intensity. They compared school to death or enslavement; if children did go to school, they would be lost to the Masai community. They would forget how to survive on the land, how to identify animals by their tracks, and how to protect the cattle. All of these things are learned by example and by experience.

David Read is a white Kenyan, fluent in Masai who said that, as a boy: "I may not have been able to read or write, but I knew how to live in the bush. I could hunt my dinner if I had to."

The first school in their territory was opened in 1919 at Narok but few children attended. The Masai scorned the other tribes, such as the Kikuyu, who later embraced Western culture and soon filled the offices of the government's bureaucracies. The distance between the Masai and the other tribes became even greater. The Masai were seen as a painful reminder of the primitivism that Europeans as well as Africans had worked so hard to erase. Today, however, many Masai families will keep one son at home to maintain traditional life, and send another one to school. In this way, they experience the benefits of literacy, opportunities for employment, money, connections to the government, and new knowledge, especially veterinary practices, while keeping their traditions intact. Masai who go to school tend to succeed, many of them graduating from college with science degrees. Some take up the study of animal diseases, and bring this knowledge back to help their communities improve the health of their cattle. The entire Masai herd was once nearly wiped out during the rinderpest epidemic in the late nineteenth century. Today, the cattle are threatened by tsetse flies. But where the Masai were able to rebuild their herds in the past, today, they would face tremendous pressure to give up cattle raising entirely.

LIVING CONDITIONS

While the Masai are admired for their great beauty, their living conditions are breeding grounds for disease. Since they keep their small livestock (sheep and goats) in the huts where they live, they are continually exposed to the animals' excrement. The cattle are just outside, in an open enclosure, and their excrement is added to the mix. Flies abound wherever cattle are kept, but with the animals living right next to the huts, they are ever-present. Like many tribal groups living in relative isolation, the Masai are highly vulnerable to diseases brought in by others. In the 1890s, when the rinderpest hit their cattle, the Masai were attacked by smallpox which, coupled with drought, reduced their numbers almost to the vanishing point.

For the most part, the Masai rely on the remedies of their traditional medicine and are renowned for their extensive knowledge and use of natural plants to treat illnesses and diseases of both people and cattle. Since they live in an area that had hardly any permanent sources of water, the Masai have learned to live without washing. They are said to have one bath at birth, another at marriage. Flies are pervasive; there is scarcely a picture of a Masai taken in their home environment that does not show flies alit on them.

Their rounded huts, looking like mushrooms growing from the ground, are built by the women. On a frame of wooden twigs, they begin to plaster mud and cow dung. Layers and layers of this are added until the roof reaches the desired thickness. Each day, cracks and holes are repaired, especially after the rains, using the readily available dung. Within the homes, they use animal hides. Everything they need can be made from the materials at hand. There are a few items such as sugar, tea, and cloth that they buy from the *dukas*, or Indian shops, in Narok, Kajiado, and other nearby towns, but money is readily obtained by selling beaded jewelry, or simply one's own image. Long ago, the Masai discovered their photogenic qualities. If they cannot survive as warriors by raiding, they will survive as icons of warriors, permitting tourists to take their pictures for a fee, and that fee is determined by hard bargaining. One does not simply take a picture of a Masai without payment; that is theft.

Their nomadic patterns have been greatly reduced; now they move only the cattle as the seasons change. During the dry season, the Masai stay on the higher parts of the escarpment and use the pastures there which they call *osukupo*. This offers a richer savannah with more trees. When the rains come, they move down to the pastures of the Rift Valley to the plains called *okpurkel*.

Their kraals are built a few miles from the water supply. The cattle drink on one day only, then are grazed the next, so they can conserve the grazing by using a larger area than they would be able to if they watered the cattle every day. But their great love of cattle has inevitably brought them to the point of overstocking. As the cattle trample their way to and from the waterhole, they destroy all vegetation near it, and the soil washes away. Scientists studying Masai land use have concluded that with the change from a totally nomadic way of life, the natural environmental resistance of this system was destroyed; there is no self-regulating mechanism left. Some Masai have permitted wheat farming on their land for the exploding Kenyan population, taking away the marginal lands that traditionally provided further grazing for their cattle.

PRESSURE TO CHANGE

In June 1901, Sir Charles Eliot, colonial governor of Kenya, said, "I regard the Masai as the most important and dangerous of the tribes with whom we have to deal in East Africa and I think it will be long necessary to maintain an adequate military force in the districts which they inhabit."

The traditional Masai way of life has been under attack ever since. The colonial British governments of Kenya and Tanzania (then Tanganyika) outlawed Masai cattle raiding and tried to stifle the initiation ceremony; the black governments that took over upon independence in the 1960s continued the process. The Masai resisted these edicts, ignored them, and did their best to circumvent them throughout the century. In some areas, they gave in entirely—cattle raiding, the principal activity of the morani—rarely occurs, but their ceremonies, the vital processes by which a boy becomes a moran and a moran becomes an elder, remain intact, although they have been banned over and over again. Stopping these ceremonies is more difficult than just proclaiming them to be over, as the Kenyan government did in 1985.

Some laws restrict the very essence of a Masai's readiness to assume the position of moran. Hunting was banned entirely in Kenya and nearly so in Tanzania (except for expensive permits issued to tourists, and restricted to designated hunting blocks), making it illegal for a moran to kill a lion to demonstrate his bravery and hunting skills. Although the Masai ignore the government whenever possible, at times such as this, conflict is unavoidable. Lions are killed occasionally, but stealthily; some modern Masai boys say, "Who needs to kill a lion? It doesn't prove anything."

The Kenyan governments requirement that Masai children go to school has also affected the traditional roles of girls and women, who traditionally married at age twelve or thirteen and left school. Now the government will send fathers and husbands to jail for taking these girls out of school. There was a case in Kenya in 1986 of a girl who wrote to the government protesting the fact that her father had removed her from school to prepare for marriage. Her mother carried the letter to the appropriate government officials, the father was tried, and the girl was allowed to return to school.

Sometimes there is cooperation between governmental policy and traditional life-style. Ceremonies are scheduled to take place in school holidays, and while government policies continue to erode traditional customs, the educated and traditional groups within the Masai community try to support each other.

TRADITION IN THE FACE OF CHANGE

Although the Masai in both countries are descended from the same people, national policies have pushed the Kenyan Masai further away from their traditions. The Tanzanian Masai, for example, still dress occasionally in animal skins, decorated with beading. The Kenyan Masai dress almost entirely in cloth, reserving skins for ceremonial occasions.

In 1977, Kenya and Tanzania closed their common border, greatly isolating the Tanzanian Masai from Western contact. Though the border has been reopened, the impact on the Masai is clear. The Kenyan Masai became one of the sights of the tourist route while the Tanzanian Masai were kept from such interaction. This has further accelerated change among the Kenyan Masai. Tepilit Ole Saitoti sees a real difference in character between the Masai of Kenya and Tanzania. "Temperamentally" he says, "the Tanzanian Masai tend to be calmer and slower than those in Kenya."

Tribal people throughout Africa are in a constant state of change, some totally urbanized, their traditions nearly forgotten; others are caught in the middle, part of the tribe living traditionally, some moving to the city and adopting Western ways. The Masai have retained their culture, their unique and distinctive way of life, longer than virtually all the other tribes of East Africa, and they have done so while living in the very middle of the tourist traffic. Rather than disappear into the bush, the Masai use their attractiveness and mystique to their own benefit. Masai Mara and Amboseli, two reserves set aside for them, are run by them for their own profit.

Few tribes in Africa still put such a clear cultural stamp on an area; few have so successfully resisted enormous efforts to change them, to modernize and "civilize" them, to make them fit into the larger society. We leave it to Tepilit Ole Saitoti to predict the future of his own people: "Through their long and difficult history, the Masai have fought to maintain their traditional way of life. Today, however, they can no longer resist the pressures of the modern world. The survival of Masai culture has ceased to be a question; in truth, it is rapidly disappearing."

BIBLIOGRAPHY

Bleeker, Sonia, *The Masai, Herders of East Africa*, 1963.

Fedders, Andrew, *Peoples and Cultures of Kenya*, TransAfrica Books, Nairobi, 1979.

Fisher, Angela, *Africa Adorned*, Harry N. Abrams Inc., New York, 1984.

Kinde, S. H., *Last of the Masai*, London, 1901.

Kipkorir, B., *Kenya's People, People of the Rift Valley*, Evans Bros. Ltd., London, 1978.

Lamb, David, *The Africans*, Vintage Books, New York, 1984.

Moravia, Alberto, *Which Tribe Do You Belong To?*, Farrar, Straus & Giroux, Inc., New York, 1974.

Ole Saitoti, Tepilit, *Masai*, Harry N. Abrams, Inc., New York, 1980.

Ricciardi, Mirella, *Vanishing Africa*, Holt, Rinehart & Winston, 1971.

Sankan, S. S., *The Masai*, Kenya Literature Bureau, Nairobi, 1971.

Thomson, Joseph, *Through Masai Land*, Sampson Low, Marstan & Co., London, 1885.

Tignor, Robert, *The Colonial Transformation of Kenya, The Kamba, Kikuyu and Masai from 1900 to 1939*, Princeton, NJ, 1976.

Ettagale Blauer is a New York-based writer who has studied the Masai culture extensively in numerous trips to Africa and who specializes in writing about Africa and jewelry.

This article originally appeared in *The World & I,* March 1987, pp. 497–513. © 1987 by Ettagale Blauer. Reprinted by permission.

Too Many Bananas, Not Enough Pineapples, and No Watermelon at All: Three Object Lessons in Living with Reciprocity

David Counts
McMaster University

NO WATERMELON AT ALL

The woman came all the way through the village, walking between the two rows of houses facing each other between the beach and the bush, to the very last house standing on a little spit of land at the mouth of the Kaini River. She was carrying a watermelon on her head, and the house she came to was the government "rest house," maintained by the villagers for the occasional use of visiting officials. Though my wife and I were graduate students, not officials, and had asked for permission to stay in the village for the coming year, we were living in the rest house while the debate went on about where a house would be built for us. When the woman offered to sell us the watermelon for two shillings, we happily agreed, and the kids were delighted at the prospect of watermelon after yet another meal of rice and bully beef. The money changed hands and the seller left to return to her village, a couple of miles along the coast to the east.

It seemed only seconds later that the woman was back, reluctantly accompanying Kolia, the man who had already made it clear to us that he was the leader of the village. Kolia had no English, and at that time, three or four days into our first stay in Kandoka Village on the island of New Britain in Papua New Guinea, we had very little Tok Pisin. Language difficulties notwithstanding, Kolia managed to make his message clear: The woman had been outrageously wrong to sell us the watermelon for two shillings and we were to return it to her and reclaim our money immediately. When we tried to explain that we thought the price to be fair and were happy with the bargain, Kolia explained again and finally made it clear that we had missed the point. The problem wasn't that we had paid too much; it was that we had paid at all. Here he was, a leader, responsible for us while we were living in his village, and we had shamed him. How would it look if he let guests in his village *buy* food? If we wanted watermelons, or bananas, or anything else, all that was necessary was to let him know. He told us that it would be all right for us to give little gifts to people who brought food to us (and they surely would), but *no one* was to sell food to us. If anyone were to try—like this woman from Lauvore—then we should refuse. There would be plenty of watermelons without us buying them.

The woman left with her watermelon, disgruntled, and we were left with our two shillings. But we had learned the first lesson of many about living in Kandoka. We didn't pay money for food again that whole year, and we did get lots of food brought to us... but we never got another watermelon. That one was the last of the season.

LESSON 1: *In a society where food is shared or gifted as part of social life, you may not buy it with money.*

TOO MANY BANANAS

In the couple of months that followed the watermelon incident, we managed to become at least marginally competent in Tok Pisin, to negotiate the construction of a house on what we hoped was neutral ground, and to settle into the routine of our fieldwork. As our village leader had predicted, plenty of food was brought to us. Indeed, seldom did a day pass without something coming in—some sweet potatoes, a few taro, a papaya, the occasional pineapple, or some bananas—lots of bananas.

We had learned our lesson about the money, though, so we never even offered to buy the things that were brought, but instead made gifts, usually of tobacco to the adults or chewing gum to the children. Nor were we so gauche as to haggle with a giver over how much of a return gift was appropriate, though the two of us sometimes conferred as to whether what had been brought was a "two-stick" or a "three-stick" stalk, bundle, or whatever. A "stick" of tobacco was a single large leaf, soaked in rum and then twisted into a ropelike form. This, wrapped in half a sheet of newsprint (torn for use as cigarette paper), sold in the local trade stores for a shilling. Nearly all of the adults in the village smoked a great deal, and they seldom had much cash, so our stocks of twist tobacco and stacks of the Sydney *Morning Herald* (all, unfortunately, the same day's issue) were seen as a real boon to those who preferred "stick" to the locally grown product.

We had established a pattern with respect to the gifts of food. When a donor appeared at our veranda we would offer our thanks and talk with them for a few minutes (usually about our children, who seemed to hold a real fascination for the villagers and for whom most of the gifts were intended) and then we would inquire whether they could use some tobacco. It was almost never refused, though occasionally a small bottle of kerosene, a box of matches, some laundry soap, a cup of rice, or a tin of meat would be requested instead of (or even in addition to) the tobacco. Everyone, even Kolia, seemed to think this arrangement had worked out well.

Now, what must be kept in mind is that while we were following their rules—or seemed to be—we were *really still buying food*. In fact we kept a running account of what came in and what we "paid" for it. Tobacco as currency got a little complicated, but since the exchange rate was one stick to one shilling, it was not too much trouble as long as everyone was happy, and meanwhile we could account for the expenditure of "in-

formant fees" and "household expenses." Another thing to keep in mind is that not only did we continue to think in terms of our buying the food that was brought, we thought of them as *selling it.* While it was true they never quoted us a price, they also never asked us if we needed or wanted whatever they had brought. It seemed clear to us that when an adult needed a stick of tobacco, or a child wanted some chewing gum (we had enormous quantities of small packets of Wrigley's for just such eventualities) they would find something surplus to their own needs and bring it along to our "store" and get what they wanted.

By late November 1966, just before the rainy season set in, the bananas were coming into flush, and whereas earlier we had received banana gifts by the "hand" (six or eight bananas in a cluster cut from the stalk), donors now began to bring bananas, "for the children," by the *stalk!* The Kaliai among whom we were living are not exactly specialists in banana cultivation—they only recognize about thirty varieties, while some of their neighbors have more than twice that many—but the kinds they produce differ considerably from each other in size, shape, and taste, so we were not dismayed when we had more than one stalk hanging on our veranda. The stalks ripen a bit at the time, and having some variety was nice. Still, by the time our accumulation had reached *four* complete stalks, the delights of variety had begun to pale a bit. The fruits were ripening progressively and it was clear that even if we and the kids ate nothing but bananas for the next week, some would still fall from the stalk onto the floor in a state of gross overripeness. This was the situation as, late one afternoon, a woman came bringing yet another stalk of bananas up the steps of the house.

Several factors determined our reaction to her approach: one was that there was literally no way we could possibly use the bananas. We hadn't quite reached the point of being crowded off our veranda by the stalks of fruit, but it was close. Another factor was that we were tired of playing the gift game. We had acquiesced in playing it—no one was permitted to sell us anything, and in turn we only gave things away, refusing un-

der any circumstances to sell tobacco (or anything else) for money. But there had to be a limit. From our perspective what was at issue was that the woman wanted something and she had come to trade for it. Further, what she had brought to trade was something we neither wanted nor could use, and it should have been obvious to her. So we decided to bite the bullet.

The woman, Rogi, climbed the stairs to the veranda, took the stalk from where it was balanced on top of her head, and laid it on the floor with the words, "Here are some bananas for the children." Dorothy and I sat near her on the floor and thanked her for her thought but explained, "You know, we really have too many bananas—we can't use these; maybe you ought to give them to someone else...." The woman looked mystified, then brightened and explained that she didn't want anything for them, she wasn't short of tobacco or anything. They were just a gift for the kids. Then she just sat there, and we sat there, and the bananas sat there, and we tried again. "Look," I said, pointing up to them and counting, "we've got four stalks already hanging here on the veranda—there are too many for us to eat now. Some are rotting already. Even if we eat only bananas, we can't keep up with what's here!"

Rogi's only response was to insist that these were a gift, and that she didn't want anything for them, so we tried yet another tack: "Don't *your* children like bananas?" When she admitted that they did, and that she had none at her house, we suggested that she should take them there. Finally, still puzzled, but convinced we weren't going to keep the bananas, she replaced them on her head, went down the stairs, and made her way back through the village toward her house.

As before, it seemed only moments before Kolia was making his way up the stairs, but this time he hadn't brought the woman in tow. "What was wrong with those bananas? Were they no good?" he demanded. We explained that there was nothing wrong with the bananas at all, but that we simply couldn't use them and it seemed foolish to take them when we had so many and Rogi's own children had none. We obviously didn't make ourselves clear because Kolia then took up the same refrain that Rogi had—he insisted that we shouldn't be worried about taking the bananas, because they were a gift for the children and Rogi hadn't wanted anything for them. There was no reason, he added, to send her away with them—she would be ashamed. I'm afraid we must have seemed as if we were hard of hearing or thought he was, for our only response was to repeat our reasons. We went through it again— there they hung, one, two, three, *four* stalks of bananas, rapidly ripening and already far beyond our capacity to eat— we just weren't ready to accept any more and let them rot (and, we added to ourselves, pay for them with tobacco, to boot).

Kolia finally realized that we were neither hard of hearing nor intentionally offensive, but merely ignorant. He stared at us for a few minutes, thinking, and then asked: "Don't you frequently have visitors during the day and evening?" We nodded. Then he asked, "Don't you usually offer them cigarettes and coffee or milo?" Again, we nodded. "Did it ever occur to you to suppose," he said, "that your visitors might be hungry?" It was at this point in the conversation, as we recall, that we began to see the depth of the pit we had dug for ourselves. We nodded, hesitantly. His last words to us before he went down the stairs and stalked away were just what we were by that time afraid they might be. "When your guests are hungry, *feed them bananas!*"

LESSON 2: *Never refuse a gift, and never fail to return a gift. If you cannot use it, you can always give it away to someone else—there is no such thing as too much—there are never too many bananas.*

NOT ENOUGH PINEAPPLES

During the fifteen years between that first visit in 1966 and our residence there in 1981 we had returned to live in Kandoka village twice during the 1970s, and though there were a great many changes in the village, and indeed for all of Papua New Guinea during that time, we continued to live according to the lessons of

reciprocity learned during those first months in the field. We bought no food for money and refused no gifts, but shared our surplus. As our family grew, we continued to be accompanied by our younger children. Our place in the village came to be something like that of educated Kaliai who worked far away in New Guinea. Our friends expected us to come "home" when we had leave, but knew that our work kept us away for long periods of time. They also credited us with knowing much more about the rules of their way of life than was our due. And we sometimes shared the delusion that we understood life in the village, but even fifteen years was not long enough to relieve the need for lessons in learning to live within the rules of gift exchange.

In the last paragraph I used the word *friends* to describe the villagers intentionally, but of course they were not all our friends. Over the years some really had become friends, others were acquaintances, others remained consultants or informants to whom we turned when we needed information. Still others, unfortunately, we did not like at all. We tried never to make an issue of these distinctions, of course, and to be even-handed and generous to all, as they were to us. Although we almost never actually refused requests that were made of us, over the long term our reciprocity in the village was balanced. More was given to those who helped us the most, while we gave assistance or donations of small items even to those who were not close or helpful.

One elderly woman in particular was a trial for us. Sara was the eldest of a group of siblings and her younger brother and sister were both generous, informative, and delightful persons. Her younger sister, Makila, was a particularly close friend and consultant, and in deference to that friendship we felt awkward in dealing with the elder sister.

Sara was neither a friend nor an informant, but she had been, since she returned to live in the village at the time of our second trip in 1971, a constant (if minor) drain on our resources. She never asked for much at a time. A bar of soap, a box of matches, a bottle of kerosene, a cup of rice, some onions, a stick or two

of tobacco, or some other small item was usually all that was at issue, but whenever she came around it was always to ask for something—or to let us know that when we left, we should give her some of the furnishings from the house. Too, unlike almost everyone else in the village, when she came, she was always empty-handed. We ate no taro from her gardens, and the kids chewed none of her sugarcane. In short, she was, as far as we could tell, a really grasping, selfish old woman—and we were not the only victims of her greed.

Having long before learned the lesson of the bananas, one day we had a stalk that was ripening so fast we couldn't keep up with it, so I pulled a few for our own use (we only had one stalk at the time) and walked down through the village to Ben's house, where his five children were playing. I sat down on his steps to talk, telling him that I intended to give the fruit to his kids. They never got them. Sara saw us from across the open plaza of the village and came rushing over, shouting, "My bananas!" Then she grabbed the stalk and went off gorging herself with them. Ben and I just looked at each other.

Finally it got to the point where it seemed to us that we had to do something. Ten years of being used was long enough. So there came the afternoon when Sara showed up to get some tobacco—again. But this time, when we gave her the two sticks she had demanded, we confronted her.

First, we noted the many times she had come to get things. We didn't mind sharing things, we explained. After all, we had plenty of tobacco and soap and rice and such, and most of it was there so that we could help our friends as they helped us, with folktales, information, or even gifts of food. The problem was that she kept coming to get things, but never came to talk, or to tell stories, or to bring some little something that the kids might like. Sara didn't argue—she agreed. "Look," we suggested, "it doesn't have to be much, and we don't mind giving you things—but you can help us. The kids like pineapples, and we don't have any—the next time you need something, bring something—like maybe a pineapple." Obviously somewhat embarrassed, she took her tobacco and left, saying that she would bring something soon. We were really pleased with ourselves. It had been a very difficult thing to do, but it was done, and we were convinced that either she would start bringing things or not come. It was as if a burden had lifted from our shoulders.

It worked. Only a couple of days passed before Sara was back, bringing her bottle to get it filled with kerosene. But this time, she came carrying the biggest, most beautiful pineapple we had seen the entire time we had been there. We had a friendly talk, filled her kerosene container, and hung the pineapple up on the veranda to ripen just a little further. A few days later we cut and ate it, and whether the satisfaction it gave came from the fruit or from its source would be hard to say, but it was delicious. That, we assumed, was the end of that irritant.

We were wrong, of course. The next afternoon, Mary, one of our best friends for years (and no relation to Sara), dropped by for a visit. As we talked, her eyes scanned the veranda. Finally she asked whether we hadn't had a pineapple there yesterday. We said we had, but that we had already eaten it. She commented that it had been a really nice-looking one, and we told her that it had been the best we had eaten in months. Then, after a pause, she asked, "Who brought it to you?" We smiled as we said, "Sara!" because Mary would appreciate our coup—she had commented many times in the past on the fact that Sara only *got* from us and never gave. She was silent for a moment, and then she said, "Well, I'm glad you enjoyed it—my father was waiting until it was fully ripe to harvest it for you, but when it went missing I thought maybe it was the one you had here. I'm glad to see you got it. I thought maybe a thief had eaten it in the bush."

LESSON 3: *Where reciprocity is the rule and gifts are the idiom, you cannot demand a gift, just as you cannot refuse a request.*

It says a great deal about the kindness and patience of the Kaliai people that they have been willing to be our hosts for all these years despite our blunders and lack of good manners. They have taught us a lot, and these three lessons are certainly not the least important things we learned.

From *The Humbled Anthropologist: Tales from the Pacific* by David Counts, 1990, pp. 18–24. Published by Wadsworth Publishing Company. © 1990 by David Counts. Reprinted by permission of the author.

Prehistory *of* Warfare

Humans have been at each others' throats since the dawn of the species.

by STEVEN A. LEBLANC

IN THE EARLY 1970s, working in the El Morro Valley of west-central New Mexico, I encountered the remains of seven large prehistoric pueblos that had once housed upwards of a thousand people each. Surrounded by two-story-high walls, the villages were perched on steep-sided mesas, suggesting that their inhabitants built them with defense in mind. At the time, the possibility that warfare occurred among the Anasazi was of little interest to me and my colleagues. Rather, we were trying to figure out what the people in these 700-year-old communities farmed and hunted, the impact of climate change, and the nature of their social systems—not the possibility of violent conflict.

One of these pueblos, it turned out, had been burned to the ground; its people had clearly fled for their lives. Pottery and valuables had been left on the floors, and bushels of burned corn still lay in the storerooms. We eventually determined that this site had been abandoned, and that immediately afterward a fortress had been built nearby. Something catastrophic had occurred at this ancient Anasazi settlement, and the survivors had almost immediately, and at great speed, set about to prevent it from happening again.

Thirty years ago, archaeologists were certainly aware that violent, organized conflicts occurred in the prehistoric cultures they studied, but they considered these incidents almost irrelevant to our understanding of past events and people. Today, some of my colleagues are realizing that the evidence I helped uncover in the El Morro Valley is indicative warfare endemic throughout the entire Southwest, with its attendant massacres, population decline, and area abandonments that forever changed the Anasazi way of life.

When excavating eight-millennia-old farm villages in southeastern Turkey in 1970, I initially marveled how similar modern villages were to ancient ones, which were occupied at a time when an abundance of plants and animals made warfare quite unnecessary. Or so I thought. I knew we had discovered some plaster sling missiles (one of our workmen showed me how shepherds used slings to hurl stones at predators threatening their sheep). Such missiles were found at many of these sites, often in great quantities, and were clearly not intended for protecting flocks of sheep; they were exactly the same size and shape as later Greek and Roman sling stones used for warfare.

The so-called "donut stones" we had uncovered at these sites were assumed to be weights for digging sticks, presumably threaded on a pole to make it heavier for digging holes to plant crops. I failed to note how much they resembled the round stone heads attached to wooden clubs—maces—used in many places of the world exclusively for fighting and still used ceremonially to signify power. Thirty years ago, I was holding mace heads and sling missiles in my hands, unaware of their use as weapons of war.

We now know that defensive walls once ringed many villages of this era, as they did the Anasazi settlements. Rooms were massed together behind solid outside walls and were entered from the roof. Other sites had mud brick defensive walls, some with elaborately defended gates. Furthermore, many of these villages had been burned to the ground, their inhabitants massacred, as indicated by nearby mass graves.

Certainly for those civilizations that kept written records or had descriptive narrative art traditions, warfare is so clearly present that no one can deny it. Think of Homer's *Iliad* or the Vedas of South India, or scenes of prisoner sacrifice on Moche pottery. There is no reason to think that warfare played any less of a role in prehistoric societies for which we have no such records, whether they be hunter-gatherers or farmers. But most scholars studying these cultures still are not seeing it. They should assume warfare occurred among the people they study, just as they assume religion and art were a normal part of human culture. Then they could ask more interesting questions, such as: What form did warfare take? Can warfare explain some of the material found in the archaeological record? What were people fighting over and why did the conflicts end?

Today, some scholars know me as Dr. Warfare. To them, I have the annoying habit of asking un-politic questions about their research. I am the one who asks why the houses at a particular site were jammed so close together and many catastrophically burned. When I suggest that the houses were crowded behind defensive walls that were not found because no one was looking for them, I am not terribly appreciated. And I don't win any popularity contests when I suggest that twenty-mile-wide zones with no sites in them imply no-man's lands—clear evidence for warfare—to archaeologists who have explained a region's history without mention of conflict.

> Scholars should assume warfare occurred among the people they study, just as they assume religion was a normal part of human culture. Then they would ask more interesting questions, such as: What form did warfare take? Why did people start and stop fighting?

Virtually all the basic textbooks on archaeology ignore the prevalence or significance of past warfare, which is usually not discussed until the formation of state-level civilizations such as ancient Sumer. Most texts either assume or actually state that for most of human history there was an abundance of available resources. There was no resource stress, and people had the means to control population, though how they accomplished this is never explained. The one archaeologist who has most explicitly railed against this hidden but pervasive attitude is Lawrence Keeley of the University of Illinois, who studies the earliest farmers in Western Europe. He has fund ample evidence of warfare as farmers spread west, yet most of his colleagues still believe the expansion was peaceful and his evidence a minor aberration, as seen in the various papers in Barry Cunliffe's *The Oxford Illustrated Prehistory of Europe* (1994) or Douglas Price's *Europe's First Farmers* (2000). Keeley contends that "prehistorians have increasingly pacified the past," presuming peace or thinking up every possible alternative explanation for the evidence they cannot ignore. In his *War Before Civilization* (1996) he accused archaeologists of being in denial on the subject.

Witness archaeologist Lisa Valkenier suggesting in 1997 that hilltop constructions along the Peruvian coast are significant because peaks are sacred in Andean cosmology. Their enclosing walls and narrow guarded entries may have more to do with restricting access to the *huacas*, or sacred shrines, on top of the hills than protecting defenders and barring entry to any potential attackers. How else but by empathy can one formulate such an interpretation in an area with a long defensive wall and hundreds of defensively located fortresses, some still containing piles of sling missiles ready to be used; where a common

artistic motif is the parading and execution of defeated enemies; where hundreds were sacrificed; and where there is ample evidence of conquest, no-man's lands, specialized weapons, and so on?

A talk I gave at the Mesa Verde National Park last summer, in which I pointed out that the over 700-year-old cliff dwellings were built in response to warfare, raised the hackles of National Park Service personnel unwilling to accept anything but the peaceful Anasazi message peddled by their superiors. In fact, in the classic book *Indians of Mesa Verde*, published in 1961 by the park service, author Don Watson first describes the Mesa Verde people as "peaceful farming Indians," and admits that the cliff dwellings had a defensive aspect, but since he had already decided that the inhabitants were peaceful, the threat must have been from a new enemy—marauding nomadic Indians. This, in spite of the fact that there is ample evidence of Southwestern warfare for more than a thousand years before the cliff dwellings were built, and there is no evidence for the intrusion of nomadic peoples at this time.

Of the hundreds of research projects in the Southwest, only one—led by Jonathan Haas and Winifred Creamer of the Field Museum and Northern Illinois University, respectively—deliberately set out to research prehistoric warfare. They demonstrated quite convincingly that the Arizona cliff dwellings of the Tsegi Canyon area (known best for Betatakin and Kiet Siel ruins) were defensive, and their locations were not selected for ideology or because they were breezier and cooler in summer and warmer in the winter, as was previously argued by almost all Southwestern archaeologists.

For most prehistoric cultures, one has to piece together the evidence for warfare from artifactual bits and pieces. Most human history involved foragers, and so they are particularly relevant. They too were not peaceful. We know from ethnography that the Inuit (Eskimo) and Australian Aborigines engaged in warfare. We've also discovered remains of prehistoric bone armor in the Arctic, and skeletal evidence of deadly blows to the head are well documented among the prehistoric Aborigines. Surprising to some is the skeletal evidence for warfare in prehistoric California, once thought of as a land of peaceful acorn gatherers. The prehistoric people who lived in southern Californian had the highest incident of warfare deaths known anywhere in the world. Thirty percent of a large sample of males dating to the first centuries A.D. had wounds or died violent deaths. About half that number of women had similar histories. When we remember that not all warfare deaths leave skeletal evidence, this is a staggering number.

There was nothing unique about the farmers of the Southwest. From the Neolithic farmers of the Middle East and Europe to the New Guinea highlanders in the twentieth century, tribally organized farmers probably had the most intense warfare of any type of society. Early villages in China, the Yucatán, present-day Pakistan, and Micronesia were well fortified. Ancient farmers in coastal Peru had plenty of forts. All Polynesian societies had warfare, from the smallest islands like Tikopia, to Tahiti, New Zealand (more than four thousand prehistoric forts), and Hawaii. No-man's lands separated farming settlements in Okinawa, Oaxaca, and the southeastern United States. Such societies took trophy heads and cannibalized their enemies. Their skeletal remains show ample evidence of violent deaths. All well-studied prehistoric farming societies had warfare. They may have had intervals of peace, but over the span of hundreds of years there is plenty of evidence for real, deadly warfare.

When farmers initially took over the world, they did so as warriors, grabbing land as they spread out from the Levant through the Middle East into Europe, or from South China down through Southeast Asia. Later complex societies like the Maya, the Inca, the Sumerians, and the Hawaiians were no less belligerent. Here, conflict took on a new dimension. Fortresses, defensive walls hundreds of miles long, and weapons and armor expertly crafted by specialists all gave the warfare of these societies a heightened visibility.

> Demonstrating the prevalence of warfare is not an end in itself. It is only the first step in understanding why there was so much of it, why it was "rational" for everyone to engage in it all the time. I believe the question of warfare links to the availability of resources.

There is a danger in making too much of the increased visibility of warfare we see in these complex societies. This is especially true for societies with writing. When there are no texts, it is easy to see no warfare. But the opposite is true. As soon as societies can write, they write about warfare. It is not a case of literate societies having warfare for the first time, but their being able to write about what had been going on for a long time. Also, many of these literate societies link to European civilization in one way or another, and so this raises the specter of Europeans being warlike and spreading war to inherently peaceful people elsewhere, a patently false but prevalent notion. Viewing warfare from their perspective of literate societies tells us nothing about the thousands of years of human societies that were not civilizations—that is, almost all of human history. So we must not rely too much on the small time slice represented by literate societies if we want to understand warfare in the past.

The Maya were once considered a peaceful society led by scholarly priests. That all changed when the texts written by their leaders could be read, revealing a long history of warfare and conquest. Most Mayanists now accept that there was warfare, but many still resist dealing with its scale or implications. Was there population growth that resulted in resource depletion, as throughout the rest of the world? We would expect the Maya to have been fighting each other over valuable farmlands as a consequence, but Mayanist Linda Schele concluded in 1984 that "I do not think it [warfare] was territorial for the most part,"

this even though texts discuss conquest, and fortifications are present at sites like El Mirador, Calakmul, Tikal, Yaxuná, Uxmal, and many others from all time periods. Why fortify them, if no one wanted to capture them?

Today, more Maya archaeologists are looking at warfare in a systematic way, by mapping defensive features, finding images of destruction, and dating these events. A new breed of younger scholars is finding evidence of warfare throughout the Maya past. Where are the no-man's lands that almost always open up between competing states because they are too dangerous to live in? Warfare must have been intimately involved in the development of Maya civilization, and resource stress must have been widespread.

Demonstrating the prevalence of warfare is not an end in itself. It is only the first step in understanding why there was so much, why it was "rational" for everyone to engage in it all the time. I believe the question of warfare links to the availability of resources.

During the 1960s, I lived in Western Samoa as a Peace Corps volunteer on what seemed to be an idyllic South Pacific Island—exactly like those painted by Paul Gauguin. Breadfruit and coconut groves grew all around my village, and I resided in a thatched-roof house with no walls beneath a giant mango tree. If ever there was a Garden of Eden, this was it. I lived with a family headed by an extremely intelligent elderly chief named Sila. One day, Sila happened to mention that the island's trees did not bear fruit as they had when he was a child. He attributed the decline to the possibility that the presence of radio transmissions had affected production, since Western Samoa (now known as Samoa) had its own radio station by then. I suggested that what had changed was not that there was less fruit but that there were more mouths to feed. Upon reflection, Sila decided I was probably right. Being an astute manager, he was already taking the precaution of expanding his farm plots into some of the last remaining farmable land on the island, at considerable cost and effort, to ensure adequate food for his growing family. Sila was aware of his escalating provisioning problems but was not quite able to grasp the overall demographic situation. Why was this?

The simple answer is that the rate of population change in our small Samoan village was so gradual that during an adult life span growth was not dramatic enough to be fully comprehended. The same thing happens to us all the time. Communities grow and change composition, and often only after the process is well advanced do we recognize just how significant the changes have been—and we have the benefit of historic documents, old photographs, long life spans, and government census surveys. All human societies can grow substantially over time, and all did whenever resources permitted. The change may seem small in one person's lifetime, but over a couple of hundred years, populations can and do double, triple, or quadruple in size.

The consequences of these changes become evident only when there is a crisis. The same can be said for environmental changes. The forests of Central America were being denuded and encroached upon for many years, but it took Hurricane Mitch, which ravaged most of the region in late October 1998, to produce the dramatic flooding and devastation that fully demonstrated the magnitude of the problem: too many people cutting down the forest and farming steep hillsides to survive. The natural environment is resilient and at the same time delicate, as modern society keeps finding out. And it was just so in the past.

From foragers to farmers to more complex societies, when people no longer have resource stress they stop fighting. When climate greatly improves, warfare declines. The great towns of Chaco Canyon were built during an extended warm– and peaceful–period.

These observations about Mother Nature are incompatible with popular myths about peaceful people living in ecological balance with nature in the past. A peaceful past is possible only if you live in ecological balance. If you live in a Garden of Eden surrounded by plenty, why fight? By this logic, warfare is a sure thing when natural resources run dry. If someone as smart as Sila couldn't perceive population growth, and if humans all over Earth continue to degrade their environments, could people living in the past have been any different?

A study by Canadian social scientists Christina Mesquida and Neil Wiener has shown that the greater the proportion of a society is composed of unmarried young men, the greater the likelihood of war. Why such a correlation? It is not because the young men are not married; it is because they cannot get married. They are too poor to support wives and families. The idea that poverty breeds war is far from original. The reason poverty exists has remained the same since the beginning of time: humans have invariably overexploited their resources because they have always outgrown them.

There is another lesson from past warfare. It stops. From foragers to farmers, to more complex societies, when people no longer have resource stress they stop fighting. When the climate greatly improves, warfare declines. For example, in a variety of places the medieval warm interval of ca. 900–1100 improved farming conditions. The great towns of Chaco Canyon were built at this time, and it was the time of archaeologist Stephen Lekson's *Pax Chaco*—the longest period of peace in the Southwest. It is no accident that the era of Gothic cathedrals was a response to similar climate improvement. Another surprising fact is that the amount of warfare has declined over time. If we count

the proportion of a society that died from warfare, and not the size of the armies, as the true measure of warfare, then we find that foragers and farmers have much higher death rates—often approaching 25 percent of the men—than more recent complex societies. No complex society, including modern states, ever approached this level of warfare.

If warfare has ultimately been a constant battle over scarce resources, then solving the resource problem will enable us to become better at ridding ourselves of conflict.

There have been several great "revolutions" in human history: control of fire, the acquisition of speech, the agricultural revolution, the development of complex societies. One of the most recent, the Industrial Revolution, has lowered the birth rate and increased available resources. History shows that peoples with strong animosities stop fighting after adequate resources are established and the benefits of cooperation recognized. The Hopi today are some of the most peaceful people on earth, yet their history is filled with warfare. The Gebusi of lowland New Guinea, the African !Kung Bushmen, the Mbuti Pygmies of central Africa, the Sanpoi and their neighbors of the southern Columbia River, and the Sirionno of Amazonia are all peoples who are noted for being peaceful, yet archaeology and historical accounts provide ample evidence of past warfare. Sometimes things changed in a generation; at other times it took longer. Adequate food and opportunity does not instantly translate into peace, but it will, given time.

The fact that it can take several generations or longer to establish peace between warring factions is little comfort for those engaged in the world's present conflicts. Add to this a recent change in the decision-making process that leads to war. In most traditional societies, be they forager bands, tribal farmers, or even complex chiefdoms, no individual held enough power to start a war on his own. A consensus was needed; pros and cons were carefully weighed and hotheads were not tolerated. The risks to all were too great. Moreover, failure of leadership was quickly recognized, and poor leaders were replaced. No Hitler or Saddam Hussein would have been tolerated. Past wars were necessary for survival, and therefore were rational; too often today this is not the case. We cannot go back to forager-band-type consensus, but the world must work harder at keeping single individuals from gaining the power to start wars. We know from archaeology that the amount of warfare has declined markedly over the course of human history and that peace can prevail under the right circumstances. In spite of the conflict we see around us, we are doing better, and there is less warfare in the world today than there ever has been. Ending it may be a slow process, but we are making headway.

©2003 *by* Steven A. LeBlanc. *Portions of this article were taken from his book* Constant Battles, *published in April 2003 by St. Martin's Press. LeBlanc is director of collections at Harvard University's Peabody Museum of Archaeology and Ethnology. For further reading visit www.archaeology.org.*

From *Indian Givers:* Chapter 8

THE FOUNDING INDIAN FATHERS

Jack Weatherford

Every day of the school year, troops of children march across the lawn of the United States Capitol perched atop the District of Columbia's highest elevation. The building dominates the Washington skyline, a model of classical symmetry and precision. Two giant wings of precisely equal proportion reach out from a Roman dome that surveys the city of Washington. If reduced to a ruin, the forest of Greek columns decorating the building would appear to be as much at home in Rome or Naples as in Athens or Corinth. The building revels in its Old World heritage.

Indian schoolchildren walking through the halls of Congress would rarely see a hint that the building sits in America overlooking the Potomac River and not along the shores of the Mediterranean Sea. The building copies European, primarily classical, styles, and its halls proudly display pictures, friezes, and busts of famous political thinkers from Hammurabi and Solomon to Rousseau and Voltaire. In the hallways stand statues of American politicians posing in Greek tunics and Roman togas as though they were Roman senators or Athenian orators. Greek busts of the vice-presidents of the United States line the halls of the Senate, lending them the aura of a classical cemetery.

The children pass under doorways that bear weighty engravings and quotations from European documents such as the Magna Carta interspersed with quotes from the United States Declaration of Independence or Constitution. The building and its appointments proudly proclaim their part in the great march of European progress and civilization. They portray the blessed dove of democracy hatching in Athens and then taking wing for a torturous flight of two millennia, pausing only momentarily over Republican Rome, the field of Runnymede, and the desk of Voltaire before finally alighting to rest permanently and securely in the virgin land of America.

A child standing squarely in the middle of the Capitol beneath the great dome sees a painted band circling the upper wall representing the history of America. In that work, the Indians appear as just one more dangerous obstacle, like the wild animals, the Appalachian Mountains, the Mississippi River, and the western deserts, that blocked the progress of European civilization and technology in the white man's march across America. The most peaceful picture with an Indian theme in the rotunda shows the baptism of Pocahontas, daughter of the Indian leader Powhatan. Surrounded by Europeans and dressed in English clothes, she symbolically renounces the savage life of the Indians for the civilization of the British.

The lesson in this august setting presents itself forcefully on every visitor. The United States government derives from European precedents, and the Americans gave civilization to the Indians. Nothing in the Capitol hints that contemporary Americans owe the slightest debt to the Indians for teaching us about democratic institutions.

Despite these civic myths surrounding the creation of American government, America's settlers from Europe knew little of democracy. The English came from a nation ruled by monarchs who claimed that God conferred their right to rule and even allowed them to wage wars of extinction against the Irish. Colonists also fled to America from France, which was wandering aimlessly through history under the extravagances of a succession of kings named Louis, most of whom pursued debauched and extravagant reigns that oppressed, exploited, and at times even starved their subjects.

Despite the ideal government sketched by Plato in *The Republic,* and the different constitutions analyzed by Aristotle in his *Politics,* the Old World offered America few democratic models for government. Democratic government had no fortress in the Old World. Despite the democratic rhetoric that came into fashion in eighteenth-century Europe, no such systems existed there at that time. The monarchy and the aristocracy of England were engaged in a protracted struggle that would eventually lead to the supremacy of Parliament (and a closely limited electoral franchise until the reforms of the nineteenth century). France had not yet begun its experiments with participatory democracy. The Founding Fathers of the United States judiciously assembled bits and pieces of many different systems to invent a completely new one. In fashioning the new system, they even borrowed some distinctive elements from the American Indians.

The Founding Fathers faced a major problem when it came time to invent the United States. They represented, under the Articles of Confederation, thirteen separate and sovereign states. How could one country be made from all thirteen without each one yielding its own power?

Reportedly, the final person to propose a union of all the colonies and to propose a federal model for it was the Iroquois chief Canassatego, speaking at an Indian-British assembly in Pennsylvania in July 1744. He complained that the Indians found it difficult to deal with so many different colonial administrations, each with its own policy. It would make life easier for everyone involved if the colonists could have a union which allowed them to speak with one voice. He not only proposed that the colonies unify themselves, but told them how they might do it. He suggested that they do as his people had done and form a union like the League of the Iroquois (Johansen, pp. 12, 61).

Hiawatha and Deganwidah founded the League of the Iroquois sometime between A.D. 1000 and 1450 under a constitution they called the *Kaianerekowa* or Great Law of Peace. When the Europeans arrived in America, the league constituted the most extensive and important political unit north of the Aztec civilization. From earliest contact the Iroquois intrigued the Europeans, and they were the subject of many amazed reports. Benjamin Franklin, however, seems to have been the first to take their system as a potentially important model by which the settlers might be able to fashion a new government.

Benjamin Franklin first became acquainted with the operation of Indian political organization in his capacity as official printer for the colony of Pennsylvania. His job included publication of the records and speeches of the various Indian assemblies and treaty negotiations, but following his instinctive curiosity, he broadened this into a study of Indian culture and institutions. Because of his expertise and interest in Indian matters, the colonial government of Pennsylvania offered him his first diplomatic assignment as their Indian commissioner. He held this post during the 1750s and became intimately familiar with the intricacies of Indian political culture and in particular with the League of the Iroquois. After this taste of Indian diplomacy, Franklin became a lifelong champion of the Indian political structure and advocated its use by the Americans. During this time he also refined his political techniques of persuasion,

compromise, and slow consensus building that proved so important to his later negotiations as the ambassador to France and as a delegate to the Constitutional Convention.

Echoing the original proposal of Canassatego, Franklin advocated that the new American government incorporate many of the same features as the government of the Iroquois (Wilson, p. 46). Speaking to the Albany Congress in 1754, Franklin called on the delegates of the various English colonies to unite and emulate the Iroquois League, a call that was not heeded until the Constitution was written three decades later (Hecht, p. 71). Even though the Founding Fathers finally adopted some of the essential features of the Iroquois League, they never followed it in quite the detail advocated by Franklin.

The Iroquois League united five principal Indian nations—the Mohawk, Onondaga, Seneca, Oneida, and Cayuga. Each of these nations had a council composed of delegates called sachems who were elected by the tribes of that nation. The Seneca Nation elected eight sachems to its council, the Mohawk and Oneida nations each had councils of nine sachems, the Cayuga Nation had a council of ten, and the Onondaga Nation had a council of fourteen. Each of these nations governed its own territory, and its own council met to decide the issues of public policy for each one. But these councils exercised jurisdiction over the internal concerns of that one nation only; in this regard they exercised powers somewhat like the individual governments of the colonies.

In addition to the individual councils of each separate nation, the sachems formed a grand Council of the League in which all fifty sachems of the six nations sat together to discuss issues of common concern. The sachems represented their individual nations, but at the same time they represented the whole League of the Iroquois, thereby making the decisions of the council the law for all five nations. In this council each sachem had equal authority and privileges, with his power dependent on his oratorical power to persuade. The council met in the autumn of at least one year in five in a longhouse in the Onondaga Nation; if needed they could be called into session at other times as well. Their power extended to all matters of common concern among the member nations. In the words of Lewis Henry Morgan, America's first modern anthropologist, the council "declared war and made peace, sent and received embassies, entered into treaties of alliance, regulated the affairs of subjugated nations, received new members into the League, extended its protection over feeble tribes, in a word, took all needful measures to promote their prosperity, and enlarge their dominion" (Morgan, pp. 66–67).

Through this government the nations of the Iroquois controlled territory from New England to the Mississippi River, and they built a league that endured for centuries. Unlike European governments, the league blended the sovereignty of several nations into one government. This model of several sovereign units united into one government presented precisely the solution to the problem confronting the writers of the United States Constitution. Today we call this a "federal" system in which each state retains power over internal affairs and the national government regulates affairs common to all. Henry Steele Commager later wrote of this crucial time that even "if Americans

77

did not actually invent federalism, they were able to take out an historical patent on it" (Commager, p. 207). The Indians invented it even though the United States patented it.

Another student of the Iroquois political organization was Charles Thomson, the perpetual secretary of the Continental Congress. He spent so much energy studying the Indians and their way of life that the Delaware Nation adopted him as a full member. Following Thomas Jefferson's request, Thomson wrote at length on Indian social and political institutions for inclusion in an appendix to Jefferson's *Notes on the State of Virginia*. According to his description of Indian political tradition, each Indian town built a council house for making local decisions and for electing delegates to the tribal council. The tribal council in turn elected delegates to the national council (Thomson, p. 203). Even though Thomson wrote this several years before the Constitutional Convention, this description reads like a blueprint for the United States Constitution, especially when we remember that the Constitution allowed the state legislatures (rather than the general populace) to elect senators. Thomson stresses that the sachems or political leaders do not acquire their positions by heredity but by election, and he adds that because outsiders can be naturalized into the Indian nation, even they can be elected to such offices.

The Americans followed the model of the Iroquois League not only in broad outline but also in many of the specific provisions of their *Kaianerekowa*. According to the *Kaianerekowa*, the sachems were not chiefs, a position frequently associated with leadership in war. As a lawmaker, the sachem could never go to war in his official capacity as a sachem. "If disposed to take the warpath, he laid aside his civil office, for the time being, and became a common warrior" (Morgan, p. 72). This followed the tradition in many Indian tribes that relied upon separate leaders for peace and for war. The colonists followed this model too in eventually separating civilian authorities from military ones. Members of Congress, judges, and other officials could not also act as military leaders without giving up their elected office; similarly, military leaders could not be elected to political office without first resigning their military position. This contrasted with British traditions; church and military leaders frequently served as members of the House of Lords and frequently played major political roles in the House of Commons as well. Similarly, this inability to separate the civil government and the military has doomed many of the imitators of American democracy, particularly in Africa and Latin America.

If the conduct of any sachem appeared improper to the populace or if he lost the confidence of his electorate, the women of his clan impeached him and expelled him by official action, whereupon the women then choose a new sachem (Goldenweiser, p. 570). This concept of impeachment ran counter to European tradition, in which the monarch ruled until death, even if he became insane or incapacitated, as in the case of George III. The Americans followed the Iroquois precedent of always providing for ways to remove leaders when necessary, but the Founding Fathers saw no reason to follow the example of the Iroquois in granting women the right to vote or any other major role in the political structure.

One of the most important characteristics of the Iroquois League permitted it to expand as needed; the council could vote to admit new members. This proved to be an important feature of the system after the Tuscarora Indians of North Carolina faced attack in 1712 by the army of Colonel John Barnwell and again in 1713 by the army of Colonel James Moore. Having thoroughly defeated the Tuscaroras, the Carolina colonists demanded reparations from the Indians to pay the colonists' expenses incurred in the war. Because the Indians had no money to pay, the colonists seized four hundred of them and sold them into slavery at the rate of ten pounds sterling apiece. The surviving Tuscaroras fled North Carolina to seek refuge among the Iroquois. In 1714 the Tuscaroras applied for formal membership in the league, and the Iroquois admitted them in 1722 as the Sixth Nation (Waldman, p. 104). Similarly the league later incorporated other decimated groups such as the Erie, but the league did not allow for an entity such as a colony, which had played such an important part in European governments since the times of the ancient Greeks.

In a radical break with Old World tradition, the emerging government of the United States emulated this Iroquois tradition of admitting new states as members rather than keeping them as colonies. The west became a series of territories and then states, but the United States treated each new territory as a future partner rather than as a colony. The new government codified this Indian practice into American law through the Congressional Resolution of 1780, the Land Ordinances of 1784 and 1785, and the Northwest Ordinance, together with similar provisions written directly into the Constitution. No direct proof links these laws with the Iroquois, but it seems likely to be more than mere coincidence that both the Iroquois and the United States governments enacted such similar procedures.

Although the Iroquois recognized no supreme leader in their system analogous to the president of the United States, the framers of the Constitution deliberately or inadvertently imitated the Great Council in establishing the electoral college system to select a president. Each state legislature selected a group of electors equal in number to that state's combined total of senators and representatives. Like the sachems, each elector then had one vote in the electoral college.

In the two centuries since the Constitution went into effect, some aspects of the system have changed. The voters rather than the state legislatures now elect both the electoral college and the senators through popular vote, but the system preserves the general features of the League of the Iroquois.

Upon election to the council, the new sachem "lost" his name and thenceforth other sachems called him by the title of his office. In much the same way, proceedings of the United States Senate do not permit the use of names such as "Senator Kennedy" or "Rudy Boschwitz." Instead the senators must be addressed by their office title as "the Senior Senator from Massachusetts" or "the Junior Senator from Minnesota." Other titles such as "Majority Leader," "Mr. Chairman," or "Mr. President" may be used, but all personal names remain strictly taboo.

Another imitation of the Iroquois came in the simple practice of allowing only one person to speak at a time in political meetings. This contrasts with the British tradition of noisy interruptions of one another as the members of Parliament shout out agreement or disagreement with the speaker. Europeans were accustomed to shouting down any speaker who displeased them; in some cases they might even stone him or inflict worse damage.

The Iroquois permitted no interruptions or shouting. They even imposed a short period of silence at the end of each oration in case the speaker had forgotten some point or wished to elaborate or change something he had said (Johansen, p. 87). Even though the American Congress and legislatures did not adopt the practice of silence at the end, they did allow speakers "to revise and extend" the written record after speaking.

The purpose of debate in Indian councils was to persuade and educate, not to confront. Unlike European parliaments, where opposing factions battle out an issue in the public arena, the council of the Indians sought to reach an agreement through compromise. This important difference in nuance led Bruce Burton to observe in his study of American law that "American democracy owes its distinctive character of debate and compromise to the principles and structures of American Indian civil government" (Burton, p. 5). Still today, this difference separates the operation of the United States Congress and the state legislatures from their European counterparts. American legislative bodies are composed primarily of individuals forming shifting factions from one issue to another, whereas the legislative bodies of Europe operate through opposing political parties that control the votes of individual representatives.

In keeping with Iroquois tradition, Franklin proposed that since the sachems did not own land or receive any financial compensation for their work, the officials of the United States should not be paid. They should perform their work as a sacred trust freely given to the communal welfare. Even though the Founding Fathers did not incorporate this, they did work to prevent property qualifications for holding office and for exercising the right to vote. They also tended to limit salaries paid to officeholders to a minimum to cover basic expenses of life rather than making public office a sinecure or a route to wealth.

In his democratic zeal to imitate the system of the Indians, Franklin even proposed that military officers should be elected by the men whom they ordered into battle. The Indians routinely fought this way, and Franklin organized such a militia himself in 1747 to protect Philadelphia from harassment by French and Dutch pirates. Even though the American army did not adopt the practice of electing officers, it gradually abandoned the European practice of allowing the purchase of commissions by the wealthy. The American system did allow for mobility within the ranks and prevented the officer corps of the army from resembling too closely an aristocratic class as in Europe or an oligarchy as in many Latin American nations.

The League of the Iroquois operated with only a single chamber in its council. Franklin became an ardent supporter of this unicameral organization, and he even wanted to use the English translation of the Iroquois term meaning "grand council" rather than the Latinism "congress." The United States government relied on only a single chamber during the years of the Continental Congress, and some states, such as Pennsylvania and Vermont, reduced their state legislatures to unicameral

bodies for a while. The unicameral congress and legislature, however, did not endure, and today only Nebraska has a unicameral legislature, instituted to save money and not to emulate the Iroquois.

In addition to Benjamin Franklin, Thomas Paine, and Charles Thomson, many of the Founding Fathers of American federalism had worked closely with the Indian political institutions. George Washington had extensive contacts with the Indians in his surveying expeditions into the western part of Virginia and fought with Indians and against Indians in the French and Indian War. Washington showed a greater interest in land speculation and making money than in observing the political life of the Indians. Thomas Jefferson, author of the Declaration of Independence, also lived close to the frontier, and he himself was the son of a pioneer. He studied and wrote numerous articles and essays on the Indians, leading a later historian to call Jefferson "the most enlightened of amateur ethnologists" (Commager, p. 179). In his recommendations for the University of Virginia, he became the first person to propose a systematic ethnological study of the Indians in order "to collect their traditions, laws, customs, languages and other circumstances" (Jefferson, p. 151).

Because of men such as Thomas Paine, Benjamin Franklin, Charles Thomson, and Thomas Jefferson, we today know a great deal about the League of the Iroquois and some of the other Indian groups of the eastern United States. Subsequent years of ethnological research into the political organizations of the New World have shown that the League of the Iroquois seems representative of political institutions throughout all of America north of Mexico and much of Central and South America as well. Councils chosen by the clans, tribes, or villages governed most Indian nations.

From Hollywood films and adventure novels Americans often conclude that strong chiefs usually commanded the Indian tribes. More often, however, as in the case of the Iroquois, a council ruled, and any person called the "head" of the tribe usually occupied a largely honorary position of respect rather than power. Chiefs mostly played ceremonial and religious roles rather than political or economic ones. Unlike the words "caucus" and "powwow," which are Indian-derived and indicative of Indian political traditions, the word "chief" is an English word of French origin that British officials tried to force onto Indian tribes in order that they might have someone with whom to trade and sign treaties.

In Massachusetts the British tried to make one leader into *King* Philip. The British imputed monarchy to the Indian system when no such institution existed. Thus while the English settlers learned from the Indians how to speak and act in group councils, they simultaneously pushed the Indians toward a monarchical and thus less democratic system.

We see the same collective system in the early 1500s in the pueblos of the southwest when one of Francisco Coronado's soldiers wrote that the Zuni had no chiefs "but are ruled by a council of the oldest men" whom they called *papas.* The Zuni word *papa* means "elder brother," and each clan probably elected its *papa* the way the Iroquois clans elected their sachems.

Even the Aztecs' government conformed to this pattern. They divided themselves into twenty *calpulli* or corporate clans, each of which owned property in common. Each *calpulli* elected a number of administrative officers to oversee the administration of property and law within its clan, and they elected a *tlatoani,* literally a "speaker," who functioned as the representative of the *calpulli* to the outside world. All the *tlatoani* met together to form the supreme council of the nation, and they elected the supreme speaker, or *huey-tlatoani,* an office with life tenure. By the time the Spanish arrived, this highest office of the nation had been reserved for a single family, but the council decided who within that family would have the office. The Spanish assumed that the Aztec system was like their own system or like that of their neighbors the Moors; they translated *huey-tlatoani* as "emperor" and called the *tlatoani* the "nobles" of the empire. Moctezuma, the Aztec leader captured by Hernando Cortés, held office as the supreme speaker of the Aztec nation, not as its emperor.

This Aztec system was no more of a democracy or a federal union because of these councils than was the Holy Roman Empire, which also had a council to elect its emperor from one family. Still, in the Aztec system we can see the outlines of a political format common throughout the Americas and in many ways closer to our democratic system in the United States today than to the systems of Europe of that time. The difference in the Aztec system and a European monarchy appeared most clearly when the Aztec people removed Moctezuma from office after the Spaniards captured him. The people even stoned him when he tried to persuade them to acquiesce to the Spanish. The Spaniards had expected the people to revere and obey their "emperor" no matter what, but they assumed erroneously that Moctezuma held the same power over the Aztec people that the Spanish king held over themselves.

The depth of democratic roots among North American Indian groups shows clearly in the detailed study of the Yaqui by historian Evelyn Hu-DeHart. Living in the present-day states of Sonora and Sinaloa of northwestern Mexico just south of the Apaches of Arizona, the Yaquis coaxed a livelihood from this desert setting through hunting and simple agriculture. In July 1739 the Yaquis sent two emissaries named Muni and Bernabe to Mexico City for a rare audience with the Spanish viceroy to plead for free elections of their own government administrators in place of the Jesuits appointed over them. After 1740 the government allowed the Yaquis to elect their own captain general as head of their tribe, but the government still sought to exercise control over the Yaquis through clerical and civilian administrators (Hu-DeHart, p. 17). Thus in the wilds of Mexico a full generation before the Revolution in the English colonies of North America, we see evidence of the Indians demanding the franchise and free elections in order to maintain their traditional political values.

In almost every North American tribe, clan, or nation for which we have detailed political information, the supreme authority rested in a group rather than in an individual. It took many generations of close interaction between colonists and Indians before the principles of group decision-making replaced the European traditions of relying on a single supreme authority. The importance of these Indian councils and groups shows clearly in the English lack of words to explain such a process.

One of the most important political institutions borrowed from the Indians was the caucus. Even though the word appears to be proper Latin and some law students with a semester of Latin occasionally decline the plural as *cauci,* the word comes from the Algonquian languages. The caucus permits informal discussion of an issue without necessitating a yea or nay vote on any particular question. This agreed with the traditional Indian way of talking through an issue or of making a powwow; it made political decisions less divisive and combative. The caucus became a mainstay of American democracy both in the Congress and in political and community groups all over the country. The caucus evolved into such an important aspect of American politics that the political parties adopted it to nominate their presidential candidates. In time this evoked into the political convention, which still functions as an important part of contemporary American politics but is largely absent from European politics.

Not all the Founding Fathers showed interest in Indian political traditions. They turned instead toward models such as the British Parliament and some of the Greek and Italian city-states. Many of them had been deeply trained in classic literature, in ways that Franklin and Paine had not been trained, and they sought to incorporate the classic notions of democracy and republicanism into the new nation.

Often this proved to be a tricky undertaking, for the ancient Greeks observed democracy far more in the breach than in its enactment. The Greeks who rhapsodized about democracy in their rhetoric rarely created democratic institutions. A few cities such as Athens occasionally attempted a system vaguely akin to democracy for a few years. These cities functioned as slave societies and were certainly not egalitarian or democratic in the Indian sense. Most of the respected political thinkers of Greece despised democracy both theoretically and in practice. The people of Athens executed Socrates during one of their democratic eras because he had conspired with the oligarchs to destroy democracy. On the other hand, Plato favored rule by a philosopher-king and even went to Syracuse to help the tyrant Dionysius rule.

In the United States, the southerners identified much more closely with the ideals of Greek democracy based on massive slavery than with Iroquois democracy, which did not permit slavery. As historian Vernon Parrington wrote, the "dream of a Greek civilization based on black slavery was discovered in the bottom of the cup of southern romanticism" (Parrington, p. 130).

Carolinians, Georgians, and Virginians identified so closely with the so-called democracies of Greece that they considered the south to be a virtual reincarnation or at least renaissance of Greek life. By the beginning of the nineteenth century, southerners had created a virtual Greek cult as an intellectual bulwark to protect their way of life. European romantics such as Lord Byron and John Keats flirted with Greek aesthetics, but the Europeans quickly dropped them in favor of a more personal form of romanticism.

The American south, however, embraced everything Greek. The southern gentleman with his leisurely life of relaxation in the study, friendly conversation in the parlor, fine meals in the dining room, courting in the ballroom, and hunting in the forest identified closely with the good life of Greek literature. At least a passing acquaintance with the Greek and Latin languages became the true mark of a gentleman in the south, and the Greek ideal of a sound mind in a sound body became the creed of the southern leisure class. Southerners wrote poems in mock-Greek style and wrote letters in a classical form. In their excess they even gave their house slaves, horses, and hunting dogs names such as Cicero, Athena, Cato, Pericles, Homer, Apollo, and Nero.

They adorned their plantations with greek names, and even built their homes in the style of Greek temples. Greek architecture prevailed so widely in the South that today the stereotyped image of a plantation house includes Corinthian columns in Greek Revival style. In their gardens they built gazebos that were styled after Greek shrines, and they set Greek statues out among the magnolia trees and the palms. Even the churches of the south added porticos and rows of columns to their fronts, topped off by very un-Greek steeples.

In making itself over in the Greek image, America neglected a major part of its democratic roots in the long house of the Iroquois and the humble caucus of the Algonquians in favor of the ostentatious props and models looted from the classical Mediterranean world. For almost the whole first century of American independence this Greek architecture and Greek oratory helped to disguise the fact that the nation was based on slavery, an institution that could never be compatible with democracy no matter how much that architectural and verbal edifice tried to cover it.

Prior to this Greek cult, most government buildings in America had been built in a very simple style, as in the state capitol of Massachusetts, Independence Hall in Philadelphia, or the government buildings of colonial Williamsburg. But with the rise of the Greek cult in the south, government architects moved away from the simple Federal style to make public buildings appear Greek. At the height of this classical obsession the United States government began work on a new Capitol. The Senate chamber took the form of a small Greek amphitheater covered in excessive classical ornaments, while the House of Representatives crowned itself with a large clock encased in a sculpture of Clio, the muse of history, riding in her winged chariot and recording the historic events below her.

Although the Greek cult spread out of the south, New Englanders never embraced it very fondly. For them mystic philosophies such as Transcendentalism, often accompanied by ideas of liberty and abolition of slavery, seemed far more alluring. For them the existence of slavery at the foundations of democracy bastardized the whole system.

Even in the south the Greek cult did not reign as the only intellectual and social fashion. In stark contrast to this indulgence of the right, the black population and the poor whites embraced a strict form of Old Testament fundamentalism closely associated with Moses, the liberator of the slaves, and of New Testament salvation focused on a very personal savior and protector.

Meanwhile in the west the process of learning democracy through experience of the frontier and Indians continued without regard to the supposed classical models. Even after the founding of the United States, the Indians continued to play a significant role in the evolution of democracy because of their sustained interactions with Americans on the frontier. The frontiersmen constantly reinvented democracy and channeled it into the eastern establishment of the United States.

Time and again the people of the frontier rebelled against the entrenched and conservative values of an ever more staid coastal elite. As the frontier gradually moved westward, the settlements on the edge sent such rebels as Henry Clay, Andrew Jackson, David Crockett, and Abraham Lincoln back to reinvest the spirit of democracy into the political institutions of the east. Some of these men, such as Sam Houston, lived for long periods with Indians. Houston spent so much time with the Cherokee that they adopted him into their nation about 1829. The influence of the Cherokees stayed with him throughout his tenure as president of Texas from 1836 to 1838 and again from 1841 to 1844. Throughout his life he maintained close working relations with a variety of Indian nations and a strong commitment to liberty.

Even Alexis de Tocqueville, who denigrated the achievements of the Indians, noticed that the settlers on the frontier "mix the ideas and customs of savage life with the civilization of their fathers." In general he found this reprehensible, for it made their "passions more intense" and "their religious morality less authoritative" (Tocqueville, Vol. I, p. 334), but these traits certainly may be interpreted by others as among the virtues of a democratic people.

Most democratic and egalitarian reforms of the past two hundred years in America originated on the frontier and not in the settled cites of the east. The frontier states dropped property and religious requirements for voters. They extended the franchise to women, and in 1916 Montana elected Jeannette Rankin as the first woman in Congress four years before the Nineteenth Amendment to the Constitution gave women the right to vote. The western states started the public election of senators in place of selection by the legislature. They also pioneered the use of primary elections of electoral recalls of unpopular officers. Even today they have more elective offices, such as judges; such offices in the east are usually filled by appointment by the governor or the legislature. This strong bias toward the electoral process and equal votes for all has been reinforced repeatedly by the people who have had the closest and the longest connections with the Indians on the frontier.

The final extension of the federal principles used in the Iroquois Nation and later in the formation of the United States came in 1918 with establishment of the League of Nations. The framers of this new league also chose the Iroquois federal system of allowing each member an equal voice no matter how small or large a country he represented. The same principle underlay creation of the General Assembly of the United Nations a generation later. By ironic coincidence, the founders of this international body located it in New York in the very territory that once belonged to the League of the Iroquois. In one respect the United Nations was an international version of that Indian league.

Washington, D.C., has never recognized the role of the Indians in the writing of the United States Constitution or in the creation of political institutions that seem so uniquely American. But an inadvertent memorial does exist. An older woman from Israel pointed this out to me one spring day as I cut across the lawn of the United States Capitol, where I then worked for Senator John Glenn. She stopped me, and in a husky voice asked me who was the Indian woman atop the Capitol dome. Suddenly looking at it through her eyes, I too saw the figure as an Indian even though I knew that it was not.

When the United States government embarked on an expansion of the Capitol in the middle of the nineteenth century, the architects proposed to cap the dome with a symbol of freedom. They chose for this a nineteen-foot bronze statue of a Roman woman who would stand on the pinnacle of the Capitol. Sculptor Thomas Crawford crowned the woman with a Phrygian cap, which in Roman history had been the sign of the freed slave. At that time Jefferson Davis, the future president of the Confederate States of America, still served as the secretary of war for the United States, and he objected strongly to what he interpreted as an antisouthern and antislavery symbol. He compelled Crawford to cap her with something less antagonistic to southern politicians. Crawford designed a helmet covered with a crown of feathers, but in putting this headdress on the figure, her whole appearance changed. Now instead of looking like a classical Greek or Roman, she looked like an Indian.

She still stands today on the pseudoclassical Capitol overlooking the city of Washington. The Washington Monument rises to the same height, but no other building has been allowed to rise higher than she. Even though no one intended her to be an Indian, she now reigns as the nearest thing to a monument that Washington ever built to honor the Indians who contributed to the building of a federal union based on democracy.

UNIT 4
Other Families, Other Ways

Unit Selections

Key Points to Consider

- Why do child-care practices vary from culture to culture?

- Why do you think "fraternal polyandry" is socially acceptable in Tibet but not in our society?

- How have dietary changes affected birth rates and women's health?

- What are the pros and cons of arranged marriages versus freedom of choice?

- Under what circumstances do "dowry deaths" occur?

- Does the stability of Japanese marriages necessarily imply compatibility and contentment?

 **Links: www.dushkin.com/online/**
These sites are annotated in the World Wide Web pages.

Kinship and Social Organization
http://www.umanitoba.ca/anthropology/tutor/kinmenu.html

Since most people of the past in small-scale societies spent their whole lives within a local area, it is understandable that their primary interactions—economic, religious, and otherwise—were with their relatives. It also makes sense that through marriage customs, they strengthened those kinship relationships that clearly defined their mutual rights and obligations. Indeed, the resulting family structure may be surprisingly flexible and adaptive, as witnessed in the essays "When Brothers Share a Wife" by Melvyn Goldstein, "Arranging a Marriage in India" by Serena Nanda and in "How Many Fathers are Best for a Child?"

For these reasons, anthropologists have looked upon family and kinship as the key mechanisms for transmitting culture from one generation to the next.

(See "Our Babies, Ourselves" by Meredith Small.) Social changes may have been slow to take place throughout the world, but as social horizons have widened, family relationships and community alliances are increasingly based upon new principles. Even as birth rates have increased, kinship networks have diminished in size and strength. As people have increasingly become involved with others as coworkers in a market economy, our associations depend more and more upon factors such as personal aptitudes, educational backgrounds, and job opportunities. Yet the family is still there. Except for some rather unusual exceptions, such as depicted in "Dowry Deaths in India: 'Let Only Your Corpse Come Out of That House'" the family is smaller, but still functions in its age-old nurturing and protective role, even under conditions where there is little affection (see "Who Needs Love! In Japan, Many Couples Don't" by Nicholas Kristof) or under conditions of extreme poverty and a high infant mortality rate (see "Death Without Weeping" by Nancy Scheper-Hughes). Beyond the immediate family, the situation is in a state of flux. Certain ethnic groups, especially those in poverty, still have a need for the broader network and in some ways seem to be reformulating those ties.

We do not know where the changes described in this section will lead us and which ones will ultimately prevail. One thing is certain: anthropologists will be there to document the trends, for the discipline of anthropology has had to change as well. One important feature of the essays in this section is the growing interest of anthropologists in the study of complex societies where old theoretical perspectives are increasingly inadequate.

Current trends, however, do not necessarily mean the eclipse of the kinship unit. The large family network is still the best guarantee of individual survival and well-being in an urban setting.

ETHNOGRAPHY

HOW MANY FATHERS ARE BEST FOR A CHILD?

After 40 years of visiting the Barí Indians in Venezuela,
anthropologists have discovered a new twist on family values

By Meredith F. Small

Anthropologist Stephen Beckerman was well into his forties before he finally understood how babies are made. He had thought, as most people do, that a sperm from one man and an egg from one woman joined to make a child. But one summer day, as he and his colleague Roberto Lizarralde lounged around in hammocks, chatting with Rachel, an elderly woman of the Barí tribe of Venezuela, she pointed out his error. Babies, she explained, can easily have more than one biological father. "My first husband was the father of my first child, my second child, and my third child," Rachel said, recalling her life. "But the fourth child, actually, he has two fathers." It was clear that Rachel didn't mean there was a stepfather hanging around or a friendly uncle who took the kid fishing every weekend. She was simply explaining the Barí version of conception to these ignorant anthropologists: A fetus is built up over time with repeated washes of sperm—which means, of course, that more than one man can contribute to the endeavor. This interview changed not only the way Beckerman and Lizarralde viewed Barí families but also brought into question the very way that anthropologists portray human coupling. If biological fatherhood can be shared—an idea accepted by many indigenous groups across South America and in many other cultures across the globe— then the nuclear family with one mom and one dad might not be the established blueprint for a family that we have been led to expect. If so, the familiar story of traditional human mating behavior, in which man the hunter brings home the bacon to his faithful wife, loses credibility. And if the Barí and other groups work perfectly well with more flexible family styles, the variety of family structures that are increasingly common in Western culture these days—everything from single-parent households to blended families—may not be as dangerous to the social fab-

ric as we are led to believe. People in this culture may simply be exercising the same family options that humans have had for millions of years, options that have been operating in other cultures while the West took a stricter view of what constitutes a family.

Women grow fat during a pregnancy, while men grow thin from all their work

STEPHEN BECKERMAN FOLDS HIS 6-FOOT-4-INCH FRAME INTO A chair and turns to the mountainous topography of papers on his desk at Pennsylvania State University. Once he manages to locate a map under all the piles, he points to a spot on the border between Venezuela and Colombia where he spent 20 years, off and on, with the indigenous Barí Indians. The traditional Barí culture, Beckerman explains, has come under attack by outside forces, starting with the conquistadors who arrived in the early 16th century. Today Catholic missionaries interact with the Barí, coal and oil companies are trying to seize their land, and drug traffickers and guerrillas are threats. Western influences are apparent: Most families have moved from traditional long-houses to single-family dwellings, and everyone wears modern Western clothes and uses Western goods. However, the Barí continue to practice their traditions of manioc farming, fishing, and hunting, according to Roberto Lizarralde, an anthropologist at the Central University of Venezuela who has been visiting the

Barí regularly since 1960. Lizarralde also says that the Barí still have great faith in traditional spirits and ancestral wisdom, including their notion that a child can have multiple biological fathers. The Barí believe that the first act of sex, which should always be between a husband and wife, plants the seed. Then the fledgling fetus must be nourished by repeated anointings of semen; the woman's body is viewed as a vessel where men do all the work. "One of the reasons women give you for taking lovers is that they don't want to wear out their husbands," Beckerman says. "They claim it's hard work for men to support a pregnancy by having enough sex, and so lovers can help." Just look, the Barí say. Women grow fat during a pregnancy, while men grow thin from all their work.

ANTHROPOLOGISTS STUDY A CULTURE'S IDEAS ABOUT conception because those ideas have a profound impact on the way people run their lives. In our culture, for example, conceiving children incurs long-term economic responsibility for both the mother and father. We take this obligation so seriously that when a parent fails to provide for a child, it is usually a violation of law. In the Barí system, when a man is named as a secondary biological father he is also placed under an obligation to the mother and the child. In addition, he is expected to give gifts of fish and game. These gifts are a significant burden because the man must also provide for his own wife and primary children. Beckerman and his colleagues have discovered that naming secondary fathers has evolutionary consequences. A team of ethnographers led by Beckerman, Roberto Lizarralde, and his son Manuel, an anthropologist at Connecticut College who has been visiting the Barí since he was 5 years old, interviewed 114 Barí women past childbearing years and asked them about their full reproductive histories. "These interviews were a lot of fun," Beckerman says, laughing. "Randy old ladies talking about their lovers." In total, the researchers recorded claims of 916 pregnancies, an average of eight pregnancies for each woman. But child mortality was high—about one-third of the children did not survive to age 15. Naming secondary fathers was a critical factor in predicting which babies made it to adulthood. Secondary fathers were involved in 25 percent of pregnancies, and the team determined that two fathers were the ideal number. Children with one father and one secondary father made it to their teens most often; kids with only one father or those with more than two fathers didn't fare as well. The researchers also found that this decrease in mortality occurred not during the child's life but during fetal development: Women were less likely to have a miscarriage or stillbirth if they had a husband and an additional male contributing food. This result was a surprise because researchers had expected that help during childhood would be more important. "The Barí are not hungry; they are not close to the bone. But it must be the extra fat and protein that they get from secondary fathers during gestation that makes the difference," Beckerman explains as he points to photographs of Barí women who look well nourished, even downright plump. Barí women seem to use this more flexible system of paternity when they need it. Within families, some children have secondary fathers, while their siblings belong to the husband alone. The team discovered that mothers are more likely to take on a secondary father when a previous child has died in infancy. Manuel Lizarralde claims the strategy makes perfect sense, given the Barí belief that the best way to cure a sick child is for the father to blow tobacco smoke over the child's body. "It is easy to imagine a bereaved mother thinking to herself that if she had only provided a secondary father and so more smoke for her dead child, she might have saved him—and vowing to provide that benefit for her next child." Beckerman says extra fathers may have always been insurance for uncertain times: "Because the Barí were once hunted as if they were game animals—by other Indians, conquistadors, oilmen, farmers, and ranchers—the odds of a woman being widowed when she still had young children were one in three, according to data we gathered about the years 1930 to 1960. The men as well as the women knew this. None of these guys can go down the street to Mutual of Omaha and buy a life insurance policy. By allowing his wife to take a lover, the husband is doing all he can to ensure the survival of his children." Barí women are also freer to do as they wish because men need their labor—having a wife is an economic necessity because women do the manioc farming, harvesting, and cooking, while men hunt and fish. "The sexual division of labor is such that you can't make it without a member of the opposite sex," says Beckerman. Initially, the researchers worried that jealousy on the part of husbands would make Barí women reticent about discussing multiple sexual partners. "In our first interviews, we would wait until the husband was out of the house," says Beckerman. "But one day we interviewed an old couple who were enjoying thinking about their lives; they were lying in their hammocks, side by side, and it was obvious he wasn't going anywhere. So we went down the list of her children and asked about other fathers. She said no, no, no for each child, and then the husband interrupted when we got to one and said, 'That's not true, don't you remember, there was that guy…' And the husband was grinning." Not all women take lovers. Manuel Lizarralde has discovered through interviews that one-third of 122 women were faithful to their husbands during their pregnancies. "These women say they don't need it, or no one asked, or they have enough support from family and don't require another father for their child," Lizarralde says. "Some even admit that their husbands were not that happy about the idea." Or it may be a sign of changing times. Based on his most recent visits to the Barí, Lizarralde thinks that under the influence of Western values, the number of people who engage in multiple fatherhood may be decreasing. But his father, who has worked with the Barí for more than 40 years, disagrees. He says the practice is as frequent but that the Barí discuss it less openly than before, knowing that Westerners object to their views. After all, it took the anthropologists 20 years to hear about other fathers, and today the Barí are probably being even more discreet because they know Westerners disapprove of their beliefs. "What this information adds up to," Beckerman says, "is that the Barí may be doing somewhat less fooling around within marriage these days but that most of them still believe that a child can have multiple fathers." More important, the Barí idea that biological paternity can be shared is not just the quirky custom of one tribe; anthropologists have found that this idea is common across South America. The same belief is shared by indigenous groups in New Guinea and India, suggesting that multiple paternity has been part of human behavior for a long time, undermining all previous descriptions of how human mating behavior evolved.

As the Barí and other cultures show, there are all sorts of ways to run a successful household

SINCE THE 1960S, WHEN ANTHROPOLOGISTS BEGAN TO construct scenarios of early human mating, they had always assumed that the model family started with a mom and dad bonded for life to raise the kids, a model that fit well with acceptable Western behavior. In 1981 in an article titled "The Origin of Man," C. Owen Lovejoy, an anthropologist at Kent State University, outlined the standard story of human evolution as it was used in the field—and is still presented in textbooks today: Human infants with their big brains and long periods of growth and learning have always been dependent on adults, a dependence that separates the humans from the apes. Mothers alone couldn't possibly find enough food for these dependent young, so women have always needed to find a mate who would stick close to home and bring in supplies for the family. Unfortunately for women, as evolutionary psychologists suggest, men are compelled by their biology to mate with as many partners as possible to pass along their genes. However, each of these men might be manipulated into staying with one woman who offered him sex and a promise of fidelity. The man, under those conditions, would be assured of paternity, and he might just stay around and make sure his kids survived. This scenario presents humans as naturally monogamous, forming nuclear families as an evolutionary necessity. The only problem is that around the world families don't always operate this way. In fact, as the Barí and other cultures show, there are all sorts of ways to run a successful household. The Na of Yunnan Province in China, for example, have a female-centric society in which husbands are not part of the picture. Women grow up and continue to live with their mothers, sisters, and brothers; they never marry or move away from the family compound. As a result, sisters and brothers rather than married pairs are the economic unit that farms and fishes together. Male lovers in this system are simply visitors. They have no place or power in the household, and children are brought up by their mothers and by the mothers' brothers. A father is identified only if there is a resemblance between him and the child, and even so, the father has no responsibilities toward the child. Often women have sex with so many partners that the biological father is unknown. "I have not found

any term that would cover the notion of father in the Na language," writes Chinese anthropologist Cai Hua in his book *A Society Without Fathers or Husbands: The Na of China*. In this case, women have complete control over their children, property, and sexuality. Across lowland South America, family systems vary because cultures put their beliefs into practice in different ways. Among some native people, such as the Canela, Mehinaku, and Araweté, women control their sex lives and their fertility, and most children have several fathers. Barí women are also sexually liberated from an early age. "Once she has completed her puberty ritual, a Barí girl can have sex with anyone she wants as long as she doesn't violate the incest taboo," Beckerman explains. "It's nobody's business, not even Mom's and Dad's business." Women can also turn down prospective husbands. In other cultures in South America, life is not so free for females, although members of these cultures also believe that babies can have more than one father. The Curripaco of Amazonia, for instance, acknowledge multiple fatherhood as a biological possibility and yet frown on women having affairs. Paul Valentine, a senior lecturer in anthropology at the University of East London who has studied the Curripaco for more than 20 years, says, "Curripaco women are in a difficult situation. The wives come into the village from different areas, and it's a very patrilineal system." If her husband dies, a widow is allowed to turn only to his brothers or to clan members on his side of the family for a new husband. The relative power of women and men over their sex lives has important consequences. "In certain social and economic systems, women are free to make mate choices," says Valentine. In these cultures women are often the foundation of society, while men have less power in the community. Sisters tend to stay in the same household as their mothers. The women, in other words, have power to make choices. "At the other extreme, somehow, it's the men who try to maximize their evolutionary success at the expense of the women," says Valentine. Men and women often have a conflict of interest when it comes to mating, marriage, and who should invest most in children, and the winners have sometimes been the men, sometimes the women. As Beckerman wryly puts it, "Anyone who believes that in a human mating relationship the man's reproductive interests always carry the day has obviously never been married." The Barí and others show that human systems are, in fact, very flexible, ready to accommodate any sort of mating system or type of family. "I think that human beings are capable of making life extremely complicated. That's our way of doing business," says Ian Tattersall, a paleoanthropologist and curator in the division of anthropology at the American Museum of Natural History in New York City. Indeed, such flexibility suggests there's no reason to assume that the nuclear family is the natural, ideal, or even most evolutionarily successful system of human grouping. As Beckerman says, "One of the things this research shows is that human beings are just as clever and creative in assembling their kin relations as they are in putting together space shuttles or symphonies."

Reprinted with permission of the author from *Discover* magazine, April 2003, pp. 54-61. Copyright © 2003 by Meredith Small.

When Brothers Share a Wife

Among Tibetans, the good life relegates many women to spinsterhood

Melvyn C. Goldstein

Eager to reach home, Dorje drives his yaks hard over the 17,000-foot mountain pass, stopping only once to rest. He and his two older brothers, Pema and Sonam, are jointly marrying a woman from the next village in a few weeks, and he has to help with the preparations.

Dorje, Pema, and Sonam are Tibetans living in Limi, a 200-square-mile area in the northwest corner of Nepal, across the border from Tibet. The form of marriage they are about to enter—fraternal polyandry in anthropological parlance—is one of the world's rarest forms of marriage but is not uncommon in Tibetan society, where it has been practiced from time immemorial. For many Tibetan social strata, it traditionally represented the ideal form of marriage and family.

The mechanics of fraternal polyandry are simple. Two, three, four, or more brothers jointly take a wife, who leaves her home to come and live with them. Traditionally, marriage was arranged by parents, with children, particularly females, having little or no say. This is changing somewhat nowadays, but it is still unusual for children to marry without their parents' consent. Marriage ceremonies vary by income and region and range from all the brothers sitting together as grooms to only the eldest one formally doing so. The age of the brothers plays an important role in determining this: very young brothers almost never participate in actual marriage ceremonies, although they typically join the marriage when they reach their mid-teens.

The eldest brother is normally dominant in terms of authority, that is, in managing the household, but all the brothers share the work and participate as sexual partners. Tibetan males and females do not find the sexual aspect of sharing a spouse the least bit unusual, repulsive, or scandalous, and the norm is for the wife to treat all the brothers the same.

Offspring are treated similarly. There is no attempt to link children biologically to particular brothers, and a brother shows no favoritism toward his child even if he knows he is the real father because, for example, his other brothers were away at the time the wife became pregnant. The children, in turn, consider all of the brothers as their fathers and treat them equally, even if they also know who is their real father. In some regions children use the term "father" for the eldest brother and "father's brother" for the others, while in other areas they call all the brothers by one term, modifying this by the use of "elder" and "younger."

Unlike our own society, where monogamy is the only form of marriage permitted, Tibetan society allows a variety of marriage types, including monogamy, fraternal polyandry, and polygyny. Fraternal polyandry and monogamy are the most common forms of marriage, while polygyny typically occurs in cases where the first wife is barren. The widespread practice of fraternal polyandry, therefore, is not the outcome of a law requiring brothers to marry jointly. There is choice, and in fact, divorce traditionally was relatively simple in Tibetan society. If a

brother in a polyandrous marriage became dissatisfied and wanted to separate, he simply left the main house and set up his own household. In such cases, all the children stayed in the main household with the remaining brother(s), even if the departing brother was known to be the real father of one or more of the children.

The Tibetans' own explanation for choosing fraternal polyandry is materialistic. For example, when I asked Dorje why he decided to marry with his two brothers rather than take his own wife, he thought for a moment, then said it prevented the division of his family's farm (and animals) and thus facilitated all of them achieving a higher standard of living. And when I later asked Dorje's bride whether it wasn't difficult for her to cope with three brothers as husbands, she laughed and echoed the rationale of avoiding fragmentation of the family and land, adding that she expected to be better off economically, since she would have three husbands working for her and her children.

Exotic as it may seem to Westerners, Tibetan fraternal polyandry is thus in many ways analogous to the way primogeniture functioned in nineteenth-century England. Primogeniture dictated that the eldest son inherited the family estate, while younger sons had to leave home and seek their own employment—for example, in the military or the clergy. Primogeniture maintained family estates intact over generations by permitting only one heir per generation. Fraternal polyandry also accomplishes this but does so by keeping all the brothers together with just one wife so that there is only one *set* of heirs per generation.

While Tibetans believe that in this way fraternal polyandry reduces the risk of family fission, monogamous marriages among brothers need not necessarily precipitate the division of the family estate: brothers could continue to live together, and the family land could continue to be worked jointly. When I asked Tibetans about this, however, they invariably responded that such joint families are unstable because each wife is primarily oriented to her own children and interested in their success and well-being over that of the children of the other wives. For example, if the youngest brother's wife had three sons while the eldest brother's wife had only one daughter, the wife of the youngest brother might begin to demand more resources for her children since, as males, they represent the future of the family. Thus, the children from different wives in the same generation are competing sets of heirs, and this makes such families inherently unstable. Tibetans perceive that conflict will spread from the wives to their husbands and consider this likely to cause family fission. Consequently, it is almost never done.

Although Tibetans see an economic advantage to fraternal polyandry, they do not value the sharing of a wife as an end in itself. On the contrary, they articulate a number of problems inherent in the practice. For example, because authority is customarily exercised by the eldest brother, his younger male siblings have to subordinate themselves with little hope of changing their status within the family. When these younger brothers are aggressive and individualistic, tensions and difficulties often occur despite there being only one set of heirs.

In addition, tension and conflict may arise in polyandrous families because of sexual favoritism. The bride normally sleeps with the eldest brother, and the two have the responsibility to see to it that the other males have opportunities for sexual access. Since the Tibetan subsistence economy requires males to travel a lot, the temporary absence of one or more brothers facilitates this, but there are also other rotation practices. The cultural ideal unambiguously calls for the wife to show equal affection and sexuality to each of the brothers (and vice versa), but deviations from this ideal occur, especially when there is a sizable difference in age between the partners in the marriage.

Dorje's family represents just such a potential situation. He is fifteen years old and his two older brothers are twenty-five and twenty-two years old. The new bride is twenty-three years old, eight years Dorje's senior. Sometimes such a bride finds the youngest husband immature and adolescent and does not treat him with equal affection; alternatively, she may find his youth attractive and lavish special attention on him. Apart from that consideration, when a younger male like Dorje grows up, he may consider his wife "ancient" and prefer the company of a woman his own age or younger. Consequently, although men and women do not find the idea of sharing a bride or bridegroom repulsive, individual likes and dislikes can cause familial discord.

Two reasons have commonly been offered for the perpetuation of fraternal polyandry in Tibet: that Tibetans practice female infanticide and therefore have to marry polyandrously, owing to a shortage of females; and that Tibet, lying at extremely high altitudes, is so barren and bleak that Tibetans would starve without resort to this mechanism. A Jesuit who lived in Tibet during the eighteenth century articulated this second view: "One reason for this most odious custom is the sterility of the soil, and the small amount of land that can be cultivated owing to the lack of water. The crops may suffice if the brothers all live together, but if they form separate families they would be reduced to beggary."

Both explanations are wrong, however. Not only has there never been institutionalized female infanticide in Tibet, but Tibetan society gives females considerable rights, including inheriting the family estate in the absence of brothers. In such cases, the woman takes a bridegroom who comes to live in her family and adopts her family's name and identity. Moreover, there is no demographic evidence of a shortage of females. In Limi, for example, there were (in 1974) sixty females and fifty-three males in the fifteen- to thirty-five-year age category, and many adult females were unmarried.

The second reason is also incorrect. The climate in Tibet is extremely harsh, and ecological factors do play a major role perpetuating polyandry, but polyandry is not a means of preventing starvation. It is characteristic, not of the poorest segments of the society, but rather of the peasant landowning families.

In the old society, the landless poor could not realistically aspire to prosperity, but they did not fear starvation. There was a persistent labor shortage throughout Tibet, and very poor families with little or no land and few animals could subsist through agricultural labor, tenant farming, craft occupations such as carpentry, or by working as servants. Although the per person family income could increase somewhat if brothers married polyandrously and pooled their wages, in the absence of inheritable land, the advantage of fraternal polyandry was not generally sufficient to prevent them from setting up their own households. A more skilled or energetic younger brother could do as well or better alone, since he would completely control his income and would not have to share it with his siblings. Consequently, while there was and is some polyandry among the poor, it is much less frequent and more prone to result in divorce and family fission.

An alternative reason for the persistence of fraternal polyandry is that it reduces population growth (and thereby reduces the pressure on resources) by relegating some females to lifetime spinsterhood. Fraternal polyandrous marriages in Limi (in 1974) averaged 2.35 men per woman, and not surprisingly, 31 percent of the females of child-bearing age (twenty to forty-nine) were unmarried. These spinsters either continued to live at home, set up their own households, or worked as servants for other families. They could also become Buddhist nuns. Being unmarried is not synonymous with exclusion from the reproductive pool. Discreet extramarital relationships are tolerated, and actually half of the adult unmarried women in Limi had one or more children. They raised these children as single mothers, working for wages or weaving cloth and blankets for sale. As a group, however, the unmarried woman had far fewer offspring than the married women, averaging only 0.7 children per woman, compared with 3.3 for married women, whether polyandrous, monogamous, or polygynous. While polyandry helps regulate population, this function of polyandry is not consciously perceived by Tibetans and is not the reason they consistently choose it.

If neither a shortage of females nor the fear of starvation perpetuates fraternal polyandry, what motivates brothers, particularly younger brothers, to opt for this system of marriage? From the perspective of the younger brother in a landholding family, the main incentive is the attainment or maintenance of the good life. With polyandry, he can expect a more secure and higher standard of living, with access not only to this family's land and animals but also to its inherited collection of clothes, jewelry, rugs, saddles, and horses. In addition, he will experience less work pressure and much greater security because all responsibility does not fall on one "father." For Tibetan brothers, the question is whether to trade off the greater personal freedom inherent in monogamy for the real or potential economic security, affluence, and social prestige associated with life in a larger, labor-rich polyandrous family.

A brother thinking of separating from his polyandrous marriage and taking his own wife would face various disadvantages. Although in the majority of Tibetan regions all brothers theoretically have rights to their family's estate, in reality Tibetans are reluctant to divide their land into small fragments. Generally, a younger brother who insists on leaving the family will receive only a small plot of land, if that. Because of its power and wealth, the rest of the family usually can block any attempt of the younger brother to increase his share of land through litigation. Moreover, a younger brother may not even get a house and cannot expect to receive much above the minimum in terms of movable possessions, such as furniture, pots, and pans. Thus, a brother contemplating going it on his own must

plan on achieving economic security and the good life not through inheritance but through his own work.

The obvious solution for younger brothers—creating new fields from virgin land—is generally not a feasible option. Most Tibetan populations live at high altitudes (above 12,000 feet), where arable land is extremely scarce. For example, in Dorje's village, agriculture ranges only from about 12,900 feet, the lowest point in the area, to 13,300 feet. Above that altitude, early frost and snow destroy the staple barley crop. Furthermore, because of the low rainfall caused by the Himalayan rain shadow, many areas in Tibet and northern Nepal that are within the appropriate altitude range for agriculture have no reliable sources of irrigation. In the end, although there is plenty of unused land in such areas, most of it is either too high or too arid.

Even where unused land capable of being farmed exists, clearing the land and building the substantial terraces necessary for irrigation constitute a great undertaking. Each plot has to be completely dug out to a depth of two to two and half feet so that the large rocks and boulders can be removed. At best, a man might be able to bring a few new fields under cultivation in the first years after separating from his brothers, but he could not expect to acquire substantial amounts of arable land this way.

In addition, because of the limited farmland, the Tibetan subsistence economy characteristically includes a strong emphasis on animal husbandry. Tibetan farmers regularly maintain cattle, yaks, goats, and sheep, grazing them in the areas too high for agriculture. These herds produce wool, milk, cheese, butter, meat, and skins. To obtain these resources, however, shepherds must accompany the animals on a daily basis. When first setting up a monogamous household, a younger brother like Dorje would find it difficult to both farm and manage animals.

In traditional Tibetan society, there was an even more critical factor that operated to perpetuate fraternal polyandry—a form of hereditary servitude

somewhat analogous to serfdom in Europe. Peasants were tied to large estates held by aristocrats, monasteries, and the Lhasa government. They were allowed the use of some farmland to produce their own subsistence but were required to provide taxes in kind and corvée (free labor) to their lords. The corvée was a substantial hardship, since a peasant household was in many cases required to furnish the lord with one laborer daily for most of the year and more on specific occasions such as the harvest. This enforced labor, along with the lack of new land and ecological pressure to pursue both agriculture and animal husbandry, made polyandrous families particularly beneficial. The polyandrous family allowed an internal division of adult labor, maximizing economic advantage. For example, while the wife worked the family fields, one brother could perform the lord's corvée, another could look after the animals, and a third could engage in trade.

Although social scientists often discount other people's explanations of why they do things, in the case of Tibetan fraternal polyandry, such explanations are very close to the truth. The custom, however, is very sensitive to changes in its political and economic milieu and, not surprisingly, is in decline in most Tibetan areas. Made less important by the elimination of the traditional serf-based economy, it is disparaged by the dominant non-Tibetan leaders of India, China, and Nepal. New opportunities for economic and social mobility in these countries, such as the tourist trade and government employment, are also eroding the rationale for polyandry, and so it may vanish within the next generation.

Melvyn C. Goldstein, now a professor of anthropology at Case Western Reserve University in Cleveland, has been interested in the Tibetan practice of fraternal polyandry (several brothers marrying one wife) since he was a graduate student in the 1960s.

Death Without Weeping

Has poverty ravaged mother love in the shantytowns of Brazil?

Nancy Scheper-Hughes

I have seen death without weeping,
The destiny of the Northeast is death,
Cattle they kill,
To the people they do
  something worse
—Anonymous Brazilian singer
  (1965)

"WHY DO THE CHURCH BELLS RING SO often?" I asked Nailza de Arruda soon after I moved into a corner of her tiny mud-walled hut near the top of the shantytown called the Alto do Cruzeiro (Crucifix Hill). I was then a Peace Corps volunteer and community development/ health worker. It was the dry and blazing hot summer of 1965, the months following the military coup in Brazil, and save for the rusty, clanging bells of N. S. das Dores Church, an eerie quiet had settled over the market town that I call Bom Jesus da Mata. Beneath the quiet, however, there was chaos and panic. "It's nothing," replied Nailza, "just another little angel gone to heaven."

Nailza had sent more than her share of little angels to heaven, and sometimes at night I could hear her engaged in a muffled but passionate discourse with one of them, two-year-old Joana. Joana's photograph, taken as she lay propped up in her tiny cardboard coffin, her eyes open, hung on a wall next to one of Nailza and Ze Antonio taken on the day they eloped.

Nailza could barely remember the other infants and babies who came and went in close succession. Most had died unnamed and were hastily baptized in their coffins. Few lived more than a month or two. Only Joana, properly bap-

tized in church at the close of her first year and placed under the protection of a powerful saint, Joan of Arc, had been expected to live. And Nailza had dangerously allowed herself to love the little girl.

In addressing the dead child, Nailza's voice would range from tearful imploring to angry recrimination: "Why did you leave me? Was your patron saint so greedy that she could not allow me one child on this earth?" Ze Antonio advised me to ignore Nailza's odd behavior, which he understood as a kind of madness that, like the birth and death of children, came and went. Indeed, the premature birth of a stillborn son some months later "cured" Nailza of her "inappropriate" grief, and the day came when she removed Joana's photo and carefully packed it away.

More than fifteen years elapsed before I returned to the Alto do Cruzeiro, and it was anthropology that provided the vehicle of my return. Since 1982 I have returned several times in order to pursue a problem that first attracted my attention in the 1960s. My involvement with the people of the Alto do Cruzeiro now spans a quarter of a century and three generations of parenting in a community where mothers and daughters are often simultaneously pregnant.

The Alto do Cruzeiro is one of three shantytowns surrounding the large market town of Bom Jesus in the sugar plantation zone of Pernambuco in Northeast Brazil, one of the many zones of neglect that have emerged in the shadow of the now tarnished economic miracle of Bra-

zil. For the women and children of the Alto do Cruzeiro the only miracle is that some of them have managed to stay alive at all.

The Northeast is a region of vast proportions (approximately twice the size of Texas) and of equally vast social and developmental problems. The nine states that make up the region are the poorest in the country and are representative of the Third World within a dynamic and rapidly industrializing nation. Despite waves of migrations from the interior to the teeming shantytowns of coastal cities, the majority still live in rural areas on farms and ranches, sugar plantations and mills.

Life expectancy in the Northeast is only forty years, largely because of the appallingly high rate of infant and child mortality. Approximately one million children in Brazil under the age of five die each year. The children of the Northeast, especially those born in shantytowns on the periphery of urban life, are at a very high risk of death. In these areas, children are born without the traditional protection of breast-feeding, subsistence gardens, stable marriages, and multiple adult caretakers that exists in the interior. In the hillside shantytowns that spring up around cities or, in this case, interior market towns, marriages are brittle, single parenting is the norm, and women are frequently forced into the shadow economy of domestic work in the homes of the rich or into unprotected and oftentimes "scab" wage labor on the surrounding sugar plantations, where they clear land for planting and weed for a pittance, sometimes less than a dollar a day. The women of the Alto may not bring their babies with them into the homes of the wealthy, where the often-sick infants are considered sources of contamination, and they cannot carry the little ones to the riverbanks where they wash clothes because the river is heavily infested with schistosomes and other deadly parasites. Nor can they carry their young children to the plantations, which are often several miles away. At wages of a dollar a day, the women of the Alto cannot hire baby sitters. Older children who are not in school will sometimes serve as somewhat indifferent caretakers. But any child not in school is also expected to find wage work. In most cases, babies are simply left at home alone, the door securely fastened. And so many also die alone and unattended.

Bom Jesus da Mata, centrally located in the plantation zone of Pernambuco, is within commuting distance of several sugar plantations and mills. Consequently, Bom Jesus has been a magnet for rural workers forced off their small subsistence plots by large landowners wanting to use every available piece of land for sugar cultivation. Initially, the rural migrants to Bom Jesus were squatters who were given tacit approval by the mayor to put up temporary straw huts on each of the three hills overlooking the town. The Alto do Cruzeiro is the oldest, the largest, and the poorest of the shantytowns. Over the past three decades many of the original migrants have become permanent residents, and the primitive and temporary straw huts have been replaced by small homes (usually of two rooms) made of wattle and daub, sometimes covered with plaster. The more affluent residents use bricks and tiles. In most Alto homes, dangerous kerosene lamps have been replaced by light bulbs. The once tattered rural garb, often fashioned from used sugar sacking, has likewise been replaced by store-brought clothes, often castoffs from a wealthy *patrão* (boss). The trappings are modern, but the hunger, sickness, and death that they conceal are traditional, deeply rooted in a history of feudalism, exploitation, and institutionalized dependency.

My research agenda never wavered. The questions I addressed first crystalized during a veritable "die-off" of Alto babies during a severe drought in 1965. The food and water shortages and the political and economic chaos occasioned by the military coup were reflected in the handwritten entries of births and deaths in the dusty, yellowed pages of the ledger books kept at the public registry office in Bom Jesus. More than 350 babies died in the Alto during 1965 alone—this from a shantytown population of little more than 5,000. But that wasn't what surprised me. There were reasons enough for the deaths in the miserable conditions of shantytown life. What puzzled me was the seeming indifference of Alto women to the death of their infants, and their willingness to attribute to their own tiny offspring an aversion to life that made their death seem wholly natural, indeed all but anticipated.

Although I found that it was possible, and hardly difficult, to rescue infants and toddlers from death by diarrhea and dehydration with a simple sugar, salt, and water solution (even bottled Coca-Cola worked fine), it was more difficult to enlist a mother herself in the rescue of a child she perceived as ill-fated for life or better off dead, or to convince her to take back into her threatened and besieged home a baby she had already come to think of as an angel rather than as a son or daughter.

I learned that the high expectancy of death, and the ability to face child death with stoicism and equanimity, produced patterns of nurturing that differentiated between those infants thought of as thrivers and survivors and those thought of as born already "wanting to die." The survivors were nurtured, while stigmatized, doomed infants were left to die, as mothers say, *a mingua*, "of neglect." Mothers stepped back and allowed nature to take its course. This pattern, which I call mortal selective neglect, is called passive infanticide by anthropologist Marvin Harris. The Alto situation, although culturally specific in the form that it takes, is not unique to Third World shantytown communities and may have its correlates in our own impoverished urban communities in some cases of "failure to thrive" infants.

I use as an example the story of Zezinho, the thirteen-month-old toddler of one of my neighbors, Lourdes. I became involved with Zezinho when I was called in to help Lourdes in the delivery of another child, this one a fair and robust little tyke with a lusty cry. I noted that while Lourdes showed great interest in the newborn, she totally ignored Zezinho who, wasted and severely malnourished, was curled up in a fetal position on a piece of urine- and feces-soaked cardboard placed under his mother's hammock. Eyes open and vacant, mouth slack, the little boy seemed doomed.

When I carried Zezinho up to the community day-care center at the top of the hill, the Alto women who took turns caring for one another's children (in order to free themselves for part-time work in the cane fields or washing clothes) laughed at my efforts to save Ze, agreeing with Lourdes that here was a baby without a ghost of a chance. Leave him alone, they cautioned. It makes no sense to fight with death. But I did do battle with Ze, and after several weeks of force-feeding (malnourished babies lose their interest in food), Ze began to succumb to my ministrations. He acquired some flesh across his taut chest bones, learned to sit up, and even tried to smile. When he seemed well enough, I returned him to Lourdes in her miserable scrap-material lean-to, but not without guilt about what I had done. I wondered whether returning Ze was at all fair to Lourdes and to his little brother. But I was busy and washed my hands of the matter. And Lourdes did seem more interested in Ze now that he was looking more human.

When I returned in 1982, there was Lourdes among the women who formed my sample of Alto mothers—still struggling to put together some semblance of life for a now grown Ze and her five other surviving children. Much was made of my reunion with Ze in 1982, and everyone enjoyed retelling the story of Ze's rescue and of how his mother had given him up for dead. Ze would laugh the loudest when told how I had had to force-feed him like a fiesta turkey. There was no hint of guilt on the part of Lourdes and no resentment on the part of Ze. In fact, when questioned in private as to who was the best friend he ever had in life, Ze took a long drag on his cigarette and answered without a trace of irony, "Why my mother, of course." "But of course," I replied.

Part of learning how to mother in the Alto do Cruzeiro is learning when to let go of a child who shows that it "wants" to die or that it has no "knack" or no "taste" for life. Another part is learning when it is safe to let oneself love a child. Frequent child death remains a powerful shaper of maternal thinking and practice. In the absence of firm expectation that a child will survive, mother love as we conceptualize it (whether in popular terms or in the psychobiological notion of maternal bonding) is attenuated and delayed with consequences for infant survival. In an environment already precarious to young life, the emotional detachment of mothers toward some of their babies contributes even further to the spiral of high mortality—high fertility in a kind of macabre lock-step dance of death.

The average woman of the Alto experiences 9.5 pregnancies, 3.5 child deaths, and 1.5 stillbirths. Seventy percent of all child deaths in the Alto occur in the first six months of life, and 82 percent by the end of the first year. Of all deaths in the community each year, about 45 percent are of children under the age of five.

Women of the Alto distinguish between child deaths understood as natural (caused by diarrhea and communicable diseases) and those resulting from sorcery, the evil eye, or other magical or supernatural afflictions. They also recognize a large category of infant deaths seen as fated and inevitable. These hopeless cases are classified by mothers under the folk terminology "child sickness" or "child attack." Women say that there are at least fourteen different types of hopeless child sickness, but most can be subsumed under two categories—chronic and acute. The chronic cases refer to infants who are born small and wasted. They are deathly pale, mothers say, as well as weak and passive. They demonstrate no vital force, no liveliness. They do not suck vigorously; they hardly cry. Such babies can be this way at birth or they can be born sound but soon show no re-

sistance, no "fight" against the common crises of infancy: diarrhea, respiratory infections, tropical fevers.

The acute cases are those doomed infants who die suddenly and violently. They are taken by stealth overnight, often following convulsions that bring on head banging, shaking, grimacing, and shrieking. Women say it is horrible to look at such a baby. If the infant begins to foam at the mouth or gnash its teeth or go rigid with its eyes turned back inside its head, there is absolutely no hope. The infant is "put aside"—left alone—often on the floor in a back room, and allowed to die. These symptoms (which accompany high fevers, dehydration, third-stage malnutrition, and encephalitis) are equated by Alto women with madness, epilepsy, and worst of all, rabies, which is greatly feared and highly stigmatized.

Most of the infants presented to me as suffering from chronic child sickness were tiny, wasted famine victims, while those labeled as victims of acute child attack seemed to be infants suffering from the deliriums of high fever or the convulsions that can accompany electrolyte imbalance in dehydrated babies.

Local midwives and traditional healers, praying women, as they are called, advise Alto women on when to allow a baby to die. One midwife explained: "If I can see that a baby was born unfortuitously, I tell the mother that she need not wash the infant or give it a cleansing tea. I tell her just to dust the infant with baby powder and wait for it to die." Allowing nature to take its course is not seen as sinful by these often very devout Catholic women. Rather, it is understood as cooperating with God's plan.

Often I have been asked how consciously women of the Alto behave in this regard. I would have to say that consciousness is always shifting between allowed and disallowed levels of awareness. For example, I was awakened early one morning in 1987 by two neighborhood children who had been sent to fetch me to a hastily organized wake for a two-month-old infant whose mother I had unsuccessfully urged to breast-feed. The infant was being sustained on sugar water, which the mother referred to as *soro* (serum), using a medical term for the infant's starvation re-

gime in light of his chronic diarrhea. I had cautioned the mother that an infant could not live on *soro* forever.

The two girls urged me to console the young mother by telling her that it was "too bad" that her infant was so weak that Jesus had to take him. They were coaching me in proper Alto etiquette. I agreed, of course, but asked, "And what do *you* think?" Xoxa, the eleven-year-old, looked down at her dusty flip-flops and blurted out, "Oh, Dona Nanci, that baby never got enough to eat, but you must never say that!" And so the death of hungry babies remains one of the best kept secrets of life in Bom Jesus da Mata.

Most victims are waked quickly and with a minimum of ceremony. No tears are shed, and the neighborhood children form a tiny procession, carrying the baby to the town graveyard where it will join a multitude of others. Although a few fresh flowers may be scattered over the tiny grave, no stone or wooden cross will mark the place, and the same spot will be reused within a few months' time. The mother will never visit the grave, which soon becomes an anonymous one.

What, then, can be said of these women? What emotions, what sentiments motivate them? How are they able to do what, in fact, must be done? What does mother love mean in this inhospitable context? Are grief, mourning, and melancholia present, although deeply repressed? If so, where shall we look for them? And if not, how are we to understand the moral visions and moral sensibilities that guide their actions?

I have been criticized more than once for presenting an unflattering portrait of poor Brazilian women, women who are, after all, themselves the victims of severe social and institutional neglect. I have described these women as allowing some of their children to die, as if this were an unnatural and inhuman act rather than, as I would assert, the way any one of us might act, reasonably and rationally, under similarly desperate conditions. Perhaps I have not emphasized enough the real pathogens in this environment of high risk: poverty, deprivation, sexism, chronic hunger, and economic exploitation. If mother love is, as many psychologists and some feminists believe, a seemingly natural and universal maternal script, what does it mean to women for whom scarcity, loss, sickness, and deprivation have made that love frantic and robbed them of their grief, seeming to turn their hearts to stone?

Throughout much of human history—as in a great deal of the impoverished Third World today—women have had to give birth and to nurture children under ecological conditions and social arrangements hostile to child survival, as well as to their own well-being. Under circumstances of high childhood mortality, patterns of selective neglect and passive infanticide may be seen as active survival strategies.

They also seem to be fairly common practices historically and across cultures. In societies characterized by high childhood mortality and by a correspondingly high (replacement) fertility, cultural practices of infant and child care tend to be organized primarily around survival goals. But what this means is a pragmatic recognition that not all of one's children can be expected to live. The nervousness about child survival in areas of northeast Brazil, northern India, or Bangladesh, where a 30 percent or 40 percent mortality rate in the first years of life is common, can lead to forms of delayed attachment and a casual or benign neglect that serves to weed out the worst bets so as to enhance the life chances of healthier siblings, including those yet to be born. Practices similar to those that I am describing have been recorded for parts of Africa, India, and Central America.

Life in the Alto do Cruzeiro resembles nothing so much as a battlefield or an emergency room in an overcrowded inner-city public hospital. Consequently, mortality is guided by a kind of "lifeboat ethics," the morality of triage. The seemingly studied indifference toward the suffering of some of their infants, conveyed in such sayings as "little critters have no feelings," is understandable in light of these women's obligation to carry on with their reproductive and nurturing lives.

In their slowness to anthropomorphize and personalize their infants, everything is mobilized so as to prevent maternal overattachment and, therefore, grief at death. The bereaved mother is

told not to cry, that her tears will dampen the wings of her little angel so that she cannot fly up to her heavenly home. Grief at the death of an angel is not only inappropriate, it is a symptom of madness and of a profound lack of faith.

Infant death becomes routine in an environment in which death is anticipated and bets are hedged. While the routinization of death in the context of shantytown life is not hard to understand, and quite possible to empathize with, its routinization in the formal institutions of public life in Bom Jesus is not as easy to accept uncritically. Here the social production of indifference takes on a different, even a malevolent, cast.

In a society where triplicates of every form are required for the most banal events (registering a car, for example), the registration of infant and child death is informal, incomplete, and rapid. It requires no documentation, takes less than five minutes, and demands no witnesses other than office clerks. No questions are asked concerning the circumstances of the death, and the cause of death is left blank, unquestioned and unexamined. A neighbor, grandmother, older sibling, or common-law husband may register the death. Since most infants die at home, there is no question of a medical record.

From the registry office, the parent proceeds to the town hall, where the mayor will give him or her a voucher for a free baby coffin. The full-time municipal coffinmaker cannot tell you exactly how many baby coffins are dispatched each week. It varies, he says, with the seasons. There are more needed during the drought months and during the big festivals of Carnaval and Christmas and São Joao's Day because people are too busy, he supposes, to take their babies to the clinic. Record keeping is sloppy.

Similarly, there is a failure on the part of city-employed doctors working at two free clinics to recognize the malnutrition of babies who are weighed, measured, and immunized without comment and as if they were not, in fact, anemic, stunted, fussy, and irritated starvation babies. At best the mothers are told to pick up free vitamins or a health "tonic" at the municipal chambers. At worst, clinic personnel will give tranquilizers and sleeping pills

to quiet the hungry cries of "sick-to-death" Alto babies.

The church, too, contributes to the routinization of, and indifference toward, child death. Traditionally, the local Catholic church taught patience and resignation to domestic tragedies that were said to reveal the imponderable workings of God's will. If an infant died suddenly, it was because a particular saint had claimed the child. The infant would be an angel in the service of his or her heavenly patron. It would be wrong, a sign of a lack of faith, to weep for a child with such good fortune. The infant funeral was, in the past, an event celebrated with joy. Today, however, under the new regime of "liberation theology," the bells of N. S. das Dores parish church no longer peal for the death of Alto babies, and no priest accompanies the procession of angels to the cemetery where their bodies are disposed of casually and without ceremony. Children bury children in Bom Jesus da Mata. In this most Catholic of communities, the coffin is handed to the disabled and irritable municipal gravedigger, who often chides the children for one reason or another. It may be that the coffin is larger than expected and the gravedigger can find no appropriate space. The children do not wait for the gravedigger to complete his task. No prayers are recited and no sign of the cross made as the tiny coffin goes into its shallow grave.

When I asked the local priest, Padre Marcos, about the lack of church ceremony surrounding infant and childhood death today in Bom Jesus, he replied; "In the old days, child death was richly celebrated. But those were the baroque customs of a conservative church that wallowed in death and misery. The new church is a church of hope and joy. We no longer celebrate the death of child angels. We try to tell mothers that Jesus doesn't want all the dead babies they send him." Similarly, the new church has changed its baptismal customs, now often refusing to baptize dying babies brought to the back door of a church or rectory. The mothers are scolded by the church attendants and told to go home and take care of their sick babies. Baptism, they are told, is for the living; it is not to be confused with the sacrament of extreme unction, which is the anointing of the dying. And so it appears to the women of the Alto that even the church has turned away from them, denying the traditional comfort of folk Catholicism.

The contemporary Catholic church is caught in the clutches of a double bind. The new theology of liberation imagines a kingdom of God on earth based on justice and equality, a world without hunger, sickness, or childhood mortality. At the same time, the church has not changed its official position on sexuality and reproduction, including its sanctions against birth control, abortion, and sterilization. The padre of Bom Jesus da Mata recognizes this contradiction intuitively, although he shies away from discussions on the topic, saying that he prefers to leave questions of family planning to the discretion and the "good consciences" of his impoverished parishioners. But this, of course, sidesteps the extent to which those good consciences have been shaped by traditional church teachings in Bom Jesus, especially by his recent predeces-

sors. Hence, we can begin to see that the seeming indifference of Alto mothers toward the death of some of their infants is but a pale reflection of the official indifference of church and state to the plight of poor women and children.

Nonetheless, the women of Bom Jesus are survivors. One woman, Biu, told me her life history, returning again and again to the themes of child death, her first husband's suicide, abandonment by her father and later by her second husband, and all the other losses and disappointments she had suffered in her long forty-five years. She concluded with great force, reflecting on the days of Carnaval '88 that were fast approaching:

> No, Dona Nanci, I won't cry, and I won't waste my life thinking about it from morning to night.... Can I argue with God for the state that I'm in? No! And so I'll dance and I'll jump and I'll play Carnaval! And yes, I'll laugh and people will wonder at a *pobre* like me who can have such a good time.

And no one did blame Biu for dancing in the streets during the four days of Carnaval—not even on Ash Wednesday, the day following Carnaval '88 when we all assembled hurriedly to assist in the burial of Mercea, Biu's beloved *casula*, her last-born daughter who had died at home of pneumonia during the festivities. The rest of the family barely had time to change out of their costumes. Severino, the child's uncle and godfather, sprinkled holy water over the little angel while he prayed: "Mercea, I don't know whether you were called, taken, or thrown out of this world. But look down at us from your heavenly home with tenderness, with pity, and with mercy." So be it.

Nancy Scheper-Hughes is a professor in the Department of Anthropology at the University of California, Berkeley. She has written Death Without Weeping: Violence of Everyday Life in Brazil *(1992).*

Our Babies, Ourselves

By Meredith F. Small

During one of his many trips to Gusii-land in southwestern Kenya, anthropologist Robert LeVine tried an experiment: he showed a group of Gusii mothers a videotape of middle-class American women tending their babies. The Gusii mothers were appalled. Why does that mother ignore the cries of her unhappy baby during a simple diaper change? And how come that grandmother does nothing to soothe the screaming baby in her lap? These American women, the Gusii concluded, are clearly incompetent

mothers. In response, the same charge might be leveled at the Gusii by American mothers. What mother hands over her tiny infant to a six-year-old sister and expects the older child to provide adequate care? And why don't those Gusii women spend more time talking to their babies, so that they will grow up smart?

Both culture—the traditional way of doing things in a particular society—and individual experience guide parents in their tasks. When a father chooses to pick up his newborn and not let it cry,

when a mother decides to bottle-feed on a schedule rather than breast-feed on demand, when a couple bring the newborn into their bed at night, they are prompted by what they believe to be the best methods of caregiving.

For decades, anthropologists have been recording how children are raised in different societies. At first, the major goals were to describe parental roles and understand how child-rearing practices and rituals helped to generate adult per-

---

Gusii Survival Skills

By Robert A. LeVine

Farming peoples of subSaharan Africa have long faced the grim reality that many babies fail to survive, often succumbing to gastrointestinal diseases, malaria, or other infections. In the 1970s, when I lived among the Gusii in a small town in southwestern Kenya, infant mortality in that nation was on the decline but was still high—about eighty deaths per thousand live births during the first years, compared with about ten in the United States at that time and six to eight in Western Europe.

The Gusii grew corn, millet, and cash crops such as coffee and tea. Women handled the more routine tasks of cultivation, food processing, and trading, while men were supervisors or entrepreneurs. Many men worked at jobs outside the village, in urban centers or on plantations. The society was

polygamous, with perhaps 10 percent of the men having two or more wives. A woman was expected to give birth every two years, from marriage to menopause, and the average married women bore about ten live children—one of the highest fertility rates in the world.

Nursing mothers slept alone with a new infant for fifteen months to insure its health. For the first three to six months, the Gusii mothers were especially vigilant for signs of ill health or slow growth, and they were quick to nurture unusually small or sick infants by feeding and holding them more often. Mothers whose newborns were deemed particularly at risk—including twins and those born prematurely—entered a ritual seclusion for several weeks, staying with their infants in a hut with a constant fire.

Mothers kept infants from crying in the early months by holding them constantly and being quick to comfort them. After three to six months—if the baby was growing normally—mothers began to entrust the baby to the care of other children (usually six to twelve years old) in order to pursue tasks that helped support the family. Fathers did not take care of infants, for this was not a traditional male activity.

Because they were so worried about their children's survival, Gusii parents did not explicitly strive to foster cognitive, social, and emotional development. These needs were not neglected, however, because from birth Gusii babies entered an active and responsive interpersonal environment, first with their mothers and young caregivers, and later as part of a group of children.

An Infant's Three Rs

By Sara Harkness and Charles M. Super

You are an American visitor spending a morning in a pleasant middle-class Dutch home to observe the normal routine of a mother and her six-month-old baby. The mother made sure you got there by 8:30 to witness the morning bath, an opportunity for playful interaction with the baby. The baby was then dressed in cozy warm clothes, her hair brushed and styled with a tiny curlicue atop her head. The mother gave her the midmorning bottle, then sang to her and played patty-cake for a few minutes before placing her in the playpen to entertain herself with a mobile while the mother attended to other things nearby. Now, about half an hour later, the baby is beginning to get fussy.

The mother watches for a minute, then offers a toy and turns away. The baby again begins to fuss. "Seems bored and in need of attention," you think. But the mother looks at the baby sympathetically and in a soothing voice says, "Oh, are you tired?" Without further ado she picks up the baby, carries her upstairs, tucks her into her crib, and pulls down the shades. To your surprise, the baby fusses for only a few more moments, then is quiet. The mother returns looking serene. "She needs plenty of sleep in order to grow," she explains. "When she doesn't have her nap or go to bed on time, we can always tell the difference—she's not so happy and playful."

Different patterns in infant sleep can be found in Western societies that seem quite similar to those of the United States. We discovered the "three R's" of Dutch child rearing—*rust* (rest), *regelmaat* (regularity) and *reinheid* (cleanliness)—while doing research on a

sample of sixty families with infants or young children in a middle-class community near Leiden and Amsterdam, the sort of community typical of Dutch life styles in all but the big cities nowadays. At six months, the Dutch babies were sleeping more than a comparison group of American babies—a total of fifteen hours per day compared with thirteen hours for the Americans. While awake at home, the Dutch babies were more often left to play quietly in their playpens or infant seats. A daily ride in the baby carriage provided time for the baby to look around at the passing scene or to doze peacefully. If the mother needed to go out for a while without the baby, she could leave it alone in bed for a short period or time her outing with the baby's nap time and ask a neighbor to monitor with a "baby phone."

To understand how Dutch families manage to establish such a restful routine by the time their babies are six months old, we made a second research visit to the same community. We found that by two weeks of age, the Dutch babies were already sleeping more than same-age American babies. In fact, a dilemma for some Dutch parents was whether to wake the baby after eight hours, as instructed by the local health care providers, or let them sleep longer. The main method for establishing and maintaining this pattern was to create a calm, regular, and restful environment for the infant throughout the day.

Far from worrying about providing "adequate stimulation," these mothers were conscientious about avoiding overstimulation in the form of late family outings, disruptions in the regularity

of eating and sleeping, or too many things to look at or listen to. Few parents were troubled by their babies' nighttime sleep routines. Babies's feeding schedules were structured following the guidelines of the local baby clinic (a national service). If a baby continued to wake up at night when feeding was no longer considered necessary, the mother (or father) would most commonly give it a pacifier and a little back rub to help it get back to sleep. Only in rare instances did parents find themselves forced to choose between letting the baby scream and allowing too much night waking.

Many aspects of Dutch society support the three Rs throughout infancy and childhood—for example, shopping is close to home, and families usually have neighbors and relatives nearby who are available to help out with child care. The small scale of neighborhoods and a network of bicycle paths provide local play sites and a safe way for children to get around easily on their own (no "soccer moms" are needed for daily transportation!). Work sites for both fathers and mothers are also generally close to home, and there are many flexible or part-time job arrangements.

National policies for health and other social benefits insure universal coverage regardless of one's employment status, and the principle of the "family wage" has prevailed in labor relations so that mothers of infants and young children rarely work more than part-time, if at all. In many ways, the three Rs of Dutch child rearing are just one aspect of a calm and unhurried life style for the whole family.

sonality. In the 1950s, for example, John and Beatrice Whiting, and their colleagues at Harvard, Yale, and Cornell Universities, launched a major comparative study of childhood, looking at six varied communities in different regions: Okinawa, the Philippines, northern India, Kenya, Mexico, and New

England. They showed that communal expectations play a major role in setting parenting styles, which in turn play a part in shaping children to become accepted adults.

More recent work by anthropologists and child-development researchers has shown that parents readily accept their

society's prevailing ideology on how babies should be treated, usually because it makes sense in their environmental or social circumstances. In the United States, for example, where individualism is valued, parents do not hold babies as much as in other cultures, and they place them in rooms of their own to

Doctor's Orders

By Edward Z. Tronick

In Boston, a pediatric resident is experiencing a vague sense of disquiet as she interviews a Puerto Rican mother who has brought her baby in for a checkup. When she is at work, the mother explains, the two older children, ages six and nine, take care of the two younger ones, a two-year-old and the three-month-old baby. Warning bells go off for the resident: young children cannot possibly be sensitive to the needs of babies and toddlers. And yet the baby is thriving; he is well over the ninetieth percentile in weight and height and is full of smiles.

The resident questions the mother in detail: How is the baby fed? Is the apartment safe for a two-year-old? The responses are all reassuring, but the resident nonetheless launches into a lecture on the importance of the mother to normal infant development. The mother falls silent, and the resident is now convinced that something is seriously wrong. And something is—the resident's model of child care.

The resident subscribes to what I call the "continuous care and contact" model of parenting, which demands a high level of contact, frequent feeding, and constant supervision, with almost all care provided by the mother. According to this model, a mother should also enhance cognitive development with play and verbal engagement. The pediatric resident is comfortable with this formula—she is not even conscious of it—because she was raised this way and treats her own child in the same manner. But at the Child Development Unit of Children's Hospital in Boston, which I direct, I want residents to abandon the idea that there is only one way to raise a child. Not to do so may interfere with patient care.

Many models of parenting are valid. Among Efe foragers of Congo's Ituri Forest, for example, a newborn is routinely cared for by several people. Babies are even nursed by many women. But few individuals ever play with the infant; as far as the Efe are concerned, the baby's job is to sleep.

In Peru, the Quechua swaddle their infants in a pouch of blankets that the mother, or a child caretaker, carries on her back. Inside the pouch, the infant cannot move, and its eyes are covered. Quechua babies are nursed in a perfunctory fashion, with three or four hours between feedings.

As I explain to novice pediatricians, such practices do not fit the continuous care and contact model; yet these babies grow up just fine. But my residents see these cultures as exotic, not relevant to the industrialized world. And so I follow up with examples closer to home: Dutch parents who leave an infant alone in order to go shopping, sometimes pinning the child's shirt to the bed to keep the baby on its back; or Japanese mothers who periodically wake a sleeping infant to teach the child who is in charge. The questions soon follow. "How could a mother leave her infant alone?" "Why would a parent ever want to wake up a sleeping baby?"

The data from cross-cultural studies indicate that child-care practices vary, and that these styles aim to make the child into a culturally appropriate adult. The Efe make future Efe. The resident makes future residents. A doctor who has a vague sense that something is wrong with how someone cares for a baby may first need to explore his or her own assumptions, the hidden "shoulds" that are based solely on tradition. Of course, pediatric residents must make sure children are cared for responsibly. I know I have helped residents broaden their views when their lectures on good mothering are replaced by such comments as "What a gorgeous baby! I can't imagine how you manage both work and three others at home!"

sleep. Pediatricians and parents alike often say this fosters independence and self-reliance. Japanese parents, in contrast, believe that individuals should be well integrated into society, and so they "indulge" their babies: Japanese infants are held more often, not left to cry, and sleep with their parents. Efe parents in Congo believe even more in a communal life, and their infants are regularly nursed, held, and comforted by any number of group members, not just parents. Whether such practices help form the anticipated adult personality traits remains to be shown, however.

Recently, a group of anthropologists, child-development experts, and pediatricians have taken the cross-cultural approach in a new direction by investigating how differing parenting styles affect infant health and growth. Instead of emphasizing the development of adult personality, these researchers, who call themselves ethnopediatricians, focus on the child as an organism. Ethnopediatricians see the human infant as a product of evolution, geared to enter a particular environment of care. What an infant actually gets is a compromise, as parents are pulled by their offspring's needs and pushed by social and personal expectations.

Compared with offspring of many other mammals, primate infants are dependent and vulnerable. Baby monkeys and apes stay close to the mother's body, clinging to her stomach or riding on her back, and nursing at will. They are protected in this way for many months, until they develop enough motor and cogni-

The Crying Game

By Ronald G. Barr

All normal human infants cry, although they vary a great deal in how much. A mysterious and still unexplained phenomenon is that crying tends to increase in the first few weeks of life, peaks in the second or third month, and then decreases. Some babies in the United States cry so much during the peak period—often in excess of three hours a day—and seem so difficult to soothe that parents come to doubt their nurturing skills or begin to fear that their offspring is suffering from a painful disease. Some mothers discontinue nursing and switch to bottle-feeding because they believe their breast milk is insufficiently nutritious and that their infants are always hungry. In extreme cases, the crying may provoke physical abuse, sometimes even precipitating the infant's death.

A look at another culture, the !Kung San hunter-gatherers of southern Africa, provides us with an opportunity to see whether caregiving strategies have any effect on infant crying. Both the !Kung San and Western infants escalate their crying during the early weeks of life, with a similar peak at two or three months. A comparison of Dutch, American, and !Kung San infants shows that the number of individual crying episodes are virtually identical. What differs is their length: !Kung San infants cry about half as long as Western babies. This implies that caregiving can influence only some aspects of crying, such as duration.

What is particularly striking about child-rearing among the !Kung San is that infants are in constant contact with a caregiver; they are carried or held most of the time, are usually in an upright position, and are breast-fed about four times an hour for one to two minutes at a time. Furthermore, the mother almost always responds to the smallest cry or fret within ten seconds.

I believe that crying was adaptive for our ancestors. As seen in the contemporary !Kung San, crying probably elicited a quick response, and thus consisted of frequent but relatively short episodes. This pattern helped keep an adult close by to provide adequate nutrition as well as protection from predators. I have also argued that crying helped an infant forge a strong attachment with the mother and—because new pregnancies are delayed by the prolongation of frequent nursing—secure more of her caregiving resources.

In the United States, where the threat of predation has receded and adequate nutrition is usually available even without breast-feeding, crying may be less adaptive. In any case, caregiving in the United States may be viewed as a cultural experiment in which the infant is relatively more separated—and separable—from the mother, both in terms of frequency of contact and actual distance.

The Western strategy is advantageous when the mother's employment outside of the home and away from the baby is necessary to sustain family resources. But the trade-off seems to be an increase in the length of crying bouts.

tive skills to move about. Human infants are at the extreme: virtually helpless as newborns, they need twelve months just to learn to walk and years of social learning before they can function on their own.

Dependence during infancy is the price we pay for being hominids, members of the group of upright-walking primates that includes humans and their extinct relatives. Four million years ago, when our ancestors became bipedal, the hominid pelvis underwent a necessary renovation. At first, this new pelvic architecture presented no problem during birth because the early hominids, known as australopithecines, still had rather small brains, one-third the present size. But starting about 1.5 million years ago, human brain size ballooned. Hominid babies now had to twist and bend to pass through the birth canal, and more important, birth had to be triggered before the skull grew too big.

As a result, the human infant is born neurologically unfinished and unable to coordinate muscle movement. Natural selection has compensated for this by favoring a close adult-infant tie that lasts years and goes beyond meeting the needs of food and shelter. In a sense, the human baby is not isolated but is part of a physiologically and emotionally entwined dyad of infant and caregiver. The adult might be male or female, a birth or adoptive parent, as long as at least one person is attuned to the infant's needs.

The signs of this interrelationship are many. Through conditioning, a mother's breast milk often begins to flow at the sound of her own infant's cries, even before the nipple is stimulated. New mothers also easily recognize the cries (and smells) of their infants over those of other babies. For their part, newborns recognize their own mother's voice and prefer it over others. One experiment showed that a baby's heart rate quickly synchronizes with Mom's or Dad's, but not with that of a friendly stranger. Babies are also predisposed to be socially engaged with caregivers. From birth, infants move their bodies in synchrony with adult speech and the general nature of language. Babies quickly recognize the arrangement of a human face—two eyes, a nose, and a mouth in the right place—over other more Picasso-like rearrangements. And mothers and infants will position themselves face-to-face when they lie down to sleep.

Babies and mothers seem to follow a typical pattern of play, a coordinated waltz that moves from attention to inattention and back again. This innate social connection was tested experimentally by

When to Wean

By Katherine A. Dettwyler

Breast-feeding in humans is a biological process grounded in our mammalian ancestry. It is also an activity modified by social and cultural constraints, including a mother's everyday work schedule and a variety of beliefs about personal autonomy, the proper relationship between mother and child (or between mother and father), and infant health and nutrition. The same may be said of the termination of breast-feeding, or weaning.

In the United States, children are commonly bottle-fed from birth or weaned within a few months. But in some societies, children as old as four or five years may still be nursed. The American Academy of Pediatrics currently advises breast-feeding for a minimum of one year (this may be revised upward), and the World Health Organization recommends two years or more. Amid conflicting advice, many wonder how long breast-feeding should last to provide an infant with optimal nutrition and health.

Nonhuman primates and other mammals give us some clues as to what the "natural" age of weaning would be if humans were less bound by cultural norms. Compared with most other orders of placental mammals, primates (including humans) have longer life spans and spend more time at each life stage, such as gestation, infant dependency, and puberty. Within the primate order itself, the trend in longevity increases from smaller-bodied, smaller-brained, often solitary prosimians through the larger-bodied, larger-brained, and usually social apes and humans. Gestation, for instance, is eighteen weeks in lemurs, twenty-four weeks in macaques, thirty-three weeks in chimpanzees, and thirty-eight weeks in humans.

Studies of nonhuman primates offer a number of different means of estimating the natural time for human weaning. First, large-bodied primates wean their offspring some months after the young have quadrupled their birth weight. In modern humans, this weight milestone is passed at about two and a half to three years of age. Second, like many other mammals, primate offspring tend to be weaned when they have attained about one third of their adult weight; humans reach this level between four and seven years of age. Third, in all species studied so far, primates also wean their offspring at the time the first permanent molars erupt; this occurs at five and a half to six years in modern humans. Fourth, in chimpanzees and gorillas, breast-feeding usually lasts about six times the duration of gestation. On this basis, a human breast-feeding would be projected to continue for four and a half years.

Taken together, these and other projections suggest that somewhat more than two and a half years is the natural minimum age of weaning for humans and seven years the maximum age, well into childhood. The high end of this range, six to seven years, closely matches both the completion of human brain growth and the maturation of the child's immune system.

In many non-Western cultures, children are routinely nursed for three to five years. Incidentally, this practice inhibits ovulation in the mother, providing a natural mechanism of family planning. Even in the United States, a significant number of children are breast-fed beyond three years of age. While not all women are able or willing to nurse each of their children for many years, those who do should be encouraged and supported. Health care professionals, family, friends, and nosy neighbors should be reassured that "extended" breast-feeding, for as long as seven years, appears physiologically normal and natural.

Substantial evidence is already available to suggest that curtailing the duration of breast-feeding far below two and a half years—when the human child has evolved to expect more—can be deleterious. Every study that includes the duration of breast-feeding as a variable shows that, on average, the longer a baby is nursed, the better its health and cognitive development. For example, breast-fed children have fewer allergies, fewer ear infections, and less diarrhea, and their risk for sudden infant death syndrome (a rare but devastating occurrence) is lower. Breast-fed children also have higher cognitive test scores and lower incidence of attention deficit hyperactivity disorder.

In many cases, specific biochemical constituents of breast milk have been identified that either protect directly against disease or help the child's body develop its own defense system. For example, in the case of many viral diseases, the baby brings the virus to the mother, and her gut-wall cells manufacture specific antibodies against the virus, which then travel to the mammary glands and go back to the baby. The docosahesanoic acid in breast milk may be responsible for improved cognitive and attention functions. And the infant's exposure to the hormones and cholesterol in the milk appears to condition the body, reducing the risk of heart disease and breast cancer in later years. These and other discoveries show that breast-feeding serves functions for which no simple substitute is available.

Jeffrey Cohn and Edward Tronick in a series of three-minute laboratory experiments at the University of Massachu-setts, in which they asked mothers to act depressed and not respond to baby's cues. When faced with a suddenly unre-sponsive mother, a baby repeatedly reaches out and flaps around, trying to catch her eye. When this tactic does not

Bedtime Story

By James J. McKenna

For as far back as you care to go, mothers have followed the protective and convenient practice of sleeping with their infants. Even now, for the vast majority of people across the globe, "cosleeping" and nighttime breast-feeding remain inseparable practices. Only in the past 200 years, and mostly in Western industrialized societies, have parents considered it normal and biologically appropriate for a mother and infant to sleep apart.

In the sleep laboratory at the University of California's Irvine School of Medicine, my colleagues and I observed mother-infant pairs as they slept both apart and together over three consecutive nights. Using a polygraph, we recorded the mother's and infant's heart rates, brain waves (EEGs), breathing, body temperature, and episodes of nursing. Infrared video photography simultaneously monitored their behavior.

We found that bed-sharing infants face their mothers for most of the night and that both mother and infants are highly responsive to each other's movements, wake more frequently, and spend more time in lighter stages of sleep than they do while sleeping alone. Bed-sharing infants nurse almost twice as often, and three times as long per bout, than they do when sleeping alone. But they rarely cry. Mothers who routinely sleep with their infants get at least as much sleep as mothers who sleep without them.

In addition to providing more nighttime nourishment and greater protection, sleeping with the mother supplies the infant with a steady stream of sensations of the mother's presence, including touch, smell, movement, and warmth. These stimuli can perhaps even compensate for the human infant's extreme neurological immaturity at birth.

Cosleeping might also turn out to give some babies protection from sudden infant death syndrome (SIDS), a heartbreaking and enigmatic killer. Cosleeping infants nurse more often, sleep more lightly, and have practice responding to maternal arousals. Arousal deficiencies are suspected in some SIDS deaths, and long periods in deep sleep may exacerbate this problem. Perhaps the physiological changes induced by cosleeping, especially when combined with nighttime breast-feeding, can benefit some infants by helping them sleep more lightly. At the same time, cosleeping makes it easier for a mother to detect and respond to an infant in crisis. Rethinking another sleeping practice has already shown a dramatic effect: In the United States, SIDS rates fell at least 30 percent after 1992, when the American Academy of Pediatrics recommended placing sleeping babies on their backs, rather than face down.

The effect of cosleeping on SIDS remains to be proved, so it would be premature to recommend it as the best arrangement for all families. The possible hazards of cosleeping must also be assessed. Is the environment otherwise safe, with appropriate bedding materials? Do the parents smoke? Do they use drugs or alcohol? (These appear to be the main factors in those rare cases in which a mother inadvertently smothers her child.) Since cosleeping was the ancestral condition, the future for our infants may well entail a borrowing back from ancient ways.

work, the baby gives up, turning away and going limp. And when the mother begins to respond again, it takes thirty seconds for the baby to reengage.

Given that human infants arrive in a state of dependency, ethnopediatricians have sought to define the care required to meet their physical, cognitive, and emotional needs. They assume there must be ways to treat babies that have proved adaptive over time and are therefore likely to be most appropriate. Surveys of parenting in different societies reveal broad patterns. In almost all cultures, infants sleep with their parents in the same room and most often in the same bed. At all other times, infants are usually carried. Caregivers also usually respond quickly to infant cries; mothers most often by offering the breast. Since most hunter-gatherer groups also follow this overall style, this is probably the ancestral pattern. If there is an exception to these generalizations, it is the industrialized West.

Nuances of caretaking, however, do vary with particular social situations. !Kung San mothers of Botswana usually carry their infants on gathering expeditions, while the forest-living Ache of Paraguay, also hunters and gatherers, usually leave infants in camp while they gather. Gusii mothers working in garden plots leave their babies in the care of older children, while working mothers in the West may turn to unrelated adults. Such choices have physiological or behavioral consequences for the infant. As parents navigate between infant needs and the constraints of making a life, they may face a series of trade-offs that set the caregiver-infant dyad at odds. The areas of greatest controversy are breast-feeding, crying, and sleep—the major preoccupations of babies and their parents.

Strapped to their mothers' sides or backs in traditional fashion, human infants have quick access to the breast. Easy access makes sense because of the nature of human milk. Compared with that of other mammals, primate milk is relatively low in fat and protein but high in carbohydrates. Such milk is biologically suitable if the infant can nurse on a frequent basis. Most Western babies are fed in a somewhat different way. At least half are bottle-fed from birth, while others are weaned from breast to bottle after only a few months. And most—whether nursed or bottle-fed—are fed at scheduled times, waiting hours between feedings. Long intervals in nursing disrupt the manufacture of breast milk, making it still lower in fat and thus less satisfying the next time the nipple is offered. And so crying over food and even the struggles of weaning result from the infant's unfulfilled expectations.

Sleep is also a major issue for new parents. In the West, babies are encouraged to sleep all through the night as soon as possible. And when infants do not do so, they merit the label "sleep problem" from both parents and pediatricians. But infants seem predisposed to sleep rather lightly, waking many times during the night. And while sleeping close to an adult allows infants to nurse more often and may have other beneficial effects, Westerners usually expect babies to sleep alone. This practice has roots in ecclesiastical laws enacted to protect against the smothering of infants by "lying over"—often a thinly disguised cover for infanticide—which was a concern in Europe beginning in the

Middle Ages. Solitary sleep is reinforced by the rather recent notion of parental privacy. Western parents are also often convinced that solitary sleep will mold strong character.

Infants' care is shaped by tradition, fads, science, and folk wisdom. Cross-cultural and evolutionary studies provide a useful perspective for parents and pediatricians as they sift through the alternatives. Where these insights fail to guide us, however, important clues are provided by the floppy but interactive babies themselves. Grinning when we talk to them, crying in distress when left alone, sleeping best when close at heart, they teach us that growth is a cooperative venture.

RECOMMENDED READING

Parents' Cultural Belief Systems: Their Origins, Expressions, and Consequences, by Sara Harkness and Charles M. Super (Guilford Press, 1996)

Child Care and Culture: Lessons from Africa, by Robert A. LeVine et al. (Cambridge University Press, 1994)

Our Babies, Ourselves, by Meredith F. Small (Anchor Books/Doubleday, 1998)

Breastfeeding: Biocultural Perspectives, edited by Patricia Stuart-Macadam and Katherine A. Dettwyler (Aldine de Gruyler, 1995)

The Family Bed: An Age Old Concept in Childrearing, by Tine Thevenin (Avery Publishing Group, 1987)

Human Birth: An Evolutionary Perspective, by Wenda R. Trevathan (Aldine de Gruyler, 1987)

Six Cultures: Studies of Child Rearing, edited by Beatrice B. Whiting (John Wiley, 1963)

A professor of anthropology at Cornell University, **Meredith F. Small** became interested in "ethnopediatrics" in 1995, after interviewing anthropologist James J. McKenna on the subject of infant sleep. Trained as a primate behaviorist, Small has observed female mating behavior in three species of macaque monkeys. She now writes about science for a general audience; her book *Our Babies, Ourselves* is published by Anchor Books/Doubleday (1998). Her previous contributions to *Natural History* include "These Animals Think, Therefore…" (August 1996) and "Read in the Bone" (June 1997).

Reprinted with permission from *Natural History*, October 1997, pp. 42–51. © 1997 by Natural History Magazine.

Arranging a Marriage in India

Serena Nanda

John Jay College of Criminal Justice

Sister and doctor brother-in-law invite correspondence from North Indian professionals only, for a beautiful, talented, sophisticated, intelligent sister, 5'3", slim, M.A. in textile design, father a senior civil officer. Would prefer immigrant doctors, between 26–29 years. Reply with full details and returnable photo. A well-settled uncle invites matrimonial correspondence from slim, fair, educated South Indian girl, for his nephew, 25 years, smart, M.B.A., green card holder, 5'6". Full particulars with returnable photo appreciated.

Matrimonial Advertisements,
India Abroad

IN INDIA, ALMOST ALL MARRIAGES ARE arranged. Even among the educated middle classes in modern, urban India, marriage is as much a concern of the families as it is of the individuals. So customary is the practice of arranged marriage that there is a special name for a marriage which is not arranged: It is called a "love match."

On my first field trip to India, I met many young men and women whose parents were in the process of "getting them married." In many cases, the bride and groom would not meet each other before the marriage. At most they might meet for a brief conversation, and this meeting would take place only after their parents had decided that the match was suitable. Parents do not compel their children to marry a person who either marriage partner finds objectionable. But only after one match is refused will another be sought.

As a young American woman in India for the first time, I found this custom of arranged marriage oppressive. How could any intelligent young person agree to such a marriage without great reluctance? It was contrary to everything I believed about the importance of romantic love as the only basis of a happy marriage. It also clashed with my strongly held notions that the choice of such an intimate and permanent relationship could be made only by the individuals involved. Had anyone tried to arrange my marriage, I would have been defiant and rebellious!

> *Young men and women do not date and have very little social life involving members of the opposite sex.*

At the first opportunity, I began, with more curiosity than tact, to question the young people I met on how they felt about this practice. Sita, one of my young informants, was a college graduate with a degree in political science. She had been waiting for over a year while her parents were arranging a match for her. I found it difficult to accept the docile manner in which this well-educated young woman awaited the outcome of a process that would result in her spending the rest of her life with a man she hardly knew, a virtual stranger, picked out by her parents.

"How can you go along with this?" I asked her, in frustration and distress. "Don't you care who you marry?"

"Of course I care," she answered." This is why I must let my parents choose a boy for me. My marriage is too important to be arranged by such an inexperienced person as myself. In such matters, it is better to have my parents' guidance."

I had learned that young men and women in India do not date and have very little social life involving members of the opposite sex. Although I could not disagree with Sita's reasoning, I continued to pursue the subject.

"But how can you marry the first man you have ever met? Not only have you missed the fun of meeting a lot of different people, but you have not given yourself the chance to know who is the right man for you."

"Meeting with a lot of different people doesn't sound like any fun at all," Sita answered. "One hears that in America the girls are spending all their time worrying about whether they will meet a man and get married. Here we have the chance to enjoy our life and let our parents do this work and worrying for us."

She had me there. The high anxiety of the competition to "be popular" with the opposite sex certainly was the most prominent feature of life as an American teenager in the late fifties. The endless worrying about the rules that governed our behavior and about our popularity ratings sapped both our self-esteem and our enjoyment of adolescence. I reflected that absence of this competition in India most certainly may have contributed to the self-confidence and natural charm of so many of the young women I met.

And yet, the idea of marrying a perfect stranger, whom one did not know and did not "love," so offended my

American ideas of individualism and romanticism, that I persisted with my objections.

"I still can't imagine it," I said. "How can you agree to marry a man you hardly know?"

"But of course he will be known. My parents would never arrange a marriage for me without knowing all about the boy's family background. Naturally we will not rely only on what the family tells us. We will check the particulars out ourselves. No one will want their daughter to marry into a family that is not good. All these things we will know beforehand."

Impatiently, I responded, "Sita, I don't mean know the family, I mean, know the man. How can you marry someone you don't know personally and don't love? How can you think of spending your life with someone you may not even like?"

"If he is a good man, why should I not like him?" she said. "With you people, you know the boy so well before you marry, where will be the fun to get married? There will be no mystery and no romance. Here we have the whole of our married life to get to know and love our husband. "This way is better, is it not?"

Her response made further sense, and I began to have second thoughts on the matter. Indeed, during months of meeting many intelligent young Indian people, both male and female, who had the same ideas as Sita, I saw arranged marriages in a different light. I also saw the importance of the family in Indian life and realized that a couple who took their marriage into their own hands was taking a big risk, particularly if their families were irreconcilably opposed to the match. In a country where every important resource in life—a job, a house, a social circle—is gained through family connections, it seemed foolhardy to cut oneself off from a supportive social network and depend solely on one person for happiness and success.

Six years later I returned to India to again do fieldwork, this time among the middle class in Bombay, a modern, sophisticated city. From the experience of my earlier visit, I decided to include a study of arranged marriages in my project. By this time I had met many Indian couples whose marriages had been arranged and who seemed very happy. Particularly in contrast to the fate of many of my married friends in the United States who were already in the process of divorce, the positive aspects of arranged marriages appeared to me to outweigh the negatives. In fact, I thought I might even participate in arranging a marriage myself. I had been fairly successful in the United States in "fixing up" many of my friends, and I was confident that my matchmaking skills could be easily applied to this new situation, once I learned the basic rules. "After all," I thought, "how complicated can it be? People want pretty much the same things in a marriage whether it is in India or America."

> *In a society where divorce is still a scandal and where, in fact, the divorce rate is exceedingly low, an arranged marriage is the beginning of a lifetime relationship not just between the bride and groom but between their families as well.*

An opportunity presented itself almost immediately. A friend from my previous Indian trip was in the process of arranging for the marriage of her eldest son. In India there is a perceived shortage of "good boys," and since my friend's family was eminently respectable and the boy himself personable, well educated, and nice looking, I was sure that by the end of my year's fieldwork, we would have found a match.

The basic rule seems to be that a family's reputation is most important. It is understood that matches would be arranged only within the same caste and general social class, although some crossing of subcastes is permissible if the class positions of the bride's and groom's families are similar. Although dowry is now prohibited by law in India, extensive gift exchanges took place with every marriage. Even when the boy's family do not "make demands," every girl's family nevertheless feels the obligation to give the traditional gifts, to the girl, to the boy, and to the boy's family. Particularly when the couple would be living in the joint family—that is, with the boy's parents and his married brothers and their families, as well as with unmarried siblings—which is still very common even among the urban, upper-middle class in India, the girls' parents are anxious to establish smooth relations between their family and that of the boy. Offering the proper gifts, even when not called "dowry," is often an important factor in influencing the relationship between the bride's and groom's families and perhaps, also, the treatment of the bride in her new home.

In a society where divorce is still a scandal and where, in fact, the divorce rate is exceedingly low, an arranged marriage is the beginning of a lifetime relationship not just between the bride and groom but between their families as well. Thus, while a girl's looks are important, her character is even more so, for she is being judged as a prospective daughter-in-law as much as a prospective bride. Where she would be living in a joint family, as was the case with my friend, the girls's ability to get along harmoniously in a family is perhaps the single most important quality in assessing her suitability.

My friend is a highly esteemed wife, mother, and daughter-in-law. She is religious, soft-spoken, modest, and deferential. She rarely gossips and never quarrels, two qualities highly desirable in a woman. A family that has the reputation for gossip and conflict among its womenfolk will not find it easy to get good wives for their sons. Parents will not want to send their daughter to a house in which there is conflict.

My friend's family were originally from North India. They had lived in Bombay, where her husband owned a business, for forty years. The family had delayed in seeking a match for their eldest son because he had been an Air Force pilot for several years, stationed in such remote places that it had seemed fruitless to try to find a girl who would be willing to accompany him. In their social class, a military career, despite its economic security, has little prestige and is considered a drawback in finding a suitable bride. Many families would not allow their daughters to marry a man in an occupation so potentially dangerous and which requires so much moving around.

The son had recently left the military and joined his father's business. Since he was a college graduate, modern, and well traveled, from such a good family, and, I thought, quite handsome, it seemed to me that he, or rather his family, was in a position to pick and choose. I said as much to my friend.

While she agreed that there were many advantages on their side, she also said, "We must keep in mind that my son is both short and dark; these are drawbacks in finding the right match." While the boy's height had not escaped my notice, "dark" seemed to me inaccurate; I would have called him "wheat" colored perhaps, and in any case, I did not realize that color would be a consideration. I discovered, however, that while a boy's skin color is a less important consideration than a girl's, it is still a factor.

An important source of contacts in trying to arrange her son's marriage was my friend's social club in Bombay. Many of the women had daughters of the right age, and some had already expressed an interest in my friend's son. I was most enthusiastic about the possibilities of one particular family who had five daughters, all of whom were pretty, demure, and well educated. Their mother had told my friend, "You can have your pick for your son, whichever one of my daughters appeals to you most."

I saw a match in sight. "Surely," I said to my friend, "we will find one there. Let's go visit and make our choice." But my friend held back; she did not seem to share my enthusiasm, for reasons I could not then fathom.

When I kept pressing for an explanation of her reluctance, she admitted, "See, Serena, here is the problem. The family has so many daughters, how will they be able to provide nicely for any of them? We are not making any demands, but still, with so many daughters to marry off, one wonders whether she will even be able to make a proper wedding. Since this is our eldest son, it's best if we marry him to a girl who is the only daughter, then the

wedding will truly be a gala affair." I argued that surely the quality of the girls themselves made up for any deficiency in the elaborateness of the wedding. My friend admitted this point but still seemed reluctant to proceed.

"Is there something else," I asked her, "some factor I have missed?" "Well," she finally said, "there is one other thing. They have one daughter already married and living in Bombay. The mother is always complaining to me that the girl's in-laws don't let her visit her own family often enough. So it makes me wonder, will she be that kind of mother who always wants her daughter at her own home? This will prevent the girl from adjusting to our house. It is not a good thing." And so, this family of five daughters was dropped as a possibility.

Somewhat disappointed, I nevertheless respected my friend's reasoning and geared up for the next prospect. This was also the daughter of a woman in my friend's social club. There was clear interest in this family and I could see why. The family's reputation was excellent; in fact, they came from a subcaste slightly higher than my friend's own. The girl, who was an only daughter, was pretty and well educated and had a brother studying in the United States. Yet, after expressing an interest to me in this family, all talk of them suddenly died down and the search began elsewhere.

"What happened to that girl as a prospect?" I asked one day. "You never mention her any more. She is so pretty and so educated, what did you find wrong?"

"She is too educated. We've decided against it. My husband's father saw the girl on the bus the other day and thought her forward. A girl who 'roams about' the city by herself is not the girl for our family." My disappointment this time was even greater, as I thought the son would have liked the girl very much. But then I thought, my friend is right, a girl who is going to live in a joint family cannot be too independent or she will make life miserable for everyone. I also learned that if the family of the girl has even a slightly higher social status than the family of the boy, the bride may think herself too good for them, and this too will cause problems. Later my friend admitted to me that this had been an impor-

tant factor in her decision not to pursue the match.

The next candidate was the daughter of a client of my friend's husband. When the client learned that the family was looking for a match for their son, he said, "Look no further, we have a daughter." This man then invited my friends to dinner to see the girl. He had already seen their son at the office and decided that "he liked the boy." We all went together for tea, rather than dinner—it was less of a commitment—and while we were there, the girl's mother showed us around the house. The girl was studying for her exams and was briefly introduced to us.

After we left, I was anxious to hear my friend's opinion. While her husband liked the family very much and was impressed with his client's business accomplishments and reputation, the wife didn't like the girl's looks. "She is short, no doubt, which is an important plus point, but she is also fat and wears glasses." My friend obviously thought she could do better for her son and asked her husband to make his excuses to his client by saying that they had decided to postpone the boy's marriage indefinitely.

"If a mistake is made we have not only ruined the life of our son or daughter, but we have spoiled the reputation of our family as well."

By this time almost six months had passed and I was becoming impatient. What I had thought would be an easy matter to arrange was turning out to be quite complicated. I began to believe that between my friend's desire for a girl who was modest enough to fit into her joint family, yet attractive and educated enough to be an acceptable partner for her son, she would not find anyone suitable. My friend laughed at my impatience: "Don't be so much in a hurry," she said. "You Americans want everything done so quickly. You get married quickly and then just as quickly get divorced. Here we take marriage more seriously. We must take all the factors into

Appendix

Further Reflections on Arranged Marriage...

This essay was written from the point of view of a family seeking a daughter-in-law. Arranged marriage looks somewhat different from the point of view of the bride and her family. Arranged marriage continues to be preferred, even among the more educated, Westernized sections of the Indian population. Many young women from these families still go along, more or less willingly, with the practice, and also with the specific choices of their families. Young women do get excited about the prospects of their marriage, but there is also ambivalence and increasing uncertainty, as the bride contemplates leaving the comfort and familiarity of her own home, where as a "temporary guest" she had often been indulged, to live among strangers. Even in the best situation she will now come under the close scrutiny of her husband's family. How she dresses, how she behaves, how she gets along with others, where she goes, how she spends her time, her domestic abilities—all of this and much more—will be observed and commented on by a whole new set of relations. Her interaction with her family of birth will be monitored and curtailed considerably. Not only will she leave their home, but with increasing geographic mobility, she may also live very far from them, perhaps even on another continent. Too much expression of her fondness for her own family, or her desire to visit them, may be interpreted as an inability to adjust to her new family, and may become a source of conflict. In an arranged marriage the burden of adjustment is clearly heavier for a woman than for a man. And that is in the best of situations.

In less happy circumstances, the bride may be a target of resentment and hostility from her husband's family, particularly her mother-in-law or her husband's unmarried sisters, for whom she is now a source of competition for the affection, loyalty, and economic resources of their son or brother. If she is psychologically, or even physically abused, her options are limited, as returning to her parents' home, or divorce, are still very stigmatized. For most Indians, marriage and motherhood are still considered the only suitable roles for a woman, even for those who have careers, and few women can comfortably contemplate remaining unmarried. Most families still consider "marrying off" their daughters as a compelling religious duty and social necessity. This increases a bride's sense of obligation to make the marriage a success, at whatever cost to her own personal happiness.

The vulnerability of a new bride may also be intensified by the issue of dowry, which although illegal, has become a more pressing issue in the consumer conscious society of contemporary urban India. In many cases, where a groom's family is not satisfied with the amount of dowry a bride brings to her marriage, the young bride will be constantly harassed to get her parents to give more. In extreme cases, the bride may even be murdered, and the murder disguised as an accident or suicide. This also offers the husband's family an opportunity to arrange another match for him, thus bringing in another dowry. This phenomena, called dowry death, calls attention not just to the "evils of dowry" but also to larger issues of the powerlessness of women as well.

Serena Nanda
March 1998

---

account. It is not enough for us to learn by our mistakes. This is too serious a business. If a mistake is made we have not only ruined the life of our son or daughter, but we have spoiled the reputation of our family as well. And that will make it much harder for their brothers and sisters to get married. So we must be very careful."

What she said was true and I promised myself to be more patient, though it was not easy. I had really hoped and expected that the match would be made before my year in India was up. But it was not to be. When I left India my friend seemed no further along in finding a suitable match for her son than when I had arrived.

Two years later, I returned to India and still my friend had not found a girl for her son. By this time, he was close to thirty, and I think she was a little worried. Since she knew I had friends all over India, and I was going to be there for a year, she asked me to "help her in this work" and keep an eye out for someone suitable. I was flattered that my judgment was respected, but knowing now how complicated the process was, I had lost my earlier confidence as a matchmaker. Nevertheless, I promised that I would try.

It was almost at the end of my year's stay in India that I met a family with a marriageable daughter whom I felt might be a good possibility for my friend's son. The girl's father was related to a good friend of mine and by coincidence came from the same village as my friend's husband. This new family had a successful business in a medium-sized city in central India and were from the same sub-caste as my friend. The daughter was pretty and chic; in fact, she had studied fashion design in college. Her parents would not allow her to go off by herself to any of the major cities in India where she could make a career, but they had compromised with her wish to work by allowing her to run a small dress-making boutique from their home. In spite of her desire to have a career, the daughter was both modest and home-loving and had had a traditional, sheltered upbringing. She had only one other sister, already married, and a brother who was in his father's business.

I mentioned the possibility of a match with my friend's son. The girl's parents were most interested. Although their daughter was not eager to marry just yet, the idea of living in Bombay—a sophisticated, extremely fashion-conscious city where she could continue her education in clothing design—was a great inducement. I gave the girl's father my friend's address and suggested that when they went to Bombay on some business or whatever, they look up the boy's family.

Returning to Bombay on my way to New York, I told my friend of this newly discovered possibility. She seemed to feel there was potential but, in spite of my urging, would not make any moves herself. She rather preferred to wait for the girl's family to call upon them. I hoped something would come of this introduction, though by now I had learned to rein in my optimism.

A year later I received a letter from my friend. The family had indeed come to visit Bombay, and their daughter and my friend's daughter, who were near in age, had become very good friends. During that year, the two girls had frequently visited each other. I thought things looked promising.

Last week I received an invitation to a wedding: My friend's son and the girl were getting married. Since I had found the match, my presence was particularly requested at the wedding. I was thrilled. Success at last! As I prepared to leave for India, I began thinking, "Now, my friend's younger son, who do I know who has a nice girl for him… ?"

Edited by Philip R. DeVita.

From *Stumbling Toward Truth: Anthropologists at Work,* edited by Philip R. DeVita, 2000, pp. 196–204. Published by Waveland Press. © 2000 by Serena Nanda. Reprinted by permission of the author.

Dowry Deaths In India

'Let only your corpse come out of that house'

Paul Mandelbaum

On the outskirts of Delhi, in the shadow of the famed Qutab Minar tower, lies the village of Saidulajab. Through its narrow rutted dirt alleyways, a local resident takes me to the home of his one-time neighbor, Manju Singh. It is there that he heard her cries of agony on July 10, 1996.

Enacting an elaborate pantomime, Manju's neighbor indicates, by pointing to the browned leaves of a backyard plant, the spot where he found her and from which he took her, in the back of his bicycle rickshaw, to a local clinic.

The next day, lying in South Delhi's Safdarjung Hospital with burns covering nearly her entire body, the twenty-seven-year-old regained consciousness long enough to tell a local police officer that her husband and in-laws had threatened to beat her the previous afternoon, haranguing her yet again over the inadequacy of her dowry. As she tried to escape—so alleges the police report—her husband and brother-in-law caught hold of her while her mother-in-law doused her with kerosene; then Manju's husband struck the match that would eventually kill her.

Manju's case is one of an alleged six thousand "dowry deaths" a year in India. The term typically refers to a newly-wed bride who, upon moving into her husband's family home, is harassed over the goods and cash she brought to the marriage, leading to her murder or suicide. Antidowry activists claim the actual death toll is much higher, and the British journal *Orbit* recently put the annual figure at fifteen thousand.

Twenty years ago, India's feminist leadership began sounding the alarm. Responding to a groundswell of pressure from women's groups and the media, in the mid-1980s India's Parliament passed sweeping amendments to the largely moribund Dowry Prohibition Act of 1961, as well as the Indian Evidence Act and the penal code. The new laws acknowledged a quasi-manslaughter crime called "dowry death," and placed the burden of proof on the accused in any situation where a bride dies unnaturally during the first seven years of marriage, if a history of dowry harassment can be shown. In the ensuing years, the violence seems only to have escalated.

As late as 1987, high concentrations of dowry-death cases were mostly confined to the corridor connecting Punjab, traditionally a very patriarchal and violent part of northwest India, to Delhi and, further east, Uttar Pradesh. But by the mid-1990s, significant per-capita concentrations of dowry death had infested half of India's thirty-two states and union territories.

Often the conflicts are not so much about material goods *per se* as about the family status such items represent. Sometimes, dowry conflicts may mask other underlying problems—infidelity, sexual incompatibility, for example—that are unthinkably intimate for many families to acknowledge and discuss.

In most cases of dowry death, the physical evidence is murky. Often a bride's death is staged to look like an accident—hence the popularity of burning.

Fire can obscure a variety of incriminating details, and the cheap kerosene stoves to which many Indian wives are virtually chained often do explode, providing offenders with a plausible scenario.

In the days before kerosene stoves, writes historian Veena Talwar Oldenburg, Indian brides fell down wells with suspicious regularity. Oldenburg has traced some of the roots of India's dowry problems to the British Raj and the economic pressures imposed by its agricultural tax system, which in turn pitted Indian farmers against one another. The parents of sons, according to Oldenburg, capitalized on the urgency felt by the parents of daughters to arrange a marriage by an acceptably early age. This urgency fueled a climate of extortion. Other cultural observers speculate that such a climate may have arrived earlier, when Hindu parents felt anxiety about protecting their daughters' honor from Muslim invaders.

In any case, modern-day dowry came to corrupt two ancient Hindu customs associated with arranged marriage. The first, *kanyadan*, called for enhancing the virgin bride with an array of jewels. The second, *stridhan*, provided the bride with a premortem inheritance from her parents. These two concepts merged and have mutated into a type of groom-price, now practiced not only by Hindus but also by some of their Muslim neighbors. Even some tribal groups who until recently preferred the inverse custom of bride-price have switched.

Today, Indian brides and their families feel compelled to buy their way into a marriage alliance with "gifts" of cash, jewels, and consumer goods for the in-laws' pleasure. This "marriage settlement" is often calculated in direct relationship to a groom's prospects. Grooms working for the elite Indian Administrative Service can sometimes command dowries equivalent to $100,000 or more. Indian grooms living in the United States seek compensation not only for their own self-perceived worth but for providing access to the American dream. In many cases, dowry is seen by both parties as an acknowledgment of the groom's desirability.

Manju Singh's parents felt obliged to present a significant endowment, even though she held a bachelor's degree from Delhi University while her fiancé was a village shopkeeper. Her father, Nawab Singh, has a thirty-one-item list of the bounty he gave, including 70,000 rupees (close to one year's salary), a scooter, a color TV, 224 grams of gold jewelry, 2 kilograms of silver, bedroom furnishings, and thirty-five suits of clothes for the groom's side. Several months after the wedding, he says, Manju's in-laws demanded a washing machine, a refrigerator, and 50,000 rupees. "So many things," the school teacher recalls for me harriedly over his lunch break. "I tried to give as much as I could." Nonetheless, he alleges, Manju's in-laws began to harass and beat her in a spiral of domestic violence leading to her death. "She was burned by them purposely for dowry," says Nawab Singh.

Even if the last quarter of the twentieth century did not create dowry death, several intersecting social and economic trends seem to have escalated the problem. For one, availability of a host of household appliances, as well as their increasing promotion on television have created a hunger among the lower-middle class and others who lack the purchasing power to afford what they are being encouraged to desire. The families of grooms have seized an opportunity, through negotiation of the customary premarital settlements, to acquire some of these items through dowry, leaving it to the bride's family to worry about the bills. At the same time, some brides' families have been doing quite well, so

well that they might wish to hide surpluses of hard currency from the tax authorities. They have seen dowry as a means to invest that money under the table and to secure their daughters a place in higher-status families. Ultimately, these two forms of dowry inflation have increased the likelihood that more and more brides' families will have a harder time fulfilling the terms of the marriage settlements they feel obliged to enter into, setting the stage for dire consequences.

The transience of the modern world has also put other pressures on arranged marriage. In the small southern town of Bangarapet, a village elder recalls for me the dowry negotiation he mediated on behalf of a local family. The prospective groom's father, visiting from New York, objected strenuously to the offer of three *lakhs*, or roughly $8,500, on the following grounds: "What do you think of me? What do you know about my status? I know the president of America. I know the president of India. What will be the state of my prestige if I collect three *lakhs* from you?"

While most Indian marriages are still made by parents as a way of ensuring a suitable match within an appropriate range of subcastes, as more Indians move from the countryside to teeming cities or abroad in pursuit of opportunity, chances have grown that a bride would marry into a family geographically removed from and previously unknown to her own parents.

Increasingly, today's marriage alliances are made blindly through brokers, classified ads, and Internet services. When it was time to marry off his twenty-nine-year-old daughter Sangeeta, who had completed her Ph.D. in solid-state physics, Bimal Agarwal of Kanpur started replying to ads in the *Sunday Times of India*. Turning to the June 27, 1993, classified section, he found one looking for a "beautiful educated match" for a "Kanpur-based handsome boy 29/173/5000 employed leading industrial house only son of senior business executive with own residence...."

Agarwal telephoned the father of this twenty-nine-year-old businessman earning 5,000 rupees per month, and over the next four days the families met several

times to negotiate marriage expenditures. On July 1, Sangeeta was engaged.

As her father and I converse on his apartment balcony, I am distracted by the anachronism of a laser eye-surgery center located across a narrow dirt street crowded with sleeping pigs. A passing woman carries atop her head the dried cow chips commonly used for cooking fires. When I get around to asking Mr. Agarwal if his daughter's engagement was decided hastily, he assures me it was quite typical.

Problems, however, began at the wedding itself, when, alleges Agarwal, the groom's family demanded a car. He adds that the ensuing pressure became a nightmare for Sangeeta. One day, roughly five months after her wedding, she and her father met for lunch. "She was weeping," he recalls. "She said, 'Father, go and talk to those people.'" But he had recently tried that, he says, and was reluctant to intervene again so soon.

Two days later, Sangeeta was found dead from "asphyxiation as a result of hanging," according to a postmortem report.

Her husband, Sanjay Goel, points out for me the ceiling fan in his family's middle-class living room. He maintains that Sangeeta committed suicide not because of any dowry demands but possibly because she had no desire to marry him in the first place.

Sangeeta's father, however, alleges that not only did dowry play a role in her death, but that she was murdered. The courts have yet to settle the case. Whatever the outcome, it seems fair to say that Sangeeta Goel, like many Indian women today, was burdened with the worst of two worlds: the marriage mandate of tradition combined with the compassionless anonymity of modern-day life.

Meanwhile, the day-to-day struggles fall to a handful of privately run women's shelters. One of the best known, Shakti Shalini, was formed thirteen years ago by mothers who were grieving for their lost daughters and who wanted to offer a haven to endangered brides. Shakti Shalini also gives counseling sessions designed to restore such troubled marriages, a service not appreciated by everyone.

"They're taking too much of a chance with somebody's life," charges Himendra Thakur, who heads the International Society against Dowry and Bride-Burning in India, an organization he runs from his home in Salem, Massachusetts. "They feel very good when they send somebody back. They think they're saving a home," says Thakur, who maintains that at the first sign of dowry harassment, "the marriage should be dissolved."

But this stance has met great resistance in India. Speaking before a Kanpur civic organization in order to pitch his dream of building a series of "residential training centers" for abused brides, Thakur is confronted by an elderly man in the front row, who stands up and demands, "What about divorce?" This strikes me as an absurd question: How could divorce conceivably approach the tragedy of dowry death? But in the mind of this gentleman and many others in India, divorce is viewed with an alarm difficult to appreciate in the United States.

In general, Hindus face a spiritual imperative to marry and remain married, with nothing less than the salvation of their forebears at stake. Furthermore, the ancient Laws of Manu enjoin a wife to suffer her husband's trespasses (thus, most marital breakdowns are viewed as the wife's fault). Such traditions serve to keep many Indian wives married, even when their safety is in danger.

As indicated by the traditional Hindu parting to a newly wed daughter ("We are sending your bridal palanquin today. Let only your corpse come out of that house."), Hindu parents have long stressed that a married daughter should refrain from returning home. A bride's parents may be especially reluctant to allow her back if there are still maiden sisters whose chances of marrying might be hurt by the reputation of coming from a "difficult" family. Sadly, this reluctance has hardened in recent years, according to Delhi University sociology professor Veena Das. "There is something that has become pathological in India," she asserts. Typically in the case of dowry death, one thing is very shocking: "The girl has gone to her parents repeatedly and says she wants to come back, but the parents refuse to take responsibility for her."

Paul Mandelbaum's journalism has appeared in the New York Times Magazine and elsewhere. He is currently completing a novel about marriage set partly in India, for which he has received a 1999 James Michener/Copernicus Society of America fellowship.

This article first appeared in *Commonweal*, October 8, 1999, pp. 18-20. © 1999 by Paul Mandelbaum. Reprinted with the permission of the author.

Who Needs Love! In Japan, Many Couples Don't

Nicholas D. Kristof

OMIYA, Japan—Yuri Uemura sat on the straw tatami mat of her living room and chatted cheerfully about her 40-year marriage to a man whom, she mused, she never particularly liked.

"There was never any love between me and my husband," she said blithely, recalling how he used to beat her. "But, well, we survived."

A 72-year-old midwife, her face as weathered as an old baseball and etched with a thousand seams, Mrs. Uemura said that her husband had never told her that he liked her, never complimented her on a meal, never told her "thank you," never held her hand, never given her a present, never shown her affection in any way. He never calls her by her name, but summons her with the equivalent of a grunt or a "Hey, you."

"Even with animals, the males cooperate to bring the females some food," Mrs. Uemura said sadly, noting the contrast to her own marriage. "When I see that, it brings tears to my eyes."

In short, the Uemuras have a marriage that is as durable as it is unhappy, one couple's tribute to the Japanese sanctity of family.

The divorce rate in Japan is at a record high but still less than half that of the United States, and Japan arguably has one of the strongest family structures in the industrialized world. As the United States and Europe fret about the disintegration of the traditional family, most Japanese families remain as solid as the small red table on which Mrs. Uemura rested her tea.

A study published last year by the Population Council, an international nonprofit group based in New York, suggested that the traditional two-parent household is on the wane not only in America but throughout most of the world. There was one prominent exception: Japan.

> *It does not seem that Japanese families survive because husbands and wives love each other more than American couples, but rather because they perhaps love each other less*

In Japan, for example, only 1.1 percent of births are to unwed mothers—virtually unchanged from 25 years ago. In the United States, the figure is 30.1 percent and rising rapidly.

Yet if one comes to a little Japanese town like Omiya to learn the secrets of the Japanese family, the people are not as happy as the statistics.

"I haven't lived for myself," Mrs. Uemura said, with a touch of melancholy, "but for my kids, and for my family, and for society."

Mrs. Uemura's marriage does not seem exceptional in Japan, whether in the big cities or here in Omiya. The people of Omiya, a community of 5,700 nestled in the rain-drenched hills of the Kii Peninsula in Mie Prefecture, nearly 200 miles southwest of Tokyo, have spoken periodically to a reporter about various aspects of their daily lives. On this visit they talked about their families.

SURVIVAL SECRETS OFTEN, THE COUPLES EXPECT LITTLE

Osamums Torida furrowed his brow and looked perplexed when he was asked if he loved his wife of 33 years.

"Yeah, so-so, I guess," said Mr. Torida, a cattle farmer. "She's like air or water. You couldn't live without it, but most of the time, you're not conscious of its existence."

The secret to the survival of the marriage, Mr. Torida acknowledged, was not mutual passion.

"Sure, we had fights about our work," he explained as he stood beside his barn. "But we were preoccupied by work and our debts, so we had no time to fool around."

That is a common theme in Omiya. It does not seem that Japanese families survive because husbands and wives love each other more than American couples, but rather because they perhaps love each other less.

"I think love marriages are more fragile than arranged marriages," said Tomika Kusukawa, 49, who married her high-school sweetheart and now runs a car repair shop with him. "In love marriages, when something happens or if the couple falls out of love, they split up."

If there is a secret to the strength of the Japanese family it consists of three ingredients: low expectations, patience, and shame.

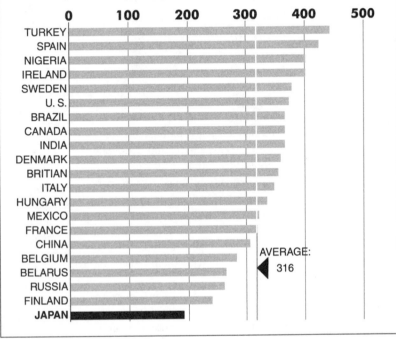

GETTING ALONG

Matchmaker, Matchmaker

How countries compare on an index of compatibility of spouses, based on answers to questions about politics, sex, social issues, religion and ethics, from a survey by the Dentsu Research Institute and Leisure Development Center in Japan. A score of 500 would indicate perfect compatibility.

TURKEY
SPAIN
NIGERIA
IRELAND
SWEDEN
U. S.
BRAZIL
CANADA
INDIA
DENMARK
BRITIAN
ITALY
HUNGARY
MEXICO
FRANCE
CHINA
BELGIUM
BELARUS
RUSSIA
FINLAND
JAPAN

AVERAGE: 316

NEW YORK TIMES

The advantage of marriages based on low expectations is that they have built in shock absorbers. If the couple discover that they have nothing in common, that they do not even like each other, then that is not so much a reason for divorce as it is par for the course.

Even the discovery that one's spouse is having an affair is often not as traumatic in a Japanese marriage as it is in the West. A little sexual infidelity on the part of a man (though not on the part of his wife) was traditionally tolerated, so long as he did not become so besotted as to pay his mistress more than he could afford.

Tsuzuya Fukuyama, who runs a convenience store and will mark her 50th wedding anniversary this year, toasted her hands on an electric heater in the front of the store and declared that a woman would be wrong to get angry if her husband had an affair.

The durability of the Japanese family is particularly wondrous because couples are, by international standards, exceptionally incompatible

---

"It's never just one side that's at fault," Mrs. Fukuyama said sternly. "Maybe the husband had an affair because his wife wasn't so hot herself. So she should look at her own faults."

Mrs. Fukuyama's daughter came to her a few years ago, suspecting that her husband was having an affair and asking what to do.

"I told her, 'Once you left this house, you can only come back if you divorce; if you're not prepared to get a divorce, then you'd better be patient,'" Mrs. Fukuyama recalled. "And so she was patient. And then she got pregnant and had a kid, and now they're close again."

The word that Mrs. Fukuyama used for patience is "gaman," a term that comes up whenever marriage is discussed in Japan. It means toughing it out, enduring hardship, and many Japanese regard gaman with pride as a national trait.

Many people complain that younger folks divorce because they do not have enough gaman, and the frequency with which the term is used suggests a rather bleak understanding of marriage.

"I didn't know my husband very well when we married, and afterward we used to get into bitter fights," said Yoshiko Hirowaki, 56, a store owner. "But then we had children, and I got very busy with the kids and with this shop. Time passed."

Now Mrs. Hirowaki has been married 34 years, and she complains about young people who do not stick to their vows.

"In the old days, wives had more gaman," she said. "Now kids just don't have enough gaman."

The durability of the Japanese family is particularly wondrous because couples are, by international standards, exceptionally incompatible.

One survey asked married men and their wives in 37 countries how they felt about politics, sex, religion, ethics and social issues. Japanese couples ranked dead last in compatibility of views, by a huge margin. Indeed, another survey found that if they were doing it over again, only about one-third of Japanese would marry the same person.

A national survey found that 30 percent of fathers spend less than 15 minutes a day on weekends talking with or playing with their children

Incompatibility might not matter so much, however, because Japanese husbands and wives spend very little time talking to each other.

"I kind of feel there's nothing new to say to her," said Masayuki Ogita, an egg farmer, explaining his reticence.

In a small town like Omiya, couples usually have dinner together, but in Japanese cities there are many "7-11 husbands," so called because they leave at 7 A.M. and return after 11 P.M.

Masahiko Kondo now lives in Omiya, working in the chamber of commerce, but he used to be a salesman in several big cities. He would leave work each morning at 7, and about four nights a week would go out for after-work drinking or mah-jongg sessions with buddies.

"I only saw my baby on Saturdays or Sundays," said Mr. Kondo, a lanky good-natured man of 37. "But in fact, I really enjoyed that life. It didn't bother me that I never spent time with my kid on weekdays."

Traditionally, many companies were reluctant to promote employees who had divorced or who had major problems at home

Mr. Kondo's wife, Keiko, had her own life, spent with her child and the wives of other workaholic husbands.

"We had birthday parties, but they were with the kids and the mothers," she remembers. "No fathers ever came."

A national survey found that 30 percent of fathers spend less than 15 minutes a day on weekdays talking with or playing with their children. Among eighth graders, 51 percent reported that they never spoke with their fathers on weekdays.

As a result, the figures in Japan for single-parent households can be deceptive. The father is often more a theoretical presence than a homework-helping reality.

Still, younger people sometimes want to see the spouses in daylight, and a result is a gradual change in focus of lives from work to family. Two decades ago, nearly half of young people said in surveys that they wanted their fathers to put priority on work rather than family. Now only one-quarter say that.

SOCIAL PRESSURES
SHAME IS KEEPING BONDS IN PLACE

For those who find themselves desperately unhappy, one source of pressure to keep plugging is shame.

"If you divorce, you lose face in society," said Tatsumi Kinoshita, a tea farmer." People say, 'His wife escaped.' So folks remain married because they hate to be gossiped about."

Shame is a powerful social sanction in Japan, and it is not just a matter of gos-

sip. Traditionally, many companies were reluctant to promote employees who had divorced or who had major problems at home.

"If you divorce, it weakens your position at work," said Akihiko Kanda, 27, who works in a local government office. "Your bosses won't give you such good ratings, and it'll always be a negative factor."

The idea, Mr. Kanda noted, is that if an employee cannot manage his own life properly, he should not be entrusted with important corporate matters.

Financial sanctions are also a major disincentive for divorce. The mother gets the children in three-quarters of divorces, but most mothers in Japan do not have careers and have few financial resources. Fathers pay child support in only 15 percent of all divorces with children, partly because women often hesitate to go to court to demand payments and partly because men often fail to pay even when the court orders it.

"The main reason for lack of divorce is that women can't support themselves," said Mizuko Kanda, a 51-year-old housewife. "My friends complain about their husbands and say that they'd divorce if they could, but they can't afford to."

The result of these social and economic pressures is clear.

Even in Japan, there are about 24 divorces for every 100 marriages, but that compares with 32 in France, and 42 in England, and 55 in the United States.

THE OUTLOOK
CHANGE CREEPS IN, IMPERILING FAMILY

But society is changing in Japan, and it is an open question whether these changes will undermine the traditional family as they have elsewhere around the globe.

The nuclear family has already largely replaced the extended family in Japan, and shame is eroding as a sanction. Haruko Okumura, for example, runs a kindergarten and speaks openly about her divorce.

"My Mom was uneasy about it, but I never had an inferiority complex about being divorced," said Mrs. Okumura, as dozens of children played in the next room. "And people accepted me easily."

Mrs. Okumura sees evidence of the changes in family patterns every day: fathers are playing more of a role in the kindergarten. At Christmas parties and sports contests, fathers have started to show up along with mothers. And Mrs. Okumura believes that divorce is on the upswing.

"If there's a weakening of the economic and social pressures to stay married," she said, "surely divorce rates will soar."

Already divorce rates are rising, approximately doubling over the last 25 years. But couples are very reluctant to divorce when they have children, and so single-parent households account for exactly the same proportion today as in 1965.

Shinsuke Kawaguchi, a young tea farmer, is one of the men for whom life is changing. Americans are not likely to be impressed by Mr. Kawaguchi's open-mindedness, but he is.

"I take good care of my wife," he said. "I may not say 'I love you,' but I do hold her hand. And I might say, after she makes dinner, 'This tastes good.'"

"Of course," Mr. Kawaguchi quickly added, "I wouldn't say that unless I'd just done something really bad."

Even Mrs. Uemura, the elderly woman whose husband used to beat her, said that her husband was treating her better.

"The other day, he tried to pour me a cup of tea," Mrs. Uemura recalled excitedly. "It was a big change. I told all my friends."

From the *New York Times*, February 11, 1996, pp. 1, 12. © 1996 by The New York Times Company. Reprinted by permission.

UNIT 5
Gender and Status

Unit Selections

Key Points to Consider

- What is it about foraging societies that encourages an egalitarian relationship between the sexes?

- What kinds of shifts, in the social relations of production, are necessary for women to achieve equality with men?

- Why do many cultures the world over treat menstruating women as taboo?

- What are the social functions of male circumcision?

- How and why do perceptions of feminine beauty vary from culture to culture?

 **Links: www.dushkin.com/online/**
These sites are annotated in the World Wide Web pages.

Arranged Marriages
http://women3rdworld.miningco.com/cs/arrangedmarriage/
Bonobo Sex and Society
http://songweaver.com/info/bonobos.html
FGM Research
http://www.amnesty.org/ailib/intcam/femgen/fgm1.htm
OMIM Home Page-Online Mendelian Inheritance in Man
http://www3.ncbi.nlm.nih.gov/omim/
Reflections on Sinai Bedouin Women
http://www.sherryart.com/women/bedouin.html

The feminist movement in the United States has had a significant impact upon the development of anthropology. Feminists have rightly charged that anthropologists have tended to gloss over the lives of women in studies of society and culture. In part this is because, until recent times, most anthropologists have been men. The result has been an undue emphasis upon male activities as well as male perspectives in descriptions of particular societies.

These charges, however, have proven to be a firm corrective. In the last few years, anthropologists have begun to study women and, more particularly, the sexual division of labor and its relation to biology as well as to social and political status. In addition, these changes in emphasis have been accompanied by an increase in the number of women in the field. (See "A Woman's Curse?" by Meredith Small.)

Feminist anthropologists have begun to critically attack many of the established anthropological beliefs. They have shown, for example, that field studies of nonhuman primates, which were often used to demonstrate the evolutionary basis of male dominance, distorted the actual evolutionary record by focusing primarily on baboons. (Male baboons are especially dominant and aggressive.) Other, less-quoted primate studies show how dominance and aggression are highly situational phenomena, sensitive to ecological variation. Feminist anthropologists have also shown that the subsistence contribution of women has likewise been ignored by anthropologists. A classic case is that of the !Kung, a hunting and gathering people in southern Africa, where women provide the bulk of the foodstuffs, including most of the available protein, and who, not coincidentally, enjoy a more egalitarian relationship than usual with men.

The most common occurrence has been male domination over women. Recent studies have concerned themselves with why there has been such gender inequality. Although the subordination of women is widespread, Martha C. Ward in "A World Full of Women," explains that the sex that controls the valued goods of exchange in a society is the dominant one. Thus, since this control is a matter of cultural variation, male authority is not biologically predetermined. In fact, women have played visibly prominent roles in many cultures. And, there are many cultures in which some men may play a more feminine or, at least, asexual role, as described in "The Berdache Tradition." As we see in "The Initiation of a Maasai Warrior" and "Where Fat Is a Mark of Beauty," gender relationships are deeply embedded in social experience.

A World Full of Women

Martha C. Ward
University of New Orleans

Work: The First Fact of Life

Women, like men, work for a living. In every human society that anthropologists ever studied, people divide the work they have to do between women and men. This is called the **sexual division of labor**, the assignment of the survival tasks of the society according to gender. Men get some of the jobs and women get some of the jobs. A few jobs may be done by both sexes. Generally, people feel strongly that their way of dividing up work is the best way or the "natural" way. Generally, some other group does it differently. That this division of work may be neither equal nor equally rewarding is quite beside the point.

Some jobs are "women's work" and others are defined as "men's work." The catch is that these tasks are not the same from group to group. For example, in cultures along the Sepik River in New Guinea, people eat flour made from sago palms. Someone must cut, haul, and process the trunk of the palm tree for the soggy flour it reluctantly yields. In some groups along the dramatic river, only men do this work. There people say, "Of course, it is naturally men's work." Downriver or upriver, women gather to strain the flour out as people in that group remark, "Naturally this is women's work." Then, just as they think they have it sorted out forever, something changes—the environment, the world economy, or historical forces beyond their control. Their division of labor by gender changes as well, predictably and irrevocably....

Value, Valued, and Valuable

Many women naively believe that if women's work and labor is so vital to human survival and comfort, then we should be treated accordingly. Our work is valuable and the reward should correspond to the importance of our contributions, we protest. Alas, women's work is not always **valued**. In fact, there is often no system for placing a value on female labor. For example, look at the concept called **use value**. This means that products made and services rendered within families are not sold and do not have a monetary value. They have a "value" only in private domestic settings. This contrasts sharply with **exchange value work**, which is the production of commodities or services for sale in the marketplace. When goods or services are exchanged for money or other financial considerations, then people say they have value.

The underlying economic principle is this: The ability to distribute, exchange, and control valuable goods and services to people who are not in our own domestic unit buys whatever we treasure: status, time, privacy, power, prestige, income, or goodies. This is true in each and every human group. Just working hard within our domestic units is only that: just working hard within our domestic units. This work, however hard, exciting, or crucial to survival it may be, does not automatically translate into power, control, status, money, or whatever. If women produce wonderful services or objects and cannot market them or keep the proceeds, then there is little or no exchange value or power. This principle applies to the products of women's bodies, too. After all, the term "labor" refers to birthing an infant. This is also why sex workers sometimes claim that offering sex in return for marriage is much the same as selling it in a free market.

But the control or power any woman has over the process and the product of her labor varies greatly between cultures. In most societies, men seem to have greater rights than women to distribute goods outside their domestic networks. So the best question is not about how hard women are working; ask instead if women control access to the resources they need. Resources typically include education, employment, child care, legal standing, land ownership, the freedom to marry and divorce, and access to the tools of survival or the means of production, as Karl Marx called them.

A related example of the sexual division of labor and the gendering of work is the **family wage ideologies**. Family wage laws and practices are still a fundamental part of gender ideologies in the Western world. They developed in nineteenth-century industrializing, capitalist societies. The premise is that a male worker (as head of a household) is hired and paid enough to support his wife and their children. Females (for example, young single women) who work the same jobs are not paid the same as males. Presumably they do not have to support families. Married women are assumed to have access to their husband's income; they are said to be working at home for him. If wives take wage-labor jobs, it is seen as supplementing their husbands' income. This cultural formulation of the sexual division of labor has been enormously instrumental, even seductive, in western European and North American societies. You may recognize the impact of this gender ideology on your own salaries and lives.

Women don't just work; we are often overworked and invisible. Sociologist Arlie Hochschild interviewed two-career couples about their own sexual division of labor; she also visited these modern working partnerships to see how they divided up their "home-work." Then she reviewed a large number of studies on who did what in contemporary households. No matter how she approached the topic, she came back to the same conclusion: the revolution is stalled. Despite the hopes and rhetoric of a generation of women, working mothers still carry the major burdens of childrearing, household maintenance, and whatever emotional work needs to be done. She averaged estimates from major studies on time use done from the 1960s on and discovered that women worked roughly fifteen hours longer each week than men do. Over a year, women worked an extra month of twenty-four days a year, and over a dozen years, they worked an extra year. Mirroring the wage gap between men and women in the workplace, there was a "leisure gap" between them at home.

*As masses of women have moved into the economy, families have been hit by a "speed-up" in work and family life. There is no more time in the day than there was when wives stayed home, but there is twice as much to get done. It is mainly women who absorb this "speed-up".... Even when couples share more equitably in the work at home, women do two-thirds of the **daily** jobs at home, like cooking and cleaning up—jobs that fix them into a rigid routine.... Beyond doing more at home, women also devote **proportionately more** of their time at home to housework and proportionately less of it to childcare. Of all the time men spend working at home, more of it goes to childcare. That is, working wives spend relatively more time "mothering the house"; husbands spend more time "mothering" the children. Since most parents prefer to tend to their children than clean house, men do more of what they'd rather do. (Hochschild 1990:8)*

Hochschild calls what happens at the end of the day in American two-career families the **second shift**. Writers about international economics usually call this the **double day**. In the double day, women do child care, household and domestic duties in addition to agricultural work, and full-time or part-time wage-labor jobs. Figure 1 is a way of diagramming these work loads. The professional career women Hochschild interviewed are supposed to "have it all." But she found that in only 20 percent of dual-career families do men share housework equally with their wives. Over and over women revealed that they accepted this inequity to keep peace and continue the connections. They also reported chronic exhaustion, low sex drive, and more frequent illnesses. They felt intense feelings of time pressure, guilt, and anxiety. "Emotionally drained" was a constant refrain. Their deepest fantasies started with getting some sleep. Low wages, lack of support services, feeling tired all the time, and the double day or the second shift compose probably the most characteristic pattern for women's work on the planet.

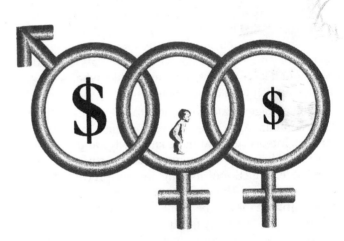

Figure 1. The Double Day or the second shift.

"What's for Dinner?": Gender and Practical Economics

All of us eat; we know that food is basic to survival and that food carries as much symbolic and practical significance as any activity humans do. Anthropologists categorize human cultures now and in the past by how people get the foods they eat. We talk about hunting and gathering, horticultural, and agricultural societies or working for wages to purchase food. Archaeologists classify and analyze cultures by the kinds of tools people make and use to survive. Tools mean actual material objects... as well as social tools such as marriage, kinship reckoning, and political organization....

Subsistence technologies, whatever they are, have critical consequences for the way work is divided and rewarded within genders and ages, and the quality and quantity of relationships between men and women. The continuum of cultural experiences in earning a living runs from our human ancestors, all of whom were gatherers and/or hunters, through cultivators, farmers, and pastoralists who care for animals to those of us who live now in complex, multicultural, urban, post-industrial nation-states. The rest of this chapter offers examples of this key proposition and the continuum of subsistence. Drawn largely from archaeology, they center on food, fibers, fabrics, and other practical technologies. The goal is to illuminate women's work in ways you may not have seen before.

Hunting, Gathering, and Being Human

The hunting-gathering or foraging way of life is extremely significant for anthropologists. All *Homo sapiens* lived this way before the beginnings of agriculture, the invention of plant and animal domestication about 10,000 years ago. A fraction of the world's peoples still earn a living this way in geographical regions where agriculture and industrialization have not reached. Foraging peoples collect wild plants; small creatures like rabbits, birds, or fish; wild fruits and berries; eggs; roots; tubers; insects; and many other delicious, healthy foods in their environment. They may also hunt large land animals like buffalo, bear, and deer or large sea mammals like whales or seals. They may fish with elaborate traps.

What foragers catch or collect to eat varies with their environment. What does not vary is their inevitable, extensive, intense, and intimate knowledge and experience with their local environments. What does not vary is the inevitable, skilled tool-making and reciprocal sharing of work and food. The significant question for us is how much latitude for independent action a woman has in her household, in her body (sexual-reproductive life), and in her pocketbook (economic matters). It is generally agreed that the sexual division of labor in foraging groups was **relatively equalitarian**.

Thanks to several generations of scholarship, we are no longer prey to popular culture's stereotypes of "man the hunter," "man the tool-maker," or the ever-popular "caveman." In this silly sexual division of labor, men brought home the bacon and women cooked it. In some accounts, women apparently hung around the campfire cooking meat, grateful for every morsel, available for sex and bearing little hunters of the future. Popular depictions show them wearing tanned animal skins and carrying tools, food, and children. Note all the work implied in this picture.

Our hunting-gathering ancestors had a small number of children and low population density. The basic social divisions they knew were age, which shifts through an individual's life, and gender, which generally doesn't shift. Men and women control some of the resources and services required by the other. Food-getting is work. It requires many tools, sharing and other social skills, wide variability in diets, and extensive knowledge of local environments. The facts of human survival offer no argument for idleness by either men or women.

Typically the group structure comes close to being equalitarian. A senior man or woman acts as a focus for collective decisions. Their taking on of serious responsibility must not be confused with power or authority. Elders and their networks of kinspeople are mobile most of the year, following the movements of game and the availability of gathered foods. As a result, foragers have no more possessions than they can comfortably carry in skin and net bags. Women carry babies or small children. For all foraging groups, there are predictable problem points: bad weather and changing seasons, vanished game, dangerous predators, sickness, childbirth, correct relationships with in-laws, and effectively bringing young people into the full knowledge and experience they will need to survive. Over time, they develop significant "religious" and "medical" experience to deal with all of these problems. Foraging cultures classically acquire knowledge and information through altered states of consciousness, dreams, trances, or other visits with the spirit world with the help of shamans who may be male or female.

The Pot-Luck Principle

Sharing, gathering, and carrying in foraging societies are complexes that shaped human life as we now know it. The pot-luck principle is one key to human survival. People contributed what they had and fed themselves and several others better than they could do it alone. In foraging cultures, a woman gathered foods from a source she knew about; then she exchanged some for a foodstuff she had not found. One day she gave foodstuffs to relatives who couldn't go out foraging that day; on another day she prepared a soft, easy-to-chew dish for an old person or an easily digestible dish for a sick person or a child. Salads, soups, and stews, for example, contain a number of ingredients put together rather flexibly. Mixing food together enhances the nutritional value for everyone. But no one person could gather and prepare his or her own bowl of salad each day. Imagine preparing a rich vegetable soup or stew from scratch for one person each day. Now imagine helping someone make a soup and sharing from a large pot. In most animal groups, individuals must find their own food each day. In sharp contrast, all known contemporary foraging groups divide subsistence tasks by gender and age. Increased sociability, sharing of resources, structured giving, and ordered social relationships would have contributed to growth and survival. Shared food is good for everybody. In some fashion or another, the metaphors of shared food around a fire are at the heart of many religions.

Sophisticated new research and analysis of contemporary foraging groups over the last 30 years reveals the complexity and contributions of gathering. Our ancestors used plants for making medicines, drinks, clothes, equipment, and tools. At the same time, females carried and nursed an infant almost continually for three to four years, did a lioness's share of food-gathering, and 90 percent of child care. A woman often walked miles carrying an equivalent of 75 percent of her body weight in baby, firewood, gathered foodstuffs, or other raw materials. Women contributed dietary proteins, clubbed turtles, and collected eggs and insects. Women made systematic observations about the availability of game or tracks and reported back to the men. Anthropologists know that women hunted as well and gathered small game and fish. Mothers often, as they still do, left small children in the care of kinfolk, sister-like cooperatives, brothers, or other adult males. Males also gathered, for themselves and in groups.

Honey, Meat, and Babies

As part of a research team, anthropologist Marjorie Shostak did fieldwork in the Kalahari desert of southern Africa (Botswana). There she listened to and recorded the life story of Nisa, a woman who was born into one of the last gathering–hunting cultures, the !Kung Bushmen. Here Nisa discusses food and her memories of childhood. The fathers brought animals home for everyone to eat. Nisa loved to eat meat dripping with fat.

> We lived, eating the animals and foods of the bush. We collected food, ground it in a mortar, and ate it. We also ate sweet nin berries and tsin beans. When I was growing up, there were no cows or goats.... Whenever my father killed an animal and I saw him coming home with meat draped over a stick, balanced on one shoulder—that's what made me happy. I'd cry out, "Mommy! Daddy's coming and he's bringing meat!" My heart would be happy when I greeted him, "Ho, ho, Daddy! We're going to eat meat!" Or honey. Sometimes he'd go out and come home with honey.... Sometimes my mother would be the one to see the honey. The two of us would be walking around gathering food and she'd find a beehive deep inside a termite mound or in a tree. (Shostak 1981:87)

Honey and animal fat are too foods deeply prized and symbolic in hunting and gathering cultures. Folklorist Megan Biesele has also worked in the Kalahari desert on the foraging ideologies of a related group called Ju/ 'hoan. She found that even symbolic and expressive domains are divided between genders. This means that art, music, poetry, mythology, and other expressive parts of the Ju/'hoan culture are codes that contain knowledge— information that helps them survive as a group. The verbal traditions are imaginative legacies strongly imprinted with ideas about work, social life, and the supernatural, which have adaptive value.

> Hunting as a male activity is typically valued and ritually elaborated over either gathering or fishing, despite the relative economic importance of the latter activities in specific instances. Men's hunting is often symbolically opposed not to the complementary female activity of gathering but rather to women's reproductive capacity. (Biesele 1993:41)

In other words, producing babies is the equivalent of producing meat in terms of making the most significant contribution to group survival. "Men have trance-curing and hunting. Women have childbirth and plant food gathering. All are indispensable ingredients of traditional Bushman subsistence and social life" (Biesele 1993:98). Men cannot produce babies. Women produce babies—itself a potentially dangerous enterprise—and make the intensive investments of raising them. They are not likely to be hunters as well. But babies were a gift to their cultures, hard as this is to image in a world full of billions of people.

Tools with a Feminine Twist

It's often difficult to find ordinary women in the archaeological record. A great irony of studying gender and work is how transitory and perishable women's productions are. Objects made of stone survive better than tools or objects made of wood, skin, bone, horn, fibers, or other perishable organic materials. Songs, stories, recipes, babies, fibers, clothes, fabrics, comfort care, or social skills may be crucial to survival but still vanish easily. This is one reason why some scientists in the past emphasized stone and saw tools only as weapons and only men as toolmakers or users. Despite the immense toil in producing clothing or children, for example, little or no evidence survives.

More and more anthropologists, however, see women in the role of tool inventors. The absolute best example is the simple act of carrying things. For starters, females carry babies in all nonhuman primate groups and in all human cultures. Slings for carrying infants are found in most human societies, so this is probably one of the earliest and most profound applications of tool use. Contemporary foragers use skin bags, fiber nets, or woven baskets for carrying food, wood, and other objects for long distances. Never mind that people in many places speak of a pregnancy as "carrying a baby." Today humans make thousands of kinds of containers. We buy them, give them as gifts, and rely on them for a thousand tasks: purses, pocketbooks, pockets, knapsacks, backpacks, shoulder bags, handbags, tin cans, paper bags, plastic sacks, boxes, baskets, briefcases, cosmetic cases, and brown paper packages wrapped up in string. These are major inventions. Frankly, I think women should boldly claim credit for inventing containers for carrying and celebrate the incredible developments that followed.

Here is a powerful example of finding women's work in the scholarly record. Elizabeth Barber is an archaeologist who has done the authoritative study of the development of cloth in the ancient and early modern worlds. She uses linguistics, anthropology, and history to reveal women's industry over the last 20,000 years. She herself spins and weaves and often recreates the fabrics found in archaeological sites to learn more about them. In most parts of the world, until the Industrial Revolution, fiber arts were an extraordinary practical force belonging primarily to women.

Our foraging ancestors gathered more than eatable wild plants. They collected plant fibers such as flax, hemp, nettle, ramie, jute, sisal, esparto, maguey, yucca, elm, linden, willow, and many others. These fibers were then processed for baskets, cordage, nets and traps for catching fish or other animals, mats for floors, roofs, beds, and fences—and thousands of other useful, necessary, everyday objects that made life safe, comfortable, and even possible. Some hunted animals like wild mountain goats for their fleece, which could be spun into warm yarns, or collected the hair other animals shed in the spring. In the great temple cave of Lascaux used 24,000 years ago, archaeologists found the remains of the string that led people into its darkness for stunning artwork and probably profound rituals and ceremonies. Should women give serious attention to something as humble and mundane as string? Barber says yes.

> We don't know how early to date this great discovery—of making string as long and as strong as needed by twisting short filaments together. But whenever it happened, it opened the door to an enormous array of new ways to save labor and improve the odds of survival, much as the harnessing of steam did for the Industrial Revolution. Soft, flexible thread of this sort is a necessary prerequisite to making woven cloth. On a far more basic level, string can be used simply to tie things up—to catch, to hold, to carry. From these notions come snares and fishlines, tethers and leashes, carrying nets, handles, and packages, not to mention a way of binding objects together to form more complex tools.... So powerful, in fact, is simple string in taming the world to human will and ingenuity that I suspect it to be the unseen weapon that allowed the human race to conquer the earth, that enabled us to move out into every econiche on the globe during the Upper Paleolithic. We could call it the String Revolution. (Barber 1994:45)

String was invented and used everywhere in the world humans went. But the women of 24,000 years ago did much more than catch fish, carry food, or lead others into caves with their practical invention. They made skirts—swinging cords fastened from a twisted hip band, some with long beaded fringes. By any standards, their skirts could not have been modest or warm. But skimpy string skirts keep appearing in the archaeological records, and always on women. From archaeological sites dating to 1300 B.C., we can see actual skirts preserved in burials of young girls. The miniskirts scandalized some European archaeologists. Well into the twentieth century, one could still find descendants of string skirts in elaborate belts and aprons in some peasant cultures of Eastern Europe.

Barber asks: What could have been so important about such impractical, eye-catching miniskirts that the style lasts for thousands of years? Her best guess is that the skirts signified something about childbearing abilities, readiness for marriage, or both. There were many times and places in our human past when how a young women dressed signaled her marriage status, even a sense of honor and specialness, and linked her with the ability to create new life—often a valuable gift to her society. A number of the so-called Venus figurines are wearing string skirts. The divine Hera in the epic poem of Homer wears a "Girdle of a hundred tassels." Her skirts are too short to do much good—except for social signaling. This may be a subtle example of a woman's language.

Planting and Harvesting: The Next Revolution

So what have anthropologists learned? The most equalitarian groups we know about are probably hunting and gathering groups. Do women and men do exactly equal work and get treated the same way? No. They do not have equality, just relatively equalitarian traditions and a sexual division of labor. No known groups allow one gender to be idle or excused from the basic work of survival. The foraging lifestyle required an amazing amount of practical intelligence; in fact, anthropologists know that horticulture and agriculture grew out of the increasingly skilled carrying, sharing, and gathering complexes of our early ancestors.

About 10,000 years ago, groups of people in various parts of the world learned how to cultivate and harvest plants and care for domestic animals as sources of food and fibers. This striking new relationship to the environment is called the **Neolithic Revolution.** But—and here is the key insight of anthropology—when people changed their patterns of earning a living and their eating habits, everything else shifted too. Eventually this key transition in food-getting would have extraordinary implications for women's work and daily lives.

Digging Sticks

The revolution didn't happen overnight. Gradually some groups adopted horticulture, the hand-cultivation system of growing food with the highly efficient but simple tools of hoes and digging sticks. Women played the major role as food producers of grain, cereal, and vegetable crops.

Men did fishing and hunting to supplement diets. Horticultural is still the basic source of subsistence for many of the rural descendants of cultivators who were neither driven off their land by colonialism nor became dependent on commercial crops and agricultural wage labor. Once our ancestors began to cultivate their food, the potential for new kinds of gender relationships exploded. These kinds of cultures have amazing variety, so it's very difficult to generalize.

Only a few things apply uniformly. In all horticultural societies, men clear the land for planting. It's heavy, dangerous work. But depending on how fast things grow, it doesn't have to be done often. Beyond that fact, there is no consistent adaptive advantage to whether females or males plant and harvest their crops. Horticulture is quite compatible with child-tending. In some places, men clear and both genders cultivate—sometimes their work is separated into "women's crops" and "men's crops." In other places, such as highland New Guinea or the island of Pohnpei, where I did fieldwork, men raise the ceremonial and prestige crops; women raise staple crops for domestic use. The common pattern in which men clear and women cultivate—like the Iroquois of Native North America—is generally associated with economic control and high status for women. In West Africa, both men and women cultivate staple crops for use value and prestige crops for exchange value. Reciprocity is still important, but trading in market arenas increases. In the advanced horticulture societies of West Africa with well-developed market systems, women handle a large share of the trading. Women rarely become wealthy or powerful, but trading the products they grow and make does give them more autonomy in their personal lives and power in their marital relationships (Clark 1994).

Horticultural societies (with some notable exceptions) do not seem to promote very amicable relationships between women and men. I can't find a convincing argument why this is true, but my theory is that men and women are freed from the mutually shared dangers of the foraging lifestyle; competition can flourish without the imperatives for cooperation. There may be within-group female solidarity as well as male group linkages. But between men and women as groups or as couples, distance, disruption, hostility, and accusations mark their common lives. The key seems to be their relationship with local environments.

In simple horticultural societies, production is largely for use value. Exchange is usually within kin groups and based on reciprocity. Such groups are not yet oriented to markets and trade outside the village. In environments with plentiful, relatively uncontested resources and abundant arable land, groups are frequently matrilineal and still relatively equalitarian. Women work and live in localized groups with their kinfolk. Matrilineal descent makes sense under these circumstances. The status and safety of women is appreciably high in matrilineal horticultural societies in which the local community is organized

around related women. When the societies practice **matrilineal descent** [tracing kinship through a female line], have high degrees of female solidarity and female economic control, and when males are absent in war or trade, women have reasonably high status. When kin groups are nearby, women are more rarely abused or beaten.

However, in circumstances in which (for whatever reason) production is increased or there is competition or environmental pressures, men tend to live in local groups and eventually move to patrilineal descent systems. In these systems, a husband and his immediate kin group are the beneficiaries of a woman's labor. Men may also take more than one wife—all the better to increase production of crops and children. When **patrilineal descent** systems, male solidarity, male economic control, population pressures, the need for local defense, and warfare complexes occur, women become second-class people.

Plows

Horticulture, with its extensive varieties, is not intrinsically predictable in its effects on women's work and lives. But the same cannot be said for **agriculture**. Women's lives overall are heavily impacted in agriculture, and it would be difficult to argue that these new systems are improvements. Agriculture is complex cultivation using a plow, domesticated draft animals, or farm machinery. Farming may involve irrigation, livestock breeding, and cash crops or farm products that have no use value and are grown for sale. This extensive means of earning a living includes all plantations, agricultural industries that produce such commodities as heroin, cocaine, tobacco, rubber, sugar, cotton, spices, and coffee. Agriculture, agribusiness, plantations, and animal husbandry are the subsistence bases for all contemporary industrial societies.

At various times and in many places in the world, people in horticultural societies needed—for whatever reason—to increase their productivity. They began to use more intensive and advanced cultivation techniques. They revitalized the soils with fertilizer; they harnessed animal power for harvesting and planting, and diverted water into fields under cultivation. These particular and increasingly widespread activities required male labor; the work was hard, long, dangerous, and strikingly incompatible with women's work styles and the demands of child care. The most spectacular new tool in intensive agriculture was plows. Plows are the tool most heavily blamed among some archaeologists for altering the balance of men and women's lives. In gathering and horticulture societies, women use hoes and digging sticks; women produce food directly, often working together in processing and distribution. But men with plows and draft animals replaced women as primary producers. Women cooked and processed food; they worked very hard at many tasks. But they did not produce food. Men increasingly did, and they did so in the company of other men. The effects on women were so dramatic that we are still living with them thousands of years later.

The realization that animals could be domesticated and used for wool, milk, and muscle power was truly a revolution. People settled down on farms and in villages; in many parts of the world, cities developed. Instead of mobility, human lives were characterized by settled village life. As you can imagine, things accumulated. Like children. The number of births per family increased. Children were very useful in subsistence tasks. There was lots of homestead work to be done: herds of sheep, goats, or cattle to shepherd, milk, and tend; barnyard animals to tend; family clothes to make; food to process to last the winter; goods to produce for trade—thousands of specialized tasks, dawn-to-darkness labor, lots of children to bear and raise. Farm life requires the most broadly skilled and hardest working women and men I've encountered on the planet. It also means concentrating intensively only on a few aspects of the environment.

Distaffs

Once again I note: It's easier than ever to lose sight of women in these male-heavy agrarian societies. So I want to add one splendid example of making women's work visible. Remember string. In settled horticultural villages and agricultural societies across the planet, from Greece and Egypt to China and Peru, women took simple string, their spun fibers, and taught each other to weave them. They invented looms and woven cloth, fabric for high-fashion clothes, home furnishings, rugs, blankets, belts, baby dresses, and the sails of ships. Once woven, cloth wrapped the dead and the newborn; it often served as currency, bedding, bandages, and the mark of social status and sacred spaces. In most nomadic cultures, women still weave the floors, the walls, and the roofs of their portable tent homes; they are architects. They spun wool from their practical sheep and beautiful flax fibers for linen. They fed exotic worms and wove their cocoons into silk—the ultimate luxury fabric and for its weight as strong as steel. In other places they grew cotton or hemp (useful for rope as well as medicines).

The folk saying claims, "Clothies make the man." But Elizabeth Barber says, "women make the clothes." She found a cloth-crazy world in the archaeological records of the Middle East and Europe. Innumerable temple walls, pottery, and paintings show women and men planting and harvesting fiber plants or tending flocks of sheep. Women are continuously shown combing, carding, spinning, dyeing, weaving, wearing, giving, trading, and selling fabrics, miles and miles of the flowing stuff, caravans of cloth. However, nowhere in the world was textile manufacture simply women's economic and household labor. Textiles became symbols of creation and fertility in some places, freedom in others. Barber says that patterned cloth

is like a language. Like clothing, it speaks of many human events or feelings.

What did ancient people try to accomplish when they deliberately made cloth bear meaning? A good look at folk customs and costumes recently in use reveals three main purposes. For one thing, it can be used to mark or announce information. It can also be used as a mnemonic device to record events and other data. Third, it can be used to invoke "magic"—to protect, to secure fertility and riches, to divine the future, perhaps even to curse. (Barber 1994:149)

Cloth was women's work and women's status, even women's language par excellence. It marked statuses such as married and dead. Social rank was coded through fabrics, designs, colors, and embellishments. Cloth marked ceremonial or ritual states and told the stories, myths, and histories of peoples. Cloth encoded women's magical, wish-fulfilling, and fantasy lives. Everywhere Barber looked women coded their common objectives into cloth: fertility, prosperity, and protection. Slave women and queens alike put their fingers to this work. Sometimes women acted as business owners; sometimes they were part of family businesses. In some places and at some times, there were free, middle-class, independent-minded women who created textiles, both beautiful and in volume, for the busy commercial markets and trade routes, working with their menfolk. There were innovations in dyes and efficiency of looms. Sometimes I think of all the hard work of cloth production and I'm glad to be spared. At other times, I glimpse something about autonomy, creativity, deep personal privacy, even a meditative healing that comes from producing fabric from scratch. It is also clear from the archaeological and anthropological record, in which women worked together or even for each other, that they had more control over their lives, more autonomy.

The history of "civilization" is woven in these extraordinary crafts. Men helped; they participated in a thousand ways. But the fiber and fabric production industries centered on and were the inspiration of women. I am impressed that in every culture in which women spin fibers into thread and yarns, spinning is associated with female economic, sexual, and spiritual freedom. Distaffs—the tool that holds the unspun fibers for spinning—are the symbol for women's work around the world. People who can spin a good yarn are valuable.

Peasants

In agriculture, women's roles changed rather dramatically from those of foraging or horticulture societies. This period, often hailed as the "dawn of civilization," undisputedly brought a loss of status and power for women relative to men of their social class, and for the majority of

A Folktale
What's for Dinner Honey?

Once upon a time, a couple lived on a farm. They quarreled constantly about the work they had to do on their homestead. Each claimed that her or his labor was the most difficult and that the other one was not properly appreciative. Finally, when there seemed no other way to settle the issue, the husband and wife agreed to trade tasks for an entire day.

Early the following morning, the wife arose and went out to plow the fields and make hay. When she returned that evening, her muscles were sore and her hands had new blisters. But she had enjoyed her quiet, simple day outside in the fields. She was fiercely hungry; the leftovers from breakfast and the small lunch her husband packed for her had not been enough. As she stepped through the carved wooden door of their cottage, she called out, "What's for dinner honey?"

But instead of dinner, she faced a disaster! Feathers coated in honey clung to the rafters. The cat, who should have been in the barn catching rats, crawled from the overturned butter churn, licking her paws with glee. Chickens cackled as they laid eggs on the mantel; they cackled as the eggs rolled off and broke on the floor. Ducks left their droppings and droolings as they marched across her handmade white quilt. From somewhere, the mooing of an unmilked and unhappy cow filled the air. The bread dough had not risen and the beer she was brewing had spilled. Flax fibers, soaking as the first stage in making linen cloth, were strewn damply about the dirty floor. Her garden was not weeded and something had happened to the fruits and vegetables she was preparing for winter. But worse, her husband, tied by his foot, hung upside down in the chimney, his face covered by her best apron and his head only inches away from a pot of uncooked soup teetering above the dead fire in the hearth.

"Don't ask," he moaned. "I've had a very bad day." Before she released him, she satisfied herself that he had a new appreciation for her work and her work skills. Then she began to clean up enough to fix dinner for them. They lived and worked together for a very long time after that.

the growing populations relative to a tiny ruling elite. A significant result of this new adaptation was the production of surpluses. People had exchangeable wealth: stored food, domesticated animals, or other products they produced, such as cloth, butter, wine, salt, and many others. They lived in permanent, larger, and denser populations. In these societies, there was still a division of labor by gender, but people had more options and statuses, more shifting by class or age or task. Plows, draft animals, fertilizing, and irrigating increased both productivity and the complexity of social organizations. But the work was strenuous, demanding, dangerous, and time-consuming. Gatherers, hunters, and horticulturalists are rightly appalled at the sheer unending physical labor of farming.

Agriculture transforms the bulk of people into **peasants**. Peasants have the highest birth rates of any group of humans on the planet. But land is always finite, and landless peasants must migrate into cities, find other occupations, or form armies. The consequences of agriculture as a way of life include social phenomena such as class oppression, slavery, caste systems, and exploited or expendable classes of people such as beggars, criminals, or the chronically unemployed. Don't forget to add in war, famine, and plague. There are always merchant or business classes, growing bureaucracies or retainer classes, and priestly classes. The world religions (Islam, Judaism, Christianity, Hinduism, and Buddhism) all spread and became institutionalized within agrarian societies. Complex trade, transportation, and communication systems as well as powerful central governments are developed. Standing armies and warfare become chronic. In short, **marked social inequality** and exploitation are built into the economies and social organizations of all the great agrarian civilizations.

In this bleak picture, where are women? If you have a family business and inherited wealth, then kinship is important. In other places, such as Europe and North America, people moved into the constellation of monogamous marriages and nuclear families. Economic productivity of wives declines, as do collective female work groups. Wives have typically left their parents' households and are living in their husbands' natal homes. Females are like cattle—the property of males and intensive breeders for the labor supply. Peasants try to produce big crops and many sons. Women in agricultural societies have the largest number of children, and their births are more closely spaced than in any other group. The hunters of the Plains of North America marveled at European farm families with eight to twelve children. "Like dogs," they whispered. Men need the labor of their wives, and women are required to have husbands—it's their work. But this is **unequal interdependence**, because males control the primary productive processes and females are relegated to secondary tasks. They are working harder than ever but are still disposable and isolated.

You will not be surprised to hear how agriculturalists value virginity for their daughters and chastity for their wives, how women are used as pawns in vast male political alliances. Women are a key reserve labor supply for intense periods like harvest or planting. The rest of the time they are available for childbearing, childrearing, extensive fiber and fabric production (spinning, weaving, sewing), and food processing. To these major activities are added jobs like small animal husbandry, nursing, and running complex households while men are away at war. On top of all of this, agrarian societies develop elaborate religious, moral, and legal justifications for their sexual stratification systems. Hammurabi's Code was the first set of laws written down and provided the basis for legal systems in the Middle East, ancient Israel, and cultures of this important region. Of the 270 laws engraved on an upright stone pillar, approximately 100 of them dealt with the problems of keeping women in line, assigning ownership and responsibility for them, and defining the boundaries of their sexuality. In the ideologies of agriculturalists, women are subordinate, unclean, and not bright enough to be trusted out alone. Women are viewed as suited only for inside and domestic tasks; they are incapable of public political and economic roles. Family units shrink. They become self-sufficient. A man's home is his castle. Women have to rely on husbands for their livelihood—in short, institutionalized dependency, subordination, and political immaturity. If some of this sounds familiar to you, that's because European-American culture and society grew from its peasant agricultural roots. Summer vacation, for example, is time off from school to help with the harvest. "Naturally," women are at home fixing their meals.

Peasant cultures do not paint a very pretty picture of women's lives. Sometimes women resist in subtle ways. They gossip or tell stories that make their work visible. In the box [on the preceding page] is a folktale about the sexual division of labor, collected from storytellers in the peasant societies of northern Europe. I think it's shamelessly a woman's story because she believes his job is simple and hers is complex and that he doesn't see or value her contributions. But you are free to interpret or rewrite it as you like.

"Over the last 500 years, many largely peasant societies have become industrialized and "developed." Some have created immense colonial empires and heavy war machinery. In the **Industrial Revolution**, factories became the work place. People worked in an assembly line, mass producing goods they couldn't sell or use at home. Only their time at work had value. Although people still need to eat, it takes only a very few to produce their food. What did the first factories of the industrialization and its capitalistic methods produce? Thread and cloth. What is the name we give to our current age? The Age of Information. Computers come from looms, based on the same binary principle: yes-no, over-under, in-out. Huge looms for Jacquard woven fabric used the first computer cards. The image of this brave new age is a web the size of the world. Were there massive changes in women's lives in each of these "revolutions"? Did marriage, family life, and economic prospects change with each new age? Of course. These are the revolutions we're currently experiencing....

Bibliography

Barber, Elizabeth 1994 *Women's Work: The First 20,000 Years. Women, Cloth, and Society in Early Times.* New York: W. W. Norton.

Biesele, Megan 1993 *Women Like Meat: The Folklore and Foraging Ideology of the Kalahari Jul'hoan.* Bloomington: Indiana University Press.

Clark, Garcia 1994 *Onions Are My Husband: Survival and Accumulation by West African Market Women.* Chicago: University of Chicago Press.

Hochschild, Arlie R. 1990 *The Second Shift: Working Parents and the Revolution at Home.* New York: Avon.

Shostak, Marjorie 1991 *Nisa: The Life and Words of !Kung Woman.* New York: Vintage Books.

The Berdache Tradition

Walter L. Williams

Because it is such a powerful force in the world today, the Western Judeo-Christian tradition is often accepted as the arbiter of "natural" behavior of humans. If Europeans and their descendant nations of North America accept something as normal, then anything different is seen as abnormal. Such a view ignores the great diversity of human existence.

This is the case of the study of gender. How many genders are there? To a modern Anglo-American, nothing might seem more definite than the answer that there are two: men and women. But not all societies around the world agree with Western culture's view that all humans are either women or men. The commonly accepted notion of "the opposite sex," based on anatomy, is itself an artifact of our society's rigid sex roles.

Among many cultures, there have existed different alternatives to "man" or "woman." An alternative role in many American Indian societies is referred to by anthropologists as *berdache*.... The role varied from one Native American culture to another, which is a reflection of the vast diversity of aboriginal New World societies. Small bands of hunter-gatherers existed in some areas, with advanced civilizations of farming peoples in other areas. With hundreds of different languages, economies, religions, and social patterns existing in North America alone, every generalization about a cultural tradition must acknowledge many exceptions.

This diversity is true for the berdache tradition as well, and must be kept in mind. My statements should be read as being specific to a particular culture, with generalizations being treated as loose patterns that might not apply to peoples even in nearby areas.

Briefly, a berdache can be defined as a morphological male who does not fill a society's standard man's role, who has a nonmasculine character. This type of person is often stereotyped as effeminate, but a more accurate characterization is androgyny. Such a person has a clearly recognized and accepted social status, often based on a secure place in the tribal mythology. Berdaches have special ceremonial roles in many Native American religions, and important economic roles in their families. They will do at least some women's work, and mix together much of the behavior, dress, and social roles of women and men. Berdaches gain social prestige by their spiritual, intel-lectual, or craftwork/artistic contributions, and by their reputation for hard work and generosity. They serve a mediating function between women and men, precisely because their character is seen as distinct from either sex. They are not seen as men, yet they are not seen as women either. They occupy an alternative gender role that is a mixture of diverse elements.

In their erotic behavior berdaches also generally (but not always) take a nonmasculine role, either being asexual or becoming the passive partner in sex with men. In some cultures the berdache might become a wife to a man. This male-male sexual behavior became the focus of an attack on berdaches as "sodomites" by the Europeans who, early on, came into contact with them. From the first Spanish conquistadors to the Western frontiersmen and the Christian missionaries and government officials, Western culture has had a considerable impact on the berdache tradition. In the last two decades, the most recent impact on the tradition is the adaptation of a modern Western gay identity.

To Western eyes berdachism is a complex and puzzling phenomenon, mixing and redefining the very concepts of what is considered male and female. In a culture with only two recognized genders, such individuals are gender nonconformist, abnormal, deviant. But to American Indians, the institution of another gender role means that berdaches are not deviant—indeed, they do conform to the requirements of a custom in which their culture tells them they fit. Berdachism is a way for society to recognize and assimilate some atypical individuals without imposing a change on them or stigmatizing them as deviant. This cultural institution confirms their legitimacy for what they are.

Societies often bestow power upon that which does not neatly fit into the usual. Since no cultural system can explain everything, a common way that many cultures deal with these inconsistencies is to imbue them with negative power, as taboo, pollution, witchcraft, or sin. That which is not understood is seen as a threat. But an alternative method of dealing with such things, or people, is to take them out of the realm of threat and to sanctify them.[1] The berdaches' role as mediator is thus not just between women and men, but also between the physical and the spiritual. American Indian cultures have taken what Western culture calls negative, and made it a positive; they have successfully utilized the different skills and insights of a class of people that Western culture has stigmatized and whose spiritual powers have been wasted.

Many Native Americans also understood that gender roles have to do with more than just biological sex. The standard Western view that one's sex is always a certainty, and that one's gender identity and sex role always conform to one's morphological sex is a view that dies hard. Western thought is typified by such dichotomies of groups perceived to be mutually exclusive: male and female, black and white, right and wrong, good and evil. Clearly, the world is not so simple; such clear divisions are not always realistic. Most American Indian worldviews generally are much more accepting of the ambiguities of life. Acceptance of gender variation in the berdache tradition is typical of many native cultures' approach to life in general.

Overall, these are generalizations based on those Native American societies that had an accepted role for berdaches. Not all cultures recognized such a respected status. Berdachism in aboriginal North America was most established among tribes in four areas: first, the Prairie and western Great Lakes, the northern and central Great Plains, and the lower Mississippi Valley; second, Florida and the Caribbean; third, the Southwest, the Great Basin, and California; and fourth, scattered areas of the Northwest, western Canada, and Alaska. For some reason it is not noticeable in eastern North America, with the exception of its southern rim....

AMERICAN INDIAN RELIGIONS

Native American religions offered an explanation for human diversity by their creation stories. In some tribal religions, the Great Spiritual Being is conceived as neither male nor female but as a combination of both. Among the Kamia of the Southwest, for example, the bearer of plant seeds and the introducer of Kamia culture was a man-woman spirit named Warharmi.[2] A key episode of the Zuni creation story involves a battle between the kachina spirits of the agricultural Zunis and the enemy hunter spirits. Every four years an elaborate ceremony commemorates this myth. In the story a kachina spirit called *ko'lhamana* was captured by the enemy spirits and transformed in the process. This transformed spirit became a mediator between the two sides, using his peacemaking skills to merge the differing lifestyles of hunters and farmers. In the ceremony, a dramatic reenactment of the myth, the part of the transformed *ko'lhamana* spirit, is performed by a berdache.[3] The Zuni word for berdache is *lhamana*, denoting its closeness to the spiritual mediator who brought hunting and farming together.[4] The moral of this story is that the berdache was created by the deities for a special purpose, and that this creation led to the improvement of society. The continual reenactment of this story provides a justification for the Zuni berdache in each generation.

In contrast to this, the lack of spiritual justification in a creation myth could denote a lack of tolerance for gender variation. The Pimas, unlike most of their Southwestern neighbors, did not respect a berdache status. *Wi-kovat*, their derogatory word, means "like a girl," but it does not signify a recognized social role. Pima mythology reflects this lack of acceptance, in a folk tale that explains male androgyny as due to Papago witchcraft. Knowing that the Papagos respected berdaches, the Pimas blamed such an occurrence on an alien influence.[5] While the Pimas' condemnatory attitude is unusual, it does point out the importance of spiritual explanations for the acceptance of gender variance in a culture.

Other Native American creation stories stand in sharp contrast to the Pima explanation. A good example is the account of the Navajos, which presents women and men as equals. The Navajo origin tale is told as a story of five worlds. The first people were First Man and First Woman, who were created equally and at the same time. The first two worlds that they lived in were bleak and unhappy, so they escaped to the third world. In the third world lived two twins, Turquoise Boy and White Shell Girl, who were the first berdaches. In the Navajo language the world for berdache is *nadle*, which means "changing one" or "one who is transformed." It is applied to hermaphrodites—those who are born with the genitals of both male and female—and also to "those who pretend to be *nadle*," who take on a social role that is distinct from either men or women.[6]

In the third world, First Man and First Woman began farming, with the help of the changing twins. One of the twins noticed some clay and, holding it in the palm of his/her hand, shaped it into the first pottery bowl. Then he/she formed a plate, a water dipper, and a pipe. The second twin observed some reeds and began to weave them, making the first basket. Together they shaped axes and grinding stones from rocks, and hoes from bone. All these new inventions made the people very happy.[7]

The message of this story is that humans are dependent for many good things on the inventiveness of *nadle*. Such individuals were present from the earliest eras of human existence, and their presence was never questioned. They were part of the natural order of the universe, with a special contribution to make.

Later on in the Navajo creation story, White Shell Girl entered the moon and became the Moon Bearer. Turquoise Boy, however, remained with the people. When First Man realized that Turquoise Boy could do all manner of women's work as well as women, all the men left the women and crossed a big river. The men hunted and planted crops. Turquoise Boy ground the corn, cooked the food, and weaved cloth for the men. Four years passed with the women and men separated, and the men were happy with the *nadle*. Later, however the women wanted to learn how to grind corn from the *nadle*, and both the men and women had decided that it was not good to continue living separately. So the women crossed the river and the people were reunited.[8]

They continued living happily in the third world, until one day a great flood began. The people ran to the highest mountaintop, but the water kept rising and they all feared they would be drowned. But just in time, the ever-inventive Turquoise Boy found a large reed. They climbed upward inside the tall hollow reed, and came out at the top into the fourth world. From there, White Shell Girl brought another reed, and the climbed again to the fifth world, which is the present world of the Navajos.[9]

These stories suggest that the very survival of humanity is dependent on the inventiveness of berdaches. With such a mythological belief system, it is no wonder that the Navajos held *nadle* in high regard. The concept of the *nadle* is well formulated in the creation story. As children were educated by these stories, and all Navajos believed in them, the high status accorded to gender variation was passed down from generation to generation. Such stories also provided instruction for *nadle* themselves to live by. A spiritual explanation guaranteed a special place for a person who was considered different but not deviant.

For American Indians, the important explanations of the world are spiritual ones. In their view, there is a deeper reality than the here-and-now. The real essence or wisdom occurs when one finally gives up trying to explain events in terms of "logic" and "reality." Many confusing aspects of existence can better be explained by actions of a multiplicity of spirits. Instead of a concept of a single god, there is an awareness of "that which we do not understand." In Lakota religion, for example, the term *Wakan Tanka* is often translated as "god." But a more proper translation, according to the medicine people who taught me, is "The Great Mystery."[10]

While rationality can explain much, there are limits to human capabilities of understanding. The English language is structured to account for cause and effect. For example, English speakers say, "It is raining," with the implication that there is a cause "it" that leads to rain. Many Indian languages, on the other hand, merely note what is most accurately translated as "raining" as an observable fact. Such an approach brings a freedom to stop worrying about causes of things, and merely to relax and accept that our human insights can go only so far. By not taking ourselves too seriously, or overinflating human importance, we can get beyond the logical world.

The emphasis of American Indian religions, then, is on the spiritual nature of all things. To understand the physical world, one must appreciate the underlying spiritual essence. Then one can begin to see that the physical is only a faint shadow, a partial reflection, of a supernatural and extrarational world. By the Indian view, everything that exists is spiritual. Every object—plants, rocks, water, air, the moon, animals, humans, the earth itself—has a spirit. The spirit of one thing (including a human) is not superior to the spirit of any other. Such a view promotes a sophisticated ecological awareness of the place that humans have in the larger environment. The function of religion is not to try to condemn or to change what exists, but to accept the realities of the world and to appreciate their contributions to life. Everything that exists has a purpose.[11]

One of the basic tenets of American Indian religion is the notion that everything in the universe is related. Nevertheless, things that exist are often seen as having a counterpart: sky and earth, plant and animal, water and fire. In all of these polarities, there exist mediators. The role of the mediator is to hold the polarities together, to keep the world from disintegrating. Polarities exist within human society also. The most important category within Indian society is gender. The notions of Woman and Man underlie much of social interaction and are comparable to the other major polarities. Women, with their nurtural qualities, are associated with the earth, while men are associated

with the sky. Women gatherers and farmers deal with plants (of the earth), while men hunters deal with animals.

The mediator between the polarities of woman and man, in the American Indian religious explanation, is a being that combines the elements of both genders. This might be a combination in a physical sense, as in the case of hermaphrodites. Many Native American religions accept this phenomenon in the same way that they accept other variations from the norm. But more important is their acceptance of the idea that gender can be combined in ways other than physical hermaphroditism. The physical aspects of a thing or a person, after all, are not nearly as important as its spirit. American Indians use the concept of a person's *spirit* in the way that other Americans use the concept of a person's *character*. Consequently, physical hermaphroditism is not necessary for the idea of gender mixing. A person's character, their spiritual essence, is the crucial thing.

THE BERDACHE'S SPIRIT

Individuals who are physically normal might have the spirit of the other sex, might range somewhere between the two sexes, or might have a spirit that is distinct from either women or men. Whatever category they fall into, they are seen as being different from men. They are accepted spiritually as "Not Man." Whichever option is chosen, Indian religions offer spiritual explanations. Among the Arapahos of the Plains, berdaches are called *haxu'xan* and are seen to be that way as a result of a supernatural gift from birds or animals. Arapaho mythology recounts the story of Nih'a'ca, the first *haxu'xan*. He pretended to be a woman and married the mountain lion, a symbol for masculinity. The myth, as recorded by ethnographer Alfred Kroeber about 1900, recounted that "These people had the natural desire to become women, and as they grew up gradually became women. They gave up the desires of men. They were married to men. They had miraculous power and could do supernatural things. For instance, it was one of them that first made an intoxicant from rainwater."[12] Besides the theme of inventiveness, similar to the Navajo creation story, the berdache role is seen as a product of a "natural desire." Berdaches "gradually became women," which underscores the notion of woman as a social category rather than as a fixed biological entity. Physical biological sex is less important in gender classification than a person's desire—one's spirit.

They myths contain no prescriptions for trying to change berdaches who are acting out their desires of the heart. Like many other cultures' myths, the Zuni origin myths simply sanction the idea that gender can be transformed independently of biological sex.[13] Indeed, myths warn of dire consequences when interference with such a transformation is attempted. Prince Alexander Maximilian of the German state of Wied, traveling in the northern Plains in the 1830s, heard a myth about a warrior who once tried to force a berdache to avoid women's clothing. The berdache resisted, and the warrior shot him with an arrow. Immediately the berdache disappeared, and the warrior saw only a pile of stones with his arrow in them. Since then, the story concluded, no intelligent person would try to coerce a berdache.[14] Making the point even more directly, a Mandan myth told of an Indian who tried to force *mihdake* (berdaches) to give up their distinctive dress and status, which led the spirits to punish many people with death. After that, no Mandans interfered with berdaches.[15]

With this kind of attitude, reinforced by myth and history, the aboriginal view accepts human diversity. The creation story of the Mohave of the Colorado River Valley speaks of a time when people were not sexually differentiated. From this perspective, it is easy to accept that certain individuals might combine elements of masculinity and femininity.[16] A respected Mohave elder, speaking in the 1930s, stated this viewpoint simply: "From the very beginning of the world it was meant that there should be [berdaches], just as it was instituted that there should be shamans. They were intended for that purpose."[17]

This elder also explained that a child's tendencies to become a berdache are apparent early, by about age nine to twelve, before the child reaches puberty: "That is the time when young persons become initiated into the functions of their sex.... None but young people will become berdaches as a rule."[18] Many tribes have a public ceremony that acknowledges the acceptance of berdache status. A Mohave shaman related the ceremony for his tribe: "When the child was about ten years old his relatives would begin discussing his strange ways. Some of them disliked it, but the more intelligent began envisaging an initiation ceremony." The relatives prepare for the ceremony without letting the boy know if it. It is meant to take him by surprise, to be both an initiation and a test of his true inclinations. People from various settlements are invited to attend. The family wants the community to see it and become accustomed to accepting the boy as an *alyha*.

On the day of the ceremony, the shaman explained, the boy is led into a circle: "If the boy showed a willingness to remain standing in the circle, exposed to the public eye, it was almost certain that he would go through with the ceremony. The singer, hidden behind the crowd, began singing the songs. As soon as the sound reached the boy he began to dance as women do." If the boy is unwilling to assume *alyha* status, he would refuse to dance. But if his character—his spirit—is *alyha*, "the song goes right to his heart and he will dance with much intensity. He cannot help it. After the fourth song he is proclaimed." After the ceremony, the boy is carefully bathed and receives a woman's skirt. He is then led back to the dance ground, dressed as an *alyha*, and announces his new feminine name to the crowd. After that he would resent being called by his old male name.[19]

Among the Yuman tribes of the Southwest, the transformation is marked by a social gathering, in which the berdache prepares a meal for the friends of the family.[20] Ethnographer Ruth Underhill, doing fieldwork among the Papago Indians in the early 1930s, wrote that berdaches were common among the Papago Indians, and were usually publicly acknowledged in childhood. She recounted that a boy's parents would test him if they noticed that he preferred female pursuits. The regular pattern, mentioned by many of Underhill's Papago informants, was to build a small brush enclosure. Inside the enclosure they placed a man's bow and arrows, and also a woman's basket. At the appointed time the boy was brought to the enclosure as the adults watched from outside. The boy was told to go inside the circle of brush. Once he was inside, the adults "set fire to the enclosure. They watched what he took with him as he ran out and if it was the basketry materials, they reconciled themselves to his being a berdache."[21]

What is important to recognize in all of these practices is that the assumption of a berdache role was not forced on the boy by others. While adults might have their suspicions, it was only when the child made the proper move that he was considered a berdache. By doing woman's dancing, preparing a meal, or taking the woman's basket he was making an important symbolic gesture. Indian children were not stupid, and they knew the implications of these ceremonies beforehand. A boy in the enclosure could have left without taking anything, or could have taken both the man's and the woman's tools. With the community standing by watching, he was well aware that his choice would mark his assumption of berdache status. Rather than being seen as an involuntary test of his reflexes, this ceremony may be interpreted as a definite statement by the child to take on the berdache role.

Indians do not see the assumption of berdache status, however, as a free will choice on the part of the boy. People felt that the boy was acting out his basic character. The Lakota shaman Lame Deer explained:

> They were not like other men, but the Great Spirit made them *winktes* and we accepted them as such.... We think that if a woman has two little ones growing inside her, if she is going to have twins, sometimes instead of giving birth to two babies they have formed up in her womb into just one, into a half-man/half-woman kind of being.... To us a man is what nature, or his dreams, make him. We accept him for what he wants to be. That's up to him.[22]

While most of the sources indicate that once a person becomes a berdache it is a lifelong status, directions from the spirits determine everything. In at least one documented case, concerning a nineteenth-century Klamath berdache named Lele'ks, he later had a supernatural experience that led him to leave the berdache role. At that time Lele'ks began dressing and acting like a man, then married women, and eventually became one of the most famous Klamath chiefs.[23] What is important is that both in assuming berdache status and in leaving it, supernatural dictate is the determining factor.

DREAMS AND VISIONS

Many tribes see the berdache role as signifying an individual's proclivities as a dreamer and a visionary....

Among the northern Plains and related Great Lakes tribes, the idea of supernatural dictate through dreaming—the vision quest—had its highest development. The goal of the vision quest is to try to get beyond the rational world by sensory deprivation and fasting. By depriving one's body of nourishment, the brain could escape from logical thought and connect with the higher reality of the supernatural. The person doing the quest simply sits and waits for a vision. But a vision might not come easily; the person might have to wait for days.

The best way that I can describe the process is to refer to my own vision quest, which I experienced when I was living on a Lakota reservation in 1982. After a long series of prayers and blessings, the shaman who had prepared me for the ceremony took me out to an isolated area where a sweat lodge had been set up for my quest. As I walked to the spot, I worried that I might not be able to stand it. Would I be overcome by hunger? Could I tolerate the thirst? What would I do if I had to go to the toilet? The shaman told me not to worry, that a whole group of holy people would be praying and singing for me while I was on my quest.

He had me remove my clothes, symbolizing my disconnection from the material would, and crawl into the sweat lodge. Before he left me I asked him, "What do I think about?" He said, "Do not think. Just pray for spiritual guidance." After a prayer he closed the flap tightly and I was left in total darkness. I still do not understand what happened to me during my vision quest, but during the day and a half that I was out there, I never once felt hungry or thirsty or the need to go to the toilet. What happened was an intensely personal experience that I cannot and do not wish to explain, a process of being that cannot be described in rational terms.

When the shaman came to get me at the end of my time, I actually resented having to end it. He did not need to ask if my vision quest were successful. He knew that it was even before seeing me, he explained, because he saw an eagle circling over me while I underwent the quest. He helped interpret the signs I had seen, then after more prayers and singing he led me back to the others. I felt relieved, cleansed, joyful, and serene. I had been through an experience that will be a part of my memories always.

If a vision quest could have such an effect on a person not even raised in Indian society, imagine its impact on a boy who from his earliest years had been waiting for the day when he could seek his vision. Gaining his spiritual power from his first vision, it would tell him what role to take in adult life. The vision might instruct him that he is going to be a great hunter, a craftsman, a warrior, or a shaman. Or it might tell him that he will be a berdache. Among the Lakotas, or Sioux, there are several symbols for various types of visions. A person becomes *wakan* (a sacred person) if she or he dreams of a bear, a wolf, thunder, a buffalo, a white buffalo calf, or Double Woman. Each dream results in a different gift, whether it is the power to cure illness or wounds, a promise of good hunting, or the exalted role of a *heyoka* (doing things backward).

A white buffalo calf is believed to be a berdache. If a person has a dream of the sacred Double Woman, this means that she or he will have the power to seduce men. Males who have a vision of Double Woman are presented with female tools. Taking such tools means that the male will become a berdache. The Lakota word *winkte* is composed of *win*, "woman," and *kte*, "would become."[24] A contemporary Lakota berdache explains, "To become a *winkte*, you have a medicine man put you up on the hill, to search for your vision. "You can become a *winkte* if

you truly are by nature. You see a vision of the White Buffalo Calf Pipe. Sometimes it varies. A vision is like a scene in a movie."[25] Another way to become a *winkte* is to have a vision given by a *winkte* from the past.[26]…

By interpreting the result of the vision as being the work of a spirit, the vision quest frees the person from feeling responsible for his transformation. The person might even claim that the change was done against his will and without his control. Such a claim does not suggest a negative attitude about berdache status, because it is common for people to claim reluctance to fulfill their spiritual duty no matter what vision appears to them. Becoming any kind of sacred person involves taking on various social responsibilities and burdens.[27]…

A story was told among the Lakotas in the 1880s of a boy who tried to resist following his vision from Double Woman. But according to Lakota informants "few men succeed in this effort after having taken the strap in the dream." Having rebelled against the instructions given him by the Moon Being, he committed suicide.[28] The moral of that story is that one should not resist spiritual guidance, because it will lead only to grief. In another case, an Omaha young man told of being addressed by a spirit as "daughter," whereupon he discovered that he was unconsciously using feminine styles of speech. He tried to use male speech patterns, but could not. As a result of this vision, when he returned to his people he resolved himself to dress as a woman.[29] Such stories function to justify personal peculiarities as due to a fate over which the individual has no control.

Despite the usual pattern in Indian societies of using ridicule to enforce conformity, receiving instructions from a vision inhibits others from trying to change the berdache. Ritual explanation provides a way out. It also excuses the community from worrying about the cause of that person's difference, or the feeling that it is society's duty to try to change him.[30] Native American religions, above all else, encourage a basic respect for nature. If nature makes a person different, many Indians conclude, a mere human should not undertake to counter this spiritual dictate. Someone who is "unusual" can be accommodated without being stigmatized as "abnormal." Berdachism is thus not alien or threatening; it is a reflection of spirituality.

NOTES

1. Mary Douglas, *Purity and Danger* (Baltimore: Penguin, 1966), p. 52. I am grateful to Theda Perdue for convincing me that Douglas's ideas apply to berdachism. For an application of Douglas's thesis to berdaches, see James Thayer, "The Berdache of the Northern Plains: A Socioreligious Perspective," *Journal of Anthropological Research 36* (1980): 292–93.

2. E. W. Gifford, "The Kamia of Imperial Valley," *Bureau of American Ethnology Bulletin 97* (1931): 12.

3. By using present tense verbs in this text, I am not implying that such activities are necessarily continuing today. I sometimes use the present tense in the "ethnographic present," unless I use the past tense when I am referring to something that has not continued. Past tense implies that all such prac-

tices have disappeared. In the absence of fieldwork to prove such disappearance, I am not prepared to make that assumption, on the historic changes in the berdache tradition.

4. Elsie Clews Parsons, "The Zuni La' Mana," *American Anthropologist* 18 (1916): 521; Matilda Coxe Stevenson, "Zuni Indians," *Bureau of American Ethnology Annual Report 23* (1903): 37; Franklin Cushing, "Zuni Creation Myths," *Bureau of American Ethnology Annual Report 13* (1894): 401–3. Will Roscoe clarified this origin story for me.

5. W. W. Hill, "Note on the Pima Berdache," *American Anthropologist 40* (1938): 339.

6. Aileen O'Bryan, "The Dine': Origin Myths of the Navaho Indians," *Bureau of American Ethnology Bulletin 163* (1956): 5; W. W. Hill, "The Status of the Hermaphrodite and Transvestite in Navaho Culture," *American Anthropologist 37* (1935): 273.

7. Martha S. Link, *The Pollen Path: A Collection of Navajo Myths* (Stanford: Stanford University Press, 1956).

8. O'Bryan, "Dine'," pp. 5, 7, 9–10.

9. Ibid.

10. Lakota informants, July 1982. See also William Powers, *Oglala Religion* (Lincoln: University of Nebraska Press, 1977).

11. For this admittedly generalized overview of American Indian religious values, I am indebted to traditionalist informants of many tribes, but especially those of the Lakotas. For a discussion of native religions see Dennis Tedlock, *Finding the Center* (New York: Dial Press, 1972); Ruth Underhill, *Red Man's Religion* (Chicago: University of Chicago Press, 1965); and Elsi Clews Parsons, *Pueblo Indian Religion* (Chicago: University of Chicago Press, 1939).

12. lfred Kroeber, "The Arapaho," *Bulletin of the American Museum of Natural History 18* (1902–7): 19.

13. Parsons, "Zuni La' Mana," p. 525.

14. Alexander Maximilian, *Travels in the interior of North America, 1832–1834*, vol. 22 of *Early Western Travels,* ed. Reuben Gold Thwaites, 32 vols. (Cleveland: A. H. Clark, 1906), pp. 283–84, 354. Maximilian was quoted in German in the early homosexual rights book by Ferdinand Karsch-Haack, *Das Gleichgeschlechtliche Leben der Naturvölker* (The same-sex life of nature peoples) (Munich: Verlag von Ernst Reinhardt, 1911; reprinted New York: Arno Press, 1975), pp. 314, 564.

15. Oscar Koch, *Der Indianishe Eros* (Berlin: Verlag Continent, 1925), p. 61.

16. George Devereux, "Institutionalized Homosexuality of the Mohave Indians," *Human Biology 9* (1937): 509.

17. Ibid., p. 501

18. Ibid.

19. Ibid., pp. 508–9.

20. C. Daryll Forde, "Ethnography of the Yuma Indians," *University of California Publications in American Archaeology and Ethnology 28* (1931): 157.

21. Ruth Underhill, *Social Organization of the Papago Indians* (New York: Columbia University Press, 1938), p. 186. This story is also mentioned in Ruth Underhill, ed., *The Autobiography of a Papago Woman* (Menasha, Wisc.: American Anthropological Association, 1936), p. 39.

22. John Fire and Richard Erdoes, *Lame Deer, Seeker of Visions* (New York: Simon and Schuster, 1972), pp. 117, 149.

23. Theodore Stern, *The Klamath Tribe: A People and Their Reservation* (Seattle: University of Washington Press, 1965), pp. 20, 24; Theodore Stern, "Some Sources of Variability in Klamath Mythology," *Journal of American Folklore 69* (1956): 242ff; Leshe Spier, *Klamath Ethnography* (Berkeley: University of California Press, 1930), p. 52.

24. Clark Wissler, "Societies and Ceremonial Associations in the Oglala Division of the Teton Dakota," *Anthoropological Papers of the american Museum of Natural History 11,* pt. 1 (1916): 92; Powers, *Oglala Religion,* pp. 57–59.

25. Ronnie Loud Hawk, Lakota informant 4, July 1982.

26. Terry Calling Eagle, Lakota informant 5, July 1982.

27. James S. Thayer, "The Berdache of the Northern Plains: A Socioreligious Perspective," *Journal of Anthropological Research 36* (1980): 289.

28. Fletcher, "Elk Mystery," p. 281.

29. Alice Fletcher and Francis La Flesche, "The Omaha Tribe," *Bureau of American Ethnology Annual Report 27* (1905–6): 132.

30. Harriet Whitehead offers a valuable discussion of this element of the vision quest in "The Bow and the Burden Strap: A New Look at Institutionalized Homosexuality in Native North America," in *Sexual Meanings,* ed. Sherry Ortner and Harriet Whitehead (Cambridge: Cambridge University Press, 1981), pp. 99–102. See also Erikson, "Childhood," p. 329.

A Woman's Curse?

Why do cultures the world over treat menstruating women as taboo?
An anthropologist offers a new answer—and a challenge to Western
ideas about contraception

By Meredith F. Small

THE PASSAGE FROM GIRLHOOD TO womanhood is marked by a flow of blood from the uterus. Without elaborate ceremony, often without discussion, girls know that when they begin to menstruate, their world is changed forever. For the next thirty years or so, they will spend much energy having babies, or trying not to, reminded at each menstruation that either way, the biology of reproduction has a major impact on their lives.

Anthropologists have underscored the universal importance of menstruation by documenting how the event is interwoven into the ideology as well as the daily activities of cultures around the world. The customs attached to menstruation take peculiarly negative forms: the so-called menstrual taboos. Those taboos may prohibit a woman from having sex with her husband or from cooking for him. They may bar her from visiting sacred places or taking part in sacred activities. They may forbid her to touch certain items used by men, such as hunting gear or weapons, or to eat certain foods or to wash at certain times. They may also require that a woman paint her face red or wear a red hip cord, or that she segregate herself in a special hut while she is menstruating. In short, the taboos set menstruating women apart from the rest of their society, marking them as impure and polluting.

Anthropologists have studied menstrual taboos for decades, focusing on the negative symbolism of the rituals as a cultural phenomenon. Perhaps, suggested one investigator, taking a Freudian perspective, such taboos reflect the anxiety that men feel about castration, an anxiety that would be prompted by women's genital bleeding. Others have suggested that the taboos serve to prevent menstrual odor from interfering with hunting, or that they protect men from microorganisms that might otherwise be transferred during sexual intercourse with a menstruating woman. Until recently, few investigators had considered the possibility that the taboos—and the very fact of menstruation—might instead exist because they conferred an evolutionary advantage.

In the mid-1980s the anthropologist Beverly I. Strassmann of the University of Michigan in Ann Arbor began to study the ways men and women have evolved to accomplish (and regulate) reproduction. Unlike traditional anthropologists, who focus on how culture affects human behavior, Strassmann was convinced that the important role played by biology was being neglected. Menstruation, she suspected, would be a key for observing and understanding the interplay of biology and culture in human reproductive behavior.

To address the issue, Strassmann decided to seek a culture in which making babies was an ongoing part of adult life. For that she had to get away from industrialized countries, with their bias toward contraception and low birthrates. In a "natural-fertility population," she reasoned, she could more clearly see the connection between the physiology of women and the strategies men and women use to exploit that physiology for their own reproductive ends.

Strassmann ended up in a remote corner of West Africa, living in close quarters with the Dogon, a traditional society whose indigenous religion of ancestor worship requires that menstruating women spend their nights at a small hut. For more than two years Strassmann kept track of the women staying at the hut, and she confirmed the menstruations by testing urine samples for the appropriate hormonal changes. In so doing, she amassed the first long-term data describing how a traditional society appropriates a physiological event—menstruation—and refracts that event through a prism of behaviors and beliefs.

What she found explicitly challenges the conclusions of earlier investigators about the cultural function of menstrual taboos. For the Dogon men, she discovered, enforcing visits to the menstrual hut serves to channel parental resources into the upbringing of their own children. But more, Strassmann, who also had training as a reproductive physiologist, proposed a new theory of why menstruation itself evolved as it did—and again, the answer is essentially a story of conserving resources. Finally, her observations pose provocative questions about women's health in industrialized societies, raising serious doubts about the tactics favored by Western medicine for developing contraceptive technology.

MENSTRUATION IS THE VISIBLE stage of the ovarian cycle, orchestrated primarily by hormones secreted by the ovaries: progesterone and a family of hormones called estrogens. At the beginning of each cycle (by convention, the first day of a woman's period) the levels of the estrogens begin to rise. After about five days, as their concentrations increase, they cause the blood- and nutrient-rich inner lining of the uterus, called the endometrium, to thicken and acquire a densely branching network of blood vessels. At about the middle of the cycle, ovulation takes place, and an egg makes its way from one of the two ovaries down one of the paired fallopian tubes to the uterus. The follicle from which the egg was released in the ovary now begins to secrete progesterone as well as estrogens, and the progesterone causes the endometrium to swell and become even richer with blood vessels—in short, fully ready for a pregnancy, should conception take place and the fertilized egg become implanted.

If conception does take place, the levels of estrogens and progesterone continue to rise throughout the pregnancy. That keeps the endometrium thick enough to support the quickening life inside the uterus. When the baby is born and the new mother begins nursing, the estrogens and progesterone fall to their initial levels, and lactation hormones keep them suppressed. The uterus thus lies quiescent until frequent lactation ends, which triggers the return to ovulation.

If conception does not take place after ovulation, all the ovarian hormones also drop to their initial levels, and menstruation—the shedding of part of the uterine lining—begins. The lining is divided into three layers: a basal layer that is constantly maintained, and two superficial layers, which shed and regrow with each menstrual cycle. All mammals undergo cyclical changes in the state of the endometrium. In most mammals the sloughed-off layers are resorbed into the body if fertilization does not take place. But in some higher primates, including

humans, some of the shed endometrium is not resorbed. The shed lining, along with some blood, flows from the body through the vaginal opening, a process that in humans typically lasts from three to five days.

OF COURSE, PHYSIOLOGICAL FACTS alone do not explain why so many human groups have infused a bodily function with symbolic meaning. And so in 1986 Strassmann found herself driving through the Sahel region of West Africa at the peak of the hot season, heading for a sandstone cliff called the Bandiagara Escarpment, in Mali. There, permanent Dogon villages of mud or stone houses dotted the rocky plateau. The menstrual huts were obvious: round, low-roofed buildings set apart from the rectangular dwellings of the rest of the village.

The Dogon are a society of millet and onion farmers who endorse polygyny, and they maintain their traditional culture despite the occasional visits of outsiders. In a few Dogon villages, in fact, tourists are fairly common, and ethnographers had frequently studied the Dogon language, religion and social structure before Strassmann's arrival. But her visit was the first time someone from the outside wanted to delve into an intimate issue in such detail.

It took Strassmann a series of hikes among villages, and long talks with male elders under the thatched-roof shelters where they typically gather, to find the appropriate sites for her research. She gained permission for her study in fourteen villages, eventually choosing two. That exceptional welcome, she thinks, emphasized the universality of her interests. "I'm working on all the things that really matter to [the Dogon]—fertility, economics—so they never questioned my motives or wondered why I would be interested in these things," she says. "It seemed obvious to them." She set up shop for the next two and a half years in a stone house in the village, with no running water or electricity. Eating the daily fare of the Dogon, millet porridge, she and a research assistant began to integrate themselves into village life, learning the language, getting to know people and tracking visits to the menstrual huts.

Following the movements of menstruating women was surprisingly easy. The menstrual huts are situated outside the walled compounds of the village, but in full view of the men's thatched-roof shelters. As the men relax under their shelters, they can readily see who leaves the huts in the morning and returns to them in the evening. And as nonmenstruating women pass the huts on their way to and from the fields or to other compounds, they too can see who is spending the night there. Strassmann found that when she left her house in the evening to take data, any of the villagers could accurately predict whom she would find in the menstrual huts.

THE HUTS THEMSELVES ARE CRAMPED, dark buildings—hardly places where a woman might go to escape the drudgery of work or to avoid an argument with her husband or a co-wife. The huts sometimes become so crowded that some occupants are forced outside—making the women even more conspicuous. Although babies and toddlers can go with their mothers to the huts, the women consigned there are not allowed to spend time with the rest of their families. They must cook with special pots, not their usual household possessions. Yet they are still expected to do their usual jobs, such as working in the fields.

Why, Strassmann wondered, would anyone put up with such conditions?

The answer, for the Dogon, is that a menstruating woman is a threat to the sanctity of religious altars, where men pray and make sacrifices for the protection of their fields, their families and their village. If menstruating women come near the altars, which are situated both indoors and outdoors, the Dogon believe that their aura of pollution will ruin the altars and bring calamities upon the village. The belief is so ingrained that the women themselves have internalized it, feeling its burden of responsibility and potential guilt. Thus violations of the taboo are rare, because a menstruating woman who breaks the rules knows that she is personally responsible if calamities occur.

NEVERTHELESS, STRASSMANN STILL thought a more functional explanation for menstrual taboos might also exist, one closely related to reproduction. As she was well aware, even before her studies among the Dogon, people around the world have a fairly sophisticated view of how reproduction works. In general, people everywhere know full well that menstruation signals the absence of a pregnancy and the possibility of another one. More precisely, Strassmann could frame her hypothesis by reasoning as follows: Across cultures, men and women recognize that a lack of menstrual cycling in a woman implies she is either pregnant, lactating or menopausal. Moreover, at least among natural-fertility cultures that do not practice birth control, continual cycles during peak reproductive years imply to people in those cultures that a woman is sterile. Thus, even though people might not be able to pinpoint ovulation, they can easily identify whether a woman will soon be ready to conceive on the basis of whether she is menstruating. And that leads straight to Strassmann's insightful hypothesis about the role of menstrual taboos: information about menstruation can be a means of tracking paternity.

"There are two important pieces of information for assessing paternity," Strassmann notes: timing of intercourse and timing of menstruation. "By forcing women to signal menstruation, men are trying to gain equal access to one part of that critical information." Such information, she explains, is crucial to Dogon men, because they invest so many resources in their own offspring. Descent is marked through the male line; land and the food that comes from the land is passed down from fathers to sons. Information about paternity is thus crucial to a man's entire lineage. And because each man has as many as four wives, he cannot possibly track them all. So forcing women to signal their menstrual periods, or lack thereof, helps men avoid cuckoldry.

TO TEST HER HYPOTHESIS, STRASSmann tracked residence in the menstrual huts for 736 consecutive days, collecting data on 477 complete cycles. She noted who was at each hut and how long each

woman stayed. She also collected urine from ninety-three women over a ten-week period, to check the correlation between residence in the menstrual hut and the fact of menstruation.

The combination of ethnographic records and urinalyses showed that the Dogon women mostly play by the rules. In 86 percent of the hormonally detected menstruations, women went to the hut. Moreover, none of the tested women went to the hut when they were not menstruating. In the remaining 14 percent of the tested menstruations, women stayed home from the hut, in violation of the taboo, but some were near menopause and so not at high risk for pregnancy. More important, none of the women who violated the taboo did it twice in a row. Even they were largely willing to comply.

Thus, Strassmann concluded, the huts do indeed convey a fairly reliable signal, to men and to everyone else, about the status of a woman's fertility. When she leaves the hut, she is considered ready to conceive. When she stops going to the hut, she is evidently pregnant or menopausal. And women of prime reproductive age who visit the hut on a regular basis are clearly infertile.

It also became clear to Strassmann that the Dogon do indeed use that information to make paternity decisions. In several cases a man was forced to marry a pregnant woman, simply because everyone knew that the man had been the woman's first sexual partner after her last visit to the menstrual hut. Strassmann followed one case in which a child was being brought up by a man because he was the mother's first sexual partner after a hut visit, even though the woman soon married a different man. (The woman already knew she was pregnant by the first man at the time of her marriage, and she did not visit the menstrual hut before she married. Thus the truth was obvious to everyone, and the real father took the child.)

In general, women are cooperative players in the game because without a man, a woman has no way to support herself or her children. But women follow the taboo reluctantly. They complain about going to the hut. And if their husbands convert from the traditional religion of the Dogon to a religion that does not impose menstrual taboos, such as Is-

lam or Christianity, the women quickly cease visiting the hut. Not that such a religious conversion quells a man's interest in his wife's fidelity: far from it. But the rules change. Perhaps the sanctions of the new religion against infidelity help keep women faithful, so the men can relax their guard. Or perhaps the men are willing to trade the reproductive advantages of the menstrual taboo for the economic benefits gained by converting to the new religion. Whatever the case, Strassmann found an almost perfect correlation between a husband's religion and his wives' attendance at the hut. In sum, the taboo is established by men, backed by supernatural forces, and internalized and accepted by women until the men release them from the belief.

BUT BEYOND THE CULTURAL MACHInations of men and women that Strassmann expected to find, her data show something even more fundamental—and surprising—about female biology. On average, she calculates, a woman in a natural-fertility population such as the Dogon has only about 110 menstrual periods in her lifetime. The rest of the time she will be prepubescent, pregnant, lactating or menopausal. Women in industrialized cultures, by contrast, have more than three times as many cycles: 350 to 400, on average, in a lifetime. They reach menarche (their first menstruation) earlier—at age twelve and a half, compared with the onset age of sixteen in natural-fertility cultures. They have fewer babies, and they lactate hardly at all. All those factors lead women in the industrialized world to a lifetime of nearly continuous menstrual cycling.

The big contrast in cycling profiles during the reproductive years can be traced specifically to lactation. Women in more traditional societies spend most of their reproductive years in lactation amenorrhea, the state in which the hormonal changes required for nursing suppress ovulation and inhibit menstruation. And it is not just that the Dogon bear more children (eight to nine on average); they also nurse each child on demand rather than in scheduled bouts, all through the night as well as the day, and intensely enough that ovulation simply stops for about twenty months per child. Women in industrialized societies typically do not breast-feed as intensely (or at all), and rarely breast-feed each child for as long as the Dogon women do. (The average for American women is four months.)

The Dogon experience with menstruation may be far more typical of the human condition over most of evolutionary history than is the standard menstrual experience in industrialized nations. If so, Strassmann's findings alter some of the most closely held beliefs about female biology. Contrary to what the Western medical establishment might think, it is not particularly "normal" to menstruate each month. The female body, according to Strassmann, is biologically designed to spend much more time in lactation amenorrhea than in menstrual cycling. That in itself suggests that oral contraceptives, which alter hormone levels to suppress ovulation and produce a bleeding, could be forcing a continual state of cycling for which the body is ill-prepared. Women might be better protected against reproductive cancers if their contraceptives mimicked lactation amenorrhea and depressed the female reproductive hormones, rather than forcing the continual ebb and flow of menstrual cycles.

Strassmann's data also call into question a recently popularized idea about menstruation: that regular menstrual cycles might be immunologically beneficial for women. In 1993 the controversial writer Margie Profet, whose ideas about evolutionary and reproductive biology have received vast media attention, proposed in *The Quarterly Review of Biology* that menstruation could have such an adaptive value. She noted that viruses and bacteria regularly enter the female body on the backs of sperm, and she hypothesized that the best way to get them out is to flush them out. Here, then, was a positive, adaptive role for something unpleasant, an evolutionary reason for suffering cramps each month. Menstruation, according to Profet, had evolved to rid the body of pathogens. The "anti-pathogen" theory was an exciting hypothesis, and it

helped win Profet a MacArthur Foundation award. But Strassmann's work soon showed that Profet's ideas could not be supported because of one simple fact: under less-industrialized conditions, women menstruate relatively rarely.

Instead, Strassmann notes, if there is an adaptive value to menstruation, it is ultimately a strategy to conserve the body's resources. She estimates that maintaining the endometrial lining during the second half of the ovarian cycle takes substantial metabolic energy. Once the endometrium is built up and ready to receive a fertilized egg, the tissue requires a sevenfold metabolic increase to remain rich in blood and ready to support a pregnancy. Hence, if no pregnancy is forthcoming, it makes a lot of sense for the body to let part of the endometrium slough off and then regenerate itself, instead of maintaining that rather costly but unneeded tissue. Such energy conservation is common among vertebrates: male rhesus monkeys have shrunken testes during their nonbreeding season, Burmese pythons shrink their guts when they are not digesting, and hibernating animals put their metabolisms on hold.

Strassmann also suggests that periodically ridding oneself of the endometrium could make a difference to a woman's long-term survival. Because female reproductive hormones affect the brain and other tissues, the metabolism of the entire body is involved during cycling. Strassmann estimates that by keeping hormonal low through half the cycle, a woman can save about six days' worth of energy for every four nonconceptive cycles. Such caloric conservation might have proved useful to early hominids who lived by hunting and gathering, and even today it might be helpful for women living in less affluent circumstances than the ones common in the industrialized West.

B UT PERHAPS THE MOST PROVOCATIVE implications of Strassmann's work have to do with women's health. In 1994 a group of physicians and anthropologists pub-

lished a paper, also in *The Quarterly Review of Biology*, suggesting that the reproductive histories and lifestyles of women in industrialized cultures are at odds with women's naturally evolved biology, and that the differences lead to greater risks of reproductive cancers. For example, the investigators estimated that women in affluent cultures may have a hundredfold greater risk of breast cancer than do women who subsist by hunting and gathering. The increased risk is probably caused not only by low levels of exercise and a high-fat diet, but also by a relatively high number of menstrual cycles over a lifetime. Repeated exposure to the hormones of the ovarian cycle—because of early menarche, late menopause, lack of pregnancy and little or no breast-feeding—is implicated in other reproductive cancers as well.

Those of us in industrialized cultures have been running an experiment on ourselves. The body evolved over millions of years to move across the landscape looking for food, to live in small kin-based groups, to make babies at intervals of four years or so and to invest heavily in each child by nursing intensely for years. How many women now follow those traditional patterns? We move little, we rely on others to get our food, and we rarely reproduce or lactate. Those culturally initiated shifts in lifestyles may pose biological risks.

Our task is not to overcome that biology, but to work with it. Now that we have a better idea of how the female body was designed, it may be time to rework our lifestyles and change some of our expectations. It may be time to borrow from our distant past or from our contemporaries in distant cultures, and treat our bodies more as nature intended.

MEREDITH F. SMALL is a professor of anthropology at Cornell University in Ithaca, New York. Her latest book, OUR BABIES, OURSELVES: HOW BIOLOGY AND CULTURE SHAPE THE WAY WE PARENT, *was published in May 1998 [see Laurence A. Marschall's review in Books in Brief, November/December 1998].*

Reprinted by permission of *The Sciences*, January/February 1999, pp. 24–29. © 1999 by the New York Academy of Science. Individual subscriptions are $28 per year. Write to: The Sciences, 2 East 63rd Street, New York, NY 10021.

Where Fat Is a Mark of Beauty

In a rite of passage, some Nigerian girls spend months gaining weight and learning customs in a special room. "To be called a 'slim princess' is an abuse," says a defender of the practice.

By Ann M. Simmons
TIMES STAFF WRITER

AKPABUYO, Nigeria—Margaret Bassey Ene currently has one mission in life: gaining weight.

The Nigerian teenager has spent every day since early June in a "fattening room" specially set aside in her father's mud-and-thatch house. Most of her waking hours are spent eating bowl after bowl of rice, yams, plantains, beans and *gari*, a porridge-like mixture of dried cassava and water.

After three more months of starchy diet and forced inactivity, Margaret will be ready to reenter society bearing the traditional mark of female beauty among her Efik people: fat.

In contrast to many Western cultures where thin is in, many culture-conscious people in the Efik and other communities in Nigeria's southeastern Cross River state hail a woman's rotundity as a sign of good health, prosperity and allure.

The fattening room is at the center of a centuries-old rite of passage from maidenhood to womanhood. The months spent in pursuit of poundage are supplemented by daily visits from elderly matrons who impart tips on how to be a successful wife and mother. Nowadays, though, girls who are not yet marriage-bound do a tour in the rooms purely as a coming-of-age ceremony. And sometimes, nursing mothers return to the rooms to put on more weight.

"The fattening room is like a kind of school where the girl is taught about motherhood," said Sylvester Odey, director of the Cultural Center Board in Calabar, capital of Cross River state. "Your daily routine is to sleep, eat and grow fat."

Like many traditional African customs, the fattening room is facing relentless pressure from Western influences. Health campaigns linking excess fat to heart disease and other illnesses are changing the eating habits of many Nigerians, and urban dwellers are opting out of the time-consuming process.

Effiong Okon Etim, an Efik village chief in the district of Akpabuyo, said some families cannot afford to constantly feed a daughter for more than a few months. That compares with a stay of up to two years, as was common earlier this century, he said.

But the practice continues partly because "people might laugh at you because you didn't have money to allow your child to pass through the rite of passage," Etim said. What's more, many believe an unfattened girl will be sickly or unable to bear children.

Etim, 65, put his two daughters in a fattening room together when they were 12 and 15 years old, but some girls undergo the process as early as age 7, after undergoing the controversial practice of genital excision.

BIGGER IS BETTER, ACCORDING TO CUSTOM

As for how fat is fat enough, there is no set standard. But the unwritten rule is the bigger the better, said Mkoyo Edet, Etim's sister.

"Beauty is in the weight," said Edet, a woman in her 50s who spent three months in a fattening room when she was 7. "To be called a 'slim princess' is an abuse. The girl is fed constantly whether she likes it or not."

In Margaret's family, there was never any question that she would enter the fattening room.

"We inherited it from our forefathers; it is one of the heritages we must continue," said Edet Essien Okon, 25, Margaret's stepfather and a language and linguistics graduate of the University of Calabar. "It's a good thing to do; it's an initiation rite."

His wife, Nkoyo Effiong, 27, agreed: "As a woman, I feel it is proper for me to put my daughter in there, so she can be educated."

Effiong, a mother of five, spent four months in a fattening room at the age of 10.

Margaret, an attractive girl with a cheerful smile and hair plaited in fluffy bumps, needs only six months in the fat-

137

tening room because she was already naturally plump, her stepfather said.

During the process, she is treated as a goddess, but the days are monotonous. To amuse herself, Margaret has only an instrument made out of a soda bottle with a hole in it, which she taps on her hand to play traditional tunes.

Still, the 16-year-old says she is enjoying the highly ritualized fattening practice.

"I'm very happy about this," she said, her belly already distended over the waist of her loincloth. "I enjoy the food, except for *gari*."

Day in, day out, Margaret must sit cross-legged on a special stool inside the secluded fattening room. When it is time to eat, she sits on the floor on a large, dried plantain leaf, which also serves as her bed. She washes down the mounds of food with huge pots of water and takes traditional medicine made from leaves and herbs to ensure proper digestion.

As part of the rite, Margaret's face is decorated with a white, claylike chalk.

"You have to prepare the child so that if a man sees her, she will be attractive," Chief Etim said.

Tufts of palm leaf fiber, braided and dyed red, are hung around Margaret's neck and tied like bangles around her wrists and ankles. They are adjusted as she grows.

Typically, Margaret would receive body massages using the white chalk powder mixed with heavy red palm oil. But the teen said her parents believe the skin-softening, blood-stimulating massages might cause her to expand further than necessary.

Margaret is barred from doing her usual chores or any other strenuous physical activities. And she is forbidden to receive visitors, save for the half a dozen matrons who school Margaret in the etiquette of the Efik clan.

They teach her such basics as how to sit, walk and talk in front of her husband. And they impart wisdom about cleaning, sewing, child care and cooking—Efik women are known throughout Nigeria for their chicken pepper soup, pounded yams and other culinary creations.

"They advise me to keep calm and quiet, to eat the *gari*, and not to have many boyfriends so that I avoid unwanted pregnancy," Margaret said of her matron teachers. "They say that unless you have passed through this, you will not be a full-grown woman."

What little exercise Margaret gets comes in dance lessons. The matrons teach her the traditional *ekombi*, which she will be expected to perform before an audience on the day she emerges from seclusion—usually on the girl's wedding day, Etim said.

But Okon said his aim is to prepare his stepdaughter for the future, not to marry her off immediately. Efik girls receive more education than girls in most parts of Nigeria, and Okon hopes Margaret will return to school and embark on a career as a seamstress before getting married.

WEDDINGS ALSO STEEPED IN TRADITION

Once she does wed, Margaret will probably honor southeastern Nigeria's rich marriage tradition. It begins with a letter from the family of the groom to the family of the bride, explaining that "our son has seen a flower, a jewel, or something beautiful in your family, that we are interested in," said Josephine Effah-Chukwuma, program officer for women and children at the Constitutional Rights Project, a law-oriented nongovernmental organization based in the Nigerian commercial capital of Lagos.

If the girl and her family consent, a meeting is arranged. The groom and his relatives arrive with alcoholic beverages, soft drinks and native brews, and the bride's parents provide the food. The would-be bride's name is never uttered, and the couple are not allowed to speak, but if all goes well, a date is set for handing over the dowry. On that occasion, the bride's parents receive about $30 as a token of appreciation for their care of the young woman. "If you make the groom pay too much, it is like selling your daughter," Effah-Chukwuma said. Then, more drinks are served, and the engagement is official.

On the day of the wedding, the bride sits on a specially built wooden throne, covered by an extravagantly decorated canopy. Maidens surround her as relatives bestow gifts such as pots, pans, brooms, plates, glasses, table covers—everything she will need to start her new home. During the festivities, the bride changes clothes three times.

The high point is the performance of the *ekombi*, in which the bride twists and twirls, shielded by maidens and resisting the advances of her husband. It is his task to break through the ring and claim his bride.

Traditionalists are glad that some wedding customs are thriving despite the onslaught of modernity.

Traditional weddings are much more prevalent in southeastern Nigeria than so-called white weddings, introduced by colonialists and conducted in a church or registry office.

"In order to be considered married, you have to be married in the traditional way," said Maureen Okon, a woman of the Qua ethnic group who wed seven years ago but skipped the fattening room because she did not want to sacrifice the time. "Tradition identifies a people. It is important to keep up a culture. There is quite a bit of beauty in Efik and Qua marriages."

The Initiation of a Maasai Warrior

Tepilit Ole Saitoti

"Tepilit, circumcision means a sharp knife cutting into the skin of the most sensitive part of your body. You must not budge; don't move a muscle or even blink. You can face only one direction until the operation is completed. The slightest movement on your part will mean you are a coward, incompetent and unworthy to be a Maasai man. Ours has always been a proud family, and we would like to keep it that way. We will not tolerate unnecessary embarrassment, so you had better be ready. If you are not, tell us now so that we will not proceed. Imagine yourself alone remaining uncircumcised like the water youth [white people]. I hear they are not circumcised. Such a thing is not known in Maasailand; therefore, circumcision will have to take place even if it means holding you down until it is completed."

My father continued to speak and every one of us kept quiet. "The pain you will feel is symbolic. There is a deeper meaning in all this. Circumcision means a break between childhood and adulthood. For the first time in your life, you are regarded as a grown-up, a complete man or woman. You will be expected to give and not just to receive. To protect the family always, not just to be protected yourself. And your wise judgment will for the first time be taken into consideration. No family affairs will be discussed without your being consulted. If you are ready for all these responsibilities, tell us now. Com-

ing into manhood is not simply a matter of growth and maturity. It is a heavy load on your shoulders and especially a burden on the mind. Too much of this—I am done. I have said all I wanted to say. Fellows, if you have anything to add, go ahead and tell your brother, because I am through. I have spoken."

After a prolonged silence, one of my half-brothers said awkwardly, "Face it, man... it's painful. I won't lie about it, but it is not the end. We all went through it, after all. Only blood will flow, not milk." There was laughter and my father left.

My brother Lellia said, "Men, there are many things we must acquire and preparations we must make before the ceremony, and we will need the cooperation and help of all of you. Ostrich feathers for the crown and wax for the arrows must be collected."

"Are you *orkirekenyi?*" one of my brothers asked. I quickly replied no, and there was laughter. *Orkirekenyi* is a person who has transgressed sexually. For you must not have sexual intercourse with any circumcised woman before you yourself are circumcised. You must wait until you are circumcised. If you have not waited, you will be fined. Your father, mother, and the circumciser will take a cow from you as punishment.

Just before we departed, one of my closest friends said, "If you kick the knife, you will be in trouble." There was laugh-

ter. "By the way, if you have decided to kick the circumciser, do it well. Silence him once and for all." "Do it the way you kick a football in school." "That will fix him," another added, and we all laughed our heads off again as we departed.

The following month was a month of preparation. I and others collected wax, ostrich feathers, honey to be made into honey beer for the elders to drink on the day of circumcision, and all the other required articles.

Three days before the ceremony my head was shaved and I discarded all my belongings, such as my necklaces, garments, spear, and sword. I even had to shave my pubic hair. Circumcision in many ways is similar to Christian baptism. You must put all the sins you have committed during childhood behind and embark as a new person with a different outlook on a new life.

The circumciser came the following day and handed the ritual knives to me. He left drinking a calabash of beer. I stared at the knives uneasily. It was hard to accept that he was going to use them on my organ. I was to sharpen them and protect them from people of ill will who might try to blunt them, thus rendering them inefficient during the ritual and thereby bringing shame on our family. The knives threw a chill down my spine; I was not sure I was sharpening them properly, so I took them to my closest brother for him to check out, and he assured me that the knives were all right. I hid them well and waited.

Tension started building between me and my relatives, most of whom worried that I wouldn't make it through the ceremony valiantly. Some even snarled at me, which was their way of encouraging me. Others threw insults and abusive words my way. My sister Loiyan in particular was more troubled by the whole affair than anyone in the whole family. She had to assume my mother's role during the circumcision. Were I to fail my initiation, she would have to face the consequences. She would be spat upon and even beaten for representing the mother of an unworthy son. The same fate would befall my father, but he seemed unconcerned. He had this weird belief that because I was not particularly handsome, I must be brave. He kept saying, "God is not so bad as to have made him ugly and a coward at the same time."

Failure to be brave during circumcision would have other unfortunate consequences: the herd of cattle belonging to the family still in the compound would be beaten until they stampeded; the slaughtered oxen and honey beer prepared during the month before the ritual would go to waste; the initiate's food would be spat upon and he would have to eat it or else get a severe beating. Everyone would call him Olkasiodoi, the knife kicker.

Kicking the knife of the circumciser would not help you anyway. If you struggle and try to get away during the ritual, you will be held down until the operation is completed. Such failure of nerve would haunt you in the future. For example, no one will choose a person who kicked the knife for a position of leadership. However, there have been instances in which a person who failed to go through circumcision successfully became very brave afterwards because he was filled with anger over the incident; no one dares to scold him or remind him of it. His agemates, particularly the warriors, will act as if nothing had happened.

During the circumcision of a woman, on the other hand, she is allowed to cry as long as she does not hinder the operation. It is common to see a woman crying and kicking during circumcision. Warriors are usually summoned to help hold her down.

For women, circumcision means an end to the company of Maasai warriors. After they recuperate, they soon get married, and often to men twice their age.

The closer it came to the hour of truth, the more I was hated, particularly by those closest to me. I was deeply troubled by the withdrawal of all the support I needed. My annoyance turned into anger and resolve. I decided not to budge or blink, even if I were to see my intestines flowing before me. My resolve was hardened when newly circumcised warriors came to sing for me. Their songs were utterly insulting, intended to annoy me further. They tucked their wax arrows under my crotch and rubbed them on my nose. They repeatedly called me names.

By the end of the singing, I was fuming. Crying would have meant I was a coward. After midnight they left me alone and I went into the house and tried to sleep but could not. I was exhausted and numb but remained awake all night.

At dawn I was summoned once again by the newly circumcised warriors. They piled more and more insults on me. They sang their weird songs with even more vigor and excitement than before. The songs praised warriorhood and encouraged one to achieve it at all costs. The songs continued until the sun shone on the cattle horns clearly. I was summoned to the main cattle gate, in my hand a ritual cowhide from a cow that had been properly slaughtered during my naming ceremony. I went past Loiyan, who was milking a cow, and she muttered something. She was shaking all over. There was so much tension that people could hardly breathe.

I laid the hide down and a boy was ordered to pour ice-cold water, known as *engare entolu* (ax water), over my head. It dripped all over my naked body and I shook furiously. In a matter of seconds I was summoned to sit down. A large crowd of boys and men formed a semi-circle in front of me; women are not allowed to watch male circumcision and vice-versa. That was the last thing I saw clearly. As soon as I sat down, the circumciser appeared, his knives at the ready. He spread my legs and said, "One cut," a pronouncement necessary to prevent an ini-

tiate from claiming that he had been taken by surprise. He splashed a white liquid, a ceremonial paint called *enturoto*, across my face. Almost immediately I felt a spark of pain under my belly as the knife cut through my penis' foreskin. I happened to choose to look in the direction of the operation. I continued to observe the circumciser's fingers working mechanically. The pain became numbness and my lower body felt heavy, as if I were weighed down by a heavy burden. After fifteen minutes or so, a man who had been supporting from behind pointed at something, as if to assist the circumciser. I came to learn later that the circumciser's eyesight had been failing him and that my brothers had been mad at him because the operation had taken longer than was usually necessary. All the same, I remained pinned down until the operation was over. I heard a call for milk to wash the knives, which signaled the end, and soon the ceremony was over.

With words of praise, I was told to wake up, but I remained seated. I waited for the customary presents in appreciation of my bravery. My father gave me a cow and so did my brother Lillia. The man who had supported my back and my brother-in-law gave me a heifer. In all I had eight animals given to me. I was carried inside the house to my own bed to recuperate as activities intensified to celebrate my bravery.

I laid on my own bed and bled profusely. The blood must be retained within the bed, for according to Maasai tradition, it must not spill to the ground. I was drenched in my own blood. I stopped bleeding after about half an hour but soon was in intolerable pain. I was supposed to squeeze my organ and force blood to flow out of the wound, but no one had told me, so the blood coagulated and caused unbearable pain. The circumciser was brought to my aid and showed me what to do, and soon the pain subsided.

The following morning, I was escorted by a small boy to a nearby valley to walk and relax, allowing my wound to drain. This was common for everyone who had been circumcised, as well as for women who had just given birth. Having lost a lot of blood, I was extremely weak. I walked very slowly, but in spite of my caution I fainted. I tried to hang on to bushes and shrubs, but I fell, irritating my wound. I came out of unconsciousness quickly, and the boy who was escorting me never realized what had happened. I was so scared that I told him to lead me back home. I could have died without there being anyone around who could have helped me. From that day on, I was selective of my company while I was feeble.

In two weeks I was able to walk and was taken to join other newly circumcised boys far away from our settlement. By tradition Maasai initiates are required to decorate their headdresses with all kinds of colorful birds they have killed. On our way to the settlement, we hunted birds and teased girls by shooting them with our wax blunt arrows. We danced and ate and were well treated wherever we went. We were protected from the cold and rain during the healing period. We were not allowed to touch food, as we were regarded as unclean, so whenever we ate we had to use specially prepared sticks instead. We remained in this pampered state until our wounds healed and our headdresses were removed. Our heads were shaved, we discarded our black cloaks and bird headdresses and embarked as newly shaven warriors, Irkeleani.

As long as I live I will never forget the day my head was shaved and I emerged a man, a Maasai warrior. I felt a sense of control over my destiny so great that no words can accurately describe it. I now stood with confidence, pride, and happiness of being, for all around me I was desired and loved by beautiful, sensuous Maasai maidens. I could now interact with women and even have sex with them, which I had not been allowed before. I was now regarded as a responsible person.

In the old days, warriors were like gods, and women and men wanted only to be the parent of a warrior. Everything else would be taken care of as a result. When a poor family had a warrior, they ceased to be poor. The warrior would go on raids and bring cattle back. The warrior would defend the family against all odds. When a society respects the individual and displays confidence in him the way the Maasai do their warriors, the individual can grow to his fullest potential. Whenever there was a task requiring physical strength or bravery, the Maasai would call

upon their warriors. They hardly ever fall short of what is demanded of them and so are characterized by pride, confidence, and an extreme sense of freedom. But there is an old saying in Maasai: "You are never a free man until your father dies." In other words, your father is paramount while he is alive and you are obligated to respect him. My father took advantage of this principle and held a tight grip on all his warriors, including myself. He always wanted to know where we all were at any given time. We fought against his restrictions, but without success. I, being the youngest of my father's five warriors, tried even harder to get loose repeatedly, but each time I was punished severely.

Roaming the plains with other warriors in pursuit of girls and adventure was a warrior's pastime. We would wander from one settlement to another, singing, wrestling, hunting, and just playing. Often I was ready to risk my father's punishment for this wonderful freedom.

One clear day my father sent me to take sick children and one of his wives to the dispensary in the Korongoro Highlands. We rode in the L. S. B. Leakey lorry. We ascended the highlands and were soon attended to in the local hospital. Near the conservation offices I met several acquaintances, and one of them told me of an unusual circumcision that was about to take place in a day or two. All the local warriors and girls were preparing to attend it.

The highlands were a lush green from the seasonal rains and the sky was a purple-blue with no clouds in sight. The land was overflowing with milk, and the warriors felt and looked their best, as they always did when there was plenty to eat and drink. Everyone was at ease. The demands the community usually made on warriors during the dry season when water was scarce and wells had to be dug were now not necessary. Herds and flocks were entrusted to youths to look after. The warriors had all the time for themselves. But my father was so strict that even at times like these he still insisted on overworking us in one way or another. He believed that by keeping us busy, he would keep us out of trouble.

When I heard about the impending ceremony, I decided to remain behind in the Korongoro Highlands and attend it now

that the children had been treated. I knew very well that I would have to make up a story for my father upon my return, but I would worry about that later. I had left my spear at home when I boarded the bus, thinking that I would be coming back that very day. I felt lighter but now regretted having left it behind; I was so used to carrying it wherever I went. In gales of laughter resulting from our continuous teasing of each other, we made our way toward a distant kraal. We walked at a leisurely pace and reveled in the breeze. As usual we talked about the women we desired, among other things.

The following day we were joined by a long line of colorfully dressed girls and warriors from the kraal and the neighborhood where we had spent the night, and we left the highland and headed to Ingorienito to the rolling hills on the lower slopes to attend the circumcision ceremony. From there one could see Oldopai Gorge, where my parents lived, and the Inaapi hills in the middle of the Serengeti Plain.

Three girls and a boy were to be initiated on the same day, an unusual occasion. Four oxen were to be slaughtered, and many people would therefore attend. As we descended, we saw the kraal where the ceremony would take place. All those people dressed in red seemed from a distance like flamingos standing in a lake. We could see lines of other guests heading to the settlements. Warriors made gallant cries of happiness known as *enkiseer*. Our line of warriors and girls responded to their cries even more gallantly.

In serpentine fashion, we entered the gates of the settlement. Holding spears in our left hands, we warriors walked proudly, taking small steps, swaying like palm trees, impressing our girls, who walked parallel to us in another line, and of course the spectators, who gazed at us approvingly.

We stopped in the center of the kraal and waited to be greeted. Women and children welcomed us. We put our hands on the children's heads, which is how children are commonly saluted. After the greetings were completed, we started dancing.

Our singing echoed off the kraal fence and nearby trees. Another line of warriors came up the hill and entered the compound, also singing and moving slowly toward us. Our singing grew in intensity. Both lines of warriors moved parallel to each other, and our feet pounded the ground with style. We stamped vigorously, as if to tell the next line and the spectators that we were the best.

The singing continued until the hot sun was overhead. We recessed and ate food already prepared for us by other warriors. Roasted meat was for those who were to eat meat, and milk for the others. By our tradition, meat and milk must not be consumed at the same time, for this would be a betrayal of the animal. It was regarded as cruel to consume a product of the animal that could be obtained while it was alive, such as milk, and meat, which was only available after the animal had been killed.

After eating we resumed singing, and I spotted a tall, beautiful *esiankiki* (young maiden) of Masiaya whose family was one of the largest and richest in our area. She stood very erect and seemed taller than the rest.

One of her breasts could be seen just above her dress, which was knotted at the shoulder. While I was supposed to dance generally to please all the spectators, I took it upon myself to please her especially. I stared at and flirted with her, and she and I danced in unison at times. We complemented each other very well.

During a break, I introduced myself to the *esiankiki* and told her I would like to see her after the dance. "Won't you need a warrior to escort you home later when the evening threatens?" I said. She replied, "Perhaps, but the evening is still far away."

I waited patiently. When the dance ended, I saw her departing with a group of other women her age. She gave me a sidelong glance, and I took that to mean come later and not now. With so many others around, I would not have been able to confer with her as I would have liked anyway.

With another warrior, I wandered around the kraal killing time until the herds returned from pasture. Before the sun dropped out of sight, we departed. As the kraal of the *esiankiki* was in the lowlands, a place called Enkoloa, we descended leisurely, our spears resting on our shoulders.

We arrived at the woman's kraal and found that cows were now being milked. One could hear the women trying to appease the cows by singing to them. Singing calms cows down, making it easier to milk them. There were no warriors in the whole kraal except for the two of us. Girls went around into warriors' houses as usual and collected milk for us. I was so eager to go and meet my *esiankiki* that I could hardly wait for nightfall. The warriors' girls were trying hard to be sociable, but my mind was not with them. I found them to be childish, loud, bothersome, and boring.

As the only warriors present, we had to keep them company and sing for them, at least for a while, as required by custom. I told the other warrior to sing while I tried to figure out how to approach my *esiankiki*. Still a novice warrior, I was not experienced with women and was in fact still afraid of them. I could flirt from a distance, of course. But sitting down with a woman and trying to seduce her was another matter. I had already tried twice to approach women soon after my circumcision and had failed. I got as far as the door of one woman's house and felt my heart beating like a Congolese drum; breathing became difficult and I had to turn back. Another time I managed to get in the house and succeeded in sitting on the bed, but then I started trembling until the whole bed was shaking, and conversation became difficult. I left the house and the woman, amazed and speechless, and never went back to her again.

Tonight I promised myself I would be brave and would not make any silly, ridiculous moves. "I must be mature and not afraid," I kept reminding myself, as I remembered an incident involving one of my relatives when he was still very young and, like me, afraid of women. He went to a woman's house and sat on a stool for a whole hour; he was afraid to awaken her, as his heart was pounding and he was having difficulty breathing.

When he finally calmed down, he woke her up, and their conversation went something like this:

"Woman, wake up."

"Why should I?"

"To light the fire."

"For what?"

"So you can see me."

"I already know who you are. Why don't *you* light the fire, as you're nearer to it than me?"

"It's your house and it's only proper that you light it yourself."

"I don't feel like it."

"At least wake up so we can talk, as I have something to tell you."

"Say it."

"I need you."

"I do not need one-eyed types like yourself."

"One-eyed people are people too."

"That might be so, but they are not to my taste."

They continued talking for quite some time, and the more they spoke, the braver he became. He did not sleep with her that night, but later on he persisted until he won her over. I doubted whether I was as strong-willed as he, but the fact that he had met with success encouraged me. I told my warrior friend where to find me should he need me, and then I departed.

When I entered the house of my *esiankiki*, I called for the woman of the house, and as luck would have it, my lady responded. She was waiting for me. I felt better, and I proceeded to talk to her like a professional. After much talking back and forth, I joined her in bed.

The night was calm, tender, and loving, like most nights after initiation ceremonies as big as this one. There must have been a lot of courting and lovemaking.

Maasai women can be very hard to deal with sometimes. They can simply reject a man outright and refuse to change their minds. Some play hard to get, but in reality are testing the man to see whether he is worth their while. Once a friend of mine while still young was powerfully attracted to a woman nearly his mother's age. He put a bold move on her. At first the woman could not believe his intention, or rather was amazed by his courage. The name of the warrior was Ngengeiya, or Drizzle.

"Drizzle, what do you want?"

The warrior stared her right in the eye and said, "You."

"For what?"

"To make love to you."

"I am your mother's age."

"The choice was either her or you."

This remark took the woman by surprise. She had underestimated the saying

"There is no such thing as a young warrior." When you are a warrior, you are expected to perform bravely in any situation. Your age and size are immaterial.

"You mean you could really love me like a grown-up man?"

"Try me, woman."

He moved in on her. Soon the woman started moaning with excitement, calling out his name. "Honey Drizzle, Honey Drizzle, you *are* a man." In a breathy, stammering voice, she said, "A real man."

Her attractiveness made Honey Drizzle ignore her relative old age. The Maasai believe that if an older and a younger person have intercourse, it is the older person who stands to gain. For instance, it is believed that an older woman having an affair with a young man starts to appear younger and healthier, while the young man grows older and unhealthy.

The following day when the initiation rites had ended, I decided to return home. I had offended my father by staying away from home without his consent, so I prepared myself for whatever punishment he might inflict on me. I walked home alone.

Originally "My Circumcision" from THE WORLDS OF A MAASAI WARRIOR by Tepilit Ole Saitoti, 1986, pp. 66–76. © 1986 by Tepilit Ole Saitoti. Reprinted by permission of Random House, Inc.

UNIT 6

Religion, Belief and Ritual

Unit Selections

Key Points to Consider

- How can modern medicine be combined with traditional healing to take advantage of the best aspects of both? In what respects do perceptions of disease affect treatment and recovery?

- How do beliefs about the supernatural contribute to a sense of personal security, individual responsibility, and social harmony?

- How has voodoo become such an important form of social control in rural Haiti?

- In what ways are magic rituals practical and rational?

- How do rituals and taboos get established in the first place?

- How important are ritual and taboo in our modern industrial society?

- What can you tell about a people by watching how they play games?

 **Links: www.dushkin.com/online/**
These sites are annotated in the World Wide Web pages.

Anthropology Resources Page
http://www.usd.edu/anth/

Masks
http://www.mpm.edu/collect/mask.html

Philosophy of Religion: Magic, Ritual, and Symbolism
http://www.kcmetro.cc.mo.us/longview/socsci/philosophy/religion/magic.htm

Yahoo: Society and Culture: Death
http://dir.yahoo.com/Society_and_Culture/Death_and_Dying/

The anthropological interest in religion, belief, and ritual is not concerned with the scientific validity of such phenomena but rather with the way in which people relate various concepts of the supernatural to their everyday lives. From this practical perspective, some anthropologists have found that traditional spiritual healing is just as helpful in the treatment of illness as is modern medicine (see "Shamans"), that voodoo is a form of social control (as in "The Secrets of Haiti's Living Dead"), and that the ritual and spiritual preparation for playing the game of baseball can be just as important as spring training (see "Baseball Magic").

Every society is composed of feeling, thinking, and acting human beings who at one time or another are either conforming to or altering the social order into which they were born. As described in "The Adaptive Value of Religious Ritual," religion is an ideological framework that gives special legitimacy and validity to human experience within any given sociocultural system. In this way, monogamy as a marriage form, or monarchy as a political form, ceases to be simply one of many alternative ways in which a society can be organized, but becomes, for

the believer, the only legitimate way. Religion considers certain human values and activities as sacred and inviolable. It is this mythic function that helps to explain the strong ideological attachments that some people have regardless of the scientific merits of their points of view.

While under some conditions religion may in fact be "the opiate of the masses," under other conditions such a belief system may be a rallying point for social and economic protest. A contemporary example of the former might be the "Moonies" (members of the Unification Church founded by Sun Myung Moon), while a good example of the latter is the role of the black church in the American civil rights movement, along with the prominence of such religious figures as Martin Luther King Jr. and Jesse Jackson. A word of caution must be set forth concerning attempts to understand belief systems of other cultures. At times the prevailing attitude seems to be, "What I believe in is religion, and what you believe in is superstition." While anthropologists generally do not subscribe to this view, some tend to explain behavior that seems, on the surface, to be incomprehensible and impractical as some form of religious ritual. The articles in this unit should serve as a strong warning concerning the pitfalls of that approach.

"Eyes of the Ngangas" shows how important a person's traditional belief systems, combined with community involvement, can be to the physical and psychological well-being of the individual. This perspective is so important that the treatment of illness is hindered without it. Thus, beliefs about the supernatural may be subtle, informal, and yet absolutely necessary for social harmony and stability.

Mystical beliefs and ritual are not absent from the modern world. "Body Ritual Among the Nacirema" reveals that our daily routines have mystic overtones and "Baseball Magic" examines the need for ritual and taboo in the "great American pastime."

In summary, the writings in this unit show religion, belief, and ritual in relationship to practical human affairs.

Eyes of the *Ngangas*: Ethnomedicine and Power in Central African Republic

People of the Third World have a variety of therapies available for combating diseases, but because of cost, availability, and cultural bias, most rely on ethnomedical traditional treatment rather than "biomedical" or Western therapies. Dr. Lehmann's field research focuses on the importance of ngangas *(traditional healers) as a source of primary health care for both the Aka Pygmy hunters and their horticultural neighbors, the Ngando of Central African Republic. Tracing the basis and locus of the* ngangas' *mystical diagnostic and healing powers, he shows that they are particularly effective with treatments for mental illness and, to an unknown extent, with herbal treatment of physical illnesses as well. The powers of the Aka* ngangas, *however, are also used to reduce the tensions between themselves and their patrons and to punish those Ngando who have caused the hunters harm. Lehmann points out the necessity of recognizing and treating the social as well as the biological aspects of illness and appeals to health care planners to establish counterpart systems that mobilize popular and biomedical specialists to improve primary health care in the Third World.*

Arthur C. Lehmann

ETHNOMEDICINE (ALSO REFERRED TO AS FOLK, TRADI-tional, or popular medicine) is the term used to describe the primary health care system of indigenous people whose medical expertise lies outside "biomedicine" the "modem" medicine of Western societies. Biomedicine does exist in the Third World, but it is unavailable to the masses of inhabitants for a number of reasons. Conversely, although popular medicine has largely been supplanted by biomedicine in the Western World, it still exists and is revived from time to time by waves of dissatisfaction with modem medicine and with the high cost of health care, by the health food movement, and by a variety of other reasons. The point is, all countries have pluralistic systems of health care, but for many members of society the combat against the diseases that have plagued mankind is restricted to the arena of popular medicine.

This is particularly true in the developing nations, such as those of the sub-Saharan regions of Africa, where over 80 percent of the population live in rural areas with a dearth of modem medical help (Bichmann 1979; Green 1980). Between 1984 and the present, I have made six field trips to one such rural area (the most recent in 1994), to study the primary health care practices of Aka Pygmy hunter-gatherers and their horticultural neighbors, the Ngando of Central African Republic (CA.R.).

The Aka and the Ngando

Several groups of the Pygmies live in a broad strip of forested territory stretching east and west across the center of Equatorial Africa. The two largest societies are the Mbuti of the Inturi Forest of Zaire and the Aka, who live in the Southern Rainforest that extends from the Lobaye River in Central African Republic into the People's Republic of the Congo and into Cameroun (Cavalli-Sforza 1971). Like the Mbuti, the Aka are long-time residents of their region. It is on the edge of the Southern Rainforest in and near the village of Bagandu that the Aka Pygmies and the Ngando come into most frequent contact. The proximity, particularly during the dry season from December to April, allows for comparisons of health care systems that would be difficult otherwise, for the Aka move deep into the forest and are relatively inaccessible for a good portion of the year.

Since Turnbull described the symbiotic relationship between Mbuti Pygmies and villagers in Zaire (1965), questions remain as to why Pygmy hunters continue their association with their sedentary neighbors. Bahuchet's work shows that the relationship between the Aka and the Ngando of C.A.R. is one of voluntary mutual dependence in which both groups benefit; indeed, the Aka consider the villagers responsible for their well-being (1985: 549). Aka provide the Ngando with labor, meat, and forest materials while the Ngando pay the Aka with plantation foods, clothes, salt, cigarettes, axes and knives, alcohol, and infrequently, money.

This mutual dependence extends to the health care practices of both societies. Ngando patrons take seriously ill Aka to the dispensary for treatment; Aka consider this service a form of payment that may be withheld by the villagers as a type of punishment. On the other hand, Aka ngangas (traditional healers) are called upon to diagnose and treat Ngando illnesses. The powers believed to be held by the ngangas are impressive, and few, particularly rural residents, question these powers or the roles they play in everyday life in Central African Republic.

Eyes of the *Ngangas*

The people believe that the ngangas intervene on their behalf with the supernatural world to combat malevolent forces and also use herbal expertise to protect them from the myriad of tropical diseases. Elisabeth Motte (1980) has recorded an extensive list of medicines extracted by the ngangas from the environment to counter both natural and supernatural illnesses; 80 percent are derived from plants and the remaining 20 percent from animals and minerals.

Both Aka and Ngando ngangas acquire their power to diagnose and cure through an extensive apprenticeship ordinarily served under the direction of their fathers, who are practicing healers themselves. This system of inheritance is based on primogeniture, although other than first sons may be chosen to become ngangas. Although Ngando ngangas may be either male or female, the vast majority are males; all Aka ngangas are males. In the absence of the father or if a younger son has the calling to become a healer, he may study under an nganga outside the immediate family.

During my six trips to the field, ngangas permitted me to question them on their training and initiation into the craft; it became apparent that important consistencies existed. First, almost all male ngangas are first sons. Second, fathers expect first sons to become ngangas; as they said, "It is natural." Third, the apprenticeship continues from boyhood until the son is himself a nganga, at which time he trains his own son. Fourth, every nganga expresses firm belief in the powers of his teacher to cure and, it follows, in his own as well. As is the case with healers around the world, despite the trickery sometimes deemed necessary to convince clients of the effectiveness of the cure, the ngangas are convinced that their healing techniques will work unless interrupted by stronger powers. Fifth, every nganga interviewed maintained strongly that other ngangas who were either envious or have a destructive spirit can destroy or weaken the power of a healer, causing him to fail. Sixth, and last, the origin and locus of the ngangas' power is believed to be in their eyes.

Over and over I was told that during the final stages of initiation, the master nganga had vaccinated the initiate's eyes and placed "medicine" in the wound, thus giving the new nganga power to divine and effectively treat illnesses. At first I interpreted the term *vaccination* to mean simply the placement of "medicine" in the eyes, but I was wrong. Using a double-edged razor blade and sometimes a needle, the master nganga may cut his apprentice's lower eyelids, the exterior corners of the eyes, or below the eyes (although making marks below the eyes is now considered "antique" I was told); he concludes the ceremony by placing magical medicine in the cuts. At this moment, the student is no longer an apprentice; he has achieved the status of an nganga and the ability to diagnose illnesses with the newly acquired power of his eyes.

Not until my last field trip in 1994 did I witness a master nganga actually cut the whites of his apprentice's eyes. At the end of an hour-long interview with an nganga, which focused on my eliciting his concept of disease etiology in treatment of illness, I casually posed the question I had asked other ngangas many times before: "Do you vaccinate your apprentice's eyes?" The nganga beckoned his apprentice seated nearby, and, to my amazement, the apprentice immediately placed his head on the master's lap. I quickly retrieved my camcorder which I had just put away! The master removed a razor blade from a match box, spread the student's eyelids apart, deftly made five cuts on the whites of each eye, and squeezed the juice of a leaf (the "medicine") into the wounds. This astounding procedure performed on perhaps the most sensitive of all human parts took less than a total of three minutes and did not appear to cause the apprentice any degree of pain, albeit his eyes were red and his tears profuse.

During the career of an nganga, his eyes will be vaccinated many times, thus, it is believed, rejuvenating the power of the eyes to correctly diagnose illness and ensure proper therapy. It is clear that the multiple powers of ngangas to cure and to protect members of their band from both physical and mental illnesses as well as from a variety of types of supernatural attacks reside in their eyes.

It follows that the actual divinatory act involves a variety of techniques, particular to each nganga, that allows him to use his powers to "see" the cause or the illness and determine its treatment. Some bum a dear, rocklike amber resin called *paka* found deep in the rain forest, staring into the flames to learn the mystery of illness and the appropriate therapy. Some stare into the rays of the sun during diagnosis or gaze into small mirrors to unlock the secret powers of the ancestors in curing. Others concentrate on plates filled with water or large, brilliant chunks of glass. The most common but certainly the most incongruous method of acquiring a vision by both Aka and Ngando ngangas today is staring into a light bulb. These are simply stuck into the ground in front of the nganga or, as is the case among many village healers, the light bulb is floated in a glass of water during consultation. The appearance of a light bulb surfacing from an Aka nganga's healing paraphernalia in the middle of a rain forest is, to say the least, unique. Western methods of divining—of knowing the unknown—were not, and to some degree are not now, significantly different from the techniques of the *ngangas*. Our ways of "seeing," involving gazing at and "reading" tea leaves, crystal balls, cards, palms, and stars, are still considered appropriate techniques by many.

Therapy Choices and Therapy Managers

A wide variety of therapies coexist in contemporary Africa, and the situation in the village of Bagandu is no exception. The major sources of treatment are Aka *ngangas*, Ngando *ngangas*, kinship therapy (family councils called to resolve illness-causing conflicts between kin), home remedies, Islamic healers (marabouts), and the local nurse at the government dispensary, who is called "doctor" by villagers and hunters alike. In addition, faith healers, herbalists, and local specialists (referred to as "fetishers") all attempt, in varying degrees, to treat mental or physical illness in Bagundu. Intennittently Westerners, such as missionaries, personnel from the U.S. Agency for International Development, and anthropologists, also treat physical ailments. Bagandu is a large village of approximately 3,400 inhabitants, however; most communities are much smaller and have little access to modem treatment. And, as Cavalli-Sforza has noted,

> If the chances of receiving Western medical help for Africans living in remote villages are very limited, those of Pygmies are practically nonexistent. They are even further removed from hospitals. African health agents usually do not treat Pygmies. Medical help comes exceptionally and almost always from rare visiting foreigners. (Cavalli-Sforza 1986: 421)

Residents of Bagandu are fortunate in having both a government dispensary and a pharmacy run by the Catholic church, but prescriptions are extremely costly relative to income, and ready cash is scarce. A more pressing problem is the availability of drugs. Frequently the "doctor" has only enough to treat the simplest ailments such as headaches and small cuts; he must refer thirty to forty patients daily to the Catholic pharmacy, which has more drugs than the dispensary but still is often unable to fill prescriptions for the most frequently prescribed drugs such as penicillin, medicine to counteract parasites, and antibiotic salves. Although the doctor does the best he can under these conditions, patients must often resort only to popular medical treatment—in spite of the fact that family members, the therapy managers, have assessed the illness as one best treated by biomedicine. In spite, too, of the regular unavailability of medicine, the doctor's diagnosis and advice is still sought out—"although many people will consent to go to the dispensary only after hav-

ing exhausted the resources of traditional medicine" (Motte 1980: 311).

Popular, ethnomedical treatment is administered by kin, *ngangas* (among both the Aka and Ngando villagers), other specialists noted for treatment of specific maladies, and Islamic marabouts, who are recent immigrants from Chad. According to both Aka and Ngando informants, the heaviest burden for health care falls to these ethnomedical systems. Ngando commonly utilize home, kin remedies for minor illnesses, but almost 100 percent indicated that for more serious illnesses they consulted either the doctor or *ngangas* (Aka, Ngando, or both); to a lesser extent they visited specialists. The choice of treatment, made by the family therapy managers, rests not only on the cause and severity of the illness, but also on the availability of therapists expert in the disease or problem, their: cost, and their proximity to the patient. Rarely do the residents of Bagandu seek the aid of the marabouts, for example, in part because of the relatively high cost of consultation. Clearly, both popular and biomedical explanations for illness play important roles in the maintenance of health among Bagandu villagers, although popular medicine is the most important therapy resource available. Popular medicine is especially vital for the Aka hunters, whose relative isolation and inferior status (in the eyes of the Ngando) have resulted in less opportunity for biomedical treatment. Yet even they seek out modem medicine for illnesses.

Whatever the system of treatment chosen, it is important to understand that "the management of illness and therapy by a set of close kin is a central aspect of the medical scene in central Africa.… The therapy managing group … exercises a brokerage function between the sufferer and the specialist" (Janzen 1978: 4). It is the kingroup that determines which therapy is to be used.

Explanations of Illness

The choice of therapy in Bagandu is determined by etiology and severity, as in the West. Unlike Western medicine, however, African ethnomedicine is not restricted to an etiology of only natural causation. Both the Aka and the Ngando spend a great deal of time, energy, and money (or other forms of payments) treating illnesses perceived as being the result of social and cultural imbalances, often described in supernatural terms. Aka and Ngando nosology has accommodated biomedicine without difficulty, but traditional etiology has not become less important to the members of these societies. Frequent supernatural explanations of illness by Aka and Ngando informants inevitably led me to the investigation of witchcraft, curses, spells, or the intervention of ancestors and nameless spirits, all of which were viewed as being responsible for poor health and misfortune. The Aka maintain, for example, that the fourth leading cause of death in Bagandu is witchcraft (diarrhea is the principal cause; measles, second, and convulsions, third [Hewlett 1986: 56]). During my research, it became apparent that a dual model of disease explanation exists among the Aka and Ngando: first, a naturalistic model that fits its Western biomedical counterpart well, and second, a supernaturalistic explanation.

Interviews with village and Pygmy *ngangas* indicated that their medical systems are not significantly different. Indeed, both groups agree that their respective categories of illness etiology are identical. Further, the categories are not mutually exclusive: an illness may be viewed as being natural, but it may be exacerbated by supernatural forces such as witchcraft and spells. Likewise, this phenomenon can be reversed: an illness episode may be caused by supernatural agents but progress into a form that is treatable through biomedical techniques. For example, my relatively educated and ambitious young field assistant, a villager, was cut on the lower leg by a piece of stone while working on a new addition to his house. The wound, eventually becoming infected, caused swelling throughout the leg and groin. As was the case in some of his children's illnesses, the explanation for the wound was witchcraft. It was clear to him that the witch was a neighbor who envied his possessions and his employment by a foreigner. Although the original cut was caused by a supernatural agent, the resulting infection fitted the biomedical model. Treatment by a single injection of penicillin quickly brought the infection under control, although my assistant believed that had the witch been stronger the medicine would not have worked. Here is a case in which, "in addition to the patient's physical signs and social relationships," the passage of time is also crucial to "the unfolding of therapeutic action" (Feierman 1985: 77). As the character of an illness changes with time as the illness runs its course, the therapy manager's decisions may change, because the perceived etiology can shift as a result of a variety of signs, such as a slow-healing wound or open conflict in the patient's social group (Janzen 1978: 9)

Studies on disease etiologies among select African societies (Bibeau 1979; Janzen 1978; Warren 1974) reported that most illnesses had natural causes, and this finding holds for the Ngando villagers as well. At first glance, these data would seem to reduce the importance of *ngangas* and of popular medicine generally, but it is necessary to recognize that *ngangas* treat both natural and supernatural illnesses utilizing both medical and mystical techniques. The question posed by Feierman, "Is popular medicine effective?" (1985: 5), is vital to the evaluation of *ngangas* as healers. Surely some traditional medicines used by these cures must in many cases work, and work regularly enough to earn the sustained support of the general public.

Illnesses of God and Illnesses of Man

Both the Ngando and Aka explanations for natural illnesses lack clarity. Some *ngangas* refer to them as "illnesses of God"; others simply identify them as "natural"; and still others frequently use both classifications, regularly assigning each label to specific ailments. Hewlett maintains that the Aka sometimes labelled unknown maladies as illnesses of God (1986: personal communication). On the other hand, the Bakongo of neighboring Zaire defined illnesses of God as those "generally, mild conditions which respond readily to therapy when no particular disturbance exists in the immediate social relationships of the sufferer.... The notion of 'god' does not imply divine intervention or retribution but simply that the cause is an affliction in the order of things unrelated to human intentions" (Janzen 1978: 9).

Both Janzen's and Hewlett's data are accurate, but my field data show as well as that the explanations of natural illnesses among the Ngando and Aka not only refer to normal mild diseases and sometimes unknown ones but also to specific illnesses named by the *ngangas* and the residents of Bagandu. The confusion surrounding these mixed explanations of disease causation is an important topic for future ethnosemantic or other techniques of emic inquiry by ethnographers.

Residents of Bagandu and both Aka and Ngando *ngangas* categorized sickness caused by witchcraft, magic, curses, spells, and spirits as "illnesses of man." This is the second major disease category. Witchcraft, for example, while not the main cause of death, is the most frequently named cause of illness in Bagandu. Informants in Bagandu cite the frequency of witchcraft accusations as proof of their viewpoint. Antisocial or troublesome neighbors are frequently accused of being witches and are jailed if the charge is proven. Maladies of all sorts, such as sterility among females, are also commonly attributed to the innate and malevolent power of witches. These types of explanations are not unusual in rural Africa. What is surprising are reports of new illnesses in the village caused by witches.

All Ngando informants claimed, furthermore, that the problem of witchcraft has not diminished over time; on the contrary, it has increased. The thinking is logical: because witchcraft is believed to be inherited, any increase in population is seen also as an inevitable increase in the number of witches in the village. Population figures in the region of the Southern Rainforest have increased somewhat in the past few decades despite epidemics such as measles; accordingly, the incidence of maladies attributed to witches has increased. One informant from Bagandu strongly insisted that witches are not only more numerous but also much more powerful today than before. Offiong (1983) reported a marked increase of witchcraft in Nigeria and adjacent states in West Africa, caused not by inflation of population but by the social strain precipitated by the frustration accompanying lack of achievement after the departure of colonial powers.

Insanity is not a major problem among the Ngando. When it does occur, it is believed to be caused by witchcraft, clan or social problems, evil spirits, and breaking taboos. Faith healers, marabouts, and *ngangas* are seen as effective in the treatment of mental illness due to witchcraft or other causes. The role of faith healers is particularly important in the lives of members of the Prophetical Christian Church in Bagandu. They have strong faith in the healing sessions and maintain that the therapy successfully treats the victims of spirits' attacks. Informants also claim the therapy lasts a long time.

The curse is a common method of venting anger in Bagandu, used by both male and female witches. Informants stated that women use curses more than men and that the subjects of their attacks are often males. The curses of witches are counted as being extremely dangerous in the intended victim. One villager accused the elderly of using the curse as a weapon most frequently. Spell-casting is also common in the area, and males often use spells as a method of seduction.

Most, if not all, residents of Bagandu use charms, portable "fetishes," and various types of magical objects placed in and around their houses for protection. Some of these objects are counter-magical: they simultaneously protect the intended victim and turn the danger away from the victim to the attackers. Counter-magic is not always immediate; results may take years to appear. Charms, fetishes, and other forms of protection are purchased from *ngangas*, marabouts, and other specialists such as herbalists. For example, the Aka and Ngando alike believe that wearing a mole's tooth on a bracelet is the most powerful protection from attacks by witches.

To a lesser extent, spirits are also believed to cause illness. It is problematic whether or not this source of illness deserves a separate category of disease causation. Bahuchet thinks not; rather, he holds that spirit-caused illnesses should be labeled illnesses of God (1986: personal communication). It is interesting to note that in addition to charms and other items put to use in Bagandu, residents supplicate ancestors for aid in times of difficulty. If the ancestors do not respond, and if the victim of the misfortune practices Christianity, he or she will seek the aid of God. Non-Christians and Christians alike commonly ask diviners the cause of their problem, after which they seek the aid of the proper specialist. Revenge for real or imagined attacks on oneself or on loved ones is common. One method is to point a claw of a mole at the wrongdoer. Ngando informants maintain the victim dies soon after. Simple possession of a claw, if discovered, means jail for the owner.

My initial survey of Aka and Ngando *ngangas* in 1984 brought out other origins of illness. Two *ngangas* in Bagandu specifically cited the devil, rather than unnamed evil spirits, as a cause for disease. The higher exposure of villagers to Christianity may account for this attribution: seven denominations are currently represented in the churches of Bagandu. Urban *ngangas* questioned in Bangui, the capital, stressed the use of poison as a cause of illness and death. Although poisonings do not figure prominently as a cause of death among the Aka and Ngando, it is common belief that *ngangas* and others do use poison.

Finally, while not a cause for illness, informants maintained that envious *ngangas* have the power to retard or halt the progress of a cure administered by another. All *ngangas* interviewed in 1984 and 1985 confirmed not only that they have the power to interrupt the healing process of a patient but also that they frequently invoke it. Interestingly, *ngangas* share this awesome power with witches, who are also believed by members of both societies to be able to spoil the "medicine" of healers. This kind of perception of the *ngangas*' power accounts, in part, for their dual character: primarily beneficial to the public, they can also be dangerous.

While the numerical differences in the frequency of physiologically and psychologically rooted illnesses in Bagandu are unknown, Ngando respondents in a small sample were able to list a number of supernaturally caused illnesses that are treatable by *ngangas*, but only a few naturally caused ones. Among the naturalistic illnesses were illnesses of the spleen; *laltungba*, deformation of the back; and *Kongo*, "illness of the rainbow." According to Hewlett (1986: 53), *Kongo* causes paralysis of the legs (and sometimes of the arms) and death after the victim steps on a dangerous mushroom growing on a damp spot in the forest where a rainbow-colored snake has rested. Had the Ngando sample been more exhaustive, it is probable that the list of natural diseases would have been greater, although perhaps not as high as the twenty natural illnesses the *ngangas* said they could treat successfully. That impressive list includes malaria, hernia, diarrhea, stomach illness, pregnancy problems, dysentery, influenza, abscesses, general fatigue, traumas (snake bite, miscellaneous wounds, and poisoning), and general and specific bodily pain (spleen, liver, ribs, head, and uterus).

Powers of the *Ngangas*

The powers of the *ngangas* are not limited to controlling and defeating supernatural or natural diseases alone. In the village of Bagandu and in the adjacent Southern Rainforest where the Ngando and Aka hunters come into frequent contact, tensions exist due to the patron-client relationship, which by its very economic nature is negative. These tensions are magnified by ethnic animosity. Without the Akas' mystical power, their economic and social inferiority would result in an even more difficult relationship with the Ngando. Here the powers of the Pygmy *ngangas* play an important part in leveling, to bearable limits, the overshadowing dominance of the

Ngando, and it is here that the *ngangas* demonstrate their leadership outside the realm of health care. Each Aka has some form of supernatural protection provided by the *nganga* of his camp to use while in the village. Still, the need exists for the extraordinary powers of the *nganga* himself for those moments of high tension when Aka are confronted by what they consider the most menacing segments of the village population: the police, the mayor, and adolescent males, all of whom, as perceived by the Aka, are dangerous to their personal safety while in the village.

In the summer of 1986, I began to study the attitudes of village patrons toward their Aka clients and, conversely, the attitudes of the so-called wayward servants (Turnbull's term for the Mbuti Pygmy of Zaire, 1965) toward the villagers. Participant observation and selective interviews of patrons, on the one hand, and of hunters, on the other, disclosed other important tangents of power of the Aka in general and of their *ngangas* in particular. First, the Aka often have visible sources of power such as scarification, cords worn on the wrist and neck, and bracelets strung with powerful charms for protection against village witches. These protective devices are provided the Aka by their *ngangas*. Second, and more powerful still, are the hidden powers of the Aka in general, bolstered by the specific powers of the *ngangas*. Although the villagers believe the hunters' power is strongest in the forest, and therefore weaker in the village setting, Aka power commands the respect of the farmers. Third, the villagers acknowledge the Aka expertise in the art of producing a variety of deadly poisons, such as *sepi*, which may be used to punish farmers capable of the most serious crimes against the Pygmies. The obvious functions of these means of protection and retribution, taken from the standpoint of the Aka, are positive. Clearly these powers reduce the tension of the Aka while in the village, but they also control behavior of villagers toward the hunters to some undefinable degree.

Villagers interpret the variety of punishments which the Aka are capable of meting out to wrongdoers as originating in their control of mystical or magical. powers. Interestingly, even poisonings are viewed m this way by villagers because of the difficulty of proving that poison rather than mystical power caused illness or death. Although the use of poison is rare, it is used and the threat remains. Georges Guille-Escuret, a French ethnohistorian working in Bagandu in 1985, reported to me that prior to my arrival in the field that year three members of the same household had died on the same day. The head of the family had been accused of repeated thefts of game from the traps and from the camp of an Aka hunter. When confronted with the evidence—a shirt the villager had left at the scene of the thefts—the family rejected the demands of the hunter for compensation for the stolen meat. Soon thereafter, the thief, his wife, and his mother died on the same day. Villagers, who knew of the accusa-tions of theft, interpreted the deaths as the result of poisoning or the mystical powers of the hunter.

Stories of Aka revenge are not uncommon, nor are the Akas' accusations of wrongdoing leveled against the villagers. To the Ngando farmers, the powers of the Aka *ngangas* include the ability to cause death through the use of fetishes, to cause illness to the culprit's eyes, and to direct lightning to strike the perpetrator. These and other impressive powers to punish are seen as real threats to villagers—but the power of the *ngangas* to cure is even more impressive.

Attempts in my research to delineate the strengths and weaknesses of the *ngangas* and other health care specialists discovered a number of qualities/ characteristics widely held to be associated with each. First, each specialist is known for specific medical abilities; that is, Aka and Ngando *ngangas* recognize the therapeutic expertise of others in a variety of cures. A *nganga* from Bangui maintained that Aka *ngangas* were generally superior to the village healers in curing. This view is shared by a number of villagers interviewed, who maintained that the power of Aka *ngangas* is greater than that of their own specialists.

The Aka strongly agree with this view, and in a sense the Aka are more propertied in the realm of curing than are the villagers. There is no question that the Aka are better hunters. Despite the Ngandos' greater political and economic power in the area and the social superiority inherent in their patron status, the Ngando need the Aka. All these elements help balance the relationship between the two societies, although the supernatural and curative powers of Aka *ngangas* have not previously been considered to be ingredients in the so-called symbiotic relationship between Pygmy hunters and their horticultural neighbors.

Second, *ngangas* noted for their ability to cure particular illnesses are often called upon for treatment by other *ngangas* who have contracted the disease. Third, with one exception, all the *ngangas* interviewed agree that European drugs, particularly those contained in hypodermic syringes and in pills, are effective in the treatment of natural diseases. One dissenting informant from the capital disdained biomedicine altogether because, as he said, "White men don't believe in us." Fourth, of the fourteen Aka and Ngando *ngangas* interviewed in 1985, only five felt that it was possible for a *nganga* to work successfully with the local doctor (male nurse) who directed the dispensary in Bagandu. All five of these *ngangas* said that if such cooperation did come about, their special contribution would be the treatment of patients having illnesses of man, including mental illness resulting from witchcraft, from magical and spiritual attacks, and from breaking taboos. None of the *ngangas* interviewed had been summoned to work in concert with the doctor. Fifth, as a group of the *ngangas* held that biomedical practitioners are unable to successfully treat mental illnesses and other illnesses resulting from attacks of supernatural agents. In this the general population of the village agree. This is a vitally important reason for the sustained confidence in popular therapy in the region— a confidence that is further strengthened by the belief that the *ngangas* can treat natural illnesses as well. Sixth, the village doctor recognized that the *ngangas* and marabouts do have more success in the treatment of mental illnesses than he does. Although the doctor confided that he has called in a village *nganga* for consultation in a case of witchcraft, he also disclosed that upon frequent occasions he had to remedy the treatment administered by popular specialists for natural diseases. It is important to recognize that unlike biomedical specialists in the capital, the local doctor does appreciate the talents of traditional therapists who successfully practice ethnopsychiatry.

All respondents to this survey recognized the value of biomedicine in the community, and little variation in the types of cures the doctor could effect was brought out. No doubts were raised regarding the necessity of both biomedicine and popular therapy to the proper maintenance of public health. The spheres of influence and expertise of both types of practitioners, while generally agreed upon by participants of the Ngando survey, did show some variation, but these were no more serious than our own estimates of the abilities of our physicians in the West. In short, all informants utilized both systems of therapy when necessary and if possible.

The continuation of supernatural explanations of illness by both the Ngando and the Aka results in part from tradition, in combination with their lack of knowledge of scientific disease etiology, and in part because of the hidden positive functions of such explanations. Accusations of witchcraft and the use of curses and malevolent magic function to express the anxiety, frustrations, and social disruptions in these societies. These are traditional explanations of disease, with more than a single focus, for they focus on both the physical illness and its sociological cause. "Witchcraft (and by extension other supernatural explanations for illness and disaster) provides an indispensable component in many philosophies of misfortune. It is the friend rather than the foe of mortality" (Lewis 1986: 16). Beyond this rationale, reliance upon practitioners of popular medicine assures the patient that medicine is available for treatment in the absence of Western drugs.

The Role of Ethnomedicine

Among the Aka and Ngando and elsewhere, systems of popular medicine have sustained African societies for centuries. The evolution of popular medicine has guaranteed its good fit to the cultures that have produced it; even as disruptive an element of the system as witchcraft can claim manifest and latent functions that contribute to social control and the promotion of proper behavior.

Unlike Western drug therapies, no quantifiable measure exists for the effectiveness of popular medicine. Good evidence from World Health Organization studies can be brought forth, however, to illustrate the relatively high percentage of success of psychotherapeutic treatment through ethnomedicine in the Third World compared to that achieved in the West. The results of my research in Bagandu also demonstrate the strong preference of villagers for popular medicine in cases involving mental illness and supernaturally caused mental problems. At the same time, the doctor is the preferred source of therapy for the many types of natural disease, while *ngangas* and other specialists still have the confidence of the public in treating other maladies; referred to as illnesses of man and some illnesses of God. Whatever the perceived etiology by kingroup therapy managers, both popular and biomedical therapists treat natural illnesses. It is in this realm of treatment that it is most important to ask, "What parts of popular medicine work?" rather than, "Does popular medicine work?" Because evidence has shown that psychotherapy is more successful in the hands of traditional curers, it is therefore most important to question the effectiveness of popular therapy in handling natural illnesses. Currently, the effectiveness of traditional drugs used for natural diseases is unknown; however, the continued support of popular therapists by both rural and urban Africans indicates a strength in the system. The effectiveness of the *ngangas* may be both psychological and pharmaceutical, and if the ecological niche does provide drugs that do cure natural illnesses, it is vital that these be determined and manufactured commercially in their countries of origin. If we can assume that some traditional drugs are effective, governments must utilize the expertise of healers in identifying these.

It is unrealistic to attempt to train popular therapists in all aspects of biomedicine, just as it is unrealistic to train biomedical specialists in the supernatural treatments applied by popular practitioners. However, neither type of therapist, nor the public, will benefit from the expertise of the other if they remain apart. The task is to make both more effective by incorporating the best of each into a counterpart system that focuses on a basic training of healers in biomedicine. This combination must certainly be a more logical and economic choice than attempting to supply biomedical specialists to every community in Central African Republic, a task too formidable for any country north or south of the Sahara. The significance of this proposal is magnified by the massive numbers for whom biomedicine is unavailable, those who must rely only upon ethnomedicine.

Even if available to all, biomedicine alone is not the final answer to disease control in the Third World. Hepburn succinctly presents strong arguments against total reliance upon the biomedical approach:

> Biomedicine is widely believed to be effective in the cure of sickness. A corollary of this is the belief that if adequate facilities could be provided in the Third World and "native" irrationalities and cultural obstacles could be overcome, the health problems of the people would largely be

eliminated. However, this belief is not true, because the effectiveness of biomedicine is limited in three ways. First, many conditions within the accepted defining properties of biomedicine (i.e., physical diseases) cannot be treated effectively. Second, by concentrating on the purely physical, biomedicine simply cannot treat the social aspects of sickness (i.e., illness). Third, cures can only be achieved under favorable environmental and political conditions: if these are not present, biomedicine will be ineffective (1988: 68).

The problems facing societies in Africa are not new. These same issues faced Westerners in the past, and our partial solutions, under unbelievably better conditions, took immense time and effort to achieve. If primary health care in the non-Western world is to improve, the evolutionary process must be quickened by the utilization of existing popular medical systems as a counterpart of biomedicine, by the expansion of biomedical systems, and by the cooperation of international funding agencies with African policymakers, who themselves must erase their antagonism toward ethnomedicine.

The Adaptive Value of Religious Ritual

Rituals promote group cohesion by requiring members to engage in behavior that is too costly to fake

Richard Sosis

I was 15 years old the first time I went to Jerusalem's Old City and visited the 2,000-year-old remains of the Second Temple, known as the Western Wall. It may have foreshadowed my future life as an anthropologist, but on my first glimpse of the ancient stones I was more taken by the people standing at the foot of the structure than by the wall itself. Women stood in the open sun, facing the Wall in solemn worship, wearing long-sleeved shirts, head coverings and heavy skirts that scraped the ground. Men in their thick beards, long black coats and fur hats also seemed oblivious to the summer heat as they swayed fervently and sang praises to God. I turned to a friend, "Why would anyone in their right mind dress for a New England winter only to spend the afternoon praying in the desert heat?" At the time I thought there was no rational explanation and decided that my fellow religious brethren might well be mad.

Of course, "strange" behavior is not unique to ultraorthodox Jews. Many religious acts appear peculiar to the outsider. Pious adherents the world over physically differentiate themselves from others: Moonies shave their heads, Jain monks of India wear contraptions on their heads and feet to avoid killing insects, and clergy almost everywhere dress in outfits that distinguish them from the rest of society. Many peoples also engage in some form of surgical alteration. Australian aborigines perform a ritual operation on adolescent boys in which a bone or a stone is inserted into the penis through an incision in the urethra. Jews and Muslims submit their sons to circumcision, and in some Muslim societies daughters are also subject to circumcision or other forms of genital mutilation. Groups as diverse as the Nuer of Sudan and the Iatmul of New Guinea force their adolescents to undergo ritual scarification. Initiation ceremonies, otherwise known as rites of passage, are often brutal. Among Native Americans, Apache boys were forced to bathe in icy water, Luiseno initiates were required to lie motionless while being bitten by hordes of ants, and Tukuna girls had their hair plucked out.

How can we begin to understand such behavior? If human beings are rational creatures, then why do we spend so much time, energy and resources on acts that can be so painful or, at the very least, uncomfortable? Archaeologists tell us that our species has engaged in ritual behavior for at least 100,000 years, and every known culture practices some form of religion. It even survives covertly in those cultures where governments have attempted to eliminate spiritual practices. And, despite the unparalleled triumph of scientific rationalism in the 20th century, religion continued to flourish. In the United States a steady 40 percent of the population attended church regularly throughout the century. A belief in God (about 96 percent), the afterlife (about 72 percent), heaven (about 72 percent) and hell (about 58 percent) remained substantial and remarkably constant. Why do religious beliefs, practices and institutions continue to be an essential component of human social life?

Such questions have intrigued me for years. Initially my training in anthropology did not provide an answer. Indeed, my studies only increased my bewilderment. I received my training in a subfield known as human behavioral ecology, which studies the adaptive design of behavior with attention to its ecological setting. Behavioral ecologists assume that natural selection has shaped the human nervous system to respond successfully to varying ecological circumstances. All organisms must balance trade-offs: Time spent doing one thing prevents them from pursuing other activities that can enhance their survival or reproductive success. Animals that maximize the rate at which they acquire resources, such as food and mates, can maximize the number of descendants, which is exactly what the game of natural selection is all about.

Behavioral ecologists assume that natural selection has designed our decision-making mechanisms to optimize the rate at which human beings accrue resources under diverse ecological conditions—a basic prediction of *optimal forag-*

ing theory. Optimality models offer predictions of the "perfectly adapted" behavioral response, given a set of environmental constraints. Of course, a perfect fit with the environment is almost never achieved because organisms rarely have perfect information and because environments are always changing. Nevertheless, this assumption has provided a powerful framework to analyze a variety of decisions, and most research (largely conducted among foraging populations) has shown that our species broadly conforms to these expectations.

If our species is designed to optimize the rate at which we extract energy from the environment, why would we engage in religious behavior that seems so counterproductive? Indeed, some religious practices, such as ritual sacrifices, are a conspicuous display of wasted resources. Anthropologists can explain why foragers regularly share their food with others in the group, but why would anyone share their food with a dead ancestor by burning it to ashes on an altar? A common response to this question is that people believe in the efficacy of the rituals and the tenets of the faith that give meaning to the ceremonies. But this response merely begs the question. We must really ask why natural selection has favored a psychology that believes in the supernatural and engages in the costly manifestations of those beliefs.

Ritual Sacrifice

Behavioral ecologists have only recently begun to consider the curiosities of religious activities, so at first I had to search other disciplines to understand these practices. The scholarly literature suggested that I wasn't the only one who believed that intense religious behavior was a sign of madness. Some of the greatest minds of the past two centuries, such as Marx and Freud, supported my thesis. And the early anthropological theorists also held that spiritual beliefs were indicative of a primitive and simple mind. In the 19th century, Edward B. Tylor, often noted as one of the founding fathers of anthropology, maintained that religion arose out of a misunderstanding among "primitives" that dreams are real. He argued that dreams about deceased ancestors might have led the primitives to believe that spirits can survive death.

Eventually the discipline of anthropology matured, and its practitioners moved beyond the equation that "primitive equals irrational." Instead, they began to seek functional explanations of religion. Most prominent among these early 20th-century theorists was the Polish-born anthropologist Bronislaw Malinowski. He argued that religion arose out of "the real tragedies of human life, out of the conflict between human plans and realities." Although religion may serve to allay our fears of death, and provide comfort from our incessant search for answers, Malinowski's thesis did not seem to explain the origin of rituals. Standing in the midday desert sun in several layers of black clothing seems more like a recipe for increasing anxiety than treating it.

The classical anthropologists didn't have the right answers to my questions. I needed to look elsewhere.

Fortunately, a new generation of anthropologists has begun to provide some explanations. It turns out that the strangeness of religious practices and their inherent costs are actually the critical features that contribute to the success of religion as a universal cultural strategy and why natural selection has favored such behavior in the human lineage. To understand this unexpected benefit we need to recognize the adaptive problem that ritual behavior solves. William Irons, a behavioral ecologist at Northwestern University, has suggested that the universal dilemma is the promotion of cooperation within a community. Irons argues that the primary adaptive benefit of religion is its ability to facilitate cooperation within a group—while hunting, sharing food, defending against attacks and waging war—all critical activities in our evolutionary history. But, as Irons points out, although everyone is better off if everybody cooperates, this ideal is often very difficult to coordinate and achieve. The problem is that an individual is even better off if everyone else does the cooperating, while he or she remains at home enjoying an afternoon siesta. Cooperation requires social mechanisms that prevent individuals from free riding on the efforts of others. Irons argues that religion is such a mechanism.

The key is that religious rituals are a form of communication, which anthropologists have long maintained. They borrowed this insight from ethologists who observed that many species engage in patterned behavior, which they referred to as "ritual." Ethologists recognized that ritualistic behaviors served as a form of communication between members of the same species, and often between members of different species. For example, the males of many avian species engage in courtship rituals—such as bowing, head wagging, wing waving and hopping (among many other gestures)—to signal their amorous intents before a prospective mate. And, of course, the vibration of a rattlesnake's tail is a powerful threat display to other species that enter its personal space.

Irons's insight is that religious activities signal commitment to other members of the group. By engaging in the ritual, the member effectively says, "I identify with the group and I believe in what the group stands for." Through its ability to signal commitment, religious behavior can overcome the problem of free riders and promote cooperation within the group. It does so because trust lies at the heart of the problem: A member must assure everyone that he or she will participate in acquiring food or in defending the group. Of course, hunters and warriors may make promises—"you have my word, I'll show up tomorrow"—but unless the trust is already established such statements are not believable.

It turns out that there is a robust way to secure trust. Israeli biologist Amotz Zahavi observes that it is often in the best interest of an animal to send a dishonest signal—perhaps to fake its size, speed, strength, health or beauty. The only signal that can be believed is one that is too costly to fake, which he referred to as a "handicap." Zahavi argues

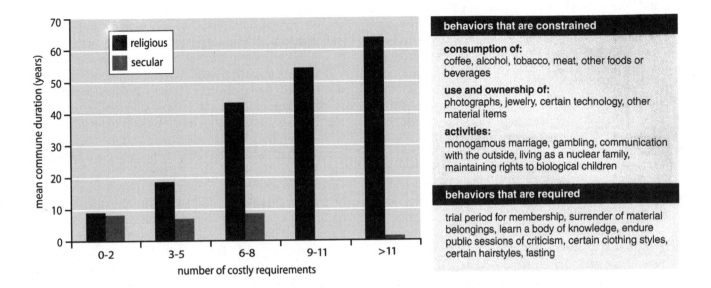

behaviors that are constrained

consumption of:
coffee, alcohol, tobacco, meat, other foods or beverages

use and ownership of:
photographs, jewelry, certain technology, other material items

activities:
monogamous marriage, gambling, communication with the outside, living as a nuclear family, maintaining rights to biological children

behaviors that are required

trial period for membership, surrender of material belongings, learn a body of knowledge, endure public sessions of criticism, certain clothing styles, certain hairstyles, fasting

that natural selection has favored the evolution of handicaps. For example, when a springbok antelope spots a predator it often *stots*—it jumps up and down. This extraordinary behavior puzzled biologists for years: Why would an antelope waste precious energy that could be used to escape the predator? And why would the animal make itself more visible to something that wants to eat it? The reason is that the springbok is displaying its quality to the predator—its ability to escape, effectively saying, "Don't bother chasing me. Look how strong my legs are, you won't be able to catch me." The only reason a predator believes the springbok is because the signal is too costly to fake. An antelope that is not quick enough to escape cannot imitate the signal because it is not strong enough to repeatedly jump to a certain height. Thus, a display can provide honest information if the signals are so costly to perform that lower quality organisms cannot benefit by imitating the signal.

In much the same way, religious behavior is also a costly signal. By donning several layers of clothing and standing out in the midday sun, ultraorthodox Jewish men are signaling to others: "Hey! Look, I'm a *haredi* Jew. If you are also a member of this group you can trust me because why else would I be dressed like this? No one would do this *unless* they believed in the teachings of ultraorthodox Judaism and were fully committed to its ideals and goals." The quality that these men are signaling is their level of commitment to a specific religious group.

Adherence to a set of religious beliefs entails a host of ritual obligations and expected behaviors. Although there may be physical or psychological benefits associated with some ritual practices, the significant time, energy and financial costs involved serve as effective deterrents for anyone who does not believe in the teachings of a particular religion. There is no incentive for nonbelievers to join or remain in a religious group, because the costs of maintaining membership—such as praying three times a day, eating only kosher food, donating a certain part of your income to charity and so on—are simply too high.

Those who engage in the suite of ritual requirements imposed by a religious group can be trusted to believe sincerely in the doctrines of their respective religious communities. As a result of increased levels of trust and commitment among group members, religious groups minimize costly monitoring mechanisms that are otherwise necessary to overcome free-rider problems that typically plague communal pursuits. Hence, the adaptive benefit of ritual behavior is its ability to promote and maintain cooperation, a challenge that our ancestors presumably faced throughout our evolutionary history.

Benefits of Membership

One prediction of the "costly signaling theory of ritual" is that groups that impose the greatest demands on their members will elicit the highest levels of devotion and commitment. Only committed members will be willing to dress and behave in ways that differ from the rest of society. Groups that maintain more-committed members can also offer more because it's easier for them to attain their collective goals than groups whose members are less committed. This may explain a paradox in the religious marketplace: Churches that require the most of their adherents are experiencing rapid rates of growth. For example, the Church of Jesus Christ of Latter-day Saints (Mormons), Seventh-day Adventists and Jehovah's Witnesses, who respectively abstain from caffeine, meat and blood transfusions (among other things), have been growing at exceptional rates. In contrast, liberal Protestant denominations such as the Episcopalians, Methodists and Presbyterians have been steadily losing members.

Economist Lawrence Iannaccone, of George Mason University, has also noted that the most demanding groups also have the greatest number of committed members. He found that the more distinct a religious group was—how much the group's lifestyle differed from mainstream America—the higher its attendance rates at services. Sociologists Roger

Finke and Rodney Stark, of Penn State and the University of Washington, respectively, have argued that when the Second Vatican Council in 1962 repealed many of the Catholic Church's prohibitions and reduced the level of strictness in the church, it initiated a decline in church attendance among American Catholics and reduced the enrollments in seminaries. Indeed, in the late 1950s almost 75 percent of American Catholics were attending Mass weekly, but since the Vatican's actions there has been a steady decline to the current rate of about 45 percent.

The costly signaling theory of ritual also predicts that greater commitment will translate into greater cooperation within groups. My colleague Eric Bressler, a graduate student at McMaster University, and I addressed this question by looking at data from the records of 19th-century communes. All communes face an inherent problem of promoting and sustaining cooperation because individuals can free ride on the efforts of others. Because cooperation is key to a commune's survival, we employed commune longevity as a measure of cooperation. Compared to their secular counterparts, the religious communes did indeed demand more of their members, including such behavior as celibacy, the surrender of all material possessions and vegetarianism. Communes that demanded more of their members survived longer, overcoming the fundamental challenges of cooperation. By placing greater demands on their members, they were presumably able to elicit greater belief in and commitment toward the community's common ideology and goals.

I also wanted to evaluate the costly signaling theory of ritual within modern communal societies. The kibbutzim I had visited in Israel as a teenager provided an ideal opportunity to examine these hypotheses. For most of their 100-year history, these communal societies have lived by the dictum, "From each according to his abilities, to each according to his needs." The majority of the more than 270 kibbutzim are secular (and often ideologically antireligious); fewer than 20 are religiously oriented. Because of a massive economic failure—a collective debt of more than $4 billion—the kibbutzim are now moving in the direction of increased privatization and reduced communality. When news of the extraordinary debt surfaced in the late 1980s, it went largely unnoticed that the religious kibbutzim were financially stable. In the words of the Religious Kibbutz Movement Federation, "the economic position of the religious kibbutzim is sound, and they remain uninvolved in the economic crisis."

The success of the religious kibbutzim is especially remarkable given that many of their rituals inhibit economic productivity. For example, Jewish law does not permit Jews to milk cows on the Sabbath. Although rabbinic rulings now permit milking by kibbutz members to prevent the cows from suffering, in the early years none of this milk was used commercially. There are also significant constraints imposed by Jewish law on agricultural productivity. Fruits are not allowed to be eaten for the first few years of the tree's life, agricultural fields must lie fallow every seven years, and the corners of fields can never be harvested—

they must be left for society's poor. Although these constraints appear detrimental to productivity, the costly signaling theory of ritual suggests that they may actually be the key to the economic success of the religious kibbutzim.

I decided to study this issue with economist Bradley Ruffle of Israel's Ben Gurion University. We developed a game to determine whether there were differences in how the members of secular and religious kibbutzim cooperated with each other. The game involves two members from the same kibbutz who remain anonymous to each other. Each member is told there are 100 shekels in an envelope to which both members have access. Each participant decides how many shekels to withdraw and keep. If the sum of both requests exceeds 100 shekels, both members receive no money and the game is over. However, if the requests are less than or equal to 100 shekels, the money remaining in the envelope is increased by 50 percent and divided evenly among the participants. Each member also keeps the original amount he or she requested. The game is an example of a common-pool resource dilemma in which publicly accessible goods are no longer available once they are consumed. Since the goods are available to more than one person, the maintenance of the resources requires individual self-restraint; in other words, cooperation.

After we controlled for a number of variables, including the age and size of the kibbutz and the amount of privatization, we found not only that religious kibbutzniks were more cooperative with each other than secular kibbutzniks, but that male religious kibbutz members were also significantly more cooperative than female members. Among secular kibbutzniks we found no sex differences at all. This result is understandable if we appreciate the types of rituals and demands imposed on religious Jews. Although there are a variety of requirements that are imposed equally on males and females, such as keeping kosher and refraining from work on the Sabbath, male rituals are largely performed in public, whereas female rituals are generally pursued privately. Indeed, none of the three major requirements imposed exclusively on women—attending a ritual bath, separating a portion of dough when baking bread and lighting Shabbat and holiday candles—are publicly performed. They are not rituals that signal commitment to a wider group; instead they appear to signal commitment to the family. Men, however, engage in highly visible rituals, most notably public prayer, which they are expected to perform three times a day. Among male religious kibbutz members, synagogue attendance is positively correlated with cooperative behavior. There is no similar correlation among females. This is not surprising given that women are not required to attend services, and so their presence does not signal commitment to the group. Here the costly signaling theory of ritual provides a unique explanation of these findings. We expect that further work will provide even more insight into the ability of ritual to promote trust, commitment and cooperation.

We know that many other species engage in ritual behaviors that appear to enhance trust and cooperation. For

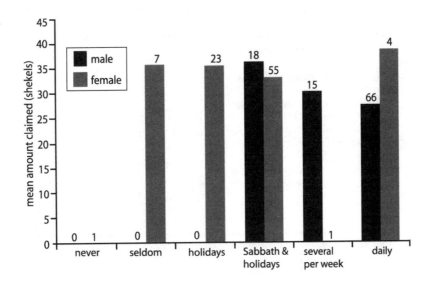

example, anthropologists John Watanabe of Dartmouth University and Barbara Smuts at the University of Michigan have shown that greetings between male olive baboons serve to signal trust and commitment between former rivals. So why are human rituals often cloaked in mystery and the supernatural? Cognitive anthropologists Scott Atran of the University of Michigan and Pascal Boyer at Washington University in St. Louis have pointed out that the counterintuitive nature of supernatural concepts are more easily remembered than mundane ideas, which facilitates their cultural transmission. Belief in supernatural agents such as gods, spirits and ghosts also appears to be critical to religion's ability to promote long-term cooperation. In our study of 19th-century communes, Eric Bressler and I found that the strong positive relationship between the number of costly requirements imposed on members and commune longevity only held for religious communes, not secular ones. We were surprised by this result because secular groups such as militaries and fraternities appear to successfully employ costly rituals to maintain cooperation. Cultural ecologist Roy Rappaport explained, however, that although religious and secular rituals can both promote cooperation, religious rituals ironically generate greater belief and commitment because they sanctify unfalsifiable statements that are beyond the possibility of examination. Since statements containing supernatural elements, such as "Jesus is the son of God," cannot be proved or disproved, believers verify them "emotionally." In contrast to religious propositions, the kibbutz's guiding dictum, taken from Karl Marx, is not beyond question; it can be evaluated by living according to its directives by distributing labor and resources appropriately. Indeed, as the economic situation on the kibbutzim has worsened, this fundamental proposition of kibbutz life has been challenged and is now disregarded by many who are pushing their communities to accept differential pay scales. The ability of religious rituals to evoke emotional experiences that can be associated with enduring supernatural concepts and symbols differentiates

them from both animal and secular rituals and lies at the heart of their efficiency in promoting and maintaining long-term group cooperation and commitment.

Evolutionary research on religious behavior is in its infancy, and many questions remain to be addressed. The costly signaling theory of ritual appears to provide some answers, and, of course, it has given me a better understanding of the questions I asked as a teenager. The real value of the costly signaling theory of ritual will be determined by its ability to explain religious phenomena across societies. Most of us, including ultraorthodox Jews, are not living in communes. Nevertheless, contemporary religious congregations that demand much of their members are able to achieve a close-knit social community—an impressive accomplishment in today's individualistic world.

Religion has probably always served to enhance the union of its practitioners; unfortunately, there is also a dark side to this unity. If the intragroup solidarity that religion promotes is one of its significant adaptive benefits, then from its beginning religion has probably always played a role in intergroup conflicts. In other words, one of the benefits for individuals of intragroup solidarity is the ability of unified groups to defend and compete against other groups. This seems to be as true today as it ever was, and is nowhere more apparent than the region I visited as a 15-year-old boy—which is where I am as I write these words. As I conduct my fieldwork in the center of this war zone, I hope that by appreciating the depth of the religious need in the human psyche, and by understanding this powerful adaptation, we can learn how to promote cooperation rather than conflict.

Bibliography

Atran, S. 2002. *In Gods We Trust.* New York: Oxford University Press.

Iannaccone, L. 1992. Sacrifice and stigma: Reducing free-riding in cults, communes, and other collectives. *Journal of Political Economy* 100:271-291.

Iannaccone, L. 1994. Why strict churches are strong. *American Journal of Sociology* 99:1180-1211.

Irons, W. 2001. Religion as a hard-to-fake sign of commitment. In *Evolution and the Capacity for Commitment,* ed. R. Nesse, pp. 292-309. New York: Russell Sage Foundation.

Rappaport, R. 1999. *Ritual and Religion in the Making of Humanity.* Cambridge: Cambridge University Press.

Sosis, R. 2003. Why aren't we all Hutterites? Costly signaling theory and religious behavior. *Human Nature* 14:91-127.

Sosis, R., and C. Alcorta. 2003. Signaling, solidarity, and the sacred: The evolution of religious behavior. *Evolutionary Anthropology* 12:264-274.

Sosis, R., and E. Bressler. 2003. Cooperation and commune longevity: A test of the costly signaling theory of religion. *Cross-Cultural Research* 37:211-239.

Sosis, R., and B. Ruffle. 2003. Religious ritual and cooperation: Testing for a relationship on Israeli religious and secular kibbutzim. *Current Anthropology* 44:713-722.

Zahavi, A., and A. Zahavi. 1997. *The Handicap Principle.* New York: Oxford University Press.

Richard Sosis is an assistant professor of anthropology at the University of Connecticut. His research interests include the evolution of cooperation, utopian societies and the behavioral ecology of religion. Address: Department of Anthropology, U-2176, University of Connecticut, Storrs, CT 06269-2176. Internet: richard.sosis@uconn.edu

Shamans

Mark J. Plotkin

Contrary to popular belief, the medicine man, or shaman (usually an accomplished botanist), represents the most ancient profession in the evolution of human culture.
        —Dr. Richard Evans Schultes, 1963

He didn't look like a medicine man to me when I first met him.

Having been raised on a steady diet of Tarzan films, I first entered the rain forest expecting to find the medicine man (or "witch doctor") outfitted in full forest regalia: grass skirts, carnivore tooth necklaces, feather headdress. And indeed I did eventually work with shamans wearing even more fantastic costumes (or almost nothing, in some instances) when I entered the jungles of the northeast Amazon in the late 1970s. But as ever-encroaching Western civilization began making its appearance throughout the most remote corners of Amazonia, the young indigenous people lost interest in the old ways. Living in a world where the cultural global icons were people like Bruce Lee, Madonna, and Michael Jordan, the young Indians showed little or no interest in their own traditional cultures. The world of the shamans, with their belief in magic spirit worlds and astral travel, seemed less useful and effective than antibiotics. And if the missionaries or government-sponsored nurses insisted that shamanism was a sham, why pay any attention to a great-grandfather who said otherwise? So I would enter villages to find ancient wizards and plant masters wearing traditional breechcloths and jaguar-tooth necklaces but their descendants dressed in National Basketball Association T-shirts and high-top tennis shoes. In fifteen years of field experience, I had met few shamans who were not at least twice as old (and, more often, thrice as old) as I was.

But this fellow was different.

It was the first day of August, 1995, and I was seated in a cotton hammock under a thatched roof in the western Amazon of Colombia. To get there, I had to fly south from the Andean city of Bogota to the burgeoning frontier town of Florencia, the capital city of the state of Caquetá; then an all-day bus ride past the military checkpoints and through the depressingly deforested landscape. In the 1960s, the national government, with the best of inten-

tions, had encouraged landless peasants to settle on the "fertile" soils of the "uninhabited" Amazon region. The peasants' inability to manage the (admittedly challenging) tropical landscape resulted in forest destruction of staggering proportions. When my mentor Richard Schultes carried out ethnobotanical research here in the 1940s and 1950s, he marveled at "the seemingly limitless forest that stretched unbroken to the far horizon." Schultes returned to the area only a decade later, and writer William Burroughs was there to record the scientist's reaction: "My God, what have they done to the forest.... It's all gone!"

I had traveled to the area at the invitation of a Colombian colleague to participate in an ayahuasca ritual, the vision-vine ceremony conducted by Amazonian shamans for purposes of curing and divination. In South and North America, ayahuasca had attained an enormous and devoted following among certain New Age groups, though none of the practitioners whom I met were Native American shamans. The invitation to the Colombian Amazon seemed to represent the opportunity to participate in a truly traditional ceremony.

On that torrid afternoon, sweat poured off me and a few mosquitoes buzzed hungrily around my ears as I conversed with a fellow who stood leaning against the wooden post from which one end of my hammock was strung. He stood about five-foot-two, the typical height of a forest Indian, though the local campesinos (peasants) were not much taller. He had jet black hair and spoke excellent Spanish, again making it difficult for me to ascertain whether he was a Native American or not (knowing that such a question can be considered extremely rude by both cultures, I would not ask him outright). He took a last, long draught of his warm beer, and asked me if I'd ever been to the jungle before. I replied that I had worked in several South American countries searching for healing plants. A brief smile flickered across his face. "Have you ever participated in a *toma*, an ayahuasca session?" he asked.

"Once," I replied, "in Peru. But I know I have much to learn about the use of the vision vine for curing purposes." A fleeting, Mona Lisa smile played across his face as he stubbed out his cigarette on the dirt floor and said,

"Then I'll see you at the ceremony tonight." And with that, he wandered off.

The session was held at a small tribal meetinghouse constructed at the edge of the village. I was crestfallen—the poured concrete floor, cinderblock walls, and corrugated aluminum roof seemed the very antithesis of rain forest culture. Where was the traditional *maloca*, the fantastic elongated conical roundhouse that was supposed to be the characteristic indigenous dwelling of the northwest Amazon? I asked a local Ingano fellow who wandered past. "The ayahuasca journey only begins there," he said, pointing with his chin at the structure. "But you will depart very quickly and travel very far away." He smiled and walked on.

The light of the moon on that clear evening was strong enough to illuminate enormous sandstone boulders that marked the edge of a small river running a few hundred meters to the west of the meetinghouse. On the other side of the water began the Andean foothills, home to the only pristine forest in the area. Surrounding the other sides of the meeting hall was nothing but depleted cattle pastures that had harbored magnificent rain forest until a few decades before.

There was an audible murmur from the other Indians as the shaman entered the hut. I marveled at the traditional *cushma*, the sky blue cotton tunic that covered him from shoulders to waist. Wrapped tightly around his thick biceps were dense strings of *shoroshoro* seeds that produced a hissing rattle as he walked. And around his neck was a magnificent necklace of jaguar teeth, the symbol of the shaman in many Amazonian tribes. It was only after admiring the medicine man's finery that I was startled to recognize him as the fellow with whom I had been chatting earlier that afternoon. In his ceremonial garb he looked every inch the great shaman, and I wondered how I could have ever thought otherwise.

The shaman took his seat on a low bench at one end of the hut while the rest of us sat in a circle on the dirt floor at his feet. A chilly breeze blew in from the Andean slopes and I shivered as much from anticipation as from the cold. The night was alive with jungle sounds: crickets buzzed and chirped, frogs croaked and trilled, night jars cooed and whooped. Howler monkeys hooted briefly, indicating that rain would fall the next day.

The shaman dipped a calabash into an earthen pot between his feet. Holding it high over his head with both hands, he mumbled a few incantations before drinking the ayahuasca in a single draught. Wiping his mouth clean with the back of his hand, he refilled the container from the pot, repeated the incantation, and passed it to me.

I looked down at the cup and saw it filled to the brim with a thick reddish brown liquid. I tried to knock it back in one swallow as I had seen the shaman do. The dreadful bitterness of the potion, however, caught me by surprise and I struggled to keep from retching. The Indian seated on the other side of the shaman noted my distress and passed me a cup of *aguardiente*, a fiery sugar cane brandy whose sweet anise aftertaste erased the disagreeable brackishness of the ayahuasca. I sat and watched the shaman slowly repeat the procedure with everyone in the circle.

All seemed quiet and peaceful until the shaman picked up a handful of *wai-rah sacha* leaves and began to shake them in a fanning motion. The leaves produced a whistling sound not unlike a high wind rushing through the rain forest canopy before a heavy thunderstorm: *shhhhhh-shhhhhh*. He shook it in a slow, rhythmic pattern that proved hypnotic, and I felt as if my brain waves were being organized in a fixed laser like pattern under his control. My body began to relax, and I lay back onto a blanket I had brought to ward off the cold. Glancing around, I noticed that everyone else had also reclined, as if the shaman had willed us to do so. Only the medicine man remained seated upright, and he began a mesmerizing chant: *Hey-yah-hey! Hey-yah-hey!*

What seems simple in retrospect was emotionally enrapturing at the time. And the shaking of the leaves added a layer of complexity and fascination that reverberated through my brain from the right front lobe to the rear left lobe to the rear right lobe to the front left lobe, and back again. By now the shaman seemed master of time, space, and my entire being.

I drifted off into a gentle trance. I felt myself lying in a tucum palm fiber hammock as comfortable as a giant feather bed. I was floating as in a dream. Looking up, I could see a beautiful blue tropical sky with only a few wisps of clouds above me. The hammock was slung between two towering columnar *epena* trees with a dark Amazonian lake below me. At the far edge of the lake I could make out the tiny figure of the shaman in this blue tunic continuing his chant. By the peaceful look on his face that I could just make out at this distance, I could tell that he was deep into his own ayahuasca visions. As I floated there with my hands propped comfortably behind my head, I peacefully reviewed scenes from my life that reenacted themselves for my analysis. Aside from a few mild waves of nausea, all seemed peaceful and calm; I was at one with the cosmos.

Soon the shaman ceased his chant, and I opened my eyes to find myself seated at his feet once more. He refilled the calabash, prayed over it, and drank it down. Repeating the first two steps, he then passed the container to me. I drained it but it didn't sit right in my stomach. I tried to ignore the volcanic nausea welling up inside. I promised myself that I would lie back down as soon as everyone had had their turn and began to feel a bit better by focusing all my attention on the shaman. I knew that he was able to feel my gaze, and he turned to me. As he did so, the beaded bracelets on his biceps produced the sound of rushing water and turned into tiny glowing diamonds that all but obscured my field of vision. As the diamonds dissipated, I could see that the shaman was staring at me with a look that combined equal parts power, disdain, humor, and kindness. I stared at his black pupils growing larger and larger, finally combining into one giant black vortex into which I was sucked. I was underwater now in waters as pitch-black as the Rio Negro. Huge black caimans and anacondas swarmed in the river, menacing me with their size and demeanor, though not attacking me directly. Running out of air, and afraid of the creatures that surrounded me in this aquatic realm, I swam desperately.

I broke the surface and crawled on all fours onto a white sandy beach along the riverbank. Having been underwater too long, I became sick, vomiting and vomiting. I was unable to stop; the life began ebbing from my body. I could not regain my feet and sank face down into the sand, rising up enough only to retch over to the side. I began weeping and begging for help as I continued to fade. Pain racked my body and my head felt as if it had exploded. I tried fighting for my life but no longer had the strength. I had managed to crawl up the riverbank toward the jungle but only made it far enough to pass out in the grass at the edge of the forest. I lay face down. I died.

I don't know how long I lay in the grass, inert, comatose, inanimate. But I could hear something in the back of my head. The shaman continued to chant, deep in the forest in front of me. With a Herculean effort, I managed to raise myself on all fours. I began weeping again because I did not have the strength to go to him. As I sat mired in this predicament, I was frightened by a deep guttural grunt in the jungle in front of me. A jaguar! Now I was weak *and* terrified. But a most extraordinary thing happened: the great cat's roar caused a wave of nausea to well up inside me and I puked as I never had before. Horrible things poured out of me: purple frogs and bloodred snakes and phosphorescent orange scorpions. I thought I was dying a second death, yet when it stopped I felt a bit stronger. So close was the jaguar that I could smell him, yet I was no longer afraid. I stumbled a bit as I followed him into the jungle; I knew that he was leading me toward the shaman. Tripping over roots, I tried to keep pace with the great cat. I momentarily worried about snakes until I realized that nothing could be worse than what I was enduring.

Falling to my knees, I looked up to see the shaman standing over me. He began a peculiar chant that made my head hurt even more until he pressed his palms against my temples and started to squeeze. As he twisted my neck to the right I felt my vertebrae pop; the pain began to abate, ever so slightly. He seated me on a tree trunk and began to dance around me. Taking a swig of an herbal tea, he circled me, spitting the aromatic liquid at me in a cold spray at each of the four cardinal points of the compass. The pain and confusion that racked my body began to subside as he massaged my arms and neck. The sun had started to rise in the east. He sang and rubbed my upper body with leaves, pausing every now and again to cast off some invisible film he seemed to be scraping off me. I managed to croak out a question: "Why did you do this to me?"

He gave a cryptic, Cheshire cat smile and replied: "You have had a glimpse of our world. You have been purged, cleaned, healed. You will never again fear death as you have now died and been reborn."

In a classic treatise on ayahuasca (1979), R. E. Schultes wrote:

> There is a magic intoxicant in northwesternmost South America which the Indians believe can free the soul from corporeal confinement, allowing it to wander free and return to the body at will. The soul, thus untrammeled, liberates its owner from the everyday life and introduces him to wondrous realms of what he considers reality and permits him to communicate with his ancestors. The Kechua term for this inebriating drink—ayahuasca ("vine of the soul")—refers to this freeing of the spirit. The plants involved are truly plants of the gods, for their powers are laid to supernatural forces residing in their tissues, and they were the divine gifts to the earliest Indians on earth. The drink employed for prophecy, divination, sorcery, and medical purposes, is so deeply rooted in native mythology and philosophy that there can be no doubt of its great age as part of aboriginal life.

In the northwest Amazon, ayahuasca represents an essential component of most—if not all—shamanic healing ceremonies. Yet there are aspects of these shamanic practices that are used by other cultures around the world, only some of which employ psychotropic plants in their healing rituals. According to Dr. Piers Vitebsky, an authority on Eurasian shamanism, the word "shaman" comes from the language of the Evenk peoples, reindeer herders in Siberia. To the Evenk, a shaman is a person who can "will his or her spirit to leave the body and journey to upper or lower world." Common elements unite the shamanic tradition found on every continent except Antarctica.

Curing disease, preventing famine, controlling the weather, entering trances, fighting evil spirits sent by malevolent shamans of other tribes, traveling up to the spirit world, or conveying souls to the underworld are common denominators among most practitioners of what we consider shamanism. In most groups, the shaman serves as the only tribal member who fully comprehends both the "real" world and the "spirit" world and is therefore responsible for maintaining the balance between the two.

Within the context of the source culture, shamanism is often considered a profoundly holy profession. Unlike in much of the industrialized world, in which healing is essentially divorced from spirituality, the shaman also functions as the priest-rabbi, which greatly augments his or her ability to heal. As Western science finally begins to study and appreciate the therapeutic benefits of spirituality, the practice and effectiveness of shamanism becomes not only more comprehensible but also more appreciated.

An integral component of shamanistic healing is what has been called "the placebo effect." Many leaders of the Western medical establishment came of age during the antibiotic revolution, the single greatest therapeutic advance of the mid-twentieth century. However, the development of these drugs also led several generations of physicians to equate (to a large degree) chemistry and healing. Spirituality (its nature and its role in healing) was part of few (if any) medical school curricula. The placebo effect, in which patients recovered because they believed they would, was not in and of itself shunned, but more often noted with bemusement rather than harnessed and put to work.

Shamans, on the other hand, are masters of the placebo effect. Much has been made of the shamanic practice of sucking the "evil darts" (or other foreign substances) out of the patient's body by the healer. References in the literature often refer to it as trickery or sleight of hand, usually in a condescending way. Two aspects, however, are overlooked. First, it often provides the patient some relief, convincing them that they are on the road to recovery and creating a mind-set that facilitates healing. Second, therapeutic compounds, usually in the form of plants, are also employed because the shaman is customarily a master botanist. The shaman's genius as a healer stems from his (or her) ability to combine the spiritual (sucking out evil darts, communing with the forces of nature, etc.) with the chemical (the plants, insects, etc.)

Chief Pierce of Flat Iron, an Oglala Sioux, explained the inextricable link between the holy and the botanical almost a century ago: "From Wakan-Tanka, the Great Mystery, comes all power.... Man knows that all healing plants are given by Wakan-Tanka: therefore they are holy.... The Great Mystery gave to men all things for their food, their clothing, their welfare. And to man he gave also the knowledge how to use these gifts ... how to find the holy healing plants."

The sophisticated botanical knowledge of these "uneducated" shamans astonishes Western researchers. In the rain forest, these healers can sometimes identify almost every single species of tree merely by the smell, appearance, or feel of the bark, a feat no university-trained botanist can accomplish. And their knowledge of the ecology of these plants—when they fruit, when they flower, what pollinates them, what disperses the seeds, what preys on them, what type of soil they prefer—is no less impressive. As nature continues to provide us with a cornucopia of new medicines, these shamans (in the rain forest and elsewhere) will prove to be the ultimate sources of knowledge about which species offer therapeutic promise and how they might best be employed.

Almost every plant species that has been put to use by Western medicine was originally discovered and utilized by indigenous cultures. Despite the fact that a single shaman may know and employ over a hundred species for medicinal purposes, or that a single tribe (which may have several shamans) may know and utilize several hundred species for medical purposes, few of the world's remaining tribal peoples have been the subject of comprehensive ethnobotanical/ethnomedical studies. Yet the more we study, the more we learn how little we know about how much they know.

Ayahuasca, the vision vine, represents a classic example. The early accounts of ayahuasca focused on a single species of vine (*Banisteriopsis caapi*). Subsequent research has revealed that other plants added to the mixture determine the actual type, intensity, and duration of the hallucinations—proving the sophistication of these shamans as both botanists and chemists. For example, leaves of a species of the *Psychotria* shrub of the coffee family are often added to the ayahuasca mixture. These leaves contain chemicals called tryptamines that induce hallucinations. The compounds, however, are inactive when taken orally unless activated by the presence of another type of chemical known as monoamine oxidase inhibitors. The psychotropic compounds in the ayahuasca vine not only induce hallucinations but also function as monoamine oxidase inhibitors. The result: a brew much more potent than one prepared from either species.

Furthermore, the shamans often have the remarkable ability to distinguish between, describe, and make use of distinct healing and/or chemical properties of different parts of the same plant. A shaman, for example, will note that bark from the upper stem of the ayahuasca vine may cause visions of jaguars, while the root bark results in scenes of anacondas. Schultes wrote:

> Among the Tukano of the Colombian Vaupes, for example, six "kinds" of Ayahuasca or Kahi are recognized.... *Kahi riama*, the strongest, produces auditory hallucinations and announces future events. It is said to cause death if improperly employed. The second strongest, *Mene-kahi-ma*, reputedly causes visions of green snakes.... These two "kinds" may not belong to Banisteriopsis or even to the family Malpighiaceae. The third in strength is called *Suana-kahi-ma* ("Kahi of the red jaguar"), producing visions in red. *Kahi-vai Bucura-rijoma* ("Kahi of the monkey head") causes monkeys to hallucinate and howl.... All of these "kinds" are referable probably to *Banisteriopsis caapi* [e.g., what to Western botanists is all the same species].

Hallucinogens, while an integral part of shamanic healing practices in the western Amazon, still represent only a very small portion of plants employed for therapeutic purposes. As we have seen before, natural products employed for a particular purpose in one culture may offer promise of a different use in our own culture. In the case of ayahuasca, for example, Western-trained physicians in both Brazil and Peru are using the vine as an experimental treatment for chronic alcoholism and crack addiction, with promising results.

An example of using one therapeutic plant for different purposes in a different culture comes to us from the tropical forests of American Samoa in the South Pacific, where the herbal healers—the *taulasea*—are primarily women. These herbalists know 200 species of plants and recognize 180 types of diseases. Ethnobotanist Dr. Paul Cox of the National Tropical Botanical Garden had been working with this culture for over a decade when, in 1984, a *taulasea* named Epenesa Mauigoa showed him an herbal treatment for acute hepatitis prepared from the inner bark of a local species of rubber tree. Cox was particularly intrigued when she insisted that only one "variety" of the tree could be employed when, in Western botanical terms, both varieties were the same species. Investigation of the plant in the laboratories of the National Cancer Institute outside Washington, D.C., yielded a new molecule that the scientists named prostratin. This compound belongs to a class of chemicals known as phorbols, many of which cause tumors in the human body. Intriguingly, however, prostratin not only inhibited the formation of tumors but, in the test tube, prevented cells from becoming infected by the HIV-1 virus and extended the life of infected cells! Of course, it is a long way from the jungle to the laboratory and, in some ways, an even longer trail from the test tube to the pharmacy. Nonetheless, research on prostratin continues. And it is precisely these finds that validate indigenous wisdom in Western eyes, leading to pharmaceutical companies' increased interest in shamanic wisdom.

Scientists continue to be astonished at the breadth and depth of indigenous wisdom. Ethnobotanists at the New York Botanical Garden recently conducted a classic comparative study of indigenous ethnobotanical sagacity in the Amazon Basin. Working with the Chacobo tribe in Bolivia, Dr. Brian Boom found they used 95 percent of the local tree species. His colleague Dr. Bill Balee learned that the Tembe peoples of Brazil employed 61.3 percent of local trees while the Ka'apoor tribe used 76.8 percent.

The effectiveness of this wisdom is being validated in the laboratory. Dr. Bernard Ortiz de Montellano of Wayne State University sifted through accounts of the ethnomedicine of the Aztec peoples of ancient Mexico and was able to identify 118 plants that they employed as medicines. When he subjected them to laboratory examination, he found that almost 85 percent were at least somewhat efficacious, strikingly similar to data gathered by Paul Cox and his colleagues in Polynesia. The joint Swedish-American research team tested the Samoan medicinal plants in the laboratory. The results: 86 percent demonstrated significant pharmacological activity.

Of course, new mechanisms must be developed to protect the intellectual property rights of these local peoples and local governments: fortunately, the colonial/neocolonial model of "Let's take what we need of local plants and wisdom and cart it off to the marketplace" is completely unacceptable as we enter the twenty-first century. New economic models and legal frameworks are being devised and put in place to share benefits from these new discoveries and avoid the "rape and run" approach to commercializing natural resources that characterized much of human history.

Nonetheless, an enormous body of shamanic knowledge remains untested (or untestable) in the laboratory because we cannot (or have not yet been able to) understand it outside of the context of indigenous culture. The Tirio Indians of the northeast Amazon, for example, employ a series of plants to treat ailments that (they claim) are caused by the breaking of hunting taboos. One ancient medicine man showed me a plant that he explained was "boiled into a tea and given to an infant who was crying at night because he couldn't sleep because his father had killed a giant anteater." Another species was used for the same purpose, except that the child suffered insomnia because the father had killed a tapir. Most Westerners would regard these ailments as imaginary. A much more effective utilitarian approach, instead of dismissing this seemingly incomprehensible claim, would be to investigate whether the plant potion contained compounds that might serve as the basis for a safe, effective, nonaddictive sleeping pill—a potion that Western medicine has been unable to devise.

In our culture, we have been taught that our system of medicine (and other things!) is the most advanced, the most successful, the most sophisticated, and so on—a valid statement, in many regards. This "lesson," however, often results in a cultural arrogance that underestimates or even denigrates other systems, either because they seem "primitive" and/or because we don't understand what they are trying to tell or teach us. In his brilliant book *Witchdoctors and Psychiatrists*, Dr. E. Fuller Torrey wrote: "A psychiatrist who tells an illiterate African that his phobia is related to fear of failure and a witch doctor who tells an American tourist that his phobia is related to possession by an ancestral spirit will be met by equally blank stares."

Our culture teaches us to "cut to the chase," to get that one plant or (better yet) one molecule that is responsible for the shaman's cure—and you can spare us the magic rattle and the sacred smoke, thank you very much. Some of these cures only work within their cultural context, be it a treatment for possession by an ancestral spirit, a cure that involves ceremony, ritual, and healing plants, or a mundane remedy that simply requires rubbing a few crushed leaves on the afflicted area. Clearly, some of these treatments harness powerful chemicals that can be used effectively far from their site of origin and within a Western (or other) clinical context.

The Western tendency to adopt a reductionist approach is not just an interest in getting to the basic chemistry (preferably a single molecule that is responsible for the therapeutic effect) or merely a question of being in a hurry—it is also a question of safety and economics. It has proven difficult, if not impossible, to patent a complex plant extract that may contain a multitude of chemicals, even if proven safe and effective. Still, our cultural propensity to reduce everything to the simplest common denominator can cause us to underestimate or even deny the shaman's healing wisdom. A recent example: two ethnobotanists were intrigued by a West African medicine man who appeared to have an extremely potent potion for reducing blood-sugar levels in diabetic patients. They asked whether he might be willing to provide them with the plants he used so they could take them back to the United States for testing. The shaman readily agreed and gave the scientists three different plants. In the lab, they tested species A, which had no effect; they tried species B, which had no effect. They tested species C, still with no positive results. Finally, they boiled them all together and analyzed the resulting potion. Nothing! A year later, back in Africa, they returned to the medicine man. "Your potion doesn't seem to work," said one of the ethnobotanists to the witch doctor.

"What do you mean?" he replied. "You saw me give it to my patients, and measured their blood-sugar levels with your instruments. You yourself told me that the blood-sugar level went down. How could you now claim it doesn't work?"

The ethnobotanists then asked the medicine man if he would be willing to prepare a batch of the potion they could then take with them. He agreed. The shaman boiled water in a big aluminum pot over a wood fire. He added the first plant species, then the second, then the third. Just as he was preparing to take the pot off the fire, he reached into a wet muslin sack, extracted a crab, and dropped it in the pot.

"What is that?" asked one of the ethnobotanists.

"What does it look like?" replied the shaman. "It is a crab!"

"Yeah, I know," responded the scientist. "But why did you add it to the pot? You didn't tell us that was part of the recipe."

The shaman smiled. "Look," he said, "you asked me if I would give you the plants used to make the potion. I did!"

The scientists took the potion back to the United States, found it to be effective at lowering blood sugar, and it is currently being investigated in the lab.

Of course, a shaman's healing wizardry does not necessarily entail the use of nature's chemistry. Dr. Charles Limbach, an American physician with extensive experience in Latin America, recently related an intriguing encounter. A friend of his, also a physician, had returned from a sojourn in the Oriente, the Amazonian territory of eastern Ecuador:

My friend was visiting a missionary acquaintance who was working with the Shuar people, also called the Jivaro, who were once renowned for their then common practice of removing and then shrinking the heads of their enemies. He was sitting on the porch of the missionary's house and chatting with his fellow American and an elderly Shuar who had a reputation as a powerful shaman. While they were conversing, another Shuar arrived and asked the missionary for help with a botfly larva (through a complicated process, botfly eggs enter the human body and hatch into larvae which feed on human flesh. The standard western treatment is to cut them out with a scalpel). The missionary, who had received some medical training, ducked into the house and came back out with alcohol, cotton swabs, a bandage, and a scalpel. The Shuar shaman asked what he planned to do with all that equipment. The American replied that he would cut out the larva. The shaman smiled, and said he would handle it. He sat the patient in a hammock, leaned over the arm with the botfly and began to sing. Within minutes, the botfly larva emerged from the man's arm, fell onto the floor of the porch, and the shaman crushed it beneath his bare foot.

Neither Limbach nor his colleague was able to explain the incident. Had the shaman sung at a particular frequency maddening to the insect, as opera singers are able to hit a note that can shatter glass? Or did the shaman surreptitiously exhale tobacco smoke into the larva's breathing hole, causing it to crawl out in search of air? In some ways, this situation is analogous to the use of aspirin for most of the past century: even though we didn't fully understand how it functioned in the human body until relatively recently, we nonetheless used the drug because it was safe, effective, and painless.

The extraordinary antiquity of shamanistic practices is well documented. Southern France has long been famous for a series of caves, the walls of which are covered with the oldest known art of human origin. Several years ago, the most ancient of all was discovered not far from other subterranean caverns that had been known and studied for over a century. This cave, christened Chauvet, contained art that was noticeably similar to that found in the earlier discoveries, with portrayals of large mammals like the cave bear and woolly rhinoceros that flourished in Europe at that time. On a hanging rock near the entrance, however, is a striking portrait of a composite creature, the bottom half of which is a human, the upper half a bison. Here, in the earliest known example of human art ever discovered, we see the portrait of the shaman.

Chauvet Cave has been dated at well over thirty thousand years old, which means that this art was created twenty-five thousand years before the more familiar paintings and sculpture of "ancient" Egypt. Similar half-man half-beast motifs are found in many caverns painted and carved in the distant past. The best known and most thoroughly studied of the caves is at Lascaux; a man in a bird mask lies next to a staff with a bird on the end of it. The bird that—unlike most humans—can soar over the forest and through the heavens represents the symbol of the shaman in many cultures. Joseph Campbell suggested that this particular figure lies "rapt in a shamanistic trance" and that "in that remote period of our species the arts of the wizard, shaman, or magician were already well developed."

The Trois Frères sanctuary dates from fourteen thousand years ago and harbors what is probably the most famous prehistoric painting of a shaman: the Dancing Sorcerer. The magnificent portrait features a male creature composed of the parts of many different animals. It has antlers on its head, yet dances on its hind legs in a clearly human manner. Adding further credence that this is a human rather than an animal is the headdress of caribou antlers worn in sacred dances by shamans of Arctic and subarctic tribes, much as Indian medicine men on the Great Plains wore headdresses of buffalo horns.

The antiquity of healing-plant knowledge is assumed to be equally great. A Neanderthal grave at Shanidar in Iraq, near the Iran border, held seven species of plants carefully buried around the corpse. People living in the region today use five of those seven species for medicinal purposes. At Monte Verde in southern Chile, recently concluded to be the site of the earliest known habitation in South America, researchers found what had been gardens of medicinal plants. A ubiquitous species was an evergreen shrub known locally as *boldo*, and widely used as a diuretic, a laxative, and a treatment for liver problems. Laboratory research has proven that this plant is an effective diuretic; investigations in Germany have led to its official approval for the treatment of stomach and intestinal cramps as well as dyspepsia.

The question then arises as to the source of ethnomedical wisdom: simply stated, how did the shamans learn which plants had healing properties? Trial and error undoubtedly played a central role. But in it place like the Amazon, with eighty thousand species of flowering plants (not to mention tens of millions of other organisms), how would the healers know not only which plant to employ but which part of the plant to use? And at what dosage? How did the shaman learn at which phase of the moon these plants should be collected? Even more curious is how they devised such clever recipes that sometimes consist of over twenty components. In the instance of the diabetes case history presented in the introduction, the shaman made the potion from four plants. What would be the odds of recreating that potion using the correct dosage, species, and particular plant parts from a forest of eighty thousand species if we tried to do it based on random collections, which has been the major approach used by most pharmaceutical companies up to the present date?

One key as to how the shamans and others have found and utilized species with therapeutic compounds is the taste test. The concept of "bitter" exists in most cultures, and bitterness often indicates the presence of alkaloids, which represent the single most important chemical components of modern medicine. Quinine and ayahuasca are some of the bitterest substances known.

Yet another clue for the shamans also serves as a lead for Western scientists like David Newman or William Fenical, who look for new medicines from marine organisms: color equals chemistry. If a plant (particularly a tree sap) has a peculiar color, it may well contain interesting chemicals. The clear red sap of the *Virola* tree led shamans of the Yanomami people of Venezuela to develop it into a powerful hallucinogenic snuff, just as the brilliant orange sap of the *Vismia* bush of Suriname led the Tirio shamans to use it as an effective treatment for fungal infections of the skin. The milky red sap of the *Croton* tree led Shuar shamans to employ it as a safe and effective agent for healing wounds.

Another key is the so-called doctrine of signatures. Simply stated, if a plant (or plant part) looks like something, it is somehow good for that something. In other words, because a walnut looks like a brain, it must be good for diseases afflicting the brain (a common belief in medieval Europe). As ludicrous as it sounds, the doctrine has yielded at least one medicinal compound in wide use until recently. The Vedas of ancient India were written about four thousand years ago and included a remedy for snakebite from the snakeroot plant, so named because the twisted roots resembled squirming serpents. Tested in the laboratory in the 1950s, it was found ineffective for countering the toxic effects of the snake venom. One of the problems associated with snakebite, however, is that the trauma of being bitten causes the heart to beat faster, thus pumping the poison throughout the system. What the alkaloid in snakeroot does do is slow down the heartbeat and, because of this, was developed into one of the first effective tranquilizers used by Western medicine.

Once again, this demonstrates why we should not reject ideas, gleaned from other medical systems without first investigating them. The Aztecs valued a Mexican species of magnolia with a heart-shaped fruit as a treatment for cardiac problems. Recent investigations in the lab have found that this fruit contains compounds with a digitalis-like activity.

The most intriguing source of ideas for which plants can be utilized medicinally is perhaps the most difficult concept for Westerners to accept: a shaman's dreams. After a ten-year hiatus, in 1995 I returned to the village of Tepoe in Suriname while searching for diabetes treatments and sought out the great shaman Mahshewah. The old healer, though he appeared pleased at my return, said that he was unable to help me. "I'm sorry," he said, "but I don't recall ever seeing that disease so I can't tell you what plant might be useful for treating it."

Six days later, Mahshewah summoned me to his hut, where he related a most interesting occurrence: "This afternoon I was sleeping in my hammock and I had a dream. And in this dream I saw a tree, and the bark of this tree may help to treat this disease that you said is killing your people. If you canoe down the river for about an hour and a half, you will find a trail on the west bank. If you walk up this trail for about an hour, you will find an enormous tree with yellowish peeling bark. That is the species whose bark may help your people."

I followed his directions down the river and found the trail. I followed his directions up the trail and found the tree. Mahshewah's legs have been paralyzed since he was born. When I asked the other Indians if the old medicine man had ever been up that trail, they told me unequivocally that he had not. How does one explain this through the prism of Western science? I gathered a few scrapings of the bark because my guide said it was a rare and sacred tree that could not be collected in bulk. We still do not know if it might prove efficacious in treating the disease.

The question as to whether something useful can be "discovered" through dreams is one that many people in our society would be inclined to answer negatively. Yet how many remember the discovery of the structure of benzene? Friedrich August Kekulé von Stradowitz, one of the greatest chemists of nineteenth-century Europe, simply could not figure out the structure of the molecule of this enormously important industrial solvent. Quitting in frustration, he decided to turn in for the night and tackle the problem again in the morning. Soon he was dreaming and in his dream he saw several snakes. One of the reptiles began chasing another and then the others joined in, forming a circle. Kekule woke up with the solution to the problem: benzene is a ring! When British scientists dream the answer to perplexing problems, they may become famous, rich, well-respected, and sometimes offered a knighthood. But when Amazonian shamans do it, we dismiss it as "unscientific."

Mother Nature herself is a great teacher. In the words of the gifted natural history writer Sy Montgomery: "In other, older cultures than our own, in which people live closer to the earth, humans do not look down on animals from an imaginary pinnacle. Life is not divided between animals and people, nonhuman and human: life is a continuum, interactive, interdependent. Humans and animals are considered companions and cop layers in the drama of life. Animals' lives, their motives and thoughts and feelings, deserve human attention and respect; dismissing their importance is a grave error."

Characteristic among indigenous cultures of North America was the famous "vision quest," in which a young man (often an apprentice shaman) would go into the wilderness to pray and fast, fast and pray. After several days, he would be visited by visions, often in the form of an animal that would, in the words of the great Inuit shaman Igjugarjuk, "open the mind of a man to all that is hidden to others." As a result of this vision quest, the boy often ended up with a totemic spirit, an animal that served as his personal symbol or protector. The shaman may conclude the process with" animal familiars" or "power animals"—an animal or animals that help him learn and heal. So close is the identification with the animal that the shaman may be perceived as part animal, an

essential component of sacred tribal dances around the world and the ancient cave paintings from Europe. In some cultures, the shamans believe that they actually become the animals, as do the Tirio shamans in the northeast Amazon, who claim the ability to turn into jaguars and roam the jungle at night. Among many tribes, the shaman becomes a bird, omniscient by virtue of his or her ability to look down from above and see things invisible to all others. In the case of the Navajo, as we saw in the last chapter, the bear is the medicinal plant master who taught the Indians about *Ligusticum* and all other healing plants.

The realization that much of shamanic knowledge is based on animals' use of plants is relatively new to Western scientific thought. As we saw in the previous chapter, many healing plants employed by tribes people have probably been learned from local animals. The legends of these cultures often feature sagas explaining how people first learned of useful plants (agricultural and medicinal) from forest creatures. In these cases, animals are, perhaps both metaphorically and literally, the bringers of wisdom.

Joseph Campbell suggested that true shamanism is the religion of the original hunting societies; with the advent of agriculture, cultures became more communally oriented and their religious beliefs changed. While this argument is somewhat hypothetical, what is more certain is that the manifestations of shamanistic religion have been seen as a threat by other organized religions, particularly Christianity, which saw itself in direct competition with belief systems that offered extraordinary experiences to the adherents: "The white goes into his church and talks about Jesus; the Indian walks into his teepee and talks to Jesus," wrote one anthropologist, describing peyote rituals among Native American peoples. But consider this passage from the Book of Job: "But ask now the beasts, and they shall teach thee; and the fowls of the air, and they shall teach thee."

The supreme irony of our suppression of, or disregard for, shamanic religions or other medical practices that rely on natural products is not only the extraordinary therapeutic gifts they have already provided us, but our undeniable need for more of these healing potions to treat "incurable" diseases. The witches of medieval Europe, burned at the stake for their heretical beliefs, were the shamans and/or herbalists of their day. It was their ethnopharmacopeia that gave us aspirin and digitalis. And if we had paid closer attention to their custom of applying moldy bread to wounds, we might have" discovered" penicillin several centuries earlier than Alexander Fleming's research in the 1920s.

A similar situation transpired in our own country. We have all heard about how Squanto and his fellow Indians taught the Pilgrims how to farm the land, but what did the settlers use for medicine? Native American medicinal plants cured the Pilgrims' ailments just as Native American crops filled the European bellies. And prior to the arrival of these Europeans, some of the original Americans had learned that mold could hasten the healing of wounds and local foxglove could treat certain heart problems. Native American healers independently invented syringes and enemas, developed a local anesthetic, and conducted head surgery. Every medicinal plant valued by the settlers was taught to them by local tribespeople. Some of these species entered into commercial, over-the-counter drugs: the yellow color of Murine eyedrops was until recently due to alkaloids extracted from the goldenseal herb. Others, like cascara sagrada (a common ingredient in many laxatives), are sold in many pharmacies. And new medicines are still being developed from plants originally employed by Native Americans: extracts of American bloodroot now serve as an antiplaque agent in toothpastes.

Even some of the most troublesome medical problems are being treated by ancient Indian medicines. Benign prostate enlargement (BPH) afflicts tens of thousands of American men. The fruits of the saw palmetto, a scrubby palm from the southeastern United States, have proven extremely effective at reducing the symptoms: as effective, it has been claimed, as a medicine marketed by Merck. Neither nature nor the shaman has all the answers to the ills that plague us, but both have some—I would say many—of these answers. Urgently needed is an approach that is more humble, more spiritual, more environmental, and more open-minded. The great anthropologist Weston LaBarre, who collaborated with R. E. Schultes on his early peyote research, wrote of the South American Indian:

> As scientists we cannot afford the luxury of an ethnocentric snobbery which assumes *a priori* that primitive cultures have nothing whatsoever to contribute to civilization. Our civilization is, in fact, a compendium of such borrowings, and it is a demonstrable error to believe that contacts of "higher" and "lower" cultures show benefits flowing exclusively in one direction. Indeed, a good case could probably be made that in the long run it is the "higher" culture which benefits the more through being enriched, while the "lower" culture not uncommonly disappears entirely as a result of the contact.

Twenty years ago, I stumbled across the most moving account of this ongoing tragedy that I have ever seen— and it was all because of an earache.

A common and painful ailment suffered by researchers working in the rain forest is fungal infection of the ear. The hot and wet environment of the tropics turns eardrums into petri dishes ripe for the cultivation of fungal invaders. When I began working in the Amazon in the late 1970s, I developed these infections on such a regular basis that before departing I would schedule appointments to have my ears examined at the university clinic upon my return to the States. I quickly learned that if I mentioned my occupation to the physician on duty, she or he would often tell me at great length that ethnobotany was what they really wanted to do with their careers but that they had student loans, a mortgage, a family, and so on, which was why they had been unable to pursue this dream.

I vividly remember going into the clinic with a terrible earache after an expedition to the jungles of southern Venezuela. After examining my ear, attending physician Dr. Jonathan Strongin asked if I had any idea where I might have picked up such a peculiar fungus. "Sure," I replied, "I've just returned from South America."

He asked what I had been doing south of the border, and I gave a distinctly noncommittal reply. He said, "You know, I lived with Indians in the Peruvian Amazon for several years while I was doing my Ph.D. in anthropology, which is how I became interested in healing."

Intrigued, I made a mental note of his name, looked up his dissertation, and found one of the most poignant statements ever recorded on the inextricable interrelationship between people, plants, healing, and belief:

> Since the time of their initial contact, the missionaries have openly discouraged the [shamans], viewing them as AntiChrists…. [Another anthropologist reported] that in the Shimaa region there was a powerful [shaman] who had to abandon his craft because he felt he no longer had the support of the Machiguenga people in his area. This shaman used ayahuasca to take the form of a bird to travel far and wide at a great height to discern the cause of illness. However, he felt that because the missionaries had so successfully eroded the traditional faith of his people, he could no longer continue to cure. For without the faith of the population, while in the avian form he would not be able to return to his body and [would] crash in the forest far from home …

The Secrets of Haiti's Living Dead

A Harvard botanist investigates mystic potions, voodoo rites, and the making of zombies.

Gino Del Guercio

Five years ago, a man walked into l'Estère, a village in central Haiti, approached a peasant woman named Angelina Narcisse, and identified himself as her brother Clairvius. If he had not introduced himself using a boyhood nickname and mentioned facts only intimate family members knew, she would not have believed him. Because, eighteen years earlier, Angelina had stood in a small cemetery north of her village and watched as her brother Clairvius was buried.

The man told Angelina he remembered that night well. He knew when he was lowered into his grave, because he was fully conscious, although he could not speak or move. As the earth was thrown over his coffin, he felt as if he were floating over the grave. The scar on his right cheek, he said, was caused by a nail driven through his casket.

The night he was buried, he told Angelina, a voodoo priest raised him from the grave. He was beaten with a sisal whip and carried off to a sugar plantation in northern Haiti where, with other zombies, he was forced to work as a slave. Only with the death of the zombie master were they able to escape, and Narcisse eventually returned home.

Legend has it that zombies are the living dead, raised from their graves and animated by malevolent voodoo sorcerers, usually for some evil purpose. Most Haitians believe in zombies, and Narcisse's claim is not unique. At about the time he reappeared, in 1980, two women turned up in other villages saying they were zombies. In the same year, in northern Haiti, the local peasants claimed to have found a group of zombies wandering aimlessly in the fields.

But Narcisse's case was different in one crucial respect; it was documented. His death had been recorded by doctors at the American-directed Schweitzer Hospital in Deschapelles. On April 30, 1962, hospital records show, Narcisse walked into the hospital's emergency room spitting up blood. He was feverish and full of aches. His doctors could not diagnose his illness, and his symptoms grew steadily worse. Three days after he entered the hospital, according to the records, he died. The attending physicians, an American among them, signed his death certificate. His body was placed in cold storage for twenty hours, and then he was buried. He said he remembered hearing his doctors pronounce him dead while his sister wept at his bedside.

At the Centre de Psychiatrie et Neurologie in Port-au-Prince, Dr. Lamarque Douyon, a Haitian-born, Canadian-trained psychiatrist, has been systematically investigating all reports of zombies since 1961. Though convinced zombies were real, he had been unable to find a scientific explanation for the phenomenon. He did not believe zombies were people raised from the dead, but that did not make them any less interesting. He speculated that victims were only made to *look* dead, probably by means of a drug that dramatically slowed metabolism. The victim was buried, dug up within a few hours, and somehow reawakened.

The Narcisse case provided Douyon with evidence strong enough to warrant a request for assistance from colleagues in New York. Douyon wanted to find an ethnobotanist, a traditional-medicines expert, who could track down the zombie potion he was sure existed. Aware of the medical potential of a drug that could dramatically lower metabolism, a group organized by the late Dr. Nathan Kline—a New York psychiatrist and pioneer in the field of psychopharmacology—raised the funds necessary to send someone to investigate.

The search for that someone led to the Harvard Botanical Museum, one of the world's foremost institutes of ethnobiology. Its director, Richard Evans Schultes, Jeffrey professor of biology, had spent thirteen years in the tropics studying native medicines. Some of his best-known work is the investigation of curare, the substance used by the nomadic people of the Amazon to poison their darts. Refined into a powerful muscle relaxant called D-tubocurarine, it is now an essential component of the anesthesia used during almost all surgery.

Schultes would have been a natural for the Haitian investigation, but he was too busy. He recommended another Harvard ethnobotanist for the assignment, Wade Davis, a 28-year-old Canadian pursuing a doctorate in biology.

Davis grew up in the tall pine forests of British Columbia and entered Harvard in 1971, influenced by a *Life* magazine story on the student strike of 1969. Before Harvard, the only Americans he had known were draft dodgers, who seemed very exotic. "I used to fight forest fires with them," Davis says. "Like everybody else, I thought America was where it was at. And I wanted to go to Harvard because of that *Life* article. When I got there, I realized it wasn't quite what I had in mind."

Davis took a course from Schultes, and when he decided to go to South America to study plants, he approached his professor for guidance. "He was an extraordinary figure," Davis remembers. "He was a man who had done it all. He had lived alone for years in the Amazon." Schultes sent Davis to the rain forest with two letters of introduction and two pieces of advice: wear a pith helmet and try ayahuasca, a powerful hallucinogenic vine. During that expedition and others, Davis proved himself an "outstanding field man," says his mentor. Now, in early 1982, Schultes called him into his office and asked if he had plans for spring break.

"I always took to Schultes's assignments like a plant takes to water," says Davis, tall and blond, with inquisitive blue eyes. "Whatever Schultes told me to do, I did. His letters of introduction opened up a whole world." This time the world was Haiti.

Davis knew nothing about the Caribbean island—and nothing about African traditions, which serve as Haiti's cultural basis. He certainly did not believe in zombies. "I thought it was a lark," he says now.

Davis landed in Haiti a week after his conversation with Schultes, armed with a hypothesis about how the zombie drug—if it existed—might be made. Setting out to explore, he discovered a country materially impoverished, but rich in culture and mystery. He was impressed by the cohesion of Haitian society; he found none of the crime, social disorder, and rampant drug and alcohol abuse so common in many of the other Caribbean islands. The cultural wealth and cohesion,

he believes, spring from the country's turbulent history.

During the French occupation of the late eighteenth century, 370,000 African-born slaves were imported to Haiti between 1780 and 1790. In 1791, the black population launched one of the few successful slave revolts in history, forming secret societies and overcoming first the French plantation owners and then a detachment of troops from Napoleon's army, sent to quell the revolt. For the next hundred years Haiti was the only independent black republic in the Caribbean, populated by people who did not forget their African heritage. "You can almost argue that Haiti is more African than Africa," Davis says. "When the west coast of Africa was being disrupted by colonialism and the slave trade, Haiti was essentially left alone. The amalgam of beliefs in Haiti is unique, but it's very, very African."

Davis discovered that the vast majority of Haitian peasants practice voodoo, a sophisticated religion with African roots. Says Davis, "It was immediately obvious that the stereotypes of voodoo weren't true. Going around the countryside, I found clues to a whole complex social world." Vodounists believe they communicate directly with, indeed are often possessed by, the many spirits who populate the everyday world. Vodoun society is a system of education, law, and medicine; it embodies a code of ethics that regulates social behavior. In rural areas, secret vodoun societies, much like those found on the west coast of Africa, are as much or more in control of everyday life as the Haitian government.

Although most outsiders dismissed the zombie phenomenon as folklore, some early investigators, convinced of its reality, tried to find a scientific explanation. The few who sought a zombie drug failed. Nathan Kline, who helped finance Davis's expedition, had searched unsuccessfully, as had Lamarque Douyon, the Haitian psychiatrist. Zora Neale Hurston, an American black woman, may have come closest. An anthropological pioneer, she went to Haiti in the Thirties, studied vodoun society, and wrote a book on the subject, *Tell My Horse*, first published in 1938. She knew about the secret societies and was con-

vinced zombies were real, but if a power existed, she too failed to obtain it.

Davis obtained a sample in a few weeks.

He arrived in Haiti with the names of several contacts. A BBC reporter familiar with the Narcisse case had suggested he talk with Marcel Pierre. Pierre owned the Eagle Bar, a bordello in the city of Saint Marc. He was also a voodoo sorcerer and had supplied the BBC with a physiologically active powder of unknown ingredients. Davis found him willing to negotiate. He told Pierre he was a representative of "powerful but anonymous interests in New York," willing to pay generously for the priest's services, provided no questions were asked. Pierre agreed to be helpful for what Davis will only say was a "sizable sum." Davis spent a day watching Pierre gather the ingredients—including human bones—and grind them together with mortar and pestle. However, from his knowledge of poison, Davis knew immediately that nothing in the formula could produce the powerful effects of zombification.

Three weeks later, Davis went back to the Eagle Bar, where he found Pierre sitting with three associates. Davis challenged him. He called him a charlatan. Enraged, the priest gave him a second vial, claiming that this was the real poison. Davis pretended to pour the powder into his palm and rub it into his skin. "You're a dead man," Pierre told him, and he might have been, because this powder proved to be genuine. But, as the substance had not actually touched him, Davis was able to maintain his bravado, and Pierre was impressed. He agreed to make the poison and show Davis how it was done.

The powder, which Davis keeps in a small vial, looks like dry black dirt. It contains parts of toads, sea worms, lizards, tarantulas, and human bones. (To obtain the last ingredient, he and Pierre unearthed a child's grave on a nocturnal trip to the cemetery.) The poison is rubbed into the victim's skin. Within hours he begins to feel nauseated and has difficulty breathing. A pins-and-needles sensation afflicts arms and legs, then progresses to body. The subject becom lips turn blue Quickly-his metabolism is lowered to a level almost indistinguishable from death.

As Davis discovered, making the poison is an inexact science. Ingredients varied in the five samples he eventually acquired, although the active agents were always the same. And the poison came with no guarantee. Davis speculates that sometimes instead of merely paralyzing the victim, the compound kills him. Sometimes the victim suffocates in the coffin before he can be resurrected. But clearly the potion works well enough often enough to make zombies more than a figment of Haitian imagination.

Analysis of the powder produced another surprise. "When I went down to Haiti originally," says Davis, "my hypothesis was that the formula would contain *concombre zombi*, the 'zombie's cucumber,' which is a *Datura* plant. I thought somehow *Datura* was used in putting people down." *Datura* is a powerful psychoactive plant, found in West Africa as well as other tropical areas and used there in ritual as well as criminal activities. Davis had found *Datura* growing in Haiti. Its popular name suggested the plant was used in creating zombies.

But, says Davis, "there were a lot of problems with the *Datura* hypothesis. Partly it was a question of how the drug was administered. *Datura* would create a stupor in huge doses, but it just wouldn't produce the kind of immobility that was key. These people had to appear dead, and there aren't many drugs that will do that."

One of the ingredients Pierre included in the second formula was a dried fish, a species of puffer or blowfish, common to most parts of the world. It gets its name from its ability to fill itself with water and swell to several times its normal size when threatened by predators. Many of these fish contain a powerful poison known as tetrodotoxin. One of the most powerful nonprotein poisons known to man, tetrodotoxin turned up in every sample of zombie powder that Davis acquired.

Numerous well-documented accounts of puffer fish poisoning exist, but the most famous accounts come from the Orient, where *fugu* fish, a species of puffer, is considered a delicacy. In Japan, special chefs are licensed to prepare *fugu*. The chef removes enough poison to make the fish nonlethal, yet enough re-

mains to create exhilarating physiological effects—tingles up and down the spine, mild prickling of the tongue and lips, euphoria. Several dozen Japanese die each year, having bitten off more than they should have.

"When I got hold of the formula and saw it was the *fugu* fish, that suddenly threw open the whole Japanese literature," says Davis. Case histories of *fugu* poisoning read like accounts of zombification. Victims remain conscious but unable to speak or move. A man who had "died" after eating *fugu* recovered seven days later in the morgue. Several summers ago, another Japanese poisoned by *fugu* revived after he was nailed into his coffin. "Almost all of Narcisse's symptoms correlated. Even strange things such as the fact that he said he was conscious and could hear himself pronounced dead. Stuff that I thought had to be magic, that seemed crazy. But, in fact, that is what people who get *fugu*-fish poisoning experience."

Davis was certain he had solved the mystery. But far from being the end of his investigation, identifying the poison was, in fact, its starting point. "The drug alone didn't make zombies," he ex-

---

Richard Schultes

His students continue his tradition of pursuing botanical research in the likeliest of unlikely places.

Richard Evans Schultes, Jeffrey professor of biology emeritus, has two homes, and they could not be more different. The first is Cambridge, where he served as director of the Harvard Botanical Museum from 1970 until last year, when he became director emeritus. During his tenure he interested generations of students in the exotic botany of the Amazon rain forest. His impact on the field through his own research is worldwide. The scholarly ethnobotanist with steel-rimmed glasses, bald head, and white lab coat is as much a part of the Botanical Museum as the thousands of plant specimens and botanical texts on the museum shelves.

In his austere office is a picture of a crew-cut, younger man stripped to the waist, his arms decorated with tribal paint. This is Schultes's other persona. Starting in 1941, he spent thirteen years in the rain

forests of South America, living with the Indians and studying the plants they use for medicinal and spiritual purposes.

Schultes is concerned that many of the people he has studied are giving up traditional ways. "The people of so-called primitive societies are becoming civilized and losing all their forefathers' knowledge of plant lore," he says. "We'll be losing the tremendous amounts of knowledge they've gained over thousands of years. We're interested in the practical aspects with the hope that new medicines and other things can be developed for our own civilization."

Schultes's exploits are legendary in the biology department. Once, while gathering South American plant specimens hundreds of miles from civilization, he contracted beri-beri. For forty days he fought creeping paralysis and overwhelming fatigue as he paddled back to a doctor. "It was an extraordinary feat of endurance," says disciple Wade Davis. "He is really one of the last nineteenth-century naturalists."

Hallucinogenic plants are one of Schultes's primary interests. As a Harvard undergraduate in the Thirties, he lived with Oklahoma's Kiowa Indians to observe their use of plants. He participated in their peyote ceremonies and wrote his thesis on the hallucinogenic cactus. He has also studied other hallucinogens, such as morning glory seeds, sacred mushrooms, and ayahuasca, a South American vision vine. Schultes's work has led to the development of anesthetics made from curare and alternative sources of natural rubber.

Schultes's main concern these days is the scientific potential of plants in the rapidly disappearing Amazon jungle. "If chemists are going to get material on 80,000 species and then analyze them, they'll never finish the job before the jungle is gone," he says. "The short cut is to find out what the [native] people have learned about the plant properties during many years of living in the very rich flora."

—G.D.G

plains. "Japanese victims of puffer-fish poisoning don't become zombies, they become poison victims. All the drug could do was set someone up for a whole series of psychological pressures that would be rooted in the culture. I wanted to know why zombification was going on," he says.

He sought a cultural answer, an explanation rooted in the structure and beliefs of Haitian society. Was zombification simply a random criminal activity? He thought not. He had discovered that Clairvius Narcisse and "Ti Femme," a second victim he interviewed, were village pariahs. Ti Femme was regarded as a thief. Narcisse had abandoned his children and deprived his brother of land that was rightfully his. Equally suggestive, Narcisse claimed that his aggrieved brother had sold him to a *bokor*, a voodoo priest who dealt in black magic; he made cryptic reference to having been tried and found guilty by the "masters of the land."

Gathering poisons from various parts of the country, Davis had come into direct contact with the vodoun secret societies. Returning to the anthropological literature on Haiti and pursuing his contacts with informants, Davis came to understand the social matrix within which zombies were created.

Davis's investigations uncovered the importance of the secret societies. These groups trace their origins to the bands of escaped slaves that organized the revolt against the French in the late eighteenth century. Open to both men and women, the societies control specific territories of the country. Their meetings take place at night, and in many rural parts of Haiti the drums and wild celebrations that characterize the gatherings can be heard for miles.

Davis believes the secret societies are responsible for policing their communities, and the threat of zombification is one way they maintain order. Says Davis, "Zombification has a material ba-

sis, but it also has a societal logic." To the uninitiated, the practice may appear a random criminal activity, but in rural vodoun society, it is exactly the opposite—a sanction imposed by recognized authorities, a form of capital punishment. For rural Haitians, zombification is an even more severe punishment than death, because it deprives the subject of his most valued possessions: his free will and independence.

The vodounists believe that when a person dies, his spirit splits into several different parts. If a priest is powerful enough, the spiritual aspect that controls a person's character and individuality, known as *ti bon ange*, the "good little angel," can be captured and the corporeal aspect, deprived of its will, held as a slave.

From studying the medical literature on tetrodotoxin poisoning, Davis discovered that if a victim survives the first few hours of the poisoning, he is likely to recover fully from the ordeal. The subject simply revives spontaneously. But zombies remain without will, in a trance-like state, a condition vodounists attribute to the power of the priest. Davis thinks it possible that the psychological trauma of zombification may be augmented by *Datura* or some other drug; he thinks zombies may be fed a *Datura* paste that accentuates their disorientation. Still, he puts the material basis of zombification in perspective: "Tetrodotoxin and *Datura* are only templates on which cultural forces and beliefs may be amplified a thousand times."

Davis has not been able to discover how prevalent zombification is in Haiti. "How many zombies there are is not the question," he says. He compares it to capital punishment in the United States: "It doesn't really matter how many people are electrocuted, as long as it's a possibility." As a sanction in Haiti, the fear is not of zombies, it's of becoming one.

Davis attributes his success in solving the zombie mystery to his approach. He

went to Haiti with an open mind and immersed himself in the culture. "My intuition unhindered by biases served me well," he says. "I didn't make any judgments." He combined this attitude with what he had learned earlier from his experiences in the Amazon. "Schultes's lesson is to go and live with the Indians as an Indian." Davis was able to participate in the vodoun society to a surprising degree, eventually even penetrating one of the Bizango societies and dancing in their nocturnal rituals. His appreciation of Haitian culture is apparent. "Everybody asks me how did a white person get this information? To ask the question means you don't understand Haitians—they don't judge you by the color of your skin."

As a result of the exotic nature of his discoveries, Davis has gained a certain notoriety. He plans to complete his dissertation soon, but he has already finished writing a popular account of his adventures. To be published in January by Simon and Schuster, it is called *The Serpent and the Rainbow*, after the serpent that vodounists believe created the earth and the rainbow spirit it married. Film rights have already been optioned; in October Davis went back to Haiti with a screenwriter. But Davis takes the notoriety in stride. "All this attention is funny," he says. "For years, not just me, but all Schultes's students have had extraordinary adventures in the line of work. The adventure is not the end point, it's just along the way of getting the data. At the Botanical Museum, Schultes created a world unto itself. We didn't think we were doing anything above the ordinary. I still don't think we do. And you know," he adds, "the Haiti episode does not begin to compare to what others have accomplished—particularly Schultes himself."

Gino Del Guercio is a national science writer for United Press International.

From *Harvard Magazine*, January/February 1986, pp. 31–37. © 1986 by Harvard Magazine, Inc. Reprinted by permission of the author.

Body Ritual Among the Nacirema

Horace Miner
University of Michigan

The anthropologist has become so familiar with the diversity of ways in which different peoples behave in similar situations that he is not apt to be surprised by even the most exotic customs. In fact, if all of the logically possible combinations of behavior have not been found somewhere in the world, he is apt to suspect that they must be present in some yet undescribed tribe. This point has, in fact, been expressed with respect to clan organization by Murdock (1949: 71). In this light, the magical beliefs and practices of the Nacirema present such unusual aspects that it seems desirable to describe them as an example of the extremes to which human behavior can go.

Professor Linton first brought the ritual of the Nacirema to the attention of anthropologists twenty years ago (1936: 326), but the culture of this people is still very poorly understood. They are a North American group living in the territory between the Canadian Cree, the Yaqui and Tarahumare of Mexico, and the Carib and Arawak of the Antilles. Little is known of their origin, though tradition states that they came from the east. According to Nacirema mythology, their nation was originated by a culture hero, Notgnishaw, who is otherwise known for two great feats of strength—the throwing of a piece of wampum across the river Pa-To-Mac and the chopping down of a cherry tree in which the Spirit of Truth resided.

Nacirema culture is characterized by a highly developed market economy which has evolved in a rich natural habitat. While much of the people's time is devoted to economic pursuits, a large part of the fruits of these labors and a considerable portion of the day are spent in ritual activity. The focus of this activity is the human body, the appearance and health of which loom as a dominant concern in the ethos of the people. While such a concern is certainly not unusual, its ceremonial aspects and associated philosophy are unique.

The fundamental belief underlying the whole system appears to be that the human body is ugly and that its natural tendency is to debility and disease. Incarcerated in such a body, man's only hope is to avert these characteristics through the use of the powerful influences of ritual and ceremony. Every household has one or more shrines devoted to this purpose. The more powerful individuals in the society have several shrines in their houses and, in fact, the opulence of a house is often referred to in terms of the number of such ritual centers it possesses. Most houses are of wattle and daub construction, but the shrine rooms of the more wealthy are walled with stone. Poorer families imitate the rich by applying pottery plaques to their shrine walls.

While each family has at least one such shrine, the rituals associated with it are not family ceremonies but are private and secret. The rites are normally only discussed with children, and then only during the period when they are being initiated into these mysteries. I was able, however, to establish sufficient rapport with the natives to examine these shrines and to have the rituals described to me.

The focal point of the shrine is a box or chest which is built into the wall. In this chest are kept the many charms and magical potions without which no native believes he could live. These preparations are secured from a variety of specialized practitioners. The most powerful of these are the medicine men, whose assistance must be rewarded with substantial gifts. However, the medicine men do not provide the curative potions for their clients, but decide what the ingredients should be and then write them down in an ancient and secret language. This writing is understood only by the medicine men and by the herbalists who, for another gift, provide the required charm.

The charm is not disposed of after it has served its purpose, but is placed in the charm-box of the household shrine. As these magical materials are specific for certain ills, and the real or imagined maladies of the people are many, the charm-box is usually full to overflowing. The magical packets are so numerous that people forget what their purposes were and fear to use them again. While the natives are very vague on this point, we can only assume that the idea in retaining all the old magical materials is that their presence in the charm-box, before which the body rituals are conducted, will in some way protect the worshipper.

Beneath the charm-box is a small font. Each day every member of the family, in succession, enters the shrine room, bows his head before the charm-box, mingles different sorts of holy water in the font, and proceeds with a brief rite of ablution.

The holy waters are secured from the Water Temple of the community, where the priests conduct elaborate ceremonies to make the liquid ritually pure.

In the hierarchy of magical practitioners, and below the medicine men in prestige, are specialists whose designation is best translated "holy-mouth-men." The Nacirema have an almost pathological horror and fascination with the mouth, the condition of which is believed to have a supernatural influence on all social relationships. Were it not for the rituals of the mouth, they believe that their teeth would fall out, their gums bleed, their jaws shrink, their friends desert them, and their lovers reject them. (They also believe that a strong relationship exists between oral and moral characteristics. For example, there is a ritual ablution of the mouth for children which is supposed to improve their moral fiber.)

The daily body ritual performed by everyone includes a mouth-rite. Despite the fact that these people are so punctilious about care of the mouth, this rite involves a practice which strikes the uninitiated stranger as revolting. It was reported to me that the ritual consists of inserting a small bundle of hog hairs into the mouth, along with certain magical powders, and then moving the bundle in a highly formalized series of gestures.

In addition to the private mouth-rite, the people seek out a holy-mouth-man once or twice a year. These practitioners have an impressive set of paraphernalia, consisting of a variety of augers, awls, probes, and prods. The use of these objects in the exorcism of the evils of the mouth involves almost unbelievable ritual torture of the client. The holy-mouth-man opens the client's mouth and, using the above mentioned tools, enlarges any holes which decay may have created in the teeth. Magical materials are put into these holes. If there are no naturally occurring holes in the teeth, large sections of one or more teeth are gouged out so that the supernatural substance can be applied. In the client's view, the purpose of these ministrations is to arrest decay and to draw friends. The extremely sacred and traditional character of the rite is evident in the fact that the natives return to the holy-mouth-men year after year, despite the fact that their teeth continue to decay.

It is to be hoped that, when a thorough study of the Nacirema is made, there will be a careful inquiry into the personality structure of these people. One has but to watch the gleam in the eye of a holy-mouth-man, as he jabs an awl into an exposed nerve, to suspect that a certain amount of sadism is involved. If this can be established, a very interesting pattern emerges, for most of the population shows definite masochistic tendencies. It was to these that Professor Linton referred in discussing a distinctive part of the daily body ritual which is performed only by men. This part of the rite involves scraping and lacerating the surface of the face with a sharp instrument. Special women's rites are performed only four times during each lunar month, but what they lack in frequency is made up in barbarity. As part of this ceremony, women bake their heads in small ovens for about an hour. The theoretically interesting point is that what seems to be a preponderantly masochistic people have developed sadistic specialists.

The medicine men have an imposing temple, or *latipso*, in every community of any size. The more elaborate ceremonies required to treat very sick patients can only be performed at this temple. These ceremonies involve not only the thaumaturge but a permanent group of vestal maidens who move sedately about the temple chambers in distinctive costume and headdress.

The *latipso* ceremonies are so harsh that it is phenomenal that a fair proportion of the really sick natives who enter the temple ever recover. Small children whose indoctrination is still incomplete have been known to resist attempts to take them to the temple because "that is where you go to die." Despite this fact, sick adults are not only willing but eager to undergo the protracted ritual purification, if they can afford to do so. No matter how ill the supplicant or how grave the emergency, the guardians of many temples will not admit a client if he cannot give a rich gift to the custodian. Even after one has gained admission and survived the ceremonies, the guardians will not permit the neophyte to leave until he makes still another gift.

The supplicant entering the temple is first stripped of all his or her clothes. In every-day life the Nacirema avoids exposure of his body and its natural functions. Bathing and excretory acts are performed only in the secrecy of the household shrine, where they are ritualized as part of the body-rites. Psychological shock results from the fact that body secrecy is suddenly lost upon entry into the *latipso*. A man, whose own wife has never seen him in an excretory act, suddenly finds himself naked and assisted by a vestal maiden while he performs his natural functions into a sacred vessel. This sort of ceremonial treatment is necessitated by the fact that the excreta are used by a diviner to ascertain the course and nature of the client's sickness. Female clients, on the other hand, find their naked bodies are subjected to the scrutiny, manipulation, and prodding of the medicine men.

Few supplicants in the temple are well enough to do anything but lie on their hard beds. The daily ceremonies, like the rites of the holy-mouth-men, involve discomfort and torture. With ritual precision, the vestals awaken their miserable charges each dawn and roll them about on their beds of pain while performing ablutions, in the formal movements of which the maidens are highly trained. At other times they insert magic wands in the supplicant's mouth or force him to eat substances which are supposed to be healing. From time to time the medicine men come to their clients and jab magically treated needles into their flesh. The fact that these temple ceremonies may not cure, and may even kill the neophyte, in no way decreases the people's faith in the medicine men.

There remains one other kind of practitioner, known as a "listener." This witch-doctor has the power to exorcise the devils that lodge in the heads of people who have been bewitched. The Nacirema believe that parents bewitch their own children. Mothers are particularly suspected of putting a curse on children while teaching them the secret body rituals. The counter-magic of the witch-doctor is unusual in its lack of ritual. The patient simply tells the "listener" all his troubles and fears, beginning with the earliest difficulties he can remember. The memory displayed by the Nacirema in these exorcism sessions is truly remarkable. It is not uncommon for the patient to bemoan the rejection he felt upon being weaned as a babe, and a few individuals even see their troubles going back to the traumatic effects of their own birth.

In conclusion, mention must be made of certain practices which have their base in native esthetics but which depend upon the pervasive aversion to the natural body and its functions. There are ritual fasts to make fat people thin and ceremonial feasts to make thin people fat. Still other rites are used to make women's breasts large if they are small, and smaller if they are large. General dissatisfaction with breast shape is symbolized in the fact that the ideal form is virtually outside the range of human variation. A few women afflicted with almost inhuman hyper-mammary development are so idolized that they make a handsome living by simply going from village to village and permitting the natives to stare at them for a fee.

Reference has already been made to the fact that excretory functions are ritualized, routinized, and relegated to secrecy. Natural reproductive functions are similarly distorted. Intercourse is taboo as a topic and scheduled as an act. Efforts are made to avoid pregnancy by the use of magical materials or by limiting intercourse to certain phases of the moon. Conception is actually very infrequent. When pregnant, women dress so as to hide their condition. Parturition takes place in secret, without friends or relatives to assist, and the majority of women do not nurse their infants.

Our review of the ritual life of the Nacirema has certainly shown them to be a magic-ridden people. It is hard to understand how they have managed to exist so long under the burdens which they have imposed upon themselves. But even such exotic customs as these take on real meaning when they are viewed with the insight provided by Malinowski when he wrote (1948:70):

> Looking from far and above, from our high places of safety in the developed civilization, it is easy to see all the crudity and irrelevance of magic. But without its power and guidance early man could not have mastered his practical difficulties as he has done, nor could man have advanced to the higher stages of civilization.

REFERENCES

Linton, Ralph. 1936. *The Study of Man*. New York, D. Appleton-Century Co.

Malinowski, Bronislaw. 1948. *Magic, Science, and Religion*. Glencoe, The Free Press.

Murdock, George P. 1949. *Social Structure*. New York, The Macmillan Co.

Baseball Magic

George Gmelch

On each pitching day for the first three months of a winning season, Dennis Grossini, a pitcher on a Detroit Tiger farm team, arose from bed at exactly 10:00 a.m. At 1:00 p.m. he went to the nearest restaurant for two glasses of iced tea and a tuna sandwich. Although the afternoon was free, he changed into the sweatshirt and supporter he wore during his last winning game, and, one hour before the game, he chewed a wad of Beech-Nut chewing tobacco. After each pitch during the game he touched the letters on his uniform and straightened his cap after each ball. Before the start of each inning he replaced the pitcher's resin bag next to the spot where it was the inning before. And after every inning in which he gave up a run, he washed his hands.

When asked which part of the ritual was most important, he said, "You can't really tell what's most important so it all becomes important. I'd be afraid to change anything. As long as I'm winning, I do everything the same."

Trobriand Islanders, according to anthropologist Bronislaw Malinowski, felt the same way about their fishing magic. Among the Trobrianders, fishing took two forms: in the *inner lagoon* where fish were plentiful and there was little danger, and on the *open sea* where fishing was dangerous and yields varied widely. Malinowski found that magic was not used in lagoon fishing, where men could rely solely on their knowledge and skill. But when fishing on the open sea, Trobrianders used a great deal of magical ritual to ensure safety and increase their catch.

Baseball, America's national pastime, is an arena in which players behave remarkably like Malinowski's Trobriand fishermen. To professional ballplayers, baseball is more than just a game. It is an occupation. Since their livelihoods depend on how well they perform, many use magic to try to control the chance that is built into baseball. There are three essential activities of the game—pitching, hitting, and fielding. In the first two, chance can play a surprisingly important role. The pitcher is the player least able to control the outcome of his own efforts. He may feel great and have good stuff warming up in the bullpen and then get into the game and not have it. He may make a bad pitch and see the batter miss it for a strike out or see it hit hard but right into the hands of a fielder for an out. His best pitch may be blooped for a base hit. He may limit the opposing team to just a few hits yet lose the game, or he may give up a dozen hits but still win. And the good and bad luck don't always average out over the course of a season. Some pitchers end the season with poor won-loss records but good earned run averages, and vice versa. For instance, this past season Andy Benes gave up over one run per game more than his teammate Omar Daal but had a better won-loss record. Benes went 14–13, while Daal was only 8–12. Both pitched for the same team—the Arizona Diamondbacks—which meant they had the same fielders behind them. Regardless of how well a pitcher performs, on every outing he depends not only on his own skill, but also upon the proficiency of his teammates, the ineptitude of the opposition, and luck.

Hitting, which many observers call the single most difficult task in the world of sports, is also full of risk and uncertainty. Unless it's a home run, no matter how well the batter hits the ball, fate determines whether it will go into a waiting glove, whistle past a fielder's diving stab, or find a gap in the outfield. The uncertainty is compounded by the low success rate of hitting: the average hitter gets only one hit in every four trips to the plate, while the very best hitters average only one hit every three trips. Fielding, as we will return to later, is the one part of baseball where chance does not play much of a role.

How does the risk and uncertainty in pitching and hitting affect players? How do they try to exercise control over the outcomes of their performance? These are questions that I first became interested in many years ago as both a ballplayer and an anthropology student. I'd devoted much of my youth to baseball, and played professionally as first baseman in the Detroit Tigers organization in the 1960s. It was shortly after the end of one baseball season that I took an anthropology course called "Magic, Religion, and Witchcraft." As I listened to my professor describe the magical rituals of the Trobriand Islanders, it occurred to me that what these so-called "primitive" people did wasn't all that different from what my teammates and I did for luck and confidence at the ball park.

ROUTINES AND RITUALS

The most common way players attempt to reduce chance and their feelings of uncertainty is to develop and follow a daily routine, a course of action which is regularly followed. Talking about the routines ballplayers follow, Pirates coach Rich Donnelly said:

They're like trained animals. They come out here [ballpark] and everything has to be the same, they don't like anything that knocks them off their routine. Just look at the dugout and you'll see every guy sitting in the same spot every night. It's amazing, everybody in the same spot. And don't you dare take someone's seat. If a guy comes up from the minors and sits here, they'll say, 'Hey, Jim sits here, find another seat.' You watch the pitcher warm up and he'll do the same thing every time. And when you go on the road it's the same way. You've got a routine and you adhere to it and you don't want anybody knocking you off it.

Routines are comforting, they bring order into a world in which players have little control. And sometimes practical elements in routines produce tangible benefits, such as helping the player concentrate. But what players often do goes beyond mere routine. Their actions become what anthropologists define as *ritual*—prescribed behaviors in which there is no empirical connection between the means (e.g., tapping home plate three times) and the desired end (e.g., getting a base hit). Because there is no real connection between the two, rituals are not rational, and sometimes they are actually irrational. Similar to rituals are the non-rational beliefs that form the basis of taboos and fetishes, which players also use to reduce chance and bring luck to their side. But first let's look more closely at rituals.

Most rituals are personal, that is, they're performed by individuals rather than by a team or group. Most are done in an unemotional manner, in much the same way players apply pine tar to their bats to improve the grip or dab eye black on their upper cheeks to reduce the sun's glare. Baseball rituals are infinitely varied. A ballplayer may ritualize any activity—eating, dressing, driving to the ballpark—that he considers important or somehow linked to good performance. For example, Yankee pitcher Denny Neagle goes to a movie on days he is scheduled to start. Pitcher Jason Bere listens to the same song on his Walkman on the days he is to pitch. Jim Ohms puts another penny in the pouch of his supporter after

each win. Clanging against the hard plastic genital cup, the pennies made a noise as he ran the bases toward the end of a winning season. Glenn Davis would chew the same gum every day during hitting streaks, saving it under his cap. Infielder Julio Gotay always played with a cheese sandwich in his back pocket (he had a big appetite, so there might also have been a measure of practicality here). Wade Boggs ate chicken before every game during his career, and that was just one of dozens of elements in his pre and post game routine, which also included leaving his house for the ballpark at precisely the same time each day (1:47 for a 7:05 game). Former Oriole pitcher Dennis Martinez would drink a small cup of water after each inning and then place it under the bench upside down, in a line. His teammates could always tell what inning it was by counting the cups.

Many hitters go through a series of preparatory rituals before stepping into the batter's box. These include tugging on their caps, touching their uniform letters or medallions, crossing themselves, tapping or bouncing the bat on the plate, or swinging the weighted warm-up bat a prescribed number of times. Consider Red Sox Nomar Garciaparra. After each pitch he steps out of the batters box, kicks the dirt with each toe, adjusts his right batting glove, adjusts his left batting glove, and touches his helmet before getting back into the box. Mike Hargrove, former Cleveland Indian first baseman, had so many time consuming elements in his batting ritual that he was known as "the human rain delay." Both players believe their batting rituals helped them regain their concentration after each pitch. But others wonder if they have become prisoners of their own superstitions. Also, players who have too many or particularly bizarre rituals risk being labeled as "flakes," and not just by teammates but by fans and media as well. For example, pitcher Turk Wendell's eccentric rituals, which included wearing a necklace of teeth from animals he had killed, made him a cover story in the *New York Times Sunday Magazine*.

Some players, especially Latin Americans, draw upon rituals from their Roman Catholic religion. Some make the sign of the cross or bless themselves be-

fore every at bat, and a few like the Rangers' Pudge Rodriguez do so before every pitch. Others, like the Detroit Tiger Juan Gonzalez, also visibly wear religious medallions around their necks, while some tuck them discretely inside their undershirts.

One ritual associated with hitting is tagging a base when leaving and returning to the dugout between innings. Some players don't "feel right" unless they tag a specific base on each trip between the dugout and the field. One of my teammates added some complexity to his ritual by tagging third base on his way to the dugout only after the third, sixth, and ninth innings. Asked if he ever purposely failed to step on the bag, he replied, "Never! I wouldn't dare. It would destroy my confidence to hit." Baseball fans observe a lot of this ritual behavior, such as fielders tagging bases, pitchers tugging on their caps or touching the resin bag after each bad pitch, or smoothing the dirt on the mound before each new batter or inning, never realizing the importance of these actions to the player. The one ritual many fans do recognize, largely because it's a favorite of TV cameramen, is the "rally cap"—players in the dugout folding their caps and wearing them bill up in hopes of sparking a rally.

Most rituals grow out of exceptionally good performances. When a player does well, he seldom attributes his success to skill alone. He knows that his skills were essentially the same the night before. He asks himself, "What was different about today which explains my three hits?" He decides to repeat what he did today in an attempt to bring more good luck. And so he attributes his success, in part, to an object, a food he ate, not having shaved, a new shirt he bought that day, or just about any behavior out of the ordinary. By repeating that behavior, he seeks to gain control over his performance. Outfielder John White explained how one of his rituals started:

I was jogging out to centerfield after the national anthem when I picked up a scrap of paper. I got some good hits that night and I guess I decided that the paper had something to do with it. The next night I picked up a gum wrapper and had another good night at the plate… I've been picking up paper every night since.

Outfielder Ron Wright of the Calgary Cannons shaves his arms once a week and plans to continue doing so until he has a bad year. It all began two years before when after an injury he shaved his arm so it could be taped, and proceeded to hit three homers over the next few games. Now he not only has one of the smoothest swings in the minor leagues, but two of the smoothest forearms. Wade Boggs' routine of eating chicken before every game began when he was a rookie in 1982. He noticed a correlation between multiple hit games and poultry plates (his wife has over 40 chicken recipes). One of Montreal Expos farmhand Mike Saccocio's rituals also concerned food, "I got three hits one night after eating at Long John Silver's. After that when we'd pull into town, my first question would be, "Do you have a Long John Silver's?" Unlike Boggs, Saccocio abandoned his ritual and looked for a new one when he stopped hitting well.

When in a slump, most players make a deliberate effort to change their rituals and routines in an attempt to shake off their bad luck. One player tried taking different routes to the ballpark; several players reported trying different combinations of tagging and not tagging particular bases in an attempt to find a successful combination. I had one manager who would rattle the bat bin when the team was not hitting well, as if the bats were in a stupor and could be aroused by a good shaking. Similarly, I have seen hitters rub their hands along the handles of the bats protruding from the bin in hopes of picking up some power or luck from bats that are getting hits for their owners. Some players switch from wearing their contact lenses to glasses. Brett Mandel described his Pioneer League team, the Ogden Raptors, trying to break a losing streak by using a new formation for their pre-game stretching.[1]

TABOO

Taboos are the opposite of rituals. The word taboo comes from a Polynesian term meaning prohibition. Breaking a taboo, players believe, leads to undesirable consequences or bad luck. Most players observe at least a few taboos, such as never stepping on the white foul lines. A few, like the Mets Turk Wendell and Red Sox Nomar Garciaparra, leap over the entire basepath. One teammate of mine would never watch a movie on a game day, despite the fact that we played nearly every day from April to September. Another teammate refused to read anything before a game because he believed it weakened his batting eye.

Many taboos take place off the field, out of public view. On the day a pitcher is scheduled to start, he is likely to avoid activities he believes will sap his strength and detract from his effectiveness. Some pitchers avoid eating certain foods, others will not shave on the day of a game, refusing to shave again as long as they are winning. Early in the 1989 season Oakland's Dave Stewart had six consecutive victories and a beard by the time he lost.

Taboos usually grow out of exceptionally poor performances, which players, in search of a reason, attribute to a particular behavior. During my first season of pro ball I ate pancakes before a game in which I struck out three times. A few weeks later I had another terrible game, again after eating pancakes. The result was a pancake taboo: I never again ate pancakes during the season. Pitcher Jason Bere has a taboo that makes more sense in dietary terms: after eating a meatball sandwich and not pitching well, he swore off them for the rest of the season.

While most taboos are idiosyncratic, there are a few that all ball players hold and that do not develop out of individual experience or misfortune. These form part of the culture of baseball, and are sometimes learned as early as Little League. Mentioning a no-hitter while one is in progress is a well-known example. It is believed that if a pitcher hears the words "no-hitter," the spell accounting for this hard to achieve feat will be broken and the no-hitter lost. This taboo is also observed by many sports broadcasters, who use various linguistic subterfuges to inform their listeners that the pitcher has not given up a hit, never saying "no-hitter."

FETISHES

Fetishes or charms are material objects believed to embody "supernatural" power that can aid or protect the owner. Good luck charms are standard equipment for some ballplayers. These include a wide assortment of objects from coins, chains, and crucifixes to a favorite baseball hat. The fetishized object may be a new possession or something a player found that happens to coincide with the start of a streak and which he holds responsible for his good fortune. While playing in the Pacific Coast League, Alan Foster forgot his baseball shoes on a road trip and borrowed a pair from a teammate. That night he pitched a no-hitter, which he attributed to the shoes. Afterwards he bought them from his teammate and they became a fetish. Expo farmhand Mark LaRosa's rock has a different origin and use:

> I found it on the field in Elmira after I had gotten bombed. It's unusual, perfectly round, and it caught my attention. I keep it to remind me of how important it is to concentrate. When I am going well I look at the rock and remember to keep my focus, the rock reminds me of what can happen when I lose my concentration.

For one season Marge Schott, former owner of the Cincinnati Reds, insisted that her field manager rub her St. Bernard "Schotzie" for good luck before each game. When the Reds were on the road, Schott would sometimes send a bag of the dog's hair to the field manager's hotel room.

During World War II, American soldiers used fetishes in much the same way. Social psychologist Samuel Stouffer and his colleagues found that in the face of great danger and uncertainty, soldiers developed magical practices, particularly the use of protective amulets and good luck charms (crosses, Bibles, rabbits' feet, medals), and jealously guarded articles of clothing they associated with past experiences of escape from danger.[2] Stouffer also found that prebattle preparations were carried out in fixed ritual-like order, similar to ballplayers preparing for a game.

Uniform numbers have special significance for some players who request their lucky number. Since the choice is usually limited, they try to at least get a uniform that contains their lucky number, such as 14, 24, 34, or 44 for the player whose lucky number is four. When Ricky Henderson came to the Blue Jays in 1993 he paid outfielder Turner Ward $25,000 for the right to wear number 24. Oddly enough, there is no consensus about the effect of wearing number 13. Some players will not wear it, others will, and a few request it. Number preferences emerge in different ways. A young player may request the number of a former star, hoping that—through what anthropologists call *imitative* magic—it will bring him the same success. Or he may request a number he associates with good luck. While with the Oakland A's Vida Blue changed his uniform number from 35 to 14, the number he wore as a high-school quarterback. When 14 did not produce better pitching performance, he switched back to 35. Former San Diego Padre first baseman Jack Clark changed his number from 25 to 00, hoping to break out of a slump. That day he got four hits in a double header, but also hurt his back. Then, three days later, he was hit in the cheekbone by a ball thrown in batting practice.

Colorado Rockies Larry Walker's fixation with the number three has become well known to baseball fans. Besides wearing 33, he takes three practice swings before stepping into the box, he showers from the third nozzle, sets his alarm for three minutes past the hour and he was wed on November 3 at 3:33 p.m. Fans in ballparks all across America rise from their seats for the seventh inning stretch before the home club comes to bat because the number seven is lucky, although the origin of this tradition has been lost.

Clothing, both the choice and the order in which they are put on, combine elements of both ritual and fetish. Some players put on their uniform in a ritualized order. Expos farmhand Jim Austin always puts on his left sleeve, left pants leg, and left shoe before the right. Most players, however, single out one or two lucky articles or quirks of dress for ritual elaboration. After hitting two home runs in a

game, for example, ex-Giant infielder Jim Davenport discovered that he had missed a buttonhole while dressing for the game. For the remainder of his career he left the same button undone. For outfielder Brian Hunter the focus is shoes, "I have a pair of high tops and a pair of low tops. Whichever shoes don't get a hit that game, I switch to the other pair." At the time of our interview, he was struggling at the plate and switching shoes almost every day. For Birmingham Baron pitcher Bo Kennedy the arrangement of the different pairs of baseball shoes in his locker is critical:

> I tell the clubies [clubhouse boys] when you hang stuff in my locker don't touch my shoes. If you bump them move them back. I want the Pony's in front, the turfs to the right, and I want them nice and neat with each pair touching each other…. Everyone on the team knows not to mess with my shoes when I pitch.

During streaks—hitting or winning—players may wear the same clothes day after day. Once I changed sweatshirts midway through the game for seven consecutive nights to keep a hitting streak going. Clothing rituals, however, can become impractical. Catcher Matt Allen was wearing a long sleeve turtle neck shirt on a cool evening in the New York-Penn League when he had a three-hit game. "I kept wearing the shirt and had a good week," he explained. "Then the weather got hot as hell, 85 degrees and muggy, but I would not take that shirt off. I wore it for another ten days—catching—and people thought I was crazy." Also taking a ritual to the extreme, Leo Durocher, managing the Brooklyn Dodgers to a pennant in 1941, is said to have spent three and a half weeks in the same gray slacks, blue coat, and knitted blue tie. During a 16-game winning streak, the 1954 New York Giants wore the same clothes in each game and refused to let them be cleaned for fear that their good fortune might be washed away with the dirt. Losing often produces the opposite effect. Several Oakland A's players, for example, went out and bought new street clothes in an attempt to break a fourteen-game losing streak.

Baseball's superstitions, like most everything else, change over time. Many of the rituals and beliefs of early baseball are no longer observed. In the 1920s and 1930s sportswriters reported that a player who tripped en route to the field would often retrace his steps and carefully walk over the stumbling block for "insurance." A century ago players spent time on and off the field intently looking for items that would bring them luck. To find a hairpin on the street, for example, assured a batter of hitting safely in that day's game. Today few women wear hairpins—a good reason the belief has died out. To catch sight of a white horse or a wagon-load of barrels were also good omens. In 1904 the manager of the New York Giants, John McGraw, hired a driver with a team of white horses to drive past the Polo Grounds around the time his players were arriving at the ballpark. He knew that if his players saw white horses, they'd have more confidence and that could only help them during the game. Belief in the power of white horses survived in a few backwaters until the 1960s. A gray haired manager of a team I played for in Drummondville, Quebec, would drive around the countryside before important games and during the playoffs looking for a white horse. When he was successful, he would announce it to everyone in the clubhouse.

One belief that appears to have died out recently is a taboo about crossed bats. Some of my Latino teammates in the 1960s took it seriously. I can still recall one Dominican player becoming agitated when another player tossed a bat from the batting cage and it landed on top of his bat. He believed that the top bat might steal hits from the lower one. In his view, bats contained a finite number of hits, a sort of baseball "image of limited good." It was once commonly believed that when the hits in a bat were used up no amount of good hitting would produce any more. Hall of Famer Honus Wagner believed each bat contained only 100 hits. Regardless of the quality of the bat, he would discard it after its 100th hit. This belief would have little relevance today, in the era of light bats with thin handles—so thin that the typical modern bat is lucky to survive a dozen hits without being broken. Other superstitions about bats do survive, however. Position players on the Class A Asheville Tourists, for example, would not let pitchers touch or swing their bats, not even to warm up. Poor-hitting players, as most pitchers are, were said to pollute or weaken the bats.

UNCERTAINTY AND MAGIC

The best evidence that players turn to rituals, taboos, and fetishes to control chance and uncertainty is found in their uneven application. They are associated mainly with pitching and hitting—the activities with the highest degree of chance—and not fielding. I met only one player who had any ritual in connection with fielding, and he was an error prone shortstop. Unlike hitting and pitching, a fielder has almost complete control over the outcome of his performance. Once a ball has been hit in his direction, no one can intervene and ruin his chances of catching it for an out (except in the unlikely event of two fielders colliding). Compared with the pitcher or the hitter, the fielder has little to worry about. He knows that, in better than 9.7 times out of 10, he will execute his task flawlessly. With odds like that there is little need for ritual.

Clearly, the rituals of American ballplayers are not unlike that of the Trobriand Islanders studied by Malinowski many years ago.[3] In professional baseball, fielding is the equivalent of the inner lagoon while hitting and pitching are like the open sea.

While Malinowski helps us understand how ballplayers respond to chance and uncertainty, behavioral psychologist B. F. Skinner sheds light on why personal rituals get established in the first place.[4] With a few grains of seed Skinner could get pigeons to do anything he wanted. He merely waited for the desired behavior (e.g. pecking) and then rewarded it with some food. Skinner then decided to see what would happen if pigeons were rewarded with food pellets regularly, every fifteen seconds, regardless of what they did. He found that the birds associate the arrival of the food with a particular action, such as tucking their head under a wing or walking in clockwise circles. About ten seconds after the arrival of the last pellet, a bird would begin doing whatever it associated with getting the food and keep doing it until the next pellet arrived. In short, the pigeons behaved as if their actions made the food appear. They learned to associate particular behaviors with the reward of being given seed.

Ballplayers also associate a reward—successful performance—with prior behavior. If a player touches his crucifix and then gets a hit, he may decide the gesture was responsible for his good fortune and touch his crucifix the next time he comes to the plate. If he gets another hit, the chances are good that he will touch his crucifix each time he bats. Unlike pigeons, however, most ballplayers are quicker to change their rituals once they no longer seem to work. Skinner found that once a pigeon associated one of its actions with the arrival of food or water, only sporadic rewards were necessary to keep the ritual going. One pigeon, believing that hopping from side to side brought pellets into its feeding cup, hopped ten thousand times without a pellet before finally giving up. But, then, didn't Wade Boggs eat chicken before every game, through slumps and good times, for seventeen years?

Obviously the rituals and superstitions of baseball do not make a pitch travel faster or a batted ball find the gaps between the fielders, nor do the Trobriand rituals calm the seas or bring fish. What both do, however, is give their practitioners a sense of control, with that added confidence, at no cost. And we all know how important that is. If you really believe eating chicken or hopping over the foul lines will make you a better hitter, it probably will.

BIBLIOGRAPHY

Malinowski, B. *Magic, Science and Religion and Other Essays* (Glencoe, Ill., 1948).

Mandel, Brett. *Minor Players, Major Dreams.* Lincoln, Nebraska: University of Nebraska Press, 1997.

Skinner, B.F. *Behavior of Organisms: An Experimental Analysis* (D. Appleton-Century Co., 1938).

Skinner, B.F. *Science and Human Behavior* (New York: Macmillan, 1953).

Stouffer, Samuel. *The American Soldier.* New York: J. Wiley, 1965.

Torrez, Danielle Gagnon. *High Inside: Memoirs of a Baseball Wife.* New York: G.P. Putnam's Sons, 1983.

NOTES

1. Mandel, *Minor Players, Major Dreams,* 156.
2. Stouffer, *The American Soldier*
3. Malinowski, B. *Magic, Science and Religion and Other Essays*
4. Skinner, B.F. *Behavior of Organisms: An Experimental Analysis*

Department of Anthropology, Union College; e-mail gmelchg@union.edu

Revised version of "Superstition and Ritual in American Baseball" from *Elysian Fields Quarterly*, Vol. 11, No. 3, 1992, pp. 25-36. © September 2000, McGraw-Hill/Dushkin, with permission of the author, George Gmelch.

UNIT 7

Sociocultural Change: The Impact of the West

Unit Selections

Key Points to Consider

- What is a subsistence system? What have been the effects of colonialism on formerly subsistence-oriented socioeconomic systems?

- How do cash crops inevitably lead to class distinctions and poverty?

- Have ecological disasters in Africa been due to drought or to Western-style political and economic institutions? Defend your answer.

- What ethical obligations do you think industrial societies have toward respecting the human rights and cultural diversity of traditional communities?

- How has the role of alcohol changed throughout Western history, and why?

- What have been the social, economic, and health consequences of the shift from the use of betel and kava to alcohol, tobacco, and marijuana in Oceania?

- What can we learn from the past about why civilizations rise and fall? How does this knowledge apply to modern America?

- What should Americans know about Native American contributions to contemporary life?

 **Links: www.dushkin.com/online/**
These sites are annotated in the World Wide Web pages.

Human Rights and Humanitarian Assistance
http://www.etown.edu/vl/humrts.html

The Indigenous Rights Movement in the Pacific
http://www.inmotionmagazine.com/pacific.html

RomNews Network—Online
http://www.romnews.com/community/index.php

WWW Virtual Library: Indigenous Studies
http://www.cwis.org/wwwvl/indig-vl.html

The origins of academic anthropology lie in the colonial and imperial ventures of the nineteenth and twentieth centuries. During these periods, many people of the world were brought into a relationship with Europe and the United States that was usually exploitative and often socially and culturally disruptive. For almost a century, anthropologists have witnessed this process and the transformations that have taken place in those social and cultural systems brought under the umbrella of a world economic order. Early anthropological studies—even those widely regarded as pure research—directly or indirectly served colonial interests. Many anthropologists certainly believed that they were extending the benefits of Western technology and society while preserving the cultural rights of those people whom they studied. But representatives of poor nations challenge this view and are far less generous in describing the past role of the anthropologist. Most contemporary anthropologists, however, have a deep moral commitment to defending the legal, political, and economic rights of the people with whom they work.

When anthropologists discuss social change, they usually mean change brought about in preindustrial societies through long-standing interaction with the nation-states of the industrialized world. In early anthropology, contact between the West and the remainder of the world was characterized by the terms "acculturation" and "culture contact." These terms were used to describe the diffusion of cultural traits between the developed and the less-developed countries. Often this was analyzed as a one-way process in which cultures of the less developed world were seen, for better or worse, as receptacles for Western cultural traits. ("When Will America be Discovered" by Jack Weatherford shows how untrue this is.) Nowadays, many anthropologists believe that the diffusion of cultural traits across social, political, and economic boundaries was emphasized at the expense of the real issues of dominance, subordinance, and dependence that characterized the colonial experience. Just as important, many anthropologists recognize that the present-day forms of cultural, economic, and political interaction between the developed and the so-called underdeveloped world are best characterized as neocolonial. (See ""The Social Psychology of Modern Slavery," "Egypt's Young and Restless" and "The Surprises of Suicide Terrorism.")

Most of the authors represented in this unit take the perspective that anthropology should be critical as well as descriptive. They raise questions about cultural contact and subsequent economic and social disruption.

In keeping with the notion that the negative impact of the West on traditional cultures began with colonial domination, this unit opens with "Why Can't People Feed Themselves?" and "The Arrow of Disease." Continuing with "The Price of Progress," we see that "progress" for the West has often meant poverty, hunger, disease, and death for traditional peoples. Indeed, "The Last Americans" warns us that current technological develop-

ments and environmental trends may even result in the collapse of Western Civilization itself.

Finally, there are essays that have to do with specific aspects of culture affected by the impact of the West. "Alcohol and the Western World" and "A Pacific Haze: Alcohol and Drugs in Oceania" deal with the traditional uses of psychoactive drugs as well as their more recent harmful applications.

Of course, traditional peoples are not the only losers in the process of cultural destruction. All of humanity stands to suffer as a vast store of human knowledge—embodied in tribal subsistence practices, language, medicine, and folklore—is obliterated, in a manner not unlike the burning of the library of Alexandria 1,600 years ago. We can only hope that it is not too late to save what is left.

Why Can't People Feed Themselves?

Frances Moore Lappé and Joseph Collins

Question: You have said that the hunger problem is not the result of overpopulation. But you have not yet answered the most basic and simple question of all: Why can't people feed themselves? As Senator Daniel P. Moynihan put it bluntly, when addressing himself to the Third World, "Food growing is the first thing you do when you come down out of the trees. The question is, how come the United States can grow food and you can't?"

Our Response: In the very first speech I, Frances, ever gave after writing *Diet for a Small Planet*, I tried to take my audience along the path that I had taken in attempting to understand why so many are hungry in this world. Here is the gist of that talk that was, in truth, a turning point in my life:

When I started I saw a world divided into two parts: a *minority* of nations that had "taken off" through their agricultural and industrial revolutions to reach a level of unparalleled material abundance and a *majority* that remained behind in a primitive, traditional, undeveloped state. This lagging behind of the majority of the world's peoples must be due, I thought, to some internal deficiency or even to several of them. It seemed obvious that the underdeveloped countries must be deficient in natural resources—particularly good land and climate—and in cultural develop-

ment, including modern attitudes conducive to work and progress.

But when looking for the historical roots of the predicament, I learned that my picture of these two separate worlds was quite false. My two separate worlds were really just different sides of the same coin. One side was on top largely because the other side was on the bottom. Could this be true? How were these separate worlds related?

Colonialism appeared to me to be the link. Colonialism destroyed the cultural patterns of production and exchange by which traditional societies in "underdeveloped" countries previously had met the needs of the people. Many precolonial social structures, while dominated by exploitative elites, had evolved a system of mutual obligations among the classes that helped to ensure at least a minimal diet for all. A friend of mine once said: "Precolonial village existence in subsistence agriculture was a limited life indeed, but it's certainly not Calcutta." The misery of starvation in the streets of Calcutta can only be understood as the end-point of a long historical process—one that has destroyed a traditional social system.

"Underdeveloped," instead of being an adjective that evokes the picture of a static society, became for me a verb (to "underdevelop")

meaning the *process* by which the minority of the world has transformed—indeed often robbed and degraded—the majority.

That was in 1972. I clearly recall my thoughts on my return home. I had stated publicly for the first time a world view that had taken me years of study to grasp. The sense of relief was tremendous. For me the breakthrough lay in realizing that today's "hunger crisis" could not be described in static, descriptive terms. Hunger and underdevelopment must always be thought of as a *process*.

To answer the question "why hunger?" it is counterproductive to simply *describe* the conditions in an underdeveloped country today. For these conditions, whether they be the degree of malnutrition, the levels of agricultural production, or even the country's ecological endowment, are not static factors—they are not "givens." They are rather the *results* of an ongoing historical process. As we dug ever deeper into that historical process for the preparation of this book, we began to discover the existence of scarcity-creating mechanisms that we had only vaguely intuited before.

We have gotten great satisfaction from probing into the past since we recognized it is the only way to approach a solution to hunger today. We have come to see that it is the *force* creating the condition, not the condition itself, that must be the target of change. Otherwise we might change the condition today, only to find tomorrow that it has been recreated—with a vengeance.

Asking the question "Why can't people feed themselves?" carries a sense of bewilderment that there are so many people in the world not able to feed themselves adequately. What astonished us, however, is that there are not *more* people in the world who are hungry—considering the weight of the centuries of effort by the few to undermine the capacity of the majority to feed themselves. No, we are not crying "conspiracy!" If these forces were entirely conspiratorial, they would be easier to detect and many more people would by now have risen up to resist. We are talking about something more subtle and insidious; a heritage of a colonial order in which people with the advantage of considerable power sought their own self-interest, often arrogantly believing they were acting in the interest of the people whose lives they were destroying.

THE COLONIAL MIND

The colonizer viewed agriculture in the subjugated lands as primitive and backward. Yet such a view contrasts sharply with documents from the colonial period now coming to light. For example, A. J. Voelker, a British agricultural scientist assigned to India during the 1890s wrote:

Nowhere would one find better instances of keeping land scrupulously clean from weeds, of ingenuity in device of water-raising appliances, of knowledge of soils and their capabilities, as well as of the exact time to sow and reap, as one would find in Indian agriculture. It is wonderful too, how much is known of rotation, the system of "mixed crops" and of fallowing.... I, at least, have never seen a more perfect picture of cultivation."[1]

None the less, viewing the agriculture of the vanquished as primitive and backward reinforced the colonizer's rationale for destroying it. To the colonizers of Africa, Asia, and Latin America, agriculture became merely a means to extract wealth—much as gold from a mine—on behalf of the colonizing power. Agriculture was no longer seen as a source of food for the local population, nor even as their livelihood. Indeed the English economist John Stuart Mill reasoned that colonies should not be thought of as civilizations or countries at all but as "agricultural establishments" whose sole purpose was to supply the "larger community to which they belong." The colonized society's agriculture was only a subdivision of the agricultural system of the metropolitan country. As Mill acknowledged, "Our West India colonies, for example, cannot be regarded as countries.... The West Indies are the place where England *finds it convenient* to carry on the production of sugar, coffee and a few other tropical commodities."[2]

Prior to European intervention, Africans practiced a diversified agriculture that included the introduction of new food plants of Asian or American origin. But colonial rule simplified this diversified production to single cash crops—often to the exclusion of staple foods —and in the process sowed the seeds of famine.[3] Rice farming once had been common in Gambia. But with colonial rule so much of the best land was taken over by peanuts (grown for the European market) that rice had to be imported to counter the mounting prospect of famine. Northern Ghana, once famous for its yams and other foodstuffs, was forced to concentrate solely on cocoa. Most of the Gold Coast thus became dependent on cocoa. Liberia was turned into a virtual plantation subsidiary of Firestone Tire and Rubber. Food production in Dahomey and southeast Nigeria was all but abandoned in favor of palm oil; Tanganyika (now Tanzania) was forced to focus on sisal and Uganda on cotton.

The same happened in Indochina. About the time of the American Civil War the French decided that the Mekong Delta in Vietnam would be ideal for producing rice for export. Through a production system based on enriching the large landowners, Vietnam became the world's third largest exporter of rice by the 1930s; yet many landless Vietnamese went hungry.[4]

Rather than helping the peasants, colonialism's public works programs only reinforced export crop production. British irrigation works built in nineteenth-century India did help increase production, but the expansion was for spring export crops at the expense of millets and legumes grown in the fall as the basic local food crops.

Because people living on the land do not easily go against their natural and adaptive drive to grow food for themselves, colonial powers had to force the production of cash crops. The first strategy was to use physical or economic force to get the local population to grow cash crops instead of food on their own plots and then turn them over to the colonizer for export. The second strategy was the direct takeover of the land by large-scale plantations growing crops for export.

FORCED PEASANT PRODUCTION

As Walter Rodney recounts in *How Europe Underdeveloped Africa*, cash crops were often grown literally under threat of guns and whips.[5] One visitor to the Sahel commented in 1928: "Cotton is an artificial crop and one the value of which is not entirely clear to the natives..." He wryly noted the "enforced enthusiasm with which the natives... have thrown themselves into... planting cotton."[6] The forced cultivation of cotton was a major grievance leading to the Maji Maji wars in Tanzania (then Tanganyika) and behind the nationalist revolt in Angola as late as 1960.[7]

Although raw force was used, taxation was the preferred colonial technique to force Africans to grow cash crops. The colonial administrations simply levied taxes on cattle, land, houses, and even the people themselves. Since the tax had to be paid in the coin of the realm, the peasants had either to grow crops to sell or to work on the plantations or in the mines of the Europeans.[8] Taxation was both an effective tool to "stimulate" cash cropping and a source of revenue that the colonial bureaucracy needed to enforce the system. To expand their production of export crops to pay the mounting taxes, peasant producers were forced to neglect the farming of food crops. In 1830, the Dutch administration in Java made the peasants an offer they could not refuse; if they would grow government-owned export crops on one fifth of their land, the Dutch would remit their land taxes.[9] If they refused and thus could not pay the taxes, they lost their land.

Marketing boards emerged in Africa in the 1930s as another technique for getting the profit from cash crop production by native producers into the hands of the colonial government and international firms. Purchases by the marketing boards were well below the world market price. Peanuts bought by the boards from peasant cultivators in West Africa were sold in Britain for more than *seven times* what the peasants received.[10]

The marketing board concept was born with the "cocoa hold-up" in the Gold Coast in 1937. Small cocoa farmers refused to sell to the large cocoa concerns like United Africa Company (a subsidiary of the Anglo-Dutch firm, Unilever—which we know as Lever Brothers) and Cadbury until they got a higher price. When the British government stepped in and agreed to buy the cocoa directly in place of the big business concerns, the smallholders must have thought they had scored at least a minor victory. But had they really? The following year the British formally set up the West African Cocoa Control Board. Theoretically, its purpose was to pay the peasants a reasonable price for their crops. In practice, however, the board, as sole purchaser, was able to hold down the prices paid the peasants for their crops when the world prices were rising. Rodney sums up the real "victory":

> None of the benefits went to Africans, but rather to the British government itself and to the private companies.... Big companies like the United African Company and John Holt were given... quotas to fulfill on behalf of the boards. As agents of the government, they were no longer exposed to direct attack, and their profits were secure.[11]

These marketing boards, set up for most export crops, were actually controlled by the companies. The chairman of the Cocoa Board was none other than John Cadbury of Cadbury Brothers (ever had a Cadbury chocolate bar?) who was part of a buying pool exploiting West African cocoa farmers.

The marketing boards funneled part of the profits from the exploitation of peasant producers indirectly into the royal treasury. While the Cocoa Board sold to the British Food Ministry at low prices, the ministry upped the price for British manufacturers, thus netting a profit as high as 11 million pounds in some years.[12]

These marketing boards of Africa were only the institutionalized rendition of what is the essence of colonialism— the extraction of wealth. While profits continued to accrue to foreign interests and local elites, prices received by those actually growing the commodities remained low.

PLANTATIONS

A second approach was direct takeover of the land either by the colonizing government or by private foreign interests. Previously self-provisioning farmers were forced to cultivate the plantation fields through either enslavement or economic coercion.

After the conquest of the Kandyan Kingdom (in present day Sri Lanka), in 1815, the British designated all the vast central part of the island as crown land. When it was determined that coffee, a profitable export crop, could be grown there, the Kandyan lands were sold off to British investors and planters at a mere five shillings per acre, the government even defraying the cost of surveying and road building.[13]

Java is also a prime example of a colonial government seizing territory and then putting it into private foreign hands. In 1870, the Dutch declared all uncultivated land—called waste land—property of the state for lease to Dutch plantation enterprises. In addition, the Agrarian Land Law of 1870 authorized foreign companies to lease village-owned land. The peasants, in chronic need of ready cash for taxes and foreign consumer goods, were only too willing to lease their land to the foreign companies for very modest sums and under terms dictated by the firms. Where land was still held communally, the village headman was tempted by high cash commissions offered by plantation companies. He would lease the village land even more cheaply than would the individual peasant or, as was frequently the case, sell out the entire village to the company.[14]

The introduction of the plantation meant the divorce of agriculture from nourishment, as the notion of food value was lost to the overriding claim of "market value" in international trade. Crops such as sugar, tobacco, and coffee were selected, not on the basis of how well they feed people, but for their high price value relative to their weight and bulk so that profit margins could be maintained even after the costs of shipping to Europe.

SUPPRESSING PEASANT FARMING

The stagnation and impoverishment of the peasant food-producing sector was not the mere by-product of benign neglect, that is, the unintended consequence of an overemphasis on export production. Plantations—just like modern "agro-industrial complexes"— needed an abundant and readily available supply of low-wage agricultural workers. Colonial administrations thus devised a variety of tactics, all to undercut self-provisioning agriculture and thus make rural populations dependent on plantation wages. Government services and even the most minimal infrastructure (access to water, roads, seeds, credit, pest and disease control information, and so on) were systematically denied. Plantations usurped most of the good land, either making much of the rural population landless or pushing them onto marginal soils. (Yet the plantations have often held much of their land idle simply to prevent the peasants from using it—even to this day. Del Monte owns 57,000 acres of Guatemala but plants only 9000. The rest lies idle except for a few thousand head of grazing cattle.)[15]

In some cases a colonial administration would go even further to guarantee itself a labor supply. In at least twelve countries in the eastern and southern parts of Africa the exploitation of mineral wealth (gold, diamonds, and copper) and the establishment of cash-crop plantations demanded a continuous supply of low-cost labor. To assure this labor supply, colonial administrations simply expropriated the land of the African communities by violence and drove the people into small reserves.[16] With neither adequate land for their traditional slash-and-burn methods nor access to the means—tools, water, and fertilizer—to make continuous farming of such limited areas viable, the indigenous population could scarcely meet subsistence needs, much less produce surplus to sell in order to cover the colonial taxes. Hundreds of thousands of Africans were forced to become the cheap labor source so "needed" by the colonial plantations. Only by laboring on plantations and in the mines could they hope to pay the colonial taxes.

The tax scheme to produce reserves of cheap plantation and mining labor was particularly effective when the Great Depression hit and the bottom dropped out of cash crop economies. In 1929 the cotton market collapsed, leaving peasant cotton producers, such as those in Upper Volta, unable to pay their colonial taxes. More and more young people, in some years as many as 80,000, were thus forced to migrate to the Gold Coast to compete with each other for low-wage jobs on cocoa plantations.[17]

The forced migration of Africa's most able-bodied workers—stripping village food farming of needed hands—was a recurring feature of colonialism. As late as 1973 the Portuguese "exported" 400,000 Mozambican peasants to work in South Africa in exchange for gold deposited in the Lisbon treasury.

The many techniques of colonialism to undercut self-provisioning agriculture in order to ensure a cheap labor supply are no better illustrated than by the story of how, in the mid-nineteenth century, sugar plantation owners in British Guiana coped with the double blow of the emancipation of slaves and the crash in the world sugar market. The story is graphically recounted by Alan Adamson in *Sugar without Slaves*.[18]

Would the ex-slaves be allowed to take over the plantation land and grow the food they needed? The planters, many ruined by the sugar slump, were determined they would not. The planter-dominated government devised several schemes for thwarting food self-sufficiency. The price of crown land was kept artificially high, and the purchase of land in parcels smaller than 100 acres was outlawed—two measures guaranteeing that newly organized ex-slave cooperatives could not hope to gain access to much land. The government also prohibited cultivation on as much as 400,000 acres—on the grounds of "uncertain property titles." Moreover, although many planters held part of their land out of sugar production due to the depressed world price, they would not allow any alternative production on them. They feared that once the ex-slaves started growing food it would be difficult to return them to sugar production when world market prices began to recover. In addition, the government taxed peasant production, then turned around and used the funds to subsidize the immigration of laborers from India and Malaysia to replace the freed slaves, thereby making sugar production again profitable for the planters. Finally, the government neglected the infrastructure for subsistence agriculture and denied credit for small farmers.

Perhaps the most insidious tactic to "lure" the peasant away from food production—and the one with profound historical consequences—was a policy of keeping the price of imported food low through the removal of tariffs and subsidies. The policy was double-edged: first, peasants were told they need not grow food because they could always buy it cheaply with their plantation wages; second, cheap food imports destroyed the market for domestic food and thereby impoverished local food producers.

Adamson relates how both the Governor of British Guiana and the Secretary for the Colonies Earl Grey favored low duties on imports in order to erode local food production and thereby release labor for the plantations. In 1851 the governor rushed through a reduction of the duty on cereals in order to "divert" labor to the sugar estates. As Adamson comments, "Without realizing it, he [the governor] had put his finger on the most mordant feature of monoculture:... its convulsive need to destroy any other sector of the economy which might compete for 'its' labor."[19]

Many colonial governments succeeded in establishing dependence on imported foodstuffs. In 1647 an observer in the West Indies wrote to Governor Winthrop of Massachusetts: "Men are so intent upon planting sugar that they had rather buy foode at very dear rates than produce it by labour, so infinite is the profitt of sugar workes...."[20] By 1770, the West Indies were importing most of the continental colonies' exports of dried fish, grain, beans, and vegetables. A dependence on imported food made the West Indian colonies vulnerable to any disruption in supply. This dependence on imported food stuffs spelled disaster when the thirteen continental colonies gained independence and food exports from the continent to the West Indies were interrupted. With no diversified food system to fall back on, 15,000 plantation workers died of famine between 1780 and 1787 in Jamaica alone.[21] The dependence of the West Indies on imported food persists to this day.

SUPPRESSING PEASANT COMPETITION

We have talked about the techniques by which indigenous populations were forced to cultivate cash crops. In some countries with large plantations, however, colonial governments found it necessary to *prevent* peasants from independently growing cash crops not out of concern for their welfare, but so that they would not compete with colonial interests growing the same crop. For peasant farmers, given a modicum of opportunity, proved themselves capable of outproducing the large plantations not only in terms of output per unit of land but, more important, in terms of capital cost per unit produced.

In the Dutch East Indies (Indonesia and Dutch New Guinea) colonial policy in the middle of the nineteenth century forbade the sugar refineries to buy sugar cane from indigenous growers and imposed a discriminatory tax on rubber produced by native smallholders.[22] A recent unpublished United Nations study of agricultural development in Africa concluded that large-scale agricultural operations owned and controlled by foreign commercial interests (such as the rubber plantations of Liberia, the sisal estates of Tanganyika [Tanzania], and the coffee estates of Angola) only survived the competition of peasant producers because "the authorities actively supported them by suppressing indigenous rural development."[23]

The suppression of indigenous agricultural development served the interests of the colonizing powers in two ways. Not only did it prevent direct competition from more efficient native producers of the same crops, but it also guaranteed a labor force to work on the foreign-owned estates. Planters and foreign investors were not unaware that peasants who could survive economically by their own production would be under less pressure to sell their labor cheaply to the large estates.

The answer to the question, then, "Why can't people feed themselves?" must begin with an understanding of how colonialism actively prevented people from doing just that.

COLONIALISM

- forced peasants to replace food crops with cash crops that were then expropriated at very low rates;
- took over the best agricultural land for export crop plantations and then forced the most able-bodied workers to leave the village fields to work as slaves or for very low wages on plantations;
- encouraged a dependence on imported food;
- blocked native peasant cash crop production from competing with

cash crops produced by settlers or foreign firms.

These are concrete examples of the development of underdevelopment that we should have perceived as such even as we read our history schoolbooks. Why didn't we? Somehow our schoolbooks always seemed to make the flow of history appear to have its own logic—as if it could not have been any other way. I, Frances, recall, in particular, a grade-school, social studies pamphlet on the idyllic life of Pedro, a nine-year-old boy on a coffee plantation in South America. The drawings of lush vegetation and "exotic" huts made his life seem romantic indeed. Wasn't it natural and proper that South America should have plantations to supply my mother and father with coffee? Isn't that the way it was *meant* to be?

NOTES

1. Radha Sinha, *Food and Poverty* (New York: Holmes and Meier, 1976), p. 26.
2. John Stuart Mill, *Political Economy*, Book 3, Chapter 25 (emphasis added).
3. Peter Feldman and David Lawrence, "Social and Economic Implications of the Large-Scale Introduction of New Varieties of Foodgrains," Africa Report, preliminary draft (Geneva: UNRISD, 1975), pp. 107–108.
4. Edgar Owens, *The Right Side of History*, unpublished manuscript, 1976.
5. Walter Rodney, *How Europe Underdeveloped Africa* (London: Bogle-L'Ouverture Publications, 1972), pp. 171–172.
6. Ferdinand Ossendowski, *Slaves of the Sun* (New York: Dutton, 1928), p. 276.
7. Rodney, *How Europe Underdeveloped Africa*, pp. 171–172.
8. Ibid., p. 181.
9. Clifford Geertz, *Agricultural Involution* (Berkeley and Los Angeles: University of California Press, 1963), pp. 52–53.
10. Rodney, *How Europe Underdeveloped Africa*, p. 185.
11. Ibid., p. 184.
12. Ibid., p. 186.
13. George L. Beckford, *Persistent Poverty: Underdevelopment in Plantation Economies of the Third World* (New York: Oxford University Press, 1972), p. 99.
14. Ibid., p. 99, quoting from Erich Jacoby, *Agrarian Unrest in Southeast Asia* (New York: Asia Publishing House, 1961), p. 66.
15. Pat Flynn and Roger Burbach, North American Congress on Latin America, Berkely, California, recent investigation.
16. Feldman and Lawrence, "Social and Economic Implications," p. 103.
17. Special Sahelian Office Report, Food and Agriculture Organization, March 28, 1974, pp. 88–89.
18. Alan Adamson, *Sugar Without Slaves: The Political Economy of British Guiana, 1838–1904* (New Haven and London: Yale University Press, 1972).
19. Ibid., p. 41.
20. Eric Williams, *Capitalism and Slavery* (New York: Putnam, 1966), p. 110.
21. Ibid., p. 121.
22. Gunnar Myrdal, *Asian Drama*, vol. 1 (New York: Pantheon, 1966), pp. 448–449.
23. Feldman and Lawrence, "Social and Economic Implications," p. 189.

Frances Moore Lappé and Dr. Joseph Collins are founders and directors of the Institute for Food and Development Policy, located in San Francisco and New York.

The Arrow of Disease

When Columbus and his successors invaded the Americas, the most potent weapon they carried was their germs. But why didn't deadly disease flow in the other direction, from the New World to the Old?

Jared Diamond

The three people talking in the hospital room were already stressed out from having to cope with a mysterious illness, and it didn't help at all that they were having trouble communicating. One of them was the patient, a small, timid man, sick with pneumonia caused by an unidentified microbe and with only a limited command of the English language. The second, acting as translator, was his wife, worried about her husband's condition and frightened by the hospital environment. The third person in the trio was an inexperienced young doctor, trying to figure out what might have brought on the strange illness. Under the stress, the doctor was forgetting everything he had been taught about patient confidentiality. He committed the awful blunder of requesting the woman to ask her husband whether he'd had any sexual experiences that might have caused the infection.

As the young doctor watched, the husband turned red, pulled himself together so that he seemed even smaller, tried to disappear under his bed sheets, and stammered in a barely audible voice. His wife suddenly screamed in rage and drew herself up to tower over him. Before the doctor could stop her, she grabbed a heavy metal bottle, slammed it onto her husband's head, and stormed out of the room. It took a while for the doctor to elicit, through the man's broken English, what he had said to so enrage his wife. The answer slowly emerged: he had admitted to repeated intercourse with sheep on a recent visit to the family farm; perhaps that was how he had contracted the mysterious microbe.

This episode, related to me by a physician friend involved in the case, sounds so bizarrely one of a kind as to be of no possible broader significance. But in fact it illustrates a subject of great importance: human diseases of animal origins. Very few of us may love sheep in the carnal sense. But most of us platonically love our pet animals, like our dogs and cats; and as a society, we certainly appear to have an inordinate fondness for sheep and other livestock, to judge from the vast numbers of them that we keep.

Some of us—most often our children—pick up infectious diseases from our pets. Usually these illnesses remain no more than a nuisance, but a few have evolved into far more. The major killers of humanity throughout our recent history—smallpox, flu, tuberculosis, malaria, plague, measles, and cholera—are all infectious diseases that arose from diseases of animals. Until World War II more victims of war died of microbes than of gunshot or sword wounds. All those military histories glorifying Alexander the Great and Napoleon ignore the ego-deflating truth: the winners of past wars were not necessarily those armies with the best generals and weapons, but those bearing the worst germs with which to smite their enemies.

The grimmest example of the role of germs in history is much on our minds this month, as we recall the European conquest of the Americas that began with Columbus's voyage of 1492. Numerous as the Indian victims of the murderous Spanish conquistadores were, they were dwarfed in number by the victims of murderous Spanish microbes. These formidable conquerors killed an estimated 95 percent of the New World's pre-Columbian Indian population.

Why was the exchange of nasty germs between the Americas and Europe so unequal? Why didn't the reverse happen instead, with Indian diseases decimating the Spanish invaders, spreading back across the Atlantic, and causing a 95 percent decline in *Europe's* human population?

Similar questions arise regarding the decimation of many other native peoples by European germs, and regarding the decimation of would-be European conquistadores in the tropics of Africa and Asia.

Naturally, we're disposed to think about diseases from our own point of view: What can we do to save ourselves and to kill the microbes? Let's stamp out the scoundrels, and never mind what *their* motives are!

In life, though, one has to understand the enemy to beat him. So for a moment, let's consider disease from the microbes' point of view. Let's look beyond our anger at their making us sick in bizarre ways, like giving us genital sores or diarrhea, and ask why it is that they do such things. After all, microbes are as much a product of natural selection as we are, and so their actions must have come about because they confer some evolutionary benefit.

Basically, of course, evolution selects those individuals that are most effective at producing babies and at helping those babies find suitable places to live. Microbes are marvels at this latter requirement. They have evolved diverse ways of spreading from one person to another, and from animals to people. Many of our symptoms of disease actually represent ways in which some clever bug modifies our bodies or our behavior such that we become enlisted to spread bugs.

The most effortless way a bug can spread is by just waiting to be transmitted passively to the next victim. That's the strategy practiced by microbes that wait for one host to be eaten by the next—salmonella bacteria, for example, which we contract by eating already-infected eggs or meat; or the worm responsible for trichinosis, which waits for us to kill a pig and eat it without properly cooking it.

As a slight modification of this strategy; some microbes don't wait for the old host to die but instead hitchhike in the saliva of an insect that bites the old host and then flies to a new one. The free ride may be provided by mosquitoes, fleas, lice, or tsetse flies, which spread malaria, plague, typhus, and sleeping sickness, respectively. The dirtiest of all passive-carriage tricks is perpetrated by microbes that pass from a woman to her fetus—microbes such as the ones responsible for syphilis, rubella (German measles), and AIDS. By their cunning these microbes can already be infecting an infant before the moment of its birth.

Other bugs take matters into their own hands, figuratively speaking. They actively modify the anatomy or habits of their host to accelerate their transmission. From our perspective, the open genital sores caused by venereal diseases such as syphilis are a vile indignity. From the microbes' point of view, however, they're just a useful device to enlist a host's help in inoculating the body cavity of another host with microbes. The skin lesions caused by smallpox similarly spread microbes by direct or indirect body contact (occasionally very

indirect, as when U.S. and Australian whites bent on wiping out "belligerent" native peoples sent them gifts of blankets previously used by smallpox patients).

More vigorous yet is the strategy practiced by the influenza, common cold, and pertussis (whooping cough) microbes, which induce the victim to cough or sneeze, thereby broadcasting the bugs toward prospective new hosts. Similarly the cholera bacterium induces a massive diarrhea that spreads bacteria into the water supplies of potential new victims. For modification of a host's behavior, though, nothing matches the rabies virus, which not only gets into the saliva of an infected dog but drives the dog into a frenzy of biting and thereby infects many new victims.

Thus, from our viewpoint, genital sores, diarrhea, and coughing are "symptoms" of disease. From a bug's viewpoint, they're clever evolutionary strategies to broadcast the bug. That's why it's in the bug's interests to make us "sick." But what does it gain by killing us? That seems self-defeating, since a microbe that kills its host kills itself.

Though you may well think it's of little consolation, our death is really just an unintended by-product of host symptoms that promote the efficient transmission of microbes. Yes, an untreated cholera patient may eventually die from producing diarrheal fluid at a rate of several gallons a day. While the patient lasts, though, the cholera bacterium profits from being massively disseminated into the water supplies of its next victims. As long as each victim thereby infects, on average, more than one new victim, the bacteria will spread, even though the first host happens to die.

So much for the dispassionate examination of the bug's interests. Now let's get back to considering our own selfish interests: to stay alive and healthy, best done by killing the damned bugs. One common response to infection is to develop a fever. Again, we consider fever a "symptom" of disease, as if it developed inevitably without serving any function. But regulation of body temperature is under our genetic control, and a fever doesn't just happen by accident. Because

some microbes are more sensitive to heat than our own bodies are, by raising our body temperature we in effect try to bake the bugs to death before we get baked ourselves.

We and our pathogens are now locked in an escalating evolutionary contest, with the death of one contestant the price of defeat, and with natural selection playing the role of umpire.

Another common response is to mobilize our immune system. White blood cells and other cells actively seek out and kill foreign microbes. The specific antibodies we gradually build up against a particular microbe make us less likely to get reinfected once we are cured. As we all know there are some illnesses, such as flu and the common cold, to which our resistance is only temporary; we can eventually contract the illness again. Against other illnesses, though—including measles, mumps, rubella, pertussis, and the now-defeated menace of smallpox—antibodies stimulated by one infection confer lifelong immunity. That's the principle behind vaccination—to stimulate our antibody production without our having to go through the actual experience of the disease.

Alas, some clever bugs don't just cave in to our immune defenses. Some have learned to trick us by changing their antigens, those molecular pieces of the microbe that our antibodies recognize. The constant evolution or recycling of new strains of flu, with differing antigens, explains why the flu you got two years ago didn't protect you against the different strain that arrived this year. Sleeping sickness is an even more slippery customer in its ability to change its antigens rapidly.

Among the slipperiest of all is the virus that causes AIDS, which evolves new antigens even as it sits within an individual patient, until it eventually overwhelms the immune system.

Our slowest defensive response is through natural selection, which changes the relative frequency with which a gene appears from generation to generation. For almost any disease some people prove to be genetically more resistant than others. In an epidemic, those people with genes for resistance to that particular microbe are more likely to survive than are people lacking such genes. As a result, over the course of history human populations repeatedly exposed to a particular pathogen tend to be made up of individuals with genes that resist the appropriate microbe just because unfortunate individuals without those genes were less likely to survive to pass their genes on to their children.

Fat consolation, you may be thinking. This evolutionary response is not one that does the genetically susceptible dying individual any good. It does mean, though, that a human population as a whole becomes better protected.

In short, many bugs have had to evolve tricks to let them spread among potential victims. We've evolved counter-tricks, to which the bugs have responded by evolving counter-counter-tricks. We and our pathogens are now locked in an escalating evolutionary contest, with the death of one contestant the price of defeat, and with natural selection playing the role of umpire.

The form that this deadly contest takes varies with the pathogens: for some it is like a guerrilla war, while for others it is a blitzkrieg. With certain diseases, like malaria or hookworm, there's a more or less steady trickle of new cases in an affected area, and they will appear in any month of any year. Epidemic diseases, though, are different: they produce no cases for a long time, then a whole wave of cases, then no more cases again for a while.

Among such epidemic diseases, influenza is the most familiar to Americans, this year having been a particularly bad one for us (but a great year for the influenza virus). Cholera epidemics come at longer intervals, the 1991 Peruvian epidemic being the first one to reach the New World during the twentieth century. Frightening as today's influenza and cholera epidemics are, through, they pale beside the far more terrifying epidemics of the past, before the rise of modern medicine. The greatest single epidemic in human history was the influenza wave that killed 21 million people at the end of the First World War. The black death, or bubonic plague, killed one-quarter of Europe's population between 1346 and 1352, with death tolls up to 70 percent in some cities.

The infectious diseases that visit us as epidemics share several characteristics. First, they spread quickly and efficiently from an infected person to nearby healthy people, with the result that the whole population gets exposed within a short time. Second, they're "acute" illnesses: within a short time, you either die or recover completely. Third, the fortunate ones of us who do recover develop antibodies that leave us immune against a recurrence of the disease for a long time, possibly our entire lives. Finally, these diseases tend to be restricted to humans; the bugs causing them tend not to live in the soil or in other animals. All four of these characteristics apply to what Americans think of as the once more-familiar acute epidemic diseases of childhood, including measles, rubella, mumps, pertussis, and smallpox.

It is easy to understand why the combination of those four characteristics tends to make a disease run in epidemics. The rapid spread of microbes and the rapid course of symptoms mean that everybody in a local human population is soon infected, and thereafter either dead or else recovered and immune. No one is left alive who could still be infected. But since the microbe can't survive except in the bodies of living people, the disease dies out until a new crop of babies reaches the susceptible age—and until an infectious person arrives from the outside to start a new epidemic.

A classic illustration of the process is given by the history of measles on the isolated Faeroe Islands in the North Atlantic. A severe epidemic of the disease reached the Faeroes in 1781, then died out, leaving the islands measles-free until an infected carpenter arrived on a ship from Denmark in 1846. Within three months almost the whole Faeroes population—7,782 people—had gotten measles and then either died or recovered, leaving the measles virus to disappear once again until the next epidemic. Studies show that measles is likely to die out in any human population numbering less than half a million people. Only in larger populations can measles shift from one local area to another, thereby persisting until enough babies have been born in the originally infected area to permit the disease's return.

Rubella in Australia provides a similar example, on a much larger scale. As of 1917 Australia's population was still only 5 million, with most people living in scattered rural areas. The sea voyage to Britain took two months, and land transport within Australia itself was slow. In effect, Australia didn't even consist of a population of 5 million, but of hundreds of much smaller populations. As a result, rubella hit Australia only as occasional epidemics, when an infected person happened to arrive from overseas and stayed in a densely populated area. By 1938, though, the city of Sydney alone had a population of over one million, and people moved frequently and quickly by air between London, Sydney, and other Australian cities. Around then, rubella for the first time was able to establish itself permanently in Australia.

What's true for rubella in Australia is true for most familiar acute infectious diseases throughout the world. To sustain themselves, they need a human population that is sufficiently numerous and densely packed that a new crop of susceptible children is available for infection by the time the disease would otherwise be waning. Hence the measles and other such diseases are also known as "crowd diseases."

Crowd diseases could not sustain themselves in small bands of hunter-gatherers and slash-and-burn farmers. As tragic recent experience with Amazonian Indians and Pacific Islanders confirms, almost an entire tribelet may be wiped out by an epidemic brought by an outside visitor, because no one in the tribelet has any antibodies against the microbe. In addition, measles and some other "childhood" diseases are more likely to kill infected adults than children, and all adults in the tribelet are susceptible. Having killed most of the tribelet, the epidemic then disappears. The small population size explains why tribelets can't sustain epidemics introduced from the outside; at the same time it explains why they could never evolve epidemic diseases of their own to give back to the visitors.

That's not to say that small human populations are free from all infectious diseases. Some of their infections are caused by microbes capable of maintaining themselves in animals or in soil, so the disease remains constantly available to infect people. For example, the yellow fever virus is carried by African wild monkeys and is constantly available to infect rural human populations of Africa. It was also available to be carried to New World monkeys and people by the trans-Atlantic slave trade.

Other infections of small human populations are chronic diseases, such as leprosy and yaws, that may take a very long time to kill a victim. The victim thus remains alive as a reservoir of microbes to infect other members of the tribelet. Finally, small human populations are susceptible to nonfatal infections against which we don't develop immunity, with the result that the same person can become reinfected after recovering. That's the case with hookworm and many other parasites.

All these types of diseases, characteristic of small, isolated populations, must be the oldest diseases of humanity. They were the ones that we could evolve and sustain through the early millions of years of our evolutionary history, when the total human population was tiny and fragmented. They are also shared with, or are similar to the diseases of, our closest wild relatives, the African great apes. In contrast, the evolution of our crowd diseases could only have occurred with the buildup of large, dense human populations, first made possible by the rise of agriculture about 10,000 years ago, then by the rise of cities several thousand years ago. Indeed, the first attested dates for many familiar infectious diseases are surprisingly recent: around 1600 B.C. for

smallpox (as deduced from pockmarks on an Egyptian mummy), 400 B.C. for mumps, 1840 for polio, and 1959 for AIDS.

Agriculture sustains much higher human population densities than does hunting and gathering—on average, 10 to 100 times higher. In addition, hunter-gatherers frequently shift camp, leaving behind their piles of feces with their accumulated microbes and worm larvae. But farmers are sedentary and live amid their own sewage, providing microbes with a quick path from one person's body into another person's drinking water. Farmers also become surrounded by disease-transmitting rodents attracted by stored food.

The explosive increase in world travel by Americans, and in immigration to the United States, is turning us into another melting pot— this time of microbes that we'd dismissed as causing disease in far-off countries.

Some human populations make it even easier for their own bacteria and worms to infect new victims, by intentionally gathering their feces and urine and spreading it as fertilizer on the fields where people work. Irrigation agriculture and fish farming provide ideal living conditions for the snails carrying schistosomes, and for other flukes that burrow through our skin as we wade through the feces-laden water.

If the rise of farming was a boon for our microbes, the rise of cities was a veritable bonanza, as still more densely packed human populations festered under even worse sanitation conditions. (Not until the beginning of the twentieth century did urban populations finally become self-sustaining; until then, constant immigration of healthy peasants from the countryside was necessary to make good the constant deaths of city dwellers from crowd diseases.) Another bonanza

was the development of world trade routes, which by late Roman times effectively joined the populations of Europe, Asia, and North Africa into one giant breeding ground for microbes. That's when smallpox finally reached Rome as the "plague of Antonius," which killed millions of Roman citizens between A.D. 165 and 180.

Similarly, bubonic plague first appeared in Europe as the plague of Justinian (A.D. 542–543). But plague didn't begin to hit Europe with full force, as the black death epidemics, until 1346, when new overland trading with China provided rapid transit for flea-infested furs from plague-ridden areas of Central Asia. Today our jet planes have made even the longest intercontinental flights briefer than the duration of any human infectious disease. That's how an Aerolíneas Argentinas airplane, stopping in Lima, Peru, earlier this year, managed to deliver dozens of cholera-infected people the same day to my city of Los Angeles, over 3,000 miles away. The explosive increase in world travel by Americans, and in immigration to the United States, is turning us into another melting pot—this time of microbes that we previously dismissed as just causing exotic diseases in far-off countries.

When the human population became sufficiently large and concentrated, we reached the stage in our history when we could at last sustain crowd diseases confined to our species. But that presents a paradox: such diseases could never have existed before. Instead they had to evolve as new diseases. Where did those new diseases come from?

Evidence emerges from studies of the disease-causing microbes themselves. In many cases molecular biologists have identified the microbe's closest relative. Those relatives also prove to be agents of infectious crowd diseases—but ones confined to various species of domestic animals and pets! Among animals too, epidemic diseases require dense populations, and they're mainly confined to social animals that provide the necessary large populations. Hence when we domesticated social animals such as cows and pigs, they were already afflicted by epidemic diseases just waiting to be transferred to us.

For example, the measles virus is most closely related to the virus causing rinderpest, a nasty epidemic disease of cattle and many wild cud-chewing mammals. Rinderpest doesn't affect humans. Measles, in turn, doesn't affect cattle. The close similarity of the measles and rinderpest viruses suggests that the rinderpest virus transferred from cattle to humans, then became the measles virus by changing its properties to adapt to us. That transfer isn't surprising, considering how closely many peasant farmers live and sleep next to cows and their accompanying feces, urine, breath, sores, and blood. Our intimacy with cattle has been going on for 8,000 years since we domesticated them—ample time for the rinderpest virus to discover us nearby. Other familiar infectious diseases can similarly be traced back to diseases of our animal friends.

Given our proximity to the animals we love, we must constantly be getting bombarded by animal microbes. Those invaders get winnowed by natural selection, and only a few succeed in establishing themselves as human diseases. A quick survey of current diseases lets us trace four stages in the evolution of a specialized human disease from an animal precursor.

In the first stage, we pick up animal-borne microbes that are still at an early stage in their evolution into specialized human pathogens. They don't get transmitted directly from one person to another, and even their transfer from animals to us remains uncommon. There are dozens of diseases like this that we get directly from pets and domestic animals. They include cat scratch fever from cats, leptospirosis from dogs, psittacosis from chickens and parrots, and brucellosis from cattle. We're similarly susceptible to picking up diseases from wild animals, such as the tularemia that hunters occasionally get from skinning wild rabbits.

In the second stage, a former animal pathogen evolves to the point where it does get transmitted directly between people and causes epidemics. However, the epidemic dies out for several reasons—being cured by modern medicine,

stopping when everybody has been infected and died, or stopping when everybody has been infected and become immune. For example, a previously unknown disease termed *o'nyong-nyong* fever appeared in East Africa in 1959 and infected several million Africans. It probably arose from a virus of monkeys and was transmitted to humans by mosquitoes. The fact that patients recovered quickly and became immune to further attack helped cause the new disease to die out quickly.

The annals of medicine are full of diseases that sound like no known disease today but that once caused terrifying epidemics before disappearing as mysteriously as they had come. Who alive today remembers the "English sweating sickness" that swept and terrified Europe between 1485 and 1578, or the "Picardy sweats" of eighteenth- and nineteenth-century France?

A third stage in the evolution of our major diseases is represented by former animal pathogens that establish themselves in humans and that do not die out; until they do, the question of whether they will become major killers of humanity remains up for grabs. The future is still very uncertain for Lassa fever, first observed in 1969 in Nigeria and caused by a virus probably derived from rodents. Better established is Lyme disease, caused by a spirochete that we get from the bite of a tick. Although the first known human cases in the United States appeared only as recently as 1962, Lyme disease is already reaching epidemic proportions in the Northeast, on the West Coast, and in the upper Midwest. The future of AIDS, derived from monkey viruses, is even more secure, from the virus's perspective.

The final stage of this evolution is represented by the major, long-established epidemic diseases confined to humans. These diseases must have been the evolutionary survivors of far more pathogens that tried to make the jump to us from animals—and mostly failed.

Diseases represent evolution in progress, as microbes adapt by natural selection to new hosts. Compared with cows' bodies, though, our bodies offer different immune defenses and different chemistry. In that new environment, a

microbe must evolve new ways to live and propagate itself.

The best-studied example of microbes evolving these new ways involves myxomatosis, which hit Australian rabbits in 1950. The myxoma virus, native to a wild species of Brazilian rabbit, was known to cause a lethal epidemic in European domestic rabbits, which are a different species. The virus was intentionally introduced to Australia in the hopes of ridding the continent of its plague of European rabbits, foolishly introduced in the nineteenth century. In the first year, myxoma produced a gratifying (to Australian farmers) 99.8 percent mortality in infected rabbits. Fortunately for the rabbits and unfortunately for the farmers, the death rate then dropped in the second year to 90 percent and eventually to 25 percent, frustrating hopes of eradicating rabbits completely from Australia. The problem was that the myxoma virus evolved to serve its own interest, which differed from the farmers' interests and those of the rabbits. The virus changed to kill fewer rabbits and to permit lethally infected ones to live longer before dying. The result was bad for Australian farmers but good for the virus: a less lethal myxoma virus spreads baby viruses to more rabbits than did the original, highly virulent myxoma.

For a similar example in humans, consider the surprising evolution of syphilis. Today we associate syphilis with genital sores and a very slowly developing disease, leading to the death of untreated victims only after many years. However, when syphilis was first definitely recorded in Europe in 1495, its pustules often covered the body from the head to the knees, caused flesh to fall off people's faces, and led to death within a few months. By 1546 syphilis had evolved into the disease with the symptoms known to us today. Apparently, just as with myxomatosis, those syphilis spirochetes evolved to keep their victims alive longer in order to transmit their spirochete offspring into more victims.

Ｈow, then, does all this explain the outcome of 1492—that Europeans conquered and depopulated the New World, instead of Native Americans conquering and depopulating Europe?

Part of the answer, of course, goes back to the invaders' technological advantages. European guns and steel swords were more effective weapons than Native American stone axes and wooden clubs. Only Europeans had ships capable of crossing the ocean and horses that could provide a decisive advantage in battle. But that's not the whole answer. Far more Native Americans died in bed than on the battlefield—the victims of germs, not of guns and swords. Those germs undermined Indian resistance by killing most Indians and their leaders and by demoralizing the survivors.

> *In the century or two following Columbus's arrival in the New World, the Indian population declined by about 95 percent. The main killers were European germs, to which the Indians had never been exposed.*

The role of disease in the Spanish conquests of the Aztec and Inca empires is especially well documented. In 1519 Cortés landed on the coast of Mexico with 600 Spaniards to conquer the fiercely militaristic Aztec Empire, which at the time had a population of many millions. That Cortés reached the Aztec capital of Tenochtitlán, escaped with the loss of "only" two-thirds of his force, and managed to fight his way back to the coast demonstrates both Spanish military advantages and the initial naïveté of the Aztecs. But when Cortés's next onslaught came, in 1521, the Aztecs were no longer naïve; they fought street by street with the utmost tenacity.

What gave the Spaniards a decisive advantage this time was smallpox, which reached Mexico in 1520 with the arrival of one infected slave from Spanish Cuba. The resulting epidemic proceeded to kill nearly half the Aztecs. The survivors were demoralized by the mysterious illness that killed Indians and spared Span-

iards, as if advertising the Spaniards' invincibility. By 1618 Mexico's initial population of 20 million had plummeted to about 1.6 million.

Pizarro had similarly grim luck when he landed on the coast of Peru in 1531 with about 200 men to conquer the Inca Empire. Fortunately for Pizarro, and unfortunately for the Incas, smallpox had arrived overland around 1524, killing much of the Inca population, including both Emperor Huayna Capac and his son and designated successor, Ninan Cuyoche. Because of the vacant throne, two other sons of Huayna Capac, Atahuallpa and Huáscar, became embroiled in a civil war that Pizarro exploited to conquer the divided Incas.

When we in the United States think of the most populous New World societies existing in 1492, only the Aztecs and Incas come to mind. We forget that North America also supported populous Indian societies in the Mississippi Valley. Sadly, these societies too would disappear. But in this case conquistadores contributed nothing directly to the societies' destruction; the conquistadores' germs, spreading in advance, did everything. When De Soto marched through the Southeast in 1540, he came across Indian towns abandoned two years previously because nearly all the inhabitants had died in epidemics. However, he was still able to see some of the densely populated towns lining the lower Mississippi. By a century and a half later, though, when French settlers returned to the lower Mississippi, almost all those towns had vanished. Their relics are the great mound sites of the Mississippi Valley. Only recently have we come to realize that the mound-building societies were still largely intact when Columbus arrived, and that they collapsed between 1492 and the systematic European exploration of the Mississippi.

When I was a child in school, we were taught that North America had originally been occupied by about one million Indians. That low number helped justify the white conquest of what could then be viewed as an almost empty continent. However, archeological excavations and descriptions left by the first

European explorers on our coasts now suggest an initial number of around 20 million. In the century or two following Columbus's arrival in the New World, the Indian population is estimated to have declined by about 95 percent.

The main killers were European germs, to which the Indians had never been exposed and against which they therefore had neither immunologic nor genetic resistance. Smallpox, measles, influenza, and typhus competed for top rank among the killers. As if those were not enough, pertussis, plague, tuberculosis, diphtheria, mumps, malaria, and yellow fever came close behind. In countless cases Europeans were actually there to witness the decimation that occurred when the germs arrived. For example, in 1837 the Mandan Indian tribe, with one of the most elaborate cultures in the Great Plains, contracted smallpox thanks to a steamboat traveling up the Missouri River from St. Louis. The population of one Mandan village crashed from 2,000 to less than 40 within a few weeks.

The one-sided exchange of lethal germs between the Old and New worlds is among the most striking and consequence-laden facts of recent history. Whereas over a dozen major infectious diseases of Old World origins became established in the New World, not a single major killer reached Europe from the Americas. The sole possible exception is syphilis, whose area of origin still remains controversial.

That one-sidedness is more striking with the knowledge that large, dense human populations are a prerequisite for the evolution of crowd diseases. If recent reappraisals of the pre-Columbian New World population are correct, that population was not far below the contemporaneous population of Eurasia. Some New World cities, like Tenochtitlán, were among the world's most populous cities at the time. Yet Tenochtitlán didn't have awful germs waiting in store for the Spaniards. Why not?

One possible factor is the rise of dense human populations began somewhat later in the New World than in the Old. Another is that the three most populous American centers—the Andes, Mexico, and the Mississippi Valley—

were never connected by regular fast trade into one gigantic breeding ground for microbes, in the way that Europe, North Africa, India, and China became connected in late Roman times.

The main reason becomes clear, however, if we ask a simple question: From what microbes could any crowd diseases of the Americas have evolved? We've seen that Eurasian crowd diseases evolved from diseases of domesticated herd animals. Significantly, there were many such animals in Eurasia. But there were only five animals that became domesticated in the Americas: the turkey in Mexico and parts of North America, the guinea pig and llama/alpaca (probably derived from the same original wild species) in the Andes, and Muscovy duck in tropical South America, and the dog throughout the Americas.

That extreme paucity of New World domestic animals reflects the paucity of wild starting material. About 80 percent of the big wild mammals of the Americas became extinct at the end of the last ice age, around 11,000 years ago, at approximately the same time that the first well-attested wave of Indian hunters spread over the Americas. Among the species that disappeared were ones that would have yielded useful domesticates, such as American horses and camels. Debate still rages as to whether those extinctions were due to climate changes or to the impact of Indian hunters on prey that had never seen humans. Whatever the reason, the extinctions removed most of the

basis for Native American animal domestication—and for crowd diseases.

The few domesticates that remained were not likely sources of such diseases. Muscovy ducks and turkeys don't live in enormous flocks, and they're not naturally endearing species (like young lambs) with which we have much physical contact. Guinea pigs may have contributed a trypanosome infection like Chagas' disease or leishmaniasis to our catalog of woes, but that's uncertain.

Initially the most surprising absence is of any human disease derived from llamas (or alpacas), which are tempting to consider as the Andean equivalent of Eurasian livestock. However, llamas had three strikes against them as a source of human pathogens: their wild relatives don't occur in big herds as do wild sheep, goats, and pigs; their total numbers were never remotely as large as the Eurasian populations of domestic livestock, since llamas never spread beyond the Andes; and llamas aren't as cuddly as piglets and lambs and aren't kept in such close association with people. (You may not think of piglets as cuddly, but human mothers in the New Guinea highlands often nurse them, and they frequently live right in the huts of peasant farmers.)

The importance of animal-derived diseases for human history extends far beyond the Americas. Eurasian germs played a key role in decimating native peoples in many other parts of the world as well, including the Pacific islands, Australia, and southern Africa. Racist Europeans used to attribute those con-

quests to their supposedly better brains. But no evidence for such better brains has been forthcoming. Instead, the conquests were made possible by Europeans nastier germs, and by the technological advances and denser populations that Europeans ultimately acquired by means of their domesticated plants and animals.

So on this 500th anniversary of Columbus's discovery, let's try to regain our sense of perspective about his hotly debated achievements. There's no doubt that Columbus was a great visionary, seaman, and leader. There's also no doubt that he and his successors often behaved as bestial murderers. But those facts alone don't fully explain why it took so few European immigrants to initially conquer and ultimately supplant so much of the native population of the Americas. Without the germs Europeans brought with them—germs that were derived from their animals—such conquests might have been impossible.

Jared Diamond is a contributing editor of DISCOVER, *a professor of physiology at the UCLA School of Medicine, a recipient of a MacArthur genius award, and a research associate in ornithology at the American Museum of Natural History. Expanded versions of many of his* DISCOVER *articles appear in his book* The Third Chimpanzee: The Evolution and Future of the Human Animal, *which won Britain's 1992* COPUS *prize for best science book. Not least among his many accomplishments was his rediscovery in 1981 of the long-lost bowerbird of New Guinea. Diamond wrote about pseudo-hermaphrodites for* DISCOVER'S *special June issue on the science of sex.*

The Price of Progress

John Bodley

In aiming at progress... you must let no one suffer by too drastic a measure, nor pay too high a price in upheaval and devastation, for your innovation.

Maunier, 1949: 725

UNTIL RECENTLY, GOVERNMENT planners have always considered economic development and progress beneficial goals that all societies should want to strive toward. The social advantage of progress—as defined in terms of increased incomes, higher standards of living, greater security, and better health—are thought to be positive, *universal* goods, to be obtained at any price. Although one may argue that tribal peoples must sacrifice their traditional cultures to obtain these benefits, government planners generally feel that this is a small price to pay for such obvious advantages.

In earlier chapters [in *Victims of Progress*, 3rd ed.], evidence was presented to demonstrate that autonomous tribal peoples have not *chosen* progress to enjoy its advantages, but that governments have *pushed* progress upon them to obtain tribal resources, not primarily to share with the tribal peoples the benefits of progress. It has also been shown that the price of forcing progress on unwilling recipients has involved the deaths of millions of tribal people, as well as their loss of land, political sovereignty, and the right to follow their own life style. This chapter does not attempt to further summarize that aspect of the cost of progress, but instead analyzes the specific effects of the participation of tribal peoples in the world-market economy. In direct opposition to the usual interpretation, it is argued here that the benefits of progress are often both illusory and detrimental to tribal peoples when they have not been allowed to control their own resources and define their relationship to the market economy.

PROGRESS AND THE QUALITY OF LIFE

One of the primary difficulties in assessing the benefits of progress and economic development for any culture is that of establishing a meaningful measure of both benefit and detriment. It is widely recognized that *standard of living*, which is the most frequently used measure of progress, is an intrinsically ethnocentric concept relying heavily upon indicators that lack universal cultural relevance. Such factors as GNP, per capita income, capital formation, employment rates, literacy, formal education, consumption of manufactured goods, number of doctors and hospital beds per thousand persons, and the amount of money spent on government welfare and health programs may be irrelevant measures of actual *quality* of life for autonomous or even semiautonomous tribal cultures. In its 1954 report, the Trust Territory government indicated that since the Micronesian population was still largely satisfying its own needs within a cashless subsistence economy, "Money income is not a significant measure of living standards, production, or well-being in this area" (TTR, 1953: 44). Unfortunately, within a short time the government began to rely on an enumeration of certain imported consumer goods as indicators of a higher standard of living in the islands, even though many tradition-oriented islanders felt that these new goods symbolized a lowering of the quality of life.

A more useful measure of the benefits of progress might be based on a formula for evaluating cultures devised by Goldschmidt (1952: 135). According to these less ethnocentric criteria, the important question to ask is: Does progress or economic development increase or decrease a given culture's ability to satisfy the physical and psychological needs of its population, or its stability? This question is a far more direct measure of quality of life than are the standard economic correlates of development, and it is universally relevant. Specific indication of this *standard* of living could be found for any society in the nutritional status and general physical and mental health of its population, the incidence of crime and delinquency, the demographic structure, family stability, and the society's relationship to its natural resource base. A society with high rates of malnutrition and crime, and one degrading its natural environment to the extent of threatening its continued existence, might be described as at a lower standard of living than is another society where these problems did not exist.

Careful examination of the data, which compare, on these specific points, the former condition of self-sufficient tribal peoples with their condition following their incorporation into the world-market economy, leads to the conclusion that their standard of living is *lowered*, not raised, by economic progress—and often to a dramatic degree. This is perhaps the most outstanding and inescapable fact to emerge from the years of research that anthropologists have devoted to the study of culture change and modernization. Despite the best intentions of those who have promoted change and improvement, all too often the results have been poverty, longer working hours, and much greater physical exertion, poor health, social disorder, discontent, discrimination, overpopulation, and environmental deterioration—

combined with the destruction of the traditional culture.

DISEASES OF DEVELOPMENT

Perhaps it would be useful for public health specialists to start talking about a new category of diseases.... Such diseases could be called the "diseases of development" and would consist of those pathological conditions which are based on the usually unanticipated consequences of the implementation of developmental schemes.

Hughes & Hunter, 1972: 93

Economic development increases the disease rate of affected peoples in at least three ways. First, to the extent that development is successful, it makes developed populations suddenly become vulnerable to all of the diseases suffered almost exclusively by "advanced" peoples. Among these are diabetes, obesity, hypertension, and a variety of circulatory problems. Second, development disturbs traditional environmental balances and may dramatically increase certain bacterial and parasite diseases. Finally, when development goals prove unattainable, an assortment of poverty diseases may appear in association with the crowded conditions of urban slums and the general breakdown in traditional socioeconomic systems.

Outstanding examples of the first situation can be seen in the Pacific, where some of the most successfully developed native peoples are found. In Micronesia, where development has progressed more rapidly than perhaps anywhere else, between 1958 and 1972 the population doubled, but the number of patients treated for heart disease in the local hospitals nearly tripled, mental disorder increased eightfold, and by 1972 hypertension and nutritional deficiencies began to make significant appearances for the first time (TTR, 1959, 1973, statistical tables).

Although some critics argue that the Micronesian figures simply represent better health monitoring due to economic progress, rigorously controlled data from Polynesia show a similar

trend. The progressive acquisition of modern degenerative diseases was documented by an eight-member team of New Zealand medical specialists, anthropologists, and nutritionists, whose research was funded by the Medical Research Council of New Zealand and the World Health Organization. These researchers investigated the health status of a genetically related population at various points along a continuum of increasing cash income, modernizing diet, and urbanization. The extremes on this acculturation continuum were represented by the relatively traditional Pukapukans of the Cook Islands and the essentially Europeanized New Zealand Maori, while the busily developing Rarotongans, also of the Cook Islands, occupied the intermediate position. In 1971, after eight years of work, the team's preliminary findings were summarized by Dr. Ian Prior, cardiologist and leader of the research, as follows:

We are beginning to observe that the more an islander takes on the ways of the West, the more prone he is to succumb to our degenerative diseases. In fact, it does not seem too much to say our evidence now shows that the farther the Pacific natives move from the quiet, carefree life of their ancestors, the closer they come to gout, diabetes, atherosclerosis, obesity, and hypertension.

Prior, 1971: 2

In Pukapuka, where progress was limited by the island's small size and its isolated location some 480 kilometers from the nearest port, the annual per capita income was only about thirty-six dollars and the economy remained essentially at a subsistence level. Resources were limited and the area was visited by trading ships only three or four times a year; thus, there was little opportunity for intensive economic development. Predictably, the population of Pukapuka was characterized by relatively low levels of imported sugar and salt intake, and a presumably related low level of heart disease, high blood pressure, and diabetes. In Rarotonga, where economic success was introducing town

life, imported food, and motorcycles, sugar and salt intakes nearly tripled, high blood pressure increased approximately ninefold, diabetes two- to threefold, and heart disease doubled for men and more than quadrupled for women, while the number of grossly obese women increased more than tenfold. Among the New Zealand Maori, sugar intake was nearly eight times that of the Pukapukans, gout in men was nearly double its rate on Pukapuka, and diabetes in men was more than fivefold higher, while heart disease in women had increased more than sixfold. The Maori were, in fact, dying of "European" diseases at a greater rate than was the average New Zealand European.

Government development policies designed to bring about changes in local hydrology, vegetation, and settlement patterns and to increase population mobility, and even programs aimed at reducing certain diseases, have frequently led to dramatic increases in disease rates because of the unforeseen effects of disturbing the preexisting order. Hughes and Hunter (1972) published an excellent survey of cases in which development led directly to increased disease rates in Africa. They concluded that hasty development intervention in relatively balanced local cultures and environments resulted in "a drastic deterioration in the social and economic conditions of life."

Traditional populations in general have presumably learned to live with the endemic pathogens of their environments, and in some cases they have evolved genetic adaptations to specific diseases, such as the sickle-cell trait, which provided an immunity to malaria. Unfortunately, however, outside intervention has entirely changed this picture. In the late 1960s, sleeping sickness suddenly increased in many areas of Africa and even spread to areas where it did not formerly occur, due to the building of new roads and migratory labor, both of which caused increased population movement. Large-scale relocation schemes, such as the Zande Scheme, had disastrous results when natives were moved from their traditional disease-free refuges into infected areas. Dams and irrigation developments inadvertently created ideal conditions for the rapid proliferation of snails carrying schistosomiasis (a liver fluke disease), and major epidemics suddenly occurred in areas where this disease had never before been a problem. DDT spraying programs have been temporarily successful in controlling malaria, but there is often a rebound effect that increases the problem when spraying is discontinued, and the malarial mosquitoes are continually evolving resistant strains.

Urbanization is one of the prime measures of development, but it is a mixed blessing for most former tribal peoples. Urban health standards are abysmally poor and generally worse than in rural areas for the detribalized individuals who have crowded into the towns and cities throughout Africa, Asia, and Latin America seeking wage employment out of new economic necessity. Infectious diseases related to crowding and poor sanitation are rampant in urban centers, while greatly increased stress and poor nutrition aggravate a variety of other health problems. Malnutrition and other diet-related conditions are, in fact, one of the characteristic hazards of progress faced by tribal peoples and are discussed in the following sections.

The Hazards of Dietary Change

The traditional diets of tribal peoples are admirably adapted to their nutritional needs and available food resources. Even though these diets may seem bizarre, absurd, and unpalatable to outsiders, they are unlikely to be improved by drastic modifications. Given the delicate balances and complexities involved in any subsistence system, change always involves risks, but for tribal people the effects of dietary change have been catastrophic.

Under normal conditions, food habits are remarkably resistant to change, and indeed people are unlikely to abandon their traditional diets voluntarily in favor of dependence on difficult-to-obtain exotic imports. In some cases it is true that imported foods may be identified with powerful outsiders and are therefore sought as symbols of greater prestige. This may lead to such absurdities as Amazonian Indians choosing to consume

imported canned tunafish when abundant high-quality fish is available in their own rivers. Another example of this situation occurs in tribes where mothers prefer to feed their infants expensive nutritionally inadequate canned milk from unsanitary, but *high status*, baby bottles. The high status of these items is often promoted by clever traders and clever advertising campaigns.

Aside from these apparently voluntary changes, it appears that more often dietary changes are forced upon unwilling tribal peoples by circumstances beyond their control. In some areas, new food crops have been introduced by government decree, or as a consequence of forced relocation or other policies designed to end hunting, pastoralism, or shifting cultivation. Food habits have also been modified by massive disruption of the natural environment by outsiders—as when sheepherders transformed the Australian Aborigines' foraging territory or when European invaders destroyed the bison herds that were the primary element in the Plains Indians' subsistence patterns. Perhaps the most frequent cause of diet change occurs when formerly self-sufficient peoples find that wage labor, cash cropping, and other economic development activities that feed tribal resources into the world-market economy must inevitably divert time and energy away from the production of subsistence foods. Many developing peoples suddenly discover that, like it or not, they are unable to secure traditional foods and must spend their newly acquired cash on costly, and often nutritionally inferior, manufactured foods.

Overall, the available data seem to indicate that the dietary changes that are linked to involvement in the world-market economy have tended to *lower* rather than raise the nutritional levels of the affected tribal peoples. Specifically, the vitamin, mineral, and protein components of their diets are often drastically reduced and replaced by enormous increases in starch and carbohydrates, often in the form of white flour and refined sugar.

Any deterioration in the quality of a given population's diet is almost certain to be reflected in an increase in deficiency diseases and a general decline in

health status. Indeed, as tribal peoples have shifted to a diet based on imported manufactured or processed foods, there has been a dramatic rise in malnutrition, a massive increase in dental problems, and a variety of other nutritional-related disorders. Nutritional physiology is so complex that even well-meaning dietary changes have had tragic consequences. In many areas of Southeast Asia, government-sponsored protein supplementation programs supplying milk to protein-deficient populations caused unexpected health problems and increased mortality. Officials failed to anticipate that in cultures where adults do not normally drink milk, the enzymes needed to digest it are no longer produced and milk *intolerance* results (Davis & Bolin, 1972). In Brazil, a similar milk distribution program caused an epidemic of permanent blindness by aggravating a preexisting vitamin A deficiency (Bunce, 1972).

Teeth and Progress

There is nothing new in the observation that savages, or peoples living under primitive conditions, have, in general, excellent teeth.... Nor is it news that most civilized populations possess wretched teeth which begin to decay almost before they have erupted completely, and that dental caries is likely to be accompanied by periodontal disease with further reaching complications.

Hooton, 1945: xviii

Anthropologists have long recognized that undisturbed tribal peoples are often in excellent physical condition. And it has often been noted specifically that dental caries and the other dental abnormalities that plague industrialized societies are absent or rare among tribal peoples who have retained their traditional diets. The fact that tribal food habits may contribute to the development of sound teeth, whereas modernized diets may do just the opposite, was illustrated as long ago as 1894 in an article in the *Journal of the Royal Anthropological Institute* that described the results of a comparison between the teeth of ten Sioux Indians were examined when they came to London as members of Buffalo Bill's Wild West Show and were found to be completely free of caries and in possession of all their teeth, even though half of the group were over thirty-nine years of age. Londoners' teeth were conspicuous for both their caries and their steady reduction in number with advancing age. The difference was attributed primarily to the wear and polishing caused by the traditional Indian diet of coarse food and the fact that they chewed their food longer, encouraged by the absence of tableware.

One of the most remarkable studies of the dental conditions of tribal peoples and the impact of dietary change was conducted in the 1930s by Weston Price (1945), an American dentist who was interested in determining what caused normal, healthy teeth. Between 1931 and 1936, Price systematically explored tribal areas throughout the world to locate and examine the most isolated peoples who were still living on traditional foods. His fieldwork covered Alaska, the Canadian Yukon, Hudson Bay, Vancouver Island, Florida, the Andes, the Amazon, Samoa, Tahiti, New Zealand, Australia, New Caledonia, Fiji, the Torres Strait, East Africa, and the Nile. The study demonstrated both the superior quality of aboriginal dentition and the devastation that occurs as modern diets are adopted. In nearly every area where traditional foods were still being eaten, Price found perfect teeth with normal dental arches and virtually no decay, whereas caries and abnormalities increased steadily as new diets were adopted. In many cases the change was sudden and striking. Among Eskimo groups subsisting entirely on traditional food he found caries totally absent, whereas in groups eating a considerable quantity of store-bought food approximately 20 percent of their teeth were decayed. This figure rose to more than 30 percent with Eskimo groups subsisting almost exclusively on purchased or government-supplied food, and reached an incredible 48 percent among the Vancouver Island Indians. Unfortunately for many of these people, modern dental treatment did not accompany the new food, and their suffering was appalling. The loss of teeth was, of course, bad

enough in itself, and it certainly undermined the population's resistance to many new diseases, including tuberculosis. But new foods were also accompanied by crowded, misplaced teeth, gum diseases, distortion of the face, and pinching of the nasal cavity. Abnormalities in the dental arch appeared in the new generation following the change in diet, while caries appeared almost immediately even in adults.

Price reported that in many areas the affected peoples were conscious of their own physical deterioration. At a mission school in Africa, the principal asked him to explain to the native schoolchildren why they were not physically as strong as children who had had no contact with schools. On an island in the Torres Strait the natives knew exactly what was causing their problems and resisted—almost to the point of bloodshed—government efforts to establish a store that would make imported food available. The government prevailed, however, and Price was able to establish a relationship between the length of time the government store had been established and the increasing incidence of caries among a population that showed an almost 100 percent immunity to them before the store had been opened.

In New Zealand, the Maori, who in their aboriginal state are often considered to have been among the healthiest, most perfectly developed of people, were found to have "advanced" the furthest. According to Price:

Their modernization was demonstrated not only by the high incidence of dental caries but also by the fact that 90 percent of the adults and 100 percent of the children had abnormalities of the dental arches.

Price, 1945: 206

Malnutrition

Malnutrition, particularly in the form of protein deficiency, has become a critical problem for tribal peoples who must adopt new economic patterns. Population pressures, cash cropping, and government programs all have tended to encourage the replacement of traditional

crops and other food sources that were rich in protein with substitutes, high in calories but low in protein. In Africa, for example, protein-rich staples such as millet and sorghum are being replaced systematically by high-yielding manioc and plantains, which have insignificant amounts of protein. The problem is increased for cash croppers and wage laborers whose earnings are too low and unpredictable to allow purchase of adequate amounts of protein. In some rural areas, agricultural laborers have been forced systematically to deprive nonproductive members (principally children) of their households of their minimal nutritional requirements to satisfy the need of the productive members. This process has been documented in northeastern Brazil following the introduction of large-scale sisal plantations (Gross & Underwood, 1971). In urban centers the difficulties of obtaining nutritionally adequate diets are even more serious for tribal immigrants, because costs are higher and poor quality foods are more tempting.

One of the most tragic, and largely overlooked, aspects of chronic malnutrition is that it can lead to abnormally undersized brain development and apparently irreversible brain damage; it has been associated with various forms of mental impairment or retardation. Malnutrition has been linked clinically with mental retardation in both Africa and Latin America (see, for example, Mönckeberg, 1968), and this appears to be a worldwide phenomenon with serious implications (Montagu, 1972).

Optimistic supporters of progress will surely say that all of these new health problems are being overstressed and that the introduction of hospitals, clinics, and the other modern health institutions will overcome or at least compensate for all of these difficulties. However, it appears that uncontrolled population growth and economic impoverishment probably will keep most of these benefits out of reach for many tribal peoples, and the intervention of modern medicine has at least partly contributed to the problem in the first place.

The generalization that civilization frequently has a broad negative impact on tribal health has found broad empirical support (see especially Kroeger & Barbira-Freedman [1982] on Amazonia; Reinhard [1976] on the Arctic; and Wirsing [1985] globally), but these conclusions have not gone unchallenged. Some critics argue that tribal health was often poor before modernization, and they point specifically to tribals' low life expectancy and high infant mortality rates. Demographic statistics on tribal populations are often problematic because precise data are scarce, but they do show a less favorable profile than that enjoyed by many industrial societies. However, it should be remembered that our present life expectancy is a recent phenomenon that has been very costly in terms of medical research and technological advances. Furthermore, the benefits of our health system are not enjoyed equally by all members of our society. High infant mortality could be viewed as a relatively inexpensive and egalitarian tribal public health program that offered the reasonable expectation of a healthy and productive life for those surviving to age fifteen.

Some critics also suggest that certain tribal populations, such as the New Guinea highlanders, were "stunted" by nutritional deficiencies created by tribal culture and are "improved" by "acculturation" and cash cropping (Dennett & Connell, 1988). Although this argument does suggest that the health question requires careful evaluation, it does not invalidate the empirical generalizations already established. Nutritional deficiencies undoubtedly occurred in densely populated zones in the central New Guinea highlands. However, the specific case cited above may not be widely representative of other tribal groups even in New Guinea, and it does not address the facts of outside intrusion or the inequities inherent in the contemporary development process.

ECOCIDE

"How is it," asked a herdsman... "how is it that these hills can no longer give pasture to my cattle? In my father's day they were green and cattle thrived there; today there is no grass and my cattle
starve." As one looked one saw that what had once been a green hill had become a raw red rock.

Jones, 1934

Progress not only brings new threats to the health of tribal peoples, but it also imposes new strains on the ecosystems upon which they must depend for their ultimate survival. The introduction of new technology, increased consumption, lowered mortality, and the eradication of all traditional controls have combined to replace what for most tribal peoples was a relatively stable balance between population and natural resources, with a new system that is imbalanced. Economic development is forcing *ecocide* on peoples who were once careful stewards of their resources. There is already a trend toward widespread environmental deterioration in tribal areas, involving resource depletion, erosion, plant and animal extinction, and a disturbing series of other previously unforeseen changes.

After the initial depopulation suffered by most tribal peoples during their engulfment by frontiers of national expansion, most tribal populations began to experience rapid growth. Authorities generally attribute this growth to the introduction of modern medicine and new health measures and the termination of intertribal warfare, which lowered morality rates, as well as to new technology, which increased food production. Certainly all of these factors played a part, but merely lowering mortality rates would not have produced the rapid population growth that most tribal areas have experienced if traditional birthspacing mechanisms had not been eliminated at the same time. Regardless of which factors were most important, it is clear that all of the natural and cultural checks on population growth have suddenly been pushed aside by culture change, while tribal lands have been steadily reduced and consumption levels have risen. In many tribal areas, environmental deterioration due to overuse of resources has set in, and in other areas such deterioration is imminent as resources continue to dwindle relative to the expanding population and increased use. Of course, population expansion by tribal peoples may have positive political

consequences, because where tribals can retain or regain their status as local majorities they may be in a more favorable position to defend their resources against intruders.

Swidden systems and pastoralism, both highly successful economic systems under traditional conditions, have proved particularly vulnerable to increased population pressures and outside efforts to raise productivity beyond its natural limits. Research in Amazonia demonstrates that population pressures and related resource depletion can be created indirectly by official policies that restrict swidden peoples to smaller territories. Resource depletion itself can then become a powerful means of forcing tribal people into participating in the world-market economy—thus leading to further resource depletion. For example, Bodley and Benson (1979) showed how the Shipibo Indians in Peru were forced to further deplete their forest resources by cash cropping in the forest area to replace the resources that had been destroyed earlier by the intensive cash cropping necessitated by the narrow confines of their reserve. In this case, certain species of palm trees that had provided critical housing materials were destroyed by forest clearing and had to be replaced by costly purchased materials. Research by Gross (1979) and other showed similar processes at work among four tribal groups in central Brazil and demonstrated that the degree of market involvement increases directly with increases in resource depletion.

The settling of nomadic herders and the removal of prior controls on herd size have often led to serious overgrazing and erosion problems where these had not previously occurred. There are indications that the desertification problem in the Sahel region of Africa was aggravated by programs designed to settle nomads. The first sign of imbalance in a swidden system appears when the planting cycles are shortened to the point that garden plots are reused before sufficient forest regrowth can occur. If reclearing and planting continue in the same area, the natural patterns of forest succession may be disturbed irreversibly and the soil can be impaired permanently. An extensive tract of tropical rainforest in the lower Amazon of Brazil was reduced to a semiarid desert in just fifty years through such a process (Ackermann, 1964). The soils in the Azande area are also now seriously threatened with laterization and other problems as a result of the government-promoted cotton development scheme (McNeil, 1972).

The dangers of overdevelopment and the vulnerability of local resource systems have long been recognized by both anthropologists and tribal peoples themselves. But the pressures for change have been overwhelming. In 1948 the Maya villagers of Chan Kom complained to Redfield (1962) about the shortening of their swidden cycles, which they correctly attributed to increasing population pressures. Redfield told them, however, that they had no choice but to go "forward with technology" (Redfield, 1962: 178). In Assam, swidden cycles were shortened from an average of twelve years to only two or three within just twenty years, and anthropologists warned that the limits of swiddening would soon be reached (Burling, 1963: 311–312). In the Pacific, anthropologists warned of population pressures on limited resources as early as the 1930s (Keesing, 1941: 64–65). These warnings seemed fully justified, considering the fact that the crowded Tikopians were prompted by population pressures on their tiny island to suggest that infanticide be legalized. The warnings have been dramatically reinforced since then by the doubling of Micronesia's population in just the fourteen years between 1958 and 1972, from 70,600 to 114,645, while consumption levels have soared. By 1985 Micronesia's population had reached 162,321.

The environmental hazards of economic development and rapid population growth have become generally recognized only since worldwide concerns over environmental issues began in the early 1970s. Unfortunately, there is as yet little indication that the leaders of the new developing nations are sufficiently concerned with environmental limitations. On the contrary, governments are forcing tribal peoples into a self-reinforcing spiral of population growth and intensified resource exploitation, which may be stopped only by environmental

disaster or the total impoverishment of the tribals.

The reality of ecocide certainly focuses attention on the fundamental contrasts between tribal and industrial systems in their use of natural resources, who controls them, and how they are managed. Tribal peoples are victimized because they control resources that outsiders demand. The resources exist because tribals managed them conservatively. However, as with the issue of the health consequences of detribalization, some anthropologists minimize the adaptive achievements of tribal groups and seem unwilling to concede that ecocide might be a consequence of cultural change. Critics attack an exaggerated "noble savage" image of tribals living in perfect harmony with nature and having no visible impact on their surroundings. They then show that tribals do in fact modify the environment, and they conclude that there is no significant difference between how tribals and industrial societies treat their environments. For example, Charles Wagley declared that Brazilian Indians such as the Tapirape

are not "natural men." They have human vices just as we do…. They do not live "in tune" with nature any more than I do; in fact, they can often be as destructive of their environment, within their limitations, as some civilized men. The Tapirape are not innocent or childlike in any way.

Wagley, 1977: 302

Anthropologist Terry Rambo demonstrated that the Semang of the Malaysian rain forests have a measurable impact on their environment. In his monograph *Primitive Polluters*, Rambo (1985) reported that the Semang live in smoke-filled houses. They sneeze and spread germs, breathe, and thus emit carbon dioxide. They clear small gardens, contributing "particulate matter" to the air and disturbing the local climate because cleared areas proved measurably warmer and drier than the shady forest. Rambo concluded that his research "demonstrates the essential functional similarity of the environmental interactions of primitive and civilized societies" (1985:

78) in contrast to a "noble savage" view (Bodley, 1983) which, according to Rambo (1985: 2), mistakenly "claims that traditional peoples almost always live in essential harmony with their environment."

This is surely a false issue. To stress, as I do, that tribals tend to manage their resources for sustained yield within relatively self-sufficient subsistence economies is not to make them either innocent children or natural men. Nor is it to deny that tribals "disrupt" their environment and may never be in absolute "balance" with nature.

The ecocide issue is perhaps most dramatically illustrated by two sets of satellite photos taken over the Brazilian rain forests of Rôndonia (Allard & McIntyre, 1988: 780–781). Photos taken in 1973, when Rôndonia was still a tribal domain, show virtually unbroken rain forest. The 1987 satellite photos, taken after just fifteen years of highway construction and "development" by outsiders, show more than 20 percent of the forest destroyed. The surviving Indians were being concentrated by FUNAI (Brazil's national Indian foundation) into what would soon become mere islands of forest in a ravaged landscape. It is irrelevant to quibble about whether tribals are noble, childlike, or innocent, or about the precise meaning of balance with nature, carrying capacity, or adaptation, to recognize that for the past 200 years rapid environmental deterioration on an unprecedented global scale has followed the wresting of control of vast areas of the world from tribal groups by resource-hungry industrial societies.

DEPRIVATION AND DISCRIMINATION

Contact with European culture has given them a knowledge of great wealth, opportunity and privilege, but only very limited avenues by which to acquire these things.

Crocombe, 1968

Unwittingly, tribal peoples have had the burden of perpetual relative deprivation thrust upon them by acceptance—either by themselves or by the governments administering them—of the standards of socioeconomic progress set for them by industrial civilizations. By comparison with the material wealth of industrial societies, tribal societies become, by definition, impoverished. They are then forced to transform their cultures and work to achieve what many economists now acknowledge to be unattainable goals. Even though in many cases the modest GNP goals set by development planners for the developing nations during the "development decade" of the 1960s were often met, the results were hardly noticeable for most of the tribal people involved. Population growth, environmental limitations, inequitable distribution of wealth, and the continued rapid growth of the industrialized nations have all meant that both the absolute and the relative gap between the rich and poor in the world is steadily widening. The prospect that tribal peoples will actually be able to attain the levels of resource consumption to which they are being encouraged to aspire is remote indeed except for those few groups who have retained effective control over strategic mineral resources.

Tribal peoples feel deprivation not only when the economic goals they have been encouraged to seek fail to materialize, but also when they discover that they are powerless, second-class citizens who are discriminated against and exploited by the dominant society. At the same time, they are denied the satisfactions of their traditional cultures, because these have been sacrificed in the process of modernization. Under the impact of major economic change family life is disrupted, traditional social controls are often lost, and many indicators of social anomie such as alcoholism, crime, delinquency, suicide, emotional disorders, and despair may increase. The inevitable frustration resulting from this continual deprivation finds expression in the cargo cults, revitalization movements, and a variety of other political and religious movements that have been widespread among tribal peoples following their disruption by industrial civilization.

Bibliography

Ackermann, F. L. 1964. *Geologia e Fisiografia da Região Bragantina, Estado do Pará*. Manaus, Brazil: Conselho Nacional de Pesquisas, Instituto Nacional de Pesquisas da Amazonia.

Allard, William Albert, and Loren McIntyre. 1988. Rondônia's settlers invade Brazil's imperiled rain forest. *National Geographic* 174(6):772–799.

Bodley, John H. 1970. *Campa Socio-Economic Adaptation*. Ann Arbor: University Microfilms.

———. 1983. *Der Weg der Zerstörung: Stammesvölker und die industrielle Zivilization*. Munich: Trickster-Verlag. (Translation of *Victims of Progress*.)

Bodley, John H., and Foley C. Benson. 1979. Cultural ecology of Amazonian palms. *Reports of Investigations*, no. 56. Pullman: Laboratory of Anthropology, Washington State University.

Bunce, George E. 1972. Aggravation of vitamin A deficiency following distribution of non-fortified skim milk: An example of nutrient interaction. In *The Careless Technology: Ecology and International Development*, ed. M. T. Farvar and John P. Milton, pp. 53–60. Garden City, N.Y.: Natural History Press.

Burling, Robbins. 1963. *Rengsanggri: Family and Kinship in a Garo Village*. Philadelphia: University of Pennsylvania Press.

Davis, A. E., and T. D. Bolin. 1972. Lactose intolerance in Southeast Asia. In *The Careless Technology: Ecology and International Development*, ed. M. T. Farvar and John P. Milton, pp. 61–68. Garden City, N.Y.: Natural History Press.

Dennett, Glenn, and John Connell. 1988. Acculturation and health in the highlands of Papua New Guinea. *Current Anthropology* 29(2):273–299.

Goldschmidt, Walter R. 1972. The interrelations between cultural factors and the acquisition of new technical skills. In *The Progress of Underdeveloped Areas*, ed. Bert F. Hoselitz, pp. 135–151. Chicago: University of Chicago Press.

Gross, Daniel R., et al. 1979. Ecology and acculturation among native peoples of Central Brazil. *Science* 206(4422): 1043–1050.

Hughes, Charles C., and John M. Hunter. 1972. The role of technological development in promoting disease in Africa. In *The Careless Technology: Ecology and International Development*, ed. M. T. Farvar and John P. Milton, pp. 69–101. Garden City, N.Y.: Natural History Press.

Keesing, Felix M. 1941. *The South Seas in the Modern World*. Institute of Pacific Relations International Research Series. New York: John Day.

Kroeger, Axel, and François Barbira-Freedman. 1982. *Culture Change and Health: The Case of South American Rainforest Indians*. Frankfurt am Main: Verlag Peter Lang. (Reprinted in Bodley, 1988a:221–236.)

McNeil, Mary. 1972. Lateritic soils in distinct tropical environments: Southern Sudan and Brazil. In *The Careless Technology: Ecology an International Development*, ed. M. T. Farvar and John P. Milton, pp. 591–608. Garden City, N.Y.: Natural History Press.

Mönckeberg, F. 1968. Mental retardation from malnutrition. *Journal of the American Medical Association* 206:30–31.

Montagu, Ashley. 1972. Sociogenic brain damage. *American Anthropologist* 74(5):1045–1061.

Rambo, A. Terry. 1985. *Primitive Polluters: Semang Impact on the Malaysian Tropical Rain Forest Ecosystem*. Anthropological Papers no. 76, Museum of Anthropology, University of Michigan.

Redfield, Robert. 1953. *The Primitive World and Its Transformations*. Ithaca, N.Y.: Cornell University Press.

———. 1962. *A Village That Chose Progress: Chan Kom Revisited*. Chicago: University of Chicago Press, Phoenix Books.

Smith, Wilberforce. 1894. The teeth of ten Sioux Indians. *Journal of the Royal Anthropological Institute* 24:109–116.

TTR: *See under* United States.

United States, Department of the Interior, Office of Territories. 1953. *Report on the Administration of the Trust Territory of the Pacific Islands* (by the United States to the United Nations) for the Period July 1, 1951, to June 30, 1952.

———. 1954. *Annual Report, High Commissioner of the Trust Territory of the Pacific Islands to the Secretary of the Interior* (for 1953).

United States, Department of State. 1955. *Seventh Annual Report to the United Nations on the Administration of the Trust Territory of the Pacific Islands* (July 1, 1953, to June 30, 1954).

———. 1959. *Eleventh Annual Report to the United Nations on the Administration of the Trust Territory of the Pacific Islands* (July 1, 1957, to June 30, 1958).

———. 1964. *Sixteenth Annual Report to the United Nations on the Administration of the Trust Territory of the Pacific Islands* (July 1, 1962 to June 30, 1963).

———. 1973. *Twenty-Fifth Annual Report to the United Nations on the Administration of the Trust Territory of the Pacific Islands* (July 1, 1971, to June 30, 1972).

The Social Psychology of Modern Slavery

Contrary to conventional wisdom, **slavery** has not disappeared from the world. Social scientists are trying to explain its **persistence**

By Kevin Bales

For Meera, the revolution began with a single rupee. When a social worker came across Meera's unmapped village in the hills of Uttar Pradesh in India three years ago, he found that the entire population was in hereditary debt bondage. It could have been in the time of their grandfathers or great-grandfathers—few in the village could remember—but at some point in their past, the families had pledged themselves to unpaid labor in return for loans of money. The debt passed down through the generations. Children as young as five years old worked in quarry pits, making sand by crushing stones with hammers. Dust, flying rock chips and heavy loads had left many villagers with silicosis and injured eyes or backs.

Calling together some of the women, the social worker proposed a radical plan. If groups of 10 women agreed to set aside a single rupee a week from the tiny sums the moneylenders gave them to buy rice, he would provide seed money and keep the funds safe. Meera and nine others formed the first group. The rupees slowly mounted up. After three months, the group had enough to pay off the loan against which Meera was bonded. She began earning money for her work, which greatly increased the amount she could contribute to the group. In another two months, another woman was freed; the following month, a third came out of bondage.

At that point, the other members, seeing that freedom was possible, simply renounced their debts and declared themselves free. The moneylenders quickly moved against them, threatening them and driving them from the quarries. But the women were able to find jobs in other quarries. New groups followed their example. The social worker has taken me to the village twice, and on my second visit, all its inhabitants were free and all their children in school.

Less than 100 kilometers away, the land turns flat and fertile. Debt bondage is common there, too. When I met Baldev in 1997, he was plowing. His master called him "my *halvaha*," meaning "my bonded plowman." Two years later I met Baldev again and learned that because of a windfall from a relative, he had freed himself from debt. But he had not freed himself from bondage. He told me:

> After my wife received this money, we paid off our debt and were free to do whatever we wanted. But I was worried all the time—what if one of the children got sick? What if our crop failed? What if the government wanted some money? Since we no longer belonged to the landlord, we didn't get food every day as before. Finally, I went to the landlord and asked him to take me back. I didn't have to borrow any money, but he agreed to let me be his *halvaha* again. Now I don't worry so much; I know what to do.

Lacking any preparation for freedom, Baldev reenrolled in slavery. Without financial or emotional support, his accidental emancipation didn't last. Although he may not bequeath any debt to his children, his family is visibly worse off than unbonded villagers in the same region.

To many people, it comes as a surprise that debt bondage and other forms of slavery persist into the 21st century. Every country, after all, has made it illegal to own and exercise total control over another human being. And yet there are people like Baldev who remain enslaved—by my estimate, which is based on a compilation of reports from governments and nongovernmental organizations, perhaps 27 million of them around the world. If slaveholders no longer own slaves in a legal sense,

THE WORLD OF SLAVERY

Slavery researchers are the first to acknowledge that their statistics are extremely unreliable. By its very nature, the subject matter is hard to detect, let alone quantify. Researchers must extrapolate from known incidence—based on reports from police, social workers, investigative reporters and freed slaves—to the broader picture. That is standard operating procedure in science: every field, from sociology to astrophysics, must make working assumptions. Unfortunately, the numerical estimates are often quoted and requoted without mentioning how provisional they are.

For instance, the International Organization for Migration recently traced one of the most widely quoted human-smuggling statistics—an estimate of 250,000 to 350,000 illegal migrant entries into western Europe in 1993—to its source. It was based on 60,000 border apprehensions and guesses by police that four to six times as many got through. Another oft-cited figure—45,000 to 50,000 women and children trafficked to the U.S. every year—originated in a classified Central Intelligence Agency briefing in April 1999. The derivation of that number has never been made public.

Kevin Bales has taken two approaches to dealing with uncertainty. First, he has collated various estimates of the numbers of slaves in individual countries (*table*), reasoning that some sources, such as governments, might tend to underestimate the problem and that others, such as human-rights groups, overestimate it. The table omits countries and regions for which researchers lack data. Second, he has prepared a scale of the relative degree of the problem in different countries, which is presumably easier to judge than the absolute number of slaves.

—George Musser, staff editor and writer

COUNTRY OR REGION	TRAFFICKING IN	OUT	ESTIMATED NUMBER OF SLAVES
Afghanistan	++	***	20,000-50,000
Albania	+	***	5,000-10,000
Algeria	++	**	1,000-2,000
Argentina	++	**	1,000-2,000
Armenia	+	**	2,000-4,000
Australia	+++	*	4,000-6,000
Austria	++		1,000-2,000
Azerbaijan	+	**	1,000-2,000
Bahrain	++	**	1,000-2,000
Bangladesh	+	****	10,000-10,000
Barbados	+	*	0-100
Belarus	+	***	2,000-3,000
Belgium	++	*	5,000-7,000
Benin	++++	****	20,000-40,000
Bosnia-Herzegovina	++	**	3,000-4,000
Brazil	++++	****	300,000-500,000
Bulgaria	++	****	2,000-4,000
Burkina Faso	+++	***	2,000-4,000
Burma	+	****	50,000-100,000
Cambodia	++	***	3,000-6,000
Cameroon	+++	***	6,000-12,000
Canada	++	*	10,000-20,000
China	+++	***	250,000-500,000
Colombia	++	***	5,000-10,000
Congo (Kinshasa)	+++	***	1,000-1,500
Costa Rica	+	**	0-100
Croatia	++	***	1,000-2,000
Czech Republic	++++	****	2,000-5,000
Denmark	+	*	1,000-2,000
Dominica	+	*	0-100
Dominican Republic	+	**	5,000-6,000
Egypt	+.	**	1,000-2,000
Equatorial Guinea	++	***	1,000-2,000
Estonia	++	**	1,000-2,000
France	+++	*	10,000-20,000
Gabon	++	***	5,000-10,000
Gambia	++++	***	3,000-6,000
Georgia	++	****	1,000-2,000
Germany	+++	*	5,000-9,000
Ghana	+++	***	10,000-20,000
Greece	++	*	5,000-9,000
Guinea-Bissau	++	***	1,000-2,000
Haiti	++	****	75,000-150,000
Hong Kong	+++	**	1,000-2,000
Hungary	+++	***	1,000-2,000
India	+++	****	18,000,000-22,000,000
Indonesia	++	***	4,000-8,000
Israel	++++	*	4,000-6,000
Italy	++++	**	30,000-40,000
Ivory Coast	++++	****	30,000-80,000
Jamaica	++	**	0-500
Japan	++++	**	5,000-10,000
Kazakhstan	+	**	1,000-2,000
Kenya	+	**	3,000-5,000
South Korea	++	**	10,000-15,000
Kuwait	++	*	1,000-2,000
Kyrgyzstan	+	*	1,000-1,500
Laos	+	***	5,000-10,000
Lebanon	++	**	1,000-1,500
Liberia	++	**	3,000-6,000
Luxembourg	++	*	2,000-3,000
Macedonia	++	***	1,000-1,500
Malaysia	+++	***	3,000-6,000
Mali	++++	****	10,000-20,000
Mauritania	++	***	250,000-300,000
Mexico	+++	***	3,000-6,000
Moldova	+++	***	1,000-1,500
Morocco	++++	****	1,000-2,000
Nepal	++	****	250,000-300,000
Netherlands	+++	*	3,000-5,000
Niger	++++	****	3,000-5,000
Nigeria	++	****	20,000-40,000
Oman	+++	**	1,000-2,000
Pakistan	+++	****	2,500,000-3,500,000
Panama	+	*	0-100
Peru	++	**	3,000-5,000
Philippines	++	****	3,000-10,000
Poland	++++	****	2,000-4,000
Portugal	+++	**	5,000-6,000
Puerto Rico	+*		0-100
Qatar	+++	**	1,000-2,000
Romania	+++	****	5,000-6,000
Russia	++++	****	8,000-10,000
SaoTome	++++	****	1,000-2,000
Saudi Arabia	++++	****	2,000-5,000
Senegal	++++	****	6,000-12,000
Sierra Leone	++++	****	3,000-6,000
Singapore	+++	***	1,000-1,500
Slovakia	+++	***	2,000-3,000
South Africa	+++	***	5,000-6,000
Spain	++	**	10,000-15,000
Sri Lanka	++	****	5,000-10,000
Sudan	++++	****	20,000-50,000
Sweden	+		2,000-3,000
Switzerland	+	*	1,000-1,500
Tajikistan	++	**	2,000-4,000
Tanzania	++**		2,000-4,000
Thailand	++++	****	30,000-60,000
Togo	++	***	6,000-10,000
Trinidad	+	*	0-100
Turkey	++++	****	20,000-30,000
Turkmenistan	+++	***	1,000-2,000
Uganda	++	***	5,000-8,000
Ukraine	++	****	3,000-5,000
U.A.E.	++++	**	1,000-2,000
U.K.	+	*	4,000-5,000
U.S.	+	*	100,000-150,000
Uzbekistan	++	**	1,000-2,000
Vietnam	++	***	5,000-7,000
Yemen	+++	**	1,000-2,000
Yugoslavia	+++	****	8,000-10,000

AMOUNT OF HUMAN TRAFFICKING (4 = SEVERE, 0 = NONE)

++++ INFLOWING   **** OUTFLOWING

how can they still exercise so much control that freed slaves sometimes deliver themselves back into bondage? This is just one of the puzzles that make slavery the greatest challenge faced by the social sciences today.

Despite being among the oldest and most persistent forms of human relationships, found in most societies at one time or another, slavery is little understood. Although historians have built up a sizable literature on antebellum American slavery, other types have barely been studied. It is as if our understanding of all arachnids were based on clues left by a single species of extinct spider. In our present state of ignorance, we have little hope of truly eradicating slavery, of making sure that Meera, rather than Baldev, becomes the model.

The New Slavery

RESEARCHERS DO KNOW that slavery is both evolving and increasing in raw numbers. Like spiders, it permeates our world, typically hidden in the dark spaces of the economy. Over the past few years, journalists and activists have documented numerous examples. Human trafficking—the involuntary smuggling of people between countries, often by organized crime—has become a huge concern, especially in Europe and Southeast Asia. Many people, lured by economic opportunities, pay smugglers to slip them across borders but then find themselves sold to sweatshops, brothels or domestic service to pay for their passage; others are kidnapped and smuggled against their will. In certain areas, notably Brazil and West Africa, laborers have been enticed into signing contracts and then taken to remote plantations and prevented from leaving. In parts of South Asia and North Africa, slavery is a millennia-old tradition that has never truly ended.

The plight of these people has drawn the attention of governments and organizations as diverse as the Vatican, the United Nations, the International Organization for Migration, and Amnesty International. Two years ago the U.S. government established a central coordinating office to deal with human trafficking. Academic researchers are beginning to conduct intensive studies. The anecdotal and journalistic approach is slowly transforming into the more rigorous inquiry of social science. For example, Urs Peter Ruf of the University of Bielefeld in Germany has documented the evolution of master-slave relations in modern Mauritania. Louise Brown of the University of Birmingham in England has studied women forced into prostitution in Asia. David Kyle of the University of California at Davis and Rey Koslowski of Rutgers University have explored human smuggling. I have posited a theory of global slavery and tested it through case studies in five countries.

A common question is why these practices should be called slavery rather than just another form of superexploitation. The answer is simple. Throughout history, slavery has meant a loss of free will and choice backed up by violence, sometimes exercised by the slaveholder, sometimes by elements of the state. That is exactly what other researchers and I have observed. Granted, workers at the bottom of the economic ladder have few options to begin with, but at some point on the continuum of ex-

ploitation, even those options are lost. These workers are unable to walk away.

> Throughout HISTORY, slavery has meant a loss of free will and choice backed up by VIOLENCE, sometimes exercised by the slaveholder, sometimes by elements of the state.

Human suffering comes in various guises, yet slavery has a distinctive horror that is evident to those of us who have seen it in the flesh. Even when it does not involve beating or other physical torture, it brings about a psychological degradation that often renders victims unable to function in the outside world. "I've worked in prisons and with cases of domestic violence," says Sydney Lytton, an American psychiatrist who has counseled freed slaves. "This is worse."

Although each of the manifestations of slavery has unique local characteristics, one of the aims of social scientists is to understand their universal features, so that therapies developed in one place can be applied elsewhere. Foremost among these commonalities is the basic economic equation. In 1850 an agricultural slave cost $1,500 in Alabama (around $30,000 in today's dollars). The equivalent laborer can be had for around $100 today. That payment might be made as part of a "loan" or as a "fee" to a trafficker. A young woman in Southeast Asia or eastern Europe might be sold several times, through a series of brokers and pimps, before she ends up in a brothel.

One should not read too much into these specific dollar amounts, because what the slaveholder purchases is somewhat different in each case. The basic point is that forced labor represents a much smaller percentage of business expenses than it used to. It took 20 years of labor for an antebellum American slave to repay his or her purchase price and maintenance costs; today it takes two years for a bonded laborer in South Asia to do the same. This fall in price has altered not only the profitability of slavery but also the relationship between slave and master. The expensive slave of the past was a protected investment; today's slave is a cheap and disposable input to low-level production. The slaveholder has little incentive to provide health care or to take care of slaves who are past their prime. Several trends could account for this shift. The world's population has tripled since World War II, producing a glut of potential slaves. Meanwhile the economic transformation of the developing world has, whatever its benefits, included the loss of community and social safety nets, matched by the erection of vast shantytowns. But the vulnerability of large numbers of people does not make them slaves; for that, you need violence. The key factor in the persistence of slavery is the weak rule of law in many regions. Widespread corruption of government and police allows violence to be used with impunity even when slavery is nominally illegal.

Free Your Mind Instead

A SECOND COMMONALITY among different forms of slavery is the psychological manipulation they all involve. The widely held conception of a slave is someone in chains who would escape if given half a chance or who simply does not know better. But Meera's and Baldev's stories, among numerous others, suggest that this view is naive. In my experience, slaves often know that their enslavement is illegal. Force, violence and psychological coercion have convinced them to accept it. When slaves begin to accept their role and identify with their master, constant physical bondage becomes unnecessary. They come to perceive their situation not as a deliberate action taken to harm them in particular but as part of the normal, if regrettable, scheme of things.

One young woman I met in northeastern Thailand, Siri, has a typical story. A woman approached her parents, offered to find their 14-year-old daughter a job, and advanced them 50,000 baht (at the time, about $2,000) against her future income. The broker transferred Siri to a low-end brothel for twice that sum. When she tried to escape, her debt was doubled again. She was told to repay it, as well as a monthly rent of 30,000 baht, from her earnings of 100 baht per customer.

Siri had little idea what it meant to be a prostitute. Her initiation took the form of assault and rape. Shattered, the teenager had to find a way to carry on with life. In the world in which she lived, there were only those with total power and those with no power. Reward and punishment came from a single source, the pimp. Young women in Siri's position often find building a relationship with the pimp to be a good survival strategy. Although pimps are thugs, they do not rely solely on violence. They are adept at fostering insecurity and dependence.

Cultural norms have prepared these young women for control and compliance. A girl will be told how her parents will suffer if she does not cooperate and work hard, how the debt is on her shoulders and must be repaid. Thai sex roles are clearly defined, and women are expected to be retiring, nonassertive and obedient—as the women are repeatedly reminded. The pimps also cite religion. The young women are encouraged to believe that they must have committed terrible sins in a past life to deserve their enslavement and abuse. They are urged to accept this karmic debt, to come to terms with it and to reconcile themselves to their fate.

To live in slavery, the young women often redefine their bondage as a duty or a job or a form of penance. To accept their role and the pimp's, they must try to diminish their view of themselves as victims who have been wronged. They must begin to see their enslavement from the point of view of the slaveholder. At the time of my visit, the women in Siri's brothel were at various stages in this process of submission. Some were even allowed to visit their families during holidays, for they always came back.

A similar psychology operates in a different form of slavery, one that involves domestic servants that African and Asian diplomats and business executives have brought with them to Europe and North America. As an employee of the Committee against Modern Slavery, Cristina Talens worked for several years to free and rehabilitate domestic slaves who had been brought to Paris. She told me that liberating the body was much easier than freeing the mind:

> In spite of the violence, and the living and working conditions, people in slavery have their own mental integrity and their own mechanisms for surviving. Some may actually like different aspects of their life, perhaps the security or their understanding of the order of things. When you disrupt this order, suddenly everything is confused. Some of the women who were freed have attempted suicide. It is easy to assume that this happened because of the abuse they had lived through. But for some of these women, slavery had been the major psychological building block in their lives. When that was destroyed, the meaning of their life was like a bit of paper crushed up and thrown away. They were told: "No, this is not the way it is supposed to be. Start all over again." It was as though their life had no meaning.

Plausible Deniability

THE PSYCHOLOGY OF THE SLAVE is mirrored by that of the slaveholder. Slavery is not a simple matter of one person holding another by force; it is an insidious mutual dependence that is remarkably difficult for slaveholder as well as slave to break out of. Branding the slaveholder as pure evil may in some way comfort us, but maintaining that definition becomes difficult when one meets actual slave masters.

Almost all the slaveholders I have met and interviewed in Pakistan, India, Brazil and Mauritania were family men who thought of themselves simply as businessmen. Pillars of the local community, they were well rewarded financially, well integrated socially, and well connected legally and politically. Their slaveholding was not seen as a social handicap except, possibly, by "outsiders" who, they felt, misunderstood the local customs of business and labor.

How is it that such nice men do such bad things? A government official in Baldev's district who held bonded workers was frank about his slaveholding:

> Of course I have bonded laborers: I'm a landlord. I keep them and their families, and they work for me. When they aren't in the fields, I have them doing the household work washing clothes, cooking, cleaning, making repairs, everything. After all, they are from the Kohl caste; that's what they do, work for Vaisyas like me. I give them food and a little land to work. They've also borrowed money, so I have to make sure that they stay on my land till it is paid back. They will work on my farm till it is all paid back. I don't care how old they get; you can't just give money away!
>
> After all, there is nothing wrong in keeping bonded labor. They benefit from the system, and so do I. Even if agriculture is completely mechanized, I'll still keep my bonded laborers. You see, the way we do it, I am like a father to these workers. It is a father-son rela-

tionship; I protect them and guide them. Of course, sometimes I have to discipline them as well, just as a father would.

Other slaveholders also have told me that their slaves are like their children, that they need close control and care. They make the argument of tradition: because the practice has been going on for so long, it must be the natural order of things. For others, it is a simple question of priorities: they say that enslaving people is unfortunate but that their own family's welfare depends on it. Often slaveholders have interposed many layers of management between themselves and the slaves. They purposely deny themselves the knowledge of what they are doing and thus the responsibility for it.

Forty Acres and a Mule

ALL THIS POINTS to the need for a highly developed system of rehabilitation for freed slaves and slaveholders alike. Physical freedom is not enough. When slaves were emancipated in the U.S. in 1865, the government enacted no such rehabilitation. General William Tecumseh Sherman's promise to give each former slave "forty acres and a mule" never materialized. The result was four million people dumped into a shattered economy without resources and with few legal protections. It can be argued that America is still suffering from this liberation without rehabilitation.

Human-rights worker Vivek Pandit of the Vidhayak Sansad organization in India has been liberating bonded laborers for more than 20 years. He is adamant that real liberation takes place in the mind, that physical freedom isn't enough—as was the case with Baldev. Conversely, mental freedom can bring about physical freedom—as it did for Meera.

> SALVERY is not a simple matter of one person holding another by force; it is an insidious MUTUAL DEPENDENCE that is remarkably difficult to break out of.

Pandit's organization has devised a program of education that prepares former bonded laborers for a life of freedom. They are taught basic science to promote their curiosity and attention to detail; role-playing to stimulate problem solving; and games to develop strategic thinking and teamwork. This training comes after a challenging public dialogue in which the laborer recounts and renounces his or her bondage. The renunciation is recorded and read out in the village. "When the ex-slave has fixed his thumbprint to this public document," Pandit says, "they can't go back."

Several models of liberation and rehabilitation are currently being field-tested. [*Editors' note: Visit* www.sciam.com/explorations/2002/031102gabon *for a case study of a program in Gabon.*] The experience of these programs suggests that a combination of economic support, counseling and education can lead to stable, sustainable freedom. This kind of work is still in its early stages, though. No systematic evaluations of these programs have been carried out. No social scientist has explored a master-slave relationship in depth.

Slave economics are another puzzle. How can would-be liberators crack the dark economy and trace the slave-made products to our homes? Why are such large numbers of people being trafficked across continents, how many of these people really are enslaved, and why are these flows apparently increasing? What is the impact of this workforce on national economies? What are the links among the traffic in people, drugs and guns?

Studying bondage can be socially and politically controversial. Researchers in the field face numerous ethical dilemmas, and clarity and objectivity are all the more difficult to achieve when individuals and governments seek to conceal what they are doing. If there is good news, it is the growing recognition of the problem. The plight of enslaved child workers has drawn significantly increased funding, and new partnerships between antislavery organizations and industries that use slave-made commodities provide an innovative model for abolition. But if our figures are correct, only a small fraction of slaves are reached and freed every year. Our ignorance of their hidden world is vast.

KEVIN BALES is a professor of sociology at the University of Surrey Roehampton in London. He is a trustee of Anti-Slavery International and a consultant to the United Nations Global Program on Trafficking of Human Beings, to the Economic Community of West African States, and to the U.S., British, Irish, Norwegian and Nepali governments. Bales began studying slavery in the early 1990s, when few Westerneres realized it still existed. Unable to secure funding for his research, he took on a commercial research project and devoted the profits to travel. The outcome—his book *Disposable People*—was nominated for the Pulitzer Prize in 2000. His work won the Premio Viareggio for services to humanity in 2000, and a television documentary based on it (shown on HBO and on Britain's Channel 4) won a Peabody Award in 2000.

Egypt's Young and Restless

Knight sketches how ordinary lives are lived in a culture that Americans have largely ignored—until they learned recently to regard virtually all Arab culture with fear and suspicion. Her focus was to understand Egyptian concerns: to learn how Egyptians were facing up to universal questions about access to high-quality education, women's evolving social roles, and career development; and to find out how their deeply held religious beliefs affect their interaction with the world at large.

By Mary Knight

Through Islam and the Internet, a new generation seeks its fair share.

Osama 'Abd al-Raheem studies engineering at Helwan University, in the southern suburbs of Cairo. He is committed to his studies, and, like most young adults, he aspires to marry, to find a decent job that puts his hard-won skills to good use, to live a fulfilling life with his family, his friends, his culture, his country. But he looks with envy on those who are fifteen or twenty years older, who were able to buy homes and furnish them during the long-vanished days of easy money. When we talked, he expressed his frustration: "If a young man takes a job in Egypt, his salary will be about 500 Egyptian pounds [less than $100] per month, so he will have to work ten years to get married; if he goes abroad, he can get married much sooner."

The disadvantage Osama must live with is that going abroad today is not the solution it was for young men twenty or more years ago. In the 1970s and 1980s, when the prospects at home were little better than they are today, Egyptian laborers, mostly male, traveled to the oil-rich Gulf states and nearby Libya for work. The income they brought or sent back home enhanced living standards for many families. Overall, in fact, poverty declined.

Then, with the collapse of OPEC's power and the crisis brought on by the 1991 Gulf War, many would-be Egyptian migrants had little choice but to stay home. For men, the blow was particularly harsh: often they could find no work in their fields of study, and what little money they did earn was not enough for the down payment on an apartment, a prerequisite for marriage. For Osama, the foreign safety valve has closed shut.

Many young Americans can probably empathize with Osama's plight. Ambitious, highly educated graduates are often thrust, when they first enter the workforce, into low-paying and exhausting dead-end jobs, just to make ends meet. But the situation in Egypt is far more desperate than it is in the United States. With 72 million people, Egypt is the most populous of the twenty-two Arab states. Officially the nation's unemployment rate is only about 9 percent. Studies that specifically track youth unemployment, however—in a nation where the median age is twenty—estimate that 25 percent of men and 59 percent

of women are without work. As in the U.S., these studies include only people who are actively seeking a job, and part-time workers are considered employed.

Unemployment, though, is only one way to understand the plight of the young people in this large Arab country. Another set of critical issues is the distribution of power—which in Egypt largely coincides with the distribution of wealth—and the perception that the distribution is unjust. The class difference is rarely discussed as such, but it is certainly noticed, and it plays a major role in gaining access to such basic social services as technical training. Social gaps everywhere—between rich and poor, young and old, educated and illiterate, urbanite and farmer—reinforce the corrosive perception that the society does not reward its citizens on merit alone. The resounding cries by youth of "it's unfair" often turn on income disparity.

Among those whose voices are raised are the Islamic militants, many of whom are men from relatively privileged backgrounds, familiar with Western ways. What often incites their anger is seeing their parents operate on principles other than those of idealistic fairness. And when these young men meet other, less privileged people who have substantial talents and abilities that are passed over by the likes of their parents, their outrage may grow to conspiratorial proportions. Last fall I traveled to Cairo, a city where I've lived and worked on and off since 1994. Because I have many friends and contacts there and am reasonably fluent in the language, I was in a good position to take the pulse of the so-called Arab street.

My aim was to sketch how ordinary lives are lived in a culture that Americans have largely ignored—ignored, that is, until they "learned" recently to regard virtually all Arab culture with fear and suspicion. The immediate questions that dog my fellow Americans—Why do they hate us? What do they think of our policies?—were not my first priority, though. My focus was to understand Egyptian concerns; to learn how Egyptians were facing up to universal questions about access to high-quality education, women's evolving social roles, and career development; and to find out how their deeply held religious beliefs affect their interaction with the world at large.

At the root of Egypt's dismal unemployment statistics are the nation's weakness in the production and dissemination of knowledge and the government's inadequate commitment to science and technology. Yet there is tremendous energy and enthusiasm for learning among Egyptian students. Every young person I spoke with acknowledged the need for job-related computer skills and for better access to information in a country where libraries are only now becoming more widely accessible.

The Ministry of Education likewise recognizes the need for computer skills, and so it has provided every public school in Egypt with at least one computer, and occasionally more than one. But school enrollments usually number in the hundreds, and the presence of one or two computers normally restricts usage to demonstrations by teachers at the front of the class. Perhaps even more detrimental is the lack of functioning, up-to-date laboratory apparatus in science education. Osama 'Abd al-Raheem and several of his friends told me that as many as sixty students typically crowd around their professor as he performs experiments for the class. The reason is that nearly all of the aging equipment is broken. "The classes are crowded," he says, "so it's hard for the students to understand. So we just memorize the lessons." Memorization is still the preferred method of learning in all disciplines, but in the sciences, the near total lack of hands-on experimental work suppresses the critical and creative skills needed to excel.

Painfully aware that their futures rest on the successful use of mouse and keyboard, Egyptian young people seek out the new technology. Cybercafés and computer training institutes now abound throughout Cairo, though all charge relatively high fees. Industrious youths save up the 2,000 to 3,000 Egyptian pounds (between $400 and $600) needed for a computer, then add peripherals, often secondhand, as their budgets permit. In the past few years, Egypt's relatively open society has helped the country surpass most of the rich Gulf states in factors that measure computer-related growth. Internet connections, for instance, are now free, though the phone charges, which are based on the amount of time spent online, are relatively expensive. That said, the percentage of all Egyptians who have ever accessed the Internet remains in the single digits.

Among those energetically devoting themselves to improving the lot of young people are what are coming to be called the "new Islamists"—Muslims who believe their primary duty is to live exemplary lives and thereby improve the community. (By contrast, militants strive first to rid the world of disbelievers, condoning violence in the process.) Hosam Muhammad, a sturdily built twenty-nine-year-old, and his colleague Hisham Muhammad, a fine-boned, quiet-mannered twenty-three-year-old, both teach English in al-Nozha Language School, a clean and orderly Islamic school on the northeastern outskirts of Cairo. The school serves about a thousand students, from kindergarten through high school. Both men use the Internet to enhance their knowledge and to make friends with English speakers around the world, particularly in the U.S.

In their jackets and ties, dress slacks, and polished shoes, the two Arabs, one clean-shaven and the other wearing a neatly trimmed beard, look like refined, educated young professionals anywhere. Polite and modest, they laugh readily and banter charmingly, in English or in Arabic. And both strongly maintain that Islam has a transformative, restorative power for their society. In the classroom they teach values through example, as a way to complement their curriculum of intensive language training. Their ultimate jihad is to push their students along the path to a better future, both economically and morally.

Another "new Islamist" is 'Abd al-Hafiz al-Sayyid Muhammad, the imam, or chief religious leader, at Omar Makram Mosque in downtown Cairo. In 1995, recognizing the need for knowledge and the traditional role of the mosque in education, 'Abd al-Hafiz initiated computer courses in rooms above the prayer hall, diverting some of the mosque's funding to the purchase of computers. (Literacy classes were already in place, for men and women.) Students—more than a thousand a year—flocked to the innovative program, not only to learn computer skills but also to learn English and a variety of vocational skills.

Women like Nermeen 'Abd al-Tawab, a vivacious twenty-eight-year-old at the University of Cairo's Faculty of Agriculture, exemplify another vibrant part of Egypt's young generation. Her specialization, agricultural research, is one of the few bright spots in Egyptian science, perhaps because 44 percent of Egyptian workers are employed in agriculture. She studies the fungal infection white rot in garlic. White rot has important economic consequences, because it often devastates the bulbs as the garlic goes to market. As part of her doctoral research, Nermeen is applying the tools of biotechnology to develop garlic that is resistant to the virus. Thus occupied, she is postponing marriage until she finds someone she loves and respects. Her family supports her plan completely.

Compared with urbanites, girls from rural areas are apt to find less family support for their education, particularly when one or both of their parents are illiterate. Rural parents encourage their daughters to marry at earlier ages, even if that means marrying a first cousin (usually not a girl's preference). But in Cairo education is a lifeline for many females, giving them hope and freedom no matter how humble (or how high) their origins. While they are in school, they don't have to compete for jobs that are unlikely to be offered to them anyway. And if they enjoy studies, they have the chance to learn more than any of their predecessors and to be respected for their achievements.

The social barriers to women in Egypt are by no means as stringent as they are in Muslim countries that impose a strict interpretation of Islamic law. Some Egyptian women even initiate divorce.

Mai Mostafa, a tall, slender thirty-two-year-old designer and artist, elaborated on the hazards of poor mate selection and divorce: "For every woman who lives in the East, marriage is very important. We've been brought up prepared to become wives later. We have a saying that the woman who dares to ask for a divorce helps the house collapse." Mai's father encouraged her to complete her education and to work for a few years, to become independent-minded and self-reliant. He did not exactly approve of her marriage partner, but assured her of his confidence in any choice she made. After the marriage failed, Mai was grateful that, again, her father supported her decision to get divorced.

In spite of the recognition of the need, attempts to establish world-class research and educational institutes in Egypt have foundered. Ahmed Zewail of the California Institute of Technology in Pasadena, the Egyptian-American who won the 1999 Nobel Prize in Chemistry, convinced the government to build a state-of-the-art university for science and technology. More than four years after the ground-breaking ceremony, however, his dream has yet to be realized.

For most young people, then, the only option is to leave the country, a choice that simply exacerbates the already pernicious brain drain. One student I met in Egypt two years ago, who received a grant to study in a computer sciences department at a U.S. university in the Midwest, assured me he would return to Egypt after completing his Ph.D. program. When I spoke with him more recently, he was equally fervent in his insistence that he has no plans to return. The reason? In the U.S. he can do research that builds on the latest developments and can produce work others will draw on. He'll stay in the loop, rather than outside it.

According to the 2003 Arab Human Development Report of the United Nations Development Programme, the uneven distribution of income is a critical obstacle to reform and progress. Estimates of extreme poverty in Egypt range from 30 to 40 percent of the population, much of it concentrated in the rural areas, where about 55 percent of the people live. In Cairo, perhaps 20 percent are truly poor; the vast majority of people are of modest means and must rely on free social services and education to improve their lot in life.

But their options are severely restricted. For example, on the basis of their grade on the *thanawiyya 'amma*, a single national test given at the end of secondary school, young people are assigned a profession, such as physician, accountant, tour guide, and so on. High scorers have the right to choose a "lesser" profession than the one they qualify for, but they normally don't, because of the social stigma attached.

Nor do they have the option of taking a year off to think about career choices. Young people entitled to go on to higher education are assigned to a university, which often involves a two-hour daily commute in each direction (and studying is nearly impossible on the overcrowded buses or trains).

None of these problems exist, of course, for the tiny minority of people who have money. The influence of wealth only begins at school; it extends to the upper echelons in all walks of life, a fact that has provoked widespread concern. In particular, the unfairness of the yawning gulf between the haves and the have-nots has engendered the outrage that has led Islamic militants to pursue their restrictive interpretation of religious law. But in conversations with militants from both modest and privileged backgrounds, I have heard a common theme: many militants would relinquish their arms if the laws already in existence were applied fairly and equally.

A comparison to the U.S. youth movement of the late 1960s and early 1970s—when, similarly, supersize cohorts of impatient, idealistic young people felt largely left out of the political process—is tempting. No, Egyptian youth are not staging sit-ins and crashing the gates of the political arena. But the reason they aren't may have more to do with the class barrier and the skewed demographics of sitting politicians than any lack of political will. A substantial number of Egyptian ministers are more than sixty-five years old, belonging to an age group that makes up just 2.2 percent of the population. Most youths cannot visualize themselves in positions of power. What they hope for is that someone they trust, whether judge or religious leader or someone else in tune with their needs, will demand and achieve for them the fairness that, in principle, the law asserts.

Although the government seems little moved by the youth crisis, there are promising signs of reform through the youth committee of the ruling National Democratic Party (NDP). The committee's head, Mohamed M. Kamal, is especially encouraged that though nearly 70 percent of the population is under thirty, qualified people are finding work in the private sector.

Leading citizens have also initiated projects not only through Islamic institutions but also through governmental and nongovernmental organizations (NGOs), and many of these reform efforts target the young. Approximately 16,000 NGOs now respond to the needs of civil society in Egypt. "We have proven as Egyptians, as Arabs, as Muslims that we can be very successful," asserts Hesham Dinana, a hard-driving thirty-nine-year-old engineer overseeing construction of a new children's cancer hospital in Cairo (it is dubbed Hospital 57357, after the number of the bank account that takes donations). Hesham spent more than a dozen years climbing the corporate ladder in the U.S. before returning to Egypt to contribute to this "people's project." With donations from across the classes, the cancer hospital, probably the largest NGO in Egypt, is proof that the Egyptian people are willing to share the burden to reduce the epidemic of childhood cancers.

Many young people do express hope for the future. Perhaps the most unusual source of optimism for the young is the media. Egyptian national television, long dominated by the monotonous recitation of news briefs and a parade of sleepy soap operas, faces a challenge in attracting the youth, who have turned to the satellite channel al-Jazeera, based in Qatar. Hussein 'Abd el-Ghani, Bureau Chief of al-Jazeera's Cairo office, boasts that the satellite channel "is the first reliable source of news for the young," and it is now the most-watched station among the youth of Egypt, according to the results of a recent survey. Young people told me they like its edgy style, its fast pace, and its no-sacred-cows approach to topics and people. Not only advertisers should be pleased by the numbers, because it's getting young people to think about politics, talk openly and critically about national and international events, and realize they deserve a place in shaping their nation's future. Although provocative for the region, al-Jazeera helps release some of the frustration felt by Egyptian youth. And it affirms their identity as young, strong, and Arab.

Mary Knight's interest in the lives of contemporary Egyptians was sparked during her tenure as a Fulbright scholar in 1994-95, studying the geography of ancient Egypt at 'Ain Shams University in Cairo. While pursuing that research, she also completed a study of the practice of female genital mutilation in antiquity, a project that led to discussions with modern Egyptians on how the practice is viewed today. Knight is a visiting scholar at New York University, and is co-editing a book on nudity in the ancient Mediterranean World.

The Surprises of Suicide Terrorism

It's not a new phenomenon, and natural selection may play a role in producing it

Josie Glausiusz

SCOTT ATRAN FELL IN LOVE with anthropology in 1970 when he went to work with Margaret Mead at the American Museum of Natural History in New York and found himself surrounded by a collection of thousands of skulls. He has spent the intervening years studying human cultures all over the world, dwelling among the secretive Druze sect in Israel, documenting conservation customs among the Maya of Guatemala, and analyzing the evolution of religion everywhere, a topic he explores in his book *In Gods We Trust*. He is based both at the National Center for Scientific Research in Paris and at the University of Michigan. His recent work has focused on suicide terrorism. He has marshaled evidence that indicates suicide bombers are not poor and crazed as depicted in the press but well-educated and often economically stable individuals with no significant psychological pathology.

Why should suicide terrorism be the object of scientific investigation?

A: Within a few days of the terrorist attacks of September 11, 2001, I started listening to the stuff that was being said in the media and by the Bush administration. I thought, "What utter nonsense"—this idea that these people were crazed or they're doing it out of despair or hopelessness. The whole history of these kinds of acts goes against this. I decided to write an article and get it into the scientific press, because governments, I believe, would take up what their scientists tell them, since there is a huge respect for science.

Why is this terrorist stereotype nonsense?

A: The CIA released a report in 2001 on the psychology and sociology of terrorism, and they basically said suicide bombers are perfectly sane. If you look at the history of these kinds of extreme acts, they're usually directed by middle-class or higher-middle-class intellectuals. They always have been. Never have they been directed by wacky, crazed, homicidal nuts. The Japanese kamikaze were, by the way, extremely intelligent guys. If you read their diaries, they were German romantics, reading Goethe and Schiller, and quite conscious of the efforts of the state to manipulate them.

What scientific research supports the notion that suicide bombers are sane?

A: Some of the earlier research was by Ariel Merari, who is a psychologist at Tel Aviv University and also a terrorism expert. He interviewed suicide bombers—survivors who were wounded and didn't die or whose bombs didn't go off—as well as their families or recruiters. Like most psychologists in the 1980s, he thought that this was individual pathology, like the idea that racists come from fatherless families. He made a 180-degree turn and found out that no, the bombers span the normal distribution and were slightly above it in terms of education and income. Nasra Hassan, a Pakistani relief worker working in Gaza for a number of years, interviewed about 250 family members, recruiters, and survivors, completely independently. She found exactly the same thing. Alan Krueger, an economist at Princeton University, has done long-term studies with Hezbollah and Hamas. His findings show that although one-third of Palestinians live in poverty, only 13 percent of Palestinian suicide bombers do; 57 percent of bombers have education beyond high school versus 15 percent of the population of comparable age. The Defense Intelligence Agency gave me profiles of all these people they were interrogating at Guantánamo Bay in Cuba. They divide them into Yemenis and Saudis. The Yemenis are sort of the foot soldiers. They found that the Saudis, their leaders especially, are from high-status families. A surprising number have graduate degrees. And they are willing to give up everything. They give up well-paying jobs, they give up their families, whom they really adore, to sacrifice themselves because they really believe that it's the only way they're going to change the world.

What's the profile of a suicide terrorist?

A: Generally, it's not someone who is off the wall—that kind of individual can't be an effective killer. Usually it is someone who is smart, who shows a willingness to give up something, who is patient, who is quiet—competent people who don't draw attention to themselves, and who are perfectly willing and able to meld into society.

How does anyone in their right mind work up the gumption to blow themselves up?

A: Exactly the same way that you get soldiers on the front line of an army to sacrifice themselves for their buddies. What these terrorist cells do is very similar to what our military, or any modern military, does. They form small groups of intimately involved "brothers" who literally sacrifice themselves for one another, the way a mother would for her child. They do it by manipulating universal, heartfelt human sentiments that I think are probably innate and part of biological evolution. In the case of something like Al Qaeda, you've got these people in groups of three to eight people for 18 months, isolated from their families, getting this intense and deep ego-stroking propaganda. You do that to anyone and you'll get them to do what you want.

You suggest that natural selection may be playing a role in generating the feelings that enable people to become suicide terrorists, but blowing yourself up is hardly a good strategy for propelling your genes into the next generation.

A: Natural selection gives us all sorts of dispositions and desires that were adaptive in ancestral environments. Now, our cultural milieu picks certain of these adaptations or their byproducts and is able to trigger them to produce behaviors that have nothing to do with what they originally evolved for. Kin altruism [the theory that individuals are willing to sacrifice their lives to save closely related kin] evolved through natural selection. If you listen to most political and religious discourse in societies, it's always done for a brotherhood—brothers and sisters. So you create a fictive family. How else are you going to get people to die for one another when they're non-kin-related? You've got to trick them into believing they are kin-related somehow.

What's the cause of suicide terrorism?

A: As a tactical weapon, it emerges when an ideologically devoted people find that they cannot possibly obtain their ends in a sort of fair fight, and when they know they're in a very weak position

Why does it matter whether we understand them?

A: There were all these harebrained schemes—they're still around—to have things like a Radio Free Arabia, bombarding these people with information about how good our society is, and that's supposed to win the war

on terrorism. If you look at the February 2003 "National Strategy for Combating Terrorism," you'll see the U.S. government plans to introduce programs against poverty and illiteracy. These ideas seem completely wrong. First, the people who carry out terrorist acts are already educated. Second, they're not poor, so reducing poverty isn't going to do a thing.

So what's your strategy?

A: I think it has to be multilayered. You've got to be able to—and this I'm all for—go after the guys who operate the cells. Jail them or kill them, because they're not willing to compromise. Another thing is to protect some of the vulnerable targets, but I think that is actually less important than trying to stop this phenomenon from becoming adopted, like a sort of virus. How do you get the people themselves to stop harboring the suicide terrorists? You've got to talk with them. You've got to address their grievances. Alan Krueger found that lack of civil liberties is a predictor of where you'll find suicide terrorism. When you don't give these people any political space to express themselves, they become radicalized.

In your book *In Gods We Trust*, you call religion an "evolutionary riddle." Why?

A: All religions require costly sacrifices that have no material rewards. Look at the Egyptian pyramids. Millions of man-hours. For what? To house dead bones? Or cathedrals. Or just going to church every Sunday and gesticulating. Or saying a Latin or Hebrew prayer, mumbling what are to many people incoherent words. Look at the things that religion is said to do. It is said to relieve people's anxieties, but it's also said to increase their anxieties so that elites can use them for political purposes. It's supposed to encourage creativity. It's supposed to stop creativity. It's supposed to explain events that can't be explained. It's supposed to prevent people from explaining them. You can find functional explanations, and their contraries, and they're all true.

Why, then, has religion managed to survive in so many cultures around the world?

A: Because humans are faced with problems they can't solve, like death. Another problem is deception. For commonsense physical events, we have ways of verifying what's real or not. For moral judgments, we have nothing. If that is so, how are people, especially non-kin, ever going to get on with one another? How are they ever going to build societies, and how are they ever going to trust one another so they won't defect? One way that humans seem to have come up with is to invent this counterintuitive world developed by these deities, who are like big brothers who watch over us and make sure that there will be no defectors.

Do you think science will ever replace religion?

A: Never. Because it doesn't solve any of the problems that religion solves, like death or deception. There is no society that survives more than a generation or two that isn't religiously based—even the Soviet Union, where half the people were religious. Thomas Jefferson's unitarian God fell by the wayside. So did the French Revolution's neutral deity. People want a personal God, for obvious reasons, to solve personal problems.

An extended version of the Discover Dialogue is available online at www.discover.com.

Alcohol in the Western World

*The role of alcohol in Western civilization has changed dramatically during this millennium.
Our current medical interpretation of alcohol as primarily an agent of
disease comes after a more complex historical relationship.*

By Bert L. Vallee

A substance, like a person, may have distinct and even contradictory aspects to its personality. Today ethyl alcohol, the drinkable species of alcohol, is a multifaceted entity; it may be social lubricant, sophisticated dining companion, cardiovascular health benefactor or agent of destruction. Throughout most of Western civilization's history, however, alcohol had a far different role. For most of the past 10 millennia, alcoholic beverages may have been the most popular and common daily drinks, indispensable sources of fluids and calories. In a world of contaminated and dangerous water supplies, alcohol truly earned the title granted it in the Middle Ages: *aqua vitae,* the "water of life."

Potent evidence exists to open a window into a societal relationship with alcohol that is simply unimaginable today. Consider this statement, issued in 1777 by Prussia's Frederick the Great, whose economic strategy was threatened by importation of coffee: "It is disgusting to notice the increase in the quantity of coffee used by my subjects, and the amount of money that goes out of the country as a consequence. Everybody is using coffee; this must be prevented. His Majesty was brought up on beer; and so were both his ancestors and officers. Many battles have been fought and won by soldiers nourished on beer, and the King does not believe that coffee-drinking soldiers can be relied upon to endure hardships in case of another war."

Surely a modern leader who urged alcohol consumption over coffee, especially by the military, would have his or her mental competence questioned. But only an eyeblink ago in historical time, a powerful head of government could describe beer in terms that make it sound like mother's milk. And indeed, that nurturing role may be the one alcohol played from the infancy of the West to the advent of safe water supplies for the masses only within the past century.

Natural processes have no doubt produced foodstuffs containing alcohol for millions of years. Yeast, in metabolizing sugar to obtain energy, creates ethyl alcohol as a by-product of its efforts. Occasionally animals acciden-tally consume alcohol that came into being as fruit "spoiled" in the natural process of fermentation; inebriated birds and mammals have been reported. Humans have a gene for the enzyme alcohol dehydrogenase; the presence of this gene at least forces the conjecture that over evolutionary time animals have encountered alcohol enough to have evolved a way to metabolize it. Ingestion of alcohol, however, was unintentional or haphazard for humans until some 10,000 years ago.

About that time, some Late Stone Age gourmand probably tasted the contents of a jar of honey that had been left unattended longer than usual. Natural fermentation had been given the opportunity to occur, and the taster, finding the effects of mild alcohol ingestion provocative, probably replicated the natural experiment. Comrades and students of this first oenologist then codified the method for creating such mead or wines from honey or dates or sap. The technique was fairly simple: leave the sweet substance alone to ferment.

Beer, which relies on large amounts of starchy grain, would wait until the origin and development of agriculture. The fertile river deltas of Egypt and Mesopotamia produced huge crops of wheat and barley; the diets of peasants, laborers and soldiers of these ancient civilizations were cereal-based. It might be viewed as a historical inevitability that fermented grain would be discovered. As in the instance of wine, natural experiments probably produced alcoholic substances that aroused the interest of those who sampled the results. Before the third millennium B.C., Egyptians and Babylonians were drinking beers made from barley and wheat.

Wine, too, would get a boost from agriculture. Most fruit juice, even wild grape juice, is naturally too low in sugar to produce wine, but the selection for sweeter grapes leading to the domestication of particular grape stock eventually led to viniculture. The practice of growing grape strains suitable for wine production has been credited to people living in what is now Armenia, at about 6000 B.C., although such dating is educated guesswork at best.

The creation of agriculture led to food surpluses, which in turn led to ever larger groups of people living in close quarters, in villages or cities. These municipalities faced a problem that still vexes, namely, how to provide inhabitants with enough clean, pure water to sustain their constant need for physiological hydration. The solution, until the 19th century, was nonexistent. The water supply of any group of people rapidly became polluted with their waste products and thereby dangerous, even fatal, to drink. How many of our progenitors died attempting to quench their thirst with water can never be known. Based on current worldwide crises of dysentery and infectious disease wrought by unclean water supplies, a safe bet is that a remarkably large portion of our ancestry succumbed to tainted water.

In addition, the lack of liquids safe for human consumption played a part in preventing long-range ocean voyages until relatively recently. Christopher Columbus made his voyage with wine on board, and the Pilgrims landed at Plymouth Rock only because their beer stores had run out. An early order of business was luring brewmasters to the colonies.

Alcohol versus Water

Negative evidence arguing against a widespread use of water for drinking can be found in perusal of the Bible and ancient Greek texts. Both the Old and New Testaments are virtually devoid of references to water as a common human beverage. Likewise, Greek writings make scant reference to water drinking, with the notable exception of positive statements regarding the quality of water from mountain springs. Hippocrates specifically cited water from springs and deep wells as safe, as was rainwater collected in cisterns. The ancients, through what must have been tragic experience, clearly understood that most of their water supply was unfit for human consumption.

In this context of contaminated water supply, ethyl alcohol may indeed have been mother's milk to a nascent Western civilization. Beer and wine were free of pathogens. And the antiseptic power of alcohol, as well as the natural acidity of wine and beer, killed many pathogens when the alcoholic drinks were diluted with the sullied water supply. Dating from the taming and conscious application of the fermentation process, people of all ages in the West have therefore consumed beer and wine, not water, as their major daily thirst quenchers.

Babylonian clay tablets more than 6,000 years old give beer recipes, complete with illustrations. The Greek *akratidzomai*, which came to mean "to breakfast," literally translates as "to drink undiluted wine." Breakfast apparently could include wine as a bread dip, and "bread and beer" connoted basic necessity much as does today's expression "bread and butter."

The experience in the East differed greatly. For at least the past 2,000 years, the practice of boiling water, usually for tea, has created a potable supply of nonalcoholic beverages. In addition, genetics played an important role in making Asia avoid alcohol: approximately half of all Asian people lack an enzyme necessary for complete alcohol metabolism, making the experience of drinking quite unpleasant. Thus, beer and wine took their place as staples only in Western societies and remained there until the end of the last century.

The traditional production of beer and wine by fermentation of cereals and grapes or other fruits produced beverages with low alcohol content compared with those familiar to present-day consumers. The beverages also contained large amounts of acetic acid and other organic acids created during fermentation. Most wines of ancient times probably would turn a modern oenophile's nose; those old-style wines in new bottles would more closely resemble today's vinegar, with some hints of cider, than a prizewinning merlot.

As the alcohol content of daily staple drinks was low, consumers focused on issues of taste, thirst quenching, hunger satisfaction and storage rather than on intoxication. Nevertheless, the "side effects" of this constant, low-level intake must have been almost universal. Indeed, throughout Western history the normal state of mind may have been one of inebriation.

The caloric value of nonperishable alcoholic beverages may also have played a significant role in meeting the daily energy requirements of societies that might have faced food shortages. In addition, they provided essential micronutrients, such as vitamins and minerals.

Alcohol also served to distract from the fatigue and numbing boredom of daily life in most cultures, while alleviating pain for which remedies were nonexistent. Today people have a plethora of handy choices against common aches and pain. But until this century, the only analgesic generally available in the West was alcohol. From the Book of Proverbs comes this prescription: "Give strong drink unto him that is ready to perish, and wine unto them that be of heavy hearts. Let him drink, and forget his poverty, and remember his misery no more." A Sumerian cuneiform tablet of a pharmacopoeia dated to about 2100 B.C. is generally cited as the oldest preserved record of medicinal alcohol, although Egyptian papyri may have preceded the tablet. Hippocrates' therapeutic system featured wines as remedies for almost all acute or chronic ailments known in his time, and the Alexandrian School of Medicine supported the medical use of alcohol.

Religion and Moderation

The beverages of ancient societies may have been far lower in alcohol than their current versions, but people of the time were aware of the potentially deleterious behavioral effects of drinking. The call for temperance began quite early in Hebrew Greek and Roman cultures and was reiterated throughout history. The Old Testament frequently disapproves of drunkenness, and the prophet Ezra and his successors integrated wine into everyday Hebrew ritual, perhaps partly to moderate undisciplined drinking custom, thus creating a religiously inspired and controlled form of prohibition.

In the New Testament, Jesus obviously sanctioned alcohol consumption, resorting to miracle in the transformation of water to wine, an act that may acknowledge the goodness of alcohol versus the polluted nature of water. His followers concentrated on extending measures to balance the use and abuse of wine but never supported total prohibition. Saint Paul and other fathers of early Christianity carried on such moderating attitudes. Rather than castigating wine for its effects on sobriety, they considered it a gift from God, both for its medicinal qualities and the tranquilizing characteristics that offered relief from pain and the anxiety of daily life.

Traditionally, beer has been the drink of the common folk, whereas wine was reserved for the more affluent. Grape wine, however, became available to the average Roman after a century of vineyard expansion that ended in about 30 B.C., a boom driven by greater profits for wine grapes compared with grain. Ultimately, the increased supply drove prices down, and the common Roman could partake in wine that was virtually free. Roman viniculture declined with the empire and was inherited by the Catholic Church and its monasteries, the only institutions with sufficient resources to maintain production.

For nearly 1,300 years the Church operated the biggest and best vineyards, to considerable profit. Throughout the Middle Ages, grain remained the basic food of peasants and beer their normal beverage, along with mead and homemade wines or ciders. The few critics of alcohol consumption were stymied by the continuing simple fact of the lack of safe alternatives. Hence, despite transitions in political systems, religions and ways of life, the West's use of and opinion toward beer and wine remained remarkably unchanged. But a technological development would alter the relationship between alcohol and humanity

After perhaps 9,000 years of experience drinking relatively low alcohol mead, beer and wine, the West was faced with alcohol in a highly concentrated form, thanks to distillation. Developed in about A.D. 700 by Arab alchemists (for whom *al kohl* signified any material's basic essence), distillation brought about the first significant change in the mode and magnitude of human alcohol consumption since the beginning of Western civilization. Although yeasts produce alcohol, they can tolerate concentrations of only about 16 percent. Fermented beverages therefore had a natural maximum proof. Distillation circumvents nature's limit by taking advantage of alcohol's 78 degree Celsius (172 degree Fahrenheit) boiling point, compared with 100 degrees C for water. Boiling a water-alcohol mixture puts more of the mix's volatile alcohol than its water in the vapor. Condensing that vapor yields liquid with a much higher alcohol level than that of the starting liquid.

The Arab method—the custom of abstinence had not yet been adopted by Islam—spread to Europe, and distillation of wine to produce spirits commenced on the Continent in about A.D. 1100. The venue was the medical school at Salerno, Italy, an important center for the transfer of medical and chemical theory and methods from Asia Minor to the West. Joining the traditional alcoholic drinks of beer and wine, which had low alcohol concentration and positive nutritional benefit, were beverages with sufficient alcohol levels to cause the widespread problems still with us today. The era of distilled spirits had begun.

Knowledge of distillation gradually spread from Italy to northern Europe; the Alsatian physician Hieronymus Brunschwig described the process in 1500 in *Liber de arte distillandi*, the first printed book on distillation. By the time Brunschwig was a best-selling author, distilled alcohol had earned its split personality as nourishing food, beneficent medicine and harmful drug. The widespread drinking of spirits followed closely on the heels of the 14th century's bouts with plague, notably the Black Death of 1347–1351. Though completely ineffective as a cure for plague, alcohol did make the victim who drank it at least feel more robust. No other known agent could accomplish even that much. The medieval physician's optimism related to spirits may be attributed to this ability to alleviate pain and enhance mood, effects that must have seemed quite remarkable during a medical crisis that saw perhaps two thirds of Europe's population culled in a single generation.

Economic recovery following the subsidence of the plague throughout Europe generated new standards of luxury and increased urbanization. This age witnessed unprecedented ostentation, gluttony, self-indulgence and inebriation. Europe, apparently relieved to have survived the pestilence of the 14th century, went on what might be described as a continentwide bender. Despite the obvious negative effects of drunkenness, and despite attempts by authorities to curtail drinking, the practice continued until the beginning of the 17th century, when nonalcoholic beverages made with boiled water became popular. Coffee, tea and cocoa thus began to break alcohol's monopoly on safety.

In the 18th century a growing religious antagonism toward alcohol, fueled largely by Quakers and Methodists and mostly in Great Britain, still lacked real effect or popular support. After all, the Thames River of the time was as dangerous a source of drinking water as the polluted streams of ancient cultures. Dysentery, cholera and typhoid, all using filthy water as a vehicle, were major killers and would remain so in the West as recently as the end of the 19th century, rivaling plague in mass destruction.

Only the realization that microorganisms caused disease and the institution of filtered and treated water supplies finally made water a safe beverage in the West. Religious anti-alcohol sentiment and potable water would combine with one other factor to make it finally possible for a significant percentage of the public to turn away from alcohol. That other factor was the recognition of alcohol dependence as an illness.

Diseases of Alcohol

Throughout the 19th century the application of scientific principles to the practice of medicine allowed clinical symptoms to be categorized into diseases that might then be understood on a rational basis. Alcohol abuse was among the earliest medical problems to receive the attention of this approach. Two graduates of the Edinburgh College of Medicine, Thomas Trotter of Britain and Benjamin Rush of the colonies and then the U.S., made the first important contributions to the clinical recognition of alcoholism as a chronic, life-threatening disease. The influence of moralistic anti-alcohol Methodism may have driven their clinical research, but their findings were nonetheless sound.

In an 1813 essay on drunkenness, Trotter described alcohol abuse as a disease and recognized that habitual and prolonged consumption of hard liquor causes liver disease, accompanied by jaundice, wasting and mental dysfunction, evident even when the patient is sober. Rush published similar ideas in America and to greater effect, as he was a prominent member of society and a signer of the Declaration of Independence. His personal fame, behind his correct diagnosis of a societal ill, helped to create viewpoints that eventually culminated in the American Prohibition (1919–1933).

Nineteenth-century studies detailed the clinical picture and pathological basis of alcohol abuse, leading to today's appreciation of it as one of the most important health problems facing America and the rest of the world. Alcohol contributes to 100,000 deaths in this country annually, making it the third leading cause of preventable mortality in the U.S. (after smoking and conditions related to poor diet and a sedentary way of life). Although the exact number of problem drinkers is difficult to estimate accurately, America is probably home to between 14 and 20 million people whose lives are disrupted by their relationship with alcohol.

The overall alcohol problem is far broader. Perhaps 40 percent of Americans have been intimately exposed to the effects of alcohol abuse through a family member. And every year some 12,000 children of drinking mothers are robbed of their potential, born with the physical signs and intellectual deficits associated with full-blown fetal alcohol syndrome; thousands more suffer lesser effects. Pharmaceutical treatments for alcoholism remain impractical and inadequate, with total abstinence still the only truly effective approach.

Society and science are at the threshold of new pharmaceutical and behavioral strategies against alcoholism, however. As with any other disease, whether of the individual or the society, a correct diagnosis is crucial to treatment. Alcoholism, in historical terms, has only just been understood and accepted as a disease; we are still coping with the historically recent arrival of concentrated alcohol. The diagnosis having been made and acknowledged, continuing research efforts can be counted on to produce new and more effective treatments based on the growing knowledge of the physiology of alcohol abuse and of addictive substances in general.

Humanity at any moment of history is inevitably caught in that time, as trapped as an insect in amber. The mores, traditions and attitudes of an era inform the individuals then living, often blinding them to the consideration of alternatives. Alcohol today is a substance primarily of relaxation, celebration and, tragically, mass destruction. To consider it as having been a primary agent for the development of an entire culture may be jolting, even offensive to some. Any good physician, however takes a history before attempting a cure.

Further Reading

DRINKING IN AMERICA: A HISTORY. Mark E. Lender and James K. Martin. Free Press (Macmillan), 1987.
TOWARD A MOLECULAR BASIS OF ALCOHOL USE AND ABUSE. Edited by B. Jansson, H. Jörnvall, U. Rydberg, L. Terenius and B. L. Vallee. Birkhäuser Verlag, Switzerland, 1994.
THE ALCOHOL DEHYDROGENASE SYSTEM. H. Jörnvall, O. Danielsson, B. Hjelmquist, B. Persson and J. Shafqat in *Advances in Experimental Medicine and Biology*, Vol. 372, pages 281–294; 1995.
KUDZU ROOT: AN ANCIENT CHINESE SOURCE OF MODERN ANTI-DIPSOTROPIC AGENTS. W. M. Keung and B. L. Vallee in *Phytochemistry*, Vol. 47, No. 4, pages 499–506; February 1998.
PATIENTS WITH ALCOHOL PROBLEMS, P. G. O'Connor and R. S. Schottenfeld in *New England Journal of Medicine*, Vol. 338, No. 9, pages 592–602; February 16, 1998.

The Author

BERT L. VALLEE received his M.D. from New York University in 1943 and held positions at the Massachusetts Institute of Technology before joining the faculty of Harvard Medical School in 1945. He is currently that institution's Edgar M. Bronfman Distinguished Senior Professor. Vallee's primary research has been in zinc enzymology, a field he is credited with establishing. His work on alcohol dehydrogenase, a zinc enzyme, led to his interest in the history of alcohol. The author of more than 600 scientific publications, Vallee is a Fellow of the National Acadmey of Sciences and holds numerous honorary degrees and professorships.

From *Scientific American*, June 1998, pp. 80-85. © 1998 by Dr. Bert L. Vallee, Department of Pathology, Harvard Medical School, Boston, MA 02115. Reprinted by permission of the author.

A Pacific Haze:
Alcohol and Drugs in Oceania

Mac Marshall
University of Iowa

All over the world people eat, drink, smoke, or blow substances up their noses in the perennial quest to alter and expand human consciousness. Most of these substances come from psychoactive plants native to different regions—coca, tobacco, and peyote, in the New World; khat, coffee, and marijuana in North Africa and the Middle East; betel and opium in Asia. Some people use hallucinogens from mushrooms or tree bark; others consume more exotic drugs. Produced by fermentation, brewing, or distillation of a remarkable variety of raw materials—ranging from fruits and grains to milk and honey—traditional alcoholic beverages were found almost everywhere before the Age of Exploration.

As European explorers trekked and sailed about the globe between 1500 and 1900, they carried many of these traditional drugs back to their homelands. Different exotic drugs became popular at different times in Europe as the explorers shared their experiences. In this manner, tea, tobacco, coffee, marijuana, and opium gained avid followers in European countries. Today, this worldwide process of drug diffusion continues at a rapid pace, with changes in attitudes toward different drugs and the introduction of new laws governing their use varying accordingly.

Oceanic peoples were no exception to the widespread quest to expand the human mind. From ancient times they used drugs to defuse tense interpersonal or intergroup relations, relax socially, and commune with the spirit world. Betel and kava were far and away the most common traditional drugs used in the Pacific Islands. The geographical distribution of these two drugs was uneven across the islands, and, in a few places (for example, Chuuk [Truk]), no drugs were used at all before the arrival of foreigners. Kava and betel were not only differentially distributed geographically, but they were also differently distributed socially. Every society had rules governing who might take them (and under what circumstances) that limited their consumption, often only to adult men.

In the four-and-a-half centuries since foreign exploration of the Pacific world began, the islanders have been introduced to several new drugs, most notably alcoholic beverages, tobacco, and marijuana. This chapter discusses substance use in the contemporary Pacific Islands by examining the history and patterns of use of the five major drugs found in the islands today: alcohol, betel, kava, marijuana, and tobacco. To the extent that reliable information exists, such recently introduced drugs as cocaine and heroin are also discussed. The primary concern of the chapter is with the negative social, economic, and health consequences that result from consumption of alcohol, tobacco, and marijuana in the contemporary Pacific Islands.

BETEL AND KAVA

"Betel" is a convenient linguistic gloss for a preparation consisting of at least three distinct substances, two of which are pharmacologically active: the nut of the *Areca catechu* palm, the leaves, stems, or catkins of the *Piper betle* vine, and slaked lime from ground seashells or coral. These substances usually are combined into a quid and chewed. In some societies, people swallow the resultant profuse saliva, while in others they spit out the blood red juice. Kava is drunk as a water-based infusion made from the pounded, grated, or chewed root of a shrub, *Piper methysticum*. Whereas betel ingredients can easily be carried on the person and quickly prepared, kava makings are not as portable, and its preparation calls for a more involved procedure. Betel is often chewed individually with little or no ceremony; kava is usually drunk communally, and frequently accompanied by elaborate ceremonial procedures.

Betel chewing appears to have originated long ago in Island Southeast Asia and to have spread into the islands of the Western Pacific from there. While betel use is widespread in Melanesia (including the New Guinea Highlands where it has recently been introduced), it is absent from the Polynesian Triangle, and it is found only on the westernmost Micronesian islands of Palau, Yap, and the Marianas (Marshall 1987a).

In most parts of the Pacific Islands where betel is chewed, its use occupies a social position akin to coffee or tea drinking in Western societies. For example, Iamo (1987) writes that betel is chewed to stimulate social activity, suppress boredom, enhance work, and increase personal enjoyment among the Keakalo people of the south coast of Papua New Guinea. Similarly, Lepowsky (1982) comments that for the people of Vanatinai Island in Papua New Guinea, shared betel symbolizes friendly and peaceful social relations. Iamo notes that betel consumption "is rampant among children, young people, and adults" in Keakalo; that is, it has few social constraints on its use, except in times of scarcity (1987:146). Similarly, "Vanatinai people chew betel many times a day," and they also begin chewing betel early in childhood: "By the age of eight to ten, boys and girls chew whenever they can find the ingredients" (Lepowsky 1982:335).

In those parts of Papua New Guinea where the betel ingredients can be produced in abundance, such as Keakalo and Vanatinai, they figure importantly as items of exchange or for sale as "exports" to surrounding peoples. The enterprising Biwat of East Sepik Province are remarkable in this regard. They trade *Areca* nut, *Piper betle*, and locally grown tobacco with other peoples in the vicinity, carry these products by canoe to the regional market town of Angoram (98 miles away), and occasionally even charter a small airplane to sell as far away as Mount Hagen in the Western Highlands Province (Watson 1987).

Traditionally, kava was drunk only in Oceania, the world region to which the plant appears native. Kava drinking occurred throughout the high islands of Polynesia (except Easter Island, New Zealand, and Rapa), on the two easternmost high islands of Micronesia (Pohnpei and Kosrae), and in various parts of Melanesia, particularly Fiji, Vanuatu, and New Guinea proper. Kava and betel were often in complementary distribution, although there were some societies where both were routinely consumed.

Whereas betel is chewed by males and females, old and young, kava is different. In most Pacific Islands societies, at least traditionally, kava drinking was restricted to men, and often to "fully adult" or high-status men. Although its consumption was thus restricted, young, uninitiated or untitled men, or young women, usually prepared it. These dis-

tinctions were notably marked in the elaborate kava ceremonies of Fiji, Tonga, and Samoa. Wherever it was used, however, kava played important parts in pre-Christian religion, political deliberations, ethnomedical systems, and general quiet social interaction among a community's adult men.

On the island of Tanna, Vanuatu, for example, Lindstrom (1987) argues that getting drunk on and exchanging kava links man to man, separates man from woman, establishes a contextual interpersonal equality among men, and determines and maintains relations of inequality between men and women. Kava is drunk every evening on Tanna at a special kava-drinking ground, separated from the village, and from which women and girls are excluded. Lindstrom argues that kava (which is grown by women) is both itself an important exchange item and symbolically represents male appropriation and control over women and their productive and reproductive capacities. Tannese men fear that women intoxicated on kava would become "crazed" and usurp men's control over them, become sexually wanton, and cease to cook. Lindstrom concludes, "Gender asymmetry in Tannese drunken practice maintains and reproduces social relations of production and exchange" (1987:116).

Among the Gebusi of Papua New Guinea's Western Province, the men of a longhouse community force their male visitors to drink several bowls of kava in rapid succession, usually to the point of nausea. This is done to prevent the chief antagonists at ritual fights or funeral feasts "from disputing or taking retaliatory action against their hosts during a particularly tense moment in the proceedings" (Knauft 1987:85). Forced smoking of home-grown tobacco is used in an analogous manner "to forestall escalation of hostilities" among a people for whom homicide tied to sorcery accusations is a leading cause of male mortality. As on Tanna, Gebusi women never drink kava. Both peoples link kava to sexuality: Lindstrom (1987:112–113) describes a Tannese-origin myth of kava that he calls "kava as dildo"; Knauft (1987:85–88) notes that kava often serves as a metaphor for semen in jokes

about heterosexual relations or the ritual homosexuality practiced by the Gebusi.

As is typically the case in human affairs, these long-known and highly valued drug substances were deeply rooted in cultural traditions and patterns of social interaction. Pacific Islands peoples had developed culturally controlled ways of using betel and kava that usually precluded abuse.[1] Users also were unlikely to develop problems because of the relatively benign physiological effects of these two substances and because neither drug by itself seems to produce serious harmful disease states when consumed in a traditional manner.

Kava drinking leads to a variety of physical effects, perhaps the most pronounced of which are analgesia, muscle relaxation, and a sense of quiet well-being. In addition to its ceremonial and recreational uses, kava is a common drug in Oceanic ethnomedicine, and kava extracts also are employed in Western biomedicine. Of the various drugs discovered by human beings around the world, kava seems to be one of the least problematic. Its physiological effects induce a state of peaceful contemplation and euphoria, with the mental faculties left clear, and it produces no serious pathology unless taken (as by some Australian Aborigines since 1980) at doses far in excess of those consumed by Pacific Islanders. The most prominent effects of prolonged heavy kava consumption among Oceanic peoples are a dry scaly skin, bloodshot eyes, possible constipation and intestinal obstruction, and occasional weight loss (Lemert 1967). Even excessive kava use does not produce withdrawal symptoms, and all of the above conditions are reversible if drinking is discontinued.

The situation with betel is somewhat more complex. The main physical effect obtained by betel chewers is central nervous system stimulation and arousal producing a sense of general well-being (Burton-Bradley 1980). Arecoline, the primary active ingredient in betel, also stimulates various glands, leading to profuse sweating and salivation, among other things. Beginners typically experience such unpleasant symptoms as nausea, diarrhea, and dizziness, and prolonged use leads to physiological addiction. There is some preliminary experimental evidence that arecoline enhances memory and learning, and it is being explored as a possible medicine for patients suffering from Alzheimer's disease (Gilbert 1986).

Considerable controversy surrounds the health risks of betel chewing, particularly as regards its possible role in the development of oral cancer (MacLennan et al. 1985). This debate has been confounded by the fact that many betel chewers in Southeast and South Asia (where most of the clinical data have been collected) add other ingredients to the betel chew, most commonly, and notably, tobacco. A summary of the epidemiological evidence available to date leads to the conclusion that chewing betel using traditional ingredients without the addition of tobacco probably does not carry any significant risk for oral cancer (Gupta et al. 1982).[2] Occasionally, a betel chewer develops what Burton-Bradley (1966) calls "betel nut psychosis," following a period of abstinence and in response to a heavy dose of the drug. This acute reversible toxic psychosis is characterized by delusions and hallucinations in predisposed individuals, but it must be emphasized that its occurrence is rare. There is thus no conclusive evidence that regular betel chewing without the addition of tobacco results in physical or mental health problems for most people. Like kava, betel appears to produce a relatively harmless "high."

As usually taken in Oceania, not only do kava and betel consumption pose few—if any—health risks, but neither drug leads to intoxicated behavior that is socially disruptive (indeed, quite the contrary). The plants from which these substances are derived are locally grown and quite readily available, and the processes for making and taking these two traditional drugs do not require commercial manufacture. In the past twenty years, some cash marketing of both drugs has developed, but this is primarily by smallholders or local concerns, and neither substance is handled by multinational corporations. Thus, kava and betel do not have negative social and economic consequences for the Pacific Islands societies where they are used.

ALCOHOLIC BEVERAGES

Pacific Islanders, like most North American Indians, had no alcoholic beverages until Europeans brought them early in the contact period. Initially, most islanders found alcohol distasteful and spat it out, but eventually they acquired a fondness for what sometimes was called "white man's kava." During the late eighteenth and first half of the nineteenth century, whalers, beachcombers, missionaries, and traders arrived in the islands in growing numbers. Many of them were drinkers and provided models of drunken behavior for the islanders to copy. Some of them established saloons in the port towns, and alcohol was widely used as an item of trade with the islanders. By at least the 1840s, missionaries to the islands, reflecting temperance politics in the United States and Great Britain, began to speak out forcefully against "the evils of drink" (Marshall and Marshall 1976).

As the European and American powers of the day consolidated colonial control over Oceania in the nineteenth century, they passed laws prohibiting islanders from consuming beverage alcohol. While such laws usually had strong missionary backing, they were also intended to maintain order, protect colonists from the possible "drunken depredations of savages," and serve what were deemed to be the islanders' own best interests. Despite prohibition, production of home brews continued in some areas, theft provided an occasional source of liquor, and the drinking of methylated spirits offered a potentially deadly alcohol alternative in some parts of the Pacific (Marshall 1988:579–582).

Colonially imposed prohibition laws remained in place until the 1950s and 1960s, when they were set aside one after another in the era of decolonization. Since then, the establishment of new Pacific nations has fostered a maze of legal regulations surrounding alcohol use, and it has also led to the encouragement of alcohol production and marketing. In many different parts of the Pacific Islands, problems have accompanied the relaxation of controls and the expansion of availability.

It is generally true around the world that more men drink alcoholic beverages than women, and that men drink greater quantities than women, but these gender differences are particularly pronounced in most of Oceania. In many of the islands, there are strong social pressures against women drinking, reinforced by church teachings, that effectively keep most women from even tasting alcoholic beverages. With a few exceptions, it is usually only Westernized women in the towns who drink on any sort of a regular basis. Boys below age fourteen or fifteen seldom, if ever, drink, but by the time they are in their late teens or early twenties, nearly all of them partake of alcohol. So much is this the case that in Chuuk (Truk) drinking and drunkenness is called "young men's work" (Marshall 1987b).

These gender differences have resulted in profoundly different attitudes toward alcohol by men and women that sometimes have resulted in outspoken social opposition by women to men's drinking and its attendant social problems (see Marshall and Marshall 1990). Weekend binge drinking by groups of young men—especially in towns—frequently leads to social disruption and confrontations that have been labeled "weekend warfare" in one Micronesian society (Marshall 1979).

For many Pacific Islanders, alcoholic beverages have come to symbolize "the good life" and active participation in a modern, sophisticated lifestyle. Beer is usually the beverage of choice in Oceania, and, in some places, it has been incorporated into ceremonial exchanges surrounding such events as bride price payments, weddings, and funerals. In the Papua New Guinea Highlands' Chuave area, beer is treated as an item of wealth and "has assumed a central role in inter- and intraclan prestations" (Warry 1982:84). Cartons of beer have been endowed with a number of social and symbolic qualities in common with pork, the most highly esteemed traditional valuable. For example, the success of a ceremony is judged, increasingly, by the amount of beer, as well as pork, available for display and distribution; beer in cartons has a known value and the twenty-four bottles are easily divisible; like pigs, the stacked cartons of beer (sometimes as many as 240!) are appropriate items for display; alcohol is a social facilitator in these sometimes tense feast situations; beer—like pork and other foodstuffs—is consumable; and, like pork, beer is used at feasts both as a tool to create relationships and as a weapon to slight rivals (Warry 1982).

The chief problems associated with alcohol use in Oceania are social ones, although it is difficult to divorce these from the interrelated public health and economic costs. Among the more prominent and widespread social problems are domestic strife, particularly wife beating; community fighting and disruption, often with attendant trauma and occasional fatalities; crime, and drunk-driving accidents.

In the post–World War II era, these alcohol-related problems have been a continuing concern of community-based and government agencies in Pacific Islands countries. For example, a seminar was held in 1977 on "Alcohol Problems with the Young People of Fiji" (Fiji National Youth Council 1977), and, in 1986, Catholic youth in the Highlands of Papua New Guinea rallied to oppose alcohol abuse (*The Times of Papua New Guinea 1986a*). Other examples of community-based concerns are church women's groups who championed a legal prohibition against alcohol on Weno, Chuuk (Moen Island, Truk) (Marshall and Marshall 1990), and an ecumenical Christian training center in Papua New Guinea (the Melanesian Institute) that has given voice to village peoples' concerns over abuse of alcohol for many years. Within a decade after it became legal for Papua New Guineans to drink, the government felt it necessary to sponsor an official Commission of Inquiry in 1971 to assess the widely perceived problems that had ensued. Less than ten years later, another investigation of alcohol use and abuse under national government auspices was launched in Papua New Guinea through its Institute for Applied Social and Economic Research (IASER). Such government commissions and groups of concerned citizens usually produce recommendations for action; however, serious and effective alcohol control policies are rarely forthcoming.

Although they have received less attention in the literature, primarily because of the absence of adequate hospital records and autopsy reports for Pacific Islands countries, the physical and mental illnesses linked to either prolonged heavy ethanol intake or binge drinking appear to be considerable. Among these are alcoholic cirrhosis, cancers of the upper respiratory and upper digestive tracts, death from ethanol overdose, alcoholic psychoses, and suicide while under the influence of alcohol.

In recent years, researchers have focused on non-insulin-dependent diabetes mellitus (NIDDM), which has increased in urbanized and migrant Pacific Islands populations (for example, Baker et al. 1986; King et al. 1984). With changes from traditional diets to "modern" diets of refined foods and higher intakes of fats, sugar, sodium, and alcoholic beverages, some Micronesian and Polynesian populations have shown what is thought to be a hereditary susceptibility to NIDDM, which apparently is only expressed with a change from the traditional rural lifestyle. Urban and migrant islanders typically engage in less physical activity and have higher levels of obesity than their rural nonmigrant counterparts. Given that individuals with diabetes are more vulnerable to the hypoglycemic effects of alcohol because alcohol interferes with hepatic gluconeogenesis (Franz 1983:149; see also Madsen 1974:52–53), heavy drinking that may produce complications for diabetics poses an added health risk.

TOBACCO

Although the Spanish and Portuguese introduced tobacco into the East Indies from the New World in the late sixteenth and early seventeenth centuries, and although this new drug spread rather quickly to the island of New Guinea via traditional trade routes, *Nicotiana tabacum* did not reach most Pacific Islands until the nineteenth century. It became a basic item of trade and even served as a kind of currency during the heyday of European exploration and colonization of Oceania. The first German plantations on the north coast of New Guinea near Madang were tobacco plan-

tations, and the crop continues to be grown commercially in Fiji and Papua New Guinea. In the 1800s, pipe and homemade cigar smoking were quite popular; today manufactured cigarettes dominate the market in most parts of the Pacific Islands. The prevalence of tobacco smoking by both men and women in Pacific Islands populations is much higher than in the developed countries of Australia, New Zealand, and the United States, and higher than in most developing nations elsewhere in the world (Marshall 1991). In some isolated rural parts of Oceania, nearly everyone in a community smokes—including children as young as eight or ten years of age.

With the decline in tobacco use in the developed nations of the West, the multinational corporations that control global production and marketing of this drug have shifted their emphasis to the huge and rapidly growing market in the Third World. Developing countries offer few restrictions to tobacco companies: most such countries have no maximum tar and nicotine levels, no laws restricting sales to minors, no advertising limits, no required health warnings, and no general public awareness of the serious health risks associated with smoking (Stebbins 1990). As a result, tobacco consumption has grown steadily in Third World countries, leading public health experts to predict and document the beginning of a major epidemic of diseases known to be linked to chronic tobacco use. During the 1980s, numerous studies have been published by health care professionals and other concerned individuals noting these alarming trends and calling for action. Studies documenting these problems exist for Africa, Latin America, and Asia, and researchers have begun to chronicle the same sad story for Oceania (Marshall 1991).

As with the upsurge in alcohol use and its aggressive marketing by multinational corporations in Pacific Islands countries, so it is, too, with the production and sale of commercial tobacco products, particularly cigarettes. Almost any store one enters in Oceania today displays tobacco advertisements prominently inside and out, and has numerous tobacco products readily available for sale. Among the many ploys used to push their brands, the tobacco companies sponsor sweepstakes contests with large cash prizes which can be entered by writing one's name and address on an empty cigarette pack and dropping it into a special box for a drawing. Tobacco firms also routinely sponsor sporting events, with trophies and prizes in cash and in kind. In other promotions, those who present fifteen empty packs of the pertinent brands are given "free" T-shirts emblazoned with the cigarette brand name.

The association of tobacco smoking with serious cardiovascular and respiratory diseases—lung cancer, chronic bronchitis, and emphysema—is by now well known. These diseases are particularly linked to the smoking of flue-cured commercial cigarettes, which now have been readily available in Oceania for about thirty years. As the Pacific Islanders who have smoked such cigarettes for many years develop health problems, more suffer from these smoking-related illnesses (Marshall 1991). One New Zealand study shows that those Maori women who smoke heavily during pregnancy produce infants of a lower average birth weight than those of Europeans or other Pacific Islanders in New Zealand (Hay and Foster 1981). Another study shows Maori women to have a lung cancer rate that is among the world's highest (Stanhope and Prior 1982).

As yet, there have been few efforts to gain control over the smoking epidemic in Pacific Islands countries. In one, the Fiji Medical Association announced a campaign to ban cigarette advertising following a directive from the Fiji Ministry of Health to stop smoking in all patient areas in government hospitals (*Pacific Islands Monthly* 1986). But the most encouraging program has been mounted in Papua New Guinea. In the early 1980s, an antismoking council was established there by members of the medical profession (Smith 1983), and, following several years of public debate, Parliament passed the Tobacco Products (Health Control) Act in November 1987. This law mandates various controls on tobacco advertising, requires health warning labels on cigarette packs and cigarette advertisements, and provides the authority to declare various public places as nonsmoking areas. As of

March 1990, these included all national and provincial government offices, the offices and buildings of all educational institutions (other than staff quarters), all hospitals, health centers, clinics and aid posts, cinemas and theatres, public motor vehicles (PMVs), and all domestic flights on scheduled airlines. While there are some enforcement problems, the Department of Health has mounted an aggressive antismoking campaign (tied to the anti-betel-chewing campaign), and this is likely to have a positive impact over the next few years.

Despite the encouraging signs in Papua New Guinea, public-health-oriented antismoking campaigns have met with relatively small success to date in the face of the large sums of money devoted to advertising by the tobacco multinationals. Much more effort is needed in community and public health education if this preventable epidemic is to be brought under control in Oceania.

MARIJUANA

Unlike the use of alcohol, betel, kava, and tobacco, marijuana smoking is uniformly illegal in Oceania. Nonetheless, the plant is now grown quite widely in the islands and has a substantial number of devotees. In part because its cultivation and use is against the law, fewer data are available on marijuana smoking than on the other four common Pacific drugs.

Native to central Asia, marijuana diffused to Oceania much more recently than alcohol or tobacco. While it doubtless was present in such places as Hawaii and New Zealand well before World War II, in other island areas like Micronesia or the New Guinea highlands, it appears to have been introduced only during the 1960s and 1970s.

While considerable controversy surrounds the long-term health effects of marijuana smoking, certain things are by now well known and give cause for concern. Marijuana induces an increased cardiovascular work load, thus posing a potential threat to individuals with hypertension and coronary atherosclerosis. Both of these health problems have been on the rise in Pacific Islands populations, especially in urban areas (Baker et al. 1986; Patrick et al. 1983; Salmond et al.

1985), and both can only be worsened by marijuana use.

Marijuana smoke is unfiltered and contains about 50 percent more cancer-causing hydrocarbons than tobacco smoke (Maugh 1982). Recent research has shown that "marijuana delivers more particulate matter to the smoker than tobacco cigarettes and with a net four-times greater burden on the respiratory system" (Addiction Research Foundation 1989:3). This same work revealed significant structural changes in the lungs of marijuana smokers, with a higher rate among those who also smoked tobacco. These changes are associated with chronic obstructive lung disease and with lung cancer. Another study has found significant short-term memory impairment in cannabis-dependent individuals that lingers for at least six weeks after use of the drug is stopped (Schwartz et al. 1989). As was discussed above for tobacco, the limited amount of research that has been done shows respiratory illnesses to be major serious diseases in Oceania. Clearly, smoking marijuana will simply raise the incidence of health problems that were already significant in the Pacific Islands even before marijuana gained popularity.

In the Pacific Islands, as in the United States, marijuana growing is attractive because it yields a higher cash return per unit of time per unit of land than other agricultural crops. Even though marijuana is grown as a cash crop and often sold by the "joint," the plant is easy to grow, requires little attention, and thrives in most island environments. As a result, most marijuana consumed in the Pacific Islands, like betel and kava, is locally grown and not imported by drug cartels or multinationals. Even so, marijuana grown in the islands is sometimes exported to larger and more lucrative markets (Nero 1985). This has become the subject of major police concern in Papua New Guinea, where there are some indications that organized crime may be involved in the purchase of marijuana grown in the highlands to be sent overseas (for example, *Niugini Nius* 1990). It will be well nigh impossible to uproot marijuana from Oceania today, but much more could be done to educate islanders about the health risks associated with its use.

OTHER DRUGS

As of 1989, hard drugs such as cocaine and heroin have made little headway in Pacific Islands communities. The most dramatic example of a place where such penetration has begun is Palau, where heroin first showed up in the early 1970s (Nero 1985:20–23). By 1985, cocaine was being used in Palau as well, and, by then, a number of Palauan heroin addicts had been sent to Honolulu for detoxification and treatment (Polloi 1985).

Although the Palauan case is somewhat unusual for the Pacific Islands at present, there are increased reports of hard drugs being shipped *through* the islands from Asia for metropolitan markets in Australia, New Zealand, and North America. Clearly, given the ease of air travel and relatively lax security and customs checks, more hard drugs will appear in the islands in the coming years.

CONCLUSIONS

Oceania's traditional drugs—betel and kava—create few if any social problems and pose minimal health risks to users. Moreover, these drugs are locally produced, and even when they are sold in the market the profits remain in islanders' hands and enrich the local economy. From an economic perspective, the cropping and selling of marijuana in most of the Pacific Islands operates in much the same way: small growers cultivate the plant for their own use or to sell in local markets. The major differences between marijuana and betel and kava are that marijuana is illegal and that smoking marijuana poses significant health risks. Oceania's other two major drug substances are produced and distributed in a very different manner and pose much more serious social and public health problems.

Over the past decade, an accumulation of studies has shown that alcoholic beverage and tobacco multinational corporations have increasingly targeted developing countries as prime markets for their products (for example, Cavanaugh and Clairmonte 1985; Muller 1978; Stebbins 1990; Wickström 1979). This marketing involves aggressive advertising, often aimed especially at young people and women. Frequently, it takes the form of joint ventures with host governments, on the grounds that large profits can be shared (which ignores the significant health and social costs involved). The multinationals also have become infamous for inducing governments (for example, the United States) to threaten trade embargoes against countries that balk at the unrestrained marketing of alcohol and tobacco products within their borders (*The Nation's Health* 1989).

The developing countries of Oceania have been subject to this "legal pushing" of harmful substances, even though their populations are small and transport poses certain logistical problems. Breweries, ultimately owned by huge overseas corporations, operate in French Polynesia, Western Samoa, Tonga, Fiji, Vanuatu, and Papua New Guinea, and there are distilled beverage producers in Fiji and Papua New Guinea.

For example, domestic production of hard liquor began in Papua New Guinea in 1985 by Fairdeal Liquors Pty. Ltd. Fairdeal imports raw materials (concentrates and ethanol) from its parent corporation based in Malaysia and from other overseas sources. The company then mixes and bottles both its own brands and selected internationally known brands on franchise (for example, Gilbey's gin, Jim Beam whiskey) in its factory in the Port Moresby suburb of Gordons. Initially, Fairdeal was able to market its own product ("Gold Cup") in small, clear plastic sachets for around 35 cents (U.S.) each. These were a marketing success but a social disaster because irresponsible storekeepers sold them to children as well as adults, and because many men drank them to excess. The ensuing public outcry led the Prime Minister to ask the company to withdraw the sachets from the market two months after they were introduced. Following the outcry from concerned citizens, especially in the highlands (*The Times of Papua New Guinea* 1986), Fairdeal briefly closed its Port Moresby factory in December 1986 because the national government also imposed a 1,200 percent increase in the import tax on the concentrate used to produce liquor (*The Times of Papua New Guinea* 1986). But even with this momentary setback, Fairdeal continues to market its own brands in bottles for half the price of comparable imports. This is possible because by bottling locally the company still avoids paying as much excise duty as that paid by importers of alcoholic beverages that are bottled abroad.

It was announced in mid-1989 that new breweries would be built in Papua New Guinea and Western Samoa (*Pacific Islands Monthly* 1989). The Papua New Guinea venture, which since has fallen through, was to be constructed at Kerowagi in Simbu Province, and represented a proposed joint venture among Danbrew Consult of Denmark and the five highlands provincial governments. At least two highlands provincial premiers had to be cajoled into committing their provinces to participation in this scheme, and the highly controversial project was opposed by women's organizations and church groups. Papua New Guinea's major brewery—South Pacific—itself a subsidiary of the Heineken Group, bought out its sole competitor (San Miguel, PNG) early in 1983. San Miguel (PNG) was a subsidiary of "the most successful conglomerate group in the Philippines," a group that held overseas interests in mining, brewing, fishing, finance, and development in nine different countries in Asia and Europe (Krinks 1987).

In 1978, War on Want published a slender volume entitled, *Tobacco and the Third World: Tomorrow's Epidemic?* Just over a decade later, the *question* in that book's title has been answered—a smoking epidemic has swept the Third World, and the Pacific Islands have not been immune to this global trend. While cigarettes and stick tobacco are locally produced in Papua New Guinea and Fiji by subsidiaries of the giant British Tobacco Company, the overwhelming majority of tobacco products sold in Oceania today are commercial cigarettes imported from the developed countries, principally Australia, New Zealand, and the United States. Promotional campaigns continue to have few, if any, restrictions placed upon them, and the costs of sweepstakes and raffle giveaways is small compared to the substantial profits to be earned once new consumers are "hooked."

A haze hangs over the Pacific Islands today, a result of widespread alcohol and tobacco abuse and of the smokescreens put up by multinationals to buy off politicians under the guise that production and marketing of these legal drugs contributes to economic development. In fact, the public health costs of alcohol and tobacco use and the social disruption surrounding alcohol abuse *undermine* economic and social development over the long run. If Pacific Islands governments do not develop more effective systems to prevent and control the aggressive marketing of alcohol and tobacco by multinationals, then the haze in the air and the glazed looks on the faces of island citizens will increase. The resultant social and health costs can only weaken Oceanic communities and make more difficult their dream of building prosperous, healthy, modern societies.

Acknowledgment: I am grateful to Linda A. Bennett for useful comments on an earlier version of this chapter.

NOTES

1. This statement remains true for Pacific Islanders; however, Australian Aborigines, to whom kava was introduced in the 1980s, and who consume it in quantities far in excess of those taken by Pacific Islanders, have developed such clinical side effects as weight loss, liver and kidney dysfunction, blood abnormalities, and possible pulmonary hypertension (Mathews et al. 1988; Riley and Mathews 1989).

2. Recently, in Papua New Guinea, and possibly elsewhere in the Pacific Islands, lime manufactured by commercial chemical firms has been substituted for lime produced in the traditional manner from ground seashells or coral. There is some evidence to suggest that the industrially manufactured lime is much more caustic than that traditionally used by Pacific betel chewers, and that this may increase the risk of oral cancer. Although controlled studies to demonstrate this have yet to be done, the Papua New Guinea Department of Health has mounted an active public health campaign advising people that if they chew betel, they run a risk of developing oral cancer.

From CONTEMPORARY PACIFIC SOCIETIES: STUDIES IN DEVELOPMENT AND CHANGE, edited by Victoria S. Lockwood and Thomas G. Harding, 1993, Chapter 17, pp. 260–272. © 1993 by Prentice Hall, Inc. Reprinted by permission.

From *Indian Givers:* Chapter 14

WHEN WILL AMERICA BE DISCOVERED?

Jack Weatherford

The old Yuqui woman jerked her head up toward me and stared blindly into my face. As flies crawled across her eyes and drank from the only moist place left on her body, her left hand scratched habitually at the lice and filth encrusted into her hair. No one knew her age, but she was the oldest survivor of a band of Yuquis living in the rain forest of the southern Amazon region. Most of her life she had wandered through the forest with her fellow Yuquis following the same culture as unknown generations had done before them. She had lived most of her life without knowledge of whites or other outsiders except that they lurked on the edges of her forest world. Like the evil spirits of the dead, the whites brought disease and death to the Yuquis, the real people.

Not until 1968 did her band make its first contact with a white, when the Protestant missionaries Bob and Mary Garland arrived in their world. In time the small band settled around the base camp of the missionaries on the Chimore River, and they wandered less and less to hunt. Anthropologist Allyn Stearman raced to record their way of life as it dissolved around her. The missionaries taught them to grow a few crops and helped them to hunt more efficiently and to use canoes. They taught them to make fire so that they would no longer have to raid another band each time their fire was lost, and they helped the women in childbirth rather than letting them disappear alone into the jungle to bear their babies as had been their tradition.

Had this woman not been contacted by the missionaries she most assuredly would have been dead long before I came across her. If the lumbermen had not captured or killed her in their periodic shootouts with the Yuquis, then perhaps the coca growers or the ranchers would have seized her in a raid and made her a cook and prostitute for the mestizo workers. Even if she had been spared all of these indignities from outsiders and managed to live alone with her band, the group would have deserted her along the trail as soon as she became too ill to travel. As nomads who traveled strictly by foot, they never developed the knowledge of how to deal with the infirm or elderly. Anyone unable to walk through the jungle was left to die alone.

Now she sits deserted all day beneath a mosquito net in her hut wrapped in a filthy rag of a dress. She lost her sight, her hearing deteriorated, and she grew too weak to walk or crawl. Gradually she became deranged and delirious. The missionaries feed her and care for her most basic needs, but her own relatives who live nearby have no idea what to do for her. In their harsh jungle life, they never had to minister to anyone like this.

When I appeared at her net with the missionary, her bony hand reached out, groping for food. She clutched my arm, and her jagged fingernails scratched my hand as her cool but dry skin rubbed against mine with a sound like sandpaper against bark. She mumbled a few words that were incoherent to me, but the missionary said she was just naming foods and uttering the names of relatives, some living and some dead. Finally in defeat, she withdrew her hand, her jaw dropped, oblivious to the gnats crawling in and out of her mouth, and she seemed to return to the stupor and the scratching that occupied most of her dying weeks.

There was nothing heroic about the poor old woman. She was now at the end of her days, and all she sought was another morsel of food, some water, and some relief from the heat and the insects that plagued her now as they had all her life. Like so many Indians today from Canada to Chile, she seemed to be the truly wretched of the earth, the abandoned, the abused, the suffering who merited nothing but pity or charity from outsiders. She lay dying as a miserable outcast from the contemporary American society that had gradually and persistently consumed her land over the past five hundred years.

This dying woman contrasted painfully with the image of the Indians as the world's greatest farmers and pharmacists, as the noble savage of Rousseau or the practical administrators who inspired Benjamin Franklin. I could not help but wonder why, if these people were really so great, they had fallen so low and been so oppressed. If they could build great cities and roads, why couldn't they defend themselves from the waves of Europeans who washed across their land?

Even though the Indian civilizations surpassed the Old World in a few areas, they lagged behind in others. The Indians developed superior agricultural skills and technology, and they surpassed the Old World in their pharmacology. They had far more sophisticated calendars than the Europeans, and the Indians of Mexico had a mathematical system based on place numbers superior to the numerical systems then in use by the Spaniards.

In their exhaustive attention to agriculture, medicine, mathematics, and religion, the Indians neglected the domestication of animals, which proved so decisive for the Old World civilizations. Because farmers in Europe, Asia, and Africa were so much less efficient in growing crops, they relied extensively on eggs, milk, cheese, and dozens of other animal products as well as on the meat of these animals. This made their Old World diet no better than that of the Americans, but it gave the people who domesticated animals a distinct advantage in that they easily learned to harness animal energy in place of human energy. The Europeans arrived in America with strong horses to help men in battle as well as oxen to pull heavy carts laden with supplies and cows and goats to give protein-rich milk to marching armies of soldiers and later to hordes of settlers.

The Indians built an elaborate civilization on human energy, but the Old World had thoroughly exploited animal energy sources that helped them in their endeavors. Additionally, the people of the Old World had begun tapping inanimate energy sources in ways that foreshadowed the coming industrial revolution. The sophisticated use of ships and sails, of windmills and waterwheels, and of cannons and gunpowder gave them a decisive advantage over the Indians.

All of these skills made the invaders better soldiers and gave them better instruments of war. Indian metallurgy lacked the variety of the Old World's and was directed mostly toward decoration rather than tools of production or war. The European invaders, however, had learned to make steel into swords and lances and to cast metal cannons, which they mounted on wheels to be pulled by animals. The Indians still fought with arrows and spears tipped with stone, and they had no war machine more sophisticated than a simple *atlatl* or spear thrower.

Together with their animals and machines, the Europeans brought horrendous epidemic diseases that had been unknown to the New World. These diseases traveled through the Indian population faster than through the European. By the time the Europeans arrived in Tenochtitlán or Cuzco or on the plains of North America, their microbes had preceded them and thoroughly decimated and weakened the native population.

The Indian civilizations crumbled in the face of the Old World not because of any intellectual or cultural inferiority. They simply succumbed in the face of disease and brute strength. While the American Indians had spent millennia becoming the world's greatest farmers and pharmacists, the people of the Old World had spent a similar period amassing the world's greatest arsenal of weapons. The strongest, but not necessarily the most creative or the most intelligent, won the day.

The inevitable defeat of Indian groups such as the Yuqui seemed so overwhelming and so final that in the process we have overlooked the contributions that they made to the world. They mined the gold and silver that made capitalism possible. Working in the mines and mints and in the plantations with the African slaves, they started the industrial revolution that then spread to Europe and on around the world. They supplied the cotton, rubber, dyes, and related chemicals that fed this new system of production. They domesticated and developed the hundreds of varieties of corn, potatoes, cassava, and peanuts that now feed much of the world. They discovered the curative powers of quinine, the anesthetizing ability of coca, and the potency of a thousand other drugs, which made possible modern medicine and pharmacology. The drugs together with their improved agriculture made possible the population explosion of the last several centuries. They developed and refined a form of democracy that has been haphazardly and inadequately adopted in many parts of the world. They were the true colonizers of America who cut the trails through the jungles and deserts, made the roads, and built the cities upon which modern America is based.

Over the past five hundred years, human beings have sculpted a new worldwide society, a new political and economic order as well as a new demographic and agricultural order. Indians played the decisive roles in each step to create this new society. Sometimes they acted as prime movers, other times they played equal roles with a set of actors, and sometimes they were mere victims. But in all cases they acted as necessary although not sufficient causes. Somewhere in the telling of modern history, the writing of the novels, the construction of textbooks and instructional programs, attention drifted away from the contribution of the Indians to the heroic stories of explorers and conquistadores, the moral lessons of missionaries, the political struggles of the colonists, the great and impersonal movements of European history, the romance of the cowboy. The modern world order came to be viewed as the product of European, not American, history. The Americans became bit players, and only their role as pathetic victims remained visible.

The Indians, such as the woman crouched before me, disintegrated into peripheral people. They became little more than beggars on the world scene, pleading for food, for the redress of land and treaty rights, for some attention. In ignoring the Indian cultures, however, we are doing far more than merely slighting the American Indians of their earned place in history. We may be hurting ourselves because of what we have all lost.

In staring at that ancient woman from the time before the white man came, I could not help but wonder what practical knowledge we were losing with her impending death. Through grubbing in the woods did she know of some plant that might serve as a key to feeding the starving masses in the tropics? From poking in ponds and bogs did she know of a concoction that might cure multiple sclerosis? From countless nights under the stars did she know of some weather-forecasting device that we had missed, or did she know something about the anatomy of the night birds that helped them to see through the dark? Had she incorporated something into her diet that prevented stomach cancer? Did her language have the capacity to express some idea more easily than ours, or could it help in the writing of new computer codes? She lived in an environment that few people in the world have ever been able to survive. What knowledge did she have that made that possible? How did she survive for so long in a place that would kill most of us within days? Soon after my visit the old woman died and now we may never know.

When she died a treasure of information went with her, for she was one of the last Yuquis to live their traditional life. In losing her and the Yuqui culture, we lose more than just a small band of people. We lose a whole world view, for each culture creates the world in a different way with unique knowledge, unique words, and unique understandings. While most of this cultural knowledge may be of no importance to us today, we have no idea what value it may yet hold for our children in generations to come. For centuries our ancestors saw no value in the potato or rubber or the Huron concoction of vitamin C to cure scurvy, but in time all of these came to have important roles to play.

The world has yet to utilize fully the gifts of the American Indians. Hundreds of plants such as amaranth and quinoa are hardly even known, much less fully utilized. Who knows how many more plants might be out there waiting to serve humans? We still do not understand the complex mathematical systems of the Mayas and the sophisticated geometric science of the Aztecs. Who knows what completely different systems of computation and calculation now lie buried in the adobe of Arizona or beneath the rocks of Inkallajta? The civilizations of Mexico and Guatemala developed a more accurate calendar than the one used in Europe, but it took decades of work for us to understand its superiority. Who knows what additional knowledge they had about the stars, the planets, the comets, and who knows how much knowledge still lies locked in the stone monuments yet to be discovered in the jungles of Guatemala or Belize?

We often know even less about the millions of American Indians surviving today, speaking their language and preserving at least some of their traditional cultural knowledge. The Quechuas of Bolivia, the Crees of Canada, the Guaranis of Paraguay, the Yanomamos of Venezuela, the Hopis of the United States, the Zapotecs of Mexico, the Shuars of Ecuador, the Mayas of Guatemala, the Cunas of Panama, the Shavantes of Brazil, and a thousand other Indian nations are not dead. They are only ignored.

In the five hundred years since Columbus's voyage to America, the people of the world have benefited greatly from the American Indians, but the world may have lost even more than it gained. Some information that died with the old Yuqui woman and with the hundreds of exterminated tribes, nations, and cities may be lost forever. Some of it may be retrieved by coming generations of scholars who have the opportunity to study our past. Sadly, however, we know much more about the building of the pyramids of Egypt, thousands of miles and years from us, than we know about the pyramid builders of the Mississippi. We know more about the language of the long-gone Hittites than we do about the still-living Quechua speakers descended from the Incas. We know more about the poetry of the ancient Chinese than about the poems of the Nahuatls. We can decipher the clay tablets of Mesopotamia better than we can the stone tablets of Mesoamerica. We understand the medical practices of ancient Babylon better than those of the living Dakotas. We understand more about the interbreeding of the Angles and the Saxons than we do about the mixing of the Indians in America with the European and African immigrants. We know more about the Greeks' mythological tribe of Amazons than we know about the dying Yuquis of the Amazon. The history and culture of America remains a mystery, still *terra incognita* after five hundred years.

Columbus arrived in the New World in 1492, but America has yet to be discovered.

THE LAST AMERICANS

Environmental collapse and the end of civilization

By Jared Diamond

I met a traveler from an antique land
Who said: Two vast and trunkless legs of stone
Stand in the desert... Near them, on the sand,
Half sunk, a shattered visage lies, whose frown,
And wrinkled lip, and sneer of cold command,
Tell that its sculptor well those passions read
Which yet survive, stamped on these lifeless
things,
The hand that mocked them, and the heart
that fed:
And on the pedestal these words appear:
"My name is Ozymandias, king of kings:
Look on my works, ye Mighty, and despair!"
Nothing beside remains. Round the decay
Of that colossal wreck, boundless and bare
The lone and level sands stretch far away.
—"Ozymandias," Percy Bysshe Shelley

One of the disturbing facts of history is that so many civilizations collapse. Few people, however, least of all our politicians, realize that a primary cause of the collapse of those societies has been the destruction of the environmental resources on which they depended. Fewer still appreciate that many of those civilizations share a sharp curve of decline. Indeed, a society's demise may begin only a decade or two after it reaches its peak population, wealth, and power.

Recent archaeological discoveries have revealed similar courses of collapse in such otherwise dissimilar ancient societies as the Maya in the Yucatán, the Anasazi in the American Southwest, the Cahokia mound builders outside St. Louis, the Greenland Norse, the statue builders of Easter Island, ancient Mesopotamia in the Fertile Crescent, Great Zimbabwe in Africa, and Angkor Wat in Cambodia. These civilizations, and many others, succumbed to various combinations of environmental degradation and climate change, aggression from enemies taking advantage of their resulting weakness, and declining trade with neighbors who faced their own environmental problems. Because peak population, wealth, resource consumption, and waste production are accompanied by peak environmental impact—approaching the limit at which impact outstrips resources—we can now understand why declines of societies tend to follow swiftly on their peaks.

These combinations of undermining factors were compounded by cultural attitudes preventing those in power from perceiving or resolving the crisis. That's a familiar problem today. Some of us are inclined to dismiss the importance of a healthy environment, or at least to suggest that it's just one of many problems facing us—an "issue." That dismissal is based on three dangerous misconceptions.

Foremost among these misconceptions is that we must balance the environment against human needs. That reasoning is exactly upside-down. Human needs and a healthy environment are not opposing claims that must be balanced; instead, they are inexorably linked by chains of cause and effect. We need a healthy environment because we need clean water, clean air, wood, and food from the ocean, plus soil and sunlight to grow crops. We need functioning natural ecosystems, with their native species of earthworms, bees, plants, and microbes, to generate and aerate our soils, pollinate our crops, decompose our wastes, and produce our oxygen. We need to prevent toxic substances from accumulating in our water and air and soil. We need to prevent weeds, germs, and other pest species from becoming established in places where they aren't native and where they cause economic damage. Our strongest arguments for a healthy environment are selfish: we want it for ourselves, not for threatened species like snail darters, spotted owls, and Furbish louseworts.

Another popular misconception is that we can trust in technology to solve our problems. Whatever environmental problem you name, you can also name some hoped-for technological solution under discussion. Some of us have faith that we shall solve our dependence on fossil fuels by developing new technologies for hydrogen engines, wind energy, or solar energy. Some of us have faith that we shall solve our food problems with new or soon-to-be-developed genetically modified crops. Some of us have faith that new technologies will succeed in cleaning up the toxic materials in our air, water, soil, and foods without the horrendous cleanup expenses that we now incur.

BEHOLD, SAY THE OPTIMISTS: WE ARE MORE PROSPEROUS THAN EVER BEFORE, AND THAT'S THE FINAL PROOF THAT OUR SYSTEM WORKS

Those with such faith assume that the new technologies will ultimately succeed, but in fact some of them may succeed and others may not. They assume that the new technologies will succeed quickly enough to make a big difference soon, but all of these major technological changes will actually take five to thirty years to develop and implement—if they catch on at all. Most of all, those with faith assume that new technology won't cause any new problems. In fact, technology merely constitutes increased power, which produces changes that can be either for the better or for the worse. All of our current environmental problems are unanticipated harmful consequences of our existing technology. There is no basis for believing that technology will miraculously stop causing new and unanticipated problems while it is solving the problems that it previously produced.

The final misconception holds that environmentalists are fear-mongering, overreacting extremists whose predictions of impending disaster have been proved wrong before and will be proved wrong again. Behold, say the optimists: water still flows from our faucets, the grass is still green, and the supermarkets are full of food. We are more prosperous than ever before, and that's the final proof that our system works.

Well, for a few billion of the world's people who are causing us increasing trouble, there isn't any clean water, there is less and less green grass, and there are no supermarkets full of food. To appreciate what the environmental problems of those billions of people mean for us Americans, compare the following two lists of countries. First ask some ivory-tower academic ecologist who knows a lot about the environment but never reads a newspaper and has no interest in politics to list the overseas countries facing some of the worst problems of environmental stress, overpopulation, or both. The ecologist would answer, "That's a no-brainer, it's obvious. Your list of environmen-

tally stressed or overpopulated countries should surely include Afghanistan, Bangladesh, Burundi, Haiti, Indonesia, Iraq, Nepal, Pakistan, the Philippines, Rwanda, the Solomon Islands, and Somalia, plus others." Then ask a First World politician who knows nothing, and cares less, about the environment and population problems to list the world's worst trouble spots: countries where state government has already been overwhelmed and has collapsed, or is now at risk of collapsing, or has been wracked by recent civil wars; and countries that, as a result of their problems, are also creating problems for us rich First World countries, which may be deluged by illegal immigrants, or have to provide foreign aid to those countries, or may decide to provide them with military assistance to deal with rebellions and terrorists, or may even (God forbid) have to send in our own troops. The politician would answer, "That's a no-brainer, it's obvious. Your list of political trouble spots should surely include Afghanistan, Bangladesh, Burundi, Haiti, Indonesia, Iraq, Nepal, Pakistan, the Philippines, Rwanda, the Solomon Islands, and Somalia, plus others."

The connection between the two lists is transparent. Today, just as in the past, countries that are environmentally stressed, overpopulated, or both are at risk of becoming politically stressed, and of seeing their governments collapse. When people are desperate and undernourished, they blame their government, which they see as responsible for failing to solve their problems. They try to emigrate at any cost. They start civil wars. They kill one another. They figure that they have nothing to lose, so they become terrorists, or they support or tolerate terrorism. The results are genocides such as the ones that already have exploded in Burundi, Indonesia, and Rwanda; civil wars, as in Afghanistan, Indonesia, Nepal, the Philippines, and the Solomon Islands; calls for the dispatch of First World troops, as to Afghanistan, Indonesia, Iraq, the Philippines, Rwanda, the Solomon Islands, and Somalia; the collapse of central government, as has already happened in Somalia; and overwhelming poverty, as in all of the countries on these lists.

But what about the United States? Some might argue that the environmental collapse of ancient societies is relevant to the modern decline of weak, far-off, overpopulated Rwanda and environmentally devastated Somalia, but isn't it ridiculous to suggest any possible relevance to the fate of our own society? After all, we might reason, those ancients didn't enjoy the wonders of modern environment-friendly technologies. Those ancients had the misfortune to suffer from the effects of climate change. They behaved stupidly and ruined their own environment by doing obviously dumb things, like cutting down their forests, watching their topsoil erode, and building cities in dry areas likely to run short of water. They had foolish leaders who didn't have books and so couldn't learn from history, and who embroiled them in destabilizing wars and didn't pay attention to problems at home. They were overwhelmed by desperate immigrants, as one society after another collapsed, sending floods of economic refugees to tax the resources of the societies that weren't collapsing. In all those respects, we modern Americans are fundamentally different from those primitive ancients, and there is nothing that we could learn from them.

Or so the argument goes. It's an argument so ingrained both in our subconscious and in public discourse that it has assumed the status of objective reality. We think we are different. In fact, of course, all of those powerful societies of the past thought that they too were unique, right up to the moment of their collapse. It's sobering to consider the swift decline of the ancient Maya, who 1,200 years ago were themselves the most advanced society in the Western Hemisphere, and who, like us now, were then at the apex of their own power and numbers. Two excellent recent books, David Webster's *The Fall of the Ancient Maya* and Richardson Gill's *The Great Maya Droughts*, help bring the trajectory of Maya civilization back to life for us. Their studies illustrate how even sophisticated societies like that of the Maya (and ours) can be undermined by details of rainfall, fanning methods, and motives of leaders.

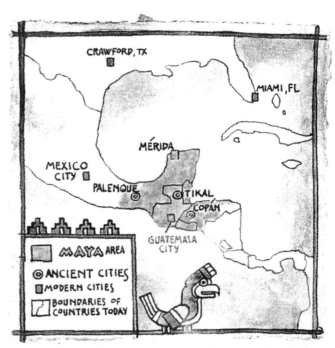

Illustration by Sam Fellows

By now, millions of modern Americans have visited Maya ruins. To do so, one need only take a direct flight from the United States to the Yucatán capital of Mérida, jump into a rental car or minibus, and drive an hour on a paved highway. Most Maya ruins, with their great temples and monuments, lie surrounded by jungles (seasonal tropical forests), far from current human settlement. They are "pure" archaeological sites. That is, their locations became depopulated, so they were not covered up by later buildings as were so many other ancient cities, like the Aztec capital of Tenochtitlán—now buried under modern Mexico City—and Rome.

One of the reasons few people live there now is that the Maya homeland poses serious environmental challenges to would-be farmers. Although it has a somewhat unpredictable rainy season from May to October, it also has a dry season from January through April. Indeed, if one focuses on the dry months, one could describe the Yucatán as a "seasonal desert."

Complicating things, from a farmer's perspective, is that the part of the Yucatán with the most rain, the south, is also the part at the highest elevation above the water table. Most of the Yucatán consists of karst—a porous, spongelike, limestone terrain—and so rain runs straight into the ground, leaving little or no surface water. The Maya in the lower-elevation regions of the north were able to reach the water table by way of deep sinkholes called cenotes, and the Maya in low coastal areas without sinkholes could reach it by digging wells up to 75 feet deep. Most Maya, however, lived in the south. How did they deal with their resulting water problem?

Technology provided an answer. The Maya plugged up leaks on karst promontories by plastering the bottoms of depressions to create reservoirs, which collected rain

and stored it for use in the dry season. The reservoirs at the Maya city of Tikal, for example, held enough water to meet the needs of about 10,000 people for eighteen months. If a drought lasted longer than that, though, the inhabitants of Tikal were in deep trouble.

Maya farmers grew mostly corn, which constituted the astonishingly high proportion of about 70 percent of their diet, as deduced from isotope analyses of ancient Maya skeletons. They grew corn by means of a modified version of swidden slash-and-burn agriculture, in which forest is cleared, crops are grown in the resulting clearing for a few years until the soil is exhausted, and then the field is abandoned for fifteen to twenty years until regrowth of wild vegetation restores the soil's fertility. Because most of the land under a swidden agricultural system is fallow at any given time, it can support only modest population densities. Thus, it was a surprise for archaeologists to discover that ancient Maya population densities, judging from numbers of stone foundations of farmhouses, were often far higher than what unmodified swidden agriculture could support: often 250 to 750 people per square mile. The Maya probably achieved those high populations by such means as shortening the fallow period and tilling the soil to restore soil fertility, or omitting the fallow period entirely and growing crops every year, or, in especially moist areas, growing two crops per year.

Socially stratified societies, ours included, consist of farmers who produce food, plus non-farmers such as bureaucrats and soldiers who do not produce food and are in effect parasites on farmers. The farmers must grow enough food to meet not only their own needs but also those of everybody else. The number of non-producing consumers who can be supported depends on the society's agricultural productivity. In the United States today, with its highly efficient agriculture, farmers make up only 2 percent of our population, and each farmer can feed, on the average, 129 other people. Ancient Egyptian agriculture was efficient enough for an Egyptian peasant to produce five times the food required for himself and his family. But a Maya peasant could produce only twice the needs of himself and his family.

Fully 80 percent of Maya society consisted of peasants. Their inability to support many non-farmers resulted from several limitations of their agriculture. It produced little protein, because corn has a much lower protein content than wheat, and because the few edible domestic animals kept by the Maya (turkeys, ducks, and dogs) included no large animals like our cows and sheep. There was little use of terracing or irrigation to increase production. In the Maya area's humid climate, stored corn would rot or become infested after a year, so the Maya couldn't get through a longer drought by eating surplus corn accumulated in good years. And unlike Old World peoples with their horses, oxen, donkeys, and camels, the Maya had no animal-powered transport. Indeed, the Maya lacked not only pack animals and animal-drawn plows but also metal tools, wheels, and boats with sails. All of those great Maya temples were built by stone and wooden tools and human muscle power alone, and all overland transport went on the backs of human porters.

Those limitations on food supply and food transport may in part explain why Maya society remained politically organized in small kingdoms that were perpetually at war with one another and that never became unified into large empires like the Aztec empire of the Valley of Mexico (fed by highly productive agriculture) or the Inca empire of the Andes (fed by diverse crops carried on llamas). Maya armies were small and unable to mount lengthy campaigns over long distances. The typical Maya kingdom held a population of only up to 50,000 people, within a radius of two or three days' walk from the king's palace. From the top of the temple of some Maya kingdoms, one could see the tops of the temples of other kingdoms.

Presiding over the temple was the king himself, who functioned both as head priest and as political leader. It was his responsibility to pray to the gods, to perform astronomical and calendrical rituals, to ensure the timely arrival of the rains on which agriculture depended, and thereby to bring prosperity. The king claimed to have the supernatural power to deliver those good things because of his asserted family relationship to the gods. Of course, that exposed him to the risk that his subjects would become disillusioned if he couldn't fulfill his boast of being able to deliver rains and prosperity.

Those are the basic outlines of Classic Maya society, which for all its limitations lasted more than 500 years. Indeed, the Maya themselves believed that it had lasted for much longer. Their remarkable Long Count calendar had its starting date (analogous to January 1, A.D. 1 of our calendar) backdated into the remote preliterate past, at August 11, 3114 B.C. The first physical evidence of civilization within the Maya area, in the form of villagers and pottery, appeared around 1400 B.C., substantial buildings around 500 B.C., and writing around 400 B.C. The so-called Classic period of Maya history arose around A.D. 250, when evidence for the first kings and dynasties emerged. From then, the Maya population increased almost exponentially, to reach peak numbers in the eighth century A.D. The largest monuments were erected toward the end of that century. All the indicators of a complex society declined throughout the ninth century, until the last date on any monument was A.D. 909. This decline of Maya population and architecture constitutes what is known as the Classic Maya collapse.

What happened? Let's consider in more detail a city whose ruins now lie in western Honduras at the world-famous site of Copán. The most fertile ground in the Copán area consists of five pockets of flat land along a river valley with a total area of only one square mile; the largest of those five pockets, known as the Copán pocket, has an area of half a square mile. Much of the land around Copán consists of steep hills with poor soil. Today, corn yields from valley-bottom fields are two or three times those of fields on hill slopes, which suffer rapid erosion and lose most of their productivity within a decade of farming.

To judge by the number of house sites, population growth in the Copán valley rose steeply from the fifth century up to a peak estimated at around 27,000 people between A.D. 750 and 900. Construction of royal monuments glorifying kings became especially massive from A.D. 650 onward. After A.D. 700, nobles other than kings got into the act and began erecting their own palaces, increasing the burden that the king and his own court already imposed on the peasants. The last big buildings at Copán were put up around A.D. 800; the last date on an incomplete altar possibly bearing a king's name is A.D. 822.

MAYA SOCIETY WAS POLITICALLY ORGANIZED IN SMALL KINGDOMS THAT WERE PERPETUALLY AT WAR WITH ONE ANOTHER

Archaeological surveys of different types of habitats in the Copán valley show that they were occupied in a regular sequence. The first area farmed was the large Copán pocket of bottomland, followed by occupation of the other four bottomland pockets. During that time the human population was growing, but the hills remained uninhabited. Hence that increased population must have been accommodated by intensifying production in the bottomland pockets: probably some combination of shorter fallow periods and double-cropping. By A.D. 500, people had started to settle the hill slopes, but those sites were occupied only briefly. The percentage of Copán's total population that was in the hills, rather than in the valleys, peaked in the year 575 and then declined, as the population again became concentrated in the pockets.

What caused that pullback of population from the hills? From excavation of building foundations on the valley floor we know that they became covered with sediment during the eighth century, meaning that the hill slopes were becoming eroded and probably also leached of nutrients. The acidic hill soils being carried down into the valley would have reduced agricultural yields. The reason for that erosion of the hillsides is clear: the forests that formerly covered them and protected their soil were being cut down. Dated pollen samples show that the pine forests originally covering the hilltops were eventually all cleared, to be burned for fuel. Besides causing sediment accumulation in the valleys and depriving valley inhabitants of wood supplies, that deforestation may have begun to cause a "man-made drought" in the valley bottom, because forests play a major role in water cycling, such that massive deforestation tends to result in lowered rainfall.

Hundreds of skeletons recovered from Copán archaeological sites have been studied for signs of disease and poor nutrition, such as porous bones and stress lines in the teeth. Those skeletal signs show that the health of Copán's inhabitants deteriorated from A.D. 650 to 850, among both the elite and commoners, though the health of commoners was worse.

Recall that Copán's population was growing rapidly while the hills were being occupied. The subsequent abandonment of all of those hill fields meant that the burden of feeding the extra population formerly dependent on the hills now fell increasingly on the valley floor, and that more and more people were competing for the food grown on that one square mile of bottomland. That would have led to fighting among the farmers themselves for the best land, or for any land, just as in modern Rwanda. Because the king was failing to deliver on his promises of rain and prosperity, he would have been the scapegoat for this agricultural failure, which explains why the last that we hear of any king is A.D. 822, and why the royal palace was burned around A.D. 850.

LIMITATIONS OF FOOD SUPPLY AND TRANSPORTATION MADE IT IMPOSSIBLE FOR MAYA KINGDOMS TO UNITE INTO AN EMPIRE

Datable pieces of obsidian, the sharp rock from which the Maya made their stone tools, suggest that Copán's total population decreased more gradually than did its signs of kings and nobles. The estimated population in the year A.D. 950 was still around 15,000, or 55 percent of the peak population of 27,000. That population continued

to dwindle, until there are few signs of anyone in the Copán valley after around A.D. 1235. The reappearance of pollen from forest trees thereafter provides independent evidence that the valley became virtually empty of people.

The Maya history that I have just related, and Copán's history in particular, illustrate why we talk about "the Maya collapse." But the story grows more complicated, for at least five reasons. There was not only that enormous Classic collapse but also at least two smaller pre-Classic collapses, around A.D. 150 and 600, as well as some post-Classic collapses. The Classic collapse was obviously not complete, because hundreds of thousands of Maya survived, in areas with stable water supplies, to meet and fight the Spaniards. The collapse of population (as gauged by numbers of house sites and of obsidian tools) was in some cases much slower than the decline in numbers of Long Count dates. Many apparent collapses of cities were nothing more than "power cycling"; i.e., particular cities becoming more powerful at the expense of neighboring cities, then declining or getting conquered by neighbors, without changes in the whole population. Finally, cities in different parts of the Maya area rose and fell on different trajectories.

Some archaeologists focus on these complications and don't want to recognize a Classic Maya collapse at all. But this overlooks the obvious fact that cries out for explanation: the disappearance of between 90 and 99 percent of the Maya population after A.D. 800, and of the institution of the kingship, Long Count calendars, and other complex political and cultural institutions. Before we can understand those disappearances, however, we need first to understand the roles of warfare and of drought.

Archaeologists for a long time believed the ancient Maya to be gentle and peaceful people. We now know that Maya warfare was intense, chronic, and unresolvable, because limitations of food supply and transportation made it impossible for any Maya principality to unite the whole region in an empire. The archaeological record shows that wars became more intense and frequent toward the time of the Classic collapse. That evidence comes from discoveries of several types since the Second World War: archaeological excavations of massive fortifications surrounding many Maya sites; vivid depictions of warfare and captives on stone monuments and on the famous painted murals discovered in 1946 at Bonampak; and the decipherment of Maya writing, much of which proved to consist of royal inscriptions boasting of conquests. Maya kings fought to capture and torture one another; an unfortunate loser was a Copán king with the to us unforgettable name of King 18 Rabbit.

Maya warfare involved well-documented types of violence: wars among separate kingdoms; attempts of cities within a kingdom to secede by revolting against the capital; and civil wars resulting from frequent violent attempts by would-be kings to usurp the throne. All of these events were described or depicted on monuments, because they involved kings and nobles. Not considered worthy of description, but probably even more frequent, were fights between commoners over land, as overpopulation became excessive and land became scarce.

The other phenomenon important to understanding all of these collapses is the repeated occurrence of droughts, as inferred by climatologists from evidence of lake evaporation preserved in lake sediments, and as summarized by Gill in *The Great Maya Droughts*. The rise of Maya civilization may have been facilitated by a rainy period beginning around 250 B.C. until a temporary drought after A.D. 125 was associated with a pre-Classic collapse at some sites. That collapse was followed by the resumption of rainy conditions and the buildup of Classic Maya cities, briefly interrupted by another drought around 600 corresponding to a decline at Tikal and some other sites. Finally, around A.D. 750 there began the worst drought in the past 7,000 years, peaking around the year A.D. 800, and suspiciously associated with the Classic collapse.

The area most affected by the Classic collapse was the southern highlands, probably for the two reasons already mentioned: it was the area with the densest population, and it also had the most severe water problems because it lay too high above the water table for cenotes or wells to provide water. The southern highlands lost more than 99 percent of its population in the course of the Classic collapse. When Cortés and his Spanish army marched in 1524 and 1525 through an area formerly inhabited by millions of Maya, he nearly starved because he encountered so few villagers from whom to acquire corn. The Spaniards passed within only a few miles of the abandoned ruins of the great Classic cities of Tikal and Palenque, but still they heard or saw nothing of them.

We can identify increasingly familiar strands in the Classic Maya collapse. One consisted of population growth outstripping available resources: the dilemma foreseen by Thomas Malthus in 1798. As Webster succinctly puts it in *The Fall of the Ancient Maya*, "Too many farmers grew too many crops on too much of the landscape." While population was increasing, the area of usable farmland paradoxically was decreasing from the effects of deforestation and hillside erosion.

The next strand consisted of increased fighting as more and more people fought over fewer resources. Maya warfare, already endemic, peaked just before the collapse. That is not surprising when one reflects that at least 5 million people, most of them farmers, were crammed into an area smaller than the state of Colorado. That's a high population by the standards of ancient farming societies, even if it wouldn't strike modern Manhattan-dwellers as crowded.

Bringing matters to a head was a drought that, although not the first one the Maya had been through, was

the most severe. At the time of previous droughts, there were still uninhabited parts of the Maya landscape, and people in a drought area or dust bowl could save themselves by moving to another site. By the time of the Classic collapse, however, there was no useful unoccupied land in the vicinity on which to begin anew, and the whole population could not be accommodated in the few areas that continued to have reliable water supplies.

The final strand is political. Why did the kings and nobles not recognize and solve these problems? A major reason was that their attention was evidently focused on the short-term concerns of enriching themselves, waging wars, erecting monuments, competing with one another, and extracting enough food from the peasants to support all those activities. Like most leaders throughout human history, the Maya kings and nobles did not have the leisure to focus on long-term problems, insofar as they perceived them.

What about those same strands today? The United States is also at the peak of its power, and it is also suffering from many environmental problems. Most of us have become aware of more crowding and stress. Most of us living in large American cities are encountering increased commuting delays, because the number of people and hence of cars is increasing faster than the number of freeway lanes. I know plenty of people who in the abstract doubt that the world has a population problem, but almost all of those same people complain to me about crowding, space issues, and traffic experienced in their personal lives.

Many parts of the United States face locally severe problems of water restriction (especially southern California, Arizona, the Everglades, and, increasingly, the Northeast); forest fires resulting from logging and forest-management practices throughout the intermontane West; and losses of farmlands to salinization, drought, and climate change in the northern Great Plains. Many of us frequently experience problems of air quality, and some of us also experience problems of water quality and taste. We are losing economically valuable natural resources. We have already lost American chestnut trees, the Grand Banks cod fishery, and the Monterey sardine fishery; we are in the process of losing swordfish and tuna and Chesapeake Bay oysters and elm trees; and we are losing topsoil.

The list goes on: All of us are experiencing personal consequences of our national dependence on imported energy, which affects us not only through higher gas prices but also through the current contraction of the national economy, itself the partial result of political problems associated with our oil dependence. We are saddled with expensive toxic cleanups at many locations, most notoriously near Montana mines, on the Hudson River, and in the Chesapeake Bay. We also face expensive eradication problems resulting from hundreds of introduced pest species—including zebra mussels, Mediterranean fruit flies, Asian longhorn beetles, water hyacinth, and spotted knapweed—that now affect our agriculture, forests, waterways, and pastures.

These particular environmental problems, and many others, are enormously expensive in terms of resources lost, cleanup and restoration costs, and the cost of finding substitutes for lost resources: a billion dollars here, 10 billion there, in dozens and dozens of cases. Some of the problems, especially those of air quality and toxic substances, also exact health costs that are large, whether measured in dollars or in lost years or in quality of life. The cost of our homegrown environmental problems adds up to a large fraction of our gross national product, even without mentioning the costs that we incur from environmental problems overseas, such as the military operations that they inspire. Even the mildest of bad scenarios for our future include a gradual economic decline, as happened to the Roman and British empires. Actually, in case you didn't notice it, our economic decline is already well under way. Just check the numbers for our national debt, yearly government budget deficit, unemployment statistics, and the value of your investment and pensions funds.

The environmental problems of the United States are still modest compared with those of the rest of the world. But the problems of environmentally devastated, overpopulated, distant countries are now our problems as well. We are accustomed to thinking of globalization in terms of us rich, advanced First Worlders sending our good things, such as the Internet and Coca-Cola, to those poor backward Third Worlders. Globalization, however, means nothing more than improved worldwide communication and transportation, which can convey many things in either direction; it is not restricted to good things carried only from the First to the Third World. They in the Third World can now, intentionally or unintentionally, send us their bad things: terrorists; diseases such as AIDS, SARS, cholera, and West Nile fever, carried inadvertently by passengers on transcontinental airplanes; unstoppable numbers of immigrants, both legal and illegal, arriving by boat, truck, train, plane, and on foot; and other consequences of their Third World problems. We in the United States are no longer the isolated Fortress America to which some of us aspired in the 1930s; instead, we are tightly and irreversibly connected to overseas countries. The United States is the world's leading importer, and it is also the world's leading exporter. Our own society opted long ago to become interlocked with the rest of the world.

That's why political stability anywhere in the world now affects us, our trade routes, and our overseas markets and suppliers. We are so dependent on the rest of the world that if a decade ago you had asked a politician to name the countries most geopolitically irrelevant to U.S.

interests because of their being so remote, poor, and weak, the list would have begun with Afghanistan and Somalia, yet these countries were subsequently considered important enough to warrant our dispatching U.S. troops. The Maya were "globalized" only within the Yucatán: the southern Yucatán Maya affected the northern Yucatán Maya and may have had some effects on the Valley of Mexico, but they had no contact with Somalia. That's because Maya transportation was slow, short-distance, on foot or else in canoes, and had low cargo capacity. Our transport today is much more rapid and has much higher cargo capacity. The Maya lived in a globalized Yucatán; we live in a globalized world.

If all of this reasoning seems straightforward when expressed so bluntly, one has to wonder: Why don't those in power today get the message? Why didn't the leaders of the Maya, Anasazi, and those other societies also recognize and solve their problems? What were the Maya thinking while they watched loggers clearing the last pine forests on the hills above Copán? Here, the past really is a useful guide to the present. It turns out that there are at least a dozen reasons why past societies failed to *anticipate* some problems before they developed, or failed to *perceive* problems that had already developed, or failed even to try to solve problems that they did perceive. All of those dozen reasons still can be seen operating today. Let me mention just three of them.

First, it's difficult to recognize a slow trend in some quantity that fluctuates widely up and down anyway, such as seasonal temperature, annual rainfall, or economic indicators. That's surely why the Maya didn't recognize the oncoming drought until it was too late, given that rainfall in the Yucatán varies several-fold from year to year. Natural fluctuations also explain why it's only within the last few years that all climatologists have become convinced of the reality of climate change, and why our president still isn't convinced but thinks that we need more research to test for it.

Second, when a problem *is* recognized, those in power may not attempt to solve it because of a clash between their short-term interests and the interests of the rest of us. Pumping that oil, cutting down those trees, and catching those fish may benefit the elite by bringing them money or prestige and yet be bad for society as a whole (including the children of the elite) in the long run. Maya kings were consumed by immediate concerns for their prestige (requiring more and bigger temples) and their success in the next war (requiring more followers); rather than for the happiness of commoners or of the next generation. Those people with the greatest power to make decisions in our own society today regularly make money from activities that may be bad for society as a whole and for their own children; those decision-makers include Enron executives, many land developers, and advocates of tax cuts for the rich.

Finally, it's difficult for us to acknowledge the wisdom of policies that clash with strongly held values. For example, a belief in individual freedom and a distrust of big government are deeply ingrained in Americans, and they make sense under some circumstances and up to a certain point. But they also make it hard for us to accept big government's legitimate role in ensuring that each individual's freedom to maximize the value of his or her land holdings doesn't decrease the value of the collective land of all Americans.

Not all societies make fatal mistakes. There are parts of the world where societies have unfolded for thousands of years without any collapse, such as Java, Tonga, and (until 1945) Japan. Today, Germany and Japan are successfully managing their forests, which are even expanding in area rather than shrinking. The Alaskan salmon fishery and the Australian lobster fishery are being managed sustainably. The Dominican Republic, hardly a rich country, nevertheless has set aside a comprehensive system of protected areas encompassing most of the country's natural habitats.

Is there any secret to explain why some societies acquire good environmental sense while others don't? Naturally, part of the answer depends on accidents of individual leaders' wisdom (or lack thereof). But part also depends upon whether a society is organized so as to minimize built-in clashes of interest between its decision-making elites and its masses. Given how our society is organized, the executives of Enron, Tyco, and Adelphi correctly calculated that their own interests would be best promoted by looting the company coffers, and that they would probably get away with most of their loot. A good example of a society that minimizes such clashes of interest is the Netherlands, whose citizens have perhaps the world's highest level of environmental awareness and of membership in environmental organizations. I never understood why, until on a recent trip to the Netherlands I posed the question to three of my Dutch friends while driving through their countryside.

Just look around you, they said. All of this farmland that you see lies below sea level. One fifth of the total area of the Netherlands is below sea level, as much as 22 feet below, because it used to be shallow bays, and we reclaimed it from the sea by surrounding the bays with dikes and then gradually pumping out the water. We call these reclaimed lands "polders." We began draining our polders nearly a thousand years ago. Today, we still have to keep pumping out the water that gradually seeps in. That's what our windmills used to be for, to drive the pumps to pump out the polders. Now we use steam, diesel, and electric pumps instead. In each polder there are lines of them, starting with those farthest from the sea, pumping the water in sequence until the last pump finally deposits it into a river or the ocean. And all of us, rich or poor, live down in the polders. It's not the case that rich people live safely up on top of the dikes while poor people live in the polder bottoms below sea level. If the dikes and pumps fail, we'll all drown together.

Throughout human history, all peoples have been connected to some other peoples, living together in virtual polders. For the ancient Maya, their polder consisted of most of the Yucatán and neighboring areas. When the Classic Maya cities collapsed in the southern Yucatán, refugees may have reached the northern Yucatán, but probably not the Valley of Mexico, and certainly not Florida. Today, our whole world has become one polder, such that events in even Afghanistan and Somalia affect Americans. We do indeed differ from the Maya, but not in ways we might like: we have a much larger population, we have more potent destructive technology, and we face the risk of a worldwide rather than a local decline. Fortunately, we also differ from the Maya in that we know their fate, and they did not. Perhaps we can learn.

Jared Diamond is a professor of geography and of environmental health sciences at UCLA. His book Guns, Germs, and Steel: the Fates of Human Societies *won a 1998 Pulitzer Prize.*

Test Your Knowledge Form

We encourage you to photocopy and use this page as a tool to assess how the articles in *Annual Editions* expand on the information in your textbook. By reflecting on the articles you will gain enhanced text information. You can also access this useful form on a product's book support Web site at *http://www.dushkin.com/online/*.

NAME: _____ DATE: _____

TITLE AND NUMBER OF ARTICLE:
_____

BRIEFLY STATE THE MAIN IDEA OF THIS ARTICLE:

_____

LIST THREE IMPORTANT FACTS THAT THE AUTHOR USES TO SUPPORT THE MAIN IDEA:

_____

WHAT INFORMATION OR IDEAS DISCUSSED IN THIS ARTICLE ARE ALSO DISCUSSED IN YOUR TEXTBOOK OR OTHER READINGS THAT YOU HAVE DONE? LIST THE TEXTBOOK CHAPTERS AND PAGE NUMBERS:

_____

LIST ANY EXAMPLES OF BIAS OR FAULTY REASONING THAT YOU FOUND IN THE ARTICLE:

_____

LIST ANY NEW TERMS/CONCEPTS THAT WERE DISCUSSED IN THE ARTICLE, AND WRITE A SHORT DEFINITION:

We Want Your Advice

ANNUAL EDITIONS revisions depend on two major opinion sources: one is our Advisory Board, listed in the front of this volume, which works with us in scanning the thousands of articles published in the public press each year; the other is you—the person actually using the book. Please help us and the users of the next edition by completing the prepaid article rating form on this page and returning it to us. Thank you for your help!

ANNUAL EDITIONS: Anthropology 05/06

ARTICLE RATING FORM

Here is an opportunity for you to have direct input into the next revision of this volume.
We would like you to rate each of the articles listed below, using the following scale:

1. **Excellent: should definitely be retained**
2. **Above average: should probably be retained**
3. **Below average: should probably be deleted**
4. **Poor: should definitely be deleted**

Your ratings will play a vital part in the next revision.
Please mail this prepaid form to us as soon as possible.
Thanks for your help!

RATING	ARTICLE
	1. Doing Fieldwork Among the Yanomamö
	2. Doctor, Lawyer, Indian Chief
	3. Eating Christmas in the Kalahari
	4. Coping with Culture Clash
	5. Fighting for Our Lives
	6. "I Can't Even Open My Mouth"
	7. Shakespeare in the Bush
	8. Body Art As Visual Language
	9. Understanding Eskimo Science
	10. Mystique of the Masai
	11. Too Many Bananas, Not Enough Pineapples, and No Watermelon at All: Three Object Lessons in Living With Reciprocity
	12. Prehistory of Warfare
	13. The Founding Indian Fathers
	14. How Many Fathers Are Best for a Child?
	15. When Brothers Share a Wife
	16. Death Without Weeping
	17. Our Babies, Ourselves
	18. Arranging a Marriage in India
	19. Dowry Deaths in India: 'Let Only Your Corpse Come Out of That House'
	20. Who Needs Love! In Japan, Many Couples Don't
	21. A World Full of Women
	22. The Berdache Tradition
	23. A Woman's Curse?
	24. Where Fat Is a Mark of Beauty
	25. The Initiation of a Maasai Warrior
	26. Eyes of the Ngangas: Ethnomedicine and Power in Central African Republic
	27. The Adaptive Value of Religious Ritual
	28. Shamans
	29. The Secrets of Haiti's Living Dead
	30. Body Ritual Among the Nacirema
	31. Baseball Magic
	32. Why Can't People Feed Themselves?
	33. The Arrow of Disease
	34. The Price of Progress
	35. The Social Psychology of Modern Slavery

RATING	ARTICLE
	36. Egypt's Young and Restless
	37. The Surprises of Suicide Terrorism
	38. Alcohol in the Western World
	39. A Pacific Haze: Alcohol and Drugs in Oceania
	40. When Will America Be Discovered?
	41. The Last Americans

(Continued on next page)

BUSINESS REPLY MAIL
FIRST CLASS MAIL PERMIT NO. 551 DUBUQUE IA

POSTAGE WILL BE PAID BY ADDRESEE

McGraw-Hill/Dushkin
2460 KERPER BLVD
DUBUQUE, IA 52001-9902

NO POSTAGE
NECESSARY
IF MAILED
IN THE
UNITED STATES

ABOUT YOU

Name   Date
_____   _____

Are you a teacher? ☐   A student? ☐
Your school's name
_____

Department
_____

Address   City   State   Zip
_____

School telephone #
_____

YOUR COMMENTS ARE IMPORTANT TO US!

Please fill in the following information:
For which course did you use this book?
_____

Did you use a text with this ANNUAL EDITION?   ☐ yes ☐ no
What was the title of the text?
_____

What are your general reactions to the *Annual Editions* concept?
_____

Have you read any pertinent articles recently that you think should be included in the next edition? Explain.
_____

Are there any articles that you feel should be replaced in the next edition? Why?
_____

Are there any World Wide Web sites that you feel should be included in the next edition? Please annotate.
_____

May we contact you for editorial input?   ☐ yes ☐ no
May we quote your comments? ☐ yes ☐ no